SO COME AND WELCOME TO JESUS CHRIST

Published by Canon Press
P.O. Box 8729, Moscow, Idaho 83843
800.488.2034 | www.canonpress.com

Douglas Wilson, *So Come and Welcome to Jesus Christ: A Morning and Evening Devotional*

Cover design by James Engerbretson
Interior design and graphics by Valerie Anne Bost

Printed in the United States of America.

Library of Congress Cataloging-in-Publication Data
Wilson, Douglas, 1953- author.
So come and welcome to Jesus Christ / Douglas Wilson.
Moscow : Canon Press, 2018. | Includes bibliographical references and index.
LCCN 2018024531 | ISBN 194450382X (pbk. : alk. paper)
LCSH: Lord's Supper--Meditations. | Devotional calendars.
Classification: LCC BV825.3 .W55 2018 | DDC 242/.2--dc23
LC record available at https://lccn.loc.gov/2018024531

23 24 25 26 27 28 9 8 7 6 5 4 3

SO COME AND WELCOME TO JESUS CHRIST

A MORNING & EVENING DEVOTIONAL

DOUGLAS WILSON

canonpress
Moscow, Idaho

This book is for Randy Booth,
and a friendship formed in a remarkable way.

PREFACE

Over the last fourteen or so years, since shortly after the time Christ Church went to a weekly observance of communion, I have been giving a short exhortation that accompanies each administration of the Supper. This devotional is a collection of those exhortations, gathered for daily use, both morning and evening.

We publish this book in the recognition that not every church practices weekly communion, but do not believe that this will affect its suitability for private devotions. I believe that it may provide a great help and blessing for saints who are preparing themselves for communion, however frequently their church observes it. Meditating on the Supper daily is a good way to gain more from the observance itself, however often it happens. And quite independent of frequency of communion, the book is intended to be used simply as a daily devotional.

So, the main thrust of this book is devotional, and should be edifying for any evangelical reader. At the same time, my doctrinal commitments with regard to the Supper do come through in places, and so I thought I should register up front what those commitments are. If I do that in this preface, a Zwinglian reader will not spend his money only to be sorely disappointed when reading in March sometime, for example. I am a sacramental Calvinist, and for the most part the teaching of the Westminster Confession of Faith summarizes my views nicely. This means that for some Baptist or Lutheran readers, certain readings will not be quite as uplifting as the one the day before was. But we must all learn that we were not put in this world for pleasure alone.

As regards broader subjects, I am a pastor in the Communion of Reformed Evangelical Churches (CREC), exhorting a congregation in the CREC, and this does come out theologically from time to time. For those unacquainted with the CREC, I am a Presbyterian, the kind that believes the Bible. While differences with saints in other traditions may be apparent, I trust the devotional will not be bristling with contentious issues.

Some of the readings are geared to the church calendar, and such readings are put in approximately the right part of the year. But because most of those days float from year to year, the chances are pretty good that there will be a number of times when a particular reading (for Pentecost, say) will not land on the exact day. Similarly, occasional references to the corporate context of a church service shouldn't be irrelevant for an individual's daily readings and may even be a blessing throughout the week.

Permission is hereby granted to any pastor who would like to use any of these meditations in leading the worship of his own congregation. I would only ask that the requirements of honesty be maintained, in that the appropriate people know the exact wording is not your own. But I do not expect to be given credit, or to be named — in fact, I would rather you didn't. The Supper is no place for footnotes. And permission is also granted to modify any of the thoughts here, putting them into your own words, and no further permission need be sought for that kind of use either.

The title of the book and the invitation at the end of each meditation is *"So come, and welcome, to Jesus Christ."* This is largely borrowed from John Bunyan, with many thanks.

Douglas Wilson
Christ Church
Christmas 2016

MORNING ✹ EAT AND BE SATISFIED

The Word of God promises that the suffering Servant will come to see the travail of His soul, and *He will be satisfied* (Is. 53:11). We too often draw the wrong conclusions from the doctrines of depravity, or from our distress over the current conditions of the Church. We *are* fallen, and the Church is in a dreadful way. We have sin to confess, and we have confessed it.

But we miss the whole point of Scripture if we do not see the *promises*. One of the promises is that after the passion of the Lord Jesus, and after His resurrection, He will look at the fruit of His cross, and He will be satisfied.

He is not ashamed to sit down at table with us. He is not ashamed to call us brothers. He is not ashamed of our table manners.

As we learn this — as we grasp what free grace really means — this sets us free to *learn* our table manners.

This table, this communion, is not a reward that we get for being worthy. It is a means of grace, it is one of the means God has ordained to make us worthy. We eat and are nourished. We are not to strive to grow healthy and strong, and then seek food as a reward. We are weak, trembling, and in need of what He gives.

But please know that He is not ashamed to give it. He is satisfied with the table He has set, and, because He is satisfied, it is possible for us to eat and be satisfied.

So come, and welcome, to Jesus Christ.

I want to explain something that I say at the conclusion of these little exhortations, and that is, "*So come, and welcome, to Jesus Christ.*" What do I mean by that?

First, the Scriptures teach us that when we partake of the bread and wine we are partakers of the Table of the Lord Jesus (1 Cor. 10:21). When we come to His Table, we are coming to Him. As we come, God in His grace has determined to grow us all up into the perfect man, the Lord Jesus, and for us to partake together in love at this meal is one of His instruments for accomplishing this. When we come here in faith, we are coming to Jesus.

Another important word I use is the word "welcome." To get to this Table, you don't have to get past a bunch of suspicious security guards with metal detectors. If you are baptized, and not under the lawful discipline of the church, then you are welcome. You are not being given bread and wine for being such a good person, you are being given bread and wine so that you might grow up into a good person. You are welcome, not for what you have done, but because of what God in His grace intends to do.

And last, I use the word "come." This is an invitation to everyone. For those not baptized, it is an invitation to be baptized. For those unrepentant, it is an invitation to repent. The only barriers to this Table are found within the confines of the sinful human heart.

So come, and welcome, to Jesus Christ.

MORNING ✵ FOOD OF THE GOSPEL

Jesus commands us to labor for the food which endures more than just a short time — food which endures to everlasting life. He tells us also *not* to give ourselves in idolatrous labor for that food which necessarily perishes.

Jesus says that the Son of man will give us the bread that does not perish because God the Father has sealed Him and gloriously honored Him beyond every name that can be given. Because of this, we honor the name of Jesus Christ as well.

But how do we work for this bread? the disciples wondered. Jesus answered that the work which the Father does in us is that we *believe* in Jesus Christ (Jn. 6:28–29).

So you are to feed, by faith. You are to sit down at this table, by faith. You are to meditate on the meaning of the table, by faith. You are to eat, by faith.

In a very real sense it is true that we are what we eat. If, by faith, you feed upon the Faithful One, then God multiplies His grace to you and in you. If you show contempt for Him in your partaking, then God uses the Table as a moment of judgment. But no sinner ought to want to hasten any day of judgment at all. Rather, we look to the one who received judgment on our behalf in His death on the cross. We look away from ourselves, and away from our own faithlessness, and to the One who gave Himself for sinners.

So look, now, in faith, and you will see the food of the gospel.

So come, and welcome, to Jesus Christ.

Jesus teaches that all men whom the Father gives to Him will in fact come (Jn 6:37). He also says that no one can come on his own authority, at his own initiative.

This meal is an "invitation only" event. At the same time, the whole world is invited—Jesus Christ is the bread of God which gives life to the *world*.

Our Lord is the bread of life. But He is also the invitation *to* that bread. No one can come in his own name. Anyone in the world can come through the name of Jesus Christ, but no one can come with a counterfeit invitation.

The reason men try to counterfeit the invitation, when the invitation was issued to the entire world, is so that they might come and sit down at this Table with their pride and self-respect intact. But this is the one impossible thing.

The flour that made this bread was ground in all humility, and so this bread and a proud stomach do not go well together. So, come, with your own name, choices, reputation, wisdom, and pride cast far away. Come, sit, at the invitation of Jesus Christ Himself.

So come, and welcome, to Jesus Christ.

MORNING ✺ EATING THE CROSS

The cross of Jesus Christ attracts those chosen by God, and that same cross repels those who are perishing (1 Cor. 1:18). The words of life are delicious to those who are being saved, and they are repulsive to those who rest in their own wisdom.

In His discussion of His body and blood, the Lord Jesus scatters the worldly wise. He gives an affront to those who want to reign over a religion that makes sense to them. His cross attracts — drawing all men to Himself. His cross repels those who are perishing. Preaching the cross calls out the elect. Preaching the cross offends the sophisticates of this world. Eating the cross, which is what we do here, nourishes the people of God. The idea of eating the cross is repellent to those who insist on separation from the people of God.

In the years since Jesus spoke these words, many have avoided this Supper in just this way. They stay away, and there is no mystery about their rebellion.

But there is another way to run from the Supper. This is to cling to the outward forms of it, while teaching or countenancing lies concerning it. One lie is that Jesus Christ is sacrificed over and over again. But another lie, much more common among evangelicals, is that our Lord does not nourish His people in any special way — the elements of the Supper do not present Christ to us so that we might respond to Him in faith. But the Supper does do this, and so we must take and eat with the mouth of faith. Not faith in bread. Not faith in wine. Faith in God, and in His Christ.

So come, and welcome, to Jesus Christ.

EVENING ◐ FAITH IS NOT UNDER YOUR SEAT

The apostle Paul tells the Corinthians that he would not that they should be ignorant. As we deal with holy things, ignorance is dangerous (1 Cor. 10:1).

Paul wanted them to know that their fathers were all under the cloud, and they all passed through the sea. The *Jews* in the wilderness are called the *fathers* of the *Gentiles* at Corinth. There was a covenantal identity between them — they, together, constituted the people of God. This is how we, who are not descended from Abraham in the ordinary way, can be considered as sons and daughters of Abraham. The thing which unites us is the covenant, and the heart of keeping this covenant is *faith*. Faith brought the Jews to the banks of the Red Sea. Faith brought them to the shores of their baptism.

But this by itself does not settle the matter. The Corinthians, and many Christians since, have assumed *automatic* blessings in the presence of God. But it was in the presence of God that Uzzah was struck down, Uzziah was afflicted with leprosy, Nadab and Abihu were consumed, and many Corinthians got sick and died.

Enormous blessings are set before us here. But we do not want you to be ignorant. Blessings are appropriated by faith, and faith is not automatic. Faith was not handed to you at the door. Faith is not under your seat.

Faith receives like a child. Faith is not up in heaven so that you might wonder how it might be retrieved. Faith comes by hearing, and hearing by the Word of God. *And this is the Word of God.* Here is the body of Christ, broken for His people. Here is the cup of the new testament, the blood shed for the remission of sin. Do you believe? Then take, and eat.

So come, and welcome, to Jesus Christ.

MORNING ☼ COVENANTAL PRESENCE

The apostle tells us that *all* the Jews in the wilderness drank the same spiritual drink. They *all* drank from the same spiritual Rock that followed them, the Rock that was Christ. But with *many,* he says, God was not pleased. They were overthrown in the wilderness (1 Cor. 10:3–5).

In the same way, certain members of the church at Corinth were overthrown in their wilderness, and did not enter into the promised land of the Christian eon. They came up out of Egypt, but (in a figure) died during the forty years between the crucifixion of Christ and the destruction of the old Jerusalem. They did not enter in because of unbelief. But the fact they did not enter in to the promised land did not keep them from communing with Christ in the wilderness. They did commune with Him in their unbelief, just as the Jews had done in a type.

When we look at the Jews in the wilderness and the Corinthians in their wilderness, we want to draw a contrast — everything must be different in the new covenant, we say — but Paul teaches that in *this* respect, everything is the same (1 Cor. 10:6, 11).

And so we reason by analogy to a third set of circumstances. The bread from heaven was Christ, but so was the bread of the land, so was the milk and honey.

This is our situation. Everyone in this room who partakes of the bread and the wine partakes of the *same* bread and the *same* wine. Christ is not present for the one who has faith, but absent from the one who does not have faith. Rather, He is present *covenantally* for both. His covenant presence is an enormous, glorious blessing for those who come in simple child-like faith. His presence is terrible for those who trifle with Him, and who think that He does not see.

So come, and welcome, to Jesus Christ.

Our presence here at this Table makes a claim on us. Because we are here, we must not become idolaters, as some of the Jews did in the wilderness. We must not eat and drink at *another* god's table, and then rise up to play.

The golden calf, however, was not called another god. Aaron tried to have it both ways—he tried to have a festival to *Jehovah* around the image that came out the fire, as he claimed, all by itself.

But this was not adequate. When Moses came down from the mountain, he was not prepared to be reasonable. He did not enter into ecumenical dialog with those who wanted to argue that the calf was not an idol, but merely a pedestal, a platform, for the invisible Creator. He jumped to conclusions, as some of our modern theologians might say. He broke the tablets of stone, and did irreparable harm to the cause of ecclesiastical and ecumenical negotiations.

His approach was so *severe,* we might want to say. He did not take the time to carefully research the arguments of those who had spoken so winsomely to Aaron. But if this is severity, then may God grant the grace of giving us more of it.

So let us guard our hearts. As we celebrate before the Lord, as we learn to rejoice before *Him,* as we learn to suck the marrow out of the bones, let us at the same time be vigilant. We often do not know what manner of spirit we are of, and when we rise up to play, if it veers toward fornication, then let us remember the twenty-three thousand who fell. God calls us to celebrate before Him, but this is to be done in the beauty of holiness.

So come, and welcome, to Jesus Christ.

MORNING ☼ DIVIDED LOYALTIES

We know from the Word of God that the ways of the flesh and the ways of the Spirit cannot be reconciled (Gal. 5:17). As long as God is holy, and as long as sin is filthy, the two will be at odds. That is to say, they will be at odds everlastingly. Paul pictures this in Corinthians as a matter of eating at one of two tables. You may not, he says, partake of the table of demons and the table of the Lord (1 Cor. 10:21). One may physically do it, certainly, but such a one may also physically die or get seriously ill.

The antithesis between good and evil extends into everything, and this antithesis is marked by how we eat and drink. The point is not that you may not eat here if you have sinned at all (for all sin is in some manner partaking of what the devil has cooked for you). The point is that you must not eat here with the formed and settled intention of continuing to eat from both tables. That is high-handed arrogance, of the kind that God strikes.

But of course, the point of such warnings is not to chase you from the Lord's Table. Realize the force of the argument here. If you are baptized, and have not been lawfully excommunicated from the Church, then you are not just invited to come and partake. Rather, we insist that you come, and we do not do this on our own authority. The Lord of the Table, the Lord Jesus, insists that you come to Him, and partake with Him, and in Him. If you are baptized, you must come.

At the same time, you may not deliberately partake of both tables. And this means that there is only one real option for you. If you are clutching to any known sin, you are not just invited to repent. Rather, this solemn and joyful moment constitutes a *command* that you repent.

Bread in hand, the name of this sin that must be forsaken is the sin of divided loyalties. Garden variety sins are confessed in the first part of the service. Divided loyalties must be dealt with here.

So come, and welcome, to Jesus Christ.

EVENING ◑ GOD IS NO MISER

The Table of the Lord is a rich Table, one that is filled with all good things. We who have been invited to that Table are not filled with all good things. The point, one that Scripture makes over and over again, is to bring about a transfer. What God has, He gives to us. What we do not have, is given to us.

One of the ways it is apparent that we are not filled with good things is the ease with which we believe lies about whether this Table is a Table of blessing. In other words, believing lies about the graciousness of God is one of the ways that we reveal how readily we tell lies.

But acknowledging this is not the same as wallowing in it. We have already confessed our sins. We have seen victory and growth over the course of our lives, as God is transforming us from glory into glory. We do not come here in order to go over our lives with morbid interest. Indeed, we come here because we serve a God who is interested in changing us so that we might stop doing this. His lovingkindness endures forever.

What this means, in practical terms, is that when you come to this Table you are charged to meditate on the goodness and greatness of God, and the goodness and the greatness of what He has given to you. You are charged to repent of unbelief, the attitude that says that God is not really giving you anything here.

But our God is a God of grace. He is no skinflint. He is no miser. His Son, our gracious Lord, is at the head of the Table, and He has given orders that ensure that the food will never run out.

So come, and welcome, to Jesus Christ.

MORNING ✵ GRUMBLING AT THE TABLE

Every manner of unconfessed sin is inconsistent with communion at this Table. But when the apostle comes to mention particular sins in conjunction with keeping our observance holy, it is notable which sins he singles out. One of them is murmuring (1 Cor. 10:10). Not only are we to avoid golden-calf-like idolatries, not only are we to avoid testing Christ, we are also told to set aside all complaining, all grumbling, all murmuring.

This means that our demeanor as we come to the Table is to be one of *contentment*. We are not permitted to grumble — even if the grumbling is over our sinfulness. He is the master of the feast; it is His business to invite, or not. If He has invited you, (and if you are baptized, He has), then it is your duty to come. And if you are not baptized, then you are invited to the water, and then to the Table after.

But we know that as we call on His name in faith, the water washes sin away. Discontent is one of those things to be washed away. And this means every form of discontent. You are at His Table, and must do what He says. Rest content then — in your marriage, in your finances, in your gifts, in your appearance, in your station, in your family, in your schoolwork, in your opportunities, in your trials, in your food, in your life.

You are seated now at His Table. He looks around from His position at the head of the Table and asks if everyone has washed up. In particular, He wants you to let Him wash away the grime of grumbling. If you have not done so, do not get up from the Table to go wash. Confess your discontent now, where you are seated. Let it go, now.

So come, and welcome, to Jesus Christ.

The various turmoils in the wilderness which the Jews experienced were all recorded, and they were recorded, Paul says, as *examples* for the new covenant believers at Corinth (1 Cor 10:6, 11). Because of this, the one who assumes that he stands needs to take heed lest he fall.

The modern evangelical world likes to draw *contrasts* between the old and new covenants at just the places where the new covenant itself draws clear and overwhelming *parallels*. And because we draw contrasts at such places, we think, somewhat presumptively, that we stand.

In the new covenant, we say, everyone knows the Lord. And since we know that no one who truly knows the Lord can fall away, we affirm the dangerous half-truth of "once saved, always saved." Now it is quite true that someone who is singled out as a recipient of God's electing and saving grace cannot be denied eternal receipt of that saving grace.

But we are not yet in glory. We live in the visible world, and God has given us a visible covenant in that world. And covenant members *do* fall away, and their bodies are scattered over the desert.

There is no temptation, Paul says, but what is common to man (1 Cor 10:13). The nature of temptation has not changed between the covenants. The nature of faithfulness has not changed. The nature of apostasy has not changed.

So you are coming now to the Table of the covenant. And so, we charge you, and we fence the Table in this manner. Come with submission. Consider your frame. You are flesh, and need to be nourished. Do not trust in theological abstractions to save you. Only the Lord Jesus Christ is your savior, and He calls you to take heed lest you fall. Come to Him.

So come, and welcome, to Jesus Christ.

MORNING ☼ THE PLOW OF GOD

God plows his people. He deals with us, and He deals with us here in the Supper. He deals with sin in the Supper.

This is very different from us trying to deal with sin on our own before we come, in order to make ourselves worthy. That misses the point, almost entirely. You do not improve yourselves, and then come here for the reward. Of course, living in known and overt sin is inconsistent with coming to the Table, and so in accordance with the Scriptures we do require you to confess your sins in the service before coming to the Table. But this does not mean you arrive at this Table in a sinless condition. God still is dealing with us, gently, patiently, for He is God our Savior.

God plows us here, and as He plows, rocks that were buried deep start coming to the surface. (The rocks that are lying on the surface should have been confessed by you already.) But when God uses this Table to cause rocks to arise from the depths of your heart, and they confront you here, do not be dismayed. God is dealing with all of us.

And when the rock is lying on the surface, it is not your job to remove it. It is not as though God's part is to point, and your part is the hard work of hauling it off. God's work in your life is to identify, and He enables you to confess, honestly and openly, surrendered to Him completely. And then *He* takes it away. He is our Savior.

Our task in this is to *be* saved. It is quite true that you have been saved already; you are freely justified through the grace of our Lord Jesus Christ. But according to the Word, we are also being saved, and at the last day, we will be saved. And each day that we live before God is part of this sovereign process that He oversees.

In this, what does He call you to? Be patient, for you *are* the patient.

So come, and welcome, to Jesus Christ.

We feed our children so that they might grow up. God feeds us for the same reason — we are His children, and He is growing us up into maturity.

This Table is therefore one of the central instruments to help us resist one of the great idols of our age — that of calculated immaturity. In fashion, in music, in manners, in desires, our culture represents a long, sustained revolt against the very idea of maturity.

The Church is not placed in the world in order to fight a rearguard action against the desire for immaturity. We are not here as simply a conservative force, to resist the general degradation. We are here to offer food to the world, for the life of the world.

We are God's children, and He summons us to His Table so that we might eat. But the intention that lies at the end of this process is God's holy intention for the Church to grow up into a perfect humanity.

We are the new humanity. We are the new human race. But we are not the complete or mature new humanity. That is the point toward which we grow. "What do you want to be when you grow up?" It is a wonderful question, and one which the Church ought to be asking herself more often.

But the old humanity, those outside the Church, are not simply discarded. We are building a new Temple to the Lord, but they are the quarry from which we are commanded to gather dead stones. God by His grace transforms them into living stones, just as He did with us, and the Temple is built, or rather, grows.

This is not a mixed metaphor. God's Temple is alive — you are that Temple — and because it is alive, it needs food. And here is your food. Take, and eat. Take, and drink. Take, and grow.

So come, and welcome, to Jesus Christ.

MORNING ✹ PRESENT OR ABSENT?

For centuries, Christians have debated the "real presence" of the Lord Jesus in the Supper. Too often it is not noted that the alternative position is necessarily a belief in His real absence. This of course is silly, and so it should cause us to reflect. All orthodox Christians believe in the real presence — the debate concerns the nature of the presence.

And by using the word *debate*, we must not show approval of the acrimony, hostility, and sometimes even bloodshed that has accompanied this debate throughout history. Never forget that this is a dinner Table discussion, a debate among sons and daughters of God, seated around the same Table — and it should be conducted accordingly.

Memorialists believe that the Lord is present here, but no more present than in any other activity conducted in faith. In other words, there is no grace available here that is not available elsewhere.

And some have come to believe in what might be called the local presence. In other words, they believe that the only way the Lord could be *really* present is if He is locally present in the Cup and on the Table, and that, of course, starts to tangle us up in physics and metaphysics.

We believe in the spiritual presence of Christ in the Supper, but remember that by spiritual we do not mean ethereal or immaterial. Following Calvin, who was following Scripture, spiritual means "by the power of the Holy Spirit." Another way of putting this is that we believe in the covenantal presence of Jesus Christ in this assigned ritual.

Taken up into the heavenlies in Christ, we do as we were instructed. As we do this, in faith, we are knit together with Jesus Christ — the resurrected Lord who is not dead — and we are being made bone of His bones, flesh of His flesh.

So come, and welcome, to Jesus Christ.

EVENING ◐ THE LORD'S SUPPER AND PRIESTCRAFT

As we develop a right approach to the Supper, which includes a weekly approach to the Supper, we have to be careful to avoid distractions. One such distraction is the charge that this "high view" of the Supper is somehow incipiently Roman Catholic.

Considering a historical debate as we come to the Supper should not be thought of as a distraction because this Supper is the embodiment of our faith in the communion of saints. You are not only partaking of the wine and bread together with the saints in this room, you are also doing this with all the saints down throughout history. This includes your fellowship with your Protestant forefathers, and their great recovery of the gospel as participated in here.

At the time of the Protestant Reformation, participation in the Supper was extremely rare for the average worshiper. The Mass was said frequently, but laymen were routinely and brutally excluded. Calvin fought for weekly participation in the sacrament for the entire congregation, but because of long-established practice, was unable to get that far. He reluctantly settled for monthly observance, but he wanted the whole congregation to come every week.

The irony is that since the Reformation, the heirs of the Reformers have begun to drift back to the assumptions and practices of medieval Catholicism — maintaining that the Supper is for the spiritual elite, and not for the spiritually hungry, that the Supper is a reward for the spiritually mature, and not food and drink for babes. To round out the irony, anyone who challenges this drift is then accused of wanting to restore medieval Catholicism.

But know this — wine for the world is not the same thing as wine for the priest only. Bread for the world is the grace of God that challenges priestcraft everywhere — whether those priests are Protestant or Catholic.

So come, and welcome, to Jesus Christ.

MORNING ✹ WHAT GOD IS LIKE

The way God reveals Himself in time and history is a revelation in some way of His eternal nature. As God created the world, He was not composing some sort of ultimate free verse. We look at the world, and unless we are suppressing the truth in unrighteousness, we see His eternal power and majesty. We see His Godhead revealed in the mountains, galaxies, fields, streams, plains, and oceans. God speaks in the world.

This being the case, how much more should we see His divine nature in the specific things He has given to us to teach us about His nature. In this category, we would of course include the Scriptures. In the Bible, God spells out for us, in big, block letters, what He is like.

But God also teaches us His nature in this aspect of worship. We have been communing with God from the beginning of the worship service down to the present moment. But this is the culmination of that communion. We do not call this communion because it alone is communion with God. It is communion because it is the summit of our communion with Him.

When God communes with us, He is revealing to us what He is like. Before the world was created, God was communing with Himself. Before we were made, He enjoyed eternal fellowship and love. He did not create us in order to fill up a void or vacuum within Himself. His creation of the world was an instance of an eternally-sufficient God overflowing. And as He overflows, what overflows is a manifestation of His nature.

And this is why, when we sit down at this Table, we are commanded to commune with one another. We are commanded to discern the body in one another. And why? Because this is what God is like.

So come, and welcome, to Jesus Christ.

The Word is prior to the world. In the beginning was the Word, and the Word was with God, and the Word was God. This means that everything about that Word was prior to everything in the world.

The world does not *constitute* reality; rather, the world *reflects* reality. Unlike the materialistic scientist, we do not look to the world to find out what is real. We look to the Word, and *there* we find what is real in the world, and what is transitory.

The Word is the image of the Father. The Word is the perfect metaphor for the Father. The Word is ultimate symbol. This means that the symbol created the world. The world is not a real ocean, with symbols coming off the top, like so much ocean spray. Rather, the world in its entirety, and all that it contains, is existent because of the Word.

We see the same thing as God is recreating the world, as He is doing in us, as He is doing through His proclaimed gospel, and as He is doing through His covenant meal here. The Word is prior. The Word is first. The Word is ultimate.

Why should we find it strange that God is summoning all the nations through the folly of preaching, through the folly of the Word? That is how He summoned the light, and the sun, and the moon, and that grass of the field. This is how God summons everything, and it does not matter that nothing is there before the Word. That is how it must be, so that the Word might have the supremacy.

The Word shapes and constitutes. The Word declares that you are one loaf, and the Word enables you to discern the body of the Lord *in one another*. The Word enables you to do this as you eat bread and drink wine. Is there magic in the bread and wine? Of course not. Is there power in the Word? Of course.

So come, and welcome, to Jesus Christ.

MORNING ☼ BITTERNESS AND BAPTISM

You are not here at the Table by yourself. Seated here with you are all the saints of God, throughout the world, and throughout history. We are called upon to discern the body, and not just the body here in this room. But this does not exclude those who are here in this room.

And so let us consider the relationship between bitterness and baptism. If you are baptized, and gathered here with us, you not only may come, but you must come. But if you are bitter and resentful toward anyone else here who is partaking with you, then you are not discerning the body as you are commanded, and coming to the Table in this condition is hazardous, and not just to your spirit.

Bitterness and baptism are inconsistent. They cannot abide one another, and they cannot abide together. One of them must go. But removing your own baptism is not something you have the authority to do. If you could do it, it would remove the inconsistency, but you cannot do it. That means you must confess the bitterness, and you must be done with it. It does not matter what the other person has done, or what you have imagined them to have done. Let none of you fall short of the grace of God. Let none of you continue to nurture that root of bitterness (Heb. 12:15).

This is hard, and so we start looking for a way of escape — and not the way of escape the Lord promised to us. And usually what we do is seek to rename our bitterness, calling it something else. We say it is righteous indignation, or a principled stand, or a thorough Christian worldview, or some other foolishness. Nevertheless, at the end of the day, we are still bent out of shape.

If you are bitter, and if you are baptized, you are about to approach this Table. The Lord Jesus is seated at the head of the Table. As you approach, remember that you do not have His permission to come in this way. Drop the bitterness. Let it go. Confess it. Repent of it. And come in gladness of heart.

So come, and welcome, to Jesus Christ.

As we approach this Table, we have to be careful. On the one hand, we are encouraged to come gladly, putting away all false scruples and morbid introspection. On the other hand, we know that coming to this Table is inconsistent with stark unrepented sin.

How can we teach against one error without encouraging the other? If we charge you all to beware of approaching this Table with defiled hands, will not the sensitive among us shrink back when they ought not? And if we encourage you to come as you are, will not unrepentant people, filled with resentments, or those who are tyrants in their homes, or those who are secretly indulging their lusts, be emboldened to come?

What are we to do? We are charged to insist that you come. The sensitive must come; they may not refrain from coming. And when they come, God strengthens them. He builds them up. He receives them, and fills their hearts with gladness, as when grain and new wine abound.

But what of the hypocrite? Do we not have a responsibility to keep *him* away from the Table? When the hypocrisy is open and defiant, the answer to this is *yes*. That is what church discipline is for, that is the meaning of excommunication. But when the hypocrisy is hidden, there is great sin in approaching the Table, and, in a certain sense, it is a sin we encourage.

Come, we say, to the Lord who sees all. Come, to the Lord who weighs hearts. Come, to the Lord who inspects grimy hands. Come, to the Table of spotless righteousness. When we come in faith, the Lord deals with our sins and sinfulness. When we come in unbelief, the Lord deals with our unbelief, either by bringing us to repentance, or by hastening the day when we come to the precipice of judgment.

And again, you tender of heart, the Lord gives *you* the strength to hear such warnings rightly.

So come, and welcome, to Jesus Christ.

MORNING ✵ DISTINCTIONS WITHIN THE COVENANT

God makes distinctions between particular congregations. He does not divide the world into two great categories, the baptized and unbaptized, and treat them all accordingly.

But neither does He treat everyone according to their individual status alone. It is true that everyone stands or falls at the Last Day one at a time, and God deals with each individual human heart. But this is not *all* He does.

God speaks to particular congregations, to particular generations, to groups of people in particular situations. So it is far too glib to invite, with great encouragement, all the baptized to approach this Table.

God speaks one way to Ephesus, and another way to Thyatira. He pronounces judgment on the Israel of the first century while at the same time rescuing the remnant. He comforts His discouraged sheep who have had burdens tied on their backs by self-important Pharisees, men who themselves carry none of the load.

You as a congregation come from a generation of recovering pietists, recovering individualists, recovering introspectionists. You are therefore summoned to come, and to come with great gladness. But do not turn this into a universal, one-size-fits-all approach.

You might wonder, what is His Word to mainstream Presbyterians? To strict, conservative Lutherans? To fundamental Baptists? But this is not the place for that question. What is that to you? You follow Christ. You must fellowship with Him here. To their master they will answer, and to your master you will answer. In the great covenant God has established, that master is the Lord Jesus, and it is sufficient for us that His wisdom distinguishes.

So come, and welcome, to Jesus Christ.

The Lord's Supper was instituted by the Lord Jesus Himself the night He was betrayed. The next scriptural example of it being observed was over a month later, on the day of Pentecost, when the disciples broke bread together (Acts 2:42). In the first, Jesus was alive and physically present with His disciples. In the second, He had come back from the dead, had ascended into Heaven, and had poured out His Holy Spirit upon the disciples. In both instances, He was *alive*. The Lord's Supper is not a memorial meal conducted over a dead body. It has never been that.

The body we partake of in this supper is *totus Christus*, the entire body of Christ, the living head and body together. This is why Paul tells us that we are the one loaf. We are the bread. And, like our Lord Jesus, we are alive.

This is a wonderful thing, but as we partake of the Lord Jesus, and as we partake of one another, we are made of one another. God knits us together. Now, what causes this knitting together? What builds us up into the Head, every joint and sinew? The apostle tells us that we are built up into Him *in love* (Eph. 4:16). Of course, all three cardinal virtues are involved — faith, hope, and love — but the greatest is love.

So you are not just to look around during the Lord's Supper in the faith that these things are so. You are not just to look around in the hope that one day the bride will be without spot or blemish. You are to look around in love. As you partake, love one another. This is the new commandment. Love your husband, your wife. Love your parents, and love your children. Love your neighbor. As you love, God uses this to accomplish what we believe and hope will be accomplished.

The bread you chew, the wine you drink, is your love for all the saints.

So come, and welcome, to Jesus Christ.

MORNING ☼ PARTAKING IN THE COVENANT

The world is covenantal. This is because the God who Himself is eternally covenanted, Father, Son, and Holy Spirit, is the Creator of this world. He could not fashion a world in which He was not the God of it, and the heavens declare His glory. In other words, the universe must display the characteristics of the one who made it.

And this is why we are not a covenant church, over against non-covenantal churches. *All* churches are covenanted with God, and therefore, all are covenanted together with us. Even non-believers are covenanted with their idols. The priests of the Old Testament were partakers of the sacrifices on the altar.

Partaking is the essential covenantal action, the central verb. Idolaters partake of their idols. Old Testament priests partake of the sacrifices. Husband and wife partake of one another. Worshipers of God in a New Covenant service partake of Jesus Christ, and all His body, which is to say, they partake of one another.

Your partaking of one another is not a secret thing — it is open and apparent to all. You put the bread in your mouth, and you raise the glass publicly. What *is* secret is whether this partaking is for blessing or not.

You are objectively partaking of all the brothers and sisters here, as you partake of Christ. He is one with them, just as He is one with you. This means that in the partaking, you are surrendering all the defensive walls you have built up against your brother, or against your sister. As far as it is possible with you, be at peace. As far as you are concerned, have a heart that is brim full of forgiveness. As far as it concerns you, partake of your brother or sister as though you are partaking of Christ, for that is exactly what you are doing.

So come, and welcome, to Jesus Christ.

The Table before us is set by God Himself. He invites us to it, and as we sit down with Him (in the person of the Lord Jesus), He deals with us. We cannot prevent this, we cannot manipulate it, we cannot turn it to our own ends.

This Table means what God says it means. It does not mean what various traditions of men declare. It is what it is, and does what it does, regardless of what men think of it.

When it comes to physical food, the various theories of nutrition and diet abound, and it appears that there is a new one arriving daily. And yet, from the beginning of the world, food does what it does, apart from any theory of nutrition in the head of the one who eats. What happens in the head is frequently of man. What happens in the stomach is of God.

It is similar here. We may contrive to think certain things so that the bread and wine will not do what God declares they will do. But what we think is ultimately irrelevant. If we are keeping covenant with God, by faith alone, then this means of grace will be used to help correct false notions. But if the false notions are devices of ours, calculated to manipulate the Supper, we will find that such covenant-breaking is chastised by the Lord Himself.

Therefore, when we come to this Supper, we are objectively submitting. God is God. God will have His way. God rules. Christ is the Lord of the covenant, and He determines what happens to His covenant people. He is the Lord. He is the shepherd. We are the sheep of His hand.

As you partake of the bread and wine, do so in evangelical faith, looking around the room in gladness and gratitude of heart. He is the Lord. We are not the Lord. We are the body of the Lord.

So come, and welcome, to Jesus Christ.

MORNING ☼ YESTERDAY'S MANNA

As you know, as we come to this meal, we are coming to Christ. Moreover, if we are doing it properly, each time we come we are coming to *more Christ*. Although we have been given all of Christ in principle, we have not yet *experienced* all of Christ in time. We are temporal, finite creatures, and so we cannot experience all of Christ in one eternal moment, one eternal present. The way God has established for us to experience all of Christ is to forever be experiencing more of Christ. Another way of saying this is that we will always be growing.

This is why we are to be spiritually ambitious. Selfish ambition leads us astray because it is directed at ungodly ends. But our problem is not the ambition, but rather where it is aimed. When we are zealous for self in a wrong direction, we are sinning. And when we are lethargic and unambitious, we are also sinning.

We were created to seek after glory, and we are being disobedient when we do not seek after glory. Paul commends those "who by patient continuance in well doing seek for glory and honour and immortality, eternal life" (Rom. 2:7).

It is not selfish to seek glory. It is selfish to refuse to seek glory. It is selfish to seek after vainglory. But glory, honor, and immortality are all a design feature. We are *intended* for it.

So never be content with yesterday's manna. Never be content to be a spiritual dry creek bed. Never settle for a comfortable liturgical routine. Do you come to the Lord's Table every week? God bless you. But do it, each week do it, seeking *more Christ*.

So come, and welcome, to Jesus Christ.

For those who are converted to God, the grace of God envelops everything, drives everything, defines everything. This includes our desire to learn how to walk in His ways, which means our desire to grow and flourish in our sanctification, which means loving and understanding His law.

This is a Table of grace. There is nothing here but undeserved favor. Christ died for the unlovely, He redeemed the inexcusable, and He secured those who were as unstable as water. This is all grace, and yet here we are, invited to come. God offers us bread from heaven.

And yet grace introduces us to a test—a test that measures whether or not we understand the potency of that grace.

"Then said the Lord unto Moses, Behold, I will rain bread from heaven for you; and the people shall go out and gather a certain rate every day, that I may prove them, whether they will walk in my law, or no" (Ex. 16:4).

Not only does God provide bread for His people, it says here that He *rains* bread from heaven upon them. But why does He do it? He is proving them—to see whether they will walk in His law, or not. And as the record of Israel in the wilderness shows us, they frequently did not.

Why did they not?

"Then Jesus said unto them, Verily, verily, I say unto you, Moses gave you not that bread from heaven; but my Father giveth you the true bread from heaven" (John 6:32).

The manna from heaven was a type, and this means that it could not accomplish what God intended for His people to do, which is to walk in His law. But what the type cannot do, the antitype does. The true bread from heaven is here because Christ is here. But Christ is only apprehended by faith. So then, the invitation is to eat and drink with the mouth of true and living faith.

So come, and welcome, to Jesus Christ.

MORNING ☼ THE CENTRAL TABLE

This is the Table, and it has its rightful place at the center of our lives. What we do here sets the tone for what we do at every other table. This Table is the rudder; it guides and directs all our other table fellowship.

If we are hypocritical here, we will be hypocritical around the dinner table at home. If we are filled with joy and gratitude here, we will be filled with joy and gratitude as we break bread with our brothers and sisters throughout the course of the week. If we think we can fool God here, we will think we can fool God with every other thing we put in our mouths. If we delight in Him at *His* Table, then He will delight in us at *our* tables.

Sin always wants to divide and separate. This over here, and that over there. Making distinctions is fine, and in a world created by the Triune God, it is most necessary. The Father is not the Son, and the Lord's Table is not my lunch table. But we may never separate, for God is one, and He encompasses and rules everything. Thus it is that the Lord's Table is set over against the table of demons, and Christians are not just required to partake here, but also required to refrain from breaking bread in any context or in any manner that is in conflict with what God is doing here.

Have you gone to lunch with a friend in order to gossip about a third person? Then reflect on this Table. Would you lean over while the cup is being passed here in order to share that particular verbal morsel? If not, then let this Table define the standard for you, and do not sin over your own cup either. This Table teaches us that whenever we eat, and whenever we drink, we should do it all to the glory of God.

So come, and welcome, to Jesus Christ.

When we come to this Table in the demeanor of faith, we are not just nourishing ourselves. Rather, the entire Body is being nourished and built up to the extent that various parts of the Body are receiving this gift in true evangelical faith. Coming to the Lord's Table rightly is *not* a way for you to get your own personal act together, independent of the rest of us. The apostle Paul teaches us that we approach the Table as *members*, and not as solitary individuals.

When members of the Body do not have genuine faith, however, what they are attempting is quite different. The faithful Christian, in eating and drinking here, is *feeding* the entire Body. The faithless Christian, in eating and drinking here, is attempting to *devour* the Body. I say attempting, because we know from the Word that all such attempts are of necessity unsuccessful.

Faithless covenant members are a cancer, attempting to feed themselves at the expense of the entire Body. For them, there are only two options. Either they must be converted into healthy members who feed themselves and the whole Body at the same time, or they must eventually be excised from the Body. Remember that by the last day, all spots, wrinkles, and blemishes will be removed from the Bride, who is the Body. This is just another way of saying the Body of Christ has a strong immune system.

How do we fight faithlessness within the Body? We do it by coming here in genuine faith and submission. We eat and drink in order to nourish. If we are not doing this in faith, then we eat and drink to our own condemnation, because we are trying to devour others instead of feeding others. We as a congregation come here now in all confidence because we know that, in the promises of God concerning the Body of Christ, health is much stronger than disease.

So come, and welcome, to Jesus Christ.

MORNING ☼ GOD DEALS WITH US

Observing the Lord's Supper on a weekly basis makes it a central event in our lives. As we have said a number of times, God deals with us here, and He deals with us according to His Word, and not according to ours.

If we are struggling against His work in us here, the temptation is to go in one of two directions. The first is the typically modern Protestant temptation, which is to get the Lord's Supper away from the center. This is done through infrequent observance, and a corresponding doctrinal minimalization of its significance.

The Roman Catholic temptation has been to keep the Lord's Supper at the center, but to corrupt it there, making it an idolatrous center.

At the time of the Reformation, it was far different, and this is what we are seeking to do here. What happens when the Word attends the Supper faithfully, and the Supper is faithfully observed often? The answer is that it creates a stir because those who do not want God to deal with His people are forced to do something to disrupt what is happening.

When Jesus began to "deal" with the Samaritan woman by telling her that she had had five husbands and was currently occupied with a sixth who was not her husband, she suddenly developed an interest in theological and liturgical questions, and wanted to talk about the best place to worship. In short, she wanted to change the subject. This is nothing but distraction, and Jesus did not allow Himself to be distracted.

It should be the same with us. Do not pay any attention to anything that takes you away from this — Word and sacrament, faithful and loving observance, and quiet, thankful rest in the goodness of God.

So come, and welcome, to Jesus Christ.

Consider this: there is no such thing as a nature/grace dichotomy. Nature is grace, and grace, rooted as it is in the very nature of God, is entirely natural. When we come to this Table, we are certainly partaking of Christ. But we are not doing this because the Table is a different kind of event, dispensing grace, over against all the other kinds of events we go through (nature).

All nature, all creation, is covenantal. This Table is at the center of that covenant reality, but it is not a different kind of thing. It is not that mystical spiritual things happen here that do not happen elsewhere. Everywhere we go, all day long, in everything we do, we are partaking covenantally. When we come to this Table, this does not change.

This is simply another way of saying that there is nothing magical about this Table. But do not draw the wrong conclusions from this. The whole world is magical, the whole world is suffused with the glory of God, the whole creation invites us to fellowship with Him.

Because God has sovereignly allowed creatures to disobey Him, those who do so reject His company, reject His fellowship. But they do not thereby escape the necessity of partaking. They are covenant creatures, living in a covenant world. They can no more reject the universal presence of covenant realities than they can escape the universal presence of gravitation.

So the choice is this. Commune with the Lord here, and in everything else you go, and the blessing of God in Christ rests upon you, and upon all your endeavors. Reject Christ here (either by refusing to come, or by coming unrepentantly), and you are partaking elsewhere, in covenant fellowship with the world, the flesh, and the devil.

You belong to Christ. Come to Him now. Come in faith, He welcomes you.

So come, and welcome, to Jesus Christ.

MORNING ✺ LOOKING FOR A CITY

The Word and the sacrament go together. Without the sacrament, the Word by turns gradually evolves into mere lecturing, or, if it is excited, a hectoring of God's people.

On the other hand, the sacrament without the Word gradually turns to superstitious and blind observance, at the end indistinguishable from rank paganism.

The two go together. But the Word is not to be understood as a brief set of instructions, or a mini-lecture. Rather, think of the Word that accompanies the sacrament as the *word of faith*.

As the word of faith, the word accomplishes that for which it was designed by God. And when the Word is faithfully stated at this point in the service, it *startles*. The means to avoid startling the people of God here are two unfaithful alternatives. The first is to change the Word so that it goes down smoothly. This is what happens when you are told that the sacrament is all about religion, with that religion defined by what you do and are in your solitude. Here the sacrament is all about you and your conscience. But the Word is adulterated by this means.

The other is to say true things, but to say them over and over again, all in the same way, in a soothing and comfortable way, so that the words wear a groove in your soul, and you no longer need pay attention. Unbelief has often masqueraded as liturgical fidelity to the old paths.

But here is the Word of God. Take and eat. Take and drink. For by this means, accompanied by a faithful word, you are building a City. And it is not an invisible, ethereal City either.

So come, and welcome, to Jesus Christ.

The Bible does not teach us that the Table must be protected from unfaithful people. Rather, the Bible teaches us that unfaithful people must be protected from the Table.

This Table is a winnowing fan, a fan that separates the wheat from the chaff. This Table deals with us as we come to it. To think that sinners could successfully defile the Table is to think that Uzzah could successfully manhandle the Ark of the covenant. To think that this Table needs protection is to think that the altar needed protection from Nadab and Abihu — but it was the other way around. Nadab and Abihu needed protection from the altar, and the presence of the Lord there.

We in our folly think that the holiness of God needs to be put under glass. We think that it is a delicate flower. We think that our grimy hands pose a threat. But the only threat posed is *to* our grimy hands, and what they are threatened with is cleansing.

But here is the next thing, baffling to us. Once we learn that the Table of the Lord needs no protection from us, we shrink back. But this is also wrong-headed. We are told to approach, consistently, regularly, confidently, approaching the throne of grace with boldness. In order to be brought to this conviction, we need the gift of faith. We may not come with an insouciant swagger, but neither may we hesitate out of false and introspective piety.

At this Table God is dealing with our cowardice and timidity. We are not given a spirit of timidity. And how is He dealing with our cowardice? He is doing it by teaching us to fear — work out our salvation, we are told, with fear and trembling. There is a fear — fear of the Lord — that drives out every fear. What is the nature of that fear? Come and taste. Come and drink, and you will see.

So come, and welcome, to Jesus Christ.

MORNING ☼ FELLOWSHIP AROUND THE TABLE

This Table is a Table of communion, and since it is offered to sinners, it presupposes forgiveness. But this has implications.

The Lord's forgiveness makes it possible to be reconciled to Him, but, as far as it is possible with us, we are also to be reconciled to one another. Reconciliation with God through Christ is easy for us to understand theologically, for He is perfect. But how are we to be reconciled to fellow Christians, coming to this Table with us, when we believe (and perhaps believe *heartily*) that they are continuing to sin against us? They have failed to see the striking ways in which they have wronged us. Or perhaps they know they have wronged us, and have confessed it, but do not appear to know the *extent* of their iniquity? The answer is that we are to cover it in love, and recognize that to his own master he stands or falls (Rom. 14:4).

Of course if it is not a matter of nuance, interpretation, he said/she said, but rather a matter of objective, verifiable sin, such a defiant sinner should be kept from the Table. That is what excommunication is for, but such things are applied to unrepentant adulterers, bank robbers, idolaters, and liars. It is not applied when someone sinfully rolls their eyes at you.

Related to this, when someone has sinned in a significant way, but has repented and been restored, that is not a time to shrink back. This is fundamental: the forgiveness we have *received* is the same kind of forgiveness we are to *extend*. Refusal to forgive the repentant is nothing but moralistic Pharisaism. Acceptance of someone back into fellowship is not to be confused with the disobedience of letting disqualified leaders continue to serve in their offices. But neither do "standards" require us to shun fellow sinners who have put things right. Not only is there fellowship *at* this Table, there is fellowship *around* this Table.

So come, and welcome, to Jesus Christ.

EVENING ◐ GOD'S LOW STANDARDS

A moment's reflection should show us that God's standards are much too low. He has graciously invited to this Table all sorts of disreputable people. When He tells us in His Word that we should show hospitality to those who cannot repay us, we need to remember that this is something which He has done.

With this thinking, centered on the concern for God's low standards, a false zeal for His holiness tempts us. We think that He will be defiled through association with people who need Him, and so we discourage repentant sinners from coming to the Table, for they might not be repentant *enough.* Another way we do this is when we withdraw the Table in a sectarian way, and make it a reward for the spiritually elite.

This bread and this wine *are* to be withheld from those who are sinning with a high hand. Those whose faces are sleek and insolent, who believe that God does not see their wickedness, who believe that this meal is somehow their automatic birthright, must be denied. Certainly, from those who pursue their adulteries, who bow down to idols, who blaspheme the name of God, we must withhold this sacred meal.

But the disconsolate must come. The discouraged must come. The one who has failed, confessed, and wept seven times in one day must come. The battered must come. The conflicted must come. The guilty must come. The one who struggles with ingratitude must come. Those in such dire straits cannot be told often enough that this bread and wine is not a reward for being good, it is grace for those who want to learn how to stop being bad.

So come, and welcome, to Jesus Christ.

MORNING ☼ TWO KINDS OF LOSERS

One of Christ's most famous parables is that of the prodigal son. It could also be called the parable of the self-righteous brother, or the parable of the longing father. What it teaches us about God the Father is quite remarkable, and to a certain kind of religious mind and heart, also quite scandalous.

Once there was a man with *two* disobedient sons. One of them was honest enough to go off and spend his inheritance on whores, while the other remained, working diligently in the fields for all the wrong reasons. The two sons are distinguished by this — the scoundrel son received a gift in order to abuse it. The other son was incapable of receiving a gift. The parable is explicit that the father divided the inheritance between the brothers at the beginning of the story, but the older brother later complained that he had received nothing. And he *had* received nothing — he was incapable of it.

Are you like the younger son? If you are, then you are an abuser of grace. You are a waster. Let us not sugarcoat it — you are a *loser*. The good news is that this is the Table that is set for you. God welcomes you to it. The fatted calf has been killed for you. You are a loser, and yet the ring has been put on your finger, and a robe has been called for. God the Father has hired a band.

But the grace of God goes still deeper than that. Are you a stuffed-shirt Pharisee? Are you a fusser? An ethical, moralistic whiner? Are you the kind of person who has no friends, and cannot recognize the grace of your Father? This just makes you a different kind of loser than your younger brother. So stop standing there in the driveway, sullenly listening to the music and dancing.

As we repent, this Table is for *both* kinds of losers.

So come, and welcome, to Jesus Christ.

This Table is what it is, and it does what it does. That is to say, it is the Table of the covenant, and it winnows out covenant keepers from covenant breakers.

Covenant keepers extend no hand to receive the elements but the hand of faith, and open no mouth to receive the bread and wine but the mouth of faith. And this is not faith in faith, it is not faith in our hand, or in our mouth. It is not faith in our heart or in our mind. Faith is a gift of God, and is a gift which He gives to enable us to receive Him. We do not receive our ability to receive; we receive *Him*.

Covenant breaking occurs here when anyone thinks to impress God by any means. He receives us, and gladly, but not because we in ourselves are impressive. His reception is all of grace; it is grace front to back, top to bottom. All grace. This is offensive to a certain kind of prim mind, and so efforts are made to combine what God offers here with something we can offer back, something we came up with on our own, and not simply what He has given in the first place. That is covenant breaking.

But we are convinced of better things concerning you. The warnings are there, and the warnings are real, but we have assembled here today in order to keep covenant, to meet with Christ, to trust in Him, and to proclaim what He has given us to proclaim.

And so we eat and drink, and consider it the ultimate eschatological toast — to the salvation of the world.

So come, and welcome, to Jesus Christ.

MORNING ☼ TREACHERY

As God writes the story of His covenant people in the world, with this Table at the center, we see that traitors and treachery are an important element in the story.

All four gospels have the story of Judas, which is certainly one indication of its importance. When Jesus talks about the Table of the Lord in John 6, He concludes this important discourse with a reference to His betrayal by Judas. The psalms prophesied the betrayal of Jesus by Judas, and how the betrayal would occur at the Table. The one who ate Christ's bread, a companion with him, was the one who lifted up his heel against Him (Ps. 41:9). The same sense of betrayal by a close companion is expressed later in the psalms (Ps. 55:12–14).

The words of institution which I repeat each week include the very important phrase "on the night in which he was betrayed."

Whenever this meal is faithfully observed, one of the signs that this is happening is that it will soon be unfaithfully betrayed. Servants are not greater than their master, and so we may expect the same sort of thing.

But when tender hearts hear this — when they hear about the possibility of betrayal — the natural reaction is like that of the first disciples. "Is it I, Lord?" No, eleven of the twelve, for all their faults, timidity, and confusion, did *not* betray the Lord. The fact that any sin is treachery "in principle" should not obscure for us the fact that there is such a thing as treachery proper, apostasy proper. So let us ask the question, as we should. "Is it I?" But then let us avoid morbid introspection in order to *hear the answer*. The Lord calls us His friends, and He summons us now. Those who are genuine traitors cannot bear to answer *that* summons for an extended period of time — while those who are tender in the Lord come at the invitation, and they come gladly.

So come, and welcome, to Jesus Christ.

The Bible teaches us that we as Christians partake of Christ. When we come to this Table, we partake of His body, and of His blood. But we do not partake of Christ in some isolated fashion, as though it were possible to partake of one narrow portion of Him.

We partake of *totus Christus*, all of Christ. All that He is, and all that He has done and will do, and all that He has united Himself to, becomes ours through His grace.

All that He is: He is the resurrected Lord. We are partaking of His body and blood, but we are not doing this with a dead body. He lives, and He lives forever — death no more has mastery over Him. We cannot come to the Table, and in any way reinstitute that death which was buried forever. We partake of the living Christ, Lord of heaven and earth.

All that He has done or will do: we are told by the apostle Peter that when we go through fiery trials, we are partaking of Christ's sufferings (1 Pet. 4:13–14). There is a genuine reciprocity here. All that we go through for His sake, He partakes of (they are His sufferings), and all that He went through for our sake, we partake of (they are *our* actions, our obedience. Theologians refer to this as the active and passive obedience of Christ imputed to us — we partake of His obedience, all of it).

All that He is united to: if we partake of Christ, and Christ partakes of my neighbor, then I am partaking of my neighbor. This is the meaning of the one loaf. You are partaking of the body of Christ, and you are the body of Christ. As you eat and drink, you are eating and drinking one another. You eat and drink the body and blood of Christ because you are the body and blood of Christ.

What does this mean? There are three answers to the question — faith, hope, and love — but the greatest is love.

So come, and welcome, to Jesus Christ.

MORNING ✵ ROUTINE

We celebrate the Lord's Supper every week, considering it the culmination of our service of covenant renewal. But to many of our fellow believers, this fact by itself smacks of ritualism or superstition. "Why do this so often? Do you keep forgetting?"

Well, on one level, yes, we keep forgetting. We believe that we are prone to sin and must constantly be called back to Christ, to be reminded of Christ, to partake of Christ—and not by mere dint of repetition, but rather by faith. This is why this word of scriptural exhortation must always accompany our observance of the sacrament.

But there is something else to realize. Repetition is inescapable, and many who object to weekly commemoration of the Lord's sacrifice for us have no problem whatever with comparable repetitions in other settings.

Christians who would object (loudly) to our recitation of the Apostles' Creed weekly—because it makes the words "meaningless"—have no problem founding Christian schools where the students recite the Pledge of Allegiance *daily*. Is that meaningless too?

When you ask a co-worker if he would like to go out for lunch together, do you expect to hear that he doesn't like to eat really, because he doesn't want it ever to become "routine." Asked how often he eats, he says that he likes to take a meal once a quarter, so that it will remain "special."

In the grip of such thinking, the *absence* of the Lord's Supper is repeated also. Week after week, the Table is consistently not there. Does that become part of the routine?

The answer to faithless routine is not to abandon the routine, but rather to embrace faith. To abandon routine is simply to establish another routine, and if faith has not been exercised, it too becomes an idol. We are Christians; this is the Table of the Lord. We are to put away our idols.

So come, and welcome, to Jesus Christ.

It is not a coincidence that the fall of our race into sin involved food. God created Adam and Eve, and placed them in a garden full of food, and placed one tree in that garden off limits. They were not to eat of that one tree.

All the other trees were open to them, and the Lord used to come down to walk with them in the cool of the day. There is at least one hint that when the Lord came down to commune with them, He would eat from the trees in the garden. The serpent urges them to eat from the prohibited tree *so that* they might become like Him. Perhaps, Adam and Eve were tempted to think, the Lord knew good and evil, not because of who He was, but simply because He was eating from this tree. And if they ate, then perhaps they could catch up. Wisdom eats, but so does folly.

It is therefore not surprising that our salvation involves food. God ate with the elders of Israel on the mountain in the days of Moses. He ate with Abraham on the great day of the promise concerning Isaac (Gen. 18). The entire sacrificial system of the Old Testament involved food. And so, now, we come to this Table.

We ought not to make Adam's mistake, thinking that we can accomplish anything simply by eating. We eat and we drink our salvation, it is true, but we also are capable of eating and drinking damnation. The chewing, tasting, and swallowing are common to both. The thing that distinguishes is evangelical heart religion. Faith, hope, and love chew and swallow. So do unbelief, cynicism, and malice. The chewing and swallowing in themselves are nothing (but also everything). What matters is love, joy, and peace in the Holy Spirit.

So come, and welcome, to Jesus Christ.

MORNING ☼ PROTECTION AND THE SACRAMENT

The Lord Jesus at the Last Supper gave bread to Judas. The apostle John says that after this identification of him, Satan entered him and he went out into the night (Jn. 13:26–27).

There is an important sense in which we should fence the Table, and this is what excommunication does. But I am afraid that too many of us want to protect the Table with the officiousness of an Uzzah protecting the ark. However, the ark did not need protecting — Uzzah needed protecting.

Charles Spurgeon was once asked how he would defend the Scriptures. "Defend the Scriptures?" he replied. "I would as soon defend a lion."

The Table the Lord established at that Last Supper did not need to be protected from the likes of Judas. *Judas* was the one who needed refuge, and he would not take refuge in the only place that could be found. Judas died shortly after his treachery settled in upon him, and the Lord's Supper is still being faithfully honored and observed two millennia later.

For those who come in simple faith, the Table fences us. The Lord is our shield and protector — it is not the other way around. And when we approach the Table in this faith, and declare the Word that accompanies the sacrament with authority, people who do not want the Lord to protect them (on *His* terms) flee from it.

But we are not in that position. We have come. We want to be fed. We gather to receive the Lord's kindness to us — and He offers it to you here.

So come, and welcome, to Jesus Christ.

We come to this Table every week. For some Christians, this repetition means that we will necessarily drift into religious complacency or sloth. This *does* happen, and so the Word must always accompany the sacrament, to keep us mindful of our responsibilities here.

But one of those responsibilities is to be repetitive. The liturgy of the worship service is the most fundamental catechism we have, particularly for our little ones. Though they do not know what I preached on five weeks ago, they do know when we came to the Table five weeks ago, and they do know when we raised our hands in the *Gloria Patri*, and they do know when we stood for the Scripture reading. They know all these things (which are important things to know) through repetition.

The entire worship service shapes us, and not only prepares us for worship next week, and the week after, but also steeps us in certain realities. We know that we do not come before a holy God without confession. We know that once we have confessed our sins, He really does forgive us and receive us. We know that all our dealings with Him must be governed according to His Word alone, and not by our own inventions and devisings. We know that we are to be a joyful people, and are to sing before Him, hearts overflowing with gratitude. We know that as a gentle Father, He feeds us and provides for us, giving us everything we need for life and godliness. All this we gain through repetition. But, let it never be said, through thoughtless repetition.

You are called, here, now, to be mindful of what Jesus Christ did for us. You are called to this, just as you were last week, and as you will be next week. Repetition, when offered in faith, is glory.

So come, and welcome, to Jesus Christ.

MORNING ✹ NOT TAKING IT FOR GRANTED

We have considered the problem posed by repetition, as well as the great blessing that flows from repetition.

Some, seeing the very real problem of getting into a liturgical groove, have sought to address the problem by changing the liturgy constantly. But this approach seeks to address a spiritual problem through mere physical means — which is like trying to help out a troubled marriage by rearranging the furniture in the living room.

Liturgy is like a dance. When you are first learning a new dance, you are not really dancing but rather counting. One, two, three, one, two, three. But once you are accustomed to the dance, and you know it, you are freed to think about the one you are dancing with. Of course, with this freedom comes the freedom (and temptation) to think about something else entirely, or someone else entirely.

This problem will not be removed by eliminating the defined dance steps. What happens with modern dances, when people simply gyrate aimlessly? Well, they are *still* free to think about something else, or someone else, only now a lot sooner, because they never have to think about counting.

The Lord's Table here is the culmination of our worship service. We have been thinking of Christ, and worshiping the Father through Christ throughout the course of the whole service. If you are used to what we do here, it is quite possible that your mind has been wandering while your body still stands and sits at the appropriate times. And now your body is here, about to partake of the bread and wine. What will keep you from taking this for granted? The means that God has assigned is the declaration of the Word that accompanies the sacrament, and repentance and faith stirred up by the Holy Spirit of God in your heart.

You are receptive to that work, so come to the Table, and welcome.

So come, and welcome, to Jesus Christ.

EVENING ◐ THE KINGDOM OF GOD IS NOT LIKE CRACKERS

The Supper of the Lord is not simply a continuation of the festival of Passover. It was instituted at that festival, and certain features of that feast are still incorporated in what we do here. For example, this cup is called by St. Paul the cup of blessing, which was the third cup in the Passover meal.

But it also encompasses far more than just the Passover meal — all the festivals of Israel are rolled into this sacrament, and find their complete fulfillment here. For example, after the institution of this sacrament (at Passover), the first observance of it recorded among Christians is the breaking of bread that occurred on the day of Pentecost. This is one of the reasons we use leavened bread here, and not the unleavened bread that was in use at the Passover.

If this sacrament were a strict Passover meal, not only would we have to use unleavened bread to partake, we would also have to ensure that there were no leaven on the premises anywhere. Leaven had to be removed from the house entirely. But when the disciples broke bread together on the day of Pentecost, they were doing so on a day when one of the required offerings to God was an offering of leavened bread — and so we see that the Lord's Supper is not a slightly modified Passover.

What does the leaven signify? Some Christians have assumed that leaven is a universally negative image in Scripture — the leaven of malice and wickedness, or the leaven of the Pharisees. But it is also used as an image of the potency of the kingdom of God. The kingdom of God is like leaven that works through the loaf.

And so this is part of what we declare in how we partake today. The kingdom of God is not like crackers. The kingdom of God is not like grape juice. We declare, as we eat and drink, the potency of obedience.

So come, and welcome, to Jesus Christ.

MORNING ☼ BECOMING ISRAEL

The Lord Jesus arrived in Israel two thousand years ago in order to show Israel a new way of being Israel. Of course this "new" way was the way that God had always intended; the new way was actually the old way. A new commandment I give you, John said, but it is not actually a new commandment (1 Jn. 2:7).

The new way of being Israel was settled however in the life, death and resurrection of Jesus because He was the only one who lived out this new way of being Israel perfectly. Others before Him — Abraham, Moses, Isaiah — had lived it out faithfully, but Jesus did it perfectly. And in doing it perfectly, He brought Israel into the maturity of the Church.

But the Church was not established in this way so that we could put all settings on autopilot, and wait for the Second Coming. As we look at the history of the Church, we see that we must constantly learn, generation after generation, what it means to be Israel.

We learn this in the worship of God, as we gather week after week. We invoke the presence and blessing of God through Christ. We confess our sins. We ascend to the heavenly Jerusalem, the church of the firstborn. We hear the word of Christ proclaimed. We sing psalms and hymns. And we come to this bread, and this cup.

In all these activities, we are becoming Israel, for we are worshiping and beholding the true Israel, the Lord Jesus Christ. It is a foundational law that you become like what you worship, and what you are actually becoming reveals to the world what you actually worship.

So we are here worshiping our Father and God through his Son Jesus Christ. We behold Him in the instruments He has given us to behold Him. These instruments are not just adequate to behold Him. If we come in faith, these instruments, these ordinances, are perfectly suited to enable us to behold. So believe, and eat. Believe, and drink.

So come, and welcome, to Jesus Christ.

EVENING ◐ EATING AND DRINKING WEAKNESS

We must be careful not to slip into the assumptions of modernity, thinking that the principalities and powers, against which we do battle, have somehow disappeared in our enlightened age. And we must also take care not to misunderstand the nature of these principalities and powers, which is always in this world, *most* respectable.

We *are* summoned to do battle against them, but too often we want to fight fire with fire. We want laws for their laws, actions for their actions, lobbyists to counter their lobbyists, and so on. But God's way is not our way; His thoughts are not our thoughts — although we are commanded to learn the process of making them our thoughts. We are engaged in the process of becoming more and more like Jesus, who is the true Israel of God.

And so, in this meal, we are partaking of the body and blood of Jesus. We declare, each week, by means of a broken body and spilt blood that God has determined before the foundation of the world to overthrow pagan power with divine weakness. The cross was the place where the weakness of God collided in a spectacular way with the strength of pagan man — and paganism and idolatry were toppled forever.

Jesus is on the throne *now*, with a name that is above every name, precisely because He suffered, bled, and died on a cross of wood. Among other things, this is what we declare each week in this meal. We preach the weakness of God, now given the name above all names.

But we do more than preach this weakness of God. We eat it. We drink it. We chew and swallow weakness. We become what we eat, and we are partaking of that weakness so that we might become weak *in the same way*. This is not the weakness of unbelief, not the weakness of *man*. We are partaking of Christ's sufferings that we might also be joined with Him in His resurrection and enthronement.

So come, and welcome, to Jesus Christ.

MORNING ☼ GOD OF SURPRISES

We serve and worship the God of surprises. Before Christ came, the Jewish people were expecting God to send His Messiah, and He would deliver His people from the Romans, overcome their enemies, and bring in the resurrection.

But God is the God of surprises. He did all this, but not in the way expected. God fulfilled *all* His promises to Israel, but He fulfilled them in Jesus, the new Israel. Jesus was betrayed in the hands of the Romans, was crucified, and then in His resurrection He was delivered from the Romans. When Jesus appeared in the upper room to His disciples, He was not worried about getting arrested again.

The resurrection of the dead, expected at the end of history, was planted squarely in the middle of history. God signaled His intent to raise everyone at the last day by giving us this down payment on the resurrection in the very middle of all our earthly affairs.

This transforms everything, and it certainly transforms our participation in this meal. When Jesus commanded us to observe this meal, He knew that we would be commemorating His death for thousands of years *after* His deliverance from that death. We now know that this is God's way. We commemorate death because death is now a defeated enemy, and has no sting.

We are participating in this death, not because Jesus is still dead, but rather because we are not yet fully dead and fully risen. We are crucified together with Him in truth, but our bodies will still die, St. Paul tells us, because of sin. This means that we must follow Jesus — if we want to be where He is, we must follow in His footsteps. And so we partake (by faith) in His death, knowing (by faith) that we will partake in His resurrection. This is why we chew and swallow weakness and death. We look forward in faith to what God *always* does with this — He vindicates His Word, His people, His way. He does this in resurrection power.

So come, and welcome, to Jesus Christ.

We are created and shaped in the image of God, and we are the crowning glory of matter. Our first father, Adam, was fashioned out of the earth, and when we die, we return to that earth. For a time, matter is organized in such a way as to love, think, sing praises to God, congregate in families, and everything else that we do.

But this returning to earth, ashes to ashes, dust to dust, is a problem. Death is an enemy. This happens because our race rebelled against God, and the warning was fulfilled. The day you eat of the tree in the midst of the garden you shall surely die.

But God is a gracious God, and right after our fall into death, He promised us that a descendant of the woman would come, and He would crush the head of the serpent. This He has done, and we are delivered. But we are still suffering some of the consequences of our first rebellion. It is hard to be the glory of matter when you only rise above it for a time, and then you return to it.

God has purposed to raise us to life everlastingly, and we will forever — flesh and bone — dwell with Him. But He has seen fit to prepare us for this over time; He does not do it all at once. So throughout the course of our lives, He gives us emblems for our salvation and sanctification — to receive, to read, to hear, to eat, and to drink. He uses these instruments to prepare us for the glory that is coming.

The point is to respond in faith to the Word of God. Are you baptized? Respond in faith. Do you hear the Word preached? Respond in faith. Is the bread in your hand? Take and eat it, in evangelical faith. Is the wine in your cup? Drink it in faith, all of it.

Why should you do this? The reason is that it is God's good pleasure that you will live forever. But as we prepare to dwell with Him, we realize that we must be acclimated, and to do *that*, we must do as we are told — in faith. God is shaping us, and so let submit to Him.

So come, and welcome, to Jesus Christ.

MORNING ☼ LIFE DEVOURING DEATH

The psalmist praises God because God prepared a table for him in the presence of his enemies (Ps. 23:5). Surely this would include the presence of the *great* enemy, death. So, rightly understood, this Table is the central example of that gracious provision.

But also, rightly understood, this Table is one of the great weapons in the arsenal of the kingdom of God. Our task in the modern world is to identify the idols that our modern culture has established, and to make a point of worshiping Jesus at just that point, through the Table.

One danger is of course the danger of syncretism, mixing our worship of Jesus with the worship of idols. But it does no good to avoid the sin of syncretism by falling into the sin of dualism, thinking somehow that Jesus is the Lord of your private thought world only. No, we are partaking of a Table at which we commune with, and partake of, the risen Lord, Jesus Christ, King of heaven and earth.

So the great danger of doing this thing, this challenging of the idols is that the idols might decide to fight back. Well, let there be no doubt — they will fight back, they are fighting back. And when we shrink from the consequences, this is usually the reason — although as Christians we cannot afford to *say* that this is the reason.

In the words of institution, we are told that in partaking of this meal we proclaim Christ's death until He comes. This proclamation is triumphant and clear. We commemorate a death, certainly, but a death in the context of resurrection. This resurrection means that this was not just any death, one death among countless billions. This death marked the death of death in the death of Jesus Christ. Death, the great enemy, death the great devourer, is now devoured.

Before the gospel, death devoured life unto death. Now, in the light of the gospel, life devours death unto life.

So come, and welcome, to Jesus Christ.

EVENING ◐ TWO QUESTIONS

There are two great questions that should be answered in your minds as you come to the Lord's Table. These questions should not just be answered at one point in your life, but rather should be part of your conscious heart and mind each time you approach the Table.

The two questions are these: what are you eating and drinking, and with whom are you eating and drinking? The answer to both questions is the same. You are eating the body of Christ, and you are sitting down to eat with the body of Christ.

This is not an appeal to superstitious magic. This is not a crude metaphysical statement about any transformation in the molecular make-up of the bread and wine. Rather, this is to see the covenant with the eyes of faith. The secret of the Lord is with them that fear Him, and those who fear Him are shown the covenant.

When we look at a man and a woman living in the same house, what is the difference between marriage, a glorious picture of the gospel, and shacking up, a vandalization of that same gospel? The difference is that in the former instance we see the covenant, and in the latter we do not. But what do we mean, *see the covenant*? How much does the covenant weigh? What color is it? What are the other dimensions? Height, breadth, width? Nonetheless, we do *see* it — this couple is married and that couple is not. It is not the case that the former couple has been transubstantiated somehow. But they have been transformed, and it is the covenant that has done it.

It is the same here. This ritual, this liturgy, commissioned by Jesus Christ Himself, is intended to strengthen us in the covenant, and to show us the covenant. When we look at the bread and wine, we should see the covenant God has made with His people. When we look at the bread and wine, we should see the people. When we look around us at all the people, we should see the bread and wine.

So come, and welcome, to Jesus Christ.

MORNING ✵ RATIONALISM AND SUPERSTITION

Consider the importance of eating. Food is not a consequence of the Fall, and the nourishment of creatures was no afterthought on the part of God. He created us as eating creatures. As we eat, and grow, and mature, and multiply, we find that God is in the process of turning inorganic matter into personal beings who love, and sing, and pray, and read, and hear, and obey.

After the Fall, God determined to restore the creation, and to bring us back from the death we had chosen through our father Adam. And again, eating is an important aspect of this. This is one of His instruments for renewing the creation.

Now of course, if we approach the Table here in unbelief, with an absence of evangelical faith in Jesus Christ who bled and died for us, then we are again approaching the Tree of the Knowledge of Good and Evil in disobedience. God's way of renewing the creation through eating is not a way of eating in disobedience. So let all superstitious tomfoolery and rationalistic minimalism be put away. We cannot please God by putting our faith in created things like bread and wine. But neither can we please God, and protect the importance of faith, by refusing to believe what He has told us.

We partake of Jesus Christ here, spiritually and covenantally, by faith. Just as the material elements are presented to your senses, so the mystical body of Christ is presented to your soul. And as you partake of the one, in genuine faith, God knits you together with His Son, bone of His bone, flesh of His flesh, enabling you to partake of Him in a glorious and merciful way.

This is the greatest of blessings, and you are charged not to corrupt it, whether with superstition or rationalism. Take, and eat. Take, and drink.

So come, and welcome, to Jesus Christ.

EVENING ◐ BROKEN BREAD

One of God's great patterns is that of taking apart, and then restoring fully. The restoration, the resurrection, is fuller, deeper, and richer than the original unity ever was. But before God tears, we consistently tend to panic, afraid that *this* time He will not be able to put anything back together. But He always does.

Jesus took a whole loaf, which represented His body, and then He gave thanks and broke it. Note what Jesus did in faith; He gave thanks for His coming brokenness. We, a Christian congregation, are an entire loaf, as St. Paul notes (1 Cor. 10:17). This loaf, this body, is torn and broken for communion, and points to the same fundamental reality. God brings life from death—but He does it according to His word. The death of Jesus was not done in our place so that we might not experience it. Jesus did not die so that we might live. He died so that we might die; He lives so that we might live.

You do not receive a fragment of bread so that you can take it off by yourself and consume it alone. That is a picture of sectarian death, not *koinonia*. The loaf is not a unified loaf, and then broken in order that we may then have a Scottish revival—an ironic term for a church blowing up into factions. There the bread is torn, but this is done in unbelief and not in faith.

But there are others who believe strongly in the institutional unity of the Church, and they therefore (in the type) will not allow the bread to be broken and distributed. Because of their fear of sectarianism, they are closed to God's pattern of reformation, which is always death and resurrection.

So the loaf is one unified loaf. In obedience to the Scriptures, I will take that loaf and break it. You will all receive broken pieces of bread. And then, in evangelical faith, you will take and eat that bread *together*. You will do this because you are one loaf, *together*.

So come, and welcome, to Jesus Christ.

MORNING ☼ DO COMMUNION? OR HAVE COMMUNION?

As we come to the Table, we are charged to flee from idolatry. We do this in two ways.

The first is that we leave all pagan idols behind. Whether these idols are actual gods made of wood or stone, or are idols of the heart and mind does not matter. We leave them behind in order to come here. In our nation, at this time, the latter case is more often necessary. We leave behind all the idols we have fashioned out of our own opinions and lusts.

But second, we also must leave idolatry behind in *how* we approach this Table. Idolatry can be found in the adverb which describes how we come. We commit idolatry whenever we come to the Table, speaking or thinking about it in a way contrary to how Scripture speaks of it.

This is a cup of blessing, and is *not* a mere memorial. When we drink the cup, we have fellowship with the blood of Christ. Note that we do not *do* communion, we *have* communion. That communion is a unity, fellowship, and identification with the blood of Christ. The same kind of thing must be said about the bread we break. The bread is fellowship or communion with Christ's body, and you are that body. You therefore have communion with one another, around the common Table. So be at peace.

The one loaf is broken, fragmented, so that a fragmented people can become one. Christ's body was broken so that we could become unbroken. And we break the bread here because we imitate Christ in His sufferings — we are this loaf, and if we are united with Him in His death, in His breaking, we will also be united with Him in His resurrection. And all things will be made whole.

So come, and welcome, to Jesus Christ.

EVENING ◐ WORDS IN THE HAND AND CUP

When we commune together, we are also communicating. When we commune, we are conversing. The words we speak are part of the food.

The words of the Lord Jesus are true nourishment. "It is the spirit that quickeneth; the flesh profiteth nothing: the words that I speak unto you, they are spirit, and they are life" (John 6:63). We hear His words when the words of institution are read, and we hear His words when exhortations are given in His name over the bread and the wine. We are not just nourished by the bread and wine in an isolated fashion. They are received by us, in faith, as tokens of God's lovingkindness toward us. We know of that lovingkindness because He tells us. This is a meal with meaning, and He is the one who tells us what it means.

But we also speak to one another. As the elements are distributed, it is our custom to sing words of encouragement to one another. This is what the apostle Paul tells us to do. "Let the word of Christ dwell in you richly in all wisdom; teaching and admonishing one another in psalms and hymns and spiritual songs, singing with grace in your hearts to the Lord" (Col. 3:16). As we sing psalm, hymns, and spiritual songs, we are told that we are teaching and admonishing one another. Moreover we are doing it as the word of Christ dwells in us richly.

So then, the audible Word is spoken over the edible Word. The musical Word is sung as the edible Word is passed and shared. And you, the body of the living Word, speak to one another. And the edible Word is eaten as we commune together. The drinkable Word follows.

So come, and welcome, to Jesus Christ.

MORNING ☼ TABLE ALLEGIANCE

We have no right to legislate morality in any area unless God has spoken to that issue clearly and directly. Apart from this, all things are lawful in their substance. The earth is the Lord's and the fullness of it.

We have already considered that all men are covenantal partakers of something. God has embodied covenantal structures deep within the world. The Jews were partakers of Christ in the Old Testament, we are partakers of Christ in the New, and heathen are covenantal partakers with their demons. No man who ever breathed is a non-partaker.

Now we who have this knowledge know that God is the only true God. This means, ultimately, that His Table is the only real Table. The other table, the table of disobedience, is a disintegrating and vanishing table. Attempts by believers to have it both ways, to shuttle between two tables, is therefore an attempt sit both at the Table of food and the table of transient vanities. Our duty is to be strengthened with this food so that we learn to identify those vanities as such.

If it is in the world, the thing itself is of course lawful. The earth really is the Lord's. But, Paul says, not everything is smart (1 Cor. 10:23). And here we see that for faithful Christians the issue is heart motive — what we might call *allegiance*. It does not answer to say that this thing or that is lawful in itself — fine, so it is — but where is your *allegiance*?

Is the privilege of sitting down at this Table everything to you? What you watch, what you eat, what you wear, what you do, where you walk — don't tell us it is lawful. We know that. Where is your *allegiance*?

So come, and welcome, to Jesus Christ.

Let no man seek his own, the apostle Paul says (1 Cor. 10:24). This is an essential part of discerning the Lord's body. We are to discern the Lord's body, among other ways, in one another.

As you partake of the Supper, do not close yourself up into a little private spiritual room. Feel free to look around at your brothers and sisters. Think of them, pray for them, consider how you might seek their best interest. In doing this, ask God to bring to mind ways that you might bring a blessing to them. Look around you in faith, and if you do, then you will see Jesus Christ.

Too often we view the Supper negatively. Of course it is important to put away all malice or envy. But do not stop there. Consider how to seek another man's well-being. Doing him good is not the same thing as not doing him evil. In turning away from sin as we approach the Supper, as we ought to do, let us be careful not to set the standard too low.

At the last day, Jesus will commend those who saw Him in the prisoner, in the hungry, in the ill-clothed. He will reject those who rejected Him in these same people. Do not be like those who are willing to defend and excuse and demand explanations, while standing before the Maker of heaven and earth, and to do this moments before their condemnation. If that kind of moral stupidity is to be avoided *then*, the best course is to avoid it now. Look to your neighbor—and don't ask who is your neighbor—and take this food to nourish you for the pleasant task of loving one another.

So come, and welcome, to Jesus Christ.

MORNING ☼ LEARNING TO EAT

The apostle Paul does not draw the kind of antithesis we might expect between the Table of the Lord and the food we eat throughout our daily lives. In 1 Corinthians 10, he talks about the Lord's Supper as a sacrament, the manna and water of the wilderness, meat eaten by the Levites from the Old Testament sacrifices, dinner parties thrown by pagans, meat previously offered to idols, and meat consumed in the context of idolatrous worship. We have food of all kinds discussed, and *all* of it relates somehow to the Table of the Lord.

Of course, the point is not that all food is strictly speaking to be thought of as the Lord's Supper. But the point is that all food is under the authority of the Lord's Supper. There is no such thing as autonomous food — everything we eat must be related by faith back to our right to sit down here, at this Table. We are disciplined by this; we are taught by it; we are fed by it.

Put another way, we receive strength here, strength and wisdom to eat properly elsewhere. If we do not understand what we are doing here, then how can we possibly understand the bewildering array of food that confronts us everywhere we look? If we do not understand these two simple elements, bread and wine, then how can we possibly be obedient Christians when it comes to sorting out all the questions and all the menu choices that face us three times a day? All of us spend a great deal of time putting food in our mouths. This is what God *wants* (He created us this way), but He wants us to do so by faith. And that means partaking rightly here, by faith, asking to be made wise.

So fence the Table here.

So come, and welcome, to Jesus Christ.

EVENING ◐ A PIOUS COCOON

The apostle tells us to do whatever we do to the glory of God. We cannot really understand this unless we have been disciplined by His Table. Whatever you eat, whatever you drink, he says, whatever you do, do it *all* to the glory of God.

But this comes at the end of a detailed discussion of how we are to honor the Table of the Lord. We cannot eat at two tables and avoid His covenant judgments. The point of learning to eat here is to teach us to spurn the food which the world offers. Like Daniel in Babylon, we are to reject the world's dainties, and eat the Lord's food only. But in doing this, all food becomes the Lord's food, and we learn that the earth is the Lord's and the fullness thereof.

But this comprehensive exuberance is not to be carnal offensiveness. Paul says to give no offense, whether to Jews, Gentiles, or to the church of God. We approach the Lord's Table, not seeking our *own* profit, but rather the profit of *many*. We are not to take the Lord's Supper looking in, but rather looking *out*.

In line with this, the elders have asked me to change the order of our service at this point. Instead of praying after the words of institution, which invites us all to close up into a pious cocoon, ignoring those others whose blessing we should be seeking by doing this, we want to thank our God *beforehand*. And then as we partake of the bread and wine, we want to ask you to keep your eyes open, looking to your brothers and sisters. We want to ask you to discern the body — look to the good of others, nourishing *them* as *you* eat. We want you to partake of the bread and wine this way because you have been made partakers together, joint-heirs, with the rest of His body.

So come, and welcome, to Jesus Christ.

MORNING ☼ THE HEAD OF THE TABLE

As the apostle Paul begins the eleventh chapter of 1 Corinthians, let us assume that he is not guilty of a radical lurch as he changes subjects, deciding finally to come back to the subject of the Lord's Supper in v. 17.

The culmination point of Christian worship is the Supper, and every disorder in the service of worship, and every disorder in our lives, is therefore ultimately a disordering of the Supper.

One such disorder was found in the marriages of Corinth. Paul tells us the head of every man is Christ, and the head of the woman is the man (1 Cor. 11:3). When we come to the Lord's Supper, we acknowledge that Christ is seated at the head of the Table because He *is* the head. But if a woman is in rebellion against her marital head, then how can she rightly acknowledge the headship of Christ? And if a man is abdicating his role as head of his wife, then how can he rightly lead his wife and family, sacrificing himself for them? Disobedience at this point cannot be corrected later on by understanding the Supper in isolation from our lives, in isolation from our lives together as men and women.

When we do not know who we are, male and female, men and women, this is nothing less than a fundamental derangement of our lives. And when our lives are deranged in this way, we must repent and ask God to nourish and teach us here.

So as you come to the Supper now, you are declaring in faith a whole series of headship relations. The head of Christ is God, the head of every man is Christ, and the head of the woman is man. You cannot separate one from another, and you should not try.

So come, and welcome, to Jesus Christ.

We want to affirm the presence of the Lord here with us now, and this presence is truly a *real* presence. We do not want to say it is an absence—a mere memorial—and neither do we say it is an ethereal, spiritualized presence, or that it is simply a raw material presence, crassly understood. Rather, God is present with His people, in His glory, through His covenant glory. And this means He is present in everything that we do.

The Lord gave ancient Israel the Shekinah glory to indicate His presence with them. This glory cloud was both a glory and a covering for them, as Isaiah says (Is. 4:5). It indicated that God was present with His people, and that all was well with them. We are called to model this as we present ourselves before the Lord. A woman's hair is given to her for a glory and a covering (1 Cor. 11:15). This is not to be understood in a simplistic or legalistic fashion, but it is to be *understood*. It is a small, individual, but nonetheless lovely reiteration of the Shekinah glory.

When we seek the Lord's presence with us, we cannot seek it for *this* portion of our lives and not for *that* portion. We cannot seek "spiritual blessings," and then return home complacently to unhappy marriages and homes. Your presence at this meal prohibits such a thing. And this means that every week, God is calling you to put things right, or keep them right, in your marriage. He is dealing with you so that you will in fact do it. And as He does this, you wives should think of how you present yourselves—you are a lovely picture of God dwelling with His people and protecting us. You want two things: you want to make that statement, and you want it to be accurate.

So come, and welcome, to Jesus Christ.

MORNING ☼ JUST COME

Because the Lord's Supper is a covenant meal, it may be abused. It is a covenant Supper, not a magic Supper. In the history of the Church, tragically, abuse has happened often. Paul says here that it is possible for the Supper to do more harm than good. He says that when the Corinthians came together, it was not for the better, but for the worse.

But notice that his solution is to address the abuses, and not to have the Corinthians shrink back from the Supper in fear. If anyone had cause to shrink back in fear — some of them had *died*, remember — it was they. But Paul notes the abuses, and urges them to reform what they do, and how they do it.

So as you come, take care to guard yourself against some contemporary abuses. You are invited to come if you have been baptized in the name of the Father, Son, and Holy Spirit. If you have not been baptized, you are invited, but not to the Supper. You are invited to be baptized, which is the invitation to the Supper.

As you come, come in faith. Do not come in perfection, for you have none. Do not come in maturity — none of us are there yet. Do not come in your own name — God gives you your true name in the Supper. Do not come clinging to any superstitious devices — the just shall live by faith. In faith, just come, and eat. Come and drink.

So come, and welcome, to Jesus Christ.

We are gathered here to eat the Lord's Supper, not our own suppers. We all have homes of our own, and kitchens in them, and dining rooms. We have left behind our own food. This is not because we are ungrateful for it, but rather because we know that our food is not the food God supplies to us in this covenant context.

We are not here to seek our own. When you are at home, you eat your own lunch, and not someone else's. But here, we share a *common* meal, taken from one loaf. Therefore, in eating and drinking here, you are acknowledging that God wants you to seek the good of others, to see Christ in your brother and sister, and to eat to the strengthening of *their* body, of which you are a part.

Your physical body does need nourishment — you have houses to eat and drink in. But you are fundamentally members of *this* house, and you are fed here. By faith, you feed on Christ. Christ is seated at the head of the Table, Christ is the meal on the Table, and Christ is present in all those who sit around the Table together with you. This can only be seen by faith, and you are charged to see it. Put away all sin, repent of it, turn away from it, and eat by faith what grace has prepared.

So come, and welcome, to Jesus Christ.

MORNING ☼ JUDAS AT THE TABLE

The apostle Paul tells us that our Lord instituted the Supper on the night He was *betrayed* (1 Cor. 11:23). The indications from the gospels are that He served the elements of that Supper to his betrayer, Judas, who was already under the influence of Satan himself. And Jesus knew this.

At the first celebration of this Supper — and it was a celebration, for Jesus' gave thanks — the Table was marred by the presence of a false one. Jesus knew this, and He established the sacrament anyway. Let God be true, and every man a liar. The sacraments are what God says about them, and never what men say about them — which is a good thing, considering the history of controversy that has swirled around what we are doing here now. We are told to *take, eat*, and not *take, speculate*.

As we think about the presence of a traitor at the first Supper, this makes us think of all the traitors present at this Table since that time, down to the present. But instead of looking around us for a Judas, we need to understand that each of us brings more than enough of Judas to the Table ourselves.

But know that the sin of Judas was not that he was at the Table, sinful as he was. His great sin was that he *departed* from that Table and went out into the night. If you obstinately cling to your sin, even if you remain in your seat, you are following him there. If you confess the goodness of God to you in His free forgiveness, then God is here giving you nourishing bread and rich wine.

So come, and welcome, to Jesus Christ.

EVENING ◐ JESUS GIVES ALCOHOL TO MINORS

For some years, we have been saying that our observance of this Supper is potent, that the gospel is like wine, and not like grape juice. Grape juice is a fitting element for the modern and moribund church to use — an inert element for an inert sacrament in an inert church. But when God moves to stir His people up, what happens? We return to a biblical observance of this Supper which can be nothing other than a *potent* declaration.

Once we had scheduled a worship service in a local college stadium in conjunction with the Trinity Festival, and some of our local adversaries officially complained. Their complaint centered on the fact that we would be serving alcohol to minors. We have seen that if we were serving grape juice in our communion service, our adversaries would not care — a tame sacrament for a domesticated church. But there is another issue as well.

The second issue is this: If we excluded you, our children, from the service, they would not care either. But because we eat and drink a potent gospel, and because we insist on including our children and grandchildren in this, their glorious inheritance, the whole thing becomes quite formidable.

When was the last time you heard about outsiders *caring* what was done inside a worship service like this? The whole affair should be greatly encouraging. God has prepared a Table for us in the presence of our enemies, and as we sit down to eat and drink, we may know by faith that God is moving in our community in wonderful ways.

We have assumed the center, and we now see our adversaries beginning to recognize that it is what is being done in faithful Christian worship that will determine the future of our town, our state, our nation, and our world. It is *here* we are formidable — and nowhere else.

So come, and welcome, to Jesus Christ.

MORNING ☼ FIGHTING WITH THE SUPPER, NOT OVER IT

As we noted previously, there is a complaint that has been brought against us — in our observance of the Lord's Supper, we serve alcohol to minors. There are many principles involved in all this, but we need to focus on just one of them right now, and bring this wisdom with us as we come to the Table next week.

The adversary wants to draw us into a position where we are fighting *over* the Lord's Supper, and away from what we are currently doing, which is fighting *with* the Lord's Supper.

What God is doing through this meal is establishing His people, His community, His kingdom. This is not done when ostensible Christians go through a perfunctory rite, not knowing what they do. That only makes our condition worse, not better. St. Paul tells us that the Lord's Supper can do more harm than good — it is a covenant meal, and this means blessings for faith and curses for disobedience.

But when God's people assemble in faith, and renew covenant with Him on a weekly basis, as we have been doing, it is not surprising that our opponents want us to come down from the wall we are building to quarrel with them. But why would we ever do *that*? We are doing a great thing — why should we come down?

This great thing I speak of is the "great thing" of Christ building His kingdom, despite all opposition. We gather together here to worship God. If our God were deaf, dumb, and blind — like theirs — this should be of no concern whatever. What should it matter to them if we all gather in a room in order to talk and sing to the ceiling?

But this is not what is happening. We worship and serve the living and ruling Christ, and those who try to ignore His sovereignty through lies are thrown into a panic when Christians rediscover the truth. And so they start caring about the next generation receiving this cup, this bread. God is good, so let us all partake *together*.

So come, and welcome, to Jesus Christ.

Paul tells us that we must not eat and drink from the Table of the New Testament unworthily. He uses the word several times, but remember the context of his warning.

The Corinthians were guilty of divisions in the church, drunkenness, sexual immorality, and greed. Paul tells them that such sins, unrepented, were inconsistent with the Table. The biblical solution to this inconsistency, always, is to repent of the sin and come to the Table. We think that an acceptable way to resolve the problem is to stay away from the Table and keep the sin. Make no mistake — unrepented sin and participation at this Table *are* fundamentally inconsistent. But we do not want to fence the Table — we want the Table to fence us, and keep us from the sin. Do not let sin keep you from the Table; seek to have the Table keep you from the sin.

It is as grievous a sin to *refrain* from the Table unworthily as it is to partake unworthily. In both cases, the sin is the same kind of thing — contemptuous ingratitude. One man eats, not recognizing or discerning the communion with Christ. Another man refrains from eating, not recognizing the obligation to commune with Christ. It is ingratitude to snatch something without saying *thank you*. It is also ingratitude to refuse such a gift, purchased at such great expense.

So guard your hearts, discern the body, and come and eat.

So come, and welcome, to Jesus Christ.

MORNING ✹ HOW MUCH MORE

The New Covenant is not a covenant that altered the fundamental nature of covenants. Throughout the Old Testament, covenants always had attendant blessings and curses. Some have wanted to imagine that the New Covenant was a covenant of *automatic* blessings, and that by its very nature, curses were impossible.

But Paul tells us that many among the Corinthians were sick and that others had died because of their abuse of the Lord's Supper (1 Cor. 11:30). The Bible tells us, contrary to our superstitions, that the curses of the New Covenant are *more* severe than those applied under Moses, and this makes sense when we consider the nature of the blessings. The blessings of the New Covenant are the fulfillment of every blessing promised in the Old Testament, and consequently, surpass them all. But it is a fixed principle in Scripture that to whom much is given, much is required.

If someone could die under Moses with the testimony of two or three witnesses, how much *worse* will it be for those sons of folly today who trample under foot the blood of the covenant by which they were sanctified (Heb. 10:28–29)? Upon learning this, our natural reaction is to shrink back from the Table—but rather we should act the part of Christians, and shrink back from our *sins*.

We are not among those who hesitate, and are lost. Neither are we among those who profane the good gift of God, set before us here.

So come, and welcome, to Jesus Christ.

If we would judge ourselves, we would not be judged (1 Cor. 11:31).

When we look *away* from ourselves, to the mirror of God's Word, and to the image of God imprinted on our brothers and sisters around us, we are brought to a true knowledge of ourselves. We cannot come to a true knowledge of ourselves through introspection, or morbid self-examination. Therefore a call to look away from your heart is not a call to ignore your own condition — rather, it is the only healthy way for you to *ascertain* your condition.

Look to God, look to your neighbor. Love God and love your neighbor. When you do this in true obedience, God grants to you a self-knowledge that is accurate, humble, contrite, and full of the confidence that comes from the Holy Spirit.

Look to yourself, and you will be sucked into a black hole that only the grace of God can free you from. This black hole is no less dangerous for acting pious and very devout — indeed, that is where the greatest danger lies. You are not permitted to look directly at yourself. How could you take out your eyeballs in order to look at them?

Those who think they are "looking at themselves" are actually looking at an acceptable, self-made filtered image, which is not in accordance with the Word.

Do you really want to know what you look like? Look to the Word. Look to the cross. Look to Christ in your neighbor. Confess your sins, and then take and eat. Take, and drink.

So come, and welcome, to Jesus Christ.

If we refuse to judge ourselves, the Word tells us, then God will undertake the task. But Paul adds that God does this so that we will not be condemned with the world. Judgment begins with the household of God (1 Pet. 4:17). Chastening *begins with* us so that it might not be the *end of* us (Heb. 12:6).

This is why we are to consider our hearts as we assemble around this Table. But as we consider our hearts, we must always take care not to abandon the standard of evaluation which God gives to us. That standard is the gospel. If you look to yourself apart from the gospel, all you will find is trouble and spiritual turmoil. So examine yourself, as Scripture does require, but if you ever examine yourself apart from reference to Christ, the examination will be a pretty dismal business, and will have sorry results.

And this is why we exhort you to look *away* as you come to the Table. Christ is on the cross. Look in hope. Christ has risen. Look *up*. Christ is on the throne. Look *around*. Christ is in your brother. Look, take and eat.

So come, and welcome, to Jesus Christ.

EVENING ◐ LOCKSTEP OR LIKEMINDEDNESS?

We are told to tarry for one another. This is why we take and eat *together*, and why we take and drink *together*. The point of this is not communion in lockstep, but rather communion in likemindedness. We are told in various places of Scripture that likemindedness is one of our great duties — we are not told to maintain diversity of opinion, but rather to strive for the unity of the Spirit in the bond of peace. Of course, this means we must have a willingness to be corrected, and not just show a willingness to correct others.

An important part of this humility is taught in *how* we take and eat, and not just in the fact that we do. We have encouraged you to look around, to discern the Lord's body in your brothers and sisters. But do not just note that they *are* your brothers and sisters, but also you are their brother or sister, and you are all here together.

When we sing a psalm, we are saying the same thing. When we say *amen*, we are vowing the same thing. When we eat together, when we drink together, this unified motion is a glorious display of likemindedness. We tarry for one another, and when we all have bread, we eat together. When we all have the cup we drink together.

These motions — holding, lifting, chewing, swallowing — are all a declaration of the glorious gospel. The Lord Jesus Christ is king of all nations, and this is something we want to declare all together. And so we tarry, waiting to manifest it together.

So come, and welcome, to Jesus Christ.

MORNING ☼ HOW MUCH BREAD AND WINE?

In order to correct some of the disorders that had crept into the worship of the saints at Corinth, the apostle tells them to deal with their hunger at home. Apparently, the love feast that accompanied the Eucharist in the first century was being used as an occasion to fill the belly, at the expense of others, rather than to nourish soul corporately and covenantally. And to all such, the apostle says that *physical* hunger should be fixed at home (1 Cor. 11:22).

This is a spiritual meal. But by this, we do not mean that it is an ethereal meal — the bread is true bread, and the wine is true wine. But at the same time, it is a meal that is also consumed in the heavens, where we are seated with the Lord Jesus Christ. He descends in the person of the Holy Spirit to be with us here, in our particular town. But we ascend to Him in that same Spirit so that we might eat heavenly bread and drink heavenly wine by faith. This happens regardless of the amount of bread or wine we have here. Too little would lead us astray, and we would begin to think that "heavenly" means "vaporous." Too much would lead us astray, as it did our Corinthian brothers and sisters, to the point where they became belly-gods, making a idol of the digestive system.

So be more concerned for the size of your faith, than the size of the loaf or cup.

So come, and welcome, to Jesus Christ.

Jesus tells us to do certain things in order to commune with Him. These things are not only to be done, they are to be done in a certain way. The service of the Passover was the time when He instituted the fellowship of the Lord's Supper, and we are to begin where we are told to begin. He told us to take and eat, take and drink. He did not say, "Here, figure this out." He commanded us nothing in regard to the metaphysics of bread. He did not urge us to develop a highly refined theology of wine. Such things are okay — in their place — but that place is not here.

In this place, we are commanded to love Jesus Christ, and to love His body. We are to show our love for His body by partaking of His body, along with the rest of His body.

As we partake, we are not partaking alone. We are communing. We commune with Jesus Christ, *and* with everyone that *He* communes with. We can (and should) fence this Table against any who want to live against God in a high-handed way, and yet still approach this Table. That is what church discipline is for. But we are not competent to fence the heavenly Table. It is *His* Table, after all.

How many people will be taking the Lord's Supper today? They number in the millions. Because it is a covenant meal, and because there is so much unfaithfulness in the Church, more than a few are eating and drinking condemnation. But what is that to us? We leave them to their own master (Rom. 14:4).

Our concern now is to remember that countless believers, from countless churches and denominations, are being *received* this morning by Jesus Christ Himself. You must, without knowing their names, receive them too, receive them in principle. And the best way to do that is by receiving your actual neighbor, the one sitting three rows back from you, the one with whom you have sometimes quarreled. Lay it all down. Put away the sin. Discern the body. Partake.

So come, and welcome, to Jesus Christ.

MORNING ✹ A TABLE, NOT A TROPHY

In the book of 1 Corinthians Paul sets a number of disorders concerning the Lord's Supper straight, presumably addressing the more significant disorders. But there were other disorders, as indicated by his closing words on the subject, where he said "the rest will I set in order when I come" (1 Cor. 11:34).

So we do not come to the Lord's Supper as a reward for having our act together. We come because it is one of God's appointed instruments for putting us together. We do not eat food as a reward for having grown big and strong, but rather as a means *for* growing. The Table is a Table, not a trophy.

Why then must some be kept from the Table? If the disorder is so great as to make edification impossible, then the Supper (because of the covenant curses attending it) does more harm to the offender than good.

But the things that Paul was intending to set in order when he came were not of this magnitude. These disorders took away from the Supper, but not so much that it would be better to abstain. Our Table manners may be poor, but if we still take, and eat, and chew, and swallow *in honest faith*, the Supper does its intended work. One of those works is the improvement of our manners. But for the one who pretends to be eating spiritually but is actively throwing the covenant food away, under the Table, then there will be a reckoning. Against such impudence, you are solemnly warned.

So come, and welcome, to Jesus Christ.

EVENING ◐ A GREAT DEAL WORSE

A few reminders are regularly necessary. This is the *Lord's* Table, and it does not belong to you. This means you are not in charge of the invitations and place cards, and have *no* authority to decline an invitation that has been graciously extended to you. Therefore, do not withdraw from the Table on your own authority. And lest there be any mistake, as a minster of Christ, authorized to do so, I invite every baptized believer who has not been lawfully excommunicated to come to the Table on Sunday with all humility and gladness.

But this relates to another common problem. We tend to think of the Lord's Supper as a reward for the good instead of as a remedy for the bad. God gave this Supper to help keep us from sin; we use sin to keep us from the Supper. The cases where someone wants to remain seated at the Table while sinning defiantly is a special case, one to be considered by the elders. We are, all of us, seated here as sinners, and we are, all of us, more sinful than we know. Ask God to reveal your sin to you through the Supper, rather than letting your sin obscure the Supper.

And this leads to the last consideration. The service of worship is where God deals with us, and He does so in all wisdom. When we according to our own lights meditate on how bad we are, this is an effective way to become a great deal worse. But through the sacraments He has established, He deals with us, and our sins, with all wisdom. As we come, invite Him to do so.

So come, and welcome, to Jesus Christ.

MORNING ☼ LOVE THEM NOW

God has given us bread and wine, but not so that we would be distracted by the bread and wine. Remember that we dwell in a universe created by the Word of God who both was God and was with God. The Word of God is the exact representation of the image and nature of God, and yet the Son is not identical to the Father. Yet the Father, and the Son, and the Holy Spirit are one triune God.

This means that Christ is the ultimate metaphor; He is the Word. He represents the Father perfectly, and yet He is not the Father. And He is God, and He is with God. These mysteries are certainly that — mysteries — but they are also invitations to understand everything else about our faith as mysterious.

Note that I said *mysterious,* not contradictory, or irrational. Our God-given reason is not offended by metaphor — rather, it is sanctified reason which understands metaphor.

Countless disputes have arisen among Christians over this meal, and this by itself is a good indication that we are not paying attention to the meal rightly. Christ did not say, "Take and dispute." He did not say, "Take, and philosophize." He said, "Take and eat. Take and drink." And we are to do so while discerning the body.

You are the body of Christ. Discern the body. The body here is fragmented and torn, so that you (also the body) would not be. Christ was crucified on the cross so that we would not crucify or pillory one another. This is the new commandment — and yet it is not new — love one another (Jn. 13:34).

When this lesson is learned, the most basic of all lessons, we may then ask (if we are reverent) some other questions. But unless we are loving one another, fervently, from the heart, we cannot be trusted with any other questions. And so, if you are struggling to love any of your brothers or sisters on Tuesdays or Fridays, humble yourself now, and learn to love them here, now.

So come, and welcome, to Jesus Christ.

The Lord's Table is a wedding feast, and unless we understand our relationship to Jesus Christ as our Bridegroom, and ourselves collectively as His chosen Bride, we will not understand what is happening here.

The book of 1 Corinthians has a great deal in it about the relationship of the two sexes, and we too often think that this is a separate question from how we relate to God through Christ. But Paul is very careful to connect the two subjects, so much so that we might be forgiven for thinking they are not two subjects at all.

In chapter six, Paul shows how sexual purity is closely related to the question of our unity with Christ. The body is not for fornication, but for the Lord. In chapter eleven, he "interrupts" his discussion of the Lord's Supper to talk about head coverings. But this is no interruption.

We are the woman; we are Eve. As Eve, *we* are the mother of all the living. Corporately, *we* are the heavenly Jerusalem, the mother of all who believe, as Paul puts it in Galatians.

So we are seated at the wedding feast, and we wear the bridal veil, the veil of which the Shekinah glory was a type. This glory is the glory of God, and yet it is bestowed on us. We therefore bear His image. We are the woman; He is the man.

As the woman, we are the glory of the man. As Eve, we were given to Adam. And as we partake of this Supper, we proclaim His death, and that proclamation is the imperishable seed by which new life comes. Our duty is therefore to observe this Supper rightly until we fill the earth with our children — the children we have borne to Him.

So come, and welcome, to Jesus Christ.

MORNING ☼ INVITED TO STAY

Jesus Christ invited Judas to this meal, knowing what was in his heart. Jesus Christ warned Judas about his peril, in much the same way that God warned Cain about sin lying in wait for him. And the greatest possible grace and the greatest act of treachery met together.

But the Table was not defiled. God's holiness is never defiled. The treachery of Judas was used by the sovereign hand of God to accomplish the salvation of the world, and when it was used, it was discarded. The Table is still here, and all over the world God's people are streaming to it, while the thirty pieces of silver have long vanished.

Along the shoreline, waves pound the rocks, but we should not worry about the rocks. Rank hypocrites by the thousands have come to this Table, only to break themselves on it. We do not need to worry about the Table.

We preach the gospel, we admonish, we warn — but we do not fence the Table for the sake of the Table.

Hearing these words, mindful of our own remaining sinfulness, we might be tempted to shrink back. We don't want to be broken on this Table. But *yes, you do*. That is precisely what you want. You don't want to be broken as Judas was, fair enough. But you should want to be broken as Peter was.

We are sinners, and God is holy. There is no way to come to Him without being broken. In just a moment, I am going to break the bread, in imitation of how Jesus broke the bread. If you are broken there, that way, in Him, the end result is resurrection and everlasting communion. But if you are here without trust and faith in Jesus, and you partake, then like Judas you have no choice but to go out into the night.

But you are invited to stay. You are invited to trust. You are invited to repent. You are invited, warmly and cordially, to believe in Jesus Christ, genuinely, from the heart.

So come, and welcome, to Jesus Christ.

EVENING ◐ THERE IS NO BETTER CHRIST

When the Lord walked with the two unnamed disciples on the road to Emmaus, the conclusion of the affair, as they narrated it, was that the Lord was known by them "in the breaking of the bread" (Lk. 24:35). The breaking of the bread in this scriptural usage clearly refers to the sacrament, and means we are also invited to come to know Christ better by this means. We do this by communing with Him in faith.

We also see this as a sacramental observance because in this incident the Lord Jesus saw to it that His Supper was made such by His Word that went before it. As the two put it, their hearts burned within them, as He talked with them by the way, and opened the Scriptures to them.

In the context of Christian worship, grace is never divided against itself. Every Christian who grows in grace is growing in Christ, and while Christ's body was broken, Christ is not divided. His body was broken in order to be restored whole in the resurrection.

This means that in this part of the service, or in that one, you will never get a better Christ. But if you are given faith to understand the flow and direction of the service, as the Word sets it forth, when we come to the Supper, you will get Christ better. Never look for a better Christ; there is none. Always look to see Christ better.

So come, and welcome, to Jesus Christ.

MORNING ☼ WHAT FAITH DOES

The Table of the Lord humbles the honest, comforts the distraught, forgives the repentant, nourishes the hungry, establishes the church, preaches the gospel, summons the world, and overwhelms the devil. And of course the Table as a mere set of physical objects does none of those things — any more than the Word of God, considered simply as paper and ink, does such things.

When the preached Word pierces the heart of a treacherous or hypocritical Christian, and he repents, no one thinks to attribute the power of the Word to the fact that it was leather-bound. Or, when some poor forsaken sinner picks up a Gideon Bible in a hotel somewhere and turns to Christ, no one thinks it was through the power of the paper or the ink. We attribute it all to the power and goodness of God, who moves and works *through* such things.

In the same way, as the Supper of the Lord deals with us — rebuking us, strengthening us, admonishing us, revealing our sin, establishing us in love for one another — no one in their right mind would attribute the power of this to the grocery store where we bought the wine, or the bakery where we obtained the bread. And neither is the power to be found in the bread or the wine. These things correspond exactly to the paper and ink of the Scriptures.

What are they apart from faith? The letter kills, but the Spirit brings life. Words *as* words bring nothing but condemnation. Bread *as* bread, wine *as* mere wine, are nothing but a ministry of death. What are they apart from faith alone? They are nothing but increasing condemnation.

As so, as children of faith, you are summoned to come. You are summoned so that your evangelical faith would be nourished and strengthened by the bread and wine, not replaced by the bread and wine. When faith comes to the Table, faith is always an essential part of the picture.

So come, and welcome, to Jesus Christ.

EVENING ◐ **THE BREAD AND WINE OF GRACE**

As the Lord Jesus taught His disciples on the Emmaus road, He showed them many glorious things out of the Scriptures. But before He did this, He rebuked them with the words "fools and slow of heart to believe" (Lk. 24:25). He then went on to show that the *entire* Old Testament was talking about Him. This is a rebuke we still need.

We have come now to the Lord's Supper, and we have it on the Lord's authority that this is also prefigured in the Old Testament in many ways. This is the heavenly manna, down from heaven. This is the meat of the Passover lamb, and the broken bread of the Passover meal. This cup is Jeremiah's new covenant. This is the meal that the elders of Israel shared on the mountain with Jehovah. This is the fruit of the tree of life.

But this morning, you are invited to think of it as a Table prepared for *you in the presence of your enemies.* In the midst of conflict, and impending war, and disaster, and terrors on every side, and rumors of battle, God invites you to sit and eat. He does not do so because your enemies are imaginary. They are present. But their role is to see that you share Table fellowship with the God of heaven, the God of battles, and they do not. They are envious, and filled with hatred. You are to be filled, but not with glee, not with malice, not with your own wisdom. You are to be filled with the bread and wine of *grace.*

So come, and welcome, to Jesus Christ.

MORNING ☼ IDENTIFIED THROUGH THE BREAD

One of the reasons the Table of the Lord has been controversial among Christians from the very beginning is the fact that the Table, faithfully observed, reveals the secrets of men. Not only does the faithful observance of the Supper nourish and strengthen the faithful, it also reveals and identifies Judas. Judas identified Jesus with his kiss, but Jesus identified Judas earlier with the *bread*.

This means that men who do not want their secrets revealed have to do something about this bread and wine. One of the things they do is observe the Supper rarely. If it is a risky business, then do it less frequently. Another thing is to engage in controversy about the Supper, and what it all means. Arguments at the Table are a great way to try to forget the food itself. Yet another response is to flee. If the Table is being faithfully observed in one place, it is time to find another place, where the Word accompanying the sacrament is somehow less threatening. Another method is to begin attacking those who are faithfully administering the Supper in a town in order to change the subject. If it is possible to get them off message, then perhaps the debate can be steered into a more political direction.

But we want to have no part of this. We want to worship God, sing to Him, hear His Word declared, and then partake of this meal in gladness and simplicity of heart. As we do this, no works at all, no effort at all, God moves in a mysterious way. How much work is expended in bringing the bread to your mouth? In drinking the wine? How much depends upon us?

And yet, we watch gratefully as God moves powerfully in our eating and drinking — moving kingdoms, spreading the gospel, revealing traitors, declaring the message of forgiveness in Christ, convicting the foolish, and establishing His kingdom.

So come, and welcome, to Jesus Christ.

In their ignorance, the disciples on the road to Emmaus besought Jesus to do something which we should all be seeking to do in all knowledge. As they came toward their home, the Lord made it look as though He was going to continue on, leaving them there. But they constrained Him, it says, and sought for Him to *abide* with them (Lk. 24:29).

But no one can stay together, even for a short time, without at some point eating together. And eating together consistently is the surest sign of living together.

Now the Scriptures say that we are to abide with Christ. This means that we are to be His companions. The word companion comes from two Latin antecedents, the first being *com,* meaning together, and the second being *panis,* bread. Companion refers to the act of taking bread together.

The two disciples traveled with Jesus along the road, but there was a wonderful moment when they sought to become His companions. The whole story has been revealed to us, and so how much more should we seek to be Christ's companions. It is not impudence—although it would be without His invitation. It is actually impudence to refuse the invitation, to decline the gracious command.

In these perilous times, we do not need any Christians seeking to advance the work of the faith without doing so as Christ's constant companions. As you take the bread and wine together, you are companions to one another. But never forget the fundamental issue here—you are companions of Christ.

So come, and welcome, to Jesus Christ.

MORNING ☼ YOU ARE THE MEAL

We gather together here at the Table of the Lord in order that He might feed us. We do not gather here on the assumption that the bread and wine constitute some kind of theological puzzle, the meaning of which we must figure out before we are qualified to take it. This is a meal — *nourishment*.

But this is not said so that we come to the meal ignorantly — meals have meaning also. But the meaning of a meal and the meaning of a theological puzzle are quite different.

Because this is a covenant meal, we have to recognize that the meaning is in the eating and in the drinking — not in the bread and wine as they sit here on the Table in their own right. The communion is in the communing, in the taking, in the chewing, in the drinking, and, here it is, in the loving.

Our lives are always part of the picture. Just as we ought not to ask if this part of Scripture is law or gospel, printed on the page, but rather to see that the response of love sees everything as gospel, and the response of hate sees everything as law, so it is with this meal.

In the giving of His Word, in the administration of His sacraments, God never simply "puts on a show." We are *never* spectators; we are *always* participants. As participants, we are either faithful or unfaithful participants. If faithful, we experience the meal one way. If unfaithful, we experience the meal another. But we may never ask what the essence of the meal is without the participants. The meal is nothing without the participants.

There is no communion without communicants. And as soon as you have communicants, you have sin that will repent, sin that won't repent, faith that will persevere, faith that staggers and will be strengthened. What is this meal? *You* are this meal.

That is why the apostle insists that you look around, and see Christ in the bread — for *you* are the bread.

So come, and welcome, to Jesus Christ.

As they walked along the road, one of the two disciples, named Cleopas, asked the Lord if He was a stranger (Lk. 24:18). *Do you not know what has gone on these past few days?* What an ironic question — "do you not know?" The other disciple is unnamed, but was probably the wife of Cleopas, who was named Mary. We know very little about both of them, and yet we do know that they were privileged to live through one of the most winsome resurrection accounts.

So let us take this lesson from it. At the Table of the Lord, there are *no little people*. Male, female, husband, wife, adult, child, slave, free, black, white, Jew, Greek — no one has to eat off in the kitchen with the servants. If you are lawfully seated at this Table, then it is for one reason only — you are called a friend of God. He does not know you simply in the aggregate. He does not invite you to sit and eat because you were standing with a certain clump of people.

Covenantally, we do constitute the Bride of Christ and that corporate, covenant reality is important. But it does not change the fact that this Bride is made up of her members, great and small. Every faithful saint has a white stone, with his name inscribed on it, and that stone marks your place here. Are you baptized? Do you believe in the Lord Jesus? You are most welcome.

So come, and welcome, to Jesus Christ.

MORNING ☼ SOLI DEO GLORIA

During His earthly ministry Jesus scandalized the "proper" crowd by sitting down and eating with sinners. Two thousand years later, He is still doing it. That is why He is here with us today, and why He is seated at this Table. I mean, look around you. Look at your own heart, and your own history. And then consider that you have been invited *here*. One of the first things that should occur to you is that Jesus doesn't seem to care about His reputation *at all*.

This meal is food for the hungry — food for the starving. It is not dessert for the well-fed. It is not a reward for the righteous. It is not a ribbon for your trophy case. This is God's soup kitchen, and we are the derelicts and winos, fresh off the street.

But imagine a wino taking pride over some of his fellows because he is *inside* the soup kitchen while they are still *outside*. "Poor, benighted heathen," he says to himself. Having imagined the picture, you have a good image of what many "proper" Christians have done — they have turned everything around, and have misunderstood the graciousness of grace.

We must never let the nobility of what we have *become* in Jesus obscure for us in the slightest a vision of what we *were*, and what we would still be apart from Him. The apostle Peter reminds us not to forget that we have been cleansed from our past sins (2 Pet. 1:9). When we forget our past sinfulness, this does not make us holy, it rather plunges us into the peculiar kind of sinfulness developed by the well-scrubbed and highly respectable Pharisee. "I thank thee, Lord, that I am not as other men. *Soli Deo gloria!*"

The human heart is slippery and bears constant watching. We can even take pride in the fact that *we* understand that we can't take pride in anything. "I thank thee, Lord, that I am not as this Arminian who boasts in his own understanding." So come. But come in grace. Come with humility of mind and heart. Come with genuine gratitude.

So come, and welcome, to Jesus Christ.

The various aspects of our worship service were shown forth in a type in the sacrificial system of the Old Testament. We come before God confessing our sins, which is the guilt offering, and we offer up the name of Jesus Christ, which cleanses all our guilt. Then our service corresponds to the ascension offering, sometimes called the burnt offering. We ascend to the Father, as smoke ascends from the altar, and through Jesus Christ, we are a sweet smelling savor to Him.

We come now to the portion of the service which corresponds to the peace offering. In this offering, God communes with the worshiper, and sits down and eats with him. When the two disciples from Emmaus recognized Jesus, they hastened back to Jerusalem that night in order to tell the others. When they got there, they heard news that the Lord had appeared to Simon. They then told their story, and how the Lord was known by them in the breaking of the bread. When they had said this, the Lord appeared to them all, and what He said to them was significant, and He says it again now. His words were, "Peace be unto you." The disciples then were terrified, but the Lord calmed their fears. Let Him do the same now.

This is a Table of peace, not war. This is a Table of resolution, not conflict. This is a Table of kindness, not malice. This is a Table of reconciliation, not estrangement. This is the Table of everlasting life. As you partake, peace be unto you.

So come, and welcome, to Jesus Christ.

MORNING ☼ HEAD AND HEART

The metaphor we use of *head* and *heart* is not really a scriptural metaphor, but we are referring to a profound scriptural truth when we use it. James points to the truth that this metaphor of ours is highlighting when he talks about hearing the word and doing the word.

But there are certain lessons from Scripture that are easy for us to grasp in a head-kind-of-way, and others are slippery because they address fundamental heart issues. In the first category, we might place learning the names of the apostles, or memorizing the ten commandments, or figuring out how to trace the missionary journeys of Paul. Pretty straightforward.

But in the second category we would have to place truths like the following: that God likes sinners and delights to forgive them, that Jesus spent time talking with prostitutes and IRS men and offered the kingdom to them, that the kingdom of the heavens is not to be propagated by main force, that the least will be the greatest, and that children are just fantastic.

We have spent so much time getting our hair combed in orthodox and acceptable ways, the part on the side being as straight as the cunning of man can make it, and yet the Holy Spirit comes in a gust and blows everything all over everywhere. And we look in the mirror and say, "I can't come to His Table looking like *this*!" Ah, but it is the only acceptable way for you to come. Do not come here because you finally have it all together. Those who do this are only kidding themselves.

But there is another temptation as well. Don't think that if it is your duty to come here in this Spirit-created disheveled state that it is somehow acceptable for you to attempt similar effects by yourself with your own hair drier. We have no autonomous control over what makes us acceptable. In our own wisdom, we cannot be put together, or taken apart. God is God — surrender it all to Him. And that means sitting down at this meal, in simple trust, now.

So come, and welcome, to Jesus Christ.

Many of our liturgical practices and beliefs rest upon a slander of God's character. We say things about Him that are certainly true in the abstract, but in context they are completely out of whack.

For example, in the course of Israel's religious calendar, God appointed for them one fast day, the Day of Atonement. He also appointed eighty feast days. That is quite a ratio, and the fact that most Christians would be surprised by this indicates that we have been bringing certain hidden assumptions about God the Killjoy to our reading of the text.

Those same assumptions have driven us to interpret this meal as a time of mourning, sadness, and virtual fasting. Since we think it is a fast, and yet because the ceremony inescapably consists of a meal, we split the difference and so we nibble and sip, minimally.

But this is a *festival*. We are to keep the festival, Paul says, by getting rid of the yeast of malice and wickedness (1 Cor. 5:8). We are to turn away from those who would pollute the feast with their licentiousness, Jude tells us (v. 12).

The word Eucharist comes from the Greek word for giving thanks. Were our November holiday of Thanksgiving celebrated in the first century, they would have called it the Eucharist.

What does this mean? Among other things, it means joy, overflow, gladness, thanksgiving, contentment, peace, and harmony.

If you need to kick yourself around a little bit for your sins, feel free. *But do it before you get here*. This is not the place for it. For those procrastinators among us, we take a moment to confess our unconfessed sins early in the service. A doormat at the front door does not accuse you of tromping in the mud, but it recognizes the possibility. Take care of business *then*. Here, rejoice in the fact that God has accepted you. He delights in you. He wants you here. Stop sulking at His dinner Table. Smile. Enjoy the company.

So come, and welcome, to Jesus Christ.

MORNING ☼ EATING THE WORLD

When we consider the image of the loaf before us, we need to remember the imagery that is brought to bear by all of Scripture, and not just the passages that deal with the Lord's Supper directly. For example, the apostle Paul teaches us that we are the one loaf of bread, and he presses this point so that we would discern one another as members of Christ (1 Cor. 10:17).

But the image is more textured than just this. In His parable of the leaven, Jesus tells us that the kingdom of God is like yeast mixed into the dough (Matt. 13:33). In this image, the world is the loaf — and the yeast is mixed in with this in a complex and messy way. But this messiness is presented in such a way as to make us realize that the yeast transforms the dough, and that the dough has no power to transform the yeast. Moreover this process has been going on since the foundation of the world. The world has never been without its yeast, although there have been centuries in which it *looked* as though it were without yeast.

We are privileged to live in a time when we can actually see the dough started to rise — but these things were true before we could see them.

So what are we doing when we eat of this loaf? Among other things, we are declaring our faith that *we* are that loaf. Looking forward in faith to the time when the present kingdom is manifested far more clearly, and the entire world is converted to God, we are preaching the gospel to a lost and forsaken world, and we are doing so by typologically eating the world.

What is it that overcomes the world? Is it not our faith? But we do not overcome the world, or conquer the world, through any sort of gun-barrel justice. We do it by speaking the Word, and eating and drinking the Word. Conducted in faith, this proclamation is *potent*. So let us come with gladness and simplicity of heart.

So come, and welcome, to Jesus Christ.

EVENING ◐ CHRIST IN THE FACE OF OTHERS

God's saints are not made out of simple and discrete blocks of wood. We are complex beings to begin with, and our sinfulness only complicates matters. As we approach the Table of the Lord this morning, take special care not to abuse it through tenaciously clutching to your own opinions about others.

Too many Christians have a high doctrine of sin when it comes to judging the thoughts, motives, and intents of other people. But rather, the true theologian in these matters is one who questions himself *first*, and then, when necessary and demanded, cautiously approaches a brother about possible sin on his part.

You can know (sometimes) what a brother has said or done. And the Bible says that it is *possible* to know that what he has done is in fact a sin. But when it comes to judging *motives* — considering *why* your brother has done or not done something — the Word teaches that you are almost certainly wrong, and if you are right, it is almost certainly an accident. The Spirit of God alone is competent here; a man cannot even know his own heart — so how can a man standing ten feet away test and try the heart and reins of another?

We are coming to the Lord's Table and have a responsibility to discern the Lord's body *in one another*. In doing this, look away from their hearts — you cannot see them anyway. Look to one another's faces, and see there the image of Jesus Christ.

So come, and welcome, to Jesus Christ.

MORNING ☼ A REAL MESS ON THE BEACH

The kingdom of heaven, Jesus taught, is like a dragnet. It hauls in *everything* that it finds in its path (Matt. 13:47). And so it is that we here, seated at this Table in history, must necessarily sit down with — to mix our metaphors — good fish, bad fish, broken beer bottles, reptiles, weeds, and old bicycle tires.

Jesus does promise us that the fish will all be sorted out at the end. The judgment at the end of history will be as exacting as promised, and in that final sorting there will be nothing that gets by Him. But this is the promised judgment at the *end* of history. We are living in the middle of history, and when we consider the state of the church today, we are up to our necks in refuse. This has made some of us think that God is not the right kind of fisherman.

But He did not say that the kingdom of God is like a fly fisherman, hand-tying his lures, and selecting just the right mountain stream, laboring faithfully to catch the rainbow trout of the elect, and only the rainbow trout of the elect, in order to bring them all home in the basket of the pure church.

No, the kingdom of God is a real *mess* on the beach. And we cannot fix everything by scootching together with other pure souls to have a "separated church" in one corner of the dragnet. Whatever makes us think that to cross the street (putting up another sign for *another* church) in any way alters the content of the dragnet? We cannot do in the midst of this process what Jesus said would only happen at the end of it.

One caveat. We do want to take all Scripture into account here. We *do* have the authority (and the competence) to excommunicate — to throw the bicycle tire out of the net before the Second Coming. But we should be very wary of our tendency in wanting to rush these things — unchecked, we want to throw other good fish out because they are speckled differently than we are.

So come, and welcome, to Jesus Christ.

As we seek to be brought to maturity through this Table, by the Lord who presides over this Table, we must take care to heed His teaching. The Word always accompanies the sacrament, and as we sit at this Table, we do not sit in silence. The Lord from His position at the head of the Table is not quiet.

He speaks to us constantly — we are held responsible to listen. When He spoke with the disciples on the Emmaus road, Luke tells us this about Jesus, who began with Moses and all the prophets: "he expounded unto them *in all the scriptures* the things concerning himself" (Lk. 24:27). Jesus is not here and there in the Old Testament; He resides on every page. This meal is the culmination of all the covenant meals of the Old Testament; it is the fulfillment of every festival; it is the place where God feeds us with manna, fruit from the tree of life; water from the rock; forgiveness from the impaled serpent; and water over the threshold of the Temple.

If the Old Testament is a closed book in your life, then when you come to this Table, in ignorance and disobedience your mouth is closed. Open your mouth, God says through the psalmist, and I will fill it (Ps. 81:10). Read your Bibles. Open your mouths, then, doing it the way you are instructed. You are the children of Israel, the offspring of Abraham, lesser sons of David — you are all invited to sit with us here. But when it comes time to eat, *open* your mouths. Open your hearts to encouragement. Open your minds to Scripture. One greater than Solomon is here.

So come, and welcome, to Jesus Christ.

MORNING ✹ THE CUP OF GOD'S FORGETFULNESS

The kingdom of heaven, Jesus taught, is a kingdom of *grace*. And this means that when we are coming into the presence of Christ, the prince over this kingdom, we are *not* coming into the presence of an unforgiving scorekeeper.

We too often project our lack of forgiveness onto Him. We assume that He is as bitter, or as unyielding, or as difficult to entreat, as we can sometimes be. But He is not like this at all. He forgives.

In the words of institution, which you have heard many times, this cup is called the cup of the new testament. This is a reference to the glorious new covenant promised by Jeremiah, and what is involved in that new covenant? Here are the words of promise: "Their sins and iniquities will I remember no more" (Heb. 10:17).

God the Father will remember no more. Jesus Christ will remember no more. The Holy Spirit will remember no more. *What* does our triune God not remember? The answer is our sins, and our iniquities. Now *iniquities* sounds pretty serious, but there it is, right in the Bible. God forgets them. You are here, worshiping Him in faith, and this means that He is unconcerned with your past sins. He does not care about your previous iniquities. They do not enter into His calculations on how to deal with you.

You have, at this Table, the greatest privilege that a sinful creature could ever have. In just a few moments, a cup will be offered to you. And what is that cup? It is the cup of the new covenant, and this means it is *the cup of God's forgetfulness*. And you are invited, summoned, *commanded*, to drink it.

Receive this in faith. You are being offered God's forgetfulness, and only the death of His Son could make such an impossible thing possible. So swallow God's kindness. Swallow His grace. Swallow His forgetfulness.

So come, and welcome, to Jesus Christ.

We are sometimes urged away from understanding the types of Scripture on the basis of authority. Yes, people say, there may be typological significance to many aspects of Scripture, but we are not the Lord, and we are not his apostles and prophets. What authority do we have to interpret this way?

This overlooks the rebukes of Scripture. The Lord Jesus, as He was teaching the disciples on the road, before He revealed Himself in the breaking of the bread, admonished them this way — "fools, and slow of heart to believe all that the prophets have spoken" (Lk. 24:25). It is true that Jesus spoke the truth when He unveiled Himself in the Old Testament, but it is also true that He expected every reader of the Old Testament to have already seen Him there, and He rebuked them when they did not.

Our task, therefore, is to throw ourselves on His mercy, and submit to His shaping of us in worship. But just as some fools lag behind in their laziness, so other fools run ahead, thinking they have peered into great mysteries when they have only spun idle fancies in their own heads. Christ is in the Old Testament, all of it, but He is not there in every conceivable way. We see Christ in the rock that accompanied the Israelites, and in the impaled serpent upon the pole, and in the manna, but we do not see Him in Pharoah, or in the golden calf.

In handling the Scriptures typologically, the common (and proper) question is this: "Where are the brakes? How do we know this, or that?" The answer is here — Christ reveals Himself to us *here,* when we come in true, evangelical faith. So, come in true and humble faith.

So come, and welcome, to Jesus Christ.

MORNING ☼ FORGET IT

So, we all accept that the cup we drink is the cup of the new covenant. One of the fundamental terms of the new covenant is the glorious promise that God will remember our sins no more. This, therefore, is the cup of God's forgetfulness.

What of the bread? We are told that the bread is the body of Christ Jesus, and that we are the body of Christ Jesus. In this Supper, we are told to look to one another, and to see Christ there.

Now as you look around the sanctuary at all the other saints gathered here, what thought comes to mind? Is it "saints, ha!"? Are you perhaps mindful of the person across the room, or perhaps sitting right next to you, who has done or said an unkind thing to you? And perhaps they did it just this morning?

But God's Word remains sure, regardless of what men do or say. You are still (all of you together) the body of Jesus Christ. When God looks at you, He sees Jesus Christ. When He looks at you, He sees the perfections of Jesus. When you look at one another, you are commanded *to see the same thing*. This can only be done by faith, and it is a lesson that even the apostle Paul spent time learning. Even though we once knew Christ after the flesh, now we do so no longer. And for this reason, we no longer know any man after the flesh either (2 Cor. 5:16). There are many things that go with this, but surely one of them is forgetfulness. Love covers a multitude of sins. This is a Table of Love. So what should be happening here? *Forget* it.

Our minds rush to the scriptural exceptions so that we can establish loopholes in principle. And once we have the loophole, we can refuse to forget petty offenses against ourselves. If we are not to simply "forget" bank robberies, or serial murders, or such things that involve the police, then we insist that we must be permitted our little grudges. No, this Table forbids that.

So come, and welcome, to Jesus Christ.

EVENING ◐ MEDIATED GLORY

Jesus tells His disciples on the Emmaus road that everything in the Old Testament pointed toward the sufferings of Christ. But He said something else as well, which is also ministered to us in this meal. He said that Christ had to suffer these things, and "enter into his glory" (Lk. 24:27).

What does this glory entail? We must not be limited by any one metaphor. He is above all things, head over heaven and earth. He is at the center of all things, everything radiates from Him. He is the one who holds all things together. He is before all things, and after them as well. He is the alpha and omega. He is beneath all things, the only foundation. Jesus Christ came to make all things new. Not only so, but the Bible tells us that this was not a vain attempt. He succeeded.

We often forget this, but we have to remember that the sun shines, regardless of how many men are blind. We live in the new heavens and the new earth. Jesus Christ is Lord of all. Jesus Christ is enthroned in His glory, and this glory is present everywhere. Do you fail to see it? Then humble yourself, take and eat.

So come, and welcome, to Jesus Christ.

MORNING ☼ GREAT JOY IN THE OPENING

In the resurrection account in Luke 24, we are told several times about the joy of the disciples. In v. 41 it says that they did not believe for joy, and after Christ's ascension, it says that they returned to Jerusalem with *great* joy (v. 57).

We are also told several times in the account that the foundation of their joy was the fulfillment of Scripture. The resurrection of Christ was not presented to the disciples as "raw data," something they could testify to on the basis of their experience alone. To the disciples from Emmaus, Jesus taught them from the Old Testament Scriptures, and then He revealed Himself to them in the breaking of the bread.

When He appeared to the disciples back in Jerusalem, He ate first in their presence (as a proof), and then He opened the Scriptures. After opening the Scriptures, it says that He opened their understanding (vv. 43–45).

God is not limited to this bread or this wine. But neither is He limited to other spiritual exercises we have cooked up on our own authority. The Spirit always moves where and as He wills, and accomplishes what He wants. In faith, we are asking Him to accomplish it here. We are asking Him to reveal Himself to us now in accordance with His Word.

We have opened the Word this morning. We are opening the bread and the wine now. May God open our hearts. The sign that He has done so is always the same—*great joy.*

So come, and welcome, to Jesus Christ.

This Table, and the Word accompanying it, are means of grace. But grace is not an invisible fluid that juices you up in your devotional life, grace is the word Scripture uses for how God imparts Himself to us. When the gracious God gives Himself, this is grace.

And we know that we are receiving this gift of God imparting Himself to the extent that we are becoming gracious ourselves. It is not the case that God is pouring out an impersonal grace fluid into so many assembled grace receptacles, so many grace buckets.

Grace is a feature of relationship. God is gracious to you, and imparts grace to you, because you are His friend. Moreover, as you function in this friendship, understanding it, you will function in friendship and brotherhood with everyone else who is receiving the same gift from Him. That would include everyone else here. You can identify them readily enough — they are the ones who eat the bread and drink the wine with you.

Being gracious to them is not the price of the ticket so that you can gain admittance to this "ritual." Rather, graciousness is the evidence that you have participated in this ritual in faith, understanding it. In this sacrament, God is dealing with all of us. Moreover, He is dealing with us according to His nature, which is gracious.

If we were gracious to begin with, we would not need this grace. But we are not gracious to begin with — we are ornery Pharisees, full of good works and all round cussedness.

To change the metaphor, we do not assemble here to take the bath as a reward for staying so clean. But neither are we here to take a bath that does nothing for us with regard to cleanliness, one way or the other.

Eat and drink, and as you do so in evangelical faith, you receive the grace of God. But beware — as you eat and drink the grace of God, you grow up into graciousness.

So come, and welcome, to Jesus Christ.

MORNING ✹ FENCING TO FEED

In Luke 22:3, we are told that Satan entered into Judas before the feast of unleavened bread drew nigh. By this, we should be reminded of what an unimpressive spiritual event the institution of the Lord's Supper appeared to be.

Judas the traitor was there, and this meant that Satan was also there. Peter was there, boastful and proud. He would never deny the Lord, and the Lord rebuked His pride. And at that same Supper, a squabble broke out among the disciples as to who would be accounted the greatest. If we were to look at the mere externals, we might be justified in thinking that Satan was presiding over that Table, and not our Lord.

And if we were to look at *our* lives over the course of this last week, at our attitudes, at our sins of omission, we might draw the same conclusion. But the central evidence of our folly is our notion that this disqualifies us from the Supper rather than the reverse.

Are you a sinner? Then you qualify. Are you a mess? Then come. Are you fearful of defiling the Supper? No man has ever successfully defiled it, and no man who ever feared defiling it ever received anything but great blessing.

Food exists to feed — it is not a reward for not being hungry. This is a covenant meal, not an awards ceremony.

Do you have scruples about coming? Are you afraid that we are not fencing the Table as we ought, since we allow you to come? You are right in this one thing — we do not fence the Table. The Table fences us in order to feed us.

So come, and welcome, to Jesus Christ.

When we assemble at this Table we are doing more than simply gathering to be nourished — although that is right at the center of what we do. We also are showing the world *where* we gather to be nourished.

When a bunch of kids are playing in the neighborhood on a summer afternoon, imagine five or six mothers appearing at their doors around the same time and calling out that dinner is ready. The kids all scatter, and run where? They run to their own homes — the Table that is set is one of the means for identifying who belongs where.

This Table is also a household Table. In fact, it is *the* household Table. But there is a difference as well. In the illustration just given, it is not infrequent that one child might be invited to come as a guest to a friend's house. If we followed the illustration out, why would we not invite "company" to this Table as well? Could we not invite members of other religious faiths here, just as company?

The answer is found in the fact that the Lord does not just feed His children; He has declared His intent to adopt all children. Because of this, it would not be right to say that other children of other households are not invited. They *are* invited — but they are not just invited to come share a meal or two. They are invited to come into the family, and to come into the family forever.

So we do not keep anyone back from this Table. Far from it. We invite everyone. But to partake of the meal is to agree that you have become a child of God, and if you agree to these terms, then you must also have submitted to what the Lord says his children need to do. The first thing they need to do before coming to the Table is wash — which is why we limit access to those who are baptized. If someone were here who wanted to come to the Table, but who did not want to be baptized, this would simply show that they think the Table is their own, and not the Lord's. But we would still invite them — to be baptized.

So come, and welcome, to Jesus Christ.

MORNING ☼ NEVERTHELESS

Jesus told His disciples that the cup of the Lord's Supper was the new testament in His blood. But later, in the Garden, when He agonized over His fast approaching death, He prayed that the cup would pass from Him. He was in such agony over this that His sweat was like blood, falling down to the ground (Lk. 22:44).

Put these things together. Jesus prayed that the new testament would not come to pass. *Nevertheless* — what an important word that is! Jesus Christ was obedient to the point of death because His Father willed it. Jesus therefore emptied Himself, taking the form of a servant. He did not cling to His own will, but rather subordinated His own will to the will of His Father in heaven. It was the Father who determined to bring you into fellowship with Himself by this means. Jesus Christ acknowledged the sovereign authority of His Father, and learned obedience through the things that He suffered, and saw clearly the joy that was set before Him.

But note carefully: that joy included you, sitting here now. The cup that is set before you now is therefore beyond all reckoning, beyond all price. Behold what manner of love is this, that we should be called children of God.

So come, and welcome, to Jesus Christ.

EVENING ◐ THE EUCHARISTIC GIFT OF THANKS

The goodness of God is seen everywhere, and in everything, but it is particularly evident in the gift of food. One of our customs is to "say grace" every time we partake of a meal, and this is actually a very sound tradition. The Bible doesn't command it anywhere, but it is truly a devout reflex that does not want any opportunity to thank God for food to pass by us.

That being the case for ordinary food, how much more should we thank God for this food. In the first place, it is a Eucharistic meal, and the word *eucharist* means thanksgiving. How could we partake of the very food of thanksgiving without being eager to give thanks?

Secondly, God has given us this food to strengthen us for our walk with Him, and so this supplies you with the grace to enjoy everything else in your life rightly. And so, if you are thankful for your marriage, your job, your home, your children, it is here that you continue to receive the grace of thanksgiving to continue your thanksgiving. Saying *thank you* takes something, and God gives you what you need in order to be able to do it.

Third, Jesus Christ did not die for you on this Table — He died outside Jerusalem, outside the camp, two thousand years ago. This Table is a memorial of that sacrifice, a memorial not only for us, but also for God. Just as the rainbow reminds God not to flood the earth again, so this Table reminds Him not to hold your sins against you. Do not allow your grasp of certain theological truths get in the way of this. Of course, God does not need any reminders — He knows everything. And this is yet another reason to be thankful. He stoops in yet another way, and gives to us the great privilege of reminding Him that we are a forgiven people.

This is all tied in with the mystery of creation, and the nature of the Creator/creature divide, for which we are also thankful.

So come, and welcome, to Jesus Christ.

MORNING ☼ RELIEF AND ANGUISH

We know that this is a covenantal Table. The cup is explicitly called the cup of the new covenant. But covenants have sanctions; when the covenants of God are abused by faithless men, He does not just sit idly by. At Corinth, Paul explains that some there were sick and some had even died because of their self-centered abuse of the Table. That abuse was measured by their willingness to squabble with fellow members of the same loaf.

Our temptation, in these days of feel good religion, is to forget that God is a jealous God, and that He guards His sacred things with sanctions. If we grow in our scriptural understanding to the point where we believe sanctions *are* a possibility, we assume that they will take the form of an unmistakable lightning bolt from the sky, and all mankind will see that "that person was bad." But the work of the Spirit is often far more subtle (not always, but often).

In some instances, the sanctions come in the form of what can easily be dismissed as "coincidental" troubles. No one could *prove* that these difficulties in the business, or marriage, or in family relations, or health are the result of hidden sin. No one knows but the Spirit, and the person who is running from the Spirit. And the person who is running should certainly stop and consider the possibilities.

In other instances, the sanction comes in the form of an increasing awareness (a tangled awareness that combines relief and anguish) that the day of repentance is gaining on you. You may now know that the day of repentance is inevitable, and that you will have to confess, and make restitution, and seek forgiveness from others you have wronged. But the strength and humility for that task seems beyond you. Yet every time you come to the Table, there it is, again.

But this is good news, not condemnation. This bread and wine remind you weekly that it *will* be put right, you *will* repent, you *will* seek forgiveness.

So come, and welcome, to Jesus Christ.

As His passion drew near, the Lord told His disciples that He desired to eat the Passover with them, but He said this in a way that emphasized that desire strongly. He said, "With desire I have desired . . ."(Lk. 22:15).

As far as it goes, it is good that we have an accurate view of ourselves and our own unworthiness. But at the same time, when God gives us this understanding by His grace, we must not cling to that understanding obstinately when He then tells us how much He rejoices in us, delights over us, wants to be with us, and how He has removed every impediment to fellowship.

We sometimes love our doctrine of depravity more than we love the one who delivered us from the reality of that depravity. We spend all our time muttering that we are not worthy to eat with Him. Of course not — that is the *point*.

We say that we cannot come, our hands are filthy. But Jesus says, come — I will wash them. We say that we cannot come, for our understanding is weak. But Jesus says, come — I will teach you. We say that we cannot come, for we are unsure of His love for us. But Jesus says, come — I bled for you. We say that we cannot come, for we have different doctrinal understandings of what happens in the Supper. But Jesus says, come — all that matters is that I meet with you in the Supper. We say that the food is not suitable for our weak stomachs. But Jesus still says come. He is the one who prepared it. Do you take issue with *Him*?

So, come. Eat and drink. You are the forgiven.

So come, and welcome, to Jesus Christ.

MORNING ✵ THE TABLE OF ACCEPTANCE

We are a conservative church. We believe the Bible. We hold to the tenets of the Reformed faith, and we have no patience with the deeds of the Nicolaitans, which God also hates. With all this being the case, this meal could easily turn into a banquet of self-congratulation.

But it is a meal for sinners. Forgiven sinners, to be sure, but still sinners for all that. This is not said so that we would somehow acquiesce in this condition — if anyone is in Christ, he is a new creation, and is summoned by the Scriptures to live that way. But this is the grace of God, mediated through faith in the Word declared.

It is not the grace of God, mediated through mere membership in a Bible-believing church. In short, conservatives can really screw up their lives, marriages, and families too. And conservatives can be tempted to look at the guilt-spattered wall of the lives and be tempted to try to hose it down with various tricks they have learned from the first Adam. Those tricks would include, but not be limited to, resolutions to get better, dedication to external good works, faithful attendance when the church doors are open, memorization of uplifting phrases, and other appalling substitutes for Jesus.

Grace does not dangle conditions in front of you. Grace does not prod you down the road with a stick. Grace is your present possession. You have it. Act like you have it.

This Table is not a reward for all you good people. This Table is nourishment for those who understand they are called to grow in what they have already been given. This Table is not the finish line; it is the body and blood of the one who already ran the race, and who already made it to the finish line, and who has bestowed that great accomplishment on you, for you to participate in.

This is not the Table of striving. This is not the Table of "I'll try to be better tomorrow." This is the Table of the Beloved, and of your complete acceptance in Him.

So come, and welcome, to Jesus Christ.

As the Lord broke the bread of life and gave the cup of the new testament, He said that the hand of the one who was to betray Him was resting on the same Table. He also said that the Son of man was going just as it had been determined in the counsel of God, but He pronounced a woe unto the man through whom it came. Thus He put all turmoil about predestination and human responsibility to rest. God's purposes *will* be done, but woe to those who do evil.

The proper response to this is to worship and bow down, and not to catch at words. Every hand on that first Table, the Lord's excepted, was a defiled hand. Everyone who has come to the Table since that first Supper has been a sinner. Peter partook and then denied the Lord. The others partook and then fled in the face of danger. All of them partook and then began arguing about which was the greatest. And when the Lord offered the Supper to them, and to us, He knew all about our folly and sinfulness. He does not demand perfection so that we might earn the right to come. He invites, so that He might fashion us into the true image of God, the image of the Lord Jesus.

The only one He pronounced a woe upon was Judas, a man in obvious high rebellion. Are you in such high rebellion? It would be better for you to drop dead where you are than to ever taste another morsel from His Table in *that* condition.

But are you simply a sinner, troubled by that sin? Then come. Are you at odds with a brother? Then come. Do you struggle with lust? Then come. Do you find yourself looking down on others? Then come. These are all manifestations of your desperate need for a different kind of food, food that is not carnal or earthly. This is bread baked in Heaven, this is wine from the vineyards of Paradise. This food from above, like wisdom from above, it is first of all peaceable.

You are a sinner, but through the gospel, you are at peace with God. So take and eat. Take and drink.

So come, and welcome, to Jesus Christ.

MORNING ☼ MEETING AT THE APPOINTED PLACE

When God feeds His people He uses means. These means are called means of grace. They do not bring grace to you the way a bucket carries water, but they are means of grace. So what does this mean?

The biblical formula is that God saves and sanctifies us by grace through faith. Different wings of the church have tried to separate these two, as though that were possible. But *sola fide* and *sola gratia* make no biblical sense apart from each other.

One error is to focus on the means of grace themselves, considered in themselves — the forms of prayer, or the reading of Scripture, or the partaking of the sacraments, or attendance at church.

Others see how foolish and superstitious this is, and they overreact in the opposite direction. True, evangelical faith is necessary in all these operations, they say, which is quite true, but then they go on to say, wrongly, that true evangelical faith does not need these appointed means. And so the person goes out into the field and "believes" God, without using the appointed means of grace.

But we believe that God meets us in the Scripture, and that He does not do so in the same way in other, uninspired books. We have to read in faith, but reading the newspaper in faith will not get the same results. God promises to meet us in that unique way in His Word, and not somewhere else.

It is the same with the Lord's Supper. The Lord has promised to meet with His people here in a unique way. Not somewhere else, but here. Does this make evangelical faith superfluous? Of course not. But if we have evangelical faith, does that make the meal superfluous? Can you exercise that faith, walk away from this meal, and receive the same spiritual blessings outside? The answer is, again, of course not.

God meets us where He has promised to meet us.

So come, and welcome, to Jesus Christ.

The Lord Jesus, as He established the sacrament of the Lord's Supper, taught His disciples about another kind of authority, one that does not depend upon who shall be reputed the greatest. He also taught that it did not depend upon how people might flatter the one who holds to carnal power — when someone exercises lordship the way the Gentiles do it is only prudent to call them beneficent benefactors.

It does not depend upon what people are accounted as — in this case the greatest. Nor does it depend upon them arranging to be called that which is spiritually correct. Rather, the one who desires to be greatest must behave as the younger, and the one who is chief must be the chief servant.

As you partake of the Lord's Supper today, and as you discern the Lord's body in the saints around you, consider how you might serve them, how you might give to them. This is not the same as seeking a *reputation* for serving, which is quite a different thing.

Connect this supper to what you will do for others this afternoon and evening. Our Lord was broken apart so that we might be put back whole. Our imitation of Him extends to this — we are to be broken apart as well, in a way that restores others and ourselves to them. Are you married to your own opinions and does it separate you from a brother? Are you convinced that you are right, and so disrupt the body? *There is a deeper right than being right.* Are you among those that serve? Some that serve have a tray in their hands and some do not. But always remember that in the kingdom of God the Table waiters in truth take the first place.

So come, and welcome, to Jesus Christ.

MORNING ☼ CONVENIENCE STORE HOLINESS

We too often want convenience store holiness. We are impatient with our sins in the wrong way, meaning that we want and demand quick fixes for our problems. We want a holiness that will straighten out the pressing problems we have created for ourselves, and we want it shrink-wrapped and hanging on a rack. We want to impulse buy our way into a better life. But our God dwells in eternity. He is not fulfilling His purposes for us on a timer, and cannot be brought to a panic.

Picture a world where the oak trees are a thousand feet high, taking thirty thousand years to grow. That is what holiness for redeemed creatures is like. And when the rain falls on such a tree, it does no good to bustle up thirty seconds later and ask, "Well, what good did that do?"

God nourishes His saints in this meal, but He is nourishing and preparing you for everlasting life with Him. He is not giving you an energy bar so that you have a little more hustle for pursuing your own impatient agenda.

As God is nourishing us, He is growing us up into His character, the fruit of His Holy Spirit. One of those characteristics is patience. It does no good to pray, "Lord, I want patience and I want it now!" You should have it now, and He is working His character into you now, but demanding it now means that you do not have what you demand — and as long as you think of it that way, you will not have it.

When you present yourself before the Lord here, week after week, He works in you every time. He nourishes every time. He confronts sin every time. He works the sin in your heart up toward the surface every time. The process is inexorable. And once we begin to feel what He is doing, we sometimes abandon our impatience, and try to resist the outworking of what His Spirit is doing. But whether we are patient, God is certainly patient. And He knows His purpose here.

So come, and welcome, to Jesus Christ.

EVENING ◐ UPSIDE-DOWN CONQUEST

At the establishment of the Lord's Supper, the Lord Himself occupied the position of the server. Who is greater, He asked, the one who sits and eats, or the one who serves? And yet, He, the Lord, was the one who served.

More than this, He has done the same thing at every celebration of this Supper since then. The Lord binds the apron of a waiter on, and brings us the meal of the new covenant. It does not matter how deficient the elements have been, or how quarrelsome and unworthy the recipients have been. He serves those who are unworthy to be served.

He did this in order to establish His kingdom. He said that He appointed unto them a kingdom—but the lesson must never be forgotten. The princes of this kingdom—apostles, prophets, ministers, elders—must be as the king of it. If He stooped to serve, what must we do?

We are strengthened by this meal of the new covenant, but it nourishes us to grow up into nature of it. Our bones are strengthened by this humility, and God does it to strengthen us *to* humility. Serve one another, therefore. Feed one another.

It is through this gospel humility that God will continue His upside-down conquest of the world.

So come, and welcome, to Jesus Christ.

MORNING ☼ REGAL COMMUNION

The disciples, Jesus said, were those who continued with Him in his temptations. And closely associated with this, He said that He appointed to them a kingdom, just as the Father had appointed one unto Him.

Confession of sin is certainly appropriate in the worship of God, but it belongs in our first approach to Him, which is why we confess our sins at the beginning of the service. The Lord's Supper is not primarily a time of introspection and confession. Jesus says at the institution of the covenant meal that it is in that context that His followers "eat and drink at my table in my kingdom," sitting on thrones judging the tribes of Israel (Lk. 22:30). This is a regal banquet, where the sons and daughters of the Prince of peace fellowship with Him, and exercise a godly and humble authority.

This has a tremendous impact on the world around us. This is how the Word of God spreads throughout the world. The Word of the apostles is preached, the apostolic bread is broken, and the world, by the decree of God, must submit to it.

It is therefore in the strategic interest of our adversary to keep us from coming to this Table, or to keep us from coming with this full understanding of faith. Hence many professing Christian churches have abandoned the Supper, while others have structured it as a rare event. Still others tamper with the elements so that the grape juice may match the impotence of the grape juice gospel they have adopted.

But by far the most common problem is that the saints come to this Table in order to grovel instead of to rule. A greater misconception can scarcely be imagined.

So come, and welcome, to Jesus Christ.

EVENING ◐ DO NOT SHRINK BACK

You have not come to a mountain that can be touched. You have not come to a mountain covered with smoke and fire, and with a backdrop of gun-metal thunderheads. You have not come to a mountain that is cordoned off, so that if even an animal strays onto the holy ground it must be impaled with a spear. You have not come to a mountain where even the saints of God had to shrink back.

You have come to the heavenly Jerusalem, mount Zion. This mountain is a mountain that can be approached. This mountain is no less holy than Sinai was — the transformation is elsewhere. The sacrifice has been offered. The propitiation has been made. For those who come with faith in Christ, the anger of God is completely and entirely abated. You are the saints of God, and so you must not shrink back. You must not come with hesitation. You must not come with fear of punishment, for love has cast out that fear.

Faith approaches. Faith believes. Faith trembles, but it is another kind of trembling — we tremble as the Jews did coming out of exile, as those who were hoping against hope that it was not all a dream. They had been delivered; they had been saved; they had been brought near. This is not an invitation "too good to be true." This is the next level beyond that — "too good to be false."

In Christ, and in fellowship with Him, there is absolutely no reason to be fearful or diffident here. He has forgiven and saved you. He already knows what a sinner you are — He forgave all that, remember? He knows what He did when He forgave you. He knows what a sinner you are, and so there is no need for *you* to remind Him.

Are there then no covenant members who should be fearful of this Supper and its sanctions then? There are, many of them. But if you are concerned about it, you are not one of them.

So come, and welcome, to Jesus Christ.

MORNING ☼ OUR LORD THE WAITER

At the establishment of the Lord's Supper, the Lord Himself occupied the position of the server. Who is greater, He asked, the one who sits and eats, or the one who serves? And yet, He, the Lord, was the one who served.

More than this, He has done the same thing at every celebration of this Supper since then. The Lord binds the apron of a waiter on, and brings us the meal of the new covenant. It does not matter how deficient the elements have been, or how quarrelsome and unworthy the recipients have been. He serves those who are unworthy to be served.

He did this in order to establish His kingdom. He said that He appointed unto them a kingdom — but the lesson must never be forgotten. The princes of this kingdom — apostles, prophets, ministers, elders — must be as the king of it. If *He* stooped to serve, what must we do?

We are strengthened by this meal of the new covenant, but it nourishes us to grow up into the nature of it. Our bones are strengthened by this humility, and God does it to strengthen us *to* humility. Serve one another, therefore. Feed one another.

It is through this gospel humility that God will continue His conquest of the world.

So come, and welcome, to Jesus Christ.

This Table is the culmination point of all that we have done in assembled worship. Here all the hymns, psalms, prayers, amens, confessions, and heedings converge.

As we never tire of reminding you, it does not do this because it is a magic Table, or because it is some kind of machine grinding away by itself. No, this is the place where God promises to meet His faithful disciples, with His blessing. And *faithful* means just that — full of faith, coming in faith, arriving in faith, expectant joy in faith.

If a husband promised to meet his wife for lunch at a certain restaurant, she could arrive there with every expectation of seeing him. But this would not involve any ideas of it being a magic restaurant, or a place that would drag her husband there if he forgot. It is the meeting that blesses, it is the relationship that strengthens.

We are taught this in many ways. The bread is before you, but Jesus is really the bread. The bread is before you, but you are really the one loaf. The blessing here is the promised meeting of the Lord with His people.

If the wife shows up at the restaurant only to quarrel with her husband, or resolved to hide certain things from him, the restaurant remains a meeting place, but not for blessing. It is the same here. This meeting is intended for blessing; the cup is called a cup of blessing. We assemble, not in terror or fear, but in expectation of blessing. There have been those who willfully hide their sin, or stubbornly cling to it, but that kind of willfulness *does not define the Table.*

Those who minimize the use of this Table through fear of abusing it are like wives who never agree to meet with their husbands for fear of saying something wrong in the conversation. But we come weekly to meet with our Lord, and we do so according to His appointment. If we fear that we are coming wrongly, then it is apparent that we need to practice it more.

So come, and welcome, to Jesus Christ.

MORNING ☼ DEALING WITH OBSTACLES

This observance does not just knit believers together in the great *koinonia*—although it certainly does that. It also deals with obstacles to us being knit together, and if we keep coming to the Table in faith, it overcomes those obstacles.

We partake of Christ as we eat and drink here. But we partake of the entire Christ—head and body together, *totus Christus*—as we do so. This means that you can never commune with Jesus all by yourself. If we walk in the light as He is in the light, we have fellowship with one another (1 Jn. 1:7). In that context of mutual fellowship, mutual partaking, the blood of Jesus cleanses us from all sin.

This means that God deals with us here, and when He deals with us, He deals also with all the sins, faults, quirks, and foibles that interrupt our fellowship with our brothers and sisters. Sometimes the problem is in them, and we think it is in us. Sometimes, more frequently, the problem is in us, and we think it is in them. Sometimes we think the problem is in them, and we are right—it is in them. Sometimes we realize that we are the problem, and we really are the problem. But the location of the problem doesn't really matter. What matters is the location of the solution.

The solution is here, in the grace of God. We come here to be knit more closely together. And the true prayer of evangelical faith is, "Lord, do what it takes. Change me, if that is what it takes."

The Lord, as you can see, put everything on the Table. You come in response and do the same—you also are to put everything on the Table. As you do, the Lord will strengthen and establish what is right in you, and correct and remove that which is not right. This is not the time of confession we have at the beginning of the service, so your demeanor ought not to be one of guilt, gloom, and sadness. Rather, this is the time of edification and a positive kind of discipline. Rejoice in it.

So come, and welcome, to Jesus Christ.

In the institution of the Last Supper, our Lord warned Peter about the spiritual peril he was in. He said, "Simon, Simon, behold, Satan hath desired to have you" (Lk. 22:31). The Lord went on to say that He had prayed for Peter, that after his return from failure, he would strengthen his brethren.

We live in a perilous world. The Lord in His grace warns us, as He warned Cain — sin is crouching at the door, and this sin is hungry and would devour us.

At the point of every crisis, at every temptation, we must understand the situation as God declares it. Sin is the lion, and we are the antelope. Instead of taking heed as we ought, we flatter ourselves, as Peter did, although he was restored, and as Cain did, although he was not. Look down at your hands as you hold the bread and then the cup. Do you look in faithful submission? Then you hold life in your hands.

Do you look at this provision with your back up? Are you wiser than God? Are you going to outwit Him? Are you going to be the first hypocrite in the history of redemption to successfully sneak by the Lord? If you really think so, then it is clear that God has already begun the process of judicially blinding you.

If this frightens you, as it should, the right response is not to abstain from the Supper. You hold bread and wine in your hands that is death to you. But to put it away, or refuse to take it, is an even greater sin and even more death. You are baptized, and so you must come. If you are rebelling against that baptism, then you must repent.

Do not trifle with the things of God.

So come, and welcome, to Jesus Christ.

MORNING ☼ NOTHING CAN STOP HIM

The Lord's Supper is not impotent. The Lord's Supper does not need our protection. If I were standing up here with an enormous lion, I do not expect that I would get many questions after the service, wondering "how I protected it." In fact, I might not get any questions at all. But if I did, the questions would be along the lines of "how may *we* be protected from the lion?"

Now this is strange. How can the Lord's Supper, which is given to us for *blessing*, be thought of this way? The Lord's Supper is not endangered by our sin; rather, the Lord's Supper is dangerous to our sin. But how may we reckon this danger and at the same time see the Supper as a place we are to approach gladly, freely, with boldness, with simplicity and singing?

The Lord's Supper is not dangerous to the children of God, but it is dangerous to that which threatens the children of God. That is, the Lord's Supper deals with their remaining sin. It does so potently, powerful, disruptively, and in all holiness. If we have made an accommodation with sin in our lives, nothing is more intrusive than this meal. If we have surrendered all sin in principle, we approach gladly. We are no more threatened by how God deals with us here than a patient is threatened by having a life-threatening cancer removed.

But many professing Christians have worked out an accommodation between their sin and weekly attendance at church. Many generations have learned to tune the preachers out, often with the connivance and help of the preachers themselves. But when the messages deal with sin, and we come to close the deal every week with the Supper, which also deals with us, what are the two possible responses? One response is repentance, and the other is changing the subject.

Here God *deals* with us. Not by argument, or charges, or finger-pointing, and not by recriminations. God deals with us in grace and love, and nothing can stop Him.

So come, and welcome, to Jesus Christ.

The world is a perilous place, and we do not make it any safer by pretending. The sacred things of God are always accompanied by many warnings, but for the faithful, and rightly understood, these warnings only serve to strengthen our faith in Him.

The sovereign covenantal purposes of God are the only security we may ever have. And we do not have security through knowing the secret *content* of those purposes, but rather through having faith and trust in the one whose good counsels they are. Trust *Him*.

While Peter denied the Lord, just as Jesus had predicted, the fact remained that Jesus had *prayed* for him, and so he returned from his sin in humility and faith. The Bible teaches that Jesus Christ is our high priest, who ever lives to make intercession for us. Jesus Christ is praying for you, *today*. He knows us each by name, and He prays for His Church.

Take heart — though you stumble in many ways, though you are humiliated by your temptations and sins, though you have not done as you have resolved to do, *take heart*. Jesus Christ prays for you, and you hear this promise with gladness and faith.

But if the words fill you with repugnance or fear, then *take heed*. All twelve of the disciples were scattered, but only eleven returned. That is a glorious majority, but such majorities are no comfort to the one. And remember that those who returned did so because Christ prayed for them. And Christ prays for you. So come, take and eat.

So come, and welcome, to Jesus Christ.

MORNING ☼ STAY, AND BELIEVE

Quite a number of years ago, we began observing the Lord's Supper on a weekly basis. Quite a bit went into that discussion beforehand, but one of the striking things about our preparations for it was the warning I got from an experienced minister. He said that when we went to weekly communion, we should expect a great deal of sin to be flushed out of the system. In the Supper, God deals with us. In the Supper, God brings things to a head. And, as it turns out, he was right.

Without the Supper, a Christian worship service can come to resemble a college classroom, or a lecture series, or a civic meeting. And of course, in none of those settings is deep fellowship necessary. But we have been breaking bread together, and drinking the cup of the new covenant together now, for quite a number of years. Not only is this a means of grace for you—when you come in genuine faith—it is also a covenantal affront to those who are not walking in that genuine faith. And so, not surprisingly, sins, affronts, disputes, differences, and offenses can all come bubbling to the surface.

One of the reasons they do this is that the affront gives an excuse for departing, and when we depart we no longer have to deal with the demand that the Supper places upon us. Look around you. These are your brothers and sisters in Christ. They will eat from the same loaf. They will drink from the cup. The Lord Jesus is communing with them just as He is doing with you. This places a weighty responsibility upon you. If we walk in the light, as He is in the light, we have fellowship with one another. And the blood of Jesus Christ cleanses us from all sin (1 Jn. 1:7).

So let the Supper bring things to head. Do not flee. Do not stay, but then suppress the work of the Spirit in your heart. Stay, and eat. Stay, and drink. Stay, *and believe in Jesus.*

So come, and welcome, to Jesus Christ.

As we learn from Tertullian, our word sacrament comes from *sacramentum*, a term that was used to describe the oath of enlistment that a soldier would take. This is a covenant meal, and covenants are God-given bonds and obligations. These bonds are not burdensome—His yoke is easy and His burden is light—but His bonds are in fact bonds. We are engaged to His service.

When we come to this meal, we are engaging to be faithful. We have already confessed those sins and occasions where we were not faithful, and we come here in order grow in our commitments to Him. We gather here in order to cinch the knots tighter.

We do this self-consciously, knowing what we do. The battles we are fighting are difficult, and we need sustenance. What happens here is that we renew our commitment to be faithful and at the same time, for those who come to it honestly, we are given grace to be faithful. We obligate ourselves to be strong, and we are given strength.

The Lord is present in the person of His Spirit, and one of His offices is to quicken those who are lagging. The Servant in Isaiah says, "The Lord God hath given me the tongue of the learned, That I should know *how to speak a word in season to him that is weary*" (Is. 50:4). Are you weary? This word is for you. The bread is for you. The wine is yours.

This is not something that could arise from a mere ritual. The Lord is present here with us. He shows us the way, and He equips us to go on that way. The Lord is present, and Scripture tells us what that presence means. "Thou wilt shew me the path of life: *In thy presence is fulness of joy*; At thy right hand there are pleasures for evermore" (Ps. 16:11).

The Lord gives us joy, and the Lord in His kindness instructs us on what to do with it.

So come, and welcome, to Jesus Christ.

MORNING ☼ LOVED AND SHAPED IN THE SUPPER

Christians are accustomed to think that a worldview consists of the things that you think. What are your "views" about the world? Your opinions about this and that? But this is a very truncated view of what it means to have a worldview. We need to develop this at length some other time, but a worldview consists of your dogma, your manner of life, your story, and your symbols. What do you believe? How do you treat your family and friends? Where do you understand your place in history to be? And what symbols and rituals do you honor?

This is a ritual in which we eat the body of Jesus Christ, who is alive this moment at the right hand of God, and in which we drink His blood, which is the cup of blessing, the cup of the new testament. Our worldview includes what we are eating and drinking here.

This is therefore part of *who you are*. You are not defined simply as a thinking machine who entertains certain thoughts. You are defined, bounded, shaped, organized, and loved as a member of this community, this church, this body. And you are loved in this way by what you eat and drink and by the fact that we are eating and drinking (at the same moment) the same.

Many people have thought that they could join (or separate) themselves by thinking certain propositions in their head. What we think is certainly part of all this, but it is by no means the only part.

If a husband were to think the thought in his head that he "is now unmarried," he remains married, despite what he thinks. Marriage is objective, as is membership in the body of Christ.

What we think will help define whether we are being faithful or unfaithful to our objective connections, but our objective connections remain. And they remain as part of our worldview. Another way of putting this is that we do not just have a worldview; a worldview has us. If you doubt it, consider the bread and wine.

So come, and welcome, to Jesus Christ.

We now observe the Supper of the Lord at the conclusion of every worship service. Do not drift into the sin of thinking that this is a *mere* routine.

What is actually happening is that God is performing the spiritual equivalent of open-heart surgery on you, and He is doing it now on a weekly basis. He does not do this because all His previous operations were failures, but rather because a whole series of reconstructive surgeries are necessary. Before the operations began, we were a mess. Apart from Him, our condition was desperate.

Are you a sinner? This is no barrier to the Table. Are you unworthy? Then welcome, it is just for you. Are you crushed with your failures, and do you need His hand to put it all right? Then this is a Table set for you, in the presence of all your enemies, including the internal ones.

But if you are fighting and hating Him as you partake, then a deep fear should overtake you. When rebellion looks into the cup, rebellion sees damnation there. But even in this situation, the solution is not to refrain from eating and drinking. If you are a covenant member, you have an obligation to eat and drink. But you also have a profound obligation to repent as you do so.

So in a real sense, *we* do not fence the Table. The Table is the fence, and it was not established by us. The Body does not protect the Table; the Table protects the Body.

So come, and welcome, to Jesus Christ.

MORNING ☼ AWAY FROM ALIEN TABLES

We know, in coming to this Table, that we are solemnly and joyfully renewing our vows, and those vows include a deep commitment to stay far away from all alien tables. We cannot commune here, and at the table of demons, as St. Paul teaches. We are also committing ourselves to stay far away from men of iniquity; we do not intend to eat any of their dainties, as David puts it (Ps. 141:4). Men of iniquity would include those of licentious life, of course. But it also includes those who are respectable in the world's eyes, but who do not remember God because their barns and bank accounts are full. It includes as well those who have leprosy of the heart and mind, men who traffic in vain philosophies and heresies. So we do not eat there.

What do we do here? We walk in the land of the living (Ps. 116:9). We believe in the Lord, and therefore we speak about Him (v. 10). Because we believe, and speak, we are greatly afflicted (v. 10). The world wants nothing more than to shut this up. We take care not to over-react. The fact that persecution comes to the righteous does not mean that all men are liars (v. 11). What then do we render to the Lord? What do we give to Him for all His saving benefits to us (v. 12)? We take here the cup of salvation (v. 13), and we call upon the name of the Lord. This is our task — to call upon Him.

This is truly the Eucharistic meal; we offer up to the Lord, here, the sacrifice of *thanksgiving* (v. 17). We do not offer up the blood of bulls and goats because we are members of the New Israel, and the ultimate Pascal lamb has been slain. We do not pretend to offer the physical body and blood of Jesus, because that ultimate Lamb was slain once, one offering for the entire world, and does not need to be repeatedly offered as though He could be continually dead.

Rather, we offer thanksgiving and praise (Heb. 13:15); this is our sacrifice. And as we do this, we really partake of the living Christ, and we do this by faith, in the power of the Holy Spirit.

So come, and welcome, to Jesus Christ.

EVENING ◐ LETTING VAINGLORY GO

Scripture reminds us that we are to think of others in a way that is very difficult to do. "Let nothing be done through strife or vainglory; but in lowliness of mind let each esteem other better than themselves" (Phil. 2:3).

Now the sense of this is not that we are to pretend that others are better than we are in things that we can do and they can't. If you can play the piano and they cannot, if you know how to do differential equations and they can't, if you know how to dunk a basketball and they can't, considering someone else better than yourself does not mean telling yourself lies about it. Nor does it mean telling *them* lies about it.

Rather, the position of the other is more important to you than your own. You are not competing with them. You are not striving. Remember the first part of the verse. Do nothing from strife or vainglory. If you have a relationship with someone, and in your mind you have a running tally of points, and it is important to you that your number is always higher than theirs, then you have a problem.

So you play the piano better. Fine. Their playing is more important to you than yours is. You run a business better. Fine. Their business matters more to you than your own does. Sometimes competition is unavoidable, just in the nature of the case. They set up shop after you did, and their establishment is right across the street. That is the way it goes sometimes. But competition *in the ego* is never unavoidable. That is what must be laid down. *That* is what we must consider as cross fodder.

When we strive, we are trying to pick things up with our right hand, instead of receiving them with our left. Are you in any kind of adversarial set-up with anyone else in the body, at any level? Then there is a sense in which you must let it go. Whoever it is, you are seated at this Table with him, and so it is time to let the vainglory go.

So come, and welcome, to Jesus Christ.

MORNING ☼ FROM TORQUEMADA TO STALIN

At this Table, we remember Christ and Him crucified. In the death of Jesus, it was not sufficient for Him simply to die — He could not have died in His sleep for our sins. It was *necessary* for Him to be betrayed by the chief priests, and to be run through a kangaroo trial. It was necessary for His enemies to hate Him without a cause.

The kind of death He died is crucial, and relates to why He died. He was dying for our sins; particularly for those sins that we had become convinced were virtues. This is one thing we commemorate in this meal — the death of the worldview of all persecutors. When Jesus died, so did the commonly received idea of the scapegoat.

Before the execution of Jesus, unruly crowds could demand the death of any assigned victim, and they could demand that the victim's name would go down in infamy. This is because the accuser, the persecutor, always has a serene confidence in his own "rightness." The guilt of the victim is always "self-evident." And the crowd shouting at Pilate was no different with regard to the first part of this. They could demand, and get, the death of the victim.

But what was different in this account was the preaching of the gospel afterwards. In the proclamation of the death of Jesus, the scandal of the cross as central to our faith, we Christians wrested control of the persecutors' vision from them. We threw it to the ground and have trampled on it.

The central story in the history of the world is now a story of a miscarriage of justice, of an innocent victim, of a man hated for no reason, of lying witnesses, of corrupt officials. And this will always be the center of the story.

The persecutors have attempted comebacks — from Torquemada to Stalin, they have been loathe to give it up. But Christ was slain and Christ is risen, and there is nothing that they can do about this meal.

So come, and welcome, to Jesus Christ.

EVENING ◐ IT IS NOT SO

After the Lord Jesus established the sacrament of the Supper, He asked His disciples if they had lacked anything when He sent them out. They had been commissioned to go without purse, money, or shoes. When He had done this, He asked, had they come to lack for anything? They had lacked for *nothing* was the reply.

You are being fed here at the Table of the Lord. You are *nourished* here. If you have this, you lack for nothing, and can lack for nothing. If you do not have this, it does not matter if you own the world — you have lost your own soul.

As you return to your vocations, having been fed at this Supper, recognize that, whatever the world might say, you have a blessing through faith which they cannot comprehend. If you are poor, what you have are unspeakable riches because what you do have is blessed by Jesus Christ Himself. If you are rich, as the world counts riches, then you have been fed here in such a way as to enable you to see that earthly wealth is like the grass of the field, which withers and perishes in a day. It is a blessing, but beside *this* blessing, it is to be reckoned as a small thing indeed.

Let the weak now say, "I am strong." Let the poor say, "I am rich." Let the wealthy confess that the central wealth of the kingdom is open and available to all who come by faith in Jesus Christ. This Supper is your central nourishment, regardless of who you are. This Supper puts everything in perspective.

Is God going to give you *this*, but then deny *any* of you *anything* else that you might need? It is not so.

So come, and welcome, to Jesus Christ.

MORNING ☼ ENACTING OUR AGREEMENT

We have said before that in this meal we are being knit together into the body of Christ, muscle and bone, sinew and tendon, joint and marrow. But too many Christians have reversed the order in this, wanting doctrinal assent or understanding to be the thing that knits us together, so that we may then come to the meal. But this is backwards. Our hearts and minds do not knit us together in the meal; the meal knits our hearts and minds together. Jesus did not say, "take, hold, figure it out." He said, "take, eat."

This is why, if you are baptized, a principled willingness to come to this Table (even when you have significant differences with others at the same Table) is so important. Everyone who comes to this Table is objectively enacting a statement of their willingness to change, their willingness to repent, their willingness to agree (in principle) that they might be the problem. They might be the reason there is disagreement or division

Their hearts and minds might be far from this, but the meal still does its knitting work. And because we observe the supper weekly, we are all saying (objectively) that we acknowledge that *we* might be the problem. This puts tremendous pressure (the right kind of pressure) on those who really are the problem, and draws inexorably them to repentance. Ultimately, there are two options — repent or run. Repentance always looks the way it looks in Scripture, and is characterized by the fruit of the Spirit — love, joy, and peace. Running need not be physical — departing the church — although that is frequently done. It could also consist of trying to change the subject through disputing, or checking out in attempted apathy.

But our responses are not the fundamental thing here. We are mostly interested in what God is doing with the fundamental statement of submission that He has assigned to us. And what is He doing? He is building us up into a perfect agreement, in perfect agreement.

So come, and welcome, to Jesus Christ.

EVENING — THE FUTURE FAILURE OF PETER

As the Lord established the sacrament of the Supper, He did a very interesting thing — He predicted the *future* failure of Peter. And yet He still administered it to him. We would tend to think that the blessing was wasted on Peter, when we should really be thinking that without it he might have fallen as Judas did. The grace of God is not a wage or paycheck, and not an occasion for us to make self-willed promises — as Peter did.

Too often we view the Supper as a reward for having been good, or a promise on our part that we will never commit a particular sin. But this is not what it is — it is a sign and seal of the *grace* of God.

Of course, God commands us not to sin, but the Lord's Supper is not the moment when we steel our resolve and make our vows. It is the moment when we sit and marvel at what God has done and is doing. In the gospel, God speaks to sinners. In the waters of baptism, He washes sinners. In the bread and wine, He feeds sinners. Never forget the object of His kindness – sinners. And never forget the point of His intentions — to transform us into His everlasting saints.

Are we there yet? Not until the resurrection. Are we there yet? Yes, of course — we are seated at a heavenly Table, with heavenly bread and heavenly wine. And what brought us there? The sovereign and conquering grace of God.

So come, and welcome, to Jesus Christ.

MORNING ☼ ONE PROVISO OF HIS WILL

God has brought us together into the household of faith, and, like all households, we share a Table together. But one common feature of most household tables going back into antiquity is the feature of sibling rivalry.

At the first Lord's Supper, there were two sets of physical brothers—Peter and Andrew (Matt. 4:18), and James and John (4:21)—and all the disciples were brothers in the new household that Jesus was gathering.

From ancient times, brothers are famous for their striving, and not for the shoulder-to-shoulder solidarity that the Scriptures require of them. In pagan mythologies, we see representative examples like Romulus and Remus. And we have to confess also that this is one of the major themes throughout all Scripture. We think of Ishmael and Isaac, and Jacob and Esau, and Perez and Zerah, sons of Tamar, and David with his brothers. And the striving and scuffling that characterized Christ's disciples is also notable in this regard.

Scripture says that a friend loves at all times, and a brother is made for the day of adversity (Prov. 17:17). That is what a brother is supposed to be. But we in our rivalries have distorted this terribly.

What we need to take care to do, then, is come to this Table with the desire and expectation that God will give us our full inheritance here. There is more than enough for everyone. If you struggle with sin in this area, then confess your sins, but seek to do it throughout the week, and at the *beginning* of the service, not here.

The author of Hebrews compares the covenant with a last will and testament, and so may we. This meal is our inheritance, and often the place where rivalries erupt is at the reading of the last will and testament. But our older brother, who died for us, has come back to life, and He is present at the reading of His will. And His will is that we love one another.

So come, and welcome, to Jesus Christ.

Jesus taught us that we should not labor for the meat that perishes, but rather for that meat which endures unto everlasting life, and this meat is the food which the Lord Jesus gives to us now. He is authorized to do this because God the Father has sealed us in Him. We do not trust the food of the Supper as mere food, any more than we trust the words of the gospel preached as mere words.

The Bible teaches there is a three-fold heavenly witness of Christ, which is of course the Father, the Word, and the Spirit. But this heavenly witness does us no good *here* unless God in His kindness stoops to give us an earthly witness. And this He does also — 1 John 5 teaches us the importance of the witness of the Spirit, the witness of the water of baptism, and the witness of the blood of the covenant (1 Jn. 5:6, 8).

Without the life-giving work of the Spirit, creating true faith in us, our religious practices will be just so much ritualistic mummery and hollow ceremony. But God did not give us this Supper so that we could start imitating the initiation ceremonies of the Moose Lodge. He gave us this bread and wine as the life of the world.

We do not look *at* it, as though saving power is resident in grain or grapes. We do not look *at* the water of baptism, as though the cleansing of the flesh were in view. Those who fall into this folly drown in their baptism, and choke on the bread of life.

Rather, when the Spirit is present, as He has promised to be this morning, we look *through and in* the Word, we look *through and in* the water, and *through and in* the bread and wine. And what do we see? By the grace of God, we see Christ and all His benefits.

So come, and welcome, to Jesus Christ.

MORNING ☼ NADAB AND ABIHU AT THE TABLE

When Jesus established the Lord's Supper, Judas was there. And because Satan had entered into Judas, Satan was also there. The sacrament here is not a reward for the already arrived. Not only so, but it is also used in driving away those who will never arrive. We don't need to drive anyone away. We don't need to defend the Table; fencing the Table (as we do) is a matter of guarding ourselves.

In Exodus, when the Lord invited Moses and seventy elders, to come up on the mountain, and eat and drink in His presence (Ex. 24:11), they all did so. Aaron also came, as did Nadab and Abihu, his sons who would later perish. It says that these men saw God, and did eat and drink. And then they went down the mountain, went on with their lives, which ended badly.

We may not say, without horrible contradictions, that God was somehow surprised by how Nadab and Abihu ended their lives. God is God, and knows the end from the beginning. But neither may we say that Nabab and Abihu were not really on the mountain, that they did not really eat and drink, and that they did not really see God. They did all these things. Apostasy is a real sin, committed by real people. It is not a sin committed by those set apart in the love of the Father before the foundation of the world, but it is a sin committed by visible and real members of His covenant people.

But we are not told to sort out the eternal decrees in order to determine who may come to the Table. Rather, the Table (along with other means of grace like the preaching of the gospel) sorts out us. *Because* Judas partook, he was driven away the way he was. *Because* Nadab and Abihu partook, their lives ended the way they did.

As we come, therefore, we should be filled with fear, awe, and trembling. For those who love Christ, this is not inconsistent with love, joy, and peace.

So come, and welcome, to Jesus Christ.

When Jesus taught His disciples that they should not labor for the meat that perishes, their response was to ask what work they should do in order to work the works of God. Jesus replied that the work of God was that they would believe on the one whom God had sent (1 Jn. 6:27). They asked what work *they* should do, and Jesus replied that the work *God* does is that they would believe.

We slip off the point so readily, so easily. We want to turn the Supper into a statement of our good intentions toward God, when it is actually a statement of God's good intentions toward us. And so we ask, how shall we approach the Supper so that we get the most out of it? The question we should be asking is how does God approach the Supper so that we get the most out of it? When we look to ourselves, we always stagger. We stand in faith when we see God, and His love, His delight, His invitation, His kindness.

We feel we must look to ourselves, for have not many shipwrecked their faith? Yes, they have — by looking to themselves. Look to God, look to His Christ, look to His Spirit.

This is not *our* Supper; it is the Lord's. Like a helpless and foolish toddler, we are strapped in the high chair, wondering what great and mighty works we should do in order to deserve our Supper. One work only — open your mouth, and God promises to fill it. What is it to open your mouth? It is to believe. This work cannot be done if you look at yourself opening your mouth. If I may speak in such a homely way, look to the One who holds the spoon.

So come, and welcome, to Jesus Christ.

MORNING ☼ BELIEVING IS SEEING

After Jesus told His followers that they must believe God since *this* was the work of God, they immediately asked for a sign.

They were asking for a sign when the one signified by any possible sign was standing right there in front of them. And from this we learn that without possession of the thing signified, the sign by itself only brings judgment. Jesus goes on to tell them that while they had seen Him, they still believed not. In this case, seeing was *not* believing. Seeing is not believing; rather believing is seeing.

These people asked for the sign because Moses gave their fathers bread from heaven to eat. Jesus responded that Moses had not given them that bread. Rather, the Father in heaven gave them the true bread, the bread of God was Jesus Christ Himself (Jn. 6:32). *He* comes down into the world and gives life to the world.

The bread of life gives life to the world, and those who do not receive this life — because of their unbelief — are thrust out from the world, and fall headlong into the outer darkness, the everlasting horror of man's own wisdom. God gives bread without price, and foolish men still want to set up their own autonomous bakeries, so that their mouths may be filled with ash forever.

But Jesus nevertheless exults in this: all that are given to Him by the Father *will* come to Him. And whoever comes to Him will be in no way cast out. You have come; you are here in faith. You have the sign and the one signified.

So come, and welcome, to Jesus Christ.

The world is full of losers, and there is no one who is not a loser. And yet, left to our own devices, we always construct religious systems based on work, striving, earning, *winning*. Perpetual losers, bred to the bone losers, we insist on devising and pursuing the calculus of success and winning.

Jesus is the only person who ever lived who was not a loser. And what was His calculus? To do the will of the Father, which was to go to the cross, suffer there, bleed and die, and to have His cooling body laid in a cold tomb. He was crucified, died, and was buried, as we confess every week. His resurrection from the dead was God's vindication of Him, God's justification of Jesus in the Spirit. God says, in this great event, that His ways are not our ways.

In this meal, we are summoned to remember what Jesus did. But do not content yourself with simply remembering the *fact* of it. We must remember here (for in remembering, we are declaring) that Jesus the winner died for losers. In doing what He did the way He did it, He declared forever that the first will be last, and the last first. Whoever wants to be great in the kingdom must become the servant of all.

But we have real problems in this area, for as soon as we are told we must become the servant of all, we treat this as nothing more than the requirement to change the goals halfway through the football game. But striving to stay alive on your own terms and death and resurrection are quite different, and not at all like a mere shift of direction, focus, or emphasis.

Since we have such trouble with this, what are we to do? The answer is set before you, on this Table. You cannot die and be raised all by yourself. You must partake, in evangelical faith, in the death and resurrection of Another. The word is declared, the elements are hearing, we will partake in a moment. And the thing that makes it efficacious for blessing is simple, God-given *faith*.

So come, and welcome, to Jesus Christ.

MORNING ✵ GETTING THE DIRECT OBJECTS RIGHT

Jesus said that it was the Father's will that He, Jesus, lose no one that had been given to Him. He said further that it was the will of God that such individuals be raised up at the last day. Who receives this gift? Jesus said that it applied to everyone who sees the Son and believes on Him. Such a one will have everlasting life, and will be raised at the last day (Jn. 6:39–40).

We cannot overemphasize this, or pay too much attention to what He actually says here. He says everyone who sees the Son, not everyone who sees himself seeing the Son. He says everyone who believes on Him, not everyone who believes himself to be believing.

The direct object of the verb *see* is Jesus Christ. The direct object of the verb *believe* is Jesus Christ. Reject every attempt to make you look somewhere else. It is an attempt to undermine your faith and confidence. When you look at Jesus Christ, like Peter, you can walk on water. When you look *anywhere* else — at the waves, at your feet, at the motives of your heart — you will sink like an anvil.

Everlasting life is set before you. Salvation is on the Table. Do not close your eyes to look inward as you eat — your Table manners will suffer. Look to the food. Look away from yourself. This is bread from outside this world. This is wine from the vineyards of God in heaven. Look to Jesus Christ in heaven. Believe on the one God has sent. Look forward to everlasting life.

So come, and welcome, to Jesus Christ.

The Lord Jesus is seated at the head of this Table, in His resurrected triumph, and yet this is also a meal where His body and blood are on the Table. Not only this, but He teaches us that we are His body, we are of His flesh and of His bone. We are one loaf, St. Paul tells us.

This means that *we* are also on the Table. This is not a magic trick, as though we were talking about some kind of substantive alteration in the chemistry of wine and bread. This is covenantal; this is ritual; this is spiritual; this is real. We become what we eat, and we are eating and drinking *one another*. We are being knit together in this fashion. This is possible because we are being knit together in the Head from which every joint, muscle, and sinew obtains its life.

This is *koinonia,* the only alternative to covetousness. We are imitative creatures; God has made us this way. And the only way to imitate without it becoming the imitation of destructive and covetous rivals is to imitate from within the life of the Trinity.

You *will* imitate. If you imitate your neighbor apart from faith, the end result will be ungodly conflict—biting and devouring. If you imitate your Lord, and your brothers and your sisters in faith, then the result is harmony. And if you receive the harmony of God, the grace of Jesus Christ, the gifts and blessings of the Holy Spirit, this will be a provocation for those who do not want another way of imitating to make its presence known in the world—and there will be conflict. But it will not be conflict that arises from your lusts, and so you must take care not to be lured back into that way of disintegration.

Receive the grace of God. Rejoice in the grace of God. Refuse to earn the grace of God. Chew and swallow the grace of God. Drink and enjoy the grace of God. This is not a race, not a competition. This is the Table of a household. This is a family meal. We are being drawn together, like it or not, by the *koinonia* of Christ.

So come, and welcome, to Jesus Christ.

When Jesus taught that He was the bread of life, come down from heaven, His listeners grumbled at Him. How was this possible, they asked? This was Jesus, after all, and they knew Joseph and Mary. How was it possible that He came down from heaven?

Jesus answered them as said that they should not murmur, and the reason for this is that no one can come to Christ unless the Father draws him. And if the Father draws him, then Jesus Christ will raise him up on the last day (Jn. 6:40–44).

We see in this that faith is a gift, sovereignly bestowed by a gracious Father. If it were to depend on scientific research, these listeners could get no earlier than Bethlehem. If it were to depend on human science, you could only trace this bread back to a particular grain field, and this vine back to a particular vineyard. But nonetheless, this is a heavenly banquet. How do we know this? All that the Father gives come to Christ, and they see Him. They see Him in the bread and wine; they see Him in the gospel; they see Him in the Old Testament; they see Him in their marriages; they see Him everywhere — for everyone that confesses that Jesus is Lord, and believes in his heart that God raised Him from the dead, will be saved.

Abandon all superstitions, and all false gods. Christ alone is your Savior, and He is visiting you with His kindness now, a kindness that will extend to the last day.

So come, and welcome, to Jesus Christ.

EVENING ◐ THEY SHALL ALL BE TAUGHT OF GOD

Our Lord quoted the prophets, saying that it is written there that "they shall all be taught of God." Jesus interpreted this as meaning that everyone who had heard, and has learned from the Father, comes necessarily to Jesus Christ. This is not to be taken as meaning that anyone can just snap their fingers and say that he is of God. Only one man has seen God, and that is Jesus Christ. *He* has seen the Father. The man who believes therefore in this Jesus, this one has eternal life.

And Jesus adds here that *He* is the bread of life. He is the one who came down from heaven. He is the living bread, and the one who eats it lives forever.

But this everlasting life is not accomplished with your mouth when your heart is elsewhere. The oldest hypocrisy in the book is the practice of feigning heart allegiance while making a great deal out of the externals required by God. To all such, the Word says that sacrifices and burnt offerings are not required, but a humble and a contrite heart (Ps. 51:17). With such a heart — for no other kind is received kindly — come and partake.

So come, and welcome, to Jesus Christ.

MORNING ☼ THE AISLE OF HEAVEN'S CATHEDRAL

The glory that is developing at this Table is far greater than any mortal man can imagine. We do not know the height, or breadth, or depth of it—although the apostle prays that we might begin our lessons. He prays that the saints would be able to know that which surpasses knowledge, to grasp the ungraspable, to comprehend the incomprehensible. This is not an exercise in futility or hopelessness; it occurs in the context of Paul's recognition that the Holy Spirit is working into the history of the world one of the greatest miracles ever performed—the unveiling of the bride of Christ, without spot, or wrinkle, or any such blemish.

We are that bride of Christ, and corporately, together, we look forward to that great Day when we shall walk down the aisle of heaven's cathedral. Until then, there are many preparations to make and mundane things to accomplish. But one of the greatest preparations is the matter of becoming truly human again so that we might marry the True Man.

But this is not a work that we can do. How could *we* arrange to grow up into a perfect bride? But God has seen to it. In and through this meal, at the culmination of the worship service, where the gospel has been declared and set forth plainly, the Holy Spirit does His work of knitting us together, bone, muscle, and sinew. We are being grown up, and it is all a very great mystery, as Paul understates it.

We do not seek to explain the miracle, but we may *describe* it. This is not a mere memorial, and it is not a form of ritual cannibalism. This is the day of resurrection, the day the Lord has made, and we will rejoice and be glad in it. On this day, in our corporate worship, the Holy Spirit lifts us up to heaven, where we presently are, and by evangelical faith we partake of the *living* Christ, and, as we do, His life continues to be imparted to us.

So come, and welcome, to Jesus Christ.

EVENING ◐ CAN'T EVEN SEE THE TABLECLOTH

The eating of this meal is annexed to a great promise made by Jesus Christ. He says that unless we eat the flesh of the Son of man, and drink His blood, we have no life in us. Conversely, if we partake, then Jesus Christ promises to raise us up at the last day (Jn. 6:53–54).

"This is a hard saying," some of His disciples muttered. "Who can hear it?" (v. 60). Only those who to whom it is given—Jesus knew that some of *His* disciples there did not believe. *What* did they not believe? The object of their disbelief was His words, which were spirit and life. The flesh profits in no way, the Spirit quickens, and brings to life (v. 63).

When Jesus points to His words, this is not an invitation for us to look away at words spoken elsewhere, by somebody else. He is talking about His words right there, the words they had just finished stumbling over. And in stumbling over them, they were tripping over eternal life. They were abusing a Table that had so many promises on it that it was not possible to see the tablecloth. What are we to do with these promises? We eat them.

Is Jesus inviting us to a superstitious use of the Supper? Not a bit of it—in fact this is precisely what He excludes. The Supper consists of simple bread and wine—and when the Word of Christ accompanies them, they become edible and drinkable words. How do you chew them? How do you swallow them? With eternal life in view, the answer is *sola fide*, by faith alone. But this is not faith placed in your own faith as the object. It is faith in *what Jesus said*.

So come, and welcome, to Jesus Christ.

MORNING ☼ GOD GIVES MORE GRACE

When we come to the Table of the Lord, we are not coming to receive any kind of reward. This is not the laurel crown for winners of the race. This is the meal you eat *before* the race. And all are invited equally to partake of this meal — indeed, since, if you are baptized, you are registered to run the race, then you are summoned to this meal.

Do not waste any of your time comparing yourself to any of the other runners. What is that to you? You follow Christ? He feeds you. He nourishes you. He strengthens you.

You may want to turn it into a trick to improve your performance, relative to others. But this is to miss the point. You do want to improve your baptism. You do want to do better. You do want to walk worthy of the name by which you were called. But you don't want to do any of it with sidelong glances at anyone else. To do this is to stumble.

But how are you to strive in your growing if you don't compare? There are two things to note. First, you can compare how you *are* doing with how you *were* doing. And it is hard to develop vainglory when your rival is the "you" of last March.

Second, we are called and created to imitate others. There is nothing wrong with this; indeed it is impossible to avoid. But we are not called to imitate as rivals, to imitate competitively. You daughters should want to be like your mothers; you should not want to surpass them and draw attention to yourself. You sons should be imitating your fathers self-consciously; but you must not be striving against them.

These are difficult things to understand, and to master. We are so caught up in imitative striving, it is so much the air we breathe, that we have a hard time even seeing it. But God strengthens you here. He feeds you here. He summons to you to grow up into His goodness. The spirit in us does tend toward imitative envy, but God gives more grace. This is one of the places He gives it.

So come, and welcome, to Jesus Christ.

Jesus delivered some hard sayings to His disciples concerning the eating of His flesh and the drinking of His blood. John says, "from that time many of his disciples went back" (Jn. 6:66). But they went back, not because Jesus told them of the overwhelming works they would have to do in order to be worthy of eating His flesh and drinking His blood. Rather, it was just the reverse. They left because it did not depend upon works, but rather upon the sheer grace of God. Much of the time religious men exult in the strain of trying to become worthy, and the rest of the time they wallow in being unworthy. And so they pulled back because of the sovereignty of grace. No man can come to me, Jesus said, unless it is *given* to him (Jn. 6:44). There it is—*gift*.

So, are you unworthy? Then you qualify. Are you sinful? Then you have need. Are you at the end of yourself? Glory to God. Are you a mess? Then a place here is reserved just for you. May God the Spirit soften our hardness of heart. How could we possibly *earn* hunger?

One of our great sins is that of looking at this meal as some sort of reward or trophy. There are such blessings, but not here. We are like a toddler in a high chair, less than a year old, looking up at another spoonful of food from our gracious mother the Church, and we ask, "Is there anything I can do? Mow the lawn? Get a job? After all, I do need to be worthy!" And the answer of grace is, "No, you dear little fathead. Just open your mouth."

So come, and welcome, to Jesus Christ.

MORNING ✹ FUSSY WITH FOOD

God delights to feed His saints, and yet His family, like all families, contains children who are fussy about their food. Parents perennially struggle to get children to eat what is set before them, gratefully and simply. It can be discouraging for parents when children won't eat, or they want something else, or they just play with their food.

We are the children of God, and it sometimes appears that we are children in every sense. He sets before us a simple meal of bread and wine, and He tells us to eat and drink.

And so we go out to the cupboards and substitute elements on our own authority, thinking that grape juice is somehow godlier than what Jesus drank, and we desire a better testimony than He had.

And we don't want to simply take and eat, take and drink. We want to do so quarterly, or annually, or rarely, at any rate, in order to keep it special. But we don't do that with our ordinary food. No husband ever declined breakfast this morning, postponing that happy event until July, in order to help keep it "special."

And we play with our food too, pushing it around on the plate, thinking the whole time about what miserable sinners we are. We mutter to ourselves that we don't deserve this kindness, and how can we just *partake*? Well, we should partake because this is what we were told to do. We are not pleasing God by arguing the point with Him. If He had wanted to save somebody else instead of you, He could have done so easily, but He didn't. So that should be settled.

When we come to this Table, we are to come with a glad and settled heart. God has invited us, we have every right to be here, and we have no right to not be here. We have no right to show up at His dinner, and try to turn it into our dinner. This is about Christ, and about His body, the Church. It is not about me, the individual. It is not about you, the individual. This Table is set by the kindness of God, and it is set with the kindness of God. Eat. Drink.

So come, and welcome, to Jesus Christ.

Jesus asked His disciples if they would also go away. "Where could we go?" Peter replied. "You have the words of eternal life" (Jn. 6:68). He said this confessing that Jesus was the Christ, the Son of the living God. And this is what we also confess. When we do, we are confessing what God has already declared Himself — in the Incarnation, at the baptism of Christ, and with His resurrection. All these realities are also declared of us in our baptism — which is not our declaration concerning God, but God's declaration concerning His Son and all who are in Him.

Ultimately, there are only two tables at which we may sit down — the Table of the Lord and the table of demons — and we do not want any of our children to partake with devils. And so I want particularly to invite some of you covenant children who may have been holding back from this Table. You are *with* us — you may partake. If you are baptized, and if you can hear these words that "this is the Table of the Lord," you are welcome. You may be worried because you do not understand the Table fully yet, but do not be concerned about this — neither does your pastor.

We grow up into Christ and into a right wisdom *because we are fed*. We do not grow up strong, and then earn the right to eat at His Table as a reward. We eat and consequently grow. We do not grow and consequently eat. So all you, from the least to the greatest, the people of God in whom He delights — come, sit down, take and eat, take and drink. Grace is dangerous, but not in the way we think.

So come, and welcome, to Jesus Christ.

MORNING ☼ THAT STRENGTH IS HERE

All homes have places where discipline occurs. As I was growing up, it was the basement. When we were "sent to the basement," this is where my father would admonish us, discipline us, pray with us afterward, and graciously invite us to rejoin the fellowship of the family. In other homes it may be one of the back bedrooms, or the bathroom. But I have never heard of a godly home where the point of discipline was the dining room, during the course of dinner. Sometimes during dinner a child has to be taken from the table for discipline, but no one that I know of brings a child to the table for discipline. We bring our children to the table for food.

Discipline is important. Confession of sin is important. Working through hard issues of sin and restitution is important. But this Table is the place for fellowship, kindness, laughter, and joy. So come, and receive the gracious nourishment offered.

Some might object to this as too casual. They might say that Jesus said that if your brother had something against you, leave your gift on the altar, and go, put it right. Yes, and we really should do this. But notice that He said we should not give in this condition, not that we should not receive in this condition. So stop tithing, stop putting your gifts in the offering box in the back until you have put things right with your brother (as far as it is possible with you). Let this be your reminder to get things right. Leave your gift envelope in your Bible until you get things right. But churches rarely tell the saints to stop giving them money until the donor is back in fellowship.

But this is a radical gospel message. Until you put things right, we will not stop offering the grace of God to you. But if you have the power to do so, and you do not put things right with your brother, then stop tithing. Stop bringing your offerings. God would rather have your obedience than your money. Is the obedience hard? Do you need strength to undertake it? That strength is here.

So come, and welcome, to Jesus Christ.

Our Lord, who knew the hearts of men, served the Lord's Supper to Judas, one in whose heart the devil was already at work. Not only this, but the Lord also took off His outer garments, took a basin, and washed the disciples' feet, including the feet of Judas — the same feet that were shortly to go out into the night in order to complete his betrayal.

Jesus did this expressly to provide an example for us. The Lord knew, and said, that not all of them were clean. But He washed their feet regardless. This does not mean that someone can never be excluded from the Supper — as Judas eventually was. But it does mean that we ought not to be so scrupulous over the Supper (on the basis of our clear readings of *other* people's hearts) that we wind up destroying the meaning of it.

The Corinthians were chided by Paul for dividing up into factions, and for excluding some of their number from the Supper. He said that when you do this, you are not discerning the Lord's body — the Lord's body and the Lord's Supper are *coextensive.* Why do we say that the Lord's body extends to every member of that body, but then through selfishness refuse to send the bread and wine that far?

Of course, reapplying this ancient error, we have taken these words as the basis for refusing the Lord's Supper to certain parts of the body. Children of God, *discern the Lord's body!* Look around you. Look down your row. While you are at it, do not look over the heads of some of the humbler members of it.

God is not a cosmic miser of grace. He pours out His grace upon His people. He is doing so now. Are you baptized? Then do not *dare* hold back.

So come, and welcome, to Jesus Christ.

MORNING ☼ COME AS YOU ARE TOLD

When Jesus was assembled with His disciples at their last meal together, He identified the one who was to betray Him with a sop of bread. When He gave the bread to Judas, Satan entered into him, and Jesus said, "That thou doest, do quickly" (Jn. 13:27).

The Lord's Supper is a sign and a seal of the new covenant. But as a sign it does what every sign always does — and this includes words, sacraments, symbols, and anything else that carries meaning. In this fallen world, before anything communicates, it first *divides*. As a sign from God, it does its work sovereignly. Every sign, every word, every symbol is in the first place an identifier of loyalty, love, and affection. The cognitive aspect of every sign comes in the second place, after love. Anselm once said *credo ut intelligam* — "I believe that I might understand." This is wonderful, but let us edit it just a bit — *amo ut intelligam.* "I love that I might understand."

The Lord offers this bread and wine to you. If you refuse it, this is not a sign of humility, but rather of hatred. If you take it, and go off into the night to follow your rebellions, as Judas did, then this is a sign of an even deeper hatred. But if you receive it, as you are invited and commanded to do, asking God to have His way with you, and you take the bread and wine — despite whatever scruples, anxieties, worries, or troubles you may have — you are receiving His gift with affection, humility, love, and an appropriate combination of worth and unworth. God knew we were sinners when He established this meal for us. Is He dismayed when we sinners come as we are told?

So come, and welcome, to Jesus Christ.

EVENING ◐ HUMILITY IS AN INFERENCE

When it comes to the duty of humility, the body is generally divided into two large sections. There are those who do not think of humility much, for the whole thing seems entirely unrealistic, and then there are those who pay a great deal of direct attention to this duty, and it is that kind of *direct* attention that is fatal to their efforts.

The first group makes no attempt to do the right thing, and the second group spends a lot of well-intentioned effort trying to accomplish the wrong thing. "Be clothed with humility: for God resisteth the proud, and giveth grace to the humble" (1 Pet. 5:5).

What we must come to learn is that *humility is an inference*. It is always and everywhere a comparative inference.

If you gaze directly at yourself, trying hard to see a lowly worm, what you will wind up seeing is a very proud worm, a worm who fills up the whole screen. Not only is this not humility, it is the very antithesis of it. But when your thoughts are full of God, when your vision is occupied with Christ, and when you make much of Him, you know and see yourself in true perspective, and it is a delight to do so. There is a great pleasure in being small. When you stand looking out over the Grand Canyon, or if you gaze at the night sky through a powerful telescope, you see yourself as small precisely because you are seeing something that is enormous. And in seeing something magnificent, you readily make the inference that humility loves to make.

Not only is there pleasure in being small, there is pleasure in being lifted up from that small position and recognized. "Humble yourselves therefore under the mighty hand of God, that he may exalt you in due time" (1 Pet. 5:6).

Let us come then to humble ourselves in the presence of God. As we reflect on what is involved in this meal, we are wonderfully humbled.

So come, and welcome, to Jesus Christ.

MORNING ☼ HE HATH FILLED THE HUNGRY WITH GOOD THINGS

Idolaters are hungry, and idolaters have the kind of hunger that cannot be filled. The prophet Isaiah says it this way: "The smith with the tongs both worketh in the coals, and fashioneth it with hammers, and worketh it with the strength of his arms: yea, he is hungry, and his strength faileth: he drinketh no water, and is faint" (Is. 44:12).

Those who fight against Zion, the city of God, think that they are able to fill themselves — but they cannot. "It shall even be as when an hungry man dreameth, and, behold, he eateth; but he awaketh, and his soul is empty" (Is. 29:8). Our Lord's mother spoke of this also. "He hath filled the hungry with good things; and the rich he hath sent empty away" (Luke 1:53).

You come to this Table to be filled, and God promises to do it. The only way you may come to this Table and not be filled is through attempting to bring any idols with you. If you are Isaiah's smith, fashioning idols with your tongs, then your strength will fail. If you are fighting against Ariel, against Zion, all your eating is just dream food, and when you awaken, the gnawing in your belly will be worse than ever before. If you come to this Table *rich* in your own conceits, then you will be sent empty away.

Blessed are the poor in spirit. Blessed are the hungry, for they shall be filled. The food is here; the food is good; the food is all of grace. You cannot earn a bit of it, and the only way to forfeit the blessing that is here is through *trying* to earn it. That is the heart of all idolatry.

You are not here because you bought a ticket. You are not here because you registered in time. You are not here because you met the deadline. You are not here because you have season tickets. You are here because you have *been* bought, and you have *been* brought.

We are fed because we do not feed ourselves.

So come, and welcome, to Jesus Christ.

EVENING ◐ LIKE SHEEP IN A THUNDERSTORM

At the first Supper, the Lord delivered a new commandment to His disciples — which was that they were love one another the same way He has loved them. He said further that this would be the mark by which they would be identified as His, by their love for one another, a love that was the same as His love (Jn. 13:34–35).

A central place where this love is to be declared, proclaimed, acted out, chewed and swallowed is in the Lord's Supper. That is the context. But we are still slow of heart to believe, and this shows up, not surprisingly, in how we observe the Supper. The apostle Paul spends virtually the entire book of 1 Corinthians chastising them for their cultivation of divisions which despised the weaker members of the congregation — and we take him to be requiring us to withhold the Supper from the weaker members of the congregation. He commands us to examine ourselves, and we take him to mean that we are to examine other people.

We use our lack of knowledge of hearts as a firm foundation for rejecting others. Christ, in His full knowledge of hearts, received and accepted the weak and lowly. To whom did He administer the Supper? We have already considered Judas. But He gave also to Peter, who boasted vainly about his dedication. He gave to the other disciples, who within hours scattered like sheep in a thunderstorm. He gave to men who took the solemn occasion to have a quarrel about who was the greatest.

Jesus said, as I have loved you, so love one another. No one in this room has offended any other person here the way the disciples offended Christ. And yet, unspeakable kindness, He fed them anyway. So come, and eat together.

So come, and welcome, to Jesus Christ.

MORNING ✻ THE ANSWER TO SACRIFICIAL CRISIS

The same night that the Jesus established the Lord's Supper, He sang with His disciples before He went to His betrayal. Because He established the Lord's Supper at a Passover Seder, we know that He sang the Hallel Psalms (113–118). This means that He sang Psalm 116, which contains these words. "I will take the cup of salvation, and call upon the name of the Lord" (v. 13). And again, "I will pay my vows unto the Lord now in the presence of all his people. Precious in the sight of the Lord is the death of his saints" (vv. 14–15).

Jesus is the preeminent holy one, the preeminent Saint, and His death was precious in the sight of God. His death was a substitution for all His people, and because of this, He is now present with us, cup of salvation in hand. He is with us, having paid all His vows in the presence of all God's people.

This means *forgiveness*. Not "forgiveness" as a word you hear at church. Not "forgiveness" as a doctrinal category in a catechism. Not "forgiveness" as an abstract ideal. Not "forgiveness" for everybody in a vague corporate way. No, this means *forgiveness* for you, now, and for the specific sins you have committed this last week.

When God's covenant people shy away from receiving this absolute cleansing, this hot, soapy bath for the soul, the result is accumulating and accumulated guilt. And guilt must always be addressed, either through the gospel or through the conflicts of paganism. When guilt goes unaddressed in a church for any length of time, the result is conflict, moral crusading and posturing, scapegoating, and more. When the sacrifice of Christ on the cross is neglected through unbelief, the result is a corporate crisis, a sacrificial crisis. And that is the condition of the Church at large today — we are in the midst of a sacrificial crisis. And the only gospel that can really resolve such a crisis is the gospel proclaimed in this bread and wine.

So come, and welcome, to Jesus Christ.

EVENING ◐ THE LOWER DUTY IS HIGHER

The Lord told His disciples that He was going somewhere, and that the disciples could not come with Him. Instead of coming with Him, He commanded them to love one another — the new commandment. But Peter wanted to accompany the Lord, which was apparently far more appealing than loving the other disciples (Jn. 13:33–37). So look around *this* room as you discern the Lord's body here. Wouldn't it be easier to ascend into the heavenly places and be with the Lord than to be down here with all the petty wrangles and quarrels that tend to break out among us? Yes, it would be, which is why the Lord told us that we are to stay here and address the question of loving one another. His immediate concern is not to get us up into heaven, but rather to get heaven down into us.

And heaven has gotten into us when the demeanor of heaven is there, and *this means loving one another*. Cast your thoughts around the room again. Can you think of others here whom you believe to be afflicted with envy, cowardice, compromise, inability to see it your way, lack of wisdom, pride, worldliness, and so on? You may well be right in the details; you are certainly right if it is taken as a generalization. We are *sinners*. But what are we commanded to do with these sinners that surround us on every hand? *We are to love them* as we chew and swallow the bread, and drink the blood-red wine.

If we shirk from this immediate duty, as Peter did, in the name of a higher and more heavenly calling — claiming that we will follow Christ to the point of death if necessary — we set ourselves to follow Peter in what he actually did, and not what he claimed he would do.

So here is the Lord's Table — you are to love everyone seated at it.

So come, and welcome, to Jesus Christ.

MORNING ☼ BURGUNDY DISHWATER

This Supper is not a covenantal meal in the midst of a non-covenantal world. Everything we do is covenantal, which is another way of saying that everything we do is a form of fellowship, or a form of partaking.

This even includes our sin. When we sin, we are trying to eat at another table in addition to this one here. But we cannot *commune* in two directions at once. One of the blessings that God gives us in this Table is an increased understanding and awareness of the radical antithesis between this Table and any of the fare offered by the world.

God offers bread and wine. The world offers you dishwater and sawdust cakes. But you must know this — the difference between the two is not apparent to *us,* if we labor to understand it in our own power. The dishwater often has a deep burgundy color, the result of a lying use of food coloring. The package on the sawdust cakes tells you that it is rich in fiber, and the simple are taken in.

But as the grace of God feeds you, He strengthens you, and you start to perceive the world's wisdom, all its wisdom, as just lying and deceitful scraps. You do not need vain speculation — feed on Christ. You do not need the entertainments of Vanity Fair — feed on Christ. You do not need worldly philosophy — feed on Christ. You do not need anything derived from the other Table except a spirit of repentance for having ever been attracted to it.

Open your mouth. Ask Christ to feed you and strengthen you to be able to see *anything* in your life that you should be tired of by now.

So come, and welcome, to Jesus Christ.

In the words of institution that we use, the apostle Paul says that as often as we eat this bread and drink this cup, we show the Lord's death until He comes. Now the verb *show* here means to proclaim or declare.

This means that the entire communicant Church preaches or announces or declares. What do we declare? Paul says that we declare or preach the Lord's death, and that we do so as long as we are eating and drinking this bread and wine until the Lord comes again.

But notice what we are *not* doing. We are not seeking out discussion partners. We are not engaging in fruitful dialog. We are not meeting anyone in the middle. We are not seeking to find out how the demands of the new postmodern *milieu* require us to reconfigure what it means to do church. We are not arguing. We are not debating. We are not lobbying in Congress.

We declare. We proclaim. We do so with *authority*.

But secularists and unbelievers ask, "How dare you by-pass all the troublesome questions of epistemology?" And we just chew and swallow, loving one another, discerning Christ in the body, seeing Christ in one another, and the world somehow *knows* that Christ is from God.

And in our own midst, we often find baptized Christians who are comfortable with this meal as "a tradition within their own faith community," but they become radically agitated whenever we declare the death and resurrection of Jesus to the world with any kind of authority.

But we are not told to go out into all the world and tell the nations that they might have a point. We are not told to find out what the philosophers are muttering about these days and try to understand this meal in the light of that. We are not told to blend the Table of the Lord with the tables of the baals. In fact, we are told not to.

So come, and welcome, to Jesus Christ.

MORNING ☼ RESTING UPON THE SACRIFICE

What you see before you is a Table, and not an altar. It is a sacrificial meal, and apart from the sacrifices of praise we offer, it is not a sacrifice. In the Old Testament, after the sacrifices were offered, the worshiper was invited to sit down at a sacrificial meal which depended on the sacrifice, but was not to be identified with it.

Our Lord Jesus was sacrificed *once*, thousands of years ago. This once for all sacrifice was sufficient to set this Table every week, in every congregation, until the end of the world. Without that sacrifice, there would be no meal, and so this must therefore be understood as a sacrificial meal. But if we were to make this the sacrifice itself, then we have fallen into the error of the Judaizers, who trampled the blood of the covenant underfoot. But the blood of the covenant belongs under your tongue, not under your feet. The bread of heaven should be in your hands, in your mouth, in your heart, and not thrown under the Table for the dogs.

With this said, take care that your *children* are not exiled under the Table, scavenging down there with the dogs. If they are covenant children, bring them to the Table — feeding and teaching them. How is it possible to do this right? Only with humility and faith.

The faith is in Jesus Christ, crucified once for all. The humility is the child-like willingness to open your mouth, look to Him for nourishment.

So come, and welcome, to Jesus Christ.

We serve and worship a *merciful* God. One of the central lessons as we approach this Table is that God loves us and wants us here.

This is a hard lesson to learn — sinful men know how to flatter themselves, and they can readily believe (in their own conceits) that God loves them just the way they are, with maybe some touch-up paint here and there, which is of course the work of grace. Such men do not understand God at all. And other men know the depth of their own sinfulness, and they have come to understand something of the holiness of God, and so they shrink back in dread, and are reluctant to come to this Table. Those who do not know God approach Him jauntily, hands in pockets, whistling. "Of course God loves me. *I* love me — why wouldn't He?" Those who do know (something of) God are terrified of this kind of impiety, and they dread the possibility of ever falling into it.

This second group knows more of God than the first, but they do not yet know as they ought. Not only is the wrath of God visited upon the arrogant sons of men, but also we learn in the gospel that the wrath of God was visited upon the Son of Man. And this was simultaneously the greatest act of God's wrath in human history and the greatest act of love in human history. *Simultaneously.*

This act of wrath/love, this pouring out of justice/mercy, this indescribable gift can only be understood by the grace of God. And that grace is what we are proclaiming here, now. That grace is what we are eating and drinking. That grace is near you — it is in your mouth and in your heart.

Grace is the only thing that knows how to weave together the words *salvation* and *fear and trembling*. Grace alone can combine forgiveness and fear. Only grace embraces justice and mercy in one embrace. Only grace enables us, forgiven sinners, to sit down at a Table like this one, and rejoice, giving thanks.

So come, and welcome, to Jesus Christ.

MORNING ☼ GLADNESS AND STRENGTH

God delights to feed His people. In Psalm 104:15, we learn that wine has been given to make glad the heart of man. We learn in the same verse that bread was given to strengthen the heart of man.

Strength and gladness are therefore here on this Table before us. God has given us the wine of the new covenant, the covenant through which all our sins are washed away, and our response is therefore one of joyful thanksgiving and gladness. This is a Eucharistic Table, a Table of Thanksgiving. Thanksgiving for what? You sins are forgiven. Your guilt is washed away. God has taken away your heart of stone and given you a heart of flesh, on which His perfect law is inscribed. We are glad because we have been justified in Christ, and we therefore have peace with God.

But we also have bread here, and bread was given to strengthen the heart of man. This is a sign of God's work in our midst to sanctify us. He does not just forgive us, and then leave us filthy. He forgives us, and He blesses us, and He washes us, and He equips us. This equipping can be seen in the bread — substantive strength for the way. You will all leave here this morning, and you will face various challenges and temptations. You need strength for the way. Remember also that the bread is the one loaf of the body of Christ, and this means that your strength is not to be thought of as individual strength. As you grow stronger, you are doing so as a member of the others here.

Wine and bread. Gladness and strength. Justification and sanctification. Forgiveness and holiness. All given to us as a flat out *gift*, none of it learned. This is the hardest thing for us to grasp. How can gladness come from another? How can strength come from outside? We are troubled by these things because we are still in the grip of radical Enlightenment individualism. We think it all must arise from within. But we are not individuals; we are interdividuals. So take and eat, take and drink.

So come, and welcome, to Jesus Christ.

The Christian faith is not divided, because Christ is not divided. There is no division here — whether Jew or Gentile, slave or free, male or female, black or white, young or old. Neither is there a division between *internal* and *external*. There are those who seek to introduce such distinctions, just as there have been those who have sought to establish ethnic distinctions.

But you come to this Table as an entire person. All of you is here. You do not feed in your heart only. You do not feed with your body only. You do not master this meal by mastering certain intellectual distinctions. You come as you are, all of you.

The only thing that seeks to divide you up in pieces is sin. Sin, the divider, is therefore to be divided *from*. There is to be no disunity here, and so we must divide from that which takes disunity everywhere it goes. Sin is your enemy, your adversary. Repent of it, and let it go.

You are coming to the Table of the Lord. At this Table, our God is establishing a new humanity, He is rebuilding our race from a spectacular ruin. Every member is to be built up, every ligament is to be brought together, and we do this by being built up into our head, the Lord Jesus Christ. Come to the Table, therefore, and come *together*.

So come, and welcome, to Jesus Christ.

MORNING ✹ BAKED INTO A LOAF

It is no accident, and no coincidence, that the elements of the bread and wine will in just a few moments pass over your lips and tongue. It is also no secret that we all fail in many ways, as James tells us, and not least with our speech. The elements of the sacrament, therefore, come in direct contact, on a weekly basis, with that part of your body which gives you the most trouble. Not only does it give *us* the most trouble, in many cases *our* speech gives others the most trouble.

This is no argument for shrinking back from the Supper. But it is an argument for coming to this Supper with a demeanor of humility — a willingness and eagerness to be corrected and forgiven. And this is what the Supper represents to you. Forgiveness of *sins,* baked into a loaf. Forgiveness of *sins,* poured into a cup.

This is a covenant meal for sinners. This means that if you come to it while stubbornly clinging to your right to speak sinfully the way you do, then the contact of these elements with your sinning organs of speech brings chastisement and discipline. And it is no wonder that you struggle as you do.

But the alternative is not to become sinlessly perfect before you partake. This meal is not a reward for having been so good. It is a sacrament that declares forgiveness of *sin*. Are you a mess? Come, and welcome. Have you been harsh with your children? Come, and welcome. Were you harsh with them this *morning*? Come, and welcome. Have you been critical of your husband? Come, and welcome. Have you been harsh with your wife? Come, and welcome. Have you spoken of any brothers and sisters here with a hard and bitter edge? Come, and welcome.

But to receive this welcome, to come in such humility, means that you come submitting yourselves to the work of God in you. Come in faith — not in fatalistic despair, and not in stubborn resistance. Come in faith, for God is at work here and now, sanctifying your tongue.

So come, and welcome, to Jesus Christ.

God has never, in the history of the world, called a people out from the world in order to starve them. It sometimes looked that way, but this was because it was God's intention to not only fed their bodies, but also to feed their faith.

This is why the manna fell from the sky. If He had wanted, God could have delivered more ordinary food for the Israelites, and arranged to do it in a more ordinary way. Everyone knows that bread is supposed to come up from the dirt, and not down out of the sky. Up out of the dirt is natural law, and down from the sky seems suspiciously like a miracle. But of course, bread from heaven is no more unusual that bread from dirt. God just alternated the pattern in order to feed the Israelites in another way.

If you were to spend all your time looking for the ordinary delivery trucks, then it did appear as though God had taken them out in the wilderness in order to starve them. As I said, it looked that way.

But God did not do this in order to feed them less, to put them on starvation rations. God was not being stingy with the food. Rather, God wanted to give them fat souls. There is a way of demanding the ordinary means of eating that obtains our request, but leanness of soul with it.

Those who rejoiced in the bread from the sky had bread on the Table, but they also had bread in their hearts. This is why you Christians are heirs of the Israelites. You are being invited to rejoice the same way. God gives you food. He does not deliver you from sin in order to take you out into a wilderness and starve you. He saves you from Egypt in order that you might see His mighty works in the desert.

Water from the Rock that was Christ. Bread from heaven, and Christ again. For those who have faith, Christ is over all, in all, and through all. He is here with us this morning, and He is here in fulfillment of His promise. So let us partake together with Him.

So come, and welcome, to Jesus Christ.

MORNING ☼ THE REAL TRANSFORMATION AT THE TABLE

When we come to this Table, we do not believe (with some) that Jesus Christ is locally present in the elements in a crude physical way, or that the bread and the wine have been in any way transformed into something else. The physical body of Jesus Christ is at the right hand of God the Father, where He has been exalted, and where He will remain until all His enemies have been made His footstool.

But we do believe that *we* are being transformed into something else, and what that is would be the perfect man, the image of the Lord Jesus Christ. For we are His body, flesh of His flesh, and bone of His bones. And when we gather around His Table in worship, He does not descend to turn Himself into bread. Rather, we *ascend* into the heavenly places to be turned into Him. Do not worry: this heavenly Table is a large heavenly one where every saint can gather around it, with room to spare.

We are *nourished* in this meal by faith alone. And by faith alone we are made glorious partakers of the *humanity* of Jesus Christ, and are being knit together as His perfect bride.

So this meal is far more than a mere reminder. It is designed to make you think of the cross and resurrection, of course, but it goes far beyond a mere mental recollection. This is the focal point of your fellowship with Him, the *koinonia* that all saints share in Jesus Christ. You are united with Him at all times, and with one another at all times, but in this meal that *koinonia* is renewed, strengthened, and grown up into God's larger and more glorious purpose. The presence of the Lord Jesus with us here is no static thing—He is dealing with us, changing us, renewing us, growing us up to maturity. Turn to Him in faith as He does so.

So come, and welcome, to Jesus Christ.

EVENING ◐ FAITH SEES BETTER THAN THAT

As we come to the Lord's Table, we are seeking to be fed. The food and drink available to us here are the body and blood of the Lord Jesus Christ. Put another way, we are being made partakers of His perfect humanity as we come, and are being nourished up into that humanity, bone of His bone and flesh of His flesh. This is all a great mystery, Paul says, and so we need to take care that we do not do anything that would empty it of its mysterious or sacramental character.

This means we must avoid the error of Rome on the one hand, which simplistically destroys the sacrament by saying that the substance of the bread and wine are changed into the physical the body and blood of the Lord. We also need to avoid the widespread error among Protestants that says this Supper is nothing but a mere reminder, and that if we already "remembered" the cross of Christ with our brains, this Supper adds nothing to the remembrance. This "mere memorialist" position does not do justice to God's cosmic purposes. This says we eat with our minds, by gnawing on propositional bones.

But we hold that as we come to this Table *in faith*, God uses our actions of eating and drinking to accomplish a heavenly transaction — and that transaction is nourishment and growth up into our shared human nature with Jesus Christ. We are being made new, transformed into a new humanity. If we come to the Table in unbelief or hypocrisy, the sin is that of holding these objective realities in contempt, and so we incur the chastisements of the covenant. We eat and drink damnation. We participate in the body of Jesus Christ in such a way as to invite removal from it.

The body of Christ does not descend to this Table. He is seated at the right hand of God. Rather, this Table, and those gathered around it, ascend into the heavenly places to be nourished there. This spiritual feeding on the body of Christ must not be taken as an imaginary feeding. True faith sees better than that.

So come, and welcome, to Jesus Christ.

MORNING ☼ THE REAL MIRACLE

The God of all creation, heaven and earth, sea and dry land, is a wonder-working God. He is the God of extraordinary miracles, and He is the God of all the ordinary miracles as well. What is more miraculous than all the ordinary things that surround us on every hand. God is the author of all this, and we cannot begin to thank Him for all that He does.

But though He works wonders, and is the God of an almost infinite number of miracles, He is not to be thought of as a ninth-rate magician, doing tricks on a table. At this meal, He meets with us in the person of His Son, and He does this by escorting us all, in the power of His Spirit, into His heavenly courts. As we commune with Him there, we are being transformed from one degree of glory to another. As we partake in evangelical faith, we are being knit together in love, the way He has determined to do it.

This is not a magic show. He is not turning bread and wine into something else. Rather He turning *us* into something else. What are we being changed into? We are being transformed into — and this is truly shocking — we are being transformed into genuine human beings, men and women. God, from the wreckage of humanity made by Adam's sin, is making a new humanity, growing us up into the image of Jesus Christ. This is not a sideshow transformation. It is a transformation that is the *point* of universal history.

When the bride of Christ is presented to Him, without spot, or wrinkle, or any other blemish, that presentation will be the result of God's work throughout history as He fashions a perfect bride — and will do so from completely unsuitable materials. How can a spotless bride be fashioned from a diseased whore? But it has been done; it is being done; it will be done.

That is the miracle. That is what you should see. *That* is what you should know by faith.

So come, and welcome, to Jesus Christ.

EVENING ◐ THIS IS A GREAT MYSTERY

As we meditate on the Word of God that accompanies the sacrament, we have to take care that we pray for the Word to teach us fully, which is to say, richly and mysteriously.

You commune with the Lord, one with Him through the agency of the Holy Spirit, and in this communion, this partaking, this *koinonia*, you are being built up into a perfect bride, without spot or wrinkle, or any other blemish. There is a particular communion in this Supper, a particular grace, that is not available elsewhere in other settings.

The apostle Paul compares union with Christ, with some hesitant qualification, to sexual communion within marriage (Eph. 5:32). We want to speak about this carefully, because St. Paul does, but we also want to speak about it clearly, because Paul does. Just as a married couple are married all the time, and are one with one another all the time, so also there are particular times when that union is particularly expressed in sexual communion.

There is a comparison that must be made to the Lord's Supper. You are one with Christ all the time. You have fellowship with Him all the time. You may pray to Him at any time. You are part of the bride of Christ all the time. But God in His grace has given us the privilege of renewing covenant with Him in this way, regularly, not because we are any less married to Christ if we do not, but because that marriage is languishing if we do not.

Again, this is all a great mystery, and all the more reason, therefore, to approach God in this way, seeking to be edified and built up in that mystery.

So come, and welcome, to Jesus Christ.

MORNING ☼ THE SABBATH CORNERSTONE

As we seek to return to an observance of a Christian calendar, we need to be careful to avoid the mistake that our fathers made. In the course of the medieval period, the year filled up with so many saints days that they had the effect that barnacles have on a ship that at one time was swift. We do not want to make that mistake again. If everything is special, then nothing is special. If everything is set apart, there is nothing left for it to be set apart from.

We are following the example here of the continental Reformers, who returned to a marking of the evangelical feast days. So, for example, Palm Sunday — the week before Easter — is a high Sabbath. Two things should be said about this. The first is that we are resisting the idolatry of *our* age in this (as distinct from those of 600 years ago), and that is the idolatry of secular statism. We refuse to measure our days in terms of Labor Day, or Memorial Day, or MLK Day. There is nothing wrong with a barbecue on such civil holidays, but they do not define our year. It is in Christ that we live and move and have our being. We want to measure our days aright, and so we structure our annual worship around the major events in our Lord's life. This is 2007, A.D. *not* C.E. We have celebrated Christmas, we have come to the threshold of Easter, we will celebrate the Ascension and the outpouring of the Holy Spirit at Pentecost. Our religious holidays are fundamental; our civil holidays are not.

The second thing that must be said is this — we have no right to establish holidays not explicitly required in the Word if that in any way impinges on the one day that God has established, which is the weekly Sabbath, the Lord's Day. *This* is the day that the Lord has made; we will rejoice and be glad in it. We have no right to set aside the Word of God for the sake of our traditions. Worship the Lord weekly, come to His Supper weekly — this worship service is the foundation. If that is so, then let us feel free to build on that foundation together.

So come, and welcome, to Jesus Christ.

EVENING ◐ GOD CONTINUES TO DEAL WITH US

Since we have begun the practice of weekly communion, sometime ago now, we have periodically said that one of the blessings that comes from this is the identification of sins, the flushing out of sins. This is never pleasant, and we are sometimes tempted to think that before the sins were revealed to us, they weren't really there. But this is not at all the case.

We have to acknowledge that there are many things in each of our lives that are out of sync with the teaching of the Word of God. We also have to acknowledge that if it were not for the imputation of Christ's righteousness to everyone that believes, not one of us could stand. This is our confidence; this is our justification.

But sanctification is not separable from justification. A husband is not a wife, but if there is no wife, there is no husband. In the same way, justification is not sanctification, but if there is no sanctification, there is no justification. And part of this sanctifying process is the gracious way that God reveals His holiness to us more and more over the years in such a way as to reveal to us, more and more, what we would be without Him, and what we are in our own nature.

This is no cause for despair. Rather, God is doing his work. God is *dealing* with us. He disciplines us, not so that we would lose heart and become faint, but rather so that we would come to understand the work He has undertaken, for His glory and our good. So as you come to the Table, expect to learn, and taste, the goodness of the Lord Your God.

So come, and welcome, to Jesus Christ.

MORNING ☼ A CONVERTING ORDINANCE?

One of the debates that the Church has had about this ordinance (and there have been many) is the debate over whether this is a converting ordinance. And the debate itself reveals the problem we have in formulating out theological opinions when it comes to the matter of saving grace. We want a tame God. We want an obedient God, who always does the same thing every time. But He will not. He does not cooperate with this.

Our Lord taught us that the Holy Spirit of God is like a wind that blows. When He moves, we cannot tell where He came from or where He is going (Jn. 3:8). We cannot package Him, and then open the package up whenever we want someone to get saved.

So is it a converting ordinance? Well, it is when someone is converted. Why would someone receive baptism, grow up in the Church, and then, one day, it just makes *sense*? The same thing happens when a man has heard a thousand sermons, and yes, I know, I've heard it before, and then, one day, the lights come on. It suddenly turns into good, glorious sense.

But we are not supposed to take the sacraments of God and try to use them as though they were techniques of ours. These have no handles on them, we cannot manipulate them. Whenever we try, all we get are vain superstitions.

Salvation is declared to the world. How many different ways can that salvation *arrive*? When the water's of Noah's flood covered the earth, in how many different ways did the water arrive? It filled some gullies, carved great canyons and filled them, it covered mountain ranges, it rushed through great forests, washing the trees away. It was not an event to be marketed. It is the same here.

God's grace comes to the world. We preach Christ crucified every time we are privileged to sit here. And that proclamation is what God uses, together with all His other means of grace, to bring salvation.

So come, and welcome, to Jesus Christ.

EVENING ◐ A MEMORIAL BEFORE THE LORD

There are two fundamental errors to avoid in coming to the Table of the Lord. We readily recognize the first, and so there is a temptation to think that this is the only possible error—so we will consider it in the second place.

The error that characterizes modernity is the sin of *arid rationalism*. In the grip of this error, the memorial of the Supper becomes little more than a string tied around our finger, designed to make us remember certain propositions. This remembrance, it is thought, could readily be accomplished by other means.

But of course, while we do remember the Lord's death by this means, this does not exhaust what Jesus meant when He spoke of this remembrance, or this memorial. Remember Your Old Testaments. Memorials were offered before the Lord as memorials to the Lord. We are not just remembering, we are reminding. But why should we remind a God who never forgets anything? This is the question posed by arid rationalism. Note where it leads—why should we pray, preach the gospel, or feed the hungry? You are *Christians*; do *nothing* in the grip of an idea. You are Christians—do as you are told. Remind the Lord of His covenant to save you.

The other error is the swamp of superstition. In the grip of this, the Table of the Lord is reduced to a simple magic trick, outside of you, there on the Table. But of course, it is not that.

There is a miracle here, a wonder, a mystery. But the mystery involves all of our faith, our life, our identity. How can you all be one with Christ? How can you be the body of Christ? How can Christ be completely identified with you? We cannot do the calculus, but still know this is true. If this is not the case, then we are all still dead in our trespasses and sins.

But this is not our condition. Rather, we live. And those who live, eat, and drink. So come, in faith, to the Table of the Lord.

So come, and welcome, to Jesus Christ.

MORNING ☼ REFUGE FROM GOD IN GOD

We come before the Lord as His people, and we commune with the Lord through the means that He has established. If this is disconcerting, we may reject these means, and flee from Him, as the open infidel does.

But we may also be *cowardly* infidels, and think that we cannot risk open flight — after all, God the Judge might see us. When this is the case, we often take refuge in the subtleties of our own heart, and we turn the means He gave us to *approach* Him into a means of *shrinking back*.

The Word of God says that the Lord has no pleasure in the one who hesitates and shrinks back. The just live by faith, the Word says, and the only alternative to faith in Hebrews 10 is just this shrinking back. Drawing back, hesitating, the erecting of barriers, all of them end in perdition. But those who believe, those who have faith, are ones who believe to the saving of the soul (Heb. 10:38–9).

If your hand holds the bread of the Lord in faith, it can hold nothing else. If your hand holds the cup of the new testament, you cannot believe and drink anything else alongside that new testament. And to make the attempt is to break covenant. So this is a call to faith, and not to a mental trick. Be warned that all mental tricks are accommodations to the flesh, and are designed to get you removed from the presence of God, into a position of relative safety. But the safety is illusory.

The only refuge *from* God is *in* God. If you would flee from Him successfully, you must meet with Him. Not only so, but you must do this by sitting down at Table with His Son. That is why we are here. Come, your place is set.

So come, and welcome, to Jesus Christ.

We are seeking to return to a full and biblical view of the sacraments, and, as we do so, we have to guard against the temptations that attend this endeavor. One of the temptations is to set Word and sacraments against one another, as though they were somehow competitors. "What is more important," the question is asked, "the sermon or the Table?" Even to pose the question illustrates that a false theology has crept in already.

What is more important, cooking or eating? What is more important, the first story of a house or the second story? What is more important for walking, your right leg or your left leg?

What God has joined together, no man may dare to separate. The Word without the sacrament is like cooking all day, and then throwing the food away. Preaching of the Word that does not come at the end to communion has forgotten the point.

But coming to the sacrament without the Word is coming to an empty table, for there has been no cooking, and once there, pretending to eat. This hardly constitutes a high view of food.

When you hear the Word, you are charged to hear with faith, and *this same faith* enables you be nourished here at the Table of the Lord.

So come, and welcome, to Jesus Christ.

MORNING ☼ THE DISLOCATED CENTER

The center of the Christian life is union with Christ. This means that the center of the Christian faith is the Incarnation.

Mankind was created in Adam to be the center of all the created order—everything in this world is meaningless without the part to be played by man. There is no point without us. We are no afterthought, but rather God created us, and set us over the work of His hands. What is man, that God was so mindful of him?

But man, the center of this created order, rebelled against God. He remained the center, but the reality of our sin meant that center was now dislocated, and everything was put out of joint. When Adam fell, all the created order fell beneath him in a heap, and since that time has been groaning and longing for the restoration.

This restoration is found in Jesus Christ, the ultimate and absolute man. But Jesus Christ does us no good at all unless we are united to Him, fully and completely. He is not God's wonder worker, off to the side. Rather, He is the second Adam, the one who restored the dislocated center, and who authoritatively summons every creature to be united to Him. You have been united to Him by faith, and you have obeyed His summons in coming here.

But you also should know that the faith which unites you to Him needs to be nourished, and needs to grow. At this Table, in this moment, God nourishes your faith, strengthens it, and makes you fit for His purposes in you. Do not neglect the observance of His sacraments—but also remember that one of the most common ways of neglecting them is to forget the point of them. God is restoring the human race in Jesus Christ. You are in Him, so continue to grow up to maturity in Him. God is making us into true human beings. So eat, and be satisfied.

So come, and welcome, to Jesus Christ.

EVENING ◐ EATING WHAT IS SET BEFORE YOU

I have preached before that this Table is the arbiter of disputes. This is what Table fellowship means; this is what true Table fellowship *does*.

You were no doubt taught by your mother that good manners involves learning how to eat what is set before you. It is no different here, and this is true on two levels. First, on a mere physical level, realize that according to the Word of God, bread and wine are set before us. We make grape juice available for those who are tender in their consciences and would have trouble if they were to drink wine, but please know that for everyone else, we should drink what is set before us. If it is not a matter of conscience, then remember that you are coming to *His* Table. For example, if your children simply do not like the *taste* of wine, then this is clearly a taste they need to acquire. If you refuse the wine for simple reasons of mere convenience, then let me exhort you to drink what Christ established.

Second, on a spiritual level, realize that God is dealing with us as we come to this Table. This means that every form of shrinking back reveals that there is something in *your* life that you do not want Him to deal with. Recognize this, admit it, and lay whatever it is at His feet. There is no obstacle with Him. What is your obstacle?

Come, have a seat. The place is set for you. The wine is poured, the bread is prepared. Lady Wisdom has set the Table of wisdom, and if you shrink back from it, it is because you are longing in some way to partake of the table set by Folly. So come now, eat. Come and drink.

So come, and welcome, to Jesus Christ.

MORNING ☼ GRATITUDE, BEFORE AND AFTER

The Church has an eating disorder. We do not come to the Table as we ought to do. We do not come frequently enough, though we are graciously invited every week. We do not come cheerfully enough, though this is a Table of thanksgiving, not of morbid introspection. We do not come with enough of our people—though children are welcome, and we do not need to get a sitter.

One of the things that reveals how important this Table is would be the many different devices we have figured out to stay away. Just as a thoughtful Christian knows how important prayer is from how difficult it can be to pray, so we ought to conclude that this Table is important from how difficult it is to get Christians to gather around it every week. We shy away from it.

As just mentioned, this is the *Eucharist*, the Table of thanksgiving. In part, we shy away because we don't want to be troubled with the disciplines of gratitude. While we don't want to be overtly complainy or whiny, we think we can just gravitate to some neutral place, neither grateful nor murmuring. But this is not possible—it will either be one or the other. Because murmuring is so easy, with its ever-present gravitational pull, we need to be brought up short, on a regular basis, with the delightful duty of rejoicing at the Lord's Table.

He has given us this as a delightful reminder, and He rejoices to sit with us. The Lord Jesus is at the head of the Table, and He is the Lord of the Table. He is the one who took the bread that represented His own body into His own hands, *gave thanks* for it, and then *broke* it. If He could give thanks in that setting, how much more should we give thanks in this setting? Because He thanked God for the breaking, we may thank God for the breaking and the restoration. If He could thank God by faith before the resurrection, how much more grateful should we be after the resurrection?

So come, and welcome, to Jesus Christ.

EVENING ◐ NOTHING IS A MERE METAPHOR

We are called to feed with Jesus Christ at His Table. He is the host; He is seated at the head of the Table because He is the head of the Church. But He is not seated there with His enemies, but rather with His bride, the Church, and He is one with His bride. This is not all. He is also the food set on the Table. So we are called to see Him by faith in at least these three ways. Faith sits down at this Table and expects to rise up nourished with the very life of God.

Jesus Christ is seated at the right hand of God the Father in heaven, which is His seat of universal dominion. As we consider Him there, we reflect on how it is necessary that He be considered the Lord of the Table, seated at the Head.

But His Spirit has been poured out upon the Church, making that Church His bride. His Spirit has been given to us to make us one with Him, and this necessarily makes us one with one another. And so in the Lord's Supper you are summoned to see Jesus Christ in your neighbor, in your wife, in your husband, in your children, in your parents. Do you have trouble because they are not worthy? Then you are not yet coming to this Table in the faith that sees that *no one* is worthy, no one *can* be worthy. That is the *point*. In the name of Jesus Christ, stop seeing this Table as a blue-ribbon reward for the self-righteous.

And last, you are called to see (by faith alone) that God performs these wonders, these signs and seals, by the covenantal meaning He has inseparably assigned to this bread and the wine. We ascend into heaven, transcending our earthly limits, and the bread and wine goes with us. The Holy Spirit is poured out upon us, declaring us to be God's saints on the earth, and He blesses the bread and wine.

Some may object saying that this simply makes the bread and wine a mere metaphor. But if we understand by faith, we see that *nothing* is a *mere* metaphor, and all is glory.

So come, and welcome, to Jesus Christ.

MORNING ☼ FAITH AS THE TRUE MOUTH

At this Table, we are called to meet with God. We meet with Him according to His Word, knowing that apart from faith the only thing we can accomplish is a meeting with His displeasure. All that is accomplished at this Table for blessing is accomplished through the instrumentality of faith. And when unbelief comes to the Table, that unbelief is guilty of trampling the Son of God underfoot. In hearing this warning, do not do as so many do, which is to confound tender faith with unbelief. God is far kinder to weakness than we imagine, and is far more severe with the arrogant than we can conceive.

As you come in faith, remember that you are what you eat. This short phrase has been taken by some in a crude materialistic way, and so they assume that because we eat matter we must be nothing more than matter. But we know that the world God made is not like this — far more depth is involved in all that we do, and particularly when we are nourished sacramentally.

You *do* become what you eat. And since we are called to grow up into a perfect man, to *become* restored humanity, this means that we are called to eat restored humanity. Obviously, we do not eat this restored humanity with our teeth and mouths *merely* — if we could do that, it would hardly be a restored and resurrected humanity, and we would be guilty of a grotesque cannibalism. But nevertheless, we do really partake of the body and blood of Jesus Christ, and faith is the true mouth, faith is the true tongue, teeth, and throat. Faith sees that we are being grown up into a perfect man, and the pattern for this is the resurrected, ascended, and glorified Lord of the Church.

As we partake together, fix your eyes on Jesus, the author and finisher of our faith.

So come, and welcome, to Jesus Christ.

EVENING ◐ SOME OF THE OTHER RIFFRAFF

One of the most important aspects of this Table is the guest list. The food on the Table is bread and wine. The Lord of the Table is the host, the one who set the Table, and who offered His body and blood in the heavenly places in a miraculous way, such that we could be knit together with Him by partaking in evangelical faith. The Holy Spirit ushers us into God's presence as we partake of this meal, and He is the one who is accomplishing the great sanctification, performed throughout the course of human history. By this means, the blemishes and wrinkles are being removed from the bride, so that by the last day, she will be fit to be escorted down the aisle to the Son of God.

But part of this sanctification means learning another important aspect of the Supper — the guest list. We don't mind the bread and wine. We don't mind being invited to be friends of God. Misunderstanding what God is up to, we take to it readily.

We *do* mind some of the other riffraff that apparently think they were invited too. We think the Lord's Supper is a black tie affair (with the black tie symbolic of whatever it is that makes us want to make this an exclusive event).

But eating with riffraff is one of the central things that God intends to teach us. We think that we have high standards when all we really have are petty standards. The Lord said that we were to scatter the invitations to this meal everywhere. Through mail slots, under windshield wiper blades, stuffed in shopping bags. This is a come one, come all sort of thing. The RSVP is our baptism, where we engage to come.

There *is* a winnowing, but the Lord does that. Some turn away from the gospel as proclaimed in the bread and wine. We can't help that, and shouldn't want to. We sometimes feel bad that we do not invite the lowly to some of our meals. But do we think the Lord is a hypocrite, and would not follow His own instructions?

So come, and welcome, to Jesus Christ.

MORNING ☼ YOUR NAME ON A PLACE CARD

In this fallen world, there are ultimately only two tables — the Table of the Lord and the table of demons. This being the case, unbelievers will attempt one of two things — they will overtly choose the table of demons in one form or another, or they will attempt to deny that they must make a choice, and will seek to eat from both tables.

Concerning the former, we do not have a great deal to say, at least not at this moment. God will judge those outside. Concerning the latter, we have a great deal to learn. Of course, in our allegiance we cannot partake of two tables at once. We cannot serve both God and mammon, and we cannot serve both God and our own lusts, and we cannot serve God and the devil. This seems simple enough, and it is — so long as you remember that morbid introspection is an attitude characteristic of the *other* table. Ironically, many come to this Table fearfully, not realizing that the fear is a sin to be repented of. At the great day, in the glorious banquet, in the consummation of all things, not one saint will be seated in the resurrection of the just with a bad case of the sulks, or glowering unbelief, or a spirit of introspective morbidity. But if you *cannot* have such an attitude then, you *may* not have it now. Drop it. Let it go. Come — you are most welcome.

One of the things that faithful partaking of the bread and wine does is that it enables you to begin seeing the allurements of the other table in their proper light. Remember, God is dealing with us. Come to this Table with trembling, certainly, but with *joy* and trembling. Love casts out fear, and you are to be seated in love.

You are here in faith. So you will not walk around this Table looking in vain for your name on a place card. Not only is it here, but it was written and placed before the world was created. You say you are not worthy — of course not, and it is your recognition that you are not worthy that constitutes your ability to hear the invitation. Come, sit — eat and drink.

So come, and welcome, to Jesus Christ.

When it comes to the Lord's Supper, the problem of the *haves* and the *have-nots* has always been a very pressing one. Recall that in the church at Corinth, there was this problem even with the elements of the Supper itself. But this communion is a time of unity and union, not a time for competition and vainglory.

Many sins are two-sided, and bring reciprocal temptations with them. For example, when men love to desire, and women love to *be* desired, this is an example of a reciprocal temptation. It is the same kind of thing with the haves and have-nots. The have-nots love to envy and desire, and the haves love to *be* envied.

Grace annihilates all this. There are those who envy you your place at Christ's Table, but it is deadly to rejoice in this, wanting to be envied. You will be, that will happen. But knowing this is very different than having an emotional need for it to happen.

God has chosen you to be here. But what do you have in this that is not a gift? There is a difference between being highly pleased with yourself ("what a fine fellow I must be to get this invitation") and being profoundly grateful. Both responses know something about the honor that has been conferred, but it is the second response that knows the nature of the honor — it is grace all the way down, grace from front to back, grace to the uttermost heavens. It is all sheer, unimaginable, infinite, majestic, sovereign gift.

Not only did we not merit or earn any of this, but we, all of us, actively demerited it. We forfeited it, first in our father Adam, and then again in our own career of sinning. But despite this, God, who is rich in mercy, invited us to come, to sit down with Him, to rejoice with Him, to commune with Him.

And we leap at the opportunity, although we are sometimes troubled by the fact that some of the other sinners around the Table appear to be taking advantage of the omniscient one.

So come, and welcome, to Jesus Christ.

MORNING ✵ EVERLASTING KINDNESS

God does not reveal sin to us so that we might be simply humiliated. Rather, God reveals sin to His people so that they might be humbled, and in that humbling, receive His grace that strengthens, and enables them to stand. The humbling of conviction is a small crucifixion, and the grace of forgiveness is a small resurrection. In this pattern, we embody the gospel throughout our lives.

We have said before that this Table is a revealer of sin — we expected weekly communion to bring many things to the surface, which it has in fact done. But never forget that this Table is efficacious in *dealing* with such sin as well. God does not reveal our sins to us so that in His holiness He might mock us. He is holy, but He is also kind to His people. This Table was set and prepared with an everlasting kindness.

We sometimes shrink from the revelation that conviction of sin brings because we, like the disciples in the gospels, are of little faith. We cannot see past the crucifixion to the resurrection. In eating and drinking, you are participating in the communion of Christ's body and blood, and this means that you are communing in His death. But the Bible teaches that as many of us as are united with Him in His death are also united with Him in His resurrection.

It is a terrible burden to come to this Table while trying to keep the crucifying power of this sacrament away from your pet sins — a sharp tongue, a critical spirit, a self-excusing logic-chopping, or anger with others. But you are Christians, and so still you must come. And this means you must come and die. But *believe the gospel,* which is utterly meaningless apart from resurrection. You also come in order to be raised again, and you leave this place in order to walk in newness of life — hands, tongue, feet, all of you. This Table is here and is set just for you.

So come, and welcome, to Jesus Christ.

EVENING ◐ TASTE AT THE TABLE

We know that God created food in order to nourish us. But is this all God does with food? Not at all—look at how much of the world was created in order to be tasted. In the course of a single day, we may experience and taste tangerines, mayonnaise, bacon, plums, salmon, steak, salt, salads, bread, beer, and chocolate. The list that could be made is simply enormous, to the appearance of being practically infinite.

The same God who created the world in this way also set this Table. So why do we have just two elements here, bread and wine? Where is the variation? Where are all the sauces and tastes? We know that this Supper cannot be boring, because that would dishonor God, but why does it sometimes seem boring to us?

A sacrament is never presented to us raw. As Augustine taught so clearly, Word and sacrament accompany one another, and without the Word, there is no sacrament. Now it is the Word which gives the sacrament its taste, its savor. Of course, the Lord's Supper can objectively nourish us whether it tastes like anything or not. But God does not want us to live like this. He could have made our earthly food nourishing—and boring. We could have been born into a world with nothing to eat but tasteless nutrition bars. But God did not do this.

Neither does He do it here. Everything that the Word of God contains goes with this meal—contrition, joy, grief, gladness, thanksgiving, dominion, glory, pleasure, kindness, love, severity, justice, music, pain, and through it all, worship. To separate the Word from the sacrament, whether in practice, or in the attitude of the heart, is to eat in such a way as to insult the overflowing benevolence of God. Do not settle for this. Come, taste and see.

So come, and welcome, to Jesus Christ.

MORNING ✲ DO YOU SEE WHAT ABRAHAM SAW?

A central part of what we have here in the Supper is the reality of the *koinonia* of God's people. This partaking, this communion, is the reality found in the *one* loaf of bread. You are called, in the observance of this Supper, to discern the Lord's body. This does not mean that you are to try to see the Lord's physical body at the right hand of the Father with your physical eyes. Not one of us can see that far. We do see Him by faith, and so this is part of what we do, but it is not the center of this fellowship meal. Nor are we to see the Lord's body transforming the physical bread and physical wine, as though metaphysical changes are being wrought on this Table here. We cannot see that because it is not happening.

The central duty before us is not to see the Lord's body in the bread, but rather in the ritual of all of us eating this bread together. We do not see this wine as blood, but we do see the blood of the Lord in the ritual of all of us drinking together.

If you curl up into a cocoon in order to meditate on your own spiritual problems, then you are misunderstanding the point of the Supper. Partake with your eyes open. Look around. But you do not look around in order to see all the bread, all the wine. Nor do you look around to see all the people. Rather, you look around and see all the saints of God eating bread together. You look around and see all the saints of God drinking wine together. And so what do you see? The salvation of the world.

So come, and welcome, to Jesus Christ.

The Word tells us that when it comes to this meal, we are to wait for each other. This is why we all take the bread at the same moment, and this is why we all drink the wine at the same moment. This is not an exercise in choreography, but rather a weighty theological proclamation.

When we take the bread, we are all taking bread *together*. When we take the wine, we are all taking wine *together*. When the words of institution are pronounced, at that moment, we all *act as one*.

We do this because we *are* one. One of the virtues of liturgical worship is that it gives us the opportunity many times in one service to declare that we are like-minded. We say *amen* to the same things, and at the same time. We sing the same psalms, and we sing the words together. When we harmonize with different notes, the purpose is not to compete with others, or to show off before others, but rather to showcase the harmonious way the entire body comes together. Harmony accentuates unity; it glorifies unity.

This is a Eucharistic celebration, which means it is a Table of thanksgiving. We all come here with many different reasons for giving thanks, but we all overflow with thanks in the same way. Hundreds of hands move to the mouth at the same instant, and we all chew and swallow bread together. The same thing happens with the wine. As we offer our thanksgiving to God, and our grateful petitions to Him, this is an instance of a royal family, seated at a royal banquet. And like all families at table, we offer our thoughts, our prayers, our counsel to the one seated at the head.

These thoughts and prayers come from many different directions, but in this unitary action of eating bread and drinking wine, God knits them all together and enacts what we His friends have sought for Him to do, and when He does so, this is what Scripture calls His sovereign good pleasure.

So come, and welcome, to Jesus Christ.

MORNING ☼ OLD WINESKINS IN A NEW AGE

This is the time of year we mark the glorious resurrection of Jesus from the dead, in a higher and more pronounced way than we do every week. Every Sunday is resurrection Sunday, Easter itself is Resurrection Sunday.

Many Christians observe a Lenten fast up to Easter, a custom we do not observe. While it is possible to do that in a good and edifying way, there are also reasons to be wary and cautious. Among those reasons is this — the resurrection is new wine, and new wine bursts old wineskins. When Jesus teaches on this subject, He expressly ties the old wineskins to a certain kind of fasting. He clearly identifies the older patterns of fasting with the old wineskins, and He teaches us that the new wine He is offering is utterly inconsistent with that kind of fasting (Mark 2:22; Luke 5:37). The problem was not the make of the wineskin, but rather the age in which it was made. The Lord doesn't identify the problem as Pharisaical distortion, because He also includes the fasting of John the Baptist's disciples.

At the same time, we do not want to fashion our own makeshift wineskin in the other direction, legalistically rejecting all fasts. The New Testament clearly shows that there are ways to fast that are fully consistent with this new wine (Acts 13:3; Acts 14:23; 2 Cor. 6:5). We should never pretend otherwise. So then, taking care to not return to the older order, taking care to rejoice in the new wine, we come to this Table in order to participate in an everlasting feast.

So come, and welcome, to Jesus Christ.

EVENING ◐ REMINDING THE GOD WHO NEVER FORGETS

When we come to this Table, we are fed by the Lord. When we eat the bread and drink the wine, we are nourished by Him. This is a memorial of Christ's death and resurrection, but this is not what many have assumed it to be. A memorial in scriptural language is far more than just a reminder. Of course, the reminding aspect is necessary in every memorial, but a great deal more is involved in it than just this. We do partake in remembrance of Christ, and what He did.

But we have to remember that Christ is seated at this Table as much as we are. He is the host, He is seated at the head of the Table. He *also* partakes in remembrance. But clearly more is involved than Him simply remembering what occurred on the cross. How could He forget that?

The same word is used in Hebrews to speak about the sacrifices, offered up year after year. In these sacrifices, God is being supplicated to remember His promises—promises to send the final sacrifice in Christ. Throughout the Old Testament, memorials were established in order to remind God of His covenant commitments.

We sometimes let our theology get in the way of our obedience. We know theologically that God needs no reminders, and so we don't partake of the memorial that He commanded us to use in order to remind Him. We know He doesn't need to hear our prayers for His benefit, and so we disobey, and neglect our prayers.

God wants us to learn a central lesson here—how to hold Him to His covenant promises. But, we argue, He doesn't need to be held to them. This is quite true—but regardless of what *He* needs, *we* need to hold Him to it. *We* need to plead the covenant. We need to commune with Him and pray to Him with that high level of faith, a faith that appears to outsiders as though we think God might forget us, coupled with our solemn declaration that He never will.

So come, and welcome, to Jesus Christ.

MORNING ✹ BECOMING HUMAN

The Holy Spirit is active in the sacrament of the Lord's Supper. This word sacrament that we use comes from the Latin word *sacramentum*, which in its turn is the translation of the Greek word *mysterion*, or mystery. In what way is this a mystery, and how does the power of the Holy Spirit come into it? The physical body of Jesus is at the right hand of God the Father, not locally present on this Table. In other words, you are not looking at Jesus, captured or contained by bread and wine. But the Scriptures plainly teach that we in the church are yet members of His flesh and of His bones. We partake of His body, and this partaking is a true verb. But how can we do this without Him being locally, physically present?

The Holy Spirit is the God of all miracles. He is the One who accomplished the work of Incarnation in the womb of Mary, who raised our Lord Jesus from the dead, who animates the church as the body of Christ, who escorts us into the heavenly places, so that we by faith can partake of the true humanity of Jesus Christ.

So we are what we eat. But take note here — we do not eat dead matter. By the power of the Holy Spirit, we are enabled to apprehend Christ by faith, and in the motions of eating and drinking, we are nourished and grown up into what we are eating. But we are eating resurrected, living, and true humanity, and we do so in a mystery. This is why we are becoming human.

But the mystery, the sacrament, does not happen in the front of the church, where you have to crane your necks to see it. It does not happen on the Table. It happens as we take, eat, drink, taste, and swallow. The Holy Spirit does all this, and *we* do not have to worry about making it happen. He makes it happen, and *He* understands it. We do not need to understand it — we just have to taste it and look around with gratitude as we see the rest of the body tasting as well. And so this is what we do, discerning the body.

So come, and welcome, to Jesus Christ.

EVENING ◐ STILL BEING BROKEN

We are here sitting down with Jesus Christ, and we are doing so in His kingdom. He is Messiah the Prince, and all authority has been bestowed on Him. From the River to the ends of the earth, He is the Lord. From the east to the west, He is the King over all of it. All the families of the earth are streaming to Him, and the word promised to Abraham is being fulfilled, year after year.

But He did not assume this rule granted to Him by His Father in order to fill the earth up with His peons. He has made us, the Bible tells us, kings and priests. This means that when we sit here with Him, we are sitting with Him in the kingdom, and we are partaking of the gracious rule that He is exercising over all nations, kingdoms, confederations, and tribes.

This is the establishment of His kingdom. And, as Isaiah clearly declared, of the increase of His government there will be no end. When Jesus broke the bread on the hillside during His earthly ministry, in that breaking was a multiplying. According to worldly wisdom, the more you break something up, the less you have of it.

But we have a wisdom that the rulers of darkness do not and cannot comprehend. The more this bread is broken, the more it is able to feed. Five loaves and two fish feed five thousand men. Jesus broke one loaf at the inauguration of this covenant meal, and that one loaf is still nourishing and feeding the world. We are still partaking of it.

The one who seeks to rule over all must become the least. The bread from heaven that feeds the world is taken in Jesus' hands and broken. This is my body, He says, broken for you. And as it is broken, the less it diminishes. The more it is broken, the more it is able to feed a starving world.

And so we invite the world to the waters of baptism, so that they may partake together with us. There is more than enough, and to spare. See? It is still being broken.

So come, and welcome, to Jesus Christ.

MORNING ☼ RECEIVING AT THE TABLE

In the old covenant, the sacrifices were a type of the coming sacrifice of the Messiah, our Lord Jesus. A pure animal was selected, set apart, killed, and offered up to God on an altar. In this the priest was enacting a type, a foreshadowing, of the coming propitiation accomplished by Christ when He was offered up to God. The sacramental offerings of the Old Testament were therefore a type of propitiation — an offering to God.

This Supper is also a sacramental sacrifice, but there is a marked difference. There the sacrifices were *offered*, and offered repeatedly. Here the sacrifice is *received*. God is giving to us. Our sacrifice here, therefore, is not a sacrifice of propitiation, but is rather a sacrifice of returned praise and thanksgiving. We *receive* at a Table; we do not *offer* upon an Altar.

The Greek word for rendering such thanks is the verb *eucharisto,* from which we get the Word Eucharist. In Hebrews 13:16, the apostle tells us to do good, and not to forget to communicate. By this, he does not mean communication in our sense of the word — i.e. talking. The word here is *koinonia,* the partaking of the Lord's body that is accomplished in our observance of this Supper. A better rendering would be "do not forget to come to communion." In the previous verse, he says something contextually telling. He says that we are to offer up sacrifice of praise, the fruit of our lips giving thanks to His name (v. 15).

This is the altar we have, and from which we eat. The altar is the altar of grace, established once for all two thousand years ago, and when we eat by faith, we overflow in Eucharistic thanks and praise.

So come, and welcome, to Jesus Christ.

We are the bride of Jesus Christ, and we are in the process of being knit together with Him, bone of His bone and flesh of His flesh.

This glorious and supernatural process is being accomplished by the Holy Spirit and the Word, the Holy Spirit and the sacrament. There are things being accomplished here by the Spirit which the natural man cannot and will not comprehend. The doctrine is so great that we cannot grasp the entirety of it at any one moment. Rather, God stoops for us, and gives us first this truth, then that one; first, this flavor, then that one; first, this taste, then that one.

We are joined to Christ on the *basis* of His death — which is why we have the signs of bread and wine, body and blood — but we are being joined in fact to a living Christ. We are being knit together with our living and *resurrected* Lord. We do not feed upon a dead body; rather, we are joined together with Him in the power of an indestructible life, and we are being built up into that life.

The grapes that made this wine were once alive, but now they are dead. The grain that made this bread was once alive but now it is dead. This is the mystery of physical eating. Life, death, and then another life sustained. But there is a contrast. In this Supper, we eat spiritually, by faith, but in the eating we partake of that which is alive, alive forevermore. Because Christ has died, *once for all*, death no more has dominion over Him. This is a *Table*, not a tomb. Because of His death, and the power of His resurrection, and the *nature* of that resurrection, we are privileged by God's grace to eat life itself. And in having us do this, God is bringing us up into that life, fitting us for it. What we are eating is what we are becoming — truly alive.

So come, and welcome, to Jesus Christ.

MORNING ☼ WHAT KIND OF MIRACLE?

What are we doing here? Or, more importantly, what is being done to us here?

The Church has historically been divided as to the meaning and import of this Supper. Some believe that no miracle occurs here; others believe that a miracle happens, but it is the wrong category of miracle. A third group believes that this is a miraculous meal — but know that it is a covenantal miracle, not a metaphysical one.

Many of our evangelical brothers believe that this Supper is nothing but a divinely appointed reminder. The blessing comes as the meal reminds you to think certain thoughts. Thus, if something else reminded you of them during the course of the week, at some other place and time, you would be just as blessed. This is the mere memorialist view. In the second view, a remarkable thing happens to the bread and wine. When the words of institution are spoken, Christ is manifested locally somehow in the bread and wine. This, of course, necessitates certain theories about the relationship of all the elements, turns the Table into an Altar, and so forth. The fundamental mistake is that it moves the sacrament away from the congregation and on to the Table. The first error moved the sacrament away from the congregation and into individual brains.

We believe that Christ is manifested in our presence in our action of eating and drinking in faith. If asked if we believe in the real presence of Christ, we should say certainly — we don't believe in His real absence. Christ is in the participles — eating and drinking — not in the inert and stationary objects of bread and wine.

How can an action like eating and drinking knit us together with the living Christ, seated at the right hand of the Father? This is the miracle — this is the work of the Holy Spirit, who takes us up into the heavenly places in this worship service, and there enables us by faith to partake of Christ.

So come, and welcome, to Jesus Christ.

I said another time that in the Lord's Supper we partake of a *living* Christ, not a dead Christ. Scripture teaches this in the tenth chapter of Hebrews, a chapter rich in sacramental doctrine.

We are sanctified through the offering of the body of Jesus Christ (Hebrews 10:10), which was offered once for all by our High Priest, who then sat down at the right hand of God the Father (v. 12), having been empowered to make His enemies a footstool (v. 13). By one offering, He has perfected us forever.

Our sins are therefore forgiven (v. 17), and this means that we have boldness to enter the Holiest by the blood of Jesus (v. 19). How are we to do this? Our modern and materialistic assumption is that we enter the Holy Place by rolling these sentences around in our heads. But that is not how we are told to enter. We draw near in faith (v. 22), with hearts sprinkled to a clean conscience (v. 22), with bodies washed with the pure water of baptism (v. 22). We do this as a congregation, holding fast together, not forsaking the gathering of ourselves together as some do (v. 25). We come by means of a new and living way (v. 20). Note that it is a *living* way. We come through the veil, it says, and then immediately adds that this veil is His flesh (v. 20).

When Jesus died, the veil to the Holy of Holies was torn in two, showing that sinners now had access to God. When Jesus ascended into heaven, this did not cease to be true — it became more gloriously true. So this observance is how we enter into the Holiest, and moreover, with boldness. We come because the blood was shed once for all two thousand years ago, and we are a *forgiven* people. We come because the flesh that is torn in two is alive and gives life. This is, in fact, a new and living way.

When God gives faith by means of the Holy Spirit, He gives it so that you might be built up and strengthened in this new and living way. As a living way, it is for those who are alive.

So come, and welcome, to Jesus Christ.

MORNING ☼ THE MIRACLE CONTINUES

The Incarnation was a stupendous event, a miracle of miracles. The death and resurrection of Jesus Christ, the foundation of all our hope, rest upon this foundation. Christ became a man in order to be able to die. He became a man in order to come back from the dead, leading us all out of the Egypt of sin and death, and into the Canaan of His everlasting promise.

But the Incarnation was not an event that culminated in His passion. Christ rose from the dead as a man, and ascended into the presence of the Ancient of Days as a man. He did not set aside His Deity, but rather we find two natures gloriously united *forever* in the person of our Savior, Jesus of Nazareth. And the point of the Incarnation extends beyond this. The new mankind in Christ requires an Eve, just as the old mankind did. The new mankind is not complete without that Eve — male and female created He them.

This means the Incarnation is not complete until *we* are complete, until the entire creation ceases its restless groaning at the resurrection. The work of the Incarnation is carried on in the power of the Holy Spirit as He knits us together, the Church of Jesus Christ, into the living humanity of our Lord and Savior.

This is not done by our power. How could it be? This is not done by our mental exercises. This is no rationalistic exercise. This is done as the grace of God falls down upon our heads, as bread out of heaven. How can we be knit together with Christ, bone of His bones and flesh of His flesh, by simply eating and drinking? The Spirit accomplishes this through His power, and we come to Him in the eating and drinking, objectively. In faith, we are part of His faithful bride. In sin and unbelief, we are adulteresses. There is no neutrality in this.

So the Incarnation was more than just a supernatural event — it was and remains a miracle. In the Supper of the Lord, the miracle continues.

So come, and welcome, to Jesus Christ.

We too often fall into the trap of thinking that a description is the same thing as an explanation. If confronted with the inadequacy of our description, we resort (oddly) to a more detailed and "scientific" description. But this makes no sense.

When we let go of an object, we readily assume that our scientific description of what happens is an explanation of it. But gravity is not something that pulls objects to the ground, but rather a name we give to our description of things falling to the ground. If confronted with the question as to why objects at a distance appear to act upon each other, the only honest answer is that we have no idea.

This is because *God* governs the world. It is in Christ that all things hold together. The world is not governed by a set of impersonal natural laws. Our tendency to think that the laws are running the show, with God off in the distance, has robbed us of a great deal.

And it has robbed us at this Table also. Why is this a blessing? It is not because we are being acted upon by certain spiritual forces, but rather because God has promised to meet us here. And the God who has promised to meet us here has promised to do so in the Person of Jesus Christ, who is the visible image of the invisible Father. In other words, we are encouraged and strengthened here because of our relationship with a divine Person, and not because we have figured out the right theological formula which will get things done.

This meal is a fellowship meal, it is a meeting of persons, and it is therefore a personal event. This is why we are encouraged to discern the Lord's body in the persons around us — whatever problems we might have with them, we don't tend to think of them as impersonal forces. Many errors concerning this Table are attempts to retreat from the personalism of *koinonia* into the impersonalism of theological metaphysics. Let us therefore meet with God in Person.

So come, and welcome, to Jesus Christ.

MORNING ☼ NO SUCH THING AS NOT PARTAKING

Most of our difficulties with understanding the Supper stem from philosophical assumptions that we all carry about with us. One of the principal culprits has been the division of the world we inhabit into two parts — the spiritual and mental, the material and physical.

But the world is not to be divided up like this. God *has* established a fundamental divide in this world, but the divide is ethical, and is characterized by faith and fidelity on one side and unbelief and infidelity on the other. In all that we say, do, or think, we reveal an allegiance in one direction or the other. The division is not spiritual versus physical, but rather obedient versus disobedient.

Creation is covenantal throughout. This means that we are always partaking, in a sacramental sense, of one of two tables. We partake of the Lord's body and blood in this rite. The Levites partook of the sacrifices of the altar in the old covenant. Pagans partook of their sacrifices in their temples. You do not partake of this Table, and then throughout the course of the rest of your regular life, go out into a realm where there is no such thing as partaking. In this world, *there is nothing but partaking*. The Lord's Supper is not any more "miraculous" than a pagan festival to Zeus. It is, however, far more mysterious than modern materialists assume. This is because your physical actions are every bit as covenantal as the rest of your actions.

The process of sanctification is therefore the process of learning to eat at one Table only. You eat at the Lord's Table on the Lord's Day, and you learn, as you take up the cross daily, to eat from it in another extended sense on Monday and Tuesday and so on. And a corollary of this is that you learn to refuse the offerings and tidbits that came from an alien altar. And if you do not want to give up those tidbits, that accounts for the temptation to shrink back from this Table. But do not do it. *Come.*

So come, and welcome, to Jesus Christ.

The world is governed by covenants. Covenantal law is present everywhere in a similar way to what we call the law of gravity. And as long as we understand gravity as a *personal* thing, the law of covenants is like it, and is made evident in a powerful attraction.

As we have frequently noted, there are only two tables in the world, and each table's law is contrary to the other's. This means, in principle, that we can only eat from one. Out and out pagans eat from their table of demons and seek to rejoice in it. They defy the God of heaven. Faithful Christians look forward to participation and fellowship in this Table, and seek to order the rest of their lives accordingly. They sin and stumble, but do not let this prevent them from coming — it is for them additional evidence of how much they need to come. But they come, as sinners, to *one* Table. They do not come here seeking to keep their name card reserved at the other table.

And this reveals the third option, which is not truly a third option at all. Attempts to eat from both tables simultaneously are simply attempts to disguise the fact that one's allegiance is with the rebellious. Both tables exert a powerful gravitational pull. We have a deep bond, instinctively understood, with anyone else at the same table. If we walk in the light as He is in the light, we have fellowship with one another, and the blood of Jesus His Son cleanses us.

In a comparable way, anyone who has a grievance against God instinctively recoils from His gracious invitation to eat with the Lord Jesus here, and he instinctively seeks out, and is attracted to, anyone else who is recoiling in a similar way. It is a mysterious phenomenon, and yet can be observed as clearly as objects falling down when dropped. Joyful, forgiven Christians cluster together.

All this testifies to the power of what Scripture says in this regard. The power of participation, of fellowship, of *koinonia,* is much more profound than a simple register of individual choices.

So come, and welcome, to Jesus Christ.

MORNING ☼ WHAT DID HE SING?

The Scriptures tell us that after He instituted the Supper, our Lord Jesus sang a hymn with His disciples and then they went out. We know that the psalms sung at the conclusion of the Passover meal were the *Hallel* Psalms, 114–118. So what did our Lord sing when He was facing death of an unspeakable nature?

"Tremble, thou earth, at the presence of the Lord. Our God is in the heavens; He hath done whatsoever He hath pleased. Those who make idols are like unto them. O Israel, trust thou in the Lord; He is their help and their shield. Ye that fear the Lord, trust in the Lord; He is their help and shield.

"I will take the cup of salvation, and call upon the name of the Lord. Precious in the sight of the Lord is the death of His saints. It is better to trust in the Lord than to put confidence in princes. All nations compassed me about, but in the name of the Lord will I destroy them.

"The right hand of the Lord is exalted; the right hand of the Lord doeth valiantly. The stone which the builders refused is become the head stone of the corner. This is the Lord's doing; it is marvelous in our eyes. This is the day which the Lord hath made; we will rejoice and be glad in it.

"Thou art my God, and I will praise thee; thou art my God, I will exalt thee. O give thanks unto the Lord; for He is good; for His mercy endureth forever."

And so it is that we take the cup of salvation. Precious in the sight of the Lord was the death of His Saint. We trust in the Lord, and give thanks to Him, for He is good. How good is God? Take, and eat. How good is God? Take, and drink.

So come, and welcome, to Jesus Christ.

EVENING ◐ A SACRIFICIAL MEAL

The Lord's Supper is a sacrificial meal, which is not the same thing as a sacrifice. The Lord Jesus offered Himself on the cross two thousand years ago, and when He ascended into heaven some weeks afterward, at that time He presented His sacrifice in the heavenly places, in the ultimate Holy of Holies. His sacrifice was a once for all atonement. But in the Bible, sacrifices have blessings that flow from them — which are distinct from the sacrifice, but not separable from it.

Because this is a sacrificial meal, it has to be understood as something God is giving to us. If we do not understand it this way, then we will of necessity turn it into something that we are rendering to God. Of course, the Roman church thinks of this Table as an altar, and the bread and wine and a sacrifice proper. But most of the modern evangelical world thinks of it in the same way. The offering of *man to God* in this case is a testimony, or a dedication, or a confession, or *something* offered up to Him. The thing they share in common is the view that man is somehow a priest in this, and offers a sacrifice of some sort to God.

But this is a sacrificial meal, not a sacrifice, and this means that the initiative is the other way. God feeds us, God nourishes us, God welcomes us, God sheds His love abroad in our hearts. We do not offer this meal; *He* offers this meal.

Our response to this may be described as a sacrifice — but it is a sacrifice of *response*, specifically the response of praise and thanksgiving. This keeps the order as it ought to be. The Table is God's gift to humanity as He makes us into His new humanity, built up into Jesus Christ, the perfect man. At this Table, we *submit* to His grace, and are most thankful.

So come, and welcome, to Jesus Christ.

MORNING ☼ AND THIS IS ODD TOO

One of the central things we learn as we come to this Table is the nature of our triune God, and consequently the nature of the world He created. Many of the disputes between Christians about what happens at this Table is the result of their secret agreement about the rest of the world. The world around us is a humdrum sort of affair, and we then debate whether that changes or not when we come to the Table. Is this a mere memorial, like a post-it note on the fridge, or is it a grand exception to that world of post-it notes?

The whole world is remarkable. Said with appropriate qualifications, the universe is a miracle. This is not because the universe is a violation of natural law (how could that be?) but rather because the whole universe is nothing but sheer, unadulterated gift or grace. God overflows, and He overflows infinitely into the created order. There is no such thing as the mundane.

So this Table is not a spiritual exception to the mundane, and it is not a mundane continuation of the mundane. Rather, this Table instructs us how God is *all the time*. What is God like in *everything*?

Everything is remarkable, for those who have eyes to see. And this Table, these means of grace, this bread and wine, is one of God's appointed means for giving us eyes to see. This bread strengthens your soul to resist temptation. This is odd, but no more odd than how peanut butter helps you get through your morning's work. This wine, taken in faith, knits you together with Christ, and this is odd too. But no more odd than water falling out of the sky so that your breakfast might grow in a field somewhere.

The universe is always and everywhere a personal place. It is in God that we live and move and have our being. He is a covenant-keeping God, and this aspect of His nature is reflected in everything that He does — and He does everything.

So come, and welcome, to Jesus Christ.

We are God's covenant people, and we are seated with our Lord in this covenant meal. Now covenants are, at bottom, *relationships*. Covenants are not doctrinal abstractions. *Covenant* is not a mere word that we use to distinguish ourselves from other denominational traditions. Covenants are structured in the very way that God created the world, and in the way He recreated the world in Jesus Christ. Simply put, you are never alone. Everywhere you go, in everything you do, you are always in relationship. In this meal, God is declaring and making His relationship to you explicitly obvious, but the relation is there all the time.

The question therefore is whether you are constant in this covenant, whether you are faithful. But this brings us to a central question, one that has vexed many unnecessarily. What does it mean to be faithful? It means to trust the only One who is faithful, the only One who ever kept covenant perfectly, our Lord Jesus Christ. You are to trust Him always, cling to Him always, rest in Him always, and never to look to your own performance or merit. There is nothing there but failure and self-condemnation.

But in Christ, there is no condemnation, so come. In Christ, there is forgiveness, so come. In Christ, there is pardon and cleansing, so come. In Christ, there is food for the hungry, so come. Come, be obedient. But obedience means faith, and faith means that you will take and eat, and take and drink. The meal is before you.

So come, and welcome, to Jesus Christ.

MORNING ☼ JUST COME

No man was ever condemned for trusting in the Word of the Lord. Men have been condemned for trifling with it in unbelief, but no poor beggar was ever turned away who came to Him in faith. He turns the proud and haughty away, and scatters the mighty of the earth. But for those who come to Him simply, He receives them simply, and simply receives them.

Coming to God is not complicated. Come to Him as a gracious Savior and You will find how simple it is. Self-righteous men always want to make grace complicated, and they want to make the law, considered in itself, easy. This abstracted law is what they use to construct a ladder which they think will be the way to climb up into heaven. They want the law easy. But in order to make it easy they have to turn the grace and forgiveness of God into a complicated system that no man can really understand. The whole thing gets covered in smoke and darkness.

If you want this gladness and simplicity of heart, when it comes to the Scriptures, or the providences of God, or the decrees of God, then observe this one simple charge. Do not take anything from God in order to chop it up, or divide it into pieces. The grace of God encompasses everything — the garden and our expulsion from it, the law and the gospel, faith and works, love and hate. Receive this, and the Word, a two-edged sword, divides you, and arranges the pieces on the altar, and you ascend to God in the smoke of the consecration offering. And in receiving this death, the good Lord gives back life to you. He gives, always gives, thirty-, sixty-, and a hundredfold.

So the grace of God really is simple. The kindness and forgiveness of the Lord is present. It is here today. The Holy Spirit invites you, simply, "Come." The bride, the wife of the Lamb, the church of God, extends the same invitation. "Come." There it is in one word. Come.

So come, and welcome, to Jesus Christ.

This event is a public ritual. It is a sacred meal at the center of the new city, the City that God is establishing in the earth. It is a potent meal, but it is not potent in the way a nuclear reactor is, or a great turbine engine is, or a profound magic spell. It is potent the same way saying the Pledge of Allegiance before basketball games is.

Moderns like to pretend that human beings can live without ritual, and that a city can be built without organizing rituals. This is quite false, and we have our rituals, like the Pledge, but because we are moderns, we don't think that we have them. And the result of this is that we have banished God's appointed rituals from His city, and we have done so in order to get rid of superstition. But what this has done is create a vacuum (a vacuum of disobedience) within the Church, so that our identity, our sense of time, the way we name ourselves, is all stamped by the civil order, and not by our fundamental allegiance, which is that of being *Christian*.

When the Church is living in vibrant faith, we do not have to be urged to make "political" applications of our faith. This is because the establishment of a new city in the midst of the city of man — which is what we are doing here, in this worship — is in its very nature a political act. Because of this, many believers, because they don't want a collision with the authorities, have made an accommodation with those authorities. Instead of proclaiming that the Church is the establishment of the future of all humanity, they have agreed that the Church is just one sect among many, and that we will play by the idolatrous rules, just like the others.

Put this another way. Whenever you eat this bread, and drink this cup, you are voting. Not only so, but you are voting in the most potent way possible, the way God wants His people to vote. Do you want the kingdom to come? Then eat, and drink. Do you want God's will done on earth, as it is in heaven? Then eat, and drink.

So come, and welcome, to Jesus Christ.

MORNING ✹ EVANGELICAL SACRAMENT

God has established His covenant in the world, and this covenant is visible. It has visible and external signs, and the covenant people of God gather at particular, identifiable places. They have water placed on them, they hear the Word preached, they sing songs, they pray, they eat the bread and drink the wine.

God has also established His secret elective decree, and He has done this within His own counsels. We must not confuse this election with the covenant, but neither must we divorce them. They relate to one another, but the only instrument that God has given us for making this relation is faith, not sight. In other words, we cannot *see* the decree of election in order to understand the covenant. Rather, we believe the promises of the covenant, and this faith (and only this faith) is the instrument that God uses to reveal the outworkings of His elective decree at the Last Day. Put simply, we are to trust God. We are to believe His signs and seals, we are to believe His promises, we are to rest in hope. Now hope that is seen is no hope at all. Faith is the assurance of things not seen.

This is why we do not trust in the sacraments as objects in themselves. Rather, we use them as emblems of faith, and we look through them, believing the promises through them. Do not believe the bread by itself; the bread lies by itself. Do not believe the cup either; the cup lies when you look *at* it. Believe nothing, believe no one, other than God Himself. He promises, He gives, He bestows Himself. To receive anything else, anything less, is idolatry.

But do not think you can create your own windows, your own sacraments, in order to see and hear His promises. We are to look *where* He tells us to look, and we are to look the *way* He tells us to look. In the motions of eating and drinking, sanctified by His Word, we see the ultimate reunion of heaven and earth in the *koinonia*. And we see this by faith alone.

So come, and welcome, to Jesus Christ.

Do not presume for a moment that in this meal the Lord Jesus Christ is a hapless victim. He became a victim, once for all, at a particular point in history. But God vindicated Him, raising Him from the dead, and He was ushered before the Ancient of Days, and was a given a throne there. In that throne, upon which He has been sitting for two thousand years, He exercises dominion over heaven and earth, and over every tribe, language, nation, and kingdom.

He is no victim. We do not have to fence the Table in order to keep Him from getting hurt. We do not have to fence the Table so that He will not be again victimized. We do fence notorious sinners away from the Table, but not for the Table's sake. This is the meaning of excommunication. God in His mercy drove Adam and Eve away from the tree of life so that they would not combine their rebellion with sacramental insolence.

But if you are baptized, and not lawfully excommunicated, then the Table fences you in. You do not protect the Table from becoming a victim; the Table protects you from becoming a victim. The world is a sinful place, and we all struggle with our remaining sinfulness. We need food for the journey; we need strength for the fight.

So here it is. Come, take and eat. Come, take and drink.

So come, and welcome, to Jesus Christ.

MORNING ☼ OUR TREE OF LIFE

When God created Adam and Eve, and placed them in the Garden, He also provided them with food. Not only their daily food—hanging from the branches of all the trees in the Garden—but also sacramental food, the food that was fruit of the Tree of Life. Only one tree was prohibited to them, the Tree of the Knowledge of Good and Evil, not two trees. And that one tree was only prohibited for a time, until after they had passed their probationary test.

But the point to be made is that God always feeds His people. When He created us, He created us needing food, and He provided the food along with the need. It is the same with us. All the food we receive is from God—this is why we thank Him for it before every meal. We bow our heads and acknowledge that we are sustained, necessarily and constantly, by His provision. But the same thing is true here. Not only does God supply us with our physical food, so He also supplies us with our spiritual nourishment. This is the cup of the new covenant, and the new covenant is the covenant of life and grace. This is our Tree of Life.

But sustenance does not come as a result of simply eating. Within the covenant, there is no such thing as automatic blessing. When we approach the Tree of Life *in faith*, we are also necessarily staying away from all those things that God has warned us away from. If we try to continue to eat from prohibited places, and come here as well, then by definition we are not coming here in faith.

Faith is not an exact synonym with obedience, but faith always obeys. Faith is never disobedient. If it is disobeying, then you know right away it is not faith. And so we speak freely of an obedient faith, a faith which simply takes God at His word, and does not try to eat from this Table and the prohibited tables set by idolaters who would lure us away from this, our first love. Let us now—in obedient faith—eat and drink.

So come, and welcome, to Jesus Christ.

When we come to the Table, we are coming to receive a gift. But in order to come rightly, in order to be able to enjoy receiving the gift, we must at the same time be gladly giving a gift. This is the meaning of *koinonia* fellowship.

In this meal, God gives Himself. He gives Himself in three ways, each corresponding to one of the Persons of the Trinity. First the bread and wine are the gift of the Son. Second, the Father is the giver of this gift — He is the one who determined the gift should be given, and it was His will that the Son was submitting to in the Garden. The decision to give the Son was a decision to give the exact image of Himself. And third, the gift is made possible through the presence and work of the Holy Spirit. He is the one who takes us up, weaves us together, and brings us into the heavenly places in order to partake of the living Christ. So then, God gives us Himself, and as He does so He is holding nothing back.

But to receive the gift we have to be oriented in a particular way. When Scripture tells us that we need to forgive in order to be forgiven, this is not an exhortation to a quid pro quo mentality — if you do x, then God will do y. No, this is stated because a non-forgiving soul cannot hold forgiveness, any more than a can hold water. It is the same kind of thing when we talk about receiving the gift of a person and being the gift of a person.

You cannot receive the gift of the Christ without knowing what that is. And you cannot know what that is when your two tight fists are clenching all your own personal prerogatives. Are you worried about the bad things that might come to pass if you give yourself away? Ah, but what might happen if you don't?

So come, and welcome, to Jesus Christ.

MORNING ☼ DRINKING THE NEW TESTAMENT

The covenant of the Lord is objective. It exists in the world, within the course of history. We are living in the times of Regeneration that the Lord Jesus told us about.

But in saying that the covenant is objective, we do not mean that it is to be understood as a mechanical thing, grinding away. Rather, a covenant is a relationship between persons, and the Bible teaches that there is mutuality in this covenant.

The hypocrite thinks that the covenant binds God to him, but forgets that the covenant binds him to God. The legalist remembers that he is bound to God, but thinks that his obligations are to work and labor in his own strength in order to have something to present to God. This also is covenant-breaking.

There is mutuality in the covenant, which means that a response is demanded from you. This thing that is demanded from you is also given to you, so that no one can boast. But that response is the response of faith. As we come to the Table, there is one thing needful. Believe the Lord. Listen to His Word, and believe. Chew and swallow the bread of the loaf which is the body of the Lord in the congregation surrounding you. Believe this, and be at peace with all your brothers and sisters. You are not just to read the New Testament, or to hear it read. You are to drink the New Testament, drink it down and you are to do so in faith.

It is physically possible to do all these things without faith, but if you are guilty of such a folly, you are not guilty of non-covenantal practices, you are guilty of covenant breaking — the sin of unbelief. Unbelief proceeds from a hard heart, so today if you hear His voice do not harden your hearts as you did in the wilderness.

The Table is set for you, and all the baptized are invited. But you must come believing God, you must come in faith.

So come, and welcome, to Jesus Christ.

In the covenant the Lord draws near to us. Because He draws near to us we are commanded to draw near to Him by faith.

This is the Table of the covenant, a central means which God has provided for us to draw near to Him in faith. He has engaged with us to be our God, and has bound Himself to us. But God never binds Himself to sinners without also binding those sinners to Himself. He does so with the strongest bonds possible — love, gratitude, faith, hope. So as we approach Him, we do so in love, thanksgiving, faith, and hope. But remember, the greatest is love.

You are baptized and invited. You believe in God and in His Son Jesus Christ — and are therefore invited to sit down. In this meal, God is pulling you, drawing you to Himself through His Son. The response that you must therefore offer is one of reciprocal faith. You come here in order to pull Christ to yourself. But never forget the order; we pull because He first pulled us.

You do this with the solitary instrument of faith, but this solitary instrument of faith gives necessary and immediate rise to actions of the body. In this case, those actions include taking with your hands, opening your mouth, chewing the bread, tasting the wine, and swallowing. The one who hears the words of institution without doing, deceives himself. The one who believes without chewing and swallowing has the same kind of faith that the devils do. And of course, it should go without saying that the one who chews and swallows in a spirit of unbelief in God's covenant promises is one who is chewing up and swallowing his own covenant disaster.

You are here for one reason, which is to participate by faith, through the power of the Holy Spirit, in the body and blood of the Lord Jesus Christ. Do so now with thanksgiving and gratitude.

So come, and welcome, to Jesus Christ.

MORNING ☼ THE EFFICACY OF RITUAL

This is a ritual meal, and in one sense we may say that this is all it is. The problem with the expression, though, is that such a statement would almost certainly be heard as a minimizing or reductionist statement. Those who want or need it to be more than such a "minimal meal" then resort to metaphysical speculations about what is really going on here on "the spiritual plane." One group says that this is just a ritual, and the assumption that goes along with this kind of statement is that rituals are not important, that rituals by their very nature are empty and hollow. Another group, in order to resist this minimalization, invests this meal with all kinds of importance, imported from elsewhere. Both groups believe that ritual, considered *as such*, is not efficacious or potent. One group goes along with the demotion, and the other group fights it by calling in metaphysical mercenaries from other realms and kingdoms.

But this meal is a symbol that challenges and throws down all earthly symbols. It is a ritual that offers defiance to all idolatrous rituals. It is a sacrament that defines the world with Christ at the center, instead of Caesar, or Mammon, or Amusement, or Sex, or Power.

This sacrament, when rightly understood, and offered in evangelical faith, establishes a new city center. This is where and how the believing Church assumes the center. Believers come into a town, or village, or city, and they begin worshiping God the Father through Christ. When they do this *as Christians*, as citizens of the heavenly city, they are mounting a challenge to all the gods, to all the idols. If they do it in unbelief, as practitioners of a sect or mystery religion, they are trying to have it both ways. They want the food and nourishment offered by a personal Savior, Jesus, but they do not want to claim (in public at any rate) that King Jesus has established a royal feast, the new center of the new city. But we are not among those who shrink back. As we eat and drink in meekness, we inherit the earth.

So come, and welcome, to Jesus Christ.

We come to this Table on a weekly basis. It is frequently assumed by many that the only reason for this would be because of some kind of superstitious regard for the merits of the Supper.

But superstition is a matter of the heart, a question of attitude. At the time of the Reformation, the established church had reduced communion to an annual event, and that *rarity* was the result of a superstitious and idolatrous view of the Supper. The Reformers were those who pressed for frequent communion. John Calvin tried, unsuccessfully, to establish weekly communion.

But superstition is flexible in the joints and can push the other way also. There are some who seek out opportunities for daily communion for superstitious reasons — they are afraid that grace leaks out of them too quickly. When pouring grace into a sieve, the proposed solution is pour lots more instead of looking for a bucket. So this kind of frequency is quite different from the excitement which caused the early Christians to break bread daily and from house to house.

Faith banishes superstition. And you are summoned to this Table by the faithful God, and His appointed instrument for drawing you here is the faith which He gives to you. Do not dare to come with any other motive. Teach your children to come in faith. Believing that God will do here what He promised to do is not superstition at all. Rather, superstition should be defined as any form of unbelief that keeps us away from the nourishment God has given to us. That unbelief might manifest itself through shrinking back, or by rushing headlong.

But we are confident of better things in your case. The Table is set, and you are most welcome. Come in the faith that brought you here.

So come, and welcome, to Jesus Christ.

MORNING ✺ EUCHARISTIC DUALISM

An important part of our responsibility in coming to this Table is to reject all false contrasts and inconsistencies. We reject as unscriptural every attempt at eucharistic dualism, a process which tries to pit external against internal. The superstitious come to the Table in order to fool about with mere externals, considered as such. Their mummeries do not amount to anything other than increased condemnation for them — properly due to any who believe the bread of the Lord is made entirely from their chaff. The religion of external form and show is pitted against heart religion. They retain the form but deny the power.

But another kind of superstition should also cause us great concern, perhaps even more because of its subtlety. This is the idea that we are more refined and philosophical when we come to believe that the bread and wine are mere externals and can be dispensed with. Such persons go on to commune with God in their own rarified imaginations, believing themselves to be *very* spiritual. But this is not spiritual at all; it is disobedience. Jesus said to eat and drink; He did not say to cogitate.

When the rationalist seeks to worship God with pure intellect, Jesus summons him to chew and swallow. When the magician comes to this Table in order to perform his conjuring tricks, Jesus commands him to drop the rattle and chicken bones, and believe the gospel that leads to everlasting life.

The Bible has a name for that which sets the chewing at odds with the thinking, or the thinking at odds with the chewing. It is called unbelief, and the remedy for unbelief is the gospel. Repent and believe. Chew and swallow. Think and do. Rise up and walk. God is in His heaven, His Son is on the throne, and the world is united and bound together in truth. Do not separate what God has joined together.

So come, and welcome, to Jesus Christ.

God is the Lord and He intends something in this Table. We are His covenant people, called by His name, and it is our task to intend the same thing.

Perhaps we do not know what that is, and are secretly glad for the ignorance. Or perhaps we do know, and have been shrinking from it. But as we assemble here, our Lord speaks from the head of the Table, and He speaks to each of us concerning His intentions for us. We each have a white stone with our name on it, and name known only to God.

At this Table, Jesus Christ addresses you with that name, and He says that He intends for this wine and this bread to build you up into Jesus Christ, the perfect man. In order for this to happen, certain new things will certainly grow and develop, but more to the point of our concerns, certain old things must cease.

This includes anger or bitterness at your spouse. It includes frustration with your children. It includes disrespect of your parents. It includes lust and all the attendant evil desires. It includes envy and covetousness over the good fortune of others. Jesus Christ has come down to us, but He did not do this in order to leave us as He found us. He is our *Savior,* and He is saving us from our *sins*. He is not saving us from just those sins that have gotten tiresome for us, while leaving us to enjoy those sins to which we are still attached. He saves and sanctifies us, and He does it according to His will.

So, today, if you hear His voice—and you have heard His voice—repent of any sin that His Spirit convicts you of. Come to the Table knowing that He is nourishing you, and growing you out of the pettiness that afflicts you. Life is before you, and you are invited to partake of it. But know this: all sin is death, and partaking of this true life here means, necessarily, the death of all death.

So come, and welcome, to Jesus Christ.

MORNING ☼ NOTHING BUTTERY AND THE TABLE

The Bible I preach from is a material book. That is all it is. There is nothing else there. The Bible is *nothing but* paper and ink. And of course to speak this way is to fall into the fallacy that one writer called *nothing buttery*. Of course, paper and ink is all it is in a material sense. But when we have the Scripture reading, and the elder afterwards says, "The Word of the Lord," and we say, "Thanks be to God," are we worshiping paper and ink? Of course not. When I preface the reading of the text to be preached from by saying, "These are the very words of God," are you standing in honor of the material elements that make up the book I am holding? Again, of course not. The paper that makes up this book came from a tree somewhere, and, for all we know, another part of that same tree went into the publication of some infidel newspaper. And we all know, and know without troubling ourselves about it, that this presents no problem at all.

This is bread and wine. In fact, this is *nothing but* bread and wine. But when I have said this, have I exhausted the subject? Of course not. When you come to this Table in faith, you are engaged in a blessed partaking of the living and resurrected Christ, and you are being knit together with all the saints to Him. You are no more to adore the bread and wine than you are to worship the paper and ink. But at the same time, you are summoned to *meet* with God in His Word, and to *commune* with Him in His sacraments. You don't do this by pretending that God or His grace has been reduced to the simple material elements of His appointed instruments.

The appointed means for doing this is a lively and evangelical faith. This faith is not stupid, and doesn't reduce God to the material level of His instruments. But neither is it disobedient, refusing to meet with Him and commune with Him where He told us He would be. Come, then, in evangelical faith.

So come, and welcome, to Jesus Christ.

God feeds us. He is not a negligent Father, one who fails to provide for His children. His Table is always set well, and always furnished with all that we need. Of course, like naughty children, we sometimes do not eat what is set before us. Some children do not come to the Table at all. They have backslidden, and are off in their bedroom with the sulks.

But there is another kind of naughtiness, one that masquerades as lowliness of heart. These children make a great show of humility and come to the Table, but do not really eat. They are not worthy to be God's children, they say, and are not deserving of the food He supplies. Instead of eating what they were told to eat, they reply that they have been disobedient that day, and do not deserve such wonderful food. They are right about the disobedience, certainly; God has commanded them to eat, and they refuse.

But of course the answer to disobedience is repentance and obedience, and not to continue the disobedience by adding some form of penance to it. Of course we are not worthy to be here. That is the whole *point*. Of course we do not earn our right to be seated with our Lord Jesus. How quickly we forget the point of the gospel! If you were worthy to come, you wouldn't need to. If you are not worthy, you need to come. And precisely because you are not worthy to eat and drink, you are also not worthy to set the terms for eating and drinking. The one who *is* worthy, He is the one who has commanded this observance. Take, and eat, He says. Take, and drink, He says.

And if we were *truly* convinced of our unworthiness, we wouldn't talk back to Him so much.

So come, and welcome, to Jesus Christ.

MORNING ☼ NO RITUAL OF DEATH

We gather to feed on the body of Christ, and to drink His blood, but do not make the mistake of thinking that it is some ritual form of macabre cannibalism. The Lord is risen, and we are partaking of His resurrection life. This is no corpse ritual. We are privileged to partake of the Lord's everlasting life.

The Lord told the woman at the well that He offered her living water to drink. The Lord taught His disciples that He was the bread that came down from Heaven, and that it was living bread (John 6:51). We are not stepping outside the rule of faith if we see what we are about to drink as living wine. We are a living people, and our food must be life. Dead food is for dead people.

This is why we bless the name of "the God of peace, that brought again from the dead our Lord Jesus, that great shepherd of the sheep, through the blood of the everlasting covenant" (Heb. 13:20).

What we eat and drink imparts to us what it possesses, provided we receive it with living faith. This is especially true as we approach Paschal Sunday, resurrection Sunday, and life is everywhere. The bread and wine are alive, the music lives, the Word of God is alive in our lives, and we gather here to partake of Christ because we are a living people, a living nation.

There is no incongruity in any of this because He is alive forever. He is alive because He rose again from the dead.

So come, and welcome, to Jesus Christ.

Jesus made Himself known to the disciples at Emmaus in the breaking of the bread. When they returned to Jerusalem, they made a particular point about relating this aspect of the story.

Now we know that the Lord deals with us in this Supper, but we sometimes assume that the only sins He deals with are the obvious, carnal sins—lust, anger, and so on. And of course, He does this, but note here that that Jesus was addressing a sin problem in a different place. He was correcting their *exegesis* in the breaking of the bread; He was admonishing their rigidity in how they read the Old Testament. He was rebuking their doctrine and admonishing their hermeneutic.

God deals with us in this Supper, but He does not just deal with us "morally." He deals with our minds, how we think, how we understand our duties as Christians. He does not just rebuke our vices, in other words, He also rebukes our virtues, and this includes what we think are our theological virtues.

The two disciples walking to Emmaus obviously loved the Lord Jesus, and were downcast at what had happened to Him. They were not conscious of struggling against any great temptation, and yet they were walking under a cloud of unbelief. Our Lord Jesus, in His great kindness, and with a wonderfully understated humor, came to them and dispelled that cloud.

We are seated at that same Table, and the Lord Jesus is breaking bread for us, just as He did for them. He is the Lord; He is risen. Follow Him!

So come, and welcome, to Jesus Christ.

MORNING ☼ GRACIOUS EATING AND DRINKING

The Lord's Supper is made up of participles — eating and drinking, not of material elements — bread and wine. The bread and wine are necessary, but the partaking of Christ happens in the action, motivated by evangelical faith. The common life, the *koinonia,* occurs when we partake together. If a minister were to walk into a deserted room, pronounce the words of institution over some bread and wine, and then walk out again, that would not be an observance of the Lord's Supper. The bread and wine would remain bread and wine, and the minister would remain a scoundrel.

And when the people come together to eat and drink, that is better, closer, but we are not there yet. St. Paul tells us that when the Corinthians came together to eat and drink in competition, vainglory, factions, and whatnot, he says, "this is not to eat the Lord's supper." Before, we had bread and wine, but the people were missing. Now we have the people, but they are squabbling, and so it is not the Lord's Supper they are partaking of — in evangelical faith. True, they *are* trifling with holy things, just like the minister doing tricks in an empty room. They are guilty of the body and blood of the Lord, and they are incurring some covenantal chastisements. St. Paul said that many among the Corinthians were sick and that many had died because of this. The new covenant is not an era where God decided that it was time to allow Himself to be mocked.

We are being knit together with Christ in every faithful and gracious partaking of this Supper. This is a miracle of grace, being wrought by the Holy Spirit Himself. But He is not doing something in the bread and wine, and then putting it into you that way. He is doing something in you, and in the Church, and in the ritual of bread and wine, and He works through the participles of gracious eating and drinking.

So come, and welcome, to Jesus Christ.

EVENING ◐ CLOSE FRIENDS, NOT ADVERSARIES

You are accustomed to hear two words paired, and those words are Word and sacrament. The two do go together, and are not in the slightest degree at odds with one another. But in the minds of some, they are at odds, and sides are chosen.

Some choose a rationalistic service, where the Word is never done, never eaten, and this is why such congregations deceive themselves. To hear the Word without doing, James tells us, is to be self-deceived (Jas. 1:23–24). But those who do without hearing are no better. The services they devise are a fool's errand, running off to obey the master without hearing what He has said to do.

When these two things, Word and sacrament, Word and divinely appointed ritual, are set at odds with one another, one must give way before the other. And then the one which has "conquered" promptly ceases to become itself.

In the waters of baptism, and in the bread and wine of the Supper, God has given us a divinely appointed image. But this image only remains such when it is *married* to the Word. Severed from the Word, image always becomes spectacle, ritual turns into gross spectacle. This is what we see in both pop evangelical worship and certain forms of high liturgical worship — we see spectacle, the natural idiom of paganism.

But severed from image, the Word becomes an arid set of propositions, and however much time it occupies, it can only do so by becoming thinner and thinner. At the end of the day, we have something which pretends to infinite richness through this process of homeopathic dilution, but which is nevertheless mostly water.

Test your souls. The more you hear the Word, the more you should hunger for the bread of life. The more you eat the bread of life, the more you should want to hear the Word preached and declared.

So come, and welcome, to Jesus Christ.

MORNING ☼ NOT THAT KIND OF FABRIC

The Christian Church is a commonwealth. One of the great things that we have in common is our access to this Table. It is a tremendous privilege, and we are not worthy of it *in one sense*.

But in another sense, we are commanded to walk in a manner that is worthy of it. This Supper is a sacrament of your fundamental allegiance. This wine and this bread mean that you belong, heart and soul, to Jesus Christ. You share this statement, this sacrament, with all who come to it.

There are those who are hypocritical in how they come, and this has been a source of great distress to those who love Jesus Christ. Unfortunately, it has also been a source of great confusion to them. In their zeal for the reputation of the Lord Jesus, seated at the head of this Table, they have undertaken to start managing the Table on His behalf — toddlers in high chairs rebuking the rowdy teen-agers.

But the Lord Jesus is *Lord*. He is the one who has said that His Word is true, though every man prove himself a liar. The sacrament is what God defines it as being; the sacrament is never defined by our sins or shortcomings. God has sent His kindness into a really messed-up world. What makes us think that we could learn to receive His grace without a hitch?

In this meal, just bow your heads and receive His kindness. Do not try to protect His kindness from the impudence of others. Just receive what He is giving to you. Do not become proud of what He offers here, for He is offering nothing other than grace. Grace is not the kind of fabric that can be fashioned into flags and banners.

This is the Eucharist, a name that comes from the Greek word for thanksgiving. Receive this meal with thanksgiving — not with pride, not with disdain for others who receive it wrongly, not with morbidity, not with sorrow, and not with excessive precision of mind. Just be thankful. Keep it simple.

So come, and welcome, to Jesus Christ.

In this Supper, all the benefits of Christ's death are sealed for those who partake in faith. This includes everything He has done for us: forgiveness, justification, reconciliation, and infinitely more. We have our conversions renewed and ratified before God as we partake. We have our covenant relation to God renewed as we partake.

This renewal is not renewed like a lease about to expire, but is a renewal more akin to the renewal that food provides, or sexual communion in marriage. But it is renewal nonetheless, and it is renewal of what you have already received from God, *all* that you have received from God. In this meal, your salvation is growing to maturity. How? The answer is by faith, faith alone, from first to last.

But faith receives the grace of God with eyes wide open. Realize that your salvation is growing to maturity alongside all your brothers and sisters gathered here. So look around as you partake. Do not curl up into a little holy ball, content to go to heaven by yourself. God is renewing covenant with all His people. Look around, and as God gives faith, you will also see the saints around the world doing the same thing, together with the saints in heaven.

And for those who come without faith, trifling with holy things, they do incur the chastisements of the covenant. They defile the body and blood of the Lord Jesus, trampling it underfoot. But we fence the Table for the sake of the defilers, not for the sake of the Lord. The altar did not need protection from Nadab and Abihu. The ark of the covenant did not need protection from Uzzah. The Supper of the Lord did not need protection from greedy and drunken Corinthians.

Although we say this, we are confident of better things in this instance. You are coming in faith, and you are being restored and built up. Rejoice in it, and be glad. This is the day that the Lord has made. Go, eat your bread with a merry heart, for God has accepted you in Jesus Christ our Lord.

So come, and welcome, to Jesus Christ.

MORNING ☼ WHICH INSTRUMENT ARE YOU PRACTICING?

This is a covenant meal. This means that the covenant features of blessing and cursing run right through the middle of it. In this covenant, God demands what He has always demanded from covenant-keepers, and that is faith in the only one who was a covenant-keeper completely, that is, the Lord Jesus. That is it — simple faith. Trust Him, rest in Him, come to Him, and feast in Him. He is the epitome of true humanity, and as you look to Him in faith, you are being built up into that perfect humanity.

The only alternative to this faith is unbelief. But we must be careful here, because an over-active and pious conscience has made us think that unbelief is any kind of failing, at any level. No, unbelief is rejection, not imperfection in your acceptance.

We are people of faith, we have faith. Do we have faith perfectly? Is our faith not to be improved upon? Are there sins and faults mixed in with this genuine faith? Of course, just as when you are learning to play the piano, you make mistakes. But even when you make mistakes, you are *always* playing the piano and not, say, the tuba. Such mistakes are not a disqualification for coming to the Supper — they are the precise reason why you must come. Unbelief that disqualifies is persistent, hard-hearted, obstinate, willful, and this is the most important point about it, obvious to the whole world.

So do not spend your time researching your motives over the course of this last week to determine if you are fit to come. Any baptized person who is concerned over their fitness to come is, by definition, commanded to come. We cannot be reminded too often. This meal is not your reward for being good. It is God's nourishment for those who would be good. It is God's kindness for those who would grow up into Jesus Christ. So, come, and eat. Come, and drink. You are in Jesus Christ, and this is why you are *welcome*.

So come, and welcome, to Jesus Christ.

Our God is truly good. The only attitude that does not see Him that way is unbelief — the twisted view that there could be another source of good, an alternative take on it, another way.

But only God is good. This means that anyone who would be good also must come to Him on His terms. His Word defines what is good; His holy arm establishes what is good; His righteousness extends to all generations.

Because God is good, the Table He prepares for us is good. He has led us here, and He has prepared this Table in the presence of our enemies. They are enemies, fundamentally, because they insist on another source for goodness. Whether it is man and his word, or nature and its law, or the pandemonium of postmodernism, our enemies are what they are because they hate the Word, they hate the water, they hate the bread, and they hate the wine. We love them all.

This world belongs to God; He could have assigned different sacraments, and there was a time in the older covenant when the sacraments did have another appearance. But the voice of our God, the voice of all that is good, is always recognizable in whatever He is saying. Today, He is speaking *here*. He is saying, "Come unto me, all ye that labor and are heavy-laden, and I will give you rest" (Matt. 11:24). God is good.

Never allow yourself to think that this Table is all about *your* goodness. No, it is set in the name of the goodness of God. You are to come frail, and leave strengthened. You come repentant, and leave encouraged. You come sick, and leave healthy. It is not the other way around.

Are you unworthy? Then confess it, and come. Are you unworthy? Then you *qualify*! How good is God! He has set this Table here, today, for *you* — a Table for the unworthy.

So come, and welcome, to Jesus Christ.

MORNING ☼ A SELF-CONDEMNING HEAD CASE

The Lord's Table is the place where we are to overflow with gratitude and thanksgiving. It is not a time for us to curl up into a little ball of sorrow or remorse. If there has been sin in your life, and of course there has, then there are other times to deal with that. You wash your hands before you come to the Table, not *at* the Table.

You should deal with sin in your life as it happens. When you sin, confess it immediately. Do not wait for it to accumulate in your life. Do not postpone confession until this service in order to confess in our time set-aside for confession. Confess sin during the week, and put things right with others as soon as possible.

But if you have (sinfully) postponed confession until today, then confess your sins at the beginning of the service. If something occurs to you, and you remember an unconfessed sin this morning, then do confess it at the beginning of the service.

And if you have struggled to the point where you come to this Table, and your hands are still dirty, then of course, confess your sins now. But add an additional sin that you should confess—you have disrupted a time of Eucharistic gladness and sought to make it a time of private penitence and sorrow. Such penitence is better than defiling the Supper, but at the same time, such penitence as a regular feature of this meal is itself another kind of defilement.

It is a particularly dangerous form of defilement, because people *think* that it is *holy*. This is always the case. If you have lied, or stolen, or been immoral, and then come here to partake, the whole world understands that hypocrisy. But if you sought to come to this meal every time as a self-condemning head case, you would be urged on in this great sin by a good part of the Christian church. Do not do it! Christ has died, and you are forgiven. Christ has risen, and you are justified.

So come, and welcome, to Jesus Christ.

EVENING ◑ WHAT GOOD WILL THIS DO?

Christ has been established at the right hand of God the Father, and He has been given dominion over all the nations of men. This has been established in principle, and the task of the Great Commission is not to go out and try to make this true, but rather to declare to all the nations that it already *is* true. As that declaration is made in faith, the reign of Christ (an established fact) is made increasingly visible to the eyes of men.

But Christ rules by His instruments, not by ours. He extends His scepter, and it is His kind of scepter, not our kind. His scepter is wielded over the nations of men by means of the Word, the gospel preached with authority, and the sacraments. That's it. Christ's kingdom will fill the earth because His preachers declare something, pour water on people, break bread and distribute wine. No armies, no lobbyists, no missiles, no goose-stepping millions, no marketing campaigns, no politics, and no flattery at all.

But make no mistake. It is not as though the armies and the governments and the nations (and all the other things we do) are irrelevant in this. They are very much a part of this process. The fact that we do not conquer by these carnal means does not mean that we will not come to see them as objects to be conquered. The Lordship of Jesus Christ must be acknowledged everywhere.

So how do we bring this about? Should we organize? No, we should take and eat, take and drink. But the objections come. "What good will *this* do?" said the Israelite grumbler, marching with the others around Jericho, just before the walls fell.

God tells us what to do, and He promises us what He will then do. The gospel always does what it does, which is to run free, setting men free. It cannot be bound, and earthly rulers have no countermeasures for it. Believe me, they have spent a great deal of time trying to develop countermeasures. But there are none.

So come, and welcome, to Jesus Christ.

MORNING ☼ THEN YOU QUALIFY

We gather around this Table, week after week, month after month, and year and year. The mere fact that we *do* this means that we are defining the boundaries of our lives by it. At the same time, we are responsible to understand what is happening here, so that we do not drift into a faithless observance.

Jesus said, "Take and eat," not "Take and dispute," or "Take and study," or "Take and torment yourself." This does not mean that there is no place for study or disputation or self-examination. But we must do all such things thoughtfully, that is to say, with wisdom.

If we study foolishly, or debate foolishly, or examine ourselves foolishly, we will always find ourselves, at the end of the process, disobeying the one thing we were explicitly commanded to do, which is, "Take and eat, take and drink."

Any study of obedience that ends in disobedience is to be rejected. Rather, we embrace the truth that obedience is the great opener of eyes. As we come, as we eat, as we drink, as we discern the Body of Christ in one another, we grow up into wisdom. We are not commanded to get wisdom so that we will then be qualified to come to the Table. We are commanded to come to the Table so that we might get wisdom. The wise woman of Proverbs tells the *simple* to come to her Table (Prov. 9:4–5).

This is wisdom here. Are you foolish? Then come. The wine is deep red, a deep wisdom. Are you simple? Then drink. The bread is nourishing, and designed to fill the hungry. Are you hungry? Then come. The Table is set. The place is reserved for you, and you were not invited because you have your spiritual act together. You were invited, I was invited, precisely because we *don't*.

Are you a spiritual mess? Then, glory to God, you *qualify*. This is a Table set with nothing but the grace of God. Do not dare to turn it into something else. Take and eat. Take and drink.

So come, and welcome, to Jesus Christ.

You are what you eat. And what you are eating here (by faith alone) is the covenant body of Jesus Christ. You are being knit together, growing up into Him, bone of His bones, flesh of His flesh. This is a foundational meal, the one that informs and sanctifies all the other eating and drinking that you do. This is your primary meal.

Because the church in America has drifted away from faithful eating and drinking *here,* we have simultaneously drifted into a multitude of drinking problems and eating disorders. If any aspect of your eating and drinking life is out of kilter, then do not seek to fix that problem by yourself. You need to learn to put it right here.

Drinking problems originate because the lordship of Christ over all drinking is not properly acknowledged here. Learn to drink *here,* which means surrendering everything here, and you will learn from Christ elsewhere. Obsessive eaters who are gluttons need to learn from the simplicity of Christ here. There is no wantonness at His Table. Obsessive eaters who are anorexic need to learn from the bounty of Christ, because the fat is the Lord's.

Those who believe in salvation and healing through eating and drinking whatever the latest idolatrous fad is, whether vitamins, bee pollen, vegetables alone, etc. need to look to the worship of the true God alone as the place where they may find the signs and seals of their salvation. Your cupboards at home, whatever they contain, can be saved — but they are not, and can never be, a savior.

So, then, learn from Christ here. This does not mean figuring this Supper out, as though it were a math problem. It means eating and drinking in faith, asking God to apply His nourishing wisdom to your life, your eating and drinking habits, however *He* sees fit. He is giving to us; we are not giving to Him.

So come, and welcome, to Jesus Christ.

MORNING ☼ SIMULTANEOUSLY CAREFUL AND FREE

We have a tendency to look at the wrong things when preparing ourselves for this meal — and of course, we *should* prepare ourselves for it. The Bible contains multiple warnings against trifling with the holy things of God. He warns the unrighteous about defiling this sacramental meal. But from this warning, the righteous have drawn many erroneous conclusions. Those who look to their own righteousness are unrighteous. Those who look to the righteousness of Jesus Christ are righteous in Him, and that is the only righteousness you need to be seated here — the fact that you are looking to another.

There is a place for soul searching, but that place is not here. There is a necessary place for confession of sin, but that place is not here. There is a time to be reminded that you have stumbled in your Christian walk, but that time is not now. You confessed your sin last Thursday — why bring it up again now in unbelief? God said He forgave you — do you not believe Him? You confessed your sins at the beginning of the service, did you not? Then don't worry at it now.

All such things, however pious they might appear, are designed to keep you from looking to Jesus Christ, crucified for you. All such introspective rummagings about in the heart keep you from seeing Jesus Christ in your neighbor, your spouse, your children, your parents. Discern the Lord's body, we are told. We are not told to discern all the different ways we fail to discern it. The point of this Supper is not our sinfulness. That is not what we memorialize. The point of this Supper is God's glad reception of us. We urge Him, in this memorial, to remember our cleansing, remember our forgiveness, remember that we are now His holy saints.

We call upon Him to remember the covenant He has made with us. And as we know He remembers, because we have reminded Him according to His Word, we remember it too.

So come, and welcome, to Jesus Christ.

As we engage with the powers and principalities of this age, we do so by spiritual means, and not by carnal means. We declare the gospel, and we baptize the nations, and we offer wine and bread. But that is not all. The rest of the Great Commission says that we are called to teach obedience to everything that Christ has commanded.

When we teach this obedience, we are not teaching obedience that must be offered for a mere two hours on Sunday morning. We are teaching obedience as a lifestyle. Obedience around the dinner table, obedience in front of the television set, obedience in the bedroom, obedience as we vote, obedience as we undertake our vocational calling, obedience as we invest, and obedience as we educate our children. Christ is Lord, and this means that all other competing lords must acknowledge this — and either resign their place entirely, or take their appropriate place of subordination.

This Table is not the place where this happens. Your life is *where* it happens. This Table is, however, *why* it happens. This worship service is why it happens. Worship and covenant renewal are the engine that drives the kingdom of God. They are the root that makes the tree by the river flourish. Without the root, the leaves on the tree will not provide healing for the nations. Without the root, the twelve kinds of fruit, scattered throughout every aspect of our lives, will not be there, and we will be left to figure out what to do, and how to live, as though we were pagans without God and without hope in the world.

This Table is a means of grace. Grace strengthens you for what God has called you to do. A good breakfast is necessary if you are going to work hard in the field all day. But a good breakfast is not a substitute for working hard in the field all day. Our focus on worship is not designed to make us gluttons of grace. Grace is taken in so that it might be *expended*. Work out your salvation, for God is at work in you.

So come, and welcome, to Jesus Christ.

MORNING ☼ FAITH APPREHENDS ALL THINGS

We live in a world filled with the glory and kindness of God. We also live in a world filled with sin, sin that can be defined as refusal to *see* the glory and kindness of God. Some Christians have so emphasized the presence and tenacity of sin that they have made themselves unable to see the glory and kindness of God. And of course this inability is just more sin. We cannot deal with sin by committing more of it. The way out is repentance, changing our minds, turning around. This Table is one of the central places where we are to repent—but not of our individual sins, faults, and failings. That should already be done before you get here. You wash up at the sink, not at the table.

But at the same time, this Table is a wonderful place to see (and repent of) the various ways we slander God. He has set a Table for us. Perhaps He did it, we think, because He is trying to poison us. He sent His Son to die on the cross in order to save us. Perhaps, we think, He really wants to damn us. He invites us to sit down—there is a place card here, with your name on it. That name was written in blood before the world was created. He took off His outer cloak, and stooped down to wash *our* feet. Perhaps He is doing this, we think, to mock us.

No—put away all such sinful thoughts. This is the place to learn that God really does love you, really does want to save you, and He offers the nourishment of His covenant to you. Take it, and eat. Take it, and drink. What does it all mean? Among other things, it means that you are accepted, forgiven, justified, cleansed, put right, straightened out, and beloved of God. Faith can apprehend all things, even this. Take and eat. Take and drink.

So come, and welcome, to Jesus Christ.

EVENING ◐ WE INSIST YOU COME

Different churches have different approaches to the Lord's Supper when it comes to how visitors from other believing communions are received. Some practice *closed* communion, where no one from outside that communion may partake. Some practice *close* communion, where you may partake under certain conditions. Others practice *open* communion, where the Table is open to all. There are important truths that are represented by each of these perspectives, but still, at the end of the day, you have to settle on some definite approach to visitors.

It is our custom, one that we believe to be scriptural, to practice *insistent* communion. That is, if you are here, and if you are baptized in the triune Name, then you *must* come. We insist. The Spirit and the Church together say *come*.

We are not seeking to protect the Table from sinners. The teaching of Scripture is that sinners need to be protected from the Table. And the only safe way to be protected is to come to it *humbly*.

You may say that you are not walking with God as you should be, and so perhaps you should stay away. No, you may *not* stay away. You have no permission from God to stay away, and unless you were excommunicated scripturally, you have no blessing from Christ's ministry to refrain. This is your life—you are a covenant child. But isn't sin inconsistent with coming? Yes, it is, but the point is to drop the sin, leave it there on the ground, and come. But will it not be a defilement if you come without repentance? Yes, it will be. But it is another kind of defilement to stay away without repentance. As a covenant child, you are called to repent of the sin, and not to repent of your covenant meal.

You belong here. A place at this Table was purchased for you through the blood of Jesus Christ. He invites you to come and eat, come and drink. Come. We insist.

So come, and welcome, to Jesus Christ.

MORNING ☼ COOKING AND EATING

The Word and sacrament do not compete with one another, any more than preparation and fulfillment compete. Cooking and eating are not competitors, and so we do not set up a false antithesis between the two.

It is common in the churches of the Reformation to have the pulpit occupy a central place, as ours does, in order to symbolize the centrality and sufficiency of the Word of God. Faithful churches will never neglect the central importance of declaration and exposition of the holy Scriptures, given to us for this purpose.

But the Table is also in a central place, and for the same reason. The one who hears the Word, but does not do it, deceives himself. The one who hears the word of life and who does not pick it up and eat it, is self-deceived. The one who sees the word poured into the glass, but fails to drink it is deceived in the same way.

But it is necessary to hear, eat, and drink in true evangelical faith. Otherwise, hearing sermons becomes just a ritual, as does participation in the sacrament of the Lord's Supper. The Word and sacrament are nourishment for your life. They are to occupy as central a place in your life this coming Tuesday as they occupy in the architecture of the sanctuary.

You are confronted with many things during the week. What does the Bible say? And how has God imparted strength to me so that I might obey Him? Nothing is accomplished in the kingdom of God apart from faith. So hear His Word in faith. Eat His Word in faith. Drink His Word in faith.

So come, and welcome, to Jesus Christ.

We Christians, of all people, should be prepared to overflow with gratitude to God as we gather together with family and friends to rejoice before Him. We do this, not because we have substituted a cultural holiday for what the Lord requires, but because for many years now we have been celebrating Thanksgiving on a weekly basis here, at this Table. This is the Eucharistic Table, or, directly rendered, this is *the* Table of Thanksgiving.

So this Table defines and directs what we do at every other table. If we have been coming to this Table as we ought, then when it comes to familial and national expressions of thanksgiving, which are certainly right and proper, we will really know how to get into it.

Here we thank God for our salvation, for the forgiveness of sin, for a complete cleansing, for our acceptance with Him, for our justification in the resurrection of Jesus. This puts everything in perspective — but perspective does not annihilate all the other things we have to be thankful for. This coming Thursday you will say a prayer thanking God for the turkey, and ham, and mashed potatoes, and gravy, and stuffing, and cranberry sauce, and green beans, and rolls, and honey butter, and more pies than you can take in. That prayer will represent, as a covenant representative, your gratitude for harvest, good weather, your jobs, your safety, peace in the land, your spouse, your children, your grandchildren, and far more than you can reckon.

Thanksgiving is a duty in which it is necessary to fail. Thanksgiving always staggers and falls under the weight of what God has actually given to us. There is no way to do it justice. So this is a glorious and honorable failure, but we do not settle for that. We want to fail better at this next year. And failing better means coming to the Table of the Lord to be strengthened in our gladness, joy, and thanksgiving — week after week. Come then.

So come, and welcome, to Jesus Christ.

MORNING ✵ CHARGE IT TO CHRIST'S ACCOUNT

We serve the living God. We are a people who have been ushered into new life. We have heard the word of life declared. This is the bread of life; this is living wine.

Life is a mystery, and only the dead think they understand it. Life is glory; life is movement; life is joy; life is growth; life is grace, from beginning to end. You who have been made alive, consider this. Jesus Christ died in order that you might die. He lives in order that you might live. He gives in order that you might receive, and, following that, that you might give in imitation of Him.

One of your central duties in this Supper is to discern the Lord's body in one another. *You* are the body of Christ, and when you quarrel and fight with one another, you are not discerning the fact that you are trying to set Christ at war with Christ. But He will not do that, despite your sinful attempts to get Him to, and He summons you to this Table.

When you arrive here, He tells you that you must discern the body. One loaf, one people, one body. Do not separate yourself from the body in this Supper; do not curl up into a private introspective, self-condemning cocoon. Partake of this meal as you do all others — with your eyes open. Look around, look up and down your row, look ahead of you, and behind. These are your people; you are one with them in Christ.

Are you quarreling with anyone here? Then drop it — charge it to Christ's account. Do not set one piece of this bread at war with a different piece of it. Are you at odds with your family? Drop it; a right understanding of this meal demands that you drop it.

Be at peace: you are the bread. You are the wine.

So come, and welcome, to Jesus Christ.

When the Lord established this meal, He intended for His people to proclaim His death until He comes again. And this is what we are doing. The death of Jesus is the new testament; we say this as a means of shorthand — we do not exclude the resurrection and ascension of Christ, but rather speak of the whole in terms of one of the more striking parts.

Through the death of Jesus, we come to life. Of course, more precisely, through the death of Jesus we die, and through the new life of Jesus we walk in newness of life. Strictly speaking, Jesus did not die so that we might live. He died so that we might die. He lives so that we might live. And so the entire congregation, and not just the preacher, proclaims the death of the Lord as we partake together of this meal. But take note, this Table should not be seen as a Protestant crucifix, with Jesus perpetually dying or everlastingly dead. We partake of the *living* Christ. Through the power of the Holy Spirit, we partake of Christ's death and resurrection here. We are being knit together with Him, bone of His bone, and flesh of His flesh.

We are being built up into a new humanity, which is the work of the Holy Spirit. He uses many means to accomplish this, but central among these means are Word and sacrament. The instrument that He gives to us to enable us to receive what He ministers to us through these various means is of course faith. Without such faith, no man can see, still less enter, the kingdom of God.

But objectively this remains the meal of that kingdom. This is the nourishment that is found there. And all who sit down at this Table are proclaiming, by that action, that they believe that Christ died, and that He rose again from the dead. They proclaim the gospel, in other words. So take care that your heart is proclaiming the same thing that your fellowship in the bread and wine is proclaiming. To do otherwise is to trifle with holy things.

So come, and welcome, to Jesus Christ.

MORNING ☼ FAITH CHEWS AND SWALLOWS

As we celebrate at this Table, we must always remember whose meal it is. We did not establish this Supper, but rather, the Lord Jesus did. He self-consciously sat down at the Passover meal with His disciples, which He said He had been longing to do, and in the midst of these old covenant symbols, He intruded a radical new meaning for the cup and the bread.

This new meaning was not at odds with the old meanings, any more than cooking is at odds with eating, or pregnancy at odds with giving birth, or prophecy at odds with fulfillment. He was contradicting nothing, but He most certainly was changing everything.

Jesus established this Table as a means for us to commune with Him. Raw faith doesn't do it, because God did not command faith to operate without sacraments. For faith to try to "go it alone" is actually unbelief, because biblical faith can only respond to what God has actually said He will do. Faith comes by hearing, and hearing by the word of God. Faith has no powers of invention.

At the same time, the bread and wine by themselves do not constitute a sacrament, either. We must come in true, sincere, lively evangelical faith. As the great Puritan Thomas Watson put it, speaking of this meal, those who come with only the skin of duty will have only the shell of comfort. When God told Abraham to sacrifice Isaac, it would not have been sufficient for Abraham to stay at home and say, "The essence of this command is that I give my 'all' to God, which I am happy to do." Faith obeys.

Some object to the idea of an obedient faith, suspecting that some Pharisee is trying to smuggle works-righteousness in, but the only alternative to obedient faith is disobedient faith, which is, of course, no faith at all.

So then, faith chews and swallows. But that is not all it does.

So come, and welcome, to Jesus Christ.

As we receive food that the Father gives, a right reception of it should make us more eager for His food that comes to us in other ways. When the early Christians responded to the gospel, they devoted themselves to the breaking of bread *and* to the teaching of the apostles (Acts 2:42).

If devotion to the Lord's Supper makes you less hungry for the Word as it is preached, or it makes you disinclined to read your Bible, then this means you are doing it wrong.

The reason we want food from the Father is that we are hungry for the Father Himself. If we start to play one kind of food off another, then this reveals that it is not the Father we were interested in, but rather the interest was in making an idol out of one of His gifts. We are not seeking nourishment when we do this, but rather were just playing with our food.

Sacramentalists who don't like preaching are not really sacramentalists. Devotees of preachers and preaching who don't yearn for the sacrament are not really paying attention to the sermons. Those who pursue bread and wine with dusty Bibles at home are revealing that they want a religious show and not spiritual nourishment.

The words of God feed us, and because we love Him we want to be fed by anything He sets on our plates.

So come, and welcome, to Jesus Christ.

MORNING ☼ NOT BEING GRADED

We have assembled here yet again. We do so aware of our sinfulness, and our unworthiness, and this is something we have already confessed.

But at the same time, we are commanded in Scripture to walk in a manner that is *worthy* of the name we have received. And you, as a particular congregation, need to be reminded that your elders and pastor are extremely grateful to God for you. We have pastoral problems, and difficulties with wandering sheep, as all churches do, but we are mindful of the good work that God is doing in our midst. Young men, continue in your strength. Young women, persevere in all modesty and purity. Fathers, provide for your households as you have been doing. Mothers, care for those in your charge, as we know you delight to do. Husbands, we know you love your wives. Wives, we know that you honor your husbands. And as citizens of our community, we know that you have been genuine salt and light, and we rejoice in the work of God.

This said, you do not come to this Table as a reward for being so good. Rather, you come to be nourished, so that God will continue His good work in you and through you all. More good works are planned for you *tomorrow*, and you need strength for the journey. We do not feed our children meals because they were good yesterday. We feed them simply because they *are* our children, and in doing this, we know we are equipping them to be good tomorrow. As you come to the Table, you are not being graded; you are being fed.

So rejoice in the work of God thus far, as we do, and look forward to tomorrow by faith.

So come, and welcome, to Jesus Christ.

EVENING ◐ WINE OR DITCH WATER?

There are only two tables in the world. The one is the Table of the Lord, the true Table, the place where life is offered and served. The other is the table of demons, the table of death. God has established a complete antithesis between the two, the difference between life and death, heaven and hell, wine and dirty ditch water, light and darkness, nourishment and poison.

But although God has established His Table on these terms, the fact that we are being sanctified from our remaining sins makes us frequently think that there is a possible third way. We are tempted to think that we can create a more sophisticated, urbane religion, and take what we like from both tables. Far from being sophisticated, such thinking is extremely simple-minded, and flies in the face of what God's Word expressly tells us. Friendship with the world is enmity with God. Acceptance of their dinner invitations, in this sense, is rejection of God's dinner invitation.

We ought not to over-analyze what God has given us. He has given it, we should receive it, and we should receive it on the terms He sets upon it — repentance and faith.

So come, and welcome, to Jesus Christ.

MORNING ☼ NO DIMINISHMENT OF THE WORD

The sinful heart is prone to error, even in necessary corrections. While many Christians have overemphasized the Word, to the neglect of the sacraments, if we are seeking to correct this, we must guard against an over-correction.

Many assume that we cannot honor the Table unless we minimize the Word. But the Word preached is the power of God unto salvation, to all who believe, to the Jew first, and also to the Greek. Without the Word, the sacraments are nothing but smoke and shadow. Without the sacraments, the Word is being thought about, but in the end disobeyed.

So we do not emphasize the sacraments as a preliminary move in the minimization of a verbal declaration of the will of God. The Bible is our life, but it is only our life as we do what it says. This includes gathering together for the breaking of bread. But we must also remind one another constantly, as long as it is called today, that we must be on guard against the deceitfulness of sin. So, as you hear the Word, cultivate humility of mind. As you partake of the sacrament, cultivate humility of heart. As you love one another, do so deeply, from the heart. That is our *koinonia*.

So come, and welcome, to Jesus Christ.

EVENING ◐ THE CONTEXT OF THE INSTITUTION

We know that the Lord Jesus is the one who established this meal, but when did He do so? He did this in the general context of the Passover meal, but there is also a distinction made. Luke tells us that He presented the cup of the new testament "after supper" (Luke 22:20). But He had also given a new covenant meaning to the cup in the course of the Supper (v. 17). And the bread He broke was in the course of the Supper as well (v. 19). So He looked forward to eating the Supper with His disciples (v. 15), longing for it. He declared it during the Supper, and He anchored after the Supper with the cup of the new testament in his blood. All of time is encompassed in this meal, past, present, and future.

In the words of institution, we learn something else about when He instituted the meal. In *the same night in which he was betrayed* . . . He took bread. This meal was *established* in the context of treachery and double-dealing. This is a meal established in the middle of our unholy and decentered world. The meal is given in order to reestablish the true center, but this is not accomplished without conflict or resistance.

The resistance comes in many forms. Some are openly treacherous and abandon their vows. Some overanalyze it. Some retreat into morbid introspection. Some come under false pretenses. None of this should surprise us. If the Lord could institute this meal the same night He was betrayed, then surely we can observe it though thousands betray Him to this day. Let God be true and every man a liar.

Sin does not wreck this story; it is part of the story. God anticipates it; He knows all about it. He deals with it. It is a central part of the whole *point*. The Lord looked forward to the meal, longing for it, even though He knew about the treachery, knowing it completely. Why do we somehow think His ways have changed?

So come, and welcome, to Jesus Christ.

MORNING ☼ THE COMPANIONSHIP OF SAINTS

In taking part in this meal, we are the Lord's companions. The word *companion* originally meant to share bread together with someone. The *com* means together, and *panis* is the word for bread. We are the Lord's companions.

This sounds wonderful to us, but there is a hitch. Everyone else who comes to this Table is His companion also, and it follows from this that we are companions one to another. If we walk in the Light, as He is in the Light, we have fellowship with one another (1 Jn. 1:7). In other words, our companionship with one another is dependent upon our companionship with the Lord. Moreover, it flows necessarily from that first companionship. If we love Jesus Christ, whom we have not seen with our eyes, then we must love all His brothers and sisters, whom we have seen with our eyes.

This includes everyone in your family, whether husband, wife, children, or parents, everyone in your row, in your section, in this congregation, in the congregation of our sister church, in this town, everyone throughout the world, and everyone throughout the history of the Church. We believe, as we say every week, in the communion of saints. Let us confess it gladly.

So come, and welcome, to Jesus Christ.

EVENING ◑ MORE THANKS

The predominant emotion that should be present as we partake of the Lord's Supper should be gratitude and thanksgiving. One of the ancient names for this meal is that of the Eucharist. This comes from the Greek word for thanksgiving, *eucharisto*. In fact, if our holiday of Thanksgiving were to be given a Greek name, it would be called the Eucharist.

It is therefore tragic that so many Christians have turned this time of worship and communion into an opportunity for self-flagellation and morbid introspection. The Bible does teach us to examine ourselves, but we are to do so with a right standard, and in decent proportions. If you spend all your time grubbing around in your own sinfulness, the one thing you may be assured of is that you will not deal effectively with any real sins in your life. This attitude of ingratitude, especially at the Supper, is one of the things that perpetuates a life without joy, a life of morbidity, a life of disobedience.

Disobedience is not sanctified by having a gloomy countenance. A long face is not a moral disinfectant. If you have sinned, confess it before you get here, and make restitution. If you have sinfully put this off, then confess your sins in our time of confession at the beginning of the service. But when you come to this Table, do not forget you have been washed up for dinner. Come with grateful and overflowing hearts.

So come, and welcome, to Jesus Christ.

MORNING ☀ READING OR EATING?

God has given us this meal as a sign and seal of the unity we have with Him, and consequently of the unity we have with one another. But, not surprisingly, we have responded like a nation of dufflepuds, using the meal of unity as one of the principle points of disunity. We have read, *take and eat* as *take and argue*.

Not only do we quarrel about the food, and the Table settings, but we chase away from *our* observance of the Table any who do not parse the arguments in exactly the same way we do. Thus we set aside the Word of God for the sake of our tradition. Such traditions are hard to break away from, admittedly, but we are seeking to do it. That is why any baptized Christian, who is not under the lawful discipline of the Church, is welcome here. We know that this is not *our* Table.

Some will say that certain parsings of the meaning of this Table amount to idolatry, and we agree. The disagreements that arise are not necessarily disagreements over *words*. They can amount to idolatry, and all idolatry must be repented. Not only must it be repented of, but the Word that accompanies the sacrament must identify all such idolatries.

But if it is a faithful Word, then it will identify the idolatries that *we* are in danger of committing, and not rest content with inveighing against idolatries that are being committed on the other side of the world, or even across town.

The errors of Rome are not really a temptation here. So what is? Many conservative Protestants insist on observing the Supper as though it were simply a cleverly disguised sermon—or an extension on the sermon, the part of the sermon where the minister uses some props, to help us remember certain propositions. And the idolatry here is of our own minds, our own rational capacities. If we don't feed ourselves, by teaching ourselves, we believe that we cannot be fed. But reading a nutrition text is not the same as eating.

So come, and welcome, to Jesus Christ.

Eating is one of the enormous mysteries of life, and one of the greatest aspects of this mystery is how readily we drift into assuming how ordinary it is. But there is nothing ordinary about eating at all — not even with non-sacramental eating. How is it *possible* for life to be sustained by this means?

As food grows up out of the earth, we see it gather nutrients from the environment — inorganic matter is transformed into organic matter. And then, as the food is tended by a farmer and harvested, and fed to us, the food is transformed from a lower organic order to a higher organic order. You are what you eat, but this is not a materialist dictum, but rather a glorious mystery — God is transforming the world, and He uses the instrument of eating.

He does the same kind of thing in the realm of the covenants. As we eat, we grow. As we grow and mature, our eating does not become less necessary, but rather more obviously important. We never mature past the point of needing food. An eighty-year-old man looks to his breakfast just as a newborn infant does. Maturity is sustained by food, and maturity never matures beyond food. This is because we are creatures, and God has created the world in an interdependent way. We come here to this Table as a needy people, and this is not our shame. It is our glory. We are His people, and He feeds us.

So come, and welcome, to Jesus Christ.

MORNING ☼ DOCTRINES ON A PAGE

Let us never overlook the obvious. The Lord feeds His people. He does not call out a people from the world in order to let them starve. His grace is all-sufficient, and He loves to feed us in remarkable ways, and in remarkable places. The wilderness is no barrier for Him — water flows from the Rock, the Rock being Christ, and bread falls from heaven, the bread being Christ also.

How are His people supposed to take in this food? How do we swallow? How do we chew? The answer is that we appropriate this blessing by one means only. Faith — genuine, evangelical faith.

This is not a faith that merely conforms to a certain doctrine on a page. It is a faith that looks to Jesus Christ, the one in whom we meet with God. He is the one who has shown us the Father. He is the one who reveals what God is like. He is the one who sustains us with the example of His life. He is the one who includes us in Him, for He is the new Adam, and we are all His covenant descendants.

Now everything just said can be reduced to certain doctrines on a page. If you stare at those words, as though they were a mural, then the closer you get, the further away the blessing will be. But if these words of life are seen as a window, seen through as a window is seen *through*, you will come by faith and meet with your God. And He will bless you. Jesus rebuked certain Bible students of His day with these words — "You search the Scriptures because you think that in them you have eternal life — and it is they that bear witness of me" (Jn. 5:39, ESV).

So come, and welcome, to Jesus Christ.

"And as they were eating, Jesus took bread, and blessed it, and brake it, and gave it to the disciples, and said, Take, eat; this is my body" (Matt. 26:26). As Jesus was instituting this Supper among His disciples, note in particular what He did with the bread. He picked it up, and then He *blessed* it.

In blessing *that* bread in this way, He, the Lord Himself, blessed *this* bread here in the same way. The Lord Jesus did not just establish this meal; He established it with a blessing. That blessing extends to the end of the world because the Lord promised to be with us always.

So this morning you are partaking of a meal that Jesus Christ Himself blessed. This is bread that Jesus Christ prayed over. But there is more than this. You are, the apostle Paul once declared, one loaf. The congregation of God's people is the bread that the Lord blessed.

But then note, that having blessed the bread, He broke it and gave it to the disciples. Now this bread was obviously His body, broken on the cross. But also, just as obvious once we think of it, we are also His body, broken on the cross. I have been crucified with Christ, Paul said (Gal. 2:20). We who have been baptized have been baptized into His death (Rom. 6:30).

He takes, He blesses, He breaks, and He distributes. He takes you and calls you by His own name. He blesses you, and you are blessed beyond all reckoning. He breaks you — not out of malice, but because this is His way — and then He gives you to your brothers and sisters. You, in participating in this meal, are cooperating with that same action. You are saying *amen*.

This is why squabbles within the body of Christ are so unseemly. They contradict everything else that is being done. When Jesus breaks you, it is with a blessing just before. When you bite and tear on your own, the break still happens, but the blessing is not there. There is a breaking that does not nourish others, and one that does.

So come, and welcome, to Jesus Christ.

MORNING ✹ FOR HE IS GOOD

One of the taunts that was brought against our Lord during His earthly ministry was that He ate with sinners. If you look around the room, and if you consider your own heart, you will observe that He is still doing this. He *still* eats with sinners. But as He does this, He does not become like we are — rather, we become like Him.

This is why Paul could write to the Roman church, confident, as he put it, that they were filled with goodness. They were not filled with a goodness of their own. But nevertheless, they were filled with goodness. An ordinary congregation of forgiven sinners, just like you, was declared by the apostle to be filled with goodness. And so are you. You are filled with goodness. Look around the room — you see other saints who are filled with that same goodness, the goodness of the grace of God. It has come to rest upon us, and He has sent His Spirit to indwell us. Because Jesus is good — no one being good except God alone — all those who have gathered at His Table in truth are also good. This is the goodness of grace, but it does not keep it from being goodness.

The food is good. The fellowship is good. The company is good. The results are good. The aroma is good. So as we partake, as we give thanks, offer your praises to the Lord, for He is good.

So come, and welcome, to Jesus Christ.

Meals talk. They say something. Of course, it does not follow from this that we always listen as we ought.

The Word that accompanies this sacrament is not a matter of us talking over the meal, providing some sort of soundtrack for it. Rather, when we speak here, it is really a matter of us listening to what the meal says. The meal speaks in the words of Scripture, and it is our responsibility to allow Scripture to interpret what we do here. We take and eat. We take and drink. What does this mean?

It means that we are the people of the new Exodus. It means that we are the freedom people. It means that slavery to sin is a thing of the past. It means that we are forgiven. It means that we are completely forgiven. It means that we cannot hope to earn our right to be seated at this Table. This place is not a reward for having been so good. Of course we are not good — that is the whole point of the meal. Jesus Christ eats with publicans and sinners. We do not have to protect God's grace by means of our paltry works — indeed, we cannot. Rather, God's grace, so evident here, protects and secures us.

How close is God's forgiveness to you in Christ? The answer is given us by this meal. Forgiveness is as close as the bread you eat. It is as close as the wine you drink.

So come, and welcome, to Jesus Christ.

MORNING ☼ NO COUNTERMEASURES

God in His great wisdom has determined that He will bring the nations to serve Him, and He will do so as His people gather together to hear His Word preached, and to eat and drink His Word served.

As the enemies of God rail and blaspheme, our interest is to make sure that *we* are not the cause of the blasphemy through any sins we have committed, and to follow that up with a careful refraining from ungodly responses to whatever they do. That said, there is nothing left for us to do but to sit down at the Table God has prepared for us in the presence of our enemies.

This meal is a glorious meal, and it has a potency far beyond our calculation. It is not the potency that some superstitious Christians have sometimes imagined for it — as though God were interested in performing magic tricks with the food. Manners are important. We are not here to play with the food, and our divine host does not play with the food either. Rather, He uses the food to nourish and strengthen His people.

The Word has been proclaimed. The gospel is heard by us, and we hear it with faith. Because of this, and only because of this, the meal we approach now is a great blessing, and not a curse for us. But what is that blessing? It is that we are privileged to conquer the world simply by eating what God has set before us. And though the nations rage, and the heathen imagine a vain thing, there is nothing whatever they can do about it. There are no counter-measures against this.

So come, and welcome, to Jesus Christ.

EVENING ◐ BRUISED AROMA

As we sit down together at this meal, with the Jesus at the head of the Table, we are partaking of a very simple meal — bread and wine. Because of this we may mistakenly forget one of the most important features of food and drink, which is the wonderful blessing of aroma. Smell is essential to what we call eating and drinking. You know what it is like to eat when you have a terrible cold — nothing *tastes*.

So what is the aroma here? That is simply another way of asking how this meal should taste. Just as St. Paul teaches us that *we* are the one loaf, and that *we* are the one body, so in another place he teaches that we are the aroma, we are the taste. The KJV says that *we* are "a sweet savour of Christ" (2 Cor. 2:15). Other translations render this as aroma — showing the connection between aroma and savor. We cannot savor food without smelling it.

This is the savor of "his knowledge *by us*" (v. 14). The Lord Jesus was bruised for our iniquities. As the Puritan Thomas Watson observed, it is when spices are bruised that they give off their aroma. As we follow in our imitation of Christ, when we surrender for others, sacrifice for others, lay down our lives for others, it is in this way that we manifest the aroma of life unto life. For those who are perishing, it is a stench, but this is only because they have no stomach for the bread of life, and have no taste for the wine that washes away every bitter taste that sin leaves in the mouth.

This meal is *supposed* to have an aroma. When we gather together in love like this, that aroma should strike us in the face when we enter the room. You know what it is like to walk into a home where the cook has been doing wonderful things all day. This service should far surpass that — love smells and tastes like nothing else. All the delightful smells that you have ever encountered together with food are just faint types and shadows. They point to this; in some small way they smell like this.

So come, and welcome, to Jesus Christ.

MORNING ☼ MORE FOOD

Eating is not a result of the Fall. When God created Adam and Eve, and placed them in the garden, He put them in a garden full of food. Food is not an unfortunate development. When Adam was cursed for his disobedience, the result was a curse upon the ground, a curse that meant that food was going to become *harder* to get. Thorns and thistles were to obstruct the growing of food. The Fall meant less food, not more food. The Fall meant a barrier to food, not the creation of food. In other words, plainly stated, sin did not bring about the creation of food.

In the new creation, we find that it is the same. Man is both created, and recreated, as an eating creature. God intends for us to take food into our mouths, and by this means, to restructure the world around us. Physical food is a great mystery, and spiritual food even more so. How can we restructure the world around us, evangelize our community, exercise dominion in the earth, throw down the idols, just by eating? Well, the answer is that we *cannot* do it just by eating — this is gospel food, and gospel food is always a curse unless it is received with living, active, evangelical faith. We come to this Table in faith. We sit down in faith.

We rule on the earth, as kings and priests, as we do this. If we run away from this Table in order to rule another way, we will only be humiliated. And if we get up from this Table in order to hide, afraid the of the responsibility that comes with this, then we receive God's discipline also. But come, He offers us more food.

So come, and welcome, to Jesus Christ.

EVENING ◐ THE FAMILY THAT EATS TOGETHER STAYS TOGETHER

This is not just a meal, it is a household meal. It is a family meal. This is a meal for sons and daughters, not for aliens and strangers. This may strike us as odd, because we know that in the Scriptures we are to invite *everyone* to this meal.

But there is an important qualification that must be remembered. It is true that we invite all strangers and aliens to this meal, but not with them coming in their capacity *as* strangers and aliens. Rather, we are inviting strangers and aliens to become sons and daughters, and *then* to sit down with us.

The fact that some stay away and others come hypocritically does not change the nature of the event. We are eating together as a household. We all know the cliché, the family that prays together stays together. Related to this, we have to remember that the family that eats together stays together. One of the reasons why the modern household is in trouble is the infrequency of their common meals. And one of the reasons why the church of Jesus Christ is so fragmented in our nation today is the same reason. The family that eats together stays together.

You are summoned to break bread together, and drink wine together. You are to consider *all* the saints here together with you, and discern the body. You are to be at peace with one another. For example, as you sit with the bread in your hand, next to the sister you squabbled with this morning, that bread and your faith together say that you should lean over and say, "Sorry."

So come, and welcome, to Jesus Christ.

MORNING ☼ DEATH AND RESURRECTION BOTH

This is, for us, a cup of blessing. We rejoice here, and we give thanks here, as the Scriptures teach us to. At the same time, we must remember that the cup that the Lord drank — and at a basic level, it is the same cup — was a cup of agony. Just before the Lord asked for the cup to be withheld from Him, He said, "My soul is exceeding sorrowful, even unto death" (Matt. 26:38).

When the Lord described something with a word like *exceeding,* we know that He was facing a formidable challenge. Jesus said that His soul was so overwhelmed with sorrow that He was at the point of dying, without Judas, or Pilate, or the soldiers.

Now this cup that Jesus prayed to avoid, this cup that He nevertheless received as the will of His Father, this cup that He drank obediently, down to the dregs, this cup of woe is for us a cup of blessing, of thanksgiving, of joy. How is this possible? This is the direction God works. We by our sin made a ruin out of the world. Jesus came as God's own priest for us, stepping into this wretched world. He then gathered up all the sin of all His people, and the wrath that was resting upon that sin, put it in a cup, and drank it down. He swallowed all of it, and death was swallowed up by victory.

But note the nature of the victory. It is not the kind of "victory" that carnal men would have anticipated. The cruciform shape of Christ's triumph would not lead us to anticipate, unless our eyes have been opened by the Spirit of God, the resurrection that followed. God's way of victory is death, and there is no shortcut or detour around that death. There is no going straight to resurrection.

Jesus drank this cup for the joy that was set before Him, which He saw by faith. We participate in what He did, also by faith, and we do so with the glad willingness to identify with Him in every aspect of His obedience — death and resurrection both.

So come, and welcome, to Jesus Christ.

When you were a child, you came to the dinner table, knowing that your parents would have food for you there. This child-like faith went for years, for all of us, and it was not until much later that we all learned what that provision cost. All we knew was that parents feed their children. We are born knowing this. No one has to teach a newborn how to cry for milk, or where to look for it.

The Word tells us that we, like newborn infants, should desire the pure milk of the Word, now that we have tasted that the Lord is good. Two things drive us. Like all who are born alive, we are born hungry. There is an instinct within us, an instinct that shows us born alive within the kingdom; we seek out the food of the Word. This of course applies to the Word of God preached, but it also applies to the Word of God eaten, the Word of God in a cup. We have an instinct that drives us here.

But Peter tells us that children also develop an affection for the Word through their *experience*—now that you have tasted that the Lord is good, he says. You have been coming to the Lord's Table on a weekly basis for years now. Try to imagine for a moment what it would be like to go back to what many of us experienced for years, when the Lord's Supper was observed periodically, rarely, or in some cases, never.

The Lord's children should be characterized by many things, but this should be high on the list—the Lord's children clamor for food.

So come, and welcome, to Jesus Christ.

MORNING ☼ STRENGTH FOR THE BATTLE

There are only two tables in the world — the Table of the Lord and the table of demons. Between the two is the division of light and darkness, righteousness and unrighteousness, good and evil. This means that the choice must be one of the two — the two cannot be combined or blended in order to create a third way.

Life is simple. Love God and hate sin. Life is not complicated. Love God, love His people, love His Word, love His sacraments, love His church. The fear of the Lord is to hate evil, and we are summoned to this fear, and we are strengthened at this Table for that hatred. Remember that the Ephesians were commended for their hatred of the deeds of the Nicolaitans, but were rebuked for falling from their first love. The intensity of our love for Jesus will not diminish our hatred for all that arrays itself against Him. Far from it.

This Table nourishes your love and nourishes your hatred. Love God and hate evil. If you do not feel yourself to have the strength for this, come here, to this Table, to receive the strength. You do not come to the Table as a reward for being strong, you come to the Table weak, knowing that only God can make you strong. The instrument He uses to enable you to receive this strength is *faith*. And even this faith is given to you as a gift so that no one can boast. Little children, you are coming to the Table, not because you are strong, but because God intends to make you strong. He will do this by His grace, so just come in simple faith.

So come, and welcome, to Jesus Christ.

Poor translations can sometimes create a world of difficulty. The rendering of the word repentance by "do penance" was a famous stumbling block for Luther.

In a similar way, we are all familiar with this phrase from the words of institution in the Lord's Supper—"do this in remembrance of me." This is taken as though we are to use the Supper to help us remember what Jesus did for us on the cross. While this element is necessarily involved in the Supper, and it is certainly part of what we do, much more is involved than this.

The phrase should actually be rendered as "do this as my memorial." Presenting a memorial to God is quite a different thing than remembering God. In a memorial, as with many memorials throughout the Old Testament, *we are calling upon God to remember*. As we do this, we certainly remember as well, but much more is involved in this than simply providing a reminder for *us*.

This Supper is a liturgical prayer, a ritual request. God is our covenant God, and we are pleading the covenant with Him. By partaking of this meal, we are presenting His promises back to Him. We might argue with this and say that God does not need such reminders. Of course not, but He nevertheless commands us to approach Him this way. The rainbow is a memorial before God in just this sense. He will never again destroy the world, and we are invited to plead the rainbow as we consider our sinfulness. He has determined to save the world through Jesus Christ, and so we proclaim the death of Jesus Christ every time we partake, as we do so because His death is the only possible salvation for the world.

Not only do we proclaim this to the world, but we also present it *to God*.

So come, and welcome, to Jesus Christ.

MORNING ☼ IGNORING THE P.R. DEPARTMENT

Christ was crucified between two thieves, with the apparent implication that He was the principal evildoer. The one who associated with sinners during the course of His life was also associated with them in His death, as His enemies tried to make it into a slander — He died with criminals, with criminals on either hand.

But there was nothing here that Christ would reject. It was the purpose of God that we Christians would have a message like this to preach — our Lord was tried by Bible-believing conservatives, by religious establishment liberals, by civil rulers concerned for the public peace, and then He was executed. This is the message that the Christian Church has been commanded to glory in to the end of the world. We gather weekly to proclaim it as a congregation, as we partake of the bread and wine. Nothing is plainer than that God did not consult with any of His P.R. staff or marketing experts when He came up with this. This body and blood is not a symbol of ultimate sacrifice acknowledged and applauded by everyone. This is a greater sacrifice than that. This is the body and blood of a condemned malefactor, rejected by virtually every entry in Jerusalem's *Who's Who*.

When God gave us this gospel, He gave us one that has to be preached *uphill*. When God gave us a Savior, He gave us one who would draw the animus of the worldly-wise. There is an institutional drift or mindset that is at odds with the gospel. But we are commanded to bring all the nations of men to Christ. And this is where we should see the importance of partaking of this meal rightly.

We are to bring the institutions of men into this; we are not to bring this into the institutions of men. The context of all future civilization must now be a recognition of the affinity that civilizations naturally have for conducting murderous travesties — like the one that gave us this Table.

So come, and welcome, to Jesus Christ.

As you know, we gladly welcome little children to the Table here. All baptized children are welcome to partake, with this proviso. What we require is that they have the capacity to be taught what we are doing *through the doing of it*, and that their parents faithfully instruct them every week as they partake of the Supper.

This means that there should be ongoing parental instruction on what the Supper means, what our demeanor ought to be, how they should confess any sins they need to confess prior to coming to the Table, and so forth. We are not just "letting" the children come; we are *teaching* them how to come. We are teaching them through the actions of the Supper, but we also want the Word to accompany the sacrament. Parents have a responsibility to make sure that the Word of instruction, the Word that must accompany the sacrament, gets down to their little level.

Children sometimes can be distracted by things like the taste of the wine, and want to hold their noses. They can be distracted by other incidental things as well. Parents, take care that your children are learning how to remember the Lord, thank the Lord, rejoice before the Lord, press covenant promises upon the Lord, and humble themselves before the Lord.

All parents who have the joy of seeing their children grow up in communion with all the saints need to remember that to whom much is given, much is required.

So come, and welcome, to Jesus Christ.

MORNING ☼ THE SACRAMENT IS IN THE PARTICIPLE

One of the great theological problems that has afflicted the church down through the ages is the tendency to think of the Lord's Supper in terms of a snapshot, and not in terms of the video.

There is no sacrament here on the Table. We have bread, and we have wine, but we have no sacrament. Nothing happens on this Table that would justify us calling this Table an altar. But many Protestants, having been reassured that nothing happens to the bread and wine on the Table, walk away reassured in the false notion that nothing happens at all.

But this is false. Something does happen to the bread — it is eaten by the people of God in faith. Something does happen to the wine — we drink it while believing God. The sacrament is the action of the body of Christ, and you are that body. The bread is transformed, but you are that bread. The wine is changed, but you are that cup, the cup of the new covenant. *You* are transformed; *you* are changed.

As we gather and do what God tells us to do, and we do it in faith, God uses this series of actions to knit us closer together with His Son and our Lord, the Lord Jesus. But the central thing in this is faith and unbelief. Those who go through this assigned ritual with evangelical faith in God are built up into Jesus Christ. Those who go through it in faithless unbelief are eating and drinking that unbelief, which is why they are eating and drinking damnation. Our salvation is graciously given through the instrument of faith.

So come, and welcome, to Jesus Christ.

This Table is all about grace, forgiveness, kindness, and acceptance. God receives you here. This is the normal way we ought to think of it.

Not only does He receive you here, but he does so knowing all about your sins. Jesus said that this was His blood of the new testament, which was to be shed for many for the remission of sins (Matt. 26:28). His blood was not shed in order to provide the world with yet another prohibition, another tree of the knowledge of good and evil. His death was to be a restoration of the way back to the tree of life, a tree that was not prohibited to our first parents. Neither is it prohibited to us. We are invited, summoned, called, importuned, and commanded to come, and to do so gladly.

We are not coming to yet another fault-finding accusation. That is what we are leaving behind. We are not coming to a censorious Deity, upset with us for arriving late, disheveled, or a little dirty. He is glad we have come, and He bids us welcome.

But we must know, for He has plainly told us, that we are taking our place at His Table, not as a reward for being good, or for being comparatively better than others who were worse, or for being on His side. We are accepted, completely, but we are accepted as sinners who have had their sins forgiven.

Forgiven means that your sins are washed away. Put away forever. Removed from you, as far as the east is from the west. God has taken your sins out to the middle of the ocean and deep-sixed them. We shall never hear about them again, either here or in the resurrection. That is what this cup represents. That is what this cup means.

And this is why the Table is not a place for gloomy or morbid introspection. This is a Eucharistic Table, a Table of thanksgiving and gladness. How could it be understood and be anything else? *God forgives sinners.*

So come, and welcome, to Jesus Christ.

MORNING ☼ THOSE WHO ARE BREAD SHOULD GET BREAD

As we have said before, your baptized children are welcome to this Table. All who *are* bread *get* bread. But we have also explained it with several provisos. Young children should have the Supper explained to them by their parents in each observance of the Supper, and they should be able to attend to what is said.

Please note that we are not requiring that little children be able to *explain* the Supper before they may partake. They are recipients; they have the Supper explained *to* them. We feed them the bread and wine in much the same way we begin speaking English to our children when they first arrive in our homes — not because they understand it, but rather so that they might *come* to understand it. It is similar here. We are not asking for anything to arise in the child or manifest itself before he is qualified to receive. He is receiving and learning, not giving and teaching.

The requirement that the child be able to attend is in the same category as the requirement that bread be withheld until a nursing infant can swallow bread, or drink wine. We remember our children's frame. If they are asleep in the car seat throughout the service, they cannot mentally chew any more than they can physically chew. We do not bring oblivious infants to the Table, but not because *we* exclude them. Their frame excludes them. But when you get to the point where you have to consistently explain to them why they *cannot* partake, it would be just as well if you used that time to explain to them why they are partaking.

So come, and welcome, to Jesus Christ.

We have been considering the presence of our children together here with us at this Table. We have noted that nothing is required of them except the capacity to receive, the capacity to be shaped and taught. We have seen from Scripture that all who *are* bread *get* bread. All who are the covenant get the covenant cup. This is because we are committed to the great confession of Joshua — as for me and my house, we will serve the Lord (Josh. 24:15).

In one of the great ironies of modernity, the world of unbelief has embraced the chastisement found in Scripture, and they are diligent to see to it that their principles of idolatry and unbelief are visited upon their descendants to three and four generations. They have no qualms about passing on unbelief as their heritage.

We have promises of covenant kindness, to a thousand generations. But in these modern times, the people of God, who have been given promises to a thousand generations, quail and quake in the presence of this kind of overwhelming graciousness. We do not believe what God has promised us. He has said that He will be our God, and the God of our children, and of their children's children. He has promised a shepherd David to lead us, throughout all generations, forever. The child in Mary's womb did not come in order to abrogate all God's generational blessings. *He came to fulfill them.*

We are *Christians*, and a burden therefore rests upon us to believe Jesus Christ, and to follow Him. And when you take up your cross to follow Him, you are *not* permitted to look around at your family and bid them farewell. We are disciples of Jesus Christ, household by household, family by family.

For little feet, the pilgrimage is hard, you might say. But the way of the wicked is harder. Come, we are invited to commune with Jesus Christ, and to walk with Him, *together*.

So come, and welcome, to Jesus Christ.

MORNING ☼ THE SUN IS UP

As we come to the Table together, I would like to speak a word to the children who have been gathered here with us.

You are named by the name of Jesus Christ. Just as you were born into a particular family, and no one asked you whether or not you wanted your last name, so you are being brought up in the Christian faith, in the nurture and admonition of the Lord. This is not the result of anyone infringing on your rights, but rather the result of your parents' obedience. This is just what God has told them to do.

Now you know that it is not enough simply to be a member of the covenant—you must also be faithful to that covenant, and fruitful in it. One temptation you will encounter is that of trying to peer into the depths of your heart to find out if you are *truly* being faithful, if you are *truly* a member of the covenant. But looking into your own heart this way will only bring confusion.

Rather, you should always look in faith to Jesus Christ. When you do that, it strengthens your faith. When you look to yourself, all you will encounter are doubts and confusions.

You do not need to know what time the sun rose this morning to know that it is up. You do not need to know what time of your life the sun rose in your hearts to know that it is up. You are here in this Christian congregation. You love Jesus Christ. You look forward to singing praise to Him. You look forward to learning from His Word. You know that you need the blessing and strengthening that comes from partaking of this Table. What does all this mean?

It means the sun is up. So come, together with the rest of us, and enjoy the blessing of God in Christ. This is true faith.

So come, and welcome, to Jesus Christ.

EVENING ◐ PREPARING FOOD, PREPARING PEOPLE

The Holy Spirit does not seek to motivate His people into positive godliness by means of guilt. The only thing that guilt motivates us to is confession. Once confession is made, the central motive force for all that we do is to be love and gratitude.

This Table is here to nourish, equip, and strengthen you for the tasks that God has assigned to you. He does not want you to come to this Table out of some guilty obligation. You are obligated, that is true, but the obligation is more like your obligation to breathe. It is not on your daily "to do" list. You have an obligation to take regular meals, but that obligation arises internally, and you do not pursue it in order to "be good." You eat because you're hungry.

In the same way, we gather here, a hungry people. We look forward to what God has prepared *for* us, and we also look forward to what God is preparing us to do. He prepares the meal, and by preparing the meal, He is preparing His people. A mother who cooks a good breakfast for her children before sending them off to school is not just preparing *food*. She is also preparing *children*.

God has established good works for you to do this coming week. He wants you to walk by faith in those good works, and He fits the work to you, and fits you to the work. One of His central instrument for equipping you for your assigned tasks this coming week is this service of worship, culminating in this meal. He strengthens you by His grace so that you might walk in His grace.

All of this is from grace, in grace, and unto grace. At no place in the process can we detach ourselves from His kindness and claim that we have done anything meritorious in ourselves. We have been saved by grace through faith, and we are God's workmanship. As His workmanship, we should be grateful for His tools. This Table is one of those tools.

So come, and welcome, to Jesus Christ.

MORNING ☼ THERE ARE ONLY TWO MEN IN THE WORLD

As we eat and drink in the fellowship of God, we need to remember that in this time of worship and communion, God is constituting and forming a new society. He is not just encouraging us in our private lives — although this *is* one result of what we do.

There are only two men in the world — Adam and Christ. There are only two cities — the city of man and the city of God. There are only two tables — the table of demons and the Table of the Lord. This is the meaning of the antithesis.

Now the formation of this new society is by no means a secret and invisible event. It is most public, and has public ramifications, and presents a potent challenge to those who claim secular ownership of the public square. When the state is god, its central liturgy is, of necessity, political posturing and positioning. But this meal is not given to us so that we might have the strength to participate in their liturgy. Rather, this meal is our liturgy, and it is a rival liturgy, serving a rival God, in the name of a rival city, and forming a rival culture.

One of the negative results of the Enlightenment — and there have been many — is that interest in Christian liturgy became much more textual, and much less enacted. But when it is enacted, and those enacting it understand what they do in faith, it is the most political thing we can do. Why? Because it is the means that God uses to form His new *polis*, His city, His society. This threatens the old order, and they always react to it. But that does not matter. God is in His heaven, Christ is on His throne, His people are assembled in response to His command, and He blesses us in full accordance with His Word.

So let the secularists have their petitions — a liturgy before a deaf and dumb idol. Let confused and compromised traditionalists sign their autonomous petitions — although we do pray for their repentance. We have a Table that strengthens and feeds the people of God.

So come, and welcome, to Jesus Christ.

One of the things that we learn from this meal is that we are a kingdom of priests. Just as the priests of the Old Testament were ordained, and afterward had access to the holy food of the sanctuary, so we are all ordained to the priesthood in our baptism. And consequently, we have access to the Table.

Now we learn this from the way the Table is arranged, and how the invitations are given. But it is important not to view this Table as an audio-visual aid from which we learn a lesson. We *do* learn a lesson, but far more is going on than just this intellectual reflection. The priestly families of the Old Testament could reflect on the food they were eating, and learn lessons from the fact that they were allowed to eat it. But the primary thing was that they eat, and be nourished.

Having said this, the arrangement is important. Before a priest was ordained in the order of Aaron, he was no priest. After he was ordained, he was. This was not because a magical act had occurred — rather it was because God has fashioned the world in such a way that words and ceremonies have the capacity to change someone's status. We see this everyday, and so it should not be difficult. Because of words spoken in a particular context, a single man becomes a husband. Because of words, a civilian becomes an enlisted solder. Because of words, a candidate becomes an office holder. All such words are a performative act. They accomplish something in the world.

When you were baptized, this same kind of performative act occurred, and you were made a priest. The Christian church is composed of kings and priests on the earth. Now whether you are a righteous priest like Phineas, or an evil priest like Caiphas, or a bumbling priest like Eli — well, there is no ceremony for *that.*

Do you believe God? Do you believe His Word? Do you trust His Spirit?

So come, and welcome, to Jesus Christ.

MORNING ☼ BREAKING A BAD HABIT

For many centuries, the Church has been cultivating the bad habit of seeing this time of communion a time of introspection.

But if there is anything that is a barrier to communion, it is the self-absorption that we have come to associate with this meal. So, as you come, do not curl up into a little ball and do not think about your shortcomings. You already confessed your sins an hour ago. This is dinner; you have already washed up, some time ago.

Do not close your eyes. Look around at all the saints that are gathered here. They are the body of Christ, together with you, and when you look at them this way, you are discerning the body of Christ.

You are not to be looking at the bread, or the wine in the cup, trying to do some theological metaphysics. You are being knit together, into a perfect man, all of you together, and you are united to the head of the body, the Lord Jesus Christ. You best assume this role when you are aware of how others are doing the same.

You are serving as an eye when you gladly reflect on how others are an ear, or fingers, or a foot. When we see the diversity that exists in the unified body of Christ, you are learning true spiritual wisdom.

You will not learn this if you spend this time reflecting on what a poor eye you have been all week. That may be, but that is no reason to continue sinning in just the same way as you approach the Table. If you have been selfish during the week, confess it, and forsake it. Particularly, forsake it here.

This meal is a communal meal. It is not about you in solitary. This meal was established by the grace of God, and is therefore all about Him, and all about us *together*. Whenever you see your morbid individualism creeping to disrupt this meal, chase it away with loud shouts. Chase it down the road, throwing rocks at it. Then come back to the Table — come back and commune with us.

So come, and welcome, to Jesus Christ.

EVENING ◐ RIGHT OUT OF CENTRAL CASTING

This is a covenant Table. God has established Jesus Christ as the Lord of the covenant Table, and one of the central features of covenant living is the feature of blessings and curses.

The sinful mind and the foolish heart war against this. But God is not mocked — men reap what they sow. Of course God teaches us not to view this woodenly or simplistically, as Job's comforters tried to do, or the Lord's disciples when they asked why a particular man was born blind. The pattern of cause and effect in covenant blessings and curses is *not* mechanical. But it is still real and open and obvious. A man cannot plant barley and think to harvest potatoes. Still less can he plant morning glory and pray for a crop of wheat. So how can a husband diligently plant his marriage full of weeds and pray for anything other than marital disaster?

God writes His story so that evil men fall into the pit that they have dug for others. Haman is hanged on the gallows he prepared for Mordecai. Sodom and Gomorrah blow up to the satisfaction of all the godly. God's villains are often right out of central casting. These things are written as examples for us, so that we might learn to think this way. But we search instead for stories with depth and ambiguity and complexity. This in itself is fine, so long as we do not lose the moral imagination, so long as we do not tumble down into moral confusion. We must remember that at the Day of Judgment there will be no ambiguity whatever. God will be terrifyingly simplistic there, with His talk of sheep and goats, and no other alternative categories.

We are a sinful people and subtleties are lost on us. We are not as intelligent as we think we are. We have not graduated as we think we have. Take and eat; it is your salvation. Take and drink; it is your redemption. Do this without evangelical faith, and it is nothing of the kind. So, come, in simple, child-like faith. Believe God. Love God, hate sin. God loves you, and He feeds you here.

So come, and welcome, to Jesus Christ.

MORNING ✹ NO MORBID FASCINATION

In Exodus 16, when manna first fell from the sky, the people called it manna for, as it says, they did not know what it was (Ex. 16:15).

This is the way of the fleshly heart. God feeds us; He surrounds us with food, but we do not know what He is doing. We do not know what His food actually is. The people in the wilderness also drank from the rock that accompanied them, and that Rock was Christ (1 Cor. 10:4). The fact that they drank from Christ does not mean that they knew or understood this in true faith. In the next verse, immediately after we are told that they drank from Christ, we are told that "with many of them God was not well pleased" (v. 5).

One of the central themes in these exhortations from the Table is that we Christians must put away all morbid introspection. But how can we do *that* when the Bible tells us that these things were written as examples for us (v. 6)? Don't these scary stories drive us into introspection?

They shouldn't. If the bad example of the Israelites is that they did not look to Christ, then how are we learning the right lesson from that bad example if we, in morbid introspection, refuse to look to Christ? The power of the bad example should cause us to see Christ in the manna, Christ in the water, Christ in the camp, Christ in our brothers and sisters. This is what we are called to, this is what God summons us to.

Do not look inside your own heart with morbid fascination — that is the way to deep spiritual trouble. Look to *Christ*. He has been preached and declared in the Word this morning. We have worshiped the Father through Him throughout this entire service. We are gathered at His Table. His body was broken for you; His blood was shed for you. The Bible does say to examine yourself, but looking away to Christ is the only real way to accomplish this. All other paths are not really self-examination at all.

So come, and welcome, to Jesus Christ.

When we come to this Table, we are not just coming to it, but rather learning how to come to it. This is particularly true of your children. The law of prayer is the law of belief. *Lex orandi, lex credendi.* The way we worship shapes the way we think. And the way we grow up worshiping shapes the way we will live for the rest of our lives.

As we have told you many times before, your baptized children are welcome to the Table here, provided that you as their parents instruct them carefully each time we partake, and they are capable of tracking with the instruction. We know that a one-year-old comes with a different level of maturity, but he should be coming the same way we do, in accordance with his ability.

When they come to the Table, our children should be doing the same basic thing that the rest of us are doing — participating in the entire service, worshiping the Lord. So if your child is asleep, do not wake them up just in time to receive the elements. They are learning by what they are doing and how they are doing it — and what they are learning this way is that coming to the Supper is no big deal, and that thoughtless, unprepared approaches to the Lord are just fine.

At the same time, you remember their frame. It is not a problem if a little one falls asleep — but if he does, they should be awakened in time to do what the rest of us do. That is, reflect, sing, hear the Word, and take the elements. If your child sleeps in the sermon, that is fine (*provided he is not sixteen*), but they should be awakened shortly before the end of the message. You should teach them why, which is that the Word is always to accompany the sacrament, and a thoughtless, disheveled approach to the Table is never appropriate.

If he is exhausted, then let him sleep through the Lord's Supper also. If, upon waking, he would be really distressed at having missed it, then wake him up in time to hear a part of the message. He is learning, not just by what we do, but also by what *he* does.

So come, and welcome, to Jesus Christ.

MORNING ☼ HE PREPARES A TABLE

Our practice of taking a day to honor our mothers is certainly a practice in accord with Scripture. It is not a holy day, marking an important event in the life of Christ, but it is a fine cultural practice. But what could it have to do with the Lord's Supper?

Everything in the world teaches us something about God, if we have ears to hear it. Every relationship we have reveals something important about God, and this includes our relationships with our mothers. This is not to accommodate the feminist conceit that God has "a feminine side," but rather to acknowledge that all things declare His glory.

For example, one of the things that our mothers do is prepare food for us. They think ahead, they prepare the menu, they shop, they set the table, and they cook. This happens so routinely that for many children it takes years to realize that this is not something that happens by itself. And God also does this. Scripture says that He prepares a Table for us, even if in the presence of our enemies. External obstacles do not deter Him.

God prepares a Table, and this is that Table. The fare is simple, but it is wisdom for the upright. The bread and wine might seem like the preparations were spare, but this meal cost more than any other meal possibly could. Our redemption, Scripture teaches, was not secured by means of precious gold or jewels, but rather through the blood of Jesus Christ — offered for blessing through this cup to those who have sincere faith.

So come, and welcome, to Jesus Christ.

EVENING ◐ INTIMACY AND AWE

How can intimacy and awe coexist? It is the work of God alone. The Holy Spirit enables us to cry out, "Abba, Father!" and the same Spirit is the one who teaches us to *hallow* God's name as we pray to Him. The Holy Spirit is, after all, a *holy* Spirit. He could no more lead us into irreverence than water can be dry.

This Table is one more instance of how God bestows upon us a demeanor of intimacy and awe. This is a familial Table; we are here because we are sons and daughters. Behold, what manner of love the Father has given to us, that we should be called children of God.

At the same time, we are not oblivious to this position of privilege and grace. We know that God has made us kings and priests on the earth, and we do not dismiss this as a light or trivial thing. We know that we are approaching the God who dwells in inapproachable light. We know that we are holding that which cannot be grasped. We understand that we are pondering mysteries that cannot be understood.

Our privilege is precisely here. We know what we have because we know that in ourselves we cannot have it. We hold nothing in our own hands, cup or bread, that is not there as a sheer and overwhelming gift from our gracious and sovereign God. We hold nothing in our hands in our own name. In the holding, in the eating, in the drinking, we are *named*. What is that name that we bear? It is the name of Jesus Christ, the name that is above every name, the name at which every knee shall bow, whether in heaven, or on earth, or under the earth. In addition to this, every tongue confesses that Jesus Christ is Lord, to the glory of God the Father.

Here, in this place, the tongues which make this confession do so, in part, because they are the same tongues which are used in this glorious eating and drinking. We do proclaim the Lord's death by singing and praying, it is true. But we also proclaim the universal lordship of Jesus through tasting and swallowing.

So come, and welcome, to Jesus Christ.

MORNING ☼ THE WHOLE THING IS BEYOND US

How does anything happen? It takes very little reflection to conclude that the world, and everything in it, is quite remarkable. How can a kernel of wheat germinate in the ground? How is a child knit together in the womb of his mother? How is it that a plant can feed on inanimate nutrients, and that a child can then feed on the plant, and grow into a mature man? How is it that, as the population grows, God turns inanimate chemicals into men and women who bear His image? We don't know; the whole thing is beyond us.

It is the same here. How is it that by faith, we feed on the living Christ, and are being transformed daily, weekly, yearly, into increasing conformity to His image? Does the spiritual world grind away mechanically, blindly? Not a bit of it — no more than this happens in the material world.

The heavens and the earth are glorious mysteriously. We cannot pull away a certain number of layers, and find, there, under all the appearances, the way things *really* are. What you see around you is what God has given, and what God is doing.

Now, at this moment, what is that? What do you see around you? You see your brothers and sisters in Jesus. You see the body of Christ. You see His members. You see what is to Jesus Christ bone of His bone, and flesh of His flesh. But you also see a work in progress. We are His body, but, sadly, we still have many spots, wrinkles, and blemishes. What are we to do? We are to remember, in faith, that God *deals* with us here. He brings sin to the surface in order to forgive it. He reveals rebellion in order to expel it. He encourages the weary. He comforts the disconsolate. And He does not do so scientifically, or by some magic trick with the wine and bread. He does it by presenting Himself to us in the act of eating and drinking wine and bread, and He deals with us in true and everlasting evangelical faith.

So come, and welcome, to Jesus Christ.

This ritual meal is not demeaned through being a ritual. We do not say that it is *merely* ritual. After all, through rituals many remarkable things happen. A bachelor becomes a husband; a daughter becomes a wife. Through ritual, a civilian becomes a soldier. Through ritual, an Englishman becomes an American, or an American becomes and Englishman. Through ritual, a layman becomes a minister and pastor. Rituals are potent, and it is no different here.

But they can also be a potent source of confusion if the Word does not accompany it, as the Word must accompany the sacrament. We do not observe the Lord's Supper on Holy Friday — for we are not, through ritual, playing the part of cannibals. We are never commanded to feed on a dead Christ. He has risen, and He is seated at the right hand of God the Father, and by faith, we are invited to partake of Him. But we do not partake of Him on Friday, the day of His death, but rather on Sunday, the day of His resurrection. He is alive forevermore; death no more has dominion over Him. *This* is the Christ who invites us to partake of Him.

The water from the Rock was living water. The bread from heaven in the wilderness was living bread. The wine in the cup is living wine. The bread before us is living bread. And what is the animating agent? How is this life that we partake of life to us, and not death?

This too is the gift of God, lest any should boast. The animating agent is the faith that is imparted to us through the living and active Spirit of God in our hearts. And since faith comes from the living Spirit, it is necessarily living faith. And so in this ritual, through faith, we partake of the Living One, seated at the head of the Table, present here with us. Only an evangelical faith can see this. What are we eating? We are eating life itself. What are we drinking? We are drinking life itself. He is *risen*.

So come, and welcome, to Jesus Christ.

MORNING ☼ BEING MADE WORTHY

Breaking a bad habit is hard to do, and the difficulty is directly proportional to how long the bad habit was indulged. The Christian church needs to break two bad habits when it comes to the Lord's Supper. These two habits consist of looking in the wrong place as we meditate.

The first place we look where we ought not is at the wine and bread in their stationary position on the Table, wondering what happens to their material elements. The answer is that *nothing* happens to their material elements, and the sooner we learn this, the better. The Lord's Supper never sits uneaten. The Lord's Supper is always a video in motion, and never a snapshot.

The second place we look where we ought not look is deep within the recesses of our own hearts. We do this to find out if we are worthy to come to the Table. But why we would have to do any examination at all in order to get the answer to *that* question is a great mystery. Of *course* we are not worthy. That is the whole point! When we start rummaging around in our hearts, we make two mistakes. The first is that we conclude we are not worthy, and stay away. The second is that we decide (on the basis of having had what *we* think was a good week) that we are worthy, and we come to the Table for our reward. And truly, we already have our reward.

We should come because we are unworthy and we know it. We come because God uses this means to make us worthy. We do this in concert with all the saints of God everywhere, which is where we ought to set our minds. So look around as we partake. As you look at the motions of the saints as they hold, lift, take, chew, swallow, and you together with them — *that* is the Lord's Supper. The company of the unworthy is being made worthy.

So come, and welcome, to Jesus Christ.

There are three Persons in the triune Godhead, and the eternal Logos is one of those Three. He is numbered among the divine entities who mutually indwell one another, and who make up the one true and living God. This one, who is numbered among the Three, became flesh and dwelt among us, and He did so in order to be *numbered* among the transgressors. This, more than anything else, reveals the baffling nature of God to us.

Augustine profoundly said that the cross was a pulpit, from which Jesus preached. What did He say? What did He declare? The message of the cross is the great reversal. Jesus came, suffered, bled and died, so that we might worship a disreputable God. Does this sound shocking? It is supposed to.

One of the temptations that comes to us through long ecclesiastical experience — hymns, stained glass, steeples, robes, decent and respectable, traditional values — is the temptation of turning the cross of Jesus into something it was never meant to be. Jesus preaches, from the cross, that God's ways are not ours. What is reputable among men is disgusting to God, and what is highly honored by Him is incomprehensible to us. Incomprehensible, that is, unless the Spirit of God moves in our hearts, and brings us to His Word and sacraments, and does so in a way that enables us to understand what God is up to.

He is saving the lost, the least, the losers. You might flinch, and instinctively say, "But I am not a loser." *Then go away.* He is saving the deadbeats, the riffraff, the sinful, the dead. "But I am not dead," you say again. Then go away, and don't come back until you are pathetic. Jesus came for the pathetic people, not the well-dressed and shiny people — who always think God wants them to have people like Jesus executed for being troublemakers.

Are you a waster? Then come. Are you a sinner? Come, and welcome. Are you a loser?

So come, and welcome, to Jesus Christ.

MORNING ☼ TENDER HEARTS

In the name of keeping the ungodly and rebellious away from the Table, many well-intentioned Christians have only succeeded in keeping the tender-hearted away. It is analogous to the bumpersticker that says when guns are outlawed, only outlaws will have guns. When the hard-hearted are whacked, only the tender-hearted listen.

When warnings are given to you to police *yourselves* in how you come to the Table, the result is that those who are willing to do so assume the responsibility of it, and those who do not care to bother themselves continue to come. This is why we urge you to come to the Table if you are a baptized member of God's covenant household. Examining yourself does not mean excommunicating yourself. So in fact, you must come.

When the Table is honored in this way, and when the Word accompanies it rightly, those who are continuing to come even though they are engaged in secret hypocrisy are doing no harm to the Table. The Table is not threatened by sin anymore than an extremely potent herbicide is threatened by weeds in a field. We don't need to protect the Supper. We fence the Supper for the sake of those who would mock God, and not because we are fearful that the Supper of God will somehow be damaged.

If you are under lawful discipline, then you should not come. If you have sinned, but are not under discipline, then you should have confessed that sin at the beginning of the service, and you should come now. If you neglected to confess it then, then confess it now, and come. If it is significant sin, requiring significant restitution, then confess it, come to the Table, seeking strength to do what you know you have to do. In short, you ought not to be suspending yourself from the Supper — you do not have that authority.

You are quite right that sin and the Supper do not go together. But to resolve this tension, you must give up the sin. Not the Supper.

So come, and welcome, to Jesus Christ.

When the two sacraments that Jesus Christ instituted are neglected, men will always substitute in new sacraments of their own devising. God has given us this Table so that at the conclusion of our covenant renewal service, we might have *closure*. Just as the peace offering closed the cycle of Old Testament sacrifices, so the Lord's Supper closes the pattern of covenant renewal worship. We have confessed our sins, we have heard the Word, we have prayed, we have offered up psalms and hymns. But we still need to know that we have been heard, that we have been received. God graciously invites us to meet with Him here, at this Table. We are invited, summoned, to meet with Jesus.

If we do not do this, then the need to do it remains. There is still a fundamental need for closure. This is why so many evangelical churches instituted the "sacrament" of the invitation. "How do I know that 'all this' is for *me*?" It is reasonable question.

Baptism and the Lord's Supper particularize the promises of God in a wonderful way. The promises are for *you*. Now it is most necessary for you to come to the sacraments, particularized for you, in the only appropriate demeanor, which is faith. If you do not come in evangelical faith, then you are slapping at God who offers the promises. But if you believe the promises, what are you doing?

You are meeting with Him, communing with Him. Without faith, it is impossible to please Him. With faith, you come to the elements to meet Christ there. He is present, covenantally present. We believe in the Real Presence, since the only alternative to this is the Real Absence. But that presence is not in the bread and wine, it is in the *meeting*. It is only a blessing for you when it is appropriated by you in living, active, and evangelical *faith*.

So come, and welcome, to Jesus Christ.

MORNING ☼ NOT IMPERSONAL FUEL

We are not coming to the Lord's Supper as though it were a gas station, and as though the grace imparted were the fuel.

It is true that the Scriptures speak of grace, and mercy, and peace as abstract nouns. This is certainly a scriptural way of speaking, provided we do not do what sinners love to do with this kind of thing, detaching such glorious words from their context and their life.

We are not coming here for a "substance" called grace. We are coming here to meet with Christ. Everything we have that is spiritually worthwhile is found in *Him*. We may therefore speak of grace being added, or multiplied, so long as we know what we mean by it.

If we were to begin speaking of our marriages the way some Christians speak of their sanctification, we would soon be measuring the health of our relationships in Spousal Affection Units, or SAUs for short. If we resist this mechanistic way of thinking, it is certainly appropriate to speak of peace residing in a home, or graciousness being pervasive there. But all this is anchored to a right understanding of the relations that necessarily must pertain between persons.

So then, we are communing with Christ here. We are worshiping Him. We are being knit together in Him, bone of His bone and flesh of His flesh. We are not a machine that runs on grace-gas. We are a body that is nourished and cherished by love.

Here, at this Table, we have the privilege of communing together with Christ, as He accomplishes this tremendous work. He is the Lord of the Table. We are meeting with Him.

So come, and welcome, to Jesus Christ.

EVENING ◑ SOLID JOYS AND LASTING TREASURE

Food is substantive. We are alive and so we eat food that is tangible, weighty. We are not sitting down to this Table in Sheol, or Hades, a place of grim shadows and shades. We are not eating shadow food, but rather the bread of heaven. On the level of our physical senses, of course, we are eating bread and drinking wine, but God has promised us that whenever we partake of them in the name of Jesus Christ, in this setting, He will visit us, and bless us, and lift us by the power of the Holy Spirit into the heavenly places. And there we are partaking, as John Newton's hymn expresses it, of solid joys and lasting treasure.

Solid joys. The texture of this bread, and the wetness of the wine points to a realm that is *more* material, *more* real, and *more* solid than what we experience now. Too many Christians think of heaven as an ethereal place, populated luminous ghosts in white linen, standing on clouds. Too many Christians think of heaven as nothing more than a well-lit Sheol.

Christ has risen, and through the power of the Spirit, we partake of Him in His life. We do not commune on a dead body; this is not cannibalism. Now of course there are aspects of this we do not understand. It does not yet appear what we shall be, but when we see Him we will become like Him for we shall see Him as He is. But this does not just happen instantaneously, at the moment of our resurrection. We are being fitted for this solid resurrection world *now*. We are being transformed from one degree of glory to another as we behold the Lord in worship now. As we see this Table, as we approach it, sit down in faith, eat the bread, and drink the wine, God the Holy Spirit is weaving us together into the Head. Do we understand how He does this? Of course not, but we know that He is at work, because He is fashioning us according to His love, and there is nothing more solid than that love. Let us eat and drink it now.

So come, and welcome, to Jesus Christ.

MORNING ☼ BLESSED ARE THE UNCOOL

This is a Table of thanksgiving, joy, and forgiveness. Everyone here should be here in a spirit of gladness and overwhelming gratitude.

But suppose you are not? What then? The temptation is to shrink away, to hold back. This is easier when churches celebrate the meal intermittently, but when we have the Supper every week, this becomes more of a challenge.

One way to abuse this Supper is through morbid introspection. Beat yourself up. Become super-pious, and accuse yourself every chance you get. Become your very own personal Satan, accusing yourself day and night before the throne of God. Come with a grim determination to enjoy none of it and to give yourself one good kick in every observance of the Supper. I say this to you advisedly, and I say it as a minister of Jesus Christ: Knock it off. You are defiling the Supper with your sin, but it is a sin that you never get around to confessing — your joylessness. Stop it. Put it away.

Another way of corrupting the joy of the Table is more common with young people than it is with the older generation, but it should be repented of wherever it occurs. This is a Table of gladness and joy. Looking forward to worship, longing for the house of God, exulting in the opportunity to sing praises to Him — none of this is cool. In response to this we must echo and affirm the title of a recent book — *blessed are the uncool*.

Come to the Table in gladness — don't saunter. Approach with simplicity of heart, and get your hair out of your eyes. You are not a rock star. Come with childlike humility and God-given grace, and if you find that you cannot do this, perhaps you do not need to look around for some flagrant violation of God's ten commandments. Perhaps the problem is with the whole *persona* you are trying to cultivate. Perhaps opening your mouth wide to receive God's blessing is too conspicuous for you. But here it is anyway.

So come, and welcome, to Jesus Christ.

EVENING ◐ A BEAUTIFUL GARDEN AND A DRAGON TO FIGHT

The history of the human race is a story of growth and maturation. This is what it was intended to be from the beginning, whether there had ever been any sin or not. The rebellion (and subsequent repentance) of our first parents complicated the course of this story enormously, but it did not alter the basic thrust of it.

The garden of Eden was perfect before the Fall, but we must never forget that this perfection included a dragon to be fought. The potential for sin was there in the prohibition of the Tree of the Knowledge of Good and Evil, but the tree was not evil in itself. In fact, its fruit is explicitly described as the tree that would make Adam and Eve like God — on this both God and the dragon agreed. The rebellion consisted of seizing the fruit prematurely, before they were ready. Once they had committed this wickedness, God barred them from the Tree of Life (which they had been eating from before) because it now would have the effect of sealing them in their rebellious state.

In the establishment of the New Jerusalem, the Garden City, the city with the Tree of Life in the center, God has opened the way back up for us. We are gathering now at this tree of life, and we do so expectantly, eager for our God to grow us up into godly maturity. He has made us to be kings and priests on the earth, and so we gather here, longing to learn how to complete our assigned tasks.

Baptized individuals who come here without repentance and faith are trifling with something far more serious than cherubim with flaming swords. But for the faithful, this meal has the effect of equipping and strengthening you to exercise dominion in a world full of thorns and weeds. God gave weeds to Adam, it is true. But then, through the last Adam, He gave us to the weeds, and has commanded us to restore the garden. This we are privileged to do in worship, and in everything that flows out of that worship, which is to say, everything.

So come, and welcome, to Jesus Christ.

MORNING ☼ SEVEN BASKETS LEFT

We are privileged to celebrate the Supper on Pentecost Sunday, the day when God in His mercy made it abundantly clear that He had given His Son, the bread from Heaven, as the life of the world.

In the gospel of Mark, Jesus miraculously feeds the multitudes on two occasions. In chapter 6, there are twelve baskets of leftovers, a number that represented the twelve tribes of Israel. Two chapters later, seven baskets were left over, a number that Jews used to represent universality. Even the words used for the baskets are different in the two accounts. The first refers to a Jewish lunch basket, the latter to a basket used by Gentiles for shopping. This, and the location of the two miracles, indicate that the crowd was largely Jewish in the first instance, and was perhaps Gentile in the second.

This is also the import of Pentecost Sunday. By bestowing praise in multiple languages, the point was clearly made: This gospel, this grace, is for all men. If you are a Jew, you are summoned to believe in Jesus and take your seat at this Table. If you are a Gentile, you are invited to come in from your far country and take your seat, as well. The middle wall of partition has been broken down, and not that we might erect others of a similar nature. No, what God has done here, He has done forever. Red and yellow, black and white — come.

We make this statement also with leavened bread. At Passover leaven had to be absent not only from the bread, but also from the surroundings. But at Pentecost, leaven was required, which means that the Passover rules are superseded. This is our peace offering, and we use leavened bread for it (Lev. 7:13). The leaven here in this loaf represents the kingdom of God itself, working through the loaf of the whole world (Matt. 13:33), until the whole thing is transformed.

And when the Great Commission is fulfilled, and all the nations are converted to Christ, we will be glad in that day to find that seven baskets are left over.

So come, and welcome, to Jesus Christ.

EVENING ◐ THE CUP OF RECONCILIATION

You hear every week in the words of institution that this cup is the cup of the new covenant in the blood of Christ. What is the blood of Christ to us? In coming weeks, we will consider a number of truths concerning that, but let us begin with this.

This is the blood of reconciliation. The apostle teaches us in Colossians (1:21–22) that we were alienated from God. We were enemies in our minds because of our wicked deeds and works. But, he goes on to say, we have been *reconciled* in the body of His flesh through *death*. This is therefore the blood of reconciliation. It is the cup of reconciliation. That is one of the central features of this Supper.

In 1 John 2:2, we learn that Christ died as a propitiation for our sins. This means that the wrath that was resting upon our heads has been fully satisfied in the death of Jesus. Because the wrath is satisfied, because the propitiation has been accepted by God, the way is open for us to be reconciled to God.

As Thomas Watson put it, "It is one thing for a traitor to be pardoned, and another thing to be brought into favour." In this blood of reconciliation, not only is our treachery against God forgiven, but we have been brought back into His fellowship and favor. This is reconciliation. This cannot happen without the shedding of blood. Without blood, there is no remission of sins. Without human blood, no human transgression can be forgiven. And if our transgressions cannot be forgiven, there can be no reconciliation.

We were estranged, alienated. We were in rebellion. Not only that, but we had no good reason for our rebellion — we just wanted it our way. While we were still sinners, while we were in this condition, Christ died for us. He died in order that the barrier to reconciliation, which was on our side, might be removed by Him on our behalf. He, the divine Logos, became a man that He might reconcile men. Let us therefore eat and drink.

So come, and welcome, to Jesus Christ.

MORNING ✵ THE WINE OF LIFE

This cup contains the wine of reconciliation. We were reconciled to God through the death of Jesus (Col. 1:21–22). This is the cup of reconciliation. But the blood of Jesus is also quickening blood. Jesus said, "Whoso eateth my flesh, and drinketh my blood, hath eternal life, and I will raise him up at the last day" (John 6:54).

The ancient law tells us that the life of the flesh is in the blood (Lev. 17:11). When we are partakers of Christ's flesh and partakers of His blood, we are therefore partakers of His life. But His life, now that He has conquered death, is eternal life, everlasting life. *This* is the gift He offers to us.

The Bible tells us that we cannot partake of Christ *partially*. If we are joined to Him in His death, we are also joined to Him in His resurrection. If we are joined to Him effectually, we cannot accompany Him part way through that journey. He that began the good work in us *will* complete it. There are those who are united to Christ covenantally, but because of their unconverted heart, as we see in John 15, they never partake of true and efficacious union Him — and hence they bear no fruit. Therefore they are cut off, taken away and burned.

But this is not why you are here. You are here because you have trusted in Christ. He has invited you to His Table, and He has invited you to drink the wine of everlasting life. And here it is, set before you. Of course you must come in faith, and without faith it is impossible to please God. But don't make the mistake of thinking that *your* faith is the wine. No, your faith receives. Your faith drinks the wine, and it is life-giving wine.

When I hold a Bible up and say, "This is your life," not one of you thinks, "Really? Paper and ink can do that?" No, the Word is potent because God promises to meet us here, not because there is magic in the substance of the book. It is the same with bread and wine. God *meets* us here — and He meets us with eternal life.

So come, and welcome, to Jesus Christ.

Why do we sit as we partake of the Lord's Table? What is the point of that? Might it not seem disrespectful, as though we were taking this too casually? Wouldn't it be more respectful to kneel, or come to the front of the church and kneel? No, we don't believe so.

There is an appropriate time to kneel in the worship of God, but this portion of the service is not that time. We are seated in this portion of the service because this is the posture of *rule*. Yes, you heard that right — rule.

We are seated with Christ in the heavenly realms. If we are crucified with Christ, we are also buried with Him. If we are buried with Him, we are raised with Him. If we are raised with Him, we have ascended with Him, and if *that* is so, then we are seated with Him at the right hand of God the Father. God has made us kings and priests.

Christ is our Lord, and so of course we do not dictate to Him. But it is equally true that He by His grace has made us His friends and counselors. He seeks our counsel. Esther was *seated* with her husband at a meal when she gave him her counsel.

As Jim Jordan has pointedly written, this is how we are to stop the killing in Darfur. This is how the abortion carnage can be brought to an end. This is how Europe will be returned to the faith. This is how China will be overrun by the gospel.

You confessed your sins at the beginning of the service, and so now is not the time to be focusing on your own petty lusts or anxieties. If a great president or emperor invited you to dine with him, and asked for your counsel, that would not be the time to bring up your annoyance with a paper cut on your thumb.

Partaking of this sacrament rightly is therefore a geo-political act. And being seated while we partake is the liturgical expression of our faith that this is indeed what we are called to do. We are not insecure kings and priests.

So come, and welcome, to Jesus Christ.

MORNING ☼ GREATER MATTERS

We have considered why it is important for us to be seated as we partake of the Lord's kindness at this Table. This is the time when we, His people, sit with the Lord at Table, and discuss with Him the affairs of the world. He has invited us to His *Table*—not so that we would just sit abashed, afraid to speak, but so that we would discern the Body and to give counsel to the Head. How are you to do this?

First, remember that whatever you offer to Him must be offered *in faith*. You have been invited to come on the authority of the Word of God, and faith comes by hearing and hearing *by* the Word of God. So believe, and speak, as the psalmist did. I believed, therefore I have spoken.

Second, remember that what you are offering to Him is part of what the entire Body is offering to Him. This is what makes it inappropriate to us to try to slip in concerns that are highly individual or idiosyncratic. Offer that which the entire Body would (or should) say *amen* to. A cessation of the abortion carnage would be an example, and you winning the lottery would not be.

Third, God has established us as kings and priests on the earth. Our concerns should therefore not be tiny or trivial. If the president invited you to the Oval Office, and asked for your counsel, you would not waste the opportunity by advising him on the color of the curtains. We do not serve a tiny God, so use this time to ask Him for the conversion of Israel, or the repentance of the Muslims, or the humbling of American pride.

But He is also God of the details—we ask Him for our daily bread after all—and so we should feel free to pray about other things at other times. Pray for a parking space, or for relief from your minor aches and pains, or for a good grade on the quiz. But don't pray for those things while we are seated here. While we are here, seated with Christ, the discussion has turned to greater matters.

So come, and welcome, to Jesus Christ.

EVENING ◐ KINGS AND PRIESTS, NOT MARTINETS

We have been considering this Table as a place where we, the people of God, give counsel to our Lord. This is both exciting and troubling. We must never forget the Creator/creature distinction, pretending to have knowledge that God does not already have. God no more needs counsel from me on how to run the world than He needs me to help push in order to keep the earth spinning on its axis. At the same time, we have to remember that God created us in His image so that we might grow up into maturity. A wise father can seek counsel from his teenage son not because he needs to receive that counsel, but because the son needs to learn how to give it.

As part of this intent and plan, God bridged the Creator/creature divide in the Incarnation. The human race, remade, has thus been united (forever) with the Godhead. We are the Bride of Christ, and He is the Bridegroom. And what kind of husband is He? The kind that demands His wife shut up? No, He seeks our counsel, not because He is not a fit husband, but rather because He is growing us up into a fit wife, without any deficiency whatever.

God has made us kings and priests. He has not made us martinets, but rather men and women, created in His image, designed to grow up into wisdom to the point where we will judge angels.

Coming to this Table, remember who you are. You are a member of a race that was made from the dust of the ground. Do not presume to lecture God on what He should do. As you come to this Table, remember who you are. You are created in the image of God, and are being restored in that image through Jesus Christ. Part of that restoration is learning to think the way God thinks, and to submit your counsel to Him humbly. We are at the Table with our Incarnate Lord. He does not want us to eat in silence, like some browbeaten or frightened wife.

So come, and welcome, to Jesus Christ.

MORNING ☼ THE SHRINE OF ENDLESS ADOLESENCE

More than once, a reluctant young boy at the dinner table has been exhorted to eat his lima beans or his spinach, so that "he can grow up big like his daddy." Growth is one of the goals that eating serves. There are many other blessings associated with eating and drinking, but growth is certainly one of them.

Although Christians have their differences over infant baptism, we need to remember that in a certain sense all baptisms are infant baptisms. Everyone comes into the Church as a babe, desiring the milk of the Word, as the apostle Peter reminds us (1 Pet. 2:2). If we follow this out we should learn to see ourselves as a large congregation of toddlers in high chairs.

We must not get caught up in an optical illusion. The fact that most of us are physically mature sometimes distracts us. We tend to equate physical maturity with spiritual maturity, and the Bible doesn't do this at all. This is the mistake the disciples made when they tried to shoo away the little kids, provoking the Lord. "We are big and strong; we understand the ways of God." The scriptural response is clear. "You are big and strong, and that is why you have barely started."

We gather here to eat and drink. We eat and drink for many reasons, but one of them is to grow up into a godly maturity. We should come to this Table expectantly, wanting to be more and more like the one who is seated at the head of the Table, our Lord Jesus. We must stop worshiping at the shrine of endless adolescence. We must stop wanting to regress. God has set before us a glorious future, and we should be oriented to that future.

We take this meal on the first day of the week. This is a future-oriented day, the foundation of all the other days. It is a future-oriented meal, the foundation of all your other meals. Look forward, therefore, to maturity.

So come, and welcome, to Jesus Christ.

EVENING ◐ **ORGANIC ALLEGIANCE**

The world is a sacramental place. By this I do not mean to say that you should be hearing some kind of spooky music everywhere you go, but rather that God has built into the world the inescapability of what might be called "rites of allegiance." This in fact is where our word *sacrament* comes from — *sacramentum* was a Latin word that referred to the oath of allegiance that a soldier would take.

When we come to this Table, we are not only declaring our allegiance to Christ, but He is weaving us into a tighter, organic bond with Him, where the allegiance becomes more and more profound. The point of the process is for you to grow to a point where the allegiance you feel toward other parts of the body here is comparable to the allegiance your right hand has to your left hand.

But there is not a special Christian magic in this supper that makes this happen. It is creational — built into the very order of things. St. Paul tells us that pagans pursuing their idolatrous rites experience exactly the same thing. When a man and a woman come together, they become one flesh, whether or not they are Christians. This is a creational reality.

In the same way, when a man sits down at a table with his god, and eats there, he is being woven into a tight, organic allegiance to that god. The table might be a real table — a gaming table, or a fund-raising dinner for abortion rights — or it might be a metaphorical table. A bed might be the table, for example, or perhaps a television set.

The fact that this just happens because of the way God made the world is why the apostle tells us not to try to eat from two tables — the Table of the Lord and the table of demons. It can be *physically* done, for a time, but the rivalry between the competing allegiances will destroy a man. This is because, as the Lord put it, no man can serve two masters.

So come, and welcome, to Jesus Christ.

MORNING ☼ THE BODY OF CHRIST

When we refer to the body of Christ, there are at least three different senses in which we use the phrase.

The first, of course, refers to the body which was crucified for us, was raised in the power of the Spirit, and which ascended into heaven. That body is the body of a true human being, and the one whose body it is has been given true dominion over all things in heaven and earth. He sits at the right hand of God the Father.

The second sense is the sacramental body — the bread before us, and the wine in the cup. This is my body, Jesus said. There have been more disputes about this than there ought to have been, but one thing we can say for sure. No Christian will say that the bread and wine are in no sense the body of Christ. When we eat and drink, we are *partaking* of Him.

The third sense refers to the Christian church. *You* are the body of Christ. There is one loaf, Paul says, one body, and he is talking about the congregation of the Lord.

We should not be content with lining up these three definitions on a shelf in our minds. There is a mystery here concerning how the three definitions intertwine. When you eat a small bit of bread in faith, and drink the wine, you are being knit together with all your brothers and sisters, both here and around the world, so that we are all growing up into a perfect humanity, as Paul says. We are being formed into a bride, without spot or wrinkle or any other blemish. And when that is completed, the bride will be given to the bridegroom and will become bone of His bone, flesh of His flesh — one body.

These things are way beyond us, and we ought not to despair over it because even the great apostle described it all as a great mystery. But God has created the world in such a way that disparate things may indwell one another — men and women, bread and wine, and the Lord in heaven.

So come, and welcome, to Jesus Christ.

We are here primarily to eat and drink. *This do,* our Lord said.

Now it is important for us to remember certain things as we do this, of course, but we are not here primarily to remember. We can do that without the bread and wine. We should of course be clean from all known sin, but that is not what this portion of the service primarily is. We should have confessed our sins before we got here — if we didn't we should now, but that is not the central point.

Eating and drinking constitute this meal. But with the way God made the world, we have to recognize that eating and drinking are never raw, mechanical acts. To the extent we try to make them so, we are dehumanizing ourselves. You eat and drink with your people.

When Jesus established this meal, He was creating a new people, a great congregation. In short, we eat and drink together.

If you were a medieval baron with your own private chapel and your own private priest, and you went to Mass all by yourself on a daily basis, it may have been really devout, but it was also completely at odds with the point of the communal meal. If you are a modern evangelical, and when the bread and wine come to you, you withdraw to the private chapel of your heart, find a priest in your emotions, you are doing the same thing — missing the point.

Table fellowship establishes loyalties. But in the New Testament sense, it is not possible to be loyal to Christ without be loyal to one another. If we walk in the light, as He is in the light, the Word says, we have fellowship with one another. It is not possible to be on good terms with the Lord and be a loner. Depending on the extent of the problem, there is something significant there to be repented and corrected.

This meal, which we observe weekly, is a good place to do that. As you partake, look around. These are your people.

So come, and welcome, to Jesus Christ.

MORNING ✺ ALL THE TREES ARE YOURS

Our God is a God who says *no* to that which destroys us, but His character is not fundamentally negative. When He put our first parents in the Garden, He said *yes* to every tree in the Garden but one. That tree was restricted, and only for a time. It is commonly assumed by Christians that the Tree of Life was also prohibited, but the text never says that — indeed, it says exactly the opposite. All the trees were available to Adam and Eve, all but one.

We are in a similar situation. All foods are declared clean for us as Christians. The Christian faith rejects all dietary restrictions for spiritual reasons. You may restrict your diet for other reasons, like getting into a different weight class for the big fight, but you may not restrict your diet because you think that God will somehow be pleased or displeased by what you put into your mouth.

This is the tree of life here. We have all been brought back to it. All the other trees in the Garden — all your ordinary meals and snacks — are given to you. Freely, completely, and with nothing held back secretly.

You may not eat from the table of demons, the New Testament tells us, and since the earth is the Lord's and the fullness of it, this means that the only way to can eat from the table of demons is by rejecting God in your heart through unbelief. Any attempt to eat autonomously is the problem. All attempts to eat gratefully are received by God as acceptable service to Him. Take care, because it is easy to mark this distinction in your mind and still come under bondage. If you are eating a certain way for your weight, or for your health, and you experience bondage, not gratitude, then something is wrong. We must not accept any yoke of bondage. Test the fruit by its fruit.

The best way to learn how to approach all the other trees rightly (which are yours to enjoy) is by approaching the tree of life rightly, and regularly. Let us do so now.

So come, and welcome, to Jesus Christ.

We have been speaking a great deal about money, wealth, Mammon, gold. But as we come to the Lord's Table again, we should be mindful of one other thing concerning gold. You can't eat it.

God has given us a covenant we can drink. He has given us a salvation we can eat. And it doesn't have to go through any kind of currency transfer. We just come to His Table in evangelical faith, and by eating this bread and drinking this wine, He nourishes us. By eating this bread in faith, and drinking this wine in faith, we come to Him directly.

Now someone, if they wanted to argue, could say, "Yes, but you can take gold, or other forms of money, and buy food with it." Yes, you can. But the ability to change one thing into another like this is a gift of God. Exchanging money for food is a very simple form of this, but there are other more complicated forms of it. Like how a kernel of wheat has the ability to make a full grown stalk out of what it finds in the dirt and air. That's a change as well. This can all happen because the world is sacramental, suffused with the kindness of God in every direction.

But these changes occur because God does not change, and the way to approach Him does not change, and that way is always direct. When we hear His Word and believe, or when we drink His wine and believe, we are not coming in a roundabout way. We are coming to Him directly, on the direct path that He has established.

In the sacrament, nothing changes. God is true, and God is constant. He meets us here, just as He has promised. And because of that kindness, we discover that in the world around us, everything leads back to Him — even our gold if we see it rightly. Meet with God directly here so that you may come to see Him indirectly in everything else. The world is only sacramental if we always remember that *it* cannot be the sacrament.

So come, and welcome, to Jesus Christ.

MORNING ☼ AND HE WILL FLEE FROM YOU

The message today was on the right response when desire, lust, gotta-have-it-now, has you by the throat. The text does not just say, "resist the devil and he will flee from you." Many Christians have felt ripped off by God because they *did* resist the devil, and then again some more, and then they resisted still more. And when they did resist, he did not flee, he did not go away, he did not vanish. Rather, he pressed in all the more, holding their feeble efforts at resisting temptation in contempt. And in our discouragement, we ask why God lied to us.

The answer is that He said more. He said, "*Submit…to God*, resist the devil, and he will flee from you" (Jas. 4:7). Too many of us want to fight the devil as free agents, on our own terms. We don't want to obey God, we want to do what we think is the right thing, and we would do it, if the devil would only flee. But he doesn't.

The fundamental issue is orientation to God. *Submit to God.* How do we do that? We do it by coming to His Word, and coming to His ordinances, and bowing down. He does not want us to get our act together so that we might then go out and do mighty works *for* Him. We are not trying ingratiate Him or appease Him or impress Him. What He wants is for us to *serve* Him.

That means coming into His presence, bowing down, and saying, "Your servant, Lord." This is the spirit of true worship. When Isaiah said, "Here am I, send me," that was worship. When our bodies are living sacrifices, holy and acceptable to God, that is worship. When we have worshiped, we have submitted to God. And when we have submitted to God, the devil will flee. We will notice new authority in resisting temptation. We will no longer feel as though all such struggles are nothing more than hopeless fights with diabolical tarbabies.

So, come, receive His food and drink. Submit to Him. He will receive you gladly.

So come, and welcome, to Jesus Christ.

You have heard many times that this Table is not the time or place for confession of sin. If you have ignored these exhortations, and have come to the Table with unconfessed sin in your life, then confessing sin here is far better than not confessing sin at all. So take care of whatever it is, but at the same time, try to break the pattern of introspective probing as one of the spiritual exercises you do when you should be coming to commune with the Lord and with His people.

This is the Table of the Lord and His people, not the Table of you and your personal problems. One of the great temptations in worship is to make it "all about you." Of course, if you have not dealt with your problems, if you have not confessed your sin, then that will hinder any attempts to honor and worship the Lord. So dealing with "your" issues is important.

But at the same time, given the sinful bent of our hearts, it does not take much to persuade us to make whatever it is we are doing into a session designed for us. But you are here, at this Table, for the sake of the *others*. You are to look around in love, discerning the body.

How can you pray for them? How can you minister to them? How can you say something to them after the service that will really strengthen them? How can you make someone's day?

The Bible says we are being knit together in love. And we should think of the Word and the sacrament as the two knitting needles. Using His Word for you on the one hand, and His covenant love for you on the other, God knits you together with other people. You are growing up, together with them, into a perfect man, as Paul says.

But this is not being done for you while you are in solitary confinement. You are not hermits or monks or reclusives. You are Christians. This is your Table, and it is for all of you.

So come, and welcome, to Jesus Christ.

MORNING ☼ HOW FAITH KNOWS

The festival of Pentecost reminds us that the Holy Spirit has been poured out. But recall, carefully remember, that throughout the Scriptures, when God's power comes down in the person of His Spirit, He is always poured out *upon* something. He comes to rest.

In the visitation of God's Spirit, we do not find the vaporization of material things, but rather their anointing and consecration. The spiritual man is not one who finds himself becoming a ghost, but rather one who finds himself walking obediently, in step with the Spirit.

This is spiritual food, but not because of some magic going on within the elements. This is spiritual food, but not because a miracle has occurred which has transformed the substance of the bread and wine. This is spiritual food because the Holy Spirit, a Person present here with us today, uses this moment, this bread, this wine, this faith of ours, to knit us together as a perfect man. We are being built up into Christ, bone of His bone, flesh of His flesh. This is a great mystery, Paul says. Who can know it?

But not being able to know it in the sense of giving detailed mechanical explanations does not keep us from knowing it in the biblical sense of that word. We come to know God by faith. We take Him at His word. A materialist could look at the Rock that accompanied Israel in the wilderness and not see Christ there, but only Rock. And when water came from the Rock, he could explain it all as coincidence. When faithful Jews drank from Christ, and ate Christ as He fell from the heavens every morning, they would fail if they tried to give a mathematical explanation, just as we fail when we try.

But you should not be explaining this just now. You have other things to do with your mouth, like tasting, chewing, and swallowing. And the Holy Spirit, poured out upon the Church forever, will do His holy work. Trust Him.

So come, and welcome, to Jesus Christ.

When the service culminates here at the Table, as we believe it does, we are not displacing the Word, or the proclamation of it. We still have a very high view of the need for preaching. But we don't believe that declaring and hearing the Word is to be treated as an end in itself.

James tells us that the one who hears the Word but does not do it is self-deceived (Jas. 1:22–24). This means that when you listen to a sermon, personal applications should never be far from your mind. You shouldn't be wondering if personal applications are running through the minds of others who get on your nerves, but rather you should be considering yourself in the first place.

And when you are hearing the Word, and are convicted by it, and you consider what changes have to be made, you can sometimes feel beat up, overwhelmed, feeling like "that's all good, but I am not up to it." At *that* moment, the Lord comes to you and offers you strength for the journey. It is at that time that He offers to nourish you with food from His Table. You are not just offered strength, you are offered strength from the Table of the Lord.

This means that He is saying to you that by His grace, you are up to it. He is saying to you that His grace is sufficient for you.

The bread and wine here are not our gift to God; they are His gift to us. If there is something you must put right, then offer that restitution to God before giving Him any other gifts. But this is His gift to you — take it for strength to go and do what you know you must do.

God does not just tell us what to do. We do not suffer under raw obligation; we do not suffer under the law. We are Christians, and so we live by the grace of God, revealed in the face of Christ. He wants us to be equipped to do His will, and he offers you strength here. But don't think that it is any kind of magic strength. The just shall live by faith, and this means that the just shall eat and drink by faith.

So come, and welcome, to Jesus Christ.

MORNING ☼ THE TABLE AT THE CENTER OF THE WORLD

God has fashioned the human race in such a way that sitting down for a meal is the center of all family life. Guests are certainly welcome, but in the day-in and day-out pattern of living, the meal is the center. This is one of the reasons we can tell that the modern family is disintegrating ... there is so little time at the table together. For those who want to do something about that, at least one meal together daily would contribute greatly.

But this is a different Table in many respects, and so the question arises whether it is different in this way also. No, not really. We have spoken often of the Church's duty to assume the center in our culture and this is one of the basic ways we do it. When we sit down here it is a royal feast, and the King of the earth, the Lord Jesus Christ, has invited all his friends, all the nobility of the kingdom of heaven. That would be you.

You might find this laughable — *us*, kings and priests? The principalities and powers also found it risible . . . until God demonstrated His unspeakable wisdom to them as manifested in the Church. We see the Church "from underneath," so to speak, and we do not yet see all that God has done in the establishment of His Church.

But even though it is glorious, already, it is still a work in progress. For this work, we need nourishment, and this Table provides that. But never forget that the idea that food is nothing but fuel is an *impoverishing* notion. This is not just eating and drinking — it is communion, with Christ and with one another. Table fellowship is a central part of this meal. And as we fellowship together, loving one another, God sees to it that this happens in the presence of our enemies, and His kindness to His people is made evident to the entire world.

We are family. We sit down together to eat. This is assuming the center.

So come, and welcome, to Jesus Christ.

Meals together are to be a time of harmony. We are *companions* here, which comes from two words meaning "one who shares bread together with you." As companions, we should want to be companions on more than just one level. We are growing together, being knit together as we partake, and so we should really want to *go* together.

Do not suspend yourself from the Table, sending yourself to your room without supper — "so that mom and dad don't have to do it." You are not mom and dad, and you don't get to make that decision. You need the strength, you need the encouragement, you need to partake. If you did badly last week, don't try to ensure that you will do poorly next week. This Supper is not a reward for being good. It is nourishment for sinners in various states of recuperation.

You have also heard that the verse about leaving your gift on the altar, and going to be reconciled to your brother applies to tithing, and not to eating. It is "gift *on* the altar" not "food *from* the altar." But somehow churches are better at encouraging the kids to stay out of the fridge and pantry than they are at discouraging the kids from contributing money to the household budget.

But it is important that you take this nourishment for the task *assigned,* which *is* to strive for likemindedness. Do you need to refrain from this meal because you are not speaking with someone else in the body? No, not at all. But if this is a standing state of affairs, then you need to partake so that you have the strength to go speak to them and put things right. And if every time you have tried that, it only makes things worse, then you need to partake so that you will have the strength to involve others who will be part of a solution.

Maybe the other person is difficult, maybe just you are, and maybe you both are. In any case, you need the Lord's grace and help, and this Table is one of the places He supplies it. So come in faith, come with gratitude. Come, and welcome.

So come, and welcome, to Jesus Christ.

MORNING ☼ NO NEED TO CRAWL

God is kind to His people, tender with them. He forgives us, and He provided us with the means of forgiveness when He knew how desperately we needed it. While we were yet sinners, Christ died for us. He did not do this because He saw how good we were being. When we come to commune with Him here, and with all His people, He is not thrown by the fact that we have struggled with various temptations and sins in this past week. This is not news to Him. He is not astonished, and He has not decided to reject you or throw you away.

The Bible says that we are to approach the throne of grace with boldness. "Let us therefore come boldly unto the throne of grace, that we may obtain mercy, and find grace to help in time of need" (Heb. 4:16). This is truly odd to us. If it is grace we are seeking, coming to obtain mercy, then how can we possibly do it with boldness? And if we come with true boldness, then how is it mercy we are seeking? If we are seeking mercy, shouldn't we be crawling? *No.*

When we come to the Table together, we are finding grace to help us in our time of need. That time of need varies for each of us. Some of us are tempted sorely when we are traveling. Some of us struggle between dinner and the time the kids go down. Others have great difficulty with the boss at work, or with our neighbor two houses down.

By strengthening you here, at a Table of fellowship with Him, God is saying that in order to obtain the help you really need, in order to grow in strength and maturity, you do not need to crawl. God does not want you to crawl; He wants you to repent and grow.

Do you need strength? Do you need mercy? Then lift up your head. You are seated at this Table with Christ your King, and His seat is a seat made up of mercy, kindness, and grace. Tell Him what you need and don't be shy. Lift up your voice, and He will grant your request.

So come, and welcome, to Jesus Christ.

EVENING ◐ AND ME

Recently, one of my grandchildren (she is only one year old) saw the bread being distributed during this Supper, and began cheerfully saying, "And me. And me."

This is something we all need to learn how to say, because it is right at the heart of biblical faith. This is the child-like approach that Jesus required of us. It is relatively easy to believe propositions in the third person. Jesus died for sinners, and there are certainly sinners out there. *They* do this and that. God has elected certain sinners for salvation, and *they* certainly are blessed. *They* have come to Christ in truth, and have responded to the Word in faith. They are true believers, and we are glad for *them*.

This is all true enough, and quite proper to say. But we need to grow in the kind of faith that knows how to intrude itself. Christ died for sinners, the preacher says. *And me,* you say. This is my body which is broken for you, the minister declares. *And me,* you say to yourself, anchoring the point. This is the cup of the new testament, which is for the remission of the sins for many. *And me.*

But we do not stop there. Once we are assured that, yes, this includes the referent of *and me,* we learn to rest in this, growing in faith, and we learn to look around. I am not the only one. God has been kind to us, and I am only here as one of His people. It is not just *me,* but *and me.* This is for all the saints, not one solitary person. This is for all the saints gathered in this room. *And me.*

So come, and welcome, to Jesus Christ.

MORNING ☼ COMMUNICANT AND EXCOMMUNICANT

You are communicant members of the body of Christ. That means that one of the great privileges of grace you have been given is that of participating, of communing, at this Table.

When we discipline someone, this is the center of what they are being excluded from. *Ex-* means *out of,* or *away from,* so an excommunicant has been placed *out of* their privilege of communing with God's people, here, in this Supper. The barrier that is created is always our formal acknowledgment of unrepented sin, and not the person's name, face, or history. As long as life lasts, there is hope. We do desire their return to us, and we pray toward that end.

Can someone who is excommunicated attend church, sing the songs, hear the message, and so on? Certainly — unless their sin is of such a nature that their presence would be a disruption, but that is unusual. May you converse in a friendly manner with an excommunicant? Certainly, and we hope you do. What this exclusion from the Table does is place all such activities in their proper context. What you may not do is pretend that all is well, that you are fellowshipping in the Lord together. So this exclusion from this Table contextualizes everything. The Westminster Confession notes that this action does not sever natural relations — whether husband and wife, or parents and children, or brother and sister — but it moves the relationship into a different judicial setting. The person concerned is to be treated as an unbeliever, not as a leper.

God does not remove the grace of communion lightly, or for trivial reasons. He knows that all of us are sinners, and when we discipline someone, it is not because we have forgotten this. We recall the fact in the confession of sin at the beginning of the service, and every week we are reassured that God's grace is waiting for us here — the Table set. This is a glorious grace that we never want to abuse.

So come, and welcome, to Jesus Christ.

We have urged you many times not to use this glorious occasion as a time for confessing your sins. We have a time for that set apart at the beginning of the service, which only makes sense. You wash your hands, and then you come to the dinner table. This is a place for laughter, fellowship, and food, not desperate introspection.

But this presupposes that the sin is really dealt with at the beginning of the service — that it is not an ongoing issue. I am not speaking here of any sins of high defiance and hypocrisy, but of a trouble in the conscience, of a sin you committed two years ago or have confessed a thousand times. You are not still committing it, but you are afraid to get help for your conscience. You are afraid to tell your parents, or your spouse, or the pastor, because then the consequences you fear would probably come upon you. You are not defiant, but you *are* stuck. You have trouble coming to this Table with rejoicing because all you can think about is that lie you told, or your lost virginity, or the abortion you never told anyone about — not a sin that you are still clinging to, but one that is still clinging to you. If you are in this position, should you come to this Table? You have been coming, because if you refrained, someone would ask you *why*, and you are afraid of the consequences of telling. In one sense you are afraid of the relief that would follow. So what should you do if you are in this position?

You are still welcome to come to this Table and to partake fully, but with one provision. As you come, you must pray that God be using this Supper as a provision of His grace to strengthen you to do — and *soon* — what you know you need to do. Confessing sin this way is always a little like cliff diving. You can even know that you are *going* to do it, but you need to fidget on the edge just a bit more. If you come to commune this way, you are not being a hypocrite. But you *are* weak, and you need to know you are coming to a Table of Strength.

So come, and welcome, to Jesus Christ.

MORNING ☼ STRENGTH TO BE HUMBLE

Last week I urged you to come freely to this Table, even if there is a sin gnawing at your conscience that you have not yet put right. You know that you need to, and you even know that you are *going* to, but you are fearful of the consequences. You need the help of God, and here it is — the Table is set, and it is set with the help of God.

Always remember that this Table is not the reward we get for being good. It is a meal, not a prize.

Suppose in a moment of weakness you cheated on a test two years ago, and your conscience has not stopped clamoring at you since. It is dangerous to ignore that persistent voice, and the danger is that you will eventually become deaf to it. Your conscience is tired and weak and needs nourishment for the hard work of trying to talk sense into you. Well, here it is. So long as you know what you are doing, feed your conscience, and feed it freely.

That sin has to be dealt with, and you know it. Come here for help and strength in dealing with it. Take the nourishment. Part of the reason you feel so hypocritical coming to this Table is that you have been ignoring your conscience diligently, which would be enough to make anyone miserable. You are miserable not because you are coming to the Lord's Table, but because you are not coming to Him for strength. You do not want to confess the cheating because your teacher thinks highly of you. "But what about, but what about . . ."

Again, you are welcome here. But you are welcome on the Lord's terms, not your own, and you must always remember that He is dealing with you here. One of the things He is doing is providing you with the strength to be humble, the strength to put things right. Tell your sister you are sorry, tell your teacher you cheated, tell your friends that you were catty about them.

Tell God about it at the beginning of the service, tell them about it after the service, and get strength for the task here and now.

So come, and welcome, to Jesus Christ.

EVENING ◐ THE LORD'S KINDNESS IS HERE

We have been talking about the problem of the nagging conscience. If you have a besetting sin — whether it is irritation with the kids, or attitudes of envy and lust, or discontent in your job — don't assume that you ought not come to the Table. Of course you should come to the Table — here is strength to help in the task of mortification. These are the ordinary sins that ordinary Christians struggle with, and the grace available here helps you struggle with them.

The principle is the same even with far more serious recurrent temptation and sin — say, bank robberies, or adulterous affairs, or cruising gay bars. With these kinds of sins, you need to immediately is involve some pastoral accountability. If you try on your own to apply the available means of grace to great sins, chances are great that you are only kidding yourself, lying to yourself, healing the wound lightly. You shouldn't excommunicate yourself — but you *must* bust yourself. There are other means of grace beyond what we see here.

If the sin is not recurrent, if it is just weighing on your conscience regardless of how many times you confess it, either some restitution is lacking, or the sin is actually the morbid introspection. If you stole twenty bucks from your roommate ten years ago, you need to keep coming to this Table, seeking the strength you need to put that right. Don't excommunicate yourself — get strength to do the right thing.

There is one other possibility. Perhaps you have the kind of conscience that worries a subject to death. You sinned against your roommate ten years ago, sought her forgiveness, received it, and yet are still obsessing about it. The problem here is not the past sin, but the current sin of *unbelief* — God says He has forgiven, and you are maintaining that He has not. Come to the Table then, asking to be grown up into the kind of Christian who can receive forgiveness.

But one way or another, all of us have a responsibility to come. Take and eat, take and drink. The Lord's kindness is here.

So come, and welcome, to Jesus Christ.

MORNING ☼ ALL TOGETHER NOW

We have a tremendous privilege here — two congregations are seated together, partaking of the Lord's Supper together. This is a small statement of a much more glorious statement: In the power of the Spirit, all the churches of Christ throughout the world are as surely gathered together at this one Table every time it is observed as our two congregations are here this morning gathered at this one Table.

I say that we are always eating at the same Table because the apostle Paul only identifies two tables total — the Table of the Lord and the table of demons. If Christian brothers are genuinely partaking of the Lord's Table, wherever in the world they may be, they are seated together in the heavens. We tend to see the physical distance, and think that the Spirit can't overcome it. But we don't have joint services so that we can partake of the Supper together — we have joint services to be reminded that we already partake together.

As separate congregations, we have distinct church cultures, but there is no way we could *ever* get those differences to surpass the cultural differences between, say, Jew and Gentile of the first century. And the apostles insisted on the Lord's Supper being used to bridge that particular chasm, which it did.

If sin is interfering with fellowship, then you have been taught to confess your own sin long before you come to this Table — you are to rejoice here, not condemn yourself in morbid introspection. If the sin of another is interfering with fellowship, then you are to either talk to your brother about it, or let love cover a multitude of it. You don't have the option of coming here, muttering about his problems. Confront, or cover, but don't complain. But don't ever make the mistake of assuming that the differences between you must be sin. Differences of personality, church culture, wisdom issues, and the like must never be allowed to hinder the wonderful fellowship between our congregations.

So come, and welcome, to Jesus Christ.

EVENING ◐ PRIMARILY FOOD, NOT MEDICINE

We speak a great deal about the grace of contentment. But there is a discontent that can be healthy, and that of course would be a discontent with the level of Christian maturity in your life.

But even here we must be extremely careful. I said that this discontent can be healthy, but most of the time it is actually a sin compounding the problems caused by your other sins.

First, the healthy discontent. Little children should *want* to grow, they should be eager for it. Within bounds, they should be looking forward to the time when they are taller, stronger, faster, when they have the capacity to know and do more than they can at the present. And when you see a ten-year-old frustrated with the limitations of being ten, and pushing against how long this whole process is taking, your response to this is to think of it as endearing. You certainly encourage the child — take heart, it is going faster than you think. First thing you know, you'll be there. This is how God thinks of us, this is how He encourages us. Take heart. You are being grown up into the perfect man, into the image of Jesus Christ, and these things take time. Always remember that God loves to take His sweet time.

Overt sin, clear sin — malice and hatred, lust and covetousness, spite and anger — are rebellions, not immaturities. Confess them now, drop them now, be done with them now. Don't give yourselves ten years in which to try to phase these things out of your life. Decisive repentance is all that is called for.

This Table is to be thought of primarily as food, not primarily as medicine. Don't come here expecting the food to "fix you," but rather to grow you. When you sin, repent at that time. When you come to worship God, confess your sins at the door. When you sit down at the Table here, you have already been washed, you have already been cleansed. So eat and be nourished. Drink and be satisfied.

So come, and welcome, to Jesus Christ.

MORNING ☼ ORDINARY MEANS, EXTRAORDINARY RESULTS

We come here to eat and drink. But this is not food from our cupboards at home — this is heavenly food. But it is not heavenly food because there is anything ethereal or magic about the food itself. So how then is it extraordinary? If this is ordinary bread then how does it differ from the ordinary bread we eat at home? How does it differ from the ordinary wine we drink at a restaurant?

The thing that makes it special is the intent, the setting, the occasion. In short, this wine and this bread are set apart for holy use, and we use them in this ritual specified for us in the Bible. We are told that when we do this, calling on the name of the Lord, He will meet us here and commune with us. The bread and wine are not being turned into the body and blood of Jesus — rather, by the faithful use of them in this specified ritual, *we* are being turned into the body and blood of the Lord. We are being grown up into the perfect man, the Lord Jesus, the Scriptures tell us.

There is a miracle here. But God is getting these extraordinary results by ordinary means. Do not look at the Table for any miracle. The miracle is happening in all the chairs. Sinners are being made fit for everlasting communion with a holy God, and one of the means that God is using to bring this about is this simple ritual.

He does similar things with other ordinary means. Paper and ink are ordinary, and the paper and ink that make up your Bible are the same kind of paper and ink that make up ordinary books — even sinful and wicked books. That doesn't matter; what matters is that the Bible comes to you as the word of life regardless. It is the same here.

So don't have the wrong kind of faith in this ritual. It is not supercharged. But don't think of it as "just" bread and wine either. God has plans for you, and He is using these means.

So come, and welcome, to Jesus Christ.

What do we believe is happening here? We obviously think that it is important because we observe the Supper every week. But what is the nature of this importance?

Both Roman Catholics and Lutherans hold to the local presence of Jesus in this meal, localized on the Table, in the elements. The historic Calvinist position holds to the real presence of Christ in this meal, but it occurs in the power of the Spirit as He ushers us into the heavenly realms to partake of Christ spiritually, but at the same time really and actually. A fourth position is the Zwinglian position, which holds that this meal is merely memorial, enabling us to remember what Christ did for us on the cross. Most evangelicals today are Zwinglian, and that is probably the tradition you grew up with.

So what do we believe? Our position is a mix of Calvinist and Zwinglian. We agree that this is a ritual, but we do not agree that it is *merely* a ritual. You could, if you wished, call our position a high Zwinglianism. There is nothing here but ritual, but, it turns out, rituals are much more potent (and much *larger*) than many have assumed. God takes them very seriously.

The heart of this ritual is the oath-taking implicit in it. The oath is what makes this ritual a sacrament. No oath, no sacrament. As we make our vows, as we renew covenant with God, we are doing so in the heavenly places and in the power and authority of the Holy Spirit. An exchange of oaths can be formal or informal, solemn or casual, full of joy or full of foreboding. What makes it what it is has to be the oath—it has to be the meeting between God and man. In this oath, you are solemnly engaging to be the Lord's, along with all that you have and are. And God is solemnly engaging to take up your part, as you trust Him, working out His sovereign will, working and willing in accordance with His good pleasure. And *that* is a meal that you can partake in with great joy.

So come, and welcome, to Jesus Christ.

MORNING ☼ RENEWING THE OATH

This is a service of covenant renewal worship. This means that we believe we have assembled here to renew covenant with God. But it is important for us to understand the nature of this renewal.

We are not renewing covenant because "if we don't" it will somehow expire. We are not renewing covenant the way a tenant renews a lease with his landlord. Rather, we are renewing covenant the way food renews the body, the way wine renews the heart, the way lovemaking renews marriage.

When a covenant is made, it is made on the basis of an oath. That oath is then sealed in some fashion, and is periodically renewed. Every time the covenant is renewed, the oath is reaffirmed.

Whenever we bring new members into our fellowship, we ask you to renew your membership vows as you accept their membership vows, and we ask you to do this with the solemn and joyful oath — the corporate *amen*. But you are renewing your connection to Christ, and to your brothers and sisters, more often than that. Every time you come to this Table, your connections are renewed. Every time you come, the oath is renewed.

But never forget one of the central features of the new covenant. What is the work that is required of you? It is to believe in the Lord Jesus Christ. When you are vowing obedience, you are vowing reliance on His obedience on your behalf. When you are resolving to live in a manner that befits a Christian — as you should be — you are resolving to trust Him to work out in your life the good works that He is willing to instill in you, and accomplish through you.

The covenant oath we are renewing here is the covenant oath that recognizes that Christ is all. Christ is everything. Christ is master, Christ is Lord. Christ is victim, Christ is king. Christ is servant, Christ is bread and wine. You in Christ, and Christ in you, that God may be all in all.

So come, and welcome, to Jesus Christ.

EVENING ◐ INEXORABLE KINDNESS

Yearly we partake of the Lord's Supper on Pentecost, the time when we mark the pouring out of the Holy Spirit into the world, the fulfillment of the glorious prophecy of Joel. That gives us opportunity to reflect that the Lord's Supper, although it was instituted at Passover, is not simply the fulfillment of that one Jewish festival. Rather, all the festivals and sacrifices of Israel culminate in the person of the Lord Jesus, and *all* the festivals of Israel are rolled into the two sacraments of the new Israel, the Christian Church.

In fact, after Jesus left them, the first recorded observation of the disciples observing this meal was on the day of Pentecost. And while leavened bread was *not* only not used at Passover, and had to be entirely absent from the premises altogether, on the day of Pentecost one of the required offerings in the law was leavened bread. This bread was necessarily present on the day of Pentecost.

We use leavened bread in our observation of the Supper, and this raises reasonable questions. One of them is what Jesus used when He instituted the meal. On Passover, there was only one kind of bread available, and St. Paul tells us that we follow the Lord in this by getting rid of the yeast of malice and wickedness (1 Cor. 5:8).

But this image raises another question. In the Bible, doesn't leaven represent sin? Yes, sometimes. We are to beware of the leaven of the Pharisees, Jesus taught us (Matt. 16:6), and in the passage just mentioned, leaven represents malice and wickedness. But leaven also represents the kingdom of God in the world, and, just as we are the one loaf that we break (for one another), so also we are that leaven.

We affect the town and community around us the same way that leaven works through a loaf of bread. As the leaven works, silently, we do not hear clanking noises. We do not see smoke. The process is silent grace, quiet love, and inexorable kindness.

So come, and welcome, to Jesus Christ.

MORNING ☼ THE GIFT OF BODY AND BLOOD

In this Supper we partake of bread and wine, representatives of the body and blood of Jesus Christ, our Lord and Savior. This is representative of His sacrifice, of course, but it is also important to note that this rite underscores the fact that Jesus took on a body.

He did not do this right before His crucifixion, but rather three decades or more before. When Gabriel announced to Mary that she would conceive, he was marking the beginning of the Incarnation. That was the point where Jesus took on a body. That was the point when blood began to flow in his veins. His body was a true body. Jesus was no apparition, He was not a ghostly manifestation. Neither did He become human by just taking on the appearance of a man. The Lord was the Lord Incarnate — when He was conceived in His mother's womb, He lived through the entire human experience.

He did not relinquish His Deity in this — not at all. But His Deity and humanity, perfectly combined in one person, were not confused or comingled. We must say that Jesus was God, and we must say that Jesus was a man, but we must never say that Deity is humanity. This is, of course, a great mystery. Fortunately, it is not a mystery we are supposed to solve, but one we are supposed to eat and drink. *That* we can do. Christ has taken us into His body, and we, here, are taking Him into our bodies. We are being knit together with Him and in Him, and God uses our faith to accomplish this great work.

So don't puzzle over it. Don't quarrel with fellow Christians over it — that really defeats the purpose. Don't separate over that which is drawing you closer together. Come in faith, and let God do what God is doing. And remember, that at the very foundation of what God is doing in the world is the Incarnation — the point where He gave a body and blood to Jesus. And now, here, in a different way, Jesus is giving body and blood to us.

So come, and welcome, to Jesus Christ.

The greatest thing that Jesus ever did was actually the sum total of His life, and the effect was to manifest the Father. In the cosmic scheme of things, His various particular wonders were little more than attention-getters. When we get distracted by them, we are missing the point. Jesus said that a wicked and adulterous generation seeks after a sign. We are not to chase after God looking for a magic show.

When we come to this Table, we are not supposed to look for a particular marvel or miracle. We are to look for, and *see*, God's work in the world. When Philip asked to see the Father, Jesus replied, "He that hath seen Me hath seen the Father" (Jn. 14:9). He was the point of access to the Father. But Jesus is now gone, and has sent a Comforter to indwell us, so that when people see the Church, they see Jesus.

Now that does not seem like a good plan. The vision of the Father was not obscured in Jesus by any sin or blemish or foibles on His part, but when people look to the body of Christ, in order to see Christ, sometimes sin and blemishes are *all* they can see. But God is telling the world to wait. The picture is going to become increasingly clear as history unfolds. As Christians are increasingly sanctified by the Spirit, as the Word takes deeper and deeper root in our lives, as we are knit together more completely, the end of the process will be a Bride without spot or blemish. And we will say to the remaining unbelievers, "If you have seen us, you have seen Jesus. And if you have seen Jesus, you have seen the Father."

Of course, it seems semi-blasphemous to talk like this, and so we shrink back. But we are told repeatedly to present the body of Christ to the world, declaring the death and resurrection of Jesus as we do. And we have three ways of presenting that body — first in the proclamation of the Word. Second, in the love we display for one another. And third, as we come to this Table to eat that body, and drink that blood.

So come, and welcome, to Jesus Christ.

MORNING ☼ ENLARGING THE IMAGINATION OF OUR HEARTS

Suppers are frequently in conjunction with other events. We have memorial banquets, birthday celebrations, anniversary dinners, and so on. God has created us in such a way that whenever we really want to mark something as important, we attach it to a meal.

God has done the same for us in this meal. This commemorative feast marks the sacrifice of Jesus. God wanted us to be sure that we never forget it. But it is not just a remembrance for us; it is a memorial for God. As the rainbow served to remind God not to destroy the earth, so the observance of the Lord's Supper reminds God that His wrath against the world has been propitiated.

Now of course, we all know that God does not need to be reminded of anything, still less by symbols like a bit of bread and a cup of wine. Still less does God need to be corrected by us when we don't understand why He has told us to do something. He is God, and we are not. If we master *that* principle of theology, we will go far. God condescends to us. He doesn't need to hear our prayers either — He already knows. So why pray? Because He is teaching *us* to know that every good thing comes from Him. Why remind Him of the Lord's sacrifice when He knows the Lord's sacrifice perfectly already? Because *we* need to know that He knows.

He has filled His Word with things that He wants us to remind Him of. He loves it when His people argue with Him in faith. He detests it when we murmur in unbelief, but He *delights* in it when we discover a promise in His Word, and turn to Him and say, "Hey! Why aren't You doing this? We know the fault must be ours, but still, why do You talk this way in the Bible if You don't want to do it?"

As we partake of this bread and wine, God is enlarging our hearts. He is growing our imagination. And as we eat this bread and drink this wine, we are growing up into Christ.

So come, and welcome, to Jesus Christ.

You have perhaps heard the admonition that "the family that prays together, stays together." This is quite true, and families should pray together. But it is also true that families that eat together stay together. One of the signs that our culture is fragmented is that it is so easy to eat alone — in the car, in front of the television, or leaning over the sink before you rush off to work. But we in the Church cannot be cultural critics if we are doing something very similar in the Church.

This is one of the reasons for weekly communion. We eat together as often as we get together. God has created us in such a way that eating is a binding ritual. Of course, Scripture teaches us that a house of feasting can also be a house of strife — and that we should prefer peace and quiet to the food, if we have to choose. The same problem arose at Corinth, in their observance of the "Lord's Supper," which Paul said was not really the Lord's Supper at all. He said that there was a way of coming together which, when God's manners were disregarded, did more harm than good. So we do not think that automatically scheduled refueling occasions have the same blessed benefit that a *meal* does.

But the glory of it is that we do not have to choose between the love and the food. If you must have one or the other, choose love over food. But never make the mistake of thinking that love instead of food is to be a permanent arrangement. Prefer love to food just long enough to get your priorities straight so that you and your brothers and sisters might come to the Table together, in real harmony.

And when we come in harmony, God uses the occasion of eating together to ratify and seal the harmony. He uses this ritual of bread and wine as a way of knitting us together. It tightens the oaths, it binds us together in love. So as we come to this Table yet again, receive the bread and wine as God's means of drawing you all together in love. And so we come gladly.

So come, and welcome, to Jesus Christ.

MORNING ☼ LOVE THROUGHOUT THE WEEK

Jesus taught us to take and eat, not take and speculate, or take and quarrel. And not only did He tell us not to quarrel, He specifically told us not to quarrel. This covenant bond is designed by God to draw us closer and closer together in love for one another, and to deal with those sinful obstacles within us that are preventing such communion.

This is communion, and it accomplishes communion. In other words, we are not just having communion while we are eating and drinking. The fact that we eat and drink together is a covenantal fact throughout the course of the week. When you deal with one another on Wednesdays, you are doing so as people who come to this Table together.

This is true if you are sleeping together as husband and wife, it is true if you are negotiating a business deal together, it is true if you are carpooling, and it is true if you are in the same classroom together. All those separate events have a common thread, and that common thread is your union with Christ made evident here.

But this means that this love feast should be resulting in love and charity expressed when we are away from the Table. When you eat physical food, you expect it to carry you to the next meal. The strength provided by the meal is not limited to the time you are eating. You do not simply gain strength enough to eat from the eating. You gain strength for everything else as well.

In the same way, this meal strengthens you — as you come in true, evangelical faith, remember — throughout the course of the week. And as you have different vocational callings, the strength required is different. If you are a realtor, or a housewife, or a teacher, or a heavy equipment operator, or a carpenter, God gives you strength. But the attitude that drives you all is to be the same — love — and so what God gives you here is the same. Come together to receive that gift, and gladly.

So come, and welcome, to Jesus Christ.

Something we have said here many times is that this meal is not a reward for being good. This is not an awards ceremony. We sometimes draw this false conclusion from the practice of church discipline — if someone can be excluded from this meal, which excommunication most certainly does, then weren't they excluded for being bad? And doesn't that mean that we are included for being good?

No. When someone is disciplined, we should not think of it as someone being expelled from an honors society. Think of it rather as an event where one patient in a hospital ward began behaving in a disruptive manner, making it impossible to treat the other patients. Being expelled from a leper colony is bad, but it is not exactly the same thing as being expelled from Phi Beta Kappa.

But there is more. The Church is not a gathering of people who have their act together, and so God has determined to reward them with bread and wine. But at the same time, God has made us kings and priests on the earth, and He is using these instruments (and others) to grow us up into the nobility of Jesus Christ. So we are not being rewarded for being good; we are being made good.

If you were being rewarded for being good, then if you sinned this last week, that would be a problem. If you sinned big this last week, that would be a big problem. But if we are being made good, sin in our lives does not disqualify us. What disqualifies is an obstinate refusal to let the Word and the Spirit get at that sin. What disqualifies is never weakness, but rebellion.

Are you assembled here in rebellion? I warn you as a minister of Christ that if you come to the Table in that frame of mind, you are asking God to contend with you. Are you gathered here as sinners? Are you assembled here aware of your weakness and frailty? Tell me something new. Don't worry about it. Take and eat — this is for you. Take and drink — it is especially for you.

So come, and welcome, to Jesus Christ.

MORNING ☼ LIFE TO THE WORLD

In the Gospel of John, Jesus feeds the five thousand in a staggering miracle — a rare miracle that is mentioned in all four gospels. Immediately following, He teaches His disciples that He is the bread of heaven, and that his flesh is life for the world. This indicates that this is an instructive miracle, an enacted parable, an object lesson. The lesson is that Jesus is going to do for the world what He did for the five thousand. He is the bread of life that came down from heaven. He is gathering all the nations of the world, today, this morning, and He is doing so in order to feed them.

The Lord is not stingy, and the meaning of the miracle is *not* that there is only bread enough for five thousand, a typified and tiny elect. We are being invited to think and believe and pray *expansively*. The Lord is kinder than any of us imagine. The five thousand are a type of all the nations under heaven, gathered on the mountain of the Lord, in order to fellowship with their Redeemer and Lord. Would God send down bread from heaven in order to feed a tiny handful? Would God deliver the bread of life to a world full of death simply to rescue a remnant? No, all men are invited to partake.

The Lord made this manifestly plain when He told us to scatter, going into all the nations, discipling them. How do we disciple them? We baptize them, and we teach them to obey all that Jesus commanded, which includes faithful attendance at this meal. Jesus commanded us to feed the world, and to do so with spiritual food and drink.

And so this is what we do. This is not the meal for a secret and exclusive club. This is the staple meal for the future of humanity. All are invited, all may come. We invite them by faithfully partaking — because we are told that partaking of this meal faithfully proclaims the death of Jesus Christ, which is the gospel, which is the world's only hope.

So come, and welcome, to Jesus Christ.

God is the God of food. He created food, and He created it in order to bestow it on his people. He made a world full of food, and has invited us to partake of all that He has set before us.

This is His character; this is what He is like. As it says in Psalm 136, God "remembered us in our low estate: for his mercy endureth for ever: And hath redeemed us from our enemies: for his mercy endureth for ever. *Who giveth food to all flesh*: for his mercy endureth for ever. O give thanks unto the God of heaven: for his mercy endureth for ever" (Ps. 136:23–26).

So our God is the God of food. As He has undertaken the re-establishment of all humanity, the re-creation of the world in and through the Church, He has repeated this same theme that was apparent at the first creation, placing food before His children. He gives food to all flesh.

There are two things here that we should keep in mind. The first is that God gives food to all believers, and in the growth of the kingdom, this will come to be an offering to all flesh. As the Great Commission is fulfilled, and as the Church spreads to every corner of the globe, we are authorized to extend this invitation. The Spirit certainly says, "Come," but let us never forget that the bride also says, "Come." Hear the invitation, which is the Gospel, come to the door, which is the laver of baptism, and come to the Table, which is here before us now.

But the second point is that He does this because His mercy endures forever. What God gives proceeds, always, from what God is like. What is the heart of God like? He is no tightwad. He is not stingy. He is not close-fisted. Why are you here? Why are you seated here at His Table? You are here because His mercy endures forever.

So come, and welcome, to Jesus Christ.

MORNING ☼ CONFESSION & COMMUNION

We do not confess our sins here weekly so that you don't have to bother with confessing them in the aftermath of having stumbled. We are not encouraging you to "wait until Sunday to do it." Neither are we saying that an honest confession at the time the sin was committed is insufficient, and that you need a second coat of forgiveness applied here at church. When God forgives, He *forgives*.

But we confess and He forgives in time, in the midst of a story. Think of it this way: The process of sanctification is the process of moral formation. We are, all of us, in the process of putting on the coat of new man, and there are many buttons to fasten.

An individual sin is a particular sin. A series of sins or a besetting sin is or may become a vice. Our generation likes to describe vices as addictions because this helps us evade personal responsibility, treating the vice in question as a misfortune, like breaking your leg. But much more is involved. Vice is sin taking shape in you as a personal characteristic. In a similar way, successfully resisting a temptation one time is not the same thing as a virtue. Virtue is an aspect of character, which is a function of habit. Virtue is goodness taking shape in you as a personal characteristic. This means resisting temptation and confessing sin over time. And it means confessing intelligently. When you confess a particular sin, you are forgiven. You don't need to wait until next Sunday. But one of the things you should do on Sunday, during the time of confession, is recognize that you are still in the process of formation, and you always will be this side Jordan.

You will be tempted in the same area again this coming week, and you know the seeds of that particular temptation are still within you. Right now they are within you. Confess that, and prepare yourself for the coming week. But do all this as the forgiven of God, and not as someone who is haunted by your shortcomings. You will need strength for the journey.

So come, and welcome, to Jesus Christ.

When our first parents fell, the occasion of their grief and ours was food. Not only was it food, it was good food. God did not create evil and place it in the midst of the Garden (Gen. 2:9, 3:6). The prohibition of the Tree of Knowledge was clearly temporary. The disaster here was one of timing. At its heart was a refusal to hear and heed God. Sinners like to think in self-excusing and rationalizing ways. We can do as we want here at this Supper because the Lord established it Himself, and placed it at the center of the new Garden. That's right, He did do that. But have we learned nothing?

Paul tells the Corinthians that their observance of the Supper is doing more harm than good. When God rebukes Adam and Eve for disobeying Him generally, it is no answer to reply that the food they ate was *good for food,* which it was. It is no answer to point to a scriptural passage that *says* that it was good for food. In the same way, it is no answer to jab your finger at certain Bible passages, insisting that your version of the real presence is dogmatically assured. Rather, we must come when the Lord says to come and partake the way the Lord says to partake. Obedience is the great opener of eyes. We will come to see and know when we come to renew our covenant vows in the *way* God says to do.

What is that way? As you partake, don't isolate yourself. Don't curl up in a little ball. Look around the room at all your brothers and sisters, the body of Christ, and love them. God has summoned everyone here, together with you. These are your people.

We took the fruit of the knowledge of good and evil prematurely. Our heads and hearts were too young for it, so our frame has collapsed underneath the weight of it. Jesus came to restore us, to make us fit to carry that knowledge without cratering beneath it. And what is it that restores our frame? It is love, kindness, mercy, gentleness, patience, gentleness, mercy, kindness, and love.

So come, and welcome, to Jesus Christ.

MORNING ☼ HE QUICKENS THE WORLD

Life is a mystery that turns inanimate matter into animate matter. Death is a disruption of this glorious gift, turning animate matter back into inanimate. But life is always God's default option. Death entered this world only through sin and rebellion. When God created the world and declared it all very good, death was not yet in the picture. Sin caused death to come in and disrupt everything. But we must not allow the fact that death is very common now make us think that God has made His peace with it. He has not — death remains His enemy. Life is what He bestows because life is what He is.

And He bestows it through food. Food is also a great mystery. We cannot be nourished by the inanimate world directly. Except for a few minerals, everything *we* eat was once alive, and is a bearer of life to us. Herbs, grains, and fruit are all devices He has created to transform inanimate matter into animate so that it might bring life to us.

And as God is in the process of overcoming the destructive impact of our sin and rebellion, He operates in an analogous way. That which is spiritually animate is conveyed to us by means of that which is spiritually inanimate. What is this, physically? It is merely bread and wine, no more capable — in its own power — of establishing us in the grace of God than any other kind of mumbo jumbo. Yet when we come here in evangelical faith, knowing that we serve and worship a God who brings life out of death, He does a wonderful thing. We do not look to the means that He used — we look to Him, grateful to Him because He keeps His Word. He always keeps His word.

So if the power here is not a magic power, what is going on? What is happening here? We are a covenant people, and God is allowing us to approach Him in order to renew covenant with Him. We do this by renewing our covenant oaths, our covenant vows. When we do this in animate faith, using the means that He has assigned — inanimate bread and wine — He quickens the world.

So come, and welcome, to Jesus Christ.

God loves matter. He invented it; He created it. God is the God of heaven and earth, which means that He is the God of earth and heaven. This means that He is Lord over all that is *earthy*.

When we come to this Table, we feed on bread and wine, not abstractions. When we come to this Table, we feed on Christ by faith, not on a doctrine. But what does it mean to feed on Christ? The Christian faith *is* literally a faith with human sacrifice at the center of it. Is the Lord's Supper also what we would call literal cannibalism? No. What does it mean then, to eat His body and drink His blood? The Lord said, without any apparent ambiguity, that if we did not do this, we would perish. Because He is the Lord, what He says we must do.

In this worship service, we have been escorted up into the heavenly places in the power of the Holy Spirit. We are spiritually partaking of Christ there as we partake of the bread and wine by faith here. This is a glorious means that God uses in order for us to be knit together with Christ as we are grown up into the perfect man.

But when we say that we partake spiritually, this is *not* a synonym for "not really." The Westminster Confession rightly says, "Our Lord Jesus, in the night wherein He was betrayed, instituted the sacrament of His body and blood, called the Lord's Supper, to be observed in His Church, unto the end of the world, for the perpetual remembrance of the sacrifice of Himself in His death; the sealing all benefits thereof unto true believers, their spiritual nourishment and growth in Him, their further engagement in and to all duties which they owe unto Him; and, to be a bond and pledge of their communion with Him, and with each other, as members of His mystical body" (29.1).

In the exhortations to come, we will consider each of these biblical truths in turn. For now, suffice it to say that God is doing something for us here that is done for us nowhere else.

So come, and welcome, to Jesus Christ.

MORNING ✵ AN EDIBLE OATH

The Westminster Confession of Faith describes this meal as "the sacrament of His body and blood." The first purpose (or blessing) it lists for the observance is the perpetual remembrance of His sacrifice on our behalf. We have already addressed this, noting that the remembrance is for both God and His people. But there is much more to this meal than simple remembrance.

The second blessing noted is the sealing of all the benefits of the death of Christ to genuine believers. The apostle Paul uses this language of sacramental *sealing* in regard to Abraham's faith, and he says that circumcision was both a sign and seal of the righteousness that he had by faith (Rom. 4:11). Our tendency is to say that if we have the reality, then who needs the seal? Well, Abraham did, and we believers in Jesus need it, as well. And what we need God has provided for us here at this Table.

We live our Christian lives *here*, in a messed-up world. We do not live in the decrees of God. We certainly live *because* of His decrees, but we cannot live *in* them. There is no air to breathe there, no food and no drink. We are also incapable of reading the decrees, so even that comfort is not possible to us. We are creatures, we live down here, and most of us have had quite a week. And because we live here, God has shown His kindness to us by offering us this tangible pledge, this seal, of His grace and mercy. For those who do not have genuine faith, this pledge or seal is nothing. They cannot see it or apprehend it. But for those with their spiritual senses quickened and alive, this is glorious. You have before you an edible oath.

So you *can* see it. You can chew it, and you can drink it. You come in faith. You want God to grant you assurance through His sacramental kindness. And that is what He is doing — you can receive genuine assurance of salvation here. Do you doubt that this letter of invitation is really from the king? Then look at the seal.

So come, and welcome, to Jesus Christ.

The third blessing that proceeds from the Lord's Supper, according to the Westminster Confession, is our "spiritual nourishment and growth in Him."

Now nourishment and growth are meaningless concepts to a dead person. If someone has died, it is no part of wisdom to run down to the kitchen to fix them a meal. Food does nothing to death. Food presupposes a principle of life, something which can take that food and adapt it to the tasks at hand.

Now the reason this food can be offered to us here is that we have been quickened. We used to be dead in our trespasses and sins, as Paul describes it in Ephesians, but now we have been made alive. Because we have been made alive by the Spirit, food is useful to us. It nourishes us and enables us to grow.

Growth means changes, transformation. Growth is not a sensation or feeling. Growth means that things do not remain the same. When a two-year-old grows into a sixteen-year-old, no one can mistake the changes that are occurring. In the same way, worshipers of Christ are in the process of growing up. We are maturing, we are being made different. We are being grown up into resurrection life. That process is occurring now, and is all part of the preparation for the great and final transformation. But the life that works with the means of grace offered by God is life that is present now.

We are not waiting to be born again; we have been born again. Because we have been born again, we may sincerely desire the pure milk of the Word, like newborn babies. No one has to teach babies to be hungry.

And further, no one has to teach babies how to use the nourishment that is resident in the food. All the baby has to do is eat and drink. And, as we come to this Table, that is all we have to do as well.

So come, and welcome, to Jesus Christ.

MORNING ☼ EVERY CHRISTIAN IS CHRISTOPHER

We have been working through the Westminster Confession's statement on the blessings that attend a right observance of the Lord's Supper. The fourth blessing is our "further engagement in and to all duties which [we] owe unto Him." This is another way of saying that by partaking of this Supper, we are renewing our covenant obligations before the Lord, our baptismal oath to live as Christians.

The Third Commandment forbids taking the Lord's name in vain. This is commonly thought to be a prohibition of cussing, which it includes, but the center of the command is more profound than that. The word "take" does not refer primarily to *saying* the name, but to *bearing* or *carrying* it. When the Jews were established as a people, they were called by His name. When we were established as a people under the new covenant, the same thing happened. We were all baptized *into* the name of the Father, Son, and Holy Spirit. We therefore carry or bear the name of the Lord in our persons. We are Christians.

Another way to think of this is that we are all named Christopher. The *pher* comes from the Greek word meaning to bear or carry. Every Christian is Christopher, bearing the name of Christ. The Third Commandment is primarily about the need for us to not do this in vanity. Do not be called Christian in vain.

Clearly the thing we must always remember is something that is easy for us to forget. Therefore God has given us a weekly opportunity to renew or recall our covenant obligations, our covenant vows. As you eat the bread, this is further engagement in and to all duties which you owe to the Lord. As you drink the wine, you are doing the same. God sets your duties before you, and you have the opportunity to eat and drink your duties. In so doing, He nourished you in such a way that you can perform your duties. Even obedience, especially obedience, is found to be the grace of God.

So come, and welcome, to Jesus Christ.

The fifth and last blessing of the Lord's Supper, as our confession of faith notes them, is this: The Supper is to be "a bond and pledge of [our] communion with Him, and with each other, as members of His mystical body." This is why, in the observance of the Supper, we encourage you not to curl up in a spiritual cocoon, in order to mediate upon the Lord alone. You are supposed to commune with Him, but not in isolation.

This Supper is a bond and pledge, and it shows, declares, reinforces, and deepens our union and communion with Him. But in God's design, it *cannot* do this apart from doing the same between us and God's people. God's Spirit converts us by ones, but that conversion is conversion into a body, which is why there is no salvation outside the Church. This does not mean there is no salvation outside Fourth Memorial, or Antioch Baptist, or Faith Presbyterian. It is the simple recognition that salvation in the Bible is salvation of a people.

And this meal is the shared bond and pledge of that people. You, this morning, as you partake of this bond and pledge are being knit together with every person in the world who is approaching this Table in accordance with God's Word. This communion of saints is a universal reality, but it is particularly evident in the local congregation.

Just as we don't want to say that we love God, whom we have not seen, unless we are loving our brothers, whom we have seen, so also we don't want to say that we love all the saints . . . whom we have not seen . . . and not be able to handle the saints who are in the same town, the same parish, the same row as you.

So remember this. There is no union with God that is being established in this partaking that is not also being established, to the same wonderful extent, with every other believer here. This is your bond and pledge, and it is the tie that binds.

So come, and welcome, to Jesus Christ.

MORNING ☼ PERPETUAL REMEMBRANCE

There are two ways to remember. One is to avoid forgetting, and the other is to enact what you have never forgotten. We mistake when we think that the first kind of remembrance is the only kind. But when the Bible says that the Lord remembered Noah, this does not mean that He slapped His forehead—"Oh, right! Noah!"—but that He acted on what He always knew, and that action was a remembrance.

Because we are sinners, when we forget them in this second sense, we are forgetting to *do* something. God tells the Jews (and us) to remember the Sabbath, to keep it holy. More is involved in "remembering" than to be able to say, "Today is Sunday, I believe."

When Jesus says that we are to do this meal in remembrance of Him, He is appealing to something deeper than mere cognition. He is telling us to observe this as a memorial. If you remembered, halfway through the day, that it was your anniversary, but neglected to do anything about it, you are still in the doghouse, even though you "remembered." If you remember and don't do, this makes the problem worse, not better. But if you remember and take your wife out to dinner, she is observing the remembrance as much as you are, even though you took the initiative.

In a similar way, this meal is a memorial as much for the Lord, as for us. Just as the rainbow in the sky was a remembrance to Him to not destroy the earth again, so the Supper is a remembrance to Him to forgive us all our sins and preserve us forever within His covenant.

Our confession of faith echoes the biblical language at this point. We are to observe this Supper in the Church, to the end of the world, as a "perpetual remembrance of the sacrifice of [Christ] in His death" (29.1). So in this observance, in this remembrance, in this memorial, please realize that not only are you remembering what Christ has done for you, but Christ is also remembering what He has done for you. Therefore, come in all gladness.

So come, and welcome, to Jesus Christ.

EVENING ◐ ADMINISTERING THE SACRAMENTS

The sacraments are ordinances of the Church; in other words, they are one of the things that makes church into Church. As such, the authority to oversee their administration, and the teaching that accompanies their administration, lies with the government of the Church.

This is why the Westminster Confession restricts administration of the sacraments to ministers of the Word only, those who have been lawfully ordained to that task. We believe that this is appropriate to good order and government, but it is not absolutely essential to a right use of the ordinance. We hold that if the minister is out of town, it would be far better to have one of the elders administer the Supper rather than have the people go without. And if a hard providence created a difficult situation — some Christian laymen locked in prison for their faith — it would be better for them to contrive a way to observe the Supper than to do without.

At the same time, in ordinary circumstances, the man or men ordained to represent Christ to the people should ordinarily baptize and ordinarily administer the elements of the Supper. This is not because he is a priest, but to keep the liturgical symbolism straight.

So come, and welcome, to Jesus Christ.

MORNING ☼ THEN COME TO CHRIST

We are continuing to reflect on what our doctrinal standards—the teachings of the Westminster Confession of Faith—say about the sacraments.

A striking thing about our standards is that they say that the Old Testament contained sacraments, and not only the New Testament. In the New, we have two sacraments, but the number of sacraments in the Old Testament is not specified. If we reason by analogy, we would say two—circumcision and the sacred meals of the sacrificial system. But it is not so tidy as that—we would also have to consider things like manna from heaven, and the Rock that followed Israel in the wilderness, for example.

But whatever the number of sacraments, we are taught that the substance of these things, which is always Christ, was signified and exhibited in the Old Testament, just as they are in the new covenant. Christ is signified here—the bread represents His body, and the wine His blood. But the confession goes further. He is signified, true, but He is also exhibited, and as the standards say elsewhere, conferred, on those who come to this Table in true faith. You are coming in faith, are you not? Then come to Christ.

So come, and welcome, to Jesus Christ.

EVENING ◐ EFFICACY IN THE SACRAMENT

The Westminster divines taught us the true foundation of the efficacy of the sacraments, and it is an important and biblical point. The first aspect of this is to note that they taught that the sacraments were efficacious. Their concern was to note *why* the sacraments were efficacious, not *whether* they were.

They made a point of saying that the efficacy of the sacrament does not depend on the subjective state of the minister — you are strengthened and nourished independently of my piety or intention in this. They also said that there is no inherent magical power in the elements — whether in the water of baptism, or here in the bread and wine.

So why are the sacraments efficacious? The sacraments are efficacious, they said, for worthy receivers — which is defined by faith alone, not works. This happens, they said, for two reasons. The first is the work of the Holy Spirit, who is present here with us. The second is the objective word of institution, which contains the promise of benefit. This promise of benefit is objective, it is biblical, and it is the offer of God. You are therefore summoned to respond to it in faith. Come and eat. Come and drink.

So come, and welcome, to Jesus Christ.

MORNING ☼ AN EXHIBITION OF GRACE

Our confessional standards, the Westminster Standards, say that when rightly used, grace is exhibited in the sacraments.

There are two sides to this. First, note that the sacraments can be, and have been, wrongly used. When that happens, as it happened at Corinth, the apostle says the observance does more harm than good. This is a covenant meal, and covenants have oaths and standards, and therefore there is no automatic blessing for us in the sacraments. Grace does not come through the sacraments like water through a garden hose. If we come in genuine faith, we are received, blessed and strengthened, for we are using the sacrament rightly. If we do not, then we are chastised, as disobedient children.

But note also that for us — who are coming in true faith — this meal exhibits the grace of God. It does not hide the grace of God, it does not obscure the grace of God, it does not mumble the grace of God. Here the bread and wine *exhibit* the grace of God. Because you come in faith, you see and understand what God is doing. He is knitting us all together in the love of Jesus Christ our Lord. Come and eat. Come and drink.

So come, and welcome, to Jesus Christ.

We learn from the Westminster Confession that in both sacraments—baptism and the Lord's Supper—there is a spiritual and sacramental *union* between the thing and the thing signified, such that it is appropriate to speak of one under the terms of the other. We do this without confounding the thing and the thing signified, but, following Scripture, we are to do it.

Thus it is that I may lift up the loaf and say, "This is the body of Christ," or the cup and say, "This is the blood of the covenant." Because of various superstitions that crept into the Church over the centuries, many evangelicals are wary of speaking this way. Either they don't speak this way at all, or they do, but with endless qualifications. But this points to a sacramental disunion, and has its own negative effects.

Our focus in this celebration ought not to be on what the bread and wine are not. They are not many things. But to us who come in true and genuine faith, these are the body and blood of the Lord Jesus, broken and shed for our restoration. We receive that promised restoration gladly, and without qualification. So come and eat, come and drink.

So come, and welcome, to Jesus Christ.

MORNING ☼ IT WILL BE YOURS

The Westminster Confession also teaches that one of the purposes of the sacraments is to "solemnly engage" us "to the service of God in Christ, according to His Word." When we are "engaged" in this way it means that we are bound to Him by means of an oath. When we are baptized, we either take an oath, or an oath is taken on our behalf — that we will live for the service of God in Christ, according to His Word. Baptism is the oath that inaugurates the relationship — much like the oaths that a bride and groom take on their wedding day. That is the fundamental oath, the oath that is foundational to all others.

This language of "solemn engagement" applies to the Lord's Supper, as well. Every time we come to this Table, we are coming to be renewed, and on that basis to renew our commitments, to renew our solemn engagements, to make our vows, to honor our promises.

This practice of "solemn engagement," if we are not careful, can drift away from grace, and we will discover ourselves neck deep in moralistic scruples and vows, and no clear way out. But when we do this, it is not because we are keeping our vows, it is because *we are not*. What is the work that God requires of us? It is for us *to believe*.

We keep our promises by trusting in Jesus, the only man who ever kept all His promises. We remember our vows when we pray in Jesus' name, the one who fulfilled all our vows for us. We obey God when we turn to the one who obeyed Him perfectly on our behalf. We offer up recompense for our sins when we plead the blood of Jesus.

Look at the cup here. That is not *your* blood. Look at the broken body. That is not *your* body. You are not the promise keeper.

But there is something else, and this is the glorious part. That blood, which is not yours, in just a few moments, will be given to you. And when it is given to you, *it will be yours*. This broken body, which is not yours, is shortly going to be given to you. And when it is given to you, *it will be yours*.

So come, and welcome, to Jesus Christ.

Our standards also teach that one of the purposes of the sacraments is to "put a visible difference between those that belong to the Church and the rest of the world." Being a Christian means that you have been washed in the waters of baptism and that you have free access to this Table. Those who have not called out to Christ do not have this privilege. This has the effect of placing a visible difference between the new world that God is creating in Christians and the old world, which is passing away.

We confess that this visible difference is not of ultimate importance, but that does not make it unimportant. We have to be very careful at this point. We know and confess that people who have been baptized and who come to this Table can be lost and that there are some who come to everlasting life without having ever had an attachment to the visible church. But many have taken the reality of these exceptions as a basis for saying that the visible markers created by the sacraments are unimportant. This follows not at all. You have great privileges, privileges of citizenship, in coming to this Table.

When we gather around this Table as communicants, we are declaring our allegiance to God's kingdom. We are showing ourselves as those who belong to Him. We are doing this in a very public way, showing that we "go to church," that we are communicant members of a Christian church. This visible difference is something that God loves to use, and He does use it.

The visible difference between those who remember His death and those who would prefer to ignore it is very stark. As we gather at this Table, we are telling the world that Christ's death and resurrection is the foundation of our week (and theirs), and is the organizing principle of time, space, and all history. And there is a visible difference between those who enact these realities and those who would ignore these realities.

So come, and welcome, to Jesus Christ.

MORNING ☼ CONFIRM YOUR STAKE IN CHRIST

The Westminster Confession says that sacraments are given by God in order to confirm our interest in Him. The word *interest* here is the kind of interest that a stockholder has in a corporation — the stake he has in the corporation. The sacraments are immediately given by God in order to confirm our stake in Christ.

We as evangelicals often struggle with this because we know, or think that we know, that sacraments do nothing of the kind. We are so accustomed to measure everything by the abuses we see rather than by what Scripture says, that when we read, "the sacraments are immediately given by God to confirm our interest in Christ," we take this to mean that the sacraments "are immediately given by God, but not in order to confirm anything at all."

Of course, a false-hearted and idolatrous abuse of the sacraments does not fool God for a minute. But what is that to you? You are coming in genuine faith, are you not? And this means that God enables you, by faith, to confirm your stake in Christ by this means.

Some might say that if you have the faith, then that is sufficient — you can go off by yourself and do your confirming of interest away from God's people. The bread and wine are entirely optional. But if God said to meet Him here in the bread and wine, how is it faith to try to meet Him somewhere else? Detaching faith from God's appointed instruments is neither right nor safe. When Namaan was told to wash in the Jordan, it would not have been appropriate for him to conclude that another river, or no river at all, would do just as well — even if he recognized that the Jordan was nothing in itself. In the same way, we insist on the potency of faith alone, which means that the faith must do something other than what unbelief would do.

Come, the bread and wine are here. Confirm your interest in Christ by partaking now, together with your brothers and sisters.

So come, and welcome, to Jesus Christ.

Sacraments are immediately instituted by God. This means that man does not have the power to multiply them. Those who want to see a sacramental significance in everything must be careful here. The only way to see the world sacramentally is to jealously guard the two sacraments that God has given to us, applying them to everything else. Application is quite different than multiplication. If we turn everything into a sacrament, then nothing is a sacrament.

These sacraments are given immediately by God, our confession says, in order to represent Christ and His benefits. This is not all that the sacraments do, but they are established by God in order to represent Christ and His benefits. Now, here is the question. When God represents something, does He represent it *well*?

Does the washing with water represent cleansing from sin well or poorly? Do this bread and wine represent the broken body and shed blood of Christ well or poorly? When God paints, does He pick up the brush with maladroit fingers? The sacraments, down through church history, *have* been the occasion of much confusion. The representation of Christ and His benefits has frequently not gotten through. But this is to be attributed to the obtuseness of men, and not to any inadequacy in the representations that God gives.

If we want men to get it right, then we must pray that God's Spirit enable us to declare the gospel to them in power. What we must *not* do is tinker with the representations He has given to us. We must not pick up our brushes to improve upon what He has painted. We must not alter the content of the gospel to make it more palatable to sinful men. We must not surround the waters of baptism with the fences of our own traditions — lest anyone fall in and be saved. We must not refuse the bread and wine to the people out of fear that they will not "get it." What we are to do is set before you what God has done, and invite you to receive it.

So come, and welcome, to Jesus Christ.

MORNING ☼ TANGIBLE SIGNS, TANGIBLE SEALS

We can also be blessed by thinking through the biblical basis for the claims Westminster makes about sacraments generally. Of course there are two sacraments — baptism and the Lord's Supper — and both of them are signs and seals of the covenant of grace.

The covenant is made with all worthy receivers — worth defined in terms of *faith,* not in terms of any kind of self-righteous works — and it is efficaciously made, for blessing, with the elect. Now it does not follow that the covenant is invisible, just like the entire body of the elect is invisible. No, the covenant, its terms, and its signs and seals are all visible. The gospel we preach is declared in real time. The water we baptize with is really wet. The wine and bread we consecrate are baked in an oven and fashioned from the juice of grapes. These are not similitudes for the covenant of grace; they are rather manifestations of the covenant of grace.

Those who have true faith respond to these signs and seals, and are therefore brought to the reality behind them. They do not bypass the means, going straight to the reality. You must travel the road that God has built for you by trusting Him to keep the promises He made through Word, Water, and Wine. You must walk, by faith alone, in the way He established, seeing more and more clearly as you do.

The covenant of grace is made with all the elect. The extent of that body does not yet appear — there is a good bit of history yet to go, and the ranks have a good deal of filling up to do. But they will fill up here, in this world, by the means that God has established. It makes sense to say that the number of the decretally elect belongs to the secret things. But it is unbelief to say that the covenant of grace is secret. Do not say in your heart, *Who will go up to heaven to get it for us, or who will cross the sea for it?* No, the word, the gospel, the covenant, is in your mouth and in your heart. Here, today, and forever.

So come, and welcome, to Jesus Christ.

EVENING ◐ WITHOUT GUILT, SHAME, OR FEAR

Our modern world is full of eating disorders of various kinds. These range from the obvious, like gluttony, anorexia, and bulimia, to the not so obvious, like being way too obedient and servile to the latest food guru.

These problems rest on a common foundation, which is father hunger, coupled with the resultant guilt and fear. If your relationship to food is coupled with guilt or fear, that has to be dealt with, and the place to deal with it is here, at the meal God prepared for you.

It is here that God declares His pleasure with you through the sacrifice and obedience of Jesus Christ. That sacrifice and obedience cannot be improved, and so you come to sit at this Table, washed, clean, and perfect. You are clothed in the righteousness of Jesus Christ Himself. You may therefore eat and drink here without guilt, without shame, and without fear.

As you learn to do that here, extend that lesson to the rest of your life with food. You will be eating later on this afternoon, and, when you do, does the guilt and fear return? If it does, that is not a sign of spiritual health and sensitivity, but just the opposite. If guilt and fear are plucking at your sleeve when you open your mouth to eat, then return here. Learn your lessons here. Your Father accepts you here.

So come, and welcome, to Jesus Christ.

MORNING ☼ AND THE SPIRIT IS THE CAR

Last week I mentioned the very common problem of father hunger. With reference to this meal, there are still a few things that need to be said about this. Jesus teaches us, plainly and explicitly, that He is the only way to God the Father. I am the way, the truth and the life, He said. No man comes to the Father except through Him (Jn. 14:6). Notice that what He came to accomplish was us coming to the Father. The Father is the destination; the Father is the one to whom we are going. But how do we come to Him through Jesus?

The Lord has established various means for us to come "through Him." The first thing of course is to believe in Jesus, and to be baptized as He commanded. As Christians we are privileged to pray in Jesus' name, and so this is how we pray. We pray to the Father, in the power of the Holy Spirit, and in the name of Jesus. If we may speak this way, the Father is the town we are driving to, Jesus is the road there, and the Spirit is the car. And this is how we approach the Supper. The Father is the one we are coming to. The Son, Jesus, is the means. In this case the instrument is bread and wine. And the Holy Spirit is the one who works powerfully to restore us to the Father. And He fills your father hunger.

So come, and welcome, to Jesus Christ.

We live in community, which means in part that we feed one another. We live in community under God, which means that we are dependent upon God — He feeds us. If He did not give the rain, if He did not make the crops grow, we would all of us starve. We want a strong doctrine of providence so that we recognize that we are not here by ourselves, cast adrift by impersonal forces in an impersonal universe. When our society gives way to fear, as they have for example with their global warming hysterics, this is because they do not know that God is in His heaven, and that the world is in the palm of His hand.

But we also want a strong doctrine of covenant, because the God who provides for us, and who will keep the planet running, has determined that we need to be fed through cooperation with one another. If we do not form covenants, or if we break or subvert them through a lack of love, the end result of this will be that some people are not fed.

This is not just true in the physical realm; it is also true with the covenant meal that God sets before us here. As we feed ourselves while loving those around us, we are also feeding them. If we don't, we aren't, and we are trying to subvert a meal that cannot be subverted. So, take, eat, love. Take, drink, love.

So come, and welcome, to Jesus Christ.

MORNING ☼ STONES FOR BREAD?

When we ask God for bread, will He give us a stone? No, of course not. And when He has promised us bread, and we asked because of that promise, will that change anything? Still less. And when He has promised the bread of Christ, offered to every sinner who understands he needs salvation from the hand of God alone, will God pull it away from our mouths at the last moment? Again, no.

Too many debates about the Lord's Supper in church history have concentrated on what the bread and wine "are like." But our central focus should be on what *God* is like. He is our *Father* — He gives, He bestows, He provides.

God has not invited you here in order to trick you. If anyone is deceived here — and yes, there have been many — it is not because this meal was too complicated. Rather, it was because the sinful heart, self-justifying in all its ways, was too complicated. God keeps it simple. Here is bread and wine; here is Christ. Take and eat, and chew with the teeth of faith. Take and drink, and swallow the new covenant.

The blessed thing is that we don't have to figure it out. We just have to eat and drink it.

So come, and welcome, to Jesus Christ.

In Psalm 28, David asks the Lord to separate His people out from the wicked. He asks the Lord to deliver them from the judgment that is coming upon them. When he concludes this psalm, the way he puts it is striking. "Save thy people, and bless thine inheritance: feed them also, and lift them up for ever" (Ps. 28:9). When God saves and delivers His people, please note that He *feeds* them. When He lifts us up forever, He does so because He has fed us. God is our Father. He provides. God is our Father; He brings provision. God is our Father. He *feeds* us.

If we forget who He is, and what He is like, we will drift into crazy thoughts. What would you think if one of your children came to the table tonight and said that he or she did not *deserve* to be there with the rest of the family? There are two issues involved in this. First, the child is quite right, and ought to be answered with, "That's exactly right, honey. None of us do." But the second thing is that you ought to be concerned that some strange pattern of thought is developing. You come to the Table, not because you *deserve* to be there, but because you're family. That may not seem like a very good reason to you, but God finds it compelling. Come, eat and drink. You're family.

So come, and welcome, to Jesus Christ.

MORNING ✹ FEEDING US WITH JUDGMENT

In the words of the prophet Ezekiel, we read this: "I will feed my flock, and I will cause them to lie down, saith the Lord God" (Ez. 34:15). The Lord really is our Shepherd, and the Lord really does see to it that the flock is fed.

It is striking that in the passage from Ezekiel, in the next breath, God promises to feed us with judgment. We naturally tend to assume that all judgments are negative, but the Bible is full of judgments that God exercises in order to vindicate His people. We are to cry out to God for this kind of vindication and deliverance, and as we partake of the Lord's Supper together, this is one of the times we should be doing so. This is because one of the "foods" that God promises to feed us with is the food of judgment.

As we are seated here at this Table, we are ruling together with Christ. He has made us kings and priests on the earth, and He nourishes us by means of His interventions and judgments. We are living in a time when we are in great need of Him to rise up and scatter His enemies, and so, as we partake now, we should be asking God to build us up, to establish us, to settle us — by means of His great and glorious judgments. And so we come to eat and drink.

So come, and welcome, to Jesus Christ.

EVENING ◐ WANTING TO OUTSOURCE THE SACRIFICE

We have been considering the fact that God in His kindness feeds His people. And as He does so, He does this as a pattern for us to emulate and follow. The Lord offers us His broken body, and this is a figure that we imitate.

It is not the case that food just appears miraculously at supermarkets. All food is the fruit of sacrifice, and this is a truth that we should not run from or seek to evade. Our bodies cannot be broken in just the same way the Lord's was—obviously—but we are to imitate Him in all that we do. This is repeatedly urged upon us in the Scriptures.

But we are not just to imitate the Lord generically. Let us imitate how He feeds us in how we feed one another. A husband and father submits to grueling or backbreaking work in order to feed his children. A woman with child submits to the considerable demands placed upon her body so that another might be fed. A nursing mother does the same. Intensive labor in the kitchen, or at the outdoor grill, is a "giving up" that another might eat.

So much that is wrong with our culture is the result of trying to evade this. We want to outsource the sacrifice. The Lord is not like that. Come.

So come, and welcome, to Jesus Christ.

MORNING ☼ CONVICTION & COMMUNION

As we continue to pray for reformation and revival we have to take care not to neglect the true nature of conviction of sin. Given the nature of the world, it is perilously easy for us to mistake certain things for conviction of sin that are not conviction of sin at all. Those who are living without Christ are frequently miserable. Their lives appear to them to have no point or purpose. Their conscience does bother them about certain things they have done. Their attempt to reinvent a type of humanity more conducive to their lusts is a wretched failure. They are plagued with drifting ennui — however many things they try, nothing *tastes* like anything. There is a feeling of aimless malaise.

But none of this is conviction of sin. It certainly presents us with the *need* for conviction of sin, but it is not conviction at all. There is a kind of worldly sorrow that only works death (2 Cor. 7:10). That is what this is. Godly sorrow, the genuine article — conviction of sin — leads to a salvation that doesn't look back, and which has no regrets. It comes to this Table with no regrets.

But godly conviction of sin consists of certain elements that explain why people shrink back from it — an awareness of the holy law of a holy God, and His *presence*, and His *displeasure*. In short, God is here, God is angry, and God is right to be angry. This experience, this sensation of conviction, is most unwelcome. There are no secret pleasures in it the way there are secret pleasures in self-pity, boredom, ennui, and so forth. Conviction of sin is *entirely* distasteful, partly because it appears that the only legitimate way out is to run *toward* the God who is generating these feelings. The only lawful refuge from God is to be found in God.

When we pray for reformation and revival in the church, and for spiritual awakening in the unbelieving world, we are praying for this. If we want a harvest, the field must be plowed.

So come, and welcome, to Jesus Christ.

EVENING ◐ NOT TOO YOUNG TO BE CARRIED

How does God feed us? In that great passage from the servant songs in Isaiah, the prophet says, "He shall feed his flock like a shepherd: he shall gather the lambs with his arm, and carry them in his bosom, and shall gently lead those that are with young" (Is. 40:11).

Notice that God does not just sling the food at us. It is not simply that we need the food, and He has to give it to us, but it is also true that we need the food brought to us in a certain *way*. We are His flock, and He feeds us the way a shepherd does. He not only feeds the entire flock, there are some other things He does that are described here.

He gathers the lambs with His arm. And so take note you children, you little ones. The Lord is our shepherd, and this means that He is shepherd of the lambs and not just shepherd of the full grown sheep. He gathers the lambs with His arm. Have you ever wondered if you are old enough to come to this Table? You may be too much of a lamb to come on your own, but no one is too much of a lamb to be *carried* by Him. How would that argument work? I am too young and too little to be carried. More than this, He will carry too close to His chest.

So come, and welcome, to Jesus Christ.

MORNING ☼ IN THE MIDST OF THE THRONE

This meal that we are privileged to have before us is a meal of foreshadowing. God is directing all of human history toward a glorious culmination, and that culmination will be a feast.

We see a glimpse of this in how the martyrs coming out of the great tribulation were received by God.

"Therefore are they before the throne of God, and serve him day and night in his temple: and he that sitteth on the throne shall dwell among them. They shall hunger no more, neither thirst any more; neither shall the sun light on them, nor any heat. For the Lamb which is in the midst of the throne shall feed them, and shall lead them unto living fountains of waters: and God shall wipe away all tears from their eyes" (Rev. 7:15–17).

When we go to be with the Lord, note that we will *hunger no more*. This is not because food is taken away, along with the need for it. Rather, we are told that the martyrs hunger no more because the Lamb in the midst of the throne *shall feed them*.

Just as we will be fed by Christ in the consummation, so we are fed by Christ now. God reminds us every week that our destiny is to commune with Him forever, and He reminds us of this by communing with us here and now. Every week, we are being acclimated to the feasting of heaven. Every week God prepares us further. Every week, the one in the midst of the throne feeds us.

So come, and welcome, to Jesus Christ.

EVENING ◐ GROWING UP INTO GLADNESS

This is a meal of gladness, and not of gloom. We see this in many different ways, but one of them can be seen in the elements that the Lord chose for us to remember Him by. "And wine that maketh glad the heart of man, and oil to make his face to shine, and bread which strengtheneth man's heart." (Ps. 104:15).

This bread, which is the body of the Lord, is given to strengthen your heart. This wine, which is the blood of Christ, is given to gladden your heart.

Note in the first place that God is addressing your heart with both elements of the sacrament. You are not coming to this Table for the same reasons that you had breakfast this morning. You need bodily strength and God provides it by means of ordinary food — which is also addressed by this passage.

But you also need heart-strength. You need to be built up spiritually. You need to be encouraged in your sanctification, in your walk with Christ. You need to allow God to minister to you by means of all His appointed means of grace. And among those means, we are glad to include this Table.

Your heart needs to be stronger than it is — and so God supplies you with bread. Your heart needs to be gladder than it is — and so He supplies you with the wine of a Eucharistic celebration. You don't need to be able to explain the mechanics of how God accomplishes this; you just need to come in simple faith. God loves you, delights in you, accepts you, and wants you to grow up into gladness. To that end, He has set the Table for you here. So come and eat, come and drink.

So come, and welcome, to Jesus Christ.

MORNING ☼ BREAD & WINE FROM SALEM

In Genesis 14:18, Scripture tells us that Abraham was met by Melchizedek. "And Melchizedek king of Salem brought forth bread and wine: and he was the priest of the most high God."

We are expressly taught in the New Testament that Melchizedek is a type of Christ. If we take that type and apply it to God's gift to us here at the Lord's Table, we see a number of things that bless us.

Melchizedek comes to us both as a king and a priest. He is the king of Salem, which means peace, and he is the priest of the most high God.

His name means king of righteousness, and that is what God imputes to us in our justification — *His* righteousness. Melchizedek not only offers the bread and wine, but he also offers himself.

But the ultimate salvation offered to Abraham and all his descendants is offered under the elements of bread and wine — the same elements that we have before us here now. We have the same elements before us because the same salvation is before us.

And last, the bread and wine is given to Abraham. And who can come and receive this gift? Who is it for? The children of Abraham are marked out by their faith. That is what distinguishes children of Abraham from children of the devil. So here is the bread. Chew by *faith*. Here is the wine. Drink it by *faith*.

So come, and welcome, to Jesus Christ.

EVENING ◐ WINE OF ASTONISHMENT

In Psalm 60:3, the judgments of God are described as making Israel drink the "wine of astonishment." That astonishment was the result of seeing God shake everything. God makes the earth tremble and shake, and those who observe are undone.

The wine we drink here at this Table is also the wine of astonishment. The Scriptures tell us that this is the cup of the new testament, and the new covenant is established among men, we are told, through the work of God shaking down all things that can be shaken — so that what is unshakable may remain.

God is establishing His city. Abraham looked forward to this city, the city whose maker and builder is God. But before He establishes the new, He bulldozes the old. That which God removed was in terrible shape and needed to come down. That which He is building will result in the everlasting restoration of heaven and earth, and with all things united through Christ, in a glorious and unending harmony. And as He builds, He wants us to be drinking the wine of astonishment.

But there are two kinds of astonishment. The first is astonishment and dismay, as is described in Psalm 60. The second is astonishment and gladness, which is what we are privileged to participate in. We drink the wine of astonishment because of what He has done, and one of His instruments for doing all this includes drinking this wine.

So come, and welcome, to Jesus Christ.

MORNING ☼ TO BE CONSUMED

The apostle Paul plainly teaches us that when we partake of the bread in this Supper, we are partaking of the body of Christ, and by this he includes the entire congregation. "For we *being* many are one bread, *and* one body: for we are all partakers of that one bread" (1 Cor. 10:17).

But there is something contained in this passage which is often missed. We do not just eat in the Lord's Supper. In every faithful commemoration of this meal, we not only eat *but are also eaten*. If we are all part of that one loaf, and every person who partakes is partaking of that loaf, then this means that we not only consume, but that we also *are* consumed. So this meal is ritual enactment of the basic principle of body life — my life for yours.

Now of course we cannot do this without partaking of Christ, and by being taken up into Him as well. But this meal knits us together in profound ways. I have often urged our weekly commemoration of the Supper as a basis for Christians to love one another in all their basic dealings. This is broadly understood by many on a rudimentary level, but let us take it a bit deeper.

If two Christians in this congregation are on the outs with one another, and they come to the Table together, what is that saying? Their spat says that they are not interested in the other's well-being at all. But coming to the Table says that each is willing to be consumed *by* the other for the *sake* of the other. If it is false then it is robust hypocrisy. If it is true, then there is no real reason to continue the squabble. So come, and partake of all the others here. But in so doing, realize that you are coming to give yourself to all of them as well.

So come, and welcome, to Jesus Christ.

EVENING ◐ EXACTLY SO

Last week we considered the truth that we do more than consume in this meal — we are consumed as well. If the entire congregation is the loaf, as St. Paul plainly teaches, then we are — all of us — both eating and being eaten. We consume and are consumed.

Christ gives Himself to us, certainly. But we also surrender ourselves to Him in this partaking. The head of the body communicates, just as the body does. And as each part of the body eats, so each part of the body is eaten. My life for yours.

This sounds noble, and quite lovely, in this context. We are all seated in church, the bread and wine are on the Table, and we have just finished worshiping the Lord. But this reality, this Table, governs the next six days, and it does not leave any spaces. My life for yours feels quite different when the kids are tearing off in six different directions, when your business partner is being difficult, when an old friend appears to be losing it, when someone in the church badmouths you, when you can't get all your work done and others aren't helping, and when you feel misunderstood by everybody.

When such moments come — and there will likely be a number of them in the next six days — you will feel like you are being consumed. But then you should think to yourself, "ah, exactly so. I offered myself for that, just this last Sunday."

So come, and welcome, to Jesus Christ.

MORNING ☼ AND WE ARE THAT LOAF

Now as we speak of the mysteries involved in the Lord's Supper, and they are many and deep, we need to occasionally speak a word of caution against a superstitious approach to the Supper. In short, the difference between superstition and evangelical faith is a difference between an unthinking acceptance of impersonal magic throughout all the world, and a basic faith in the authority of the Word spoken.

That said, as evangelicals we have to remind ourselves that the Word has spoken to us more clearly and extensively than our traditions sometimes admit. St. Paul says that we are all the one loaf of communion. Just as plainly as Jesus said, "this is *my* body, broken for you," so also the apostle Paul said that "we being many *are* one loaf." He says this right after he has taught us that we have communion in the blood of Christ by partaking and communion in the body of Christ by partaking. Now plainly the bread on the Table does not "turn into" the Smiths, and Johnsons, and Thompsons. Paul is addressing and insisting on our *koinonia* union at a much deeper and more profound level than a magic trick on the Table. So do not make the mistake that many evangelicals have made, which is to think that because it is not happening on the Table that it must not be happening. Do not think that if the words of a priest cannot do it, then somehow it cannot be done. No, not at all. What priests and ministers cannot do, God has determined to do through the instrumentality of the Word and faith, simple evangelical faith. And the Word says that this happens as we eat and drink in love. Come, then.

So come, and welcome, to Jesus Christ.

God is our Father, and one of the things that fathers are called to do is *provide*. "The blessing of the Lord, it maketh rich, and he addeth no sorrow with it" (Prov. 10:22). Now this meal is the blessing of the Lord—we are told explicitly that the cup is the cup of blessing. Now when the Lord brings blessing, it *is* possible to receive it wrongly, to twist it in such a way that our observance of the Supper does, as Paul put it once, more harm than good.

But that ought to be the exceptional case. That is not to be the ordinary way we come to our Father to be fed. He adds no sorrow to it. And yet, why is it that so many Christians come to this Table cringing?

There are two basic reasons, and I have little doubt that they are related. The first is that a teaching has gotten abroad in the Church that the Father is pleased when we come to this Table in order to abase ourselves. But I know, as a father, that it would displease me extremely if I were to discover that my children or grandchildren were coming to my table in the conviction that the food was poisoned, and would likely do them in. Fathers don't do that—Jesus even acknowledged that evil fathers don't do that. What father would give his son a stone when he had asked for bread?

But here is the second reason, and it is likely the reason that the doctrine mentioned above has come to make any sense to people at all. Fathers don't give their children physical poison at the dinner table, but they often administer the poisons of a harsh and critical tongue, on the one hand, or a distance and detachment on the other. When fathers fail to nourish the souls of the little ones around their tables, it creates the false impression that tables are something we come to reluctantly, if at all. We think that fathers have nothing to do with fat souls, but in reality, only the Father can do this. Come then. This Table was set in fulfillment of the Father's will.

So come, and welcome, to Jesus Christ.

MORNING ☼ SUBATOMIC GOLDEN CALVES

We have often noted that the covenant renewal worship service is structured around the sacrifices of the Old Testament. Our corporate confession of sin corresponds to the guilt offering, fulfilled in the death of Jesus. Our Psalm singing, Scripture reading, and sermon listening correspond to the ascension offering—sometimes called the whole burnt offering. This is an offering of consecration, with the entire animal ascending to heaven in the smoke. And our service culminates in the Lord's Supper, which corresponds to the peace offering, where the worshiper sits down and shares a meal with his God.

So we have come to the peace offering. God meets with us, receives us, and accepts us. We have emphasized that God does receive you here, despite your sins, because you have confessed them and you acknowledge them to be sins. We have emphasized this because in conservative, evangelical, and Reformed circles, far too many Christians have used this as an occasion for beating themselves up. But this is not the part of the worship service that is designed for self-accusation. Confess your sins at the beginning of the service, and sit down at this Table with joy. Wash your hands and then come to dinner.

Not that other abuses are impossible, but we want to deal with *our* characteristic abuses first. There are those who want to keep the Supper and their sins. How did the people spend the morning before the infamous golden calf incident? "They rose up early on the morrow, and offered burnt offerings, and brought peace offerings; and the people sat down to eat and to drink, and rose up to play" (Ex. 32:6).

So of course that is not the way. Don't be dancing around the golden calf while calling it a festival to YHWH. In a congregation this size, there are some doing just that. But we are far more likely to be distracted from true communion with the Lord because we are furtively looking for subatomic golden calves that we know are residing in our hearts. Don't be doing that either.

So come, and welcome, to Jesus Christ.

EVENING ◐ THE LIQUID OATH AND EDIBLE VOW

Our fathers the Jews were baptized into Moses in the cloud and in the sea. They, like us, were inaugurated into the body of God's people. And they also had spiritual food and spiritual drink in the wilderness. The drink came from the rock that accompanied them, the rock that was Christ. They had manna, the bread of heaven that came down from heaven, just as Jesus did.

The Corinthians had begun to put on airs over against the unbelieving Jews of their day. We have a spiritual meal. We have spiritual drink. Paul makes a point of showing them that when it came to the substance of covenantal identity and covenantal nourishment, the Corinthians had nothing that the Jews did not also have. Nevertheless, with many of them God was not well pleased.

But note the structure of Paul's argument. He is not saying that God was not well-pleased with the Jews because they did not have spiritual food and drink. He was not pleased with them because they neglected the covenanted nature of the sealed oaths that these sacraments established, these sacraments being something that they had. And then Paul goes on to warn the Corinthians against committing the very same sin.

Of course the new covenant has a much higher degree of glory. But we must be careful to locate the differences where the New Testament does, and to locate the similarities where the New Testament does. As we renew covenant week after week, as we assemble before the Lord, together in our households, let us take care to remember that this wine is a liquid oath. This bread is an edible vow. And the Lord Jesus is present with us to enable us to keep covenant with Him. So come and eat. Come and drink.

So come, and welcome, to Jesus Christ.

MORNING ☼ BREAD FOR STRENGTH, WINE FOR JOY

In Psalm 104:14–15, we are told that God feeds the world. As part of this, the psalmist mentions wine and bread as part of God's great gift. He tells us that bread is given to strengthen the heart of man, and that wine is given to gladden the heart of man.

As we gather at the Lord's Table, these are two things we must remember. It is true of food generally, and it is certainly true of this sacramental food. When God gives you something to strengthen you, this means that you need to be strengthened. If you didn't need, God would not be piling superfluous gifts on you. And in the same way, when God gives you wine to gladden your heart, this means that your heart needs to be gladdened.

Christians are too often weak, and they are too often sorrowful. Because of this, God brings you what is most needful. He brings you strength in the form of bread, and He brings you joy in a cup, the joy of the new covenant.

The bread, of course, is the body of the Lord, which means that you commune with His body, and you commune with one another — for you are His body. If you want to know where a great deal of the strength is, look around you. God has given you strength in the bread He has given you. And He has done the same thing with joy. For this, just listen. Listen to the psalms, and to the harmonies, and to the words of joy. So come — bread for strength, and wine for joy.

So come, and welcome, to Jesus Christ.

When the Lord was tempted in the wilderness, one of the points of temptation was bread. The tempter said that if He was who He claimed to be, He ought to prove it by turning stones into bread (Matt. 4:3). Jesus responded by saying if He turned the stones into bread, that would not be enough because man does not live by bread alone, but by every word that comes from the mouth of God (v. 4).

It is clear from this that the temptation would have resulted in an act of power that would have resulted in mere bread, only bread, bread unadorned by that which is our life—every word that comes from God.

We must be careful then to avoid coming to this Table with an expectation of receiving mere bread, bread by itself. That is not our life. Man does not live by bread alone, or by wine alone. This is nothing to us unless we are here in conformity to the word of Christ, which summons us, and authorizes us to partake. Apart from that, we might as well be giving one another stones in the wilderness.

But we are not gathered here with mere bread and mere wine. We have the Word, here. We have the Spirit of Christ. We have one another. Come and eat. Come and drink.

So come, and welcome, to Jesus Christ.

MORNING ☼ MAKING THE PHYSICAL SPIRITUAL

The God we worship is the God of all mercy. Scripture tells us repeatedly that His mercies crown all that He does, and one aspect of this mercy is that He gives "food to all flesh: for his mercy endureth for ever" (Ps. 136:25).

One central aspect of His great mercy is His provision of food. And, at the center of this, we find His provision of *spiritual* food. Man needs more nourishment than can be provided by the food that perishes. We are invited by God to eat and to drink everlasting life. As with everything else we do on the spiritual plane, we use physical instruments.

When you sing spiritual songs, you do so with a physical throat, mouth, and tongue. When you offer spiritual worship to God, you do so by offering your physical body. When the Jews in the wilderness ate and drank spiritual food and drink, they did so by eating and drinking what God provided for them on the physical plane. And it is the same with us. This wine and bread here is as physical as anything else in the room. It is not ethereal. The wine came from a vineyard, and the bread from a wheat field.

When I say the words of institution, these elements do not become ghostly. They are not spiritual in *that* way. When we eat and drink this way, we are partaking of Christ spiritually because we are coming to Him in obedience, and God inhabits the obedience of His people. This obedience, contra many, does not make the spiritual physical, but rather makes the physical spiritual. So come, eat and drink.

So come, and welcome, to Jesus Christ.

EVENING ◐ WISDOM OFFERS BREAD AND WINE

We come to this Supper week after week, and it is tempting for us to start to assume, after a few years of it, that we are doing so as old hands. We know the ropes, we know the words, we know the theology. But one of the things we should know — if we know the theology — is that we always have a tendency to grow in our own wisdom during the week, and God has to humble us and make us simple again. The invitation here is given to the simple.

In the book of Proverbs, note what Lady Wisdom says in her invitation to eat and drink.

"Whoso is simple, let him turn in hither: as for him that wanteth understanding, she saith to him, Come, *eat of my bread*, and *drink of the wine* which I have mingled. Forsake the foolish, and live; and go in the way of understanding" (Prov. 9:4–6).

We come to this Table simple, and we should leave having forsaken the ways of the foolish. When we do this we are not relying on our own wisdom, but rather the wisdom that has been given to us in a loaf and in a cup. We then grow sophisticated again, and we have to remind ourselves to come again in simplicity.

In this Advent season, let us remember to cultivate a real simplicity of heart — a heart attitude that repents of the wrong kind of simplicity and foolishness, and embraces the right kind, which is a straight-up acceptance of the gospel.

So come, and welcome, to Jesus Christ.

MORNING ✺ ACCEPTED WEEKLY

It is no accident that our service of worship concludes, or culminates, in the Supper. In response to the summons of the Lord, we have called on His name. We have confessed our sins, knowing that we cannot enter into the holy place of worship apart from His cleansing and forgiveness. We have consecrated ourselves to Him entirely, just as a sacrificial animal ascended to heaven in the column of smoke from the altar. This is how we have heard the sermon, this is how we have offered our psalms and hymns.

This part of the service, every Lord's Day, is the place where God assures us that, for the sake of Jesus Christ and His perfections, our offerings and our worship has been accepted. This is the peace offering, this is the place where the Lord invites us to sit down with Him and share a meal. We do so gladly . . . this meal means, as we receive it in true evangelical faith, that we have been *justified*. So come then, eat and drink.

So come, and welcome, to Jesus Christ.

Our Lord was fond of *a fortiori*, "how much more" arguments. Not a sparrow falls to the ground apart from the will of the Father. That being the case, He urged, His disciples ought not to fret over whether *they* were going to be cared for.

We can reason the same way here, at this Table. The Lord feeds all His creatures, the Scriptures say. "He giveth to the beast his food, and to the young ravens which cry" (Ps. 147:9). That being true, we ought not to worry about whether He will feed us. He clothes the lily of the field, and so why would He not clothe us? We are worth more than ten million lilies.

But let's take it a step beyond that. If God gives the beasts of the field their physical food, and if He gives us our daily bread, the why would He then neglect to offer us food for our souls, food to nourish the inner man?

The answer of course is that He does not neglect to offer us this food. He spreads the Table, and sends His Spirit out into the world to issue the invitation. Come, the Spirit says. But not only does the Spirit invite everyone to this rich meal, so does the Bride. The Spirit and the Bride both say, *come*.

We can say that the offer is frequently neglected by those who hear it. But we cannot say that the offer is neglected by the one who makes it, by the one who holds out His hands to a disobedient people.

The provision is here, and more than enough. The Lord has told us to preach the gospel to every creature, and to establish churches, centers of worship, in every part of the globe. When this is finally done, there will be a Table like this, within walking distance of every sinner in the world.

So come, and welcome, to Jesus Christ.

MORNING ✺ BEFORE YOU NOW

Many unbelievers have dismissed this Table before us as a great superstition. Two thousand years after Jesus lived and died, here we are gathering to eat His flesh and drink His blood. What kind of sense does that make?

The first thing to note about this charge is the truth of Chesterton's observation — a man who refuses to believe in something does not believe in nothing, but rather he eventually come to believe in anything. The cavalier dismissal of this Table as the center of the world has not banished superstitions; rather, it has opened the door wide open to them.

Unbelievers instinctively know that we are saved by what we eat. That is quite true. But we have to eat the body of Christ, drinking His blood, and we have to do this by true faith in the Word that is declared over it. If you refuse to partake of this, then there may be a brief period of food atheism, or perhaps food agnosticism. But when that brief period is over, the superstitions will come flooding in, and people start trying to align themselves to *some* arbitrary standard of righteousness by what they put in their mouths. It is inescapable — you will either put salvation in your mouth through evangelical faith, and it will come in the form of bread and wine, or you will try to justify yourself by some other form of salvation food, some other kind of false gospel food.

If you eat and drink grace, then it will go down the way grace always does, *smoothly*, and you will be doing it with deep gratitude. If you eat and drink works — and this is the only alternative to grace — you will be trying to choke down sawdust cakes, molded and shaped by carpenter's glue. So come, here, now, in true faith. The Table is set before you. God's grace is before you.

So come, and welcome, to Jesus Christ.

Partaking of the bread and wine is a privilege that our children grow up with. It is our practice to come to this Table with our little ones.

This is of course a matter of debate in the broader Christian world, and one of the things we should do because of this is guard ourselves at all those places where those who differ with us have a point.

In other words, when someone says that bringing little ones to the Table will make them take it for granted, making it a dull routine, your response should not be to say *phhhttt*. Your response should be to pray to God that this might not happen in your family, and to encourage your children to receive the elements with gladness and joy. And this exhortation will of course fall to the ground unless you are receiving the elements with gladness and joy.

If someone says that this will make your children think that being a member of the Christian church is a low bar affair, a tiny works club, respond by teaching your children the difference between grace and tiny works. It is not a quantitative difference; it is a qualitative difference.

If someone says that this will admit a ton of unregenerate hellions into the church, admit that that *can* happen, and then bring your children up, as you promised you would do at their baptisms, in the nurture and admonition of the Lord.

Giving them these elements in the right spirit, and with evangelical faith, is part of that nurture. So come, all of you, and welcome.

So come, and welcome, to Jesus Christ.

MORNING ✵ MORE THAN WORDS CAN SAY

This is a meal, not a sermon. It is a meal with a meaning, of course, and sermons have meanings as well. Or, at any rate, some sermons do. But the fact that the meal has meaning and sermons have meaning should not make us think that a meal is a sermon — or that a sermon is a meal, for that matter.

When you are satisfied in your spirit by the preaching of the Word of God, you can and should respond to it as though you had been fed. But this is a metaphor — and a scriptural metaphor at that — but it is still a metaphor. When God feeds you with words, it is like being fed with food.

But when God feeds you with food here, it is not *like* you are eating and drinking. You *are* eating and drinking. Because it is a sacramental meal, it does more than a regular meal does, but it does not do less. God has arranged your Christian life in such a way that when you eat this bread and drink this wine, you are, in the power of the Spirit, partaking of Christ.

This is not because the meaning of the bread and wine is routed through a sermon first. This is not a sermon, cleverly disguised. This is something that stands in its own right, something that feeds us in its own way. What you are receiving here is not something that you could get by going off into the woods in order to recite Bible verses to yourself.

And so, come, eat and drink, and be satisfied.

So come, and welcome, to Jesus Christ.

EVENING ◐ SPIRITUAL BREAD, SPIRITUAL WINE

This bread is spiritual bread, and this wine is spiritual wine. But it is not spiritual in the sense that the bread and wine are somehow ethereal or non-real. The bread and wine before us is recognizably bread and wine. So what do we mean by considering it spiritual food? When Paul says that in the resurrection we will have a spiritual body, he does not mean that we will have no body — rather he means that our bodies will be fully animated by the Spirit. The Spirit quickens, enlivens, and animates our bodies. Physical things are spiritual when the Spirit works with them. And they are spiritual without ceasing to be what they are.

In the same way, we believe that we are gathered here in worship through the power of the Spirit, and that when He gathers us, He does not do this just to release us unchanged an hour and a half later. He gathers us in order to bring us into the heavenly places . . . where Christ is enthroned. The Spirit gathers us in such a way, as that by the means of eating and drinking physical bread and wine, we are privileged to partake of Christ.

He is not doing a miracle *in* the bread or *to* the wine. He is using the bread and wine to do the miracle in us. *We* are the bread that is changed. We are the wine of life. We are the body of Christ, Paul teaches. The Holy Spirit is sovereign over all of this, and He is accomplishing great things here in us. So as you come in true evangelical faith, realize that you are partaking of Christ, and you are being transformed as you do. So come, and welcome.

So come, and welcome, to Jesus Christ.

MORNING ☼ BREAKING BREAD, BREAKING SIN

This bread is the sacrament of the body of the Lord, as He put it. And when He picked it up in the institution of this meal, He took the bread that represented His own body, and He gave thanks, and He broke it. The remarkable grace and love that we see here is striking, but there is something else to be learned from this. Jesus broke the body that was to bear our sins, and in that breaking we see the salvation of the world. What else does God break? When we think about this, we should come to recognize what sorts of things are broken in the world as we commemorate this meal in true evangelical faith.

God breaks the images and idols (2 Kings 23:14). God breaks the houses of the sodomites (2 Kings 23:7). God breaks the weapons of war (Ps. 76:3). God breaks the jaws of the wicked (Ps. 3:7; Job 29:17). In short, God breaks all rebellion and sin.

In this memorial, we can see how He does this in such a way that we are not consumed. God made Him who knew no sin to become sin on our behalf (2 Cor. 5:21) so that we could be broken with Him, and restored and made whole with Him. Jesus took on the likeness of sinful flesh so that all those corruptions could be placed on Him, and there broken forever (Rom. 8:3). God condemned sin in the flesh, and in that condemnation, in that breaking, you can see your only hope.

In just a moment, I will lift the loaf of bread up and I will break it. Just as surely as you see that bread broken, so you are invited to see your sins, all of them, broken forever.

This is good news indeed. Come, and partake of it.

So come, and welcome, to Jesus Christ.

When the people of Israel sinned in the notorious golden calf incident, Moses responded by grinding their idol to powder, throwing it into the water, and making them drink it. They drank the object of their foul worship, thus becoming completely identified with it — in that case, for cursing.

We also consume what we worship, partaking of Him by faith. Jesus Christ suffered, bled and died on the cross, shedding His blood for us. This cup is the cup of the new testament, and Paul calls it the cup of blessing. We drink wine that represents the blood of the one who died for us. The Israelites in the wilderness drank the defiled water, made up of the remains of the idol that was going to consume them.

We drink death followed by resurrection. They drank death, and that was it. We drink death offered for others. They drank death that was simply the fruit of their own sin.

We drink from the rock that accompanied the Israelites in the wilderness, and that rock is Christ (1 Cor. 10: 4). They drank from a stream that was from God also, but it descended from the mount, and was a bane to them (Dt. 9:21).

If you are worshiping an idol, it does not matter that you say that your festival is to Yahweh. The dust of the idol is thrown into the drink, and you become more and more like what you partake of. But this is not what we are doing here. We have come before God with true faith in Christ, and we trust in Him alone for our salvation. We look to Him alone for the forgiveness we all seek. We do not drink judgment in the water; we drink forgiveness in the wine.

So come, and welcome, to Jesus Christ.

MORNING ☼ THE DEATH OF DEATH AND THE LIFE OF NATIONS

The Lord gives us rich food, and we must take a moment to consider how this can be. At first glance, it appears very plain — simple bread and red wine. How is this a banquet?

The Lord declared through the prophet Isaiah that in the time of the new covenant, on the mountain of the Lord where we now are, He would set a glorious meal (Is. 25:6). It would be a feast of fat things, of wine racked in the cellar, of fat things full of marrow, of fine wine racked in the cellar. When the Lord brought us to this meal, what would be the result?

What will the result of a faithful commemoration of this meal be? It is an evangelical meal, and it is an evangelistic meal. The Lord will destroy (in this mountain) the covering that has been covering over all the nations. He will remove the veil that is over the face of the nations.

Our worship, our communing, our preaching, our singing, all of it is building to a crescendo, a crescendo where the Lord will finally and utterly destroy death. He will wipe away every tear, and so consider that He has well begun the process. You are communing at a meal where death is being eaten, death is being swallowed. Look — body and blood. At the same time, this does not mean that death is triumphant — just the reverse. Life is doing the swallowing.

This is a meal where every tear should be dried. Why? Because the Lord our God has spoken it. Come, celebrate the death of death, and the life of all nations.

So come, and welcome, to Jesus Christ.

This is a meal that should be bookended with gratitude. We come to the Table in the first place because we are grateful, and we are looking for a means to overflow, a way to express that gratitude. One of the names for this meal is the Eucharist, which comes from the Greek word for *thanksgiving*. We come to the Supper thankful.

But it is a meal, and so we receive in the course of it. If it were undiluted thanksgiving, it would be sheer output. But we come to receive, and we receive bread and wine, emblems of God's kindness to us. This is a sacrament in which God offers Christ to us, and what could He offer more than that? And, as we all learned as children, when you are given something, what do you say? You say *thank you*.

And when you are given the one who fills heaven and earth, the first born over all creation, what do you say? You can't say anything more than *thank you*, but you can bow down under the *weight* of the gratitude.

So we come in gratitude, and we receive more than we had before, meaning that we leave more even grateful than we came. This is more than we can comprehend, and all of it is good. Had God determined to give us a fraction of what He did give, it would have been sufficient, and we should have been content with it. But He has given us all things in Christ, and sometimes it seems that a weekly meal of thanks is not nearly enough. But He blesses it and it is.

So come, and welcome, to Jesus Christ.

MORNING ☼ INTERPRETING OUR LIVES

The Lord spoke to the people of Israel through Moses when they were on the threshold of the land they were about to inherit. He told them, as part of a series of exhortations to remain faithful to the covenant, that the secret things belong to the Lord our God, but that the things revealed belong to us and to our children (Dt. 29:29). The phrase "secret things" refers to God's secret decrees, the way He is ordering all the events of history, not to mention the number of His elect. The "revealed things" as a phrase refers to the covenant, and contextually to the blessings and curses of the covenant.

Now this is the meal of the new covenant, and in this regard the covenants have not changed. In other respects, the new covenant is more glorious, internalized in more people, and not susceptible to an idolatrous and calamitous end as the old covenant was. Nevertheless, the secret things still belong to God, and the blessings and curses belong to us.

As finite beings, we cannot know absolutely. But we can know the Absolute, for that is what the triune God is. And He has given us warrant for interpreting history and biography and autobiography a certain way. We come to this Table to be reinforced, reestablished and sustained in our enjoyment of all God's blessings and benefits. But if we retain rebellion in the stubbornness of our hearts as we come, and God chastises us publicly, this is one of the revealed things. It is not arrogance to operate on the basis of the things revealed.

So come, and welcome, to Jesus Christ.

In this glorious meal, Jesus Christ is genuinely and truly offered. The divide between historic Protestantism and the Roman Catholic view is not over that—both sides believe that Jesus Christ is truly offered. The difference is not over whether that happens or not. The difference is one of *direction,* and concerns who receives the offering.

The Roman view is that Jesus Christ is offered again to God, in a repeated (or renewed) sacrifice. Our view is that in this meal God offers Jesus Christ to us. The difference is directional. One view is that Jesus is offered *up* again, and the other is that Jesus is offered *down*.

And so, if we were to be asked if we believed in the real presence of Christ, the answer would be that we certainly don't believe in His real absence. The Lord is present with us, in this meal. He is offered to us, and we partake of Him by faith. And of course, in order to partake of Him by faith, we have to *believe* that we are doing so. And so we do.

But there are some other important things to note. This is Easter Sunday, and we of course know that we are celebrating the resurrection. But it follows from this that in this Easter communion you are not being offered a dead Christ, but a living Christ. A dead Christ was offered to God so that a living Christ could be offered to you. You are converted. You are now Christians. Why would you want to partake of death any longer? God gave you a death to partake of by faith, so that you might partake of life now, here.

So come, and welcome, to Jesus Christ.

MORNING ☼ THE PLEASANT RAIN OF RIGHTEOUSNESS

We have reminded you on many occasions that the time set aside for confession of sin in our service is at the very beginning of the service. If we visit a friend's house, we wipe our feet at the door, not two thirds of the way through the evening. This is a time to be nourished and strengthened, not rebuked and scolded. This is a meal, not a confrontation. God is showing His kindness to us here; it is not a revelation of how stern He can be.

But this does not mean that the meal has nothing whatever to do with sin. In this meal, God is dealing with us. He — by showing us His kindness — is breaking up the fallow ground. And as the prophet Hosea says, "Sow to yourselves in righteousness, reap in mercy; break up your fallow ground: for it is time to seek the Lord, till he come and rain righteousness upon you" (Hos. 10:12). When our ground has lain fallow, there are things there that need to be broken up, that need to be dealt with. This is not said so that you will try to seat the accuser here at the Table, but rather so that the Comforter will do His work. We come in the confidence that as we continue to worship God, He will — gradually, slowly, inexorably, and *kindly* — put everything right.

This could mean bringing hidden sin to light, but you do not need to assume that. Just trust Him to do what He is doing. Sow in righteousness, reap in mercy, and break up the fallow ground. God will grow the wheat that makes up this bread, and He will do it with the pleasant rain of righteousness.

So come, and welcome, to Jesus Christ.

EVENING ◐ TOKENS OF AFFECTION

The Lord is kind to us in the tokens of His affection that He gives. He gives them in all affection and kindness, and we are to receive them in the same way. But these are tokens, not *props*. God loves us through His Word, through His sacraments, through His ordinances. He loves us *through* these things — He is not all tied *by* them.

If a husband gives his wife a bouquet of flowers, this is presumably not because he wanted to get into a debate with her over what color they actually. He offers them in a spirit of affection, and they are a great blessing when she receives them in the same way.

We should not over-analyze what God offers us. He promises to meet us, to feed us, to comfort us, to encourage us by certain institutions that He has established. He has given us precious tokens. But just as Jesus told the Pharisees that they searched the Scriptures while missing the point of them, so also too many have searched the sacraments — all while missing the whole point.

Jesus is here. He is in the body, and you, that body, are the bread. You receive the bread, and you give yourselves back to one another (in all affection), because you too are bread. You consume and you have the privilege of being consumed. This is not put before you as a mystery in metaphysics. It is the way all healthy relationships work. And the Lord's Table here is covenantal *relationship*.

So come, and welcome, to Jesus Christ.

MORNING ☼ A RITUAL, NOT A ROUTINE

The Supper of the Lord is a ritual that knits us together. We come here, week after week, to worship the Lord — to confess our sins, to sing His praises, to hear His Scriptures read aloud, to hear his Word preached and proclaimed, and to sit down with Him at Table.

Some of you may not have known what you thought of weekly communion when we first went to that practice. Some of you may not know what you think of it now. But all of you, if you are visiting another church, and the service does not end with communion, feel like something is missing.

Now this will happen with any custom — it need not be a sacramental custom. But when a sacrament is involved, it is important for us to realize that there is a covenantal aspect to it all.

This means that if we are not careful, we could come to miss something we have not really taken care to understand in the first place. This is a time in the service where we are privileged to undertake, yet again, a covenant oath. We are bound to the Lord, and He to us, and this covenant is renewed as those bonds are strengthened, cinched, worked tighter. As we do this, it is paramount that we *know* that we are doing it. Do not do it thoughtlessly, or lightly. You children, who are growing up with the privilege of coming to the Table — you are not being taught to take it lightly or as a routine. You are being taught to not take it lightly. You are being nourished to enable you to not take it lightly.

So come, and welcome, to Jesus Christ.

EVENING ◐ HONESTY AT THE TABLE

The central thing we need in the presence of God is honesty, and we cannot have it apart from Jesus Christ. Jesus was the only honest man to ever live, and unless we come to the Father through Him, we will never come honestly at all.

When we present ourselves to God in the name of Jesus, His obedience is reckoned as ours. This is our justification, and it can never be improved upon. Regardless of what kind of week you had — whether it was wonderful or horrible — your approach to God next Sunday in the name of Jesus will not be any better or any worse. The plea that we make is the perfections of Christ, and His perfections do not need to be improved upon.

But God wants us to grow in this life, day to day, and this is the process of our sanctification. It is here that our honesty can grow and flourish. We can become more clear-headed about our relationship to God as we practice simple honesty before God.

When we come to the Table honestly, this means that our conversation here is not stiff, stilted … dishonest. We can simply sit and eat, enjoying the fact that we have been invited to do so. Table fellowship is a wonderful form of fellowship, but it requires more than a simple physical presence. Judas was *present* at the Table when the Lord instituted this meal.

This is not what you have been doing. When you have sinned, you have acknowledged it honestly, repented of it sincerely, and answered the summons to come to this meal.

So come, and welcome, to Jesus Christ.

MORNING ☼ RECEIVING THE GIFT OF BEING ABLE TO GIVE

We have been talking about provision — here in this Supper God provides for His people. But God provides for us in His way, and not in the way that we might anticipate.

When God gives, He gives gifts that continue to give themselves. He doesn't give the kind of gift that makes its way to a closet in a back room somewhere. God's gifts, being what they are, are living and active, and they continue to give, continue to multiply.

We see that here in this Supper. God is the one who provides the wine and bread. But in giving us the bread, for example, He is giving us ourselves because we are the bread. And when He has given us ourselves in the bread, He expects us to imitate, which means to break the bread and give it to another.

This meal is God's provision for us, certainly, but it is also God's provision for the saints *in* the saints, and *through* the saints. This is the pattern — God became a man who was the bread from heaven. He took the bread, which was Himself, gave thanks and broke it, and gave it away. When we receive this gift, we are receiving the enormous privilege of doing exactly the same thing.

When you look at the bread in your hand, you need to think on these things. You consume because someone else was consumed. You consume, and so you recognize the honor you have in giving yourself away to be consumed. There is no way to really receive from God without giving.

So come, and welcome, to Jesus Christ.

EVENING ◐ REPLACE THEM ALL WITH DIAMONDS

I have preached often that God provides for His people. Open your mouth, God says through the psalmist, and "I will fill it." As parents and grandparents, it delights us when a child in a high chair sees the spoon and dutifully opens his mouth. God delights to feed us. He delights to provide for us. He is the one who sets abundance around us on every hand, and we are the ones who struggle far too much as we try to understand how intent He is on giving to us, and how doubly intent He is on teaching us how to receive what He gives in all gratitude.

Unbelief in the Scriptures revolves around the strange inability we have to believe that God is going to be good to us, provide for us, and give to us what He promised to give. Even when God calls us to give something up for His sake, it is always because He intends to give us something far more valuable in its place.

Now for many Christians, this meal has come to symbolize the times when God takes things away from us, or we voluntarily surrender them. We think that piety is expecting the hard things with a resigned dread, instead of looking to God with joyful expectancy. But God intends good for you, and not ill. He meets with us at this Table in order to nourish us, strengthen us, and establish us.

And whenever He makes you let go of what you have in your fist, it is because you have nothing but pebbles from the gravel in your driveway. He intends to replace them all with diamonds.

So come, and welcome, to Jesus Christ.

MORNING ☼ HIS NAME IS PROVISION

God is the one who provides for His people. Jesus told us not to worry about clothing, because God was thoughtful enough to clothe the flowers of the field. He taught us not to worry because God took care of all the animals. Jesus taught us, in our central prayer, that we are to ask Him for our daily bread. And the provision of bread really is the central provision — without food and without nourishment, we all would perish.

Food is the central provision, and this spiritual food and drink here is the standing memorial to the God who provides. You assemble, you gather your families, you come — and the food is simply here. Now God uses means, here as everywhere else, and we are grateful to those who work to prepare it. But God provides.

All human existence is conducted in uncertainty. Sometimes we know about the uncertainty, and other times we foolishly don't. But throughout our lives, God is always certain, always sure, and always there.

Will God provide for us? Will God take care of us? Whenever you have come to this Table, He has always been there. His food has always been present. How would He not provide? His *name* is Provision.

So come, and welcome, to Jesus Christ.

EVENING ◐ FREE AND FULL FORGIVENESS

As we have often told you, the designated time for confession of sin is not here at this Table. If you are walking with the Lord, you will confess sin whenever you commit it, and put it right with anyone you need to put it right with immediately. As we all need reminders to do this diligently, we have a time set aside for weekly confession at the beginning of the service. This Table, at the conclusion of the service, was not designed to serve as a time of morbid introspection.

But what of those who do not confess their sins appropriately? Week after week, they come to this Table without having prepared themselves. What happens to them in that case? Though the Table wasn't designed to foster introspection, it does have a feature that deals with those who refuse to examine themselves appropriately.

Moses warns Israel that their sin will find them out (Num. 32:23). This Table is a time of nourishment for the faithful. But for those who are not dealing with secret and hidden sin appropriately, it is a time of manifestation. This is why many Corinthians had taken sick, and had died. This Table brings things to light. Heaven and earth meet in this meal, just as they do in the great day of judgment, and this means that God is in the process of bringing all things to light. He does this inexorably and in accordance with His covenant word.

So whenever those with a double life partake of the bread and wine, it is a time of unfolding secrets. That money taken from your employer and never put right, a pattern of hidden homosexual sin or secret infidelity of other forms . . . all are being brought to light. Regardless of what we *think* we are doing here, to partake in communion is to objectively ask God to bring the hidden things to light. And He consistently answers whether or not we know we have asked and whether or not we would like His agenda. But this need not be grim news. It is, in fact, *gospel*. When God brings sin to light, there is an opportunity for free and full forgiveness.

So come, and welcome, to Jesus Christ.

MORNING ☼ LETTING THE WINE AFFECT US

The first mention of wine in the Bible is on the occasion of Noah's drunkenness. The last mention of wine in the Bible is in the context of a condemnation of Babylon's luxuriousness. It is not really surprising that many Christians have come to regard wine with suspicion. Other drinks are safer, less wild, less susceptible to dangerous corruptions. In other words, other drinks are less like the gospel.

In the message of the death, burial, and resurrection of Jesus, and in the declaration that He, the risen one, is now at the right hand of God the Father, we have massive scope for misunderstanding, abuse, confusion, and more. The gospel is a lot like wine—*potent*.

We come to this Table every week, not to domesticate it, making it more like our mundane selves, but rather so that it would make us potent. God gives us the wine of the new covenant to drink, so that *we* would be transformed, not so that it would be.

Some might want to say that the wine of the new covenant is automatically safe, that it is not possible to get drunk on it. But the behavior of the Corinthians tells us otherwise on one level, and all the strange doctrines that have spun out of the Christian faith on another level says the same. But the solution to this problem is not to retreat to a watered down gospel, or a grape juice gospel. The solution is to accept from this meal what God is giving us in it—nothing more and nothing less.

So come, and welcome, to Jesus Christ.

When we come to this Table, the Bible teaches us that we are *partaking*. In Scripture, this partaking is not a divvying up, after which each person gets a distinct and separate piece. Partaking is a movement of union and communion.

The idolater partakes of the idol when he eats the food offered to that idol in worship (1 Cor. 10:20). The Levitical priests who ate the sacrifices are described as men who partook of the *altar* (1 Cor. 9:13). And we are described as being one because we partake of one loaf (1 Cor. 10:17). This means that partaking connotes sharing, union, closeness, and identification.

And this happens throughout the world — it happens everywhere. A special miracle of transubstantiation is not necessary in order to make it happen. If an idolater ate meat that had been sacrificed to Athena, it was not necessary for the meat to be transformed into the demon in order for the worshiper to be a partaker with demons. In the same way, it is not necessary for anything to happen to the bread and wine in order for us to partake of Christ as we eat and drink. This meal is not a miracle in the midst of a mundane world. Rather it is covenantal union with Christ in a world where covenantal union with *something* is inescapable. It will either be the Table of the Lord or the Table of demons. It is covenantal partaking, covenantal union, which is ordinary. It would take a miracle for this not to happen.

So this is the Table of *Christ*. The fact that you are here means you are forsaking every other religious table.

So come, and welcome, to Jesus Christ.

MORNING ☼ THE LAST SHALL BE FIRST

One of our names for the establishment of this sacramental meal is the Last Supper. We call it this because it was the last meal that Jesus shared with His disciples before His arrest and crucifixion. But the name is more evocative than being just a reference to the chronology of Christ's life.

It was the meal at which He established this ritual, and so in that sense, of course, it was the First Supper. And He established this meal before He was crucified, and so what He did looked forward to the reality, in much the same way that the Old Testament sacrifices did. Our meal here is privileged — because Christ has died and has been raised up again — and we have the vantage of being able to look back at the once for all sacrifice, the sacrifice that was made at the end of the ages.

And of course, that is another sense in which we can refer to this as the Last Supper. The incarnation of Jesus, His death and resurrection, were an intrusion of the Last Things into the middle of history. He is the first fruits of the Last Day, which means that this is yet another way in which the last has become the first.

And so, in this meal we anticipate the consummation of all things. We are privileged to eat this meal, the last meal in the world. We are being given the last cup of wine, the last piece of bread, and this momentous meal is served to us in time and in history. In this way, each week we mark our faith in the fact that the end of the world defines the reality of it.

So come, and welcome, to Jesus Christ.

When the Lord gave food to Adam, He gave him the world as food. Only one tree was off limits, and every other tree in the garden, and from there to the world, was given into his hand. But after the arrival of sin, and the great judgment on sin that we call the flood, the picture was a little different. Noah was another founder of the human race, in a way quite similar to Adam. Everyone in this room is descended from Noah as much as from Adam, and so we should note how God gave food to Noah.

In his salvation, God provided food for Noah inside the ark when the entire world outside was under cataclysmic judgment. There was no food outside the Church, but there was food and to spare within. The apostle Peter tells us that the ark was a type of our salvation, and so here we are inside the ark, with judgment outside (1 Pet. 3:21). The food is here. We have taken refuge here, and God will preserve us. But remember that God has not shut us up into a box so that we might live here forever and ever. There comes a time when the flood is over, and the ground outside is dried, the Church opens up so that the world might be settled again.

This food is for the world, but not for the world as it is. The gospel declares that sinners must do two things — repent and believe. That repentance must come first so that it is lawful to offer the bread and wine. That repentance means that the judgment is complete in Christ, and that all foods are lawful, beginning with the tree of life, beginning with the bread and wine.

So come, and welcome, to Jesus Christ.

MORNING ☼ ROUND ABOUT

Keeping the Supper faithfully is not a matter of ginning up holy feelings. It is not a matter of introspection, figuring out a hundred and one reasons why you ought not to be partaking. Neither is it a summons to theological logic-chopping, where you try to figure out what happens to the bread and why, and what happens to the wine and how.

This moment is the time that God has assigned for us to be knit together with our brothers and sisters, not only here, but throughout the world, and throughout all history. We are called to discern the body as we partake. Through that participle, in the act of partaking, we discern that we *have* a people, and that for these others, we *are* a people. The principle of organization is the mysterious call of God, and most emphatically not the sort of friends we would naturally have picked on our own.

Look around you. The glory of the Christian church is that it is not a club, where the members are bound by a shared interest in books, or quilting, or hunting. Those are all wonderful in their place, but they are too *small* for this. That which binds us together is not a subset of our lives, but is rather the principle of life itself. We are a subset of that life.

This is what we are enacting as we partake of the bread of life, and as we drink the wine of the new covenant. The life is in the blood, recall, and so we are coming here to that life. Life encompasses us round about, and we have all been quickened, brought to life. *That* is our shared interest.

So come, and welcome, to Jesus Christ.

If a misguided father, in the interests of preventing pride from taking root in his children, offered criticism after criticism, the results would not be what he anticipated. Instead of rearing humble children, he would bring up neurotic and jumpy children. "What is it *now*?" would be their constant internal question. But another father who praised, honored, accepted, delighted in, and rejoiced over his children would be bringing up secure children, children who are able to forget themselves in the interests of others.

Now we are at the Lord's dinner Table, where many of these conversations take place. What kind of father do you think He is? Which father represents our heavenly Father best? Far too often we slander Him, as though He were like the first father in the illustration. We pretend that we are being severe with ourselves, when we are actually misrepresenting Him.

You are here, at His Table. Forgiveness has been declared over you. You have heard the Word proclaimed. You have sung psalms and hymns to Him, and all of it has been received in the Lord Jesus. You are seated here, and you are *welcome* here. You are seated in the company of the blessed, and you are not the odd man out. This is your home. This is your meal. These are your people. He is your God. Quiet your fears. Set them aside. My commission as a minister is to tell you to set them aside. Did God pay the price He paid in order to be able to bring you in here to snarl at you? Of *course* not. Come and welcome.

So come, and welcome, to Jesus Christ.

MORNING ☼ AND RATHER STARVE THAN COME

One of our hymns laments the choice that many others have made with regard to the Lord's Table.

> Why was I made to hear Thy voice,
> And enter while there's room,
> When thousands make a wretched choice,
> And rather starve than come?

The choices men make are odd, and it is even stranger that if God had not turned our hearts back to Him, we would have made the same choice that they have made. They would rather starve than partake of a certain kind of food. They want food, certainly, but on their terms, their way. This is the mystery of lawlessness; this is the reason that sin makes no sense.

And so we need to remember the grace of God at this Table, and how it is offered to us in two respects. First is the grace offered to you on the Table — the wine for cleansing and the bread for salvation. This food is for all who ask for it. This is where God has shown additional grace to us — He gave us the grace of wanting to partake of this.

He gave us the food, and He gave the ability to eat, and the desire to have it. This is all the grace of God, every bit of it. There is nothing here that was not given to you as a gift. And if as a gift, then never boast over the privilege of coming while others starve. That was your desire too, before God gave you a different heart. And recognition of this is why we see it truly as a thanksgiving meal.

So come, and welcome, to Jesus Christ.

EVENING ◐ CONSUMPTION AND THE COVENANT

Our nation's public economists usually refer to you in your capacity as consumer. This is in contrast to previous and wiser eras, when citizens were thought of as producers, and as savers. But we have departed from the way, and when disaster strikes, one of the things we think to do, is spend our way out of it. Republicans want to spend our way out this way, and Democrats that way, but we all think that consumption is king. Our understanding of consuming has become deranged.

But this is not because it is bad to consume. Your fundamental identity is wrapped up in what you consume. Here, at this Table, you assemble weekly to consume an oath, to drink a covenant. The issue is therefore an inescapable one—the question is not *whether* you will be a consumer, but rather *what* you will consume.

The world entices you to consume according to their principles, according to their law, according to their covenants. You must not. Rather, you come here in order to be disciplined according to the words of our Lord, and to have your desires and wants tamed and regulated by what you eat and drink here.

Learn consumption here. As you have done so, you will be equipped to behave like a sane person when you go out into the market. You will no longer spend as those who are without God and without hope in the world. When you learn to consume rightly, you produce more than you consume, and you do so out of love for others. When Jesus fed the multitudes, they always wound up with more afterward than they had when they started. He is doing the same thing here with us now.

So come, and welcome, to Jesus Christ.

MORNING ✺ FAITH NEEDS TO BELIEVE

We partake of this Supper every week. But we do not do this because we have some superstitious attachment to it. We do not believe that God wants us to shuffle along, looking down, our sight rising no higher than the lip of the Table. No, we are Christians, and we are called to set our minds and hearts in the heavenly places, where Christ is.

We do not partake of a dead Christ with a dead faith, in a dead ritual. No — the Spirit has gathered all of us up, and He has lifted us up into the heavenly places. We partake of a living and glorified Christ, and we do so with a faith that is living, just as He is living. The mouth that receives Christ is the mouth of faith, not the mouth that unbelievers have together with you.

But if it is the mouth of faith, and if it is the Spirit who takes us up into the heavens, then . . . the question might arise . . . why do we need the bread and wine? Why gather at a Table if faith enables us to gather in Heaven? Well, remember that faith is not an active agent all by itself. Faith responds to what God has said. Faith believes it, going beyond the appearances.

And God has said that we are to meet Him by remembering the sacrifice of Jesus through the instruments of bread and wine. To say that faith doesn't need these things is to say that because faith is faith it doesn't need to believe, which is absurd. In order to be true evangelical faith, we must not fall short of what God has declared, and we must not overshoot it in our own carnal zeal.

So come, and welcome, to Jesus Christ.

We have gathered at this Table from many different households, and we represent many different eating habits. But once a week, we all gather together in order to eat and drink the same thing, and do so in the same way, according to the same custom.

In Christ, this is a meal of shared love, and it reminds us regularly that we are not to come into conflict over food in the rest of our lives. We are not to collide because someone else took what we wanted. We are not to collide because someone served us something we didn't want. We are not to collide when other people eat things we find objectionable, whether those things are cardboard muffins on the healthy end or deep-fried twinkies on the other end. We are called to love each other, and we take a weekly oath that we shall do so. This oath, coming as it does in the form of food, has a particular application to disputes over food.

Remember the words of the apostle: "He that eateth, eateth to the Lord, for he giveth God thanks; and he that eateth not, to the Lord he eateth not, and giveth God thanks" (Rom. 14:6). That other person's presence *here* gives you a basis for bearing with them *there*.

Ironically, it is here, at the Table of the kingdom, that we learn one of the fundamental lessons of the kingdom. "For the kingdom of God is not meat and drink; but righteousness, and peace, and joy in the Holy Ghost" (Rom. 14:17).

So come, and welcome, to Jesus Christ.

MORNING ☼ THE FIRST MEAL

The Lord's Supper is the first meal and it is the last meal, because it is the meal that memorializes the Lord Jesus, revealed to us as the Alpha and the Omega, the First and Last. The first food available to our parents in Eden was eaten in communion with God, particularly the tree of life, identified with our salvation throughout Scripture—and Jesus Christ is our salvation. The first food eaten on the moon was a communion meal, taken there by Buzz Aldrin. And the first real food that you ever received was bread and wine, the meal that is before you now.

The last meal is the wedding supper of the Lamb, and we are all looking forward to that as the culmination of all meals. This meal, taken in time and in history, embodies the reality of already/not yet. God has given us Himself in salvation, and we long for the day when He will reveal Himself in our salvation.

But from beginning to end, that salvation will be accompanied by, and escorted by, food and drink. God does not offer you a detached or abstracted salvation. He saves His people in time, in history, and through the Incarnation He has declared Himself—beyond any possibility of refutation—to be the material God. God created stuff. He pronounced it all good. James tells us that the body without the spirit is dead; he does not tell us the spirit doesn't need the body—just the reverse. So come in faith, remembering that your faith quickens what is happening in this material realm. And since we are to live by faith from first to last, we come to this meal by faith, from first to last.

So come, and welcome, to Jesus Christ.

EVENING ◐ SUPERSTITION AND THE SUPPER

What is superstition? In our secular age, it is common to define it as the religious practices of someone else, practices that you don't believe in. But this is too easy.

Superstition should be best understood as any devoted spiritual practice that is mindlessly conducted and pursued, and yet tenaciously practiced. False faith would be when someone genuinely thinks about what he is doing, and really believes it, but his faith is placed in the wrong object. True faith is when the heart and mind are right, and the object of faith is faithful and true.

All three of these have been seen as approaches to the Lord's Supper. There have been those who come to this Table, and they do so while on autopilot. This is just what you do, don't ask me why. An example of false faith would be when someone comes to the Table, really and sincerely believing that the bread literally turns into the body of Jesus. He is still wrong, but his faith is real. We should not adopt the common practice around us of dismissing as superstitious any faith that we do not share. This is so that we can make helpful distinctions, and not so that we can agree with what we disagree with.

True faith understands that God has promised to meet us here, and the way we "show up" is by faith. Of course, we have to be physically present, but that is not sufficient. We show up to be blessed by God when we come here believing His Word, His gospel, His promises.

When we look at the doctrinal divisions in Christendom, we need to recognize that there is superstition on "our side" of these divisions. We have people coming on cruise control also. So we should want to come in such a way as to testify to the world that this is true Life, and we are coming to it as a true people.

So come, and welcome, to Jesus Christ.

MORNING ☼ GRACE BOTH LIFTS AND LOWERS

We have reminded you many times that this is a Table of thanksgiving, and not a table of introspection. We have come here to rejoice and be glad, not to mope in the presence of our heavenly Father.

This is not because there is no moral danger for us. Of course not. But the danger is away from the presence of the Lord. When we are with Him, as we are here, what does He do? In Psalm 36, God promises to feed us. "They shall be abundantly satisfied with the fatness of thy house; and thou shalt make them drink of the river of thy pleasures" (Ps. 36:8). Earlier in the psalm we are told that this occurs when we are under the shadow of His wings. We are protected here, as we trust Him. Later in the psalm, the prayer is that the foot of the proud be kept away. As we rejoice in God's presence, under His protection, we can afford to be glad. We can afford to rejoice.

We do not taunt the proud adversary because we have anything over him in our own names. Certainly not. As John Newton put it, "with salvation's walls surrounded, thou mayst smile at all thy foes." You may only smile at the proud and insolent who would besiege you if you know yourself to be standing on salvation's walls, and you know for a fact that they are walls *that you did not build*.

Grace is the only thing that can exalt and humble a sinful man at the same time. Every carnal alternative will either grind you down or puff you up. But *grace* . . .! Grace humbles and exalts. And grace offers you bread and wine.

So come, and welcome, to Jesus Christ.

EVENING ◐ THE SPIRIT WENT OUT OF HER

The Queen of Sheba had heard about Solomon's glory, and so she came to visit him in order to see if it was true. The fact that she came a great distance means that on one level, she certainly wanted the reports to be true. And yet she was resistant. It is very interesting to note what persuaded her.

"And the meat of his table, and the sitting of his servants, and the attendance of his ministers, and their apparel; his cupbearers also, and their apparel; and his ascent by which he went up into the house of the LORD; there was no more spirit in her" (2 Chron. 9:4).

The way the Israelites ate, the way they sat, the way Solomon's ministers performed their jobs, the way they dressed, the way the cupbearers behaved and dressed, and the way Solomon worshiped — all this did her in. There was "no more spirit in her," it says.

One of the things we should be longing for is a reformation and revival, the kind that thoroughly demoralizes nonbelievers. Everything about us will be involved, down to the way we dress, but note here the centrality of worship. The list of things that affected the queen in this peculiar way culminated in the way Solomon ascended into the house of the Lord.

Take all of this. There is no Table like this one. The cupbearers who bring you the wine of the new covenant are discharging their responsibilities in a way that God can use to declare His wonders abroad. We have ascended into the house of the Lord, and we are in His presence now — not only worshiping Him, but also communing with Him, and partaking of Him. There is nothing like this, anywhere in the world. To see it, you have to be taken up into the heavens, and you have to see with the eye of faith.

So come, and welcome, to Jesus Christ.

MORNING ☼ SIN CRUSHED AS WELL AS BROKEN

We know that God breaks all idols, and He breaks all sin, and He breaks it for our salvation in the body of Christ. And so we, as that body, are enabled by God's grace to partake of His forgiveness.

The wine is made by crushing the grapes. This kind of crushing is an image in Scripture of two things. The first is that crushing grapes is an image of great wrath and judgment (Rev. 14:18). The second is that it is the occasion of great harvest home rejoicing (Num. 13:23). We find both of these elements present in our commemoration of this sacrament.

This cup, we are told, is the cup of the new testament, and that new testament is the testament of Christ's blood. But Christ's blood was shed for sin, and it was shed under judgment (Heb. 9:14). And yet we are privileged to drink it in a Eucharistic celebration. Both elements are present; both elements are here.

Without the cross there can be no resurrection. Without the resurrection, the cross is nothing but an agony of despair. Without judgment for sin, celebration is hollow, empty, vain. Without celebration, sacrifice is hollow, empty, and vain.

This means that as we celebrate, we should be filled with solemnity, knowing the penalty that Jesus paid so that we could rejoice before Him and with Him. And as we consider His sacrifice on the cross, we should look forward, as Jesus Himself did, to the joy set before Him. And so we come in faith, knowing that our sins are broken forever in the bread, and our iniquities are crushed forever in the grapes. God has truly been good to us—come therefore with gratitude.

So come, and welcome, to Jesus Christ.

EVENING ◐ DEFERENCE OF DEATH

In Matthew 20, the mother of the sons of Zebedee came to Jesus and asked if her two sons could sit on Christ's right hand and left in the kingdom. He asked if they could participate in His baptism, and if they could drink the cup that He would drink. He replied that they would in fact do so, but that to apportion the places to His right and left was not His to give. When the other disciples heard this, they were indignant — and it was presumably not because they were filled with humility and were upset at the arrival of pride in the hearts of two of them.

Jesus takes the occasion to teach them that authority in the kingdom of God did not work the same way that striving for power works in the world's way of doing things. Remember that He said that they would in fact share in His baptism, and they would in fact drink from His cup. But they clearly had not done so yet. That is because His baptism is His death, and when we are baptized we share in His death. His cup is the cup of the new covenant, and it is a cup of death, a cup of blood. What does it mean for us to partake of Him? It means that we die. Among other things, this Supper means that we die to all angling, striving, grasping, and positioning. We die to it, which is not the same thing as taking that self-aggrandizement and trying to slow it down a little bit. Death slows it down completely.

This means that we partake of His death. It means we are called to share in His sufferings. And it means that this observance of the sacrament is a deference of death, an observance of organized deference to one another — *love.*

So come, and welcome, to Jesus Christ.

MORNING ☼ CUP AND PLATTER

When the Lord Jesus is chastising the Pharisees for their hypocrisy, He speaks to them with the image of a cup and platter (Matt. 23:25–26). We would do well to apply what He said to our use of the cup and platter here.

He said that the scribes and Pharisees liked to make a fair show on the outside, but on the inside they were full of extortion and excess.

When the Lord's Supper is observed rightly, what is on the inside of the cup? It is the blood of Christ, the blood that cleanses from all sin. What is on the platter? It is the true bread of heaven, the body of believers, with Christ as the true head.

Cleansing the inside of the cup is not accomplished by introspection. Cleansing the platter is not brought about by self-accusation. Sinners can only be cleansed because Christ their Savior died — and at this meal, we are confronted with that reality. Christ bled. Christ was broken. This broken bread cleanses the platter. This shed blood cleanses the cup. Look to that reality and respond in faith.

Responding in faith is different than acting as though you had faith by magnifying what you say is happening in this meal through various forms of ceremonial pomp. Gold cups don't automatically have the blood of Christ in them. Silver platters don't automatically have the body of Christ on them. Our observance here is dignified, but we want it to be simple. We want your faith to be simple at the same level.

So come, and welcome, to Jesus Christ.

We worship and serve Christ, who is the Incarnation of the God of all grace. We come to partake of Him here, and this means that we come to be partakers of His grace.

Now this Table is all grace. The cup is a cup of blessing, and the bread is the bread of life. But this creates a question. How can a Table of blessing bring destruction? Why had some of the Corinthians died as a result of their sacrilegious approach to the Table?

When grace is despised, it does not cease to be objectively grace, but it does cease to be experienced *as* grace by the one who despises it. When someone approaches God in unbelief, his unbelief is superficially confirmed to him — what he does not believe the sacrament to be (the blessing of God) is confirmed in his experience. He does not believe it to be the goodness of God, and for him, it is not. This does not justify his unbelief, for the gracious nature of the sacrament remains.

For those who come in faith, the reverse is true. In his *Institutes,* John Calvin points out that sacraments effect the blessings they signify, but they only do this for those who come to them in genuine faith. If you chew the sacrament with your teeth only, then you are not partaking of the blessing. You must chew and swallow Christ in Your hearts. You don't do this by any means other than what God has set forth in His Word — simple, unadulterated *faith.*

So come, and welcome, to Jesus Christ.

MORNING ✹ NEVER WALK AWAY

In the two sacraments, God presents spiritual realities to us in physical form. Unbelief looks at the physical form only — whether water, bread, or wine — and faith looks upon Christ. Some forms of unbelief look at the physical form only and deny that Christ has anything to do with it. Other forms of unbelief identify Christ with His sacramental clothing. Both are wrongheaded.

In the sacraments, there is the reality and there is the sign. The water, the bread, and the wine are the signs. Christ is the reality. Now some, wanting to be wiser than God, say that they would choose Christ, and therefore reject the signs — but these are the tokens that Christ has given to us. Christ has promised to meet us here.

There is only one way to tie the reality and sign together. This way is true, living, evangelical faith. Without faith, we have nothing here but covenantal judgment. In faith, we have a sacramental bond that holds reality and sign together. Everything else is idolatry — either crass superstition that bows before created things, or philosophical idolatry that wants to traffic in mere ideas.

Christ is in the water, Christ is in the bread, Christ is in the wine. As a minister of Christ, I have spoken these words, and Christ is in the words as well. It is not our portion to dissect these realities, trying to separate what God has joined together. We cannot do it successfully, and to the extent that we have done it (in our own hearts and minds), all we have done is walk away from Christ. So don't walk away — sit and eat. Sit and drink.

So come, and welcome, to Jesus Christ.

In the Lord's Supper, God meets with us in very ordinary things. It is the same with the sacrament of baptism — what is more plentiful than water? Bread is common, a staple. And wine is abundant — virtually every human society has rejoiced in that particular gift of God.

So what does this mean? In Deuteronomy, Moses tells the people that the Lord is not up in Heaven out of reach, nor is He across the sea. He is in our hearts, and in our mouths. The gospel is not distant; it is not esoteric. It is not *rare*.

It is striking that God did not give us sacraments to represent our salvation by means of rare elements like gold or diamonds. As tempting as it might be to hide our salvation away in a safe box, God has made a move in the opposite direction. Although we have been redeemed by the blood of Christ, which is more precious than costly jewels, at the same time we have to realize that we are dealing with a different kind of rarity.

What is more rare than gold? Well, to start, seeing water the right way — that's rare. Whenever we see water, we should be reminded of our baptism. And when we think of our baptism, we should see Christ. But we see water all the time — what should follow from this? We live in the midst of glorious wheat fields. What should we see every time we look at them? We should see bread, and in that bread we see Christ.

So water is not rare, and neither is bread or wine. But seeing them rightly, seeing them with true faith, meeting with Christ rightly — that is still rare. And so come, with the prayer that what is now rare may become exceedingly common.

So come, and welcome, to Jesus Christ.

MORNING ☼ THE SPIRIT'S WORK

You have often been reminded that in this meal we partake of the body and blood of Jesus Christ. We do not do this because He is somehow *locally* present on this Table—for He is at the right hand of the Father, and not here. But Paul is very clear that we are made *partakers* of His Table (1 Cor. 10:21). This cup is the *communion* of the blood, and this bread is the *communion* of the body (1 Cor. 10:16). So we know *that* it happens, but how does it happen?

The historic Reformed reply is that we are joined together with Christ, knit together with Him, and joined to Him, by means of the Holy Spirit's work. This is what the Holy Spirit does for us. If a man does not have the Spirit of Christ, then he is none of Christ's (Rom. 8:9). And if Christ is in you, even though your body is mortal (because of sin), the Spirit in you is still life, and communicates that life to you (Rom. 8:10). If the Holy Spirit, the one who raised Jesus from the dead, dwells in you, then He will be engaged in quickening your mortal body (Rom. 8:11). As He does this, He is knitting you together with Christ.

This means that your participation in Christ, and His indwelling of you, is established, strengthened, and completed by means of God's Holy Spirit. The *Spirit* is the one who accomplishes this great *physical* renewal. He is the one who takes all the means of grace that the Father has established, and applies it to you, both body and soul. He uses the ministry of the Word, and the ministry of the sacraments, to grow you up into Christ. So come, therefore, to eat and drink.

So come, and welcome, to Jesus Christ.

The apostle Paul tells us that this bread represents the unity of the body of Christ (1 Cor. 10:16–17). How so? Remember that the Lord's way of unity is one, one divided, and two restored into one. That is what He did in the Garden. Adam was one, then he was divided into two, so that they could then be restored to one. That restoration to one caused a child to be conceived, and again one became two—only this time it was the woman who was divided. And since that time, two have become one, so that one could become two again, and the earth fills with the sons and daughters of Adam and Eve.

The wheat field is filled with countless grains of wheat. They are brought together, ground into flour, and then baked into one loaf. But that one loaf is not a *static* picture of the body of Christ. The loaf is broken into many pieces, and distributed to all of you. As you partake in love for Christ and one another, the many pieces are used to knit you all together into one body characterized by love and harmony. And then you, the one loaf, at the benediction are taken in hand, divided into many pieces *again*, and sent out those doors so that you might become life to the world.

As you depart from here, in order to be consumed for others, those others are delivered from their fragmented and lonely lives, and through the gospel are brought to genuine faith in Christ.

One, many, and then one again. Many become one, so that one may become many. And as God does this, at the end of each round, we discover that the many *this* time are many more than the many last time. This is how the world fills up; this is how the world is blessed. This is God's way, and you, as His people are called to follow His way. So come, partake together so that we might have something to distribute to the world.

So come, and welcome, to Jesus Christ.

MORNING ☼ A PROMISE ONLY GOD CAN MAKE

Every sacrament, by definition, contains and manifests a promise of salvation. That is what a sacrament *is*. The sacrament of baptism contains a promise of salvation at its inception, and the Supper contains a promise of salvation related to perseverance. What God began God will complete. These promises are apprehended with the heart, whenever someone receives them *in faith*.

Faith alone, *sola fide*, is not only alone with regard to works. We are justified by faith alone, but never by a faith that is alone. This is the issue of faith alone related to works, which is an important issue. But there is another sense in which faith is never alone. Faith is never self-originating. Faith is something that is always responsive to something outside of itself that God offers to us. And God offers salvation in two principal places — the first is in the preaching of the Word, and the second is in the presentation of the sacraments. And so baptism and the Supper cannot justify you any more than hearing a sermon can. If you hear the sermon *in faith*, then you meet Christ. If you partake of the bread and wine in evangelical *faith*, then you meet Christ.

Because a sacrament must contain a promise of salvation, it follows from this that only God can institute a sacrament . . . because He is the only one who can promise salvation. This is why there are only two sacraments — if we could promise salvation by ritual means, we could generate as many sacraments as we wanted. But we have no authority to issue promises of salvation. We must be content with the authority we were given, which is the authority to *believe* promises of salvation.

So come, and welcome, to Jesus Christ.

EVENING ◑ JUSTICE, MERCY, AND HUMILITY

Because God is the author of sacraments, He is the one who governs and regulates them. In some matters, He doesn't care how we set the Table — He doesn't mandate a white tablecloth, for example, or silver trays for distribution. He requires that what we do in this regard is filled with reverence and godly awe, but there are various ways in which that can be communicated. He leaves that sort of thing up to us.

What does He require? He requires bread, and He requires it be broken. He requires wine, and he requires that it be blessed wine; He calls it the cup of blessing. He requires the words of institution that I am about to speak, and He requires a response of faith and love from you. He has shown you, O man, what He requires — do justice, love mercy, and walk with humility. All of that is present here.

The cross of Christ was perfect justice and Christ fulfilled the demands of that divine justice by laying down His life on your behalf. Mercy is here as well — this is the new covenant mercy seat. Humility is of course present — the eternal Son of God died on a cross in order to secure your forgiveness, and He died in such a way as to establish the sacrament that is celebrated here, so that you could be reminded, in a glorious and fulfilling way, what kind of Savior you have. Justice, mercy, and humility are all offered. It is no injustice to receive it, when you receive mercy, you also extend it, and it is grievous pride to reject the humility of God.

So come, and welcome, to Jesus Christ.

MORNING ☼ HE WHO HAS A TONGUE TO TASTE

When we say that faith comes by hearing, and hearing by the Word of God, we generally do well at not inserting any portion of the material creation in between Christ and the believing soul. We know that it is the Word preached or written that was the instrument of salvation, but we don't attribute this power to the ink on the page, or to the leather binding of the Bible, or to the mystic quality of sound waves in the air. The gospel is mediated to the believing soul by means of matter, but we know that faith matters — the matter doesn't matter. The fact that it does not matter simply means that it is not the active agent — rather, it is the carrier of God's gracious purposes, received by faith.

In the proclamation of the gospel, grace is communicated to the believing soul by material means just as much as grace is communicated to us by means of the sacramental water, or the sacramental bread and wine. The organ of efficacious reception is always faith, nothing but faith, faith to the end of the world. But how does faith receive something to believe. Sound doesn't travel in a vacuum, and neither does grace.

When a man is deaf, this is because there is something wrong with his ears, and not because he lives in a vacuum. When a man is not blessed in this Supper, it is because grace is blocked by his unbelief, and not because the grace is not extended. In this meal, Christ is offered to all. In a faithful observance of this Supper, Christ is received by the believer. He who has ears to hear, let him hear. He who has a tongue to taste, let him taste.

So come, and welcome, to Jesus Christ.

When we commune with God, it is always because He gives Himself. It is always because He reveals Himself. It is always because He meets with us in accordance with His promises, and it is because we believe those promises.

It is never because we have captured Him. It is never because God was successfully enclosed within a box. He commanded the Temple to be made, and yet the Most High does not dwell in temples made by men. He commanded the sacrifices of the old order, and yet sacrifices and burnt offerings He did not require. He commanded us to honor and revere His Scriptures, and yet when we read them with the wrong kind of heart, they are a barrier to our knowledge of Him.

It is the same here, with the bread and wine. Has God promised to meet us here? He most certainly has. And for those who think that He is contained by these little cups, or that He rests beneath these white napkins, you are missing the point entirely. Not only are you missing the point, you are missing the Christ. Your God is here, but always in accordance with His nature and character, and always as the God of Scripture. The religious wit of man has never figured out how to weave His promises into a net that can catch Him, and make Him do forgiveness tricks for us.

The only cup that really holds the blood of Christ is the cup of true evangelical faith. The only platter that truly holds His broken body is the platter of real faith. So come, commune with your God.

So come, and welcome, to Jesus Christ.

MORNING ☼ TRUE VICTIM

We have gathered here to commemorate the death of the Lord Jesus Christ, the propitiatory sacrifice of the true Victim. We have so much to learn about what He did for us in this that we could spend the rest of lives just trying to figure out how to scratch the surface.

We sometimes drift into thinking that Jesus died as a victim on behalf of all the victims throughout history. But this is one of the notions that He came to crucify. He was the true victim, and He was the only one. He did not die as victim on behalf of all victims. He died as the true victim so that we could be liberated from our perpetual tendency to play victim. Because He died for false victims, knowing what He did, He stepped into the place of the true victim, and He triumphed over that death from within.

There are only two kinds of justification. The first is the kind that God offers us in the cross of Jesus Christ. The second is the kind we offer to ourselves, in our own name. On the one hand, we have excuses, reasons, duties, strivings, exertions, explanations, and shifting. On the other, we have the blood of Jesus Christ. Put another way, we have true justification and we have false justification. True justification is the result of the innocent dying for the guilty. False justification is the result of the guilty pretending that the problem is elsewhere.

You have come to this Table because you have been sealed with the mark of baptism, which obligates you with the most solemn of vows, to look to Christ alone as the only real victim in the history of the world. And so we have come, and so we do.

So come, and welcome, to Jesus Christ.

EVENING ◐ HE KILLED THEIR VIOLENCE

The Lord Jesus died at the hands of violent men, and when He rose, He was delivered from the hands of violent men. This is one of the themes we find in Scripture — God's deliverance of His people from violence (Ps. 18:48; Ps. 140:1–4). This does not require pacifism — God's warriors are never described as violent men. Violence requires injustice.

Now this meal is a commemoration of the violent death that Jesus suffered on our behalf. This is His body; this is His blood — the body and blood of one who was murdered. The murder was conducted by sanctimonious men who made sure everything was entered into the minutes properly, but it was still a murder. When Judas returned the money, they made sure they put the money back in the right account.

When we partake of this meal by faith, we are partaking of all that Christ did on our behalf. One of the things He did was suffer at the hands of violent men, doing so in a way that put their violent and bloodthirsty ways to death forever. By allowing their violence to kill Him, He killed their violence. By partaking of this bread and wine, we are identifying with that victory by faith. This is why this can be a Table of love, communion, fellowship — indeed, why it must be so.

When we eat, we are eating the worst that enmity can do. When we drink, we are drinking what God-forsaken violence thought it could do. But Christ is risen, and love conquered violence.

So come, and welcome, to Jesus Christ.

MORNING ☼ EXTENDING WHAT HE HAS DONE

We considered last week that in His death, the Lord Jesus put all ungodly violence to death. When the lion lies down with the lamb, it will be the outworking of His passion and sacrifice. When they no longer hurt or destroy in all His holy mountain, it will be because of the death He suffered on that small mountain rise called Calvary.

That is what God has done, laying the foundation of all His purposes and plans. But let us speak for a moment about the privilege He has given to us, the privilege of extending His work in the world. We are called and chosen instruments — not for establishing this work, but rather for extending and applying it. Jesus died, and His death was once for all.

But we go out into the world, prepared to die, not because our deaths are foundational to God's purposes, but rather because our readiness to die is His instrument for extending what He has already done. This is why Paul can say that he fills up the afflictions of Christ in his body (Col. 1:24). When Christ cried out that it is finished, the foundational work was indeed finished. But the application work had just started. When we gather around this Table as we ought to do, prepared to overflow with grace to our brothers and sisters, we do so because we are applying the death of Jesus to one another. We are giving it as a gift, and it is, of course, not ours to give, at least not in our own name. But the Lord gave it to us, and He did so with this in mind. So come, partake together.

So come, and welcome, to Jesus Christ.

This is the central meal of history. This is the meal at the world's end, and it is the food that was set before our first parents in the Garden, and which they turned away from in search of their own food. This is the Table at the center. This is the food that teaches us how to partake of all food. This is the drink that quenches our thirst forever, and enables us to drink elsewhere as free men, women, and children.

Idolatry is the attempt to squeeze out of a finite thing what only the infinite can provide. When we turn away from what the infinite God has supplied for us, we are forced to try to get more from the rest of the world than it can possibly provide. This is because God has set eternity in our hearts, and we seek out eternal things wherever we go, whatever we do. If we are out of fellowship with the God who made us, then we are not trying to put a square peg in a round hole — we are trying to draw the infinite out of a finite thing. The only one who could do that kind of miracle is God Himself, and He did it by uniting God and man in one person, the Lord Jesus from Nazareth. And He, the Lord Jesus, communes with us here.

When we grasp this, or rather are grasped by it, we cease trying to get this blessing out of things that do not contain it. To use the example of food only — you cannot get peace with God from fast food, or from healthy food, or from citrus, or from vegetables, or from meat off the grill, or from anything else in your cupboards. When you go to the grocery store, or the co-op, or you order food online, you are not on trial. There is no condemnation. Here, here at this Table, there is peace with God. And when you have eaten the peace offering here in faith, you may take that peace with you everywhere you go. It is yours to keep.

So come, and welcome, to Jesus Christ.

MORNING ☼ THE LORD OF GLUTTONS AND DRUNKARDS

One of the central aspects of the ministry of Jesus — one that is continued here — was the fact that He ate with sinners.

This is actually one of the most striking things about the story that the gospel writers tell about Him. Not only did He eat with sinners, those who had been exiled from the ranks of the pious, He often did so in a celebratory way. Not only did He eat with them, but He failed to require them to maintain an appropriate demeanor for sinners in search of forgiveness. Perhaps we could understand His condescension if He agreed to eat with them while they all sat in the dark, nibbled on a cracker, and had a small glass of tepid water. But no, He ate with them in such a way as to earn for Himself a reputation for being a glutton and a drunkard. The slander was indeed a slander, but it began somewhere. It was not manufactured out of whole cloth.

What we may take away from this is that Jesus is not concerned about what your presence here today will do to His reputation. He is not distressed over the possibility that our sin might contaminate Him. It cannot and will not. As far as that is concerned, He just doesn't care.

In extreme cases, we exclude people from this Table because they are destroying themselves, not because they are destroying the forgiveness that is set before us here. We come because we need to. We partake and are built up and strengthened. We eat and drink, and are identified with Jesus, the one who is willing — by His grace — to be identified with us.

So come, and welcome, to Jesus Christ.

Last week we considered the fact that Jesus would eat with sinners. As we continue our meditation on this, we should realize that this is a simple extension from the fact that He would eat with anybody.

The gospels are full of occasions where Jesus would eat in disreputable ways, and He told a number of His parables to involve meals and/or sinners. The meals are holy, but that does not mean they are cordoned off. The meals are holy, but the guest list sure isn't.

Jesus calls Levi, a low-life tax-collector, to be a disciple, and attends a big blowout hosted by Levi (Mark 2:13–17), and attended by a roomful of his collaborator friends. Jesus feeds the five thousand and the four thousand, and that would have been a mixed crowd for sure (Mark 6:30–44; 8:1–10). As we noted last week, Jesus was accused of being a glutton and a drunkard (Matt. 11:19), and this is not a reputation that one gets from living in a hermit's cave. Jesus even eats with a Pharisee (Luke 7:36–50), and then a disreputable woman comes there to anoint Him. This is just a small sample.

Jesus ate with the downtrodden and outcast. Jesus ate with those who patriotically hated their oppressors. Jesus ate with those oppressors. Jesus would eat with anybody.

This does not mean that you can live any old way you please and come to this meal — but not because you have to achieve a certain status before you come. You can be the worst loser ever and come — just read the gospels. But you cannot come and eat without being fed. And if you are fed, then you will be transformed. This is food for the recovering sick, and not the catered meal right before we hand out the trophies. This food is grace for you, not strict merit to you.

So come, and welcome, to Jesus Christ.

MORNING ☼ JESUS WALKS RIGHT BY THIS

We have been noting that this meal is a meal with Christ and, as such, it is similar to the meals He would eat during the time of His earthly ministry. And one of the characteristics of the meals He had during His earthly ministry is that they drew criticism from the pious.

"And when the scribes and Pharisees saw him eat with publicans and sinners, they said unto his disciples, How is it that he eateth and drinketh with publicans and sinners?" (Mark 2:16).

The publicans were tax-gathering middlemen. They were collaborators with the hated Romans, and they used the political power of Rome to benefit themselves at the expense of their countrymen. They gathered the necessary tax, and anything else they got was theirs. They were turncoats, and their despised status should be no surprise to us. The "sinners" here includes the prostitutes mentioned elsewhere in the gospels and, given the nature of their profession, they would have been well-acquainted with the Roman soldiery. This is characteristic of every occupied country — and the resentments they endured are not surprising.

What is surprising is that Jesus walks right by all this. He sits down and He eats with them. Now this is a rabbi, if we are to believe His Sermon on the Mount, who taught a standard of ethical behavior that was as high as the character of the Father Himself. So how could He eat with such sinners, while teaching this standard of unreachable holiness? Well, He did it because He lived that standard Himself.

So come, and welcome, to Jesus Christ.

EVENING ◐ DON'T BRING THAT TO THE TABLE

We have been considering the Lord's odd choice of table companions. First the religious fussers are upset with Him.

"Then drew near unto him all the publicans and sinners for to hear him. And the Pharisees and scribes murmured, saying, This man receiveth sinners, and eateth with them" (Luke 15:1).

But Jesus is not in the business of stepping into our world in order to choose sides. Notice what He did in the previous chapter.

"And it came to pass, as he went into the house of one of the chief Pharisees to eat bread on the sabbath day, that they watched him" (Luke 14:1).

Not only was He eating with a Pharisee here, but with one of the *chief* Pharisees. Jesus does not choose sides between tax collector and zealot, but calls one of each to His side as part of the Twelve. Jesus does not choose between Jew or Greek, or male and female. He does not choose between centurion and freedom fighter. Jesus did not become man in order to help us with our project, whatever we thought it was.

Jesus is the new humanity, and so this is the Table of the new humanity. Jesus has called us all together—individuals who would have come together for no other reason—and at this Table all our petty differences are told to disappear. How many times when you were a child did your mother say something like, "Don't bring that to the table"? Something similar happens here. Do you have differences? Fine. But don't bring them to the Table. When you are given His welcome, always remember that others are given the same welcome.

So come, and welcome, to Jesus Christ.

MORNING ☼ HE HAS THE SAME PROBLEM

As one writer aptly put it, one of the reasons we go to church is to learn how to love people we don't like very much. And the testing point of this is here, at this Table. When you come, you are coming as a reconciled people, and this means that you are not only reconciled to God, but also to one another. You confess your sins to God at the beginning of the service (or whenever it is appropriate to do so), and you should also have made anything right with your neighbor if there is anything between you.

This does not mean that you have to become fishing buddies with everybody — you cannot be equally close to everyone. Jesus called the seventy, and out of the seventy, He chose twelve, and out of the twelve He was closer to three, and out of that three, He was closest to one. If Jesus had a best friend, there is no reason you cannot be closer to some than others.

So in what sense is this meal a testing point? If there is some sort of friction between you and another, or if you have clashed, put it right, but things are still tense, if your relationship is okay but the situation is not, it must gladden your heart that this other person is coming to the Table. And no, it must not be because you think that the other person really needs it. No, you must be delighted to be there together because you both need it. It must be an occasion of joy to you that the Spirit is in the process of knitting you together with this difficult person. It may be a help for you to recognize that He is doing the same thing for the other person — he also is being knit together with a difficult person.

So come, and welcome, to Jesus Christ.

EVENING ◐ THE BLESSING, THE BREAD, AND THE WINE

In Genesis 14, Melchizedek greets Abraham as he returns from the slaughter of the kings.

"And Melchizedek king of Salem brought forth bread and wine: and he was the priest of the most high God. And he blessed him, and said, Blessed be Abram of the most high God, possessor of heaven and earth: And blessed be the most high God, which hath delivered thine enemies into thy hand. And he gave him tithes of all" (Gen. 14:18–20).

We know from the New Testament that Melchizedek was a type of Jesus Christ. The Lord was to be a priest forever, after the order of Melchizedek — meaning that the Lord was going to do the same sorts of things that Melchizedek.

Note here, then, that Melchizedek brings the bread and wine to Abraham, not the other way around. Note that Abraham was blessed by Melchizedek, and he was blessed in the aftermath of his defeat of the pagan kings. He was also blessed for this in the presence of another unbelieving king, the king of Sodom, one that Abraham refused to receive any blessing from. Abraham spoiled the pagan kings, and gave a tithe of the spoils to Melchizedek. He refused to take any share of the spoils himself — in essence, he forced the king of Sodom to tithe, but did it in a way that would not permit anyone to slander his motives for doing so.

In exchange, he received a blessing, and the bread and wine. And that is exactly what you are receiving.

So come, and welcome, to Jesus Christ.

MORNING ☼ THE DESTROYER AND THE SACRAMENTAL PEOPLE

In his discussion of the Lord's Supper in Corinthians, Paul tells them that there is no temptation overtaking them that was not common to man. The context of this exhortation was the fact that they had apparently been putting on airs, over against the Jews. *We* have been baptized. *We* have spiritual food, they were saying. *We* have spiritual drink as well. But Paul cuts them off — the Jews were baptized also, in the cloud and in the sea. The Jews had a spiritual food, the kind that fell out of the sky. The Jews had a spiritual drink, water that came straight from Christ Himself. Nevertheless, a covenantal judgment fell on most of them, and they were overthrown in the wilderness.

Paul does not tell the Corinthians this because he believes that their situation was completely different. *They* were the ones who thought that. Paul was teaching them that the temptation of despising the sacraments by means of sexual corruption was common to man. The pattern of the wilderness wanderings was given to us so that we would learn that God provides a way of escape. As He did for them, He will do for us.

So the phrase that "no temptation has overtaken you" is not referring to the fact that if you are tempted to be impatient with family members, then you can count on the fact that others have been tempted the same way. That is quite true, but it is not what Paul is talking about here. Paul is saying that the temptation to come to God's Table of grace, and to sneak around on the side as well, is common to man. But God shows us the way out.

So come, and welcome, to Jesus Christ.

EVENING ◐ TO GLADDEN THE HEARTS OF ALL MEN

This is a meal of bread and wine, not milk and honey, but we need to talk about milk and honey anyway. The land of Canaan, the land to be inherited by Israel, is routinely described as a land flowing with milk and honey, and it is the land of blessing, the land of their inheritance, the land of promise. God has expanded all those promises in the time of the new covenant, in which we are living, but He still apportions His promises in accordance with the covenant. After all, we are receiving the promises of the new *covenant*.

Canaan was Israel's land by covenant, and solemn covenants in the Bible are sealed with an oath, and have attendant blessings and curses. The oath entails blessings and the blessings entail an oath. Note what it says in Deuteronomy. Right after the Lord tells them to walk faithfully in all that He has commanded, He tells them this: "Hear therefore, O Israel, and observe to do it; that it may be well with thee, and that ye may increase mightily, as the LORD God of thy fathers hath promised thee, in the land that floweth with milk and honey" (Dt. 6:3).

God's provision of milk and honey are a type of the antitype here before us now. God gives us sustenance, and He does so with an open hand. The type shows us that God's provision of bread and wine, and His Christ by those means of grace, is not a provision of starvation rations. It is not limited; we are not being given thin commons.

So as you eat the bread and drink the wine, remember that far more is involved than just the morsel you possess. This is bread for the world; this is wine to gladden the hearts of all men.

So come, and welcome, to Jesus Christ.

MORNING ☼ TWO KINDS OF KINGS

There are two kinds of kings in Scripture. In the gospel of Mark, chapter 6, we see them placed side by side so that we might see the stark contrast between them.

Herod had a big birthday bash, and the daughter of his illicit wife danced for them all, and Herod promised to give her anything she wanted. What she wanted, instigated by her mother, was the head of John the Baptist on a platter. John had rebuked Herod for taking his brother's wife, and Herodias had it in for him. So this is a great feast, and John's head was brought into the feast — on a dinner platter. This is one kind of king, the kind who devours his people.

Immediately after this, Jesus goes out into a desolate place, and a multitude follow Him there, about five thousand men. He has compassion for them all, for they were like sheep without a shepherd, and it says that He taught them many things. When the day was late, He tells his disciples to feed them. They say they cannot, and so Jesus does. Here is another kind of banquet, with another kind of king. This king feeds the people.

So we have a sumptuous palace, and a king who devours the substance of the people, and we have a desolate waste, and a king who miraculously feeds the people there. We live in a time of grasping and avaricious rulers, who want to take what you have earned. They want to eat you. But we are also Christians, and this means we live in time, and we serve a king, whose intent is to feed you. And here it is, bread and wine, salvation and gospel.

So come, and welcome, to Jesus Christ.

EVENING ◐ NABALS AT THE SUPPER

In 1 Samuel 25, we are told the story of Nabal, Abigail, and David. It was the time of shearing, a time of prosperity for Nabal, a prosperity made possible by David. Nabal was celebrating this by means of a drunken feast. When messengers came from David, seeking to be included in the blessing, Nabal answered them churlishly, and sent them packing. It was only through the intervention of Abigail that David was prevented from slaughtering that whole household in judgment.

In Corinth, the apostle Paul had to deal with a similar situation. There were selfish and wealthy Corinthians who were feasting selfishly, and drunkenly, at the Lord's Supper. When messengers came from the Son of David — those messengers being the Corinthian church members who were without — they were sinfully rejected and excluded. And, like Nabal, some of them paid with their lives.

Meals that are centered on gratitude and thanksgiving — like harvest home festivals and this Eucharistic meal — are never times for grabbing and getting your own. We not allowed to pretend that the blessing we enjoy begins with us. We must not refuse the son of David if the son of David is the one who set the table in the first place. And He has, and so we come with gratitude and a willingness to imitate the attitude that blessed us, which means a willingness to share and to overflow.

Freely you have received, freely give.

So come, and welcome, to Jesus Christ.

MORNING ☼ OVER YOU AND YOUR IRRITATING NEIGHBOR

The first thing that we learn about the Spirit of God in the Bible is that He hovered over matter. God the Father had spoken that matter into existence, and the Word which was powerfully spoken that way was God the Son, God the Word. And then the Spirit came, and He hovered over the spoken text, interpreting it.

God the Father was also the one who uttered the decree that the Son of God would go to the cross and die. When the Lord wrestled with this terrible will in the Garden, the will of His Father, He was wrestling with the Word that had been spoken. But, as was made evident by His glorious submission to it, He also was the Word that was spoken. And even here, no Word is without a Reader, without an interpreter. And it is the Spirit who interprets, and He reads in such a way as to accomplish what He is interpreting.

Jesus died and rose so that we might all be knit together in love. He died so that the disparate and warring factions of a fragmented humanity might be brought together in one new man. And thus it is that the Spirit is active and working in our lives, accomplishing this very thing. We are told in Colossians that our increase in grace is an increase that results from being progressively knit together into the Head, which is of course the Spirit's work. But He does not unite us in some other ethereal region; He does not unite us in the airy fairy upper reaches of the heavenlies. He hovers over matter — over us, over bread and wine, over you and your irritating neighbor.

So come, and welcome, to Jesus Christ.

EVENING ◐ BREAD AND WINE ON THEIR LEVEL

When we bring a baby home from the hospital, even though that baby doesn't speak English, we begin speaking to the baby in English anyway. In fact, we speak English to the baby at the hospital. We do this, not because we are confused on the point, but rather because we understand that this is how a child acquires native fluency. As we speak to the child, we correct mistakes as they arise, but we expect that a large portion of what we say will go right over his head.

When we bring small children to the Table here, we are doing something similar. Our church constitution does not allow parents to simply expect their kids to figure the Supper out by themselves. Some of them might be able to do so, but as they come, we ask parents to regularly and consistently remind the children what this is, what we are doing, and why.

Because we celebrate this meal every week, it is not necessary to say everything about it every week, but it is necessary to go over the basics every Lord's Day, week to week. You should be saying things like, "This bread is for you," "Jesus died for all of us," "This cup is the blood of Jesus, shed for you," "We are all one body," and "The death of Jesus is the salvation of the world."

Keep it simple. Keep it basic. Vary what you tell your children week to week—so that they will grow up into a communicant fluency. We don't want sixteen-year-old kids who have never thought about these things. We want sixteen-year-old kids who have thought about them for fifteen years.

So come, and welcome, to Jesus Christ.

MORNING ☼ IN OR OUT

Our baptized children are welcome to the Table, together with us. But just as there are pitfalls in excluding them, so also there are pitfalls in bringing them. We must always remember that covenantal blessings are received by faith; they are not dispensed automatically.

As our children come, we make necessary adjustments for their frame. God remembers our frame; He knows that we are but dust, and so we should remember and recall our children's' frame. As we do this, we should be consistent across the board.

We don't believe that at the serving of the Supper it is necessary to wake up an infant who is conked out in the car seat, and who just came home from the hospital three weeks ago. A child that age cannot chew bread or drink wine, and in a similar fashion, he cannot mentally chew or reflect. Sleeping through the Supper because you are not yet a month old is not equivalent to excommunication.

But if a child is older, and has begun to notice that the tray is passing by, and that others are partaking, and that he is not, it is not possible to continue that practice without educating him in a false doctrine, or at the very least, a schizophrenic doctrine. The fact that you baptized him says that he is *in*, but the fact that you are withholding bread and wine says that he is *out*. And because he does not remember his baptism, the present lesson is the one that is being impressed on him. So if that is your situation, you are welcome to share the bread and wine with your children.

So come, and welcome, to Jesus Christ.

We want to come to the Table in faith, and not because of superstitious attachment to ritual. At the same time, we don't want to avoid superstitious ritual by avoiding ritual itself—that would be a superstitious attachment to the arid intellectual customs of the modern age.

This stark contrast between faith and superstition can be easily seen in how we bring our children to the Table. If we feel like they have to have the bread and wine regardless of the circumstances, and we are doing it largely because that is what everyone else is doing, then we are not displaying faith—rather we are showing off the fact that herd instincts do not disappear just because you are in church.

If you are here with small children, and you are bringing them to the Table, you are most welcome to do so. But you are also called to acquaint yourselves with the promises of God for your children in the Scriptures. What did God say? Did He invite you, and are you coming for that reason? If so, then the bread and wine are among the most precious shared possessions that two or three generations can possibly share. It is a blessing that is promised to a thousand generations. But if not, then iniquity is visited to three and four generations. That solemn warning is attached to the commandment against idolatry (Ex. 20:5), and bread and wine with no Christ is an idol. Bread and wine just because does more harm than good, as Paul would say.

The bread and wine are here, and so is Jesus. Come to them all, and welcome.

So come, and welcome, to Jesus Christ.

MORNING ☼ OUR NEW BIRTHRIGHT

As you teach your children how to come to this Table, one of the things you should be cultivating is this: we come because we were invited, not because we are entitled.

The invitation proceeded from grace, and is extended to us in grace. We don't deserve any of it. The response we should have, if we "get" this, is a response of gratitude. Grace breeds gratitude.

But one of the temptations that comes from bringing our children to the Table early, as we do, is that it is very easy to take this for granted, assuming that this is just the way it has to be, because it has been this way their entire lives. Just as we take our hair color for granted, or our skin color, or our family name, or anything else we have always had, we take our access to this Table for granted. A sense of entitlement creeps in, and entitlement is always based on pride, comparisons, envy, and ingratitude. It is anti-response to the response of gratitude for grace.

When entitlement takes hold, the idea of church discipline becomes monstrous. To excommunicate someone is, in this thinking, to deny their personhood. Rather, in the biblical framework, it assumes personhood, because covenants are made and kept, or broken, by persons. When an individual is held accountable for his covenant-breaking, this honors the dignity of his responsibilities.

The bread and wine here is all grace, all gift. It is not our birthright in an entitlement sense. It is our new birthright.

So come, and welcome, to Jesus Christ.

EVENING ◐ THE RIGHT WAY TO TAKE GRACE FOR GRANTED

When we come to the Lord's Table week after week it is with the expectation that God will feed us. We come here expectantly, and we are right to do so. We bring our children with us to this meal, and they are right to be expectant also. Food and wine were promised, and food and wine are always provided.

You have been urged before not to take this for granted, and that exhortation is right and good to remember. But there is another sense in which we ought to take God's goodness for granted. What do I mean?

We resist the temptation to take it for granted wrongly when we remember that except for the grace of God, we would not be here at all. We are not here by any autonomous right, resident within ourselves. This is all gift, it is all of grace.

But once the gift is given, once the forgiveness is pronounced, it is not humility to hang back, but rather unbelief. Once the gift is given, we ought not to show up at church thinking that in order to keep from taking this for granted we have to believe that God may or may not bless us here. No. That is not cultivating a good remembrance; that is cultivating a craven spirit. You and your children are children here at the Table. Your place was purchased for you, not by you, but it was in fact *purchased*, and is now yours. You and your children are here at the Table, and are not dogs under the Table, collecting the scraps.

So come, and welcome, to Jesus Christ.

MORNING ☼ NOTHING BUT GIFT

One of the hardest lessons for us to learn is that our salvation is all of grace. We know that it is by grace; we struggle with the idea that it is all of grace. We want to shoehorn something in there that distinguishes one from another. But, though there are distinctions, and sharp ones, between the wise and foolish, the elect and the reprobate, the saved and lost, every last one of those distinctions, as far as the recipients of grace are concerned, is an unadulterated gift from the hand of the Lord. All gift, and nothing but gift.

This teaching is one of the glories of our Protestant heritage. But glory is a tricky thing — beware of taking glory in that kind of glory, because to boast in the grace of God, as though you earned it by understanding it, is the most perverse of all errors. Salvation is all of grace, and this is hard for the fallen heart to grasp. So then, have you grasped it? Well done! What have you earned? You cannot boast in the fact that you understand that boasting is excluded. To fall into this mistake is not to glory in salvation by grace; it is to confuse grace with tiny works, in this case, a tiny doctrinal work.

What does this have to do with the Lord's Supper? One of the blessings we can glean from our practice of admitting little ones to the Table is that we can begin to see how gracious God is to us. We see the nature of grace, and we rejoice to give bread and wine to our children — even though they are just now on the threshold of understanding it. When children are brought to a table, nobody thinks they are earning their keep. Mom and Dad provide what's on the table — kids just show up and receive. That is what we are doing here — showing up in order to receive.

So come, and welcome, to Jesus Christ.

The reason why faith is the grace that God uses to justify us is that faith is entirely about receiving. Hope and love are things that we actively do, and even if we grant that God is the one who gives us this hope and love, it would be easy to get confused. It would be easy to think that God was rewarding us for what we did. Our minds turn in this direction naturally. Faith, by definition, receives.

That is what we are doing here. We are being fed, receiving. We are to do this in faith, receiving the same way. But the impetus to be up and doing dies hard in the human breast, and so many have made the sacraments into pageants that we can contribute something to. And at some level, you can always find an excuse to think this way, if you really want the excuse. After all, you had to get up this morning and drive here in order to receive, and it would be possible to start thinking that preparatory work adds something to the faith that simply receives. But it does not. God wants us to open our mouths, and He will fill them.

The traffic should go the other way. The more you see this Table as simple grace, and your responsibility here to consist of receiving that grace, you will start to see how this receptive attitude is appropriate everywhere else. We are called to live from faith to faith, and the discipline of receiving God's kindness here by faith alone is an important discipline.

And again, the reality of watching how your children receive this goodness is full of important lessons for us all.

So come, and welcome, to Jesus Christ.

MORNING ☼ LIFE FROM BODIES AS GOOD AS DEAD

One of the things that a supper does is that it enables a family to gather around, and to do so as a family. One of the things that a family does in such situations is tell the story of the family. A people are shaped by the narrative that the people tell. Part of this narrative should include how the narrative trails off. Part of the story of God's covenant people concerns how God's covenant people wander off the path. We don't tell you this story because you are not God's people, but rather because you are.

As one theologian has noted, the first generation is characterized by a true and living zeal. The second generation seeks to consolidate the gains of the first, but does so by means of legalistic and oppressive rules. The third generation goes liberal, out of a reaction to the stupidity of a blind conservatism. The fourth generation goes apostate, and it is time for a revival. God specializes in bringing great spiritual vigor out of bodies that are as good as dead.

How do we maintain faithfulness across generations? The first thing to note is that it is accomplished by faith. There is *nothing* automatic about it. In other words, you are not to bring your children to this Table because they are here. You are to bring them because you believe the promises of God. You are not to bring them because you understand what is acceptable at Christ Church. You bring them because you are acting on the basis of the covenant.

So come, and welcome, to Jesus Christ.

In a number of places, the New Testament describes this meal as a feast and a festival, and the saints are told to avoid the immoral men who defile their love feasts (Jude 12; 2 Pet. 2:13). Paul tells the Corinthians to get rid of the yeast of malice and wickedness as they observe the festival (1 Cor. 5:8). So this is a feast.

But some might wonder at the simplicity of the Supper. The apostle encourages us to use small portions (1 Cor. 11:34), which we do, and the Lord instituted the meal with the two very simple ingredients of bread and wine (Luke 22:19–20). What do we have then? We have small portions, with just two elements, and the Scriptures call this a feast. The conclusion we need to draw is that the Bible is teaching us to redefine what true wealth is, what true abundance is. Rather than complaining that this "isn't really" a feast, we need to remember that the Word of God is absolute. *God* defines what a feast is.

The worldlings always think that if one's good, then two must be better. Kings and potentates always like to forget the meaning of words like "excess." They like pomp, they like fanfare, they like arabesques up near the ceiling. But the Lord is of a different mind. He has determined to remake the world, and He has decided to use simpler lines. We are His people, and so He wants us to learn to worship Him, as the early Christians did, with gladness and simplicity of heart. We do not think that a godly observance means that it must be ornate, or complicated, or something like a rococo cornice piece near the ceiling of a renaissance ballroom.

Keep the observance simple — and match it with your heart.

So come, and welcome, to Jesus Christ.

MORNING ☼ FAITH MUST HAVE SOMETHING IN ITS HANDS

When we gather at this Table, we are partaking *of* Christ and we are partaking *with* Christ. The thing that makes this an efficacious blessing is of course faith, but this faith does not work apart from what it was told to do. We were told to eat and drink, and so believing faith eats and drinks in faith. Believing faith does not jettison the bread and wine, and try to gin up the same results by means of naked faith. Naked faith is not what the Reformers meant by *sola fide*, faith alone.

When Moses was told to extend his rod over the Red Sea, he would not have been exhibiting greater faith if he had left his rod in his tent. That would have been unbelief, not greater faith. When Peter got out of the boat to walk toward Jesus, he would not have been exhibiting greater faith if he stayed in the boat so that his faith could walk out toward Jesus. Faith always deals with the appointed objects. Superstition keeps the object, and neglects the faith which we were commanded to have, while super-spiritualism dispenses with the object, and tries to keep the faith going. But this is as unbelieving as the superstition. If God tells you to do something, how could it be super-faith if you refused to do it?

We gather here to eat bread and drink wine. We gather to do this with a particular demeanor, one which God calls us to throughout all Scripture. We are called to assemble in living, vibrant, robust, evangelical faith—a faith which does what it is told, the way it is told.

So come, and welcome, to Jesus Christ.

EVENING ◐ STAYING AWAY FROM ZIBA

We are gathered here at the royal Table of the greater David, the one who has graciously invited us to take this meal together with him. As the Lord Jesus is the one greater than David, so we are like Mephibosheth, descended from an enemy of the king, and with no great power of our own — crippled in our feet. And yet, the kindness of the king is extended to us, and though we were once far away, we have now been brought near through blood of the everlasting covenant.

As Mephibosheth discovered, to his dismay, if there is one thing worse than to be a defeated enemy, it is to be a defeated enemy, graciously forgiven, and then to be accused of treachery in response to that kindness. In his case, the accusation was a false one, but there are two lessons for us to draw from it as we gather at this Table.

The first is obviously that we should refrain from all sin, for what is sin but treachery against the one who has cleansed and forgiven us? He did all this when He didn't have to, and we should always remember this. The other is to guard ourselves from situations that could plausibly result in us being accused of such treachery. There will often be a Ziba around somewhere, ready to take advantage.

This is a Table of thanksgiving. This is a Eucharistic meal. It is our responsibility, therefore, to avoid ingratitude, to give thanks to God, and to look like we are offering and giving thanks.

So come, and welcome, to Jesus Christ.

MORNING ☼ DON'T COME UNLESS YOU WANT SOME

There are many complementary contrasts between the old and new covenants, and one of them has to do with the relative potency of sin. In the old covenant, sin is contagious. In the new covenant, holiness is.

In the old covenant, God's people were consistently warned against coming into contact with the unclean — with dead bodies, lepers, or those with other forms of ritual uncleanness. You might think that when the Messiah came, He would be the only one who was ever able to maintain these ritual purity codes . . . but when He arrived, what He did was go around Israel touching the unclean. This was not because God had changed His mind, and it was now alright to be unclean. No. What had changed was the direction of the flow, the direction of the current. Now holiness is contagious.

Those Christians who put this Table behind a mine field and a ring of concertina wire, fearful that it might be defiled, have missed an important transition in the flow of redemptive history. In the great conflict between unholiness and holiness, the battle has turned. Have you not heard?

Those who fence the Table out of concern that the one who abuses it might be struck down are more biblical. That has happened from time to time. There is never an era where it is wise to trifle with God. But the great danger in coming close to God, or the things of God, is that His white-hot holiness is catching. Don't come unless you want some.

So come, and welcome, to Jesus Christ.

EVENING HAMAN BROUGHT THE TREACHERY WITH HIM

This meal is a royal feast; the Lord Jesus is the king, and He has invited us all to sit down and partake with Him. But the fact that we are seated at this Table should not make us careless of our manners.

Haman was invited to a meal by a queen, and he sat down to eat and drink with a king and queen. But because there was treachery in his heart, he was eating and drinking his own condemnation. Consequently those who come to this meal with covenantal treachery in their hearts should take heed to themselves.

But if you love Jesus Christ, and there is no base treachery, then you should come, take, and eat, and come, take, and drink as though you have been invited, as indeed you have been invited. You should come as though there is no trap — for there is no trap.

The only ones who are caught in a trap at this Table are those who bring their own trap. This cup is the cup of blessing — not the cup of blessing and cursing. This is the bread of Heaven, not the bread of Heaven and Hell. Just as marriage is a blessed institution, so this meal is a blessed institution. Some, because they bring their own traps to their marriages, entangle themselves, but the problem is not the fact that God created us male and female.

In the same way, there is nothing here but blessing, and this blessing is received by faith, simply and honestly. If you want something other than that here, then you are the one that has to bring it.

What shall we say then?

So come, and welcome, to Jesus Christ.

MORNING ☼ A TABLE THAT DISCIPLINES ALL WE BRING TO IT

As you bring your little ones to this Table, take care in two areas.

The first is to remember that you as parents don't hold the power of the keys. This means that you should not be conducting church discipline in your family row, withholding the bread, for example, if your child was being fussy or fidgety earlier in the service. If your child is a communicant, your child is a communicant.

At the same time, just as this weekly observance reminds us to keep short accounts with God and with one another, so also this weekly observance may be revealing to you that you need to get some help in how you love, teach, and discipline your child. If the approach of the Lord's Table reminds you to be reconciled to your brother — as it ought to — so also the approach of the Table ought to highlight that you need some help with some aspects of your parental teaching. If your child is flipping out during the Supper, for example, and doing so routinely, how is that not a disgrace? This Table is a Table of discipline, by definition.

We cannot argue for paedocommunion, urging that little children be allowed to come to the Table that disciplines us all, and then protest if when this discipline starts to take effect. Just realize that it takes effect, in this instance, with the parents. Bringing your children to the Table involves far more than bringing them to bread and wine. It means bringing the whole family, heart and soul, hugs and swats, mom and dad, the whole fam, to the Lord Jesus, and He receives us here.

So come, and welcome, to Jesus Christ.

The Lord comes to us in order to deal with our sinfulness, and our resultant sins. The Lord deals with us; He does not let us continue on as before. But at the same time, God deals us with in surprising ways. He deals with us by means of His grace. He washes us, teaches us, and sets us down at His Table. After all, here we are.

And what does God offer us here? When God gives us food, what is He giving to us? Psalm 36 gives us a glorious picture: "They shall be abundantly satisfied with the fatness of thy house; and thou shalt make them drink of the river of thy pleasures. For with thee is the fountain of life: in thy light shall we see light" (Ps. 36:8–9).

You are welcome here through the grace of God, plus nothing else. But the fact that you earned nothing does not mean that you receive, by grace, barely nothing. The fact that you have no works to offer does not mean that God responds with tiny grace. No, what happens here when you come by faith? You are abundantly satisfied. What is it that accomplishes this? It is the fatness of God's house. You do not come here for tiny rations. You do not come here for thin commons.

And what do you drink from? You drink from the river of God's pleasures, a river that another psalm tells us flows at God's right hand. You drink from a river of infinite pleasure, and you do so in a place of privilege — God's right hand. When God sets the Table, we do not just "get by."

So come, and welcome, to Jesus Christ.

MORNING ☼ REVEALED IN MEALS

The Lord loves to reveal Himself in meals. The Lord loves to feed us with food, which is not surprising, but He also loves to feed our souls when we sit together to break bread. This is true on an ordinary level, in each of our families, and it true here, as we sit down as members of God's family.

"He hath made his wonderful works to be remembered: the Lord is gracious and full of compassion. He hath given meat unto them that fear him: he will ever be mindful of his covenant" (Ps. 111:4–5).

One of functions of a meal is to enable us to tell family stories, so that we remember who we are. In this passage from the Psalms, God makes His wonderful works to be remembered, and we see how He is gracious and full of compassion. And in the next breath, we are being told that God gives us food. When God gives us food, we are reminded that God will always be mindful of His covenant.

The rainbow, the sign of another covenant, was not just so that we would remember that God would not destroy the earth again with a flood — it was a memorial, so that God would remember. Now of course, this is not included in Scripture so that we would conclude that God is absent-minded, and needs to leave little reminders around for Himself. But it is so that we will see that He is remembering.

It is the same with this Supper. It is a memorial. God sees it, and He remembers that you are under the blood, you are accepted, you are forgiven. God sees what He has done for you, and He rejoices in it.

So come, and welcome, to Jesus Christ.

The apostle Paul teaches us that ultimately there are only two tables in the world — the Table of the Lord and the table of demons. These tables are set in a way calculated to exclude one another — it is not possible to eat from both with any kind of consistency.

We see the same thing in the book of Proverbs. Lady Wisdom sets her Table, and Lady Folly sets hers. The whole point of the contrast is to set before the reader a choice, an alternative. Either you go this way, or you go that way. The prophet Elijah on Mt. Carmel speaks the same way — if YHWH is God, serve Him. If Baal is God, serve him. But do not dither in between.

So you are invited here to sit down and taste the bread and wine that the eternal wisdom of God set for you. What He has promised, He has provided. Wisdom in Proverbs sets the Table, and tells us exactly what is there (Prov. 9:2). Folly is a bit more vague, promising only that stolen water and bread eaten in secret will be "delicious" (Prov. 9:17).

Wisdom promises a true banquet, and what she promises is likely in the background when Jesus describes His great feast (Luke 14:16–24). This bread that you can chew is what wisdom tastes like. This red wine gives you the chance to taste, savor, and swallow wisdom.

But these are invitations and promises, and the only way to receive them is to believe them.

So come, and welcome, to Jesus Christ.

MORNING ☼ THE GIFT OF FAITH AND JOY

If there is any good in this life, it is enjoyed as the gift of God. If God gives the gift, and the capacity to do more than just hold that gift in your hand, then joy is possible. This is true of our physical life, our physical food, and it is true of our spiritual life and our spiritual food.

"I know that there is no good in them, but for a man to rejoice, and to do good in his life. And also that every man should eat and drink, and enjoy the good of all his labour, it is the gift of God" (Ecc. 3:12–13). A man should eat and drink, but to enjoy the good of our labor is not ours to command. God must give it. Just as a man might have millions of dollars, and no capacity to enjoy, so also many have come to this Table, with the riches of Christ set before them, and it is all useless because they have no faith. And even that faith is the gift of God, lest any should boast.

What does that faith do? It sees, knows, and understands that God is the giver of all things. This is the first day of the week, the weekly anniversary of the creation of the material universe. This is the day when God first spoke everything that is into being. This is also the day when God recreated the whole universe in the resurrection of Jesus. This being the case, how is possible for us to enjoy anything unless God gives us that gift? The grace of God is here — and in blessing you, the bread is more than just bread, and the wine more than just wine. Your faith receives God's grace.

So come, and welcome, to Jesus Christ.

EVENING ◑ ALREADY ACCEPTED

We gather at this Table because we are accepted in Christ Jesus. We cannot pay in order to come here, and we cannot earn an invitation in any way. This Table is a Table which is based entirely and solely on grace. This is why we can eat and drink—grace from top to bottom, and from front to back.

"Go thy way, eat thy bread with joy, and drink thy wine with a merry heart; for God now accepteth thy works" (Ecc. 9:7).

This is why this is not a place for morbid introspection. We are invited to eat all our bread with joy, and that would certainly include this bread. We are invited to drink all our wine with a merry heart, and so that would clearly include this wine. And why? Because God has accepted us, and has accepted our works. If you are coming here in order to get God to accept you somehow, then you can never know if you are doing things perfectly. But if God has already accepted you, then come with joy, then come with a merry heart.

This is only possible because of the perfect righteousness of Jesus Christ, imputed to us, given as a gift, straight across. God has already accepted you. This is why you can eat this bread and drink this wine with gladness and simplicity of heart. This is why you can come here with nothing to prove, and everything to receive. This is why we can invite you to come to Jesus Christ, and how His grace is offered here.

So come, and welcome, to Jesus Christ.

MORNING ☼ FEEDING ON, EATING WITH

The ancient prophets looked forward to the time of the Messiah, and one of the ways they did this was through the imagery of the messianic banquet. Isaiah in particular describes the mountain of the Lord, on which the best wine would be served, and the table would be covered with the best meat (Is. 25:6).

This glorious time would be brought in by the Christ, and not only would He provide us with glorious food, but also with odd Table companions. One of the ways this is pictured, in Isaiah 11, is that wild animals, that used to feed on one another, would begin to feed with one another. The cow would feed with the bear, and the lion would eat straw like an ox, perhaps sharing it with the ox. In the first century, we saw the beginning of this fulfillment when Jews and Gentiles had the middle wall of partition torn down so that they could share Table fellowship. The final fulfillment of this will certainly include the animal kingdom, but the real work of reconciliation begins where the animal kingdom's troubles first began — with human sin and hostility.

Part of the reason we are enabled to partake of the body of Christ as we eat and drink, and all by faith, is because we are enabled see Christ in the one we are eating with. We eat the body of Christ to the extent, by faith, we are eating with the body of Christ — including that person here you are having an attitude about. We drink the blood of Christ the same way — everyone here is a blood brother or sister. So when I say, come, and welcome, I mean all of you.

So come, and welcome, to Jesus Christ.

In Daniel 1:8–16, Belshazzar holds a great feast, on the night when the great city of Babylon fell. There was eating and drinking, and there were even sacred vessels from the Temple in use there—but not for blessing. That was the night when a hand appeared and wrote on the wall that "you have been weighed in the balances and found wanting" (Dan. 5:27). There was a feast, and there was food and drink, but there was no blessing, only judgment.

We are gathered in a banqueting hall as well, and God Himself summons us to His Table. But while warnings about this Table are certainly appropriate in their place, the handwriting on the wall here says that you are accepted. It says that the penalty has been paid. It says that the judgment is long past, two thousand years ago.

If it had not been for Jesus and His sacrifice, we would gather at a feasting hall, like Belshazzar, only to find it a hall of slaughter, a hall of judicial blindness. But with His sacrifice, we are clean, we are accepted. With His sacrifice, there is no need for fear, no need for panic, no need to have your knees knock together, as Belshazzar's did. This is not a place for that. This is not Babylon. This city cannot fall.

So then, we are weighed in the balances, and the measurement is perfect. We are found to have the measurements of Jesus Himself. This is a meal of blessing, a meal of kindness. This is the grace of God.

So come, and welcome, to Jesus Christ.

MORNING ☼ TABLE OF PLENTY

In the Old Testament, one of the things that we learn about meals is that they draw boundaries. They define the limit between who is in and who is out. This is the first, the rudimentary lesson. The New Testament does not set this lesson aside but rather builds on it. The New Testament does not erase these boundaries, but rather expands them. The Table of the Lord is what it always was — the dividing line between the saints and the infidels. But now that the Spirit has been poured out at Pentecost, we have been instructed to take this bread to the world. We do not do this because the boundary line between holiness and unholiness has been made blurry, but rather because holiness is in the process of conquering the world. Holiness is expanding — but there is always a boundary. Until the last day, there will always be a frontier.

As we celebrate this meal, this means we have to make a sharp distinction between the holiness of God in its imperial phase, and the holiness of God surrendering to the tenets of worldliness. The former is the truth; the latter is a lie. The expansion of God's ways into the world is not intended to dilute those ways. The growth of the kingdom does not spread it thinner. The more we break this bread, the more of it there is. We offer this to the world — but we are not offering less and less of it as we go. We are not going to run out. We break the loaves, and as we are passing it out in the back rows of the multitudes of all the earth, we will discover that we end with more than we started with. So, come. This is a Table of plenty.

So come, and welcome, to Jesus Christ.

EVENING ◐ THE SPIRIT WHO BONDS

There is a communion we Christians experience with one another all the time. The ritual enactment of that everyday fellowship that we experience weekly in church is also called, unsurprisingly, communion. We take communion because we *are* a communion. And we are a communion because of the gift of the Holy Spirit. Consider this benediction that Paul gives. "The *grace* of the Lord Jesus Christ, and the *love* of God, and the *communion* of the Holy Ghost, be with you all. Amen" (2 Cor. 13:14). Notice what is happening here. Every member of the Trinity is named, and a particular gift or grace is associated with each. The Father is associated with love, the Son with grace, and the Holy Spirit with *communion*. Now you know, perfectly well, that what each person of the Trinity has, the other two have as well. It is not as though the Spirit is unloving, or the Father ungracious.

But this is a description of what theologians call the "economic Trinity," or the Trinity "at work." When God gives Himself to us, what does He do? Well, He sends His love, and He gives us His grace, but none of this would stick to us unless the Holy Spirit served as the bonding agent. The Holy Spirit brings communion. Communion of what? Well, among other things, the love of the Father, and the grace of the Lord Jesus Christ.

We are different individuals, and the Holy Spirit binds us together. That binding is love, that binding is grace, that binding is God Himself. And this is why you are invited, warmly, to come.

So come, and welcome, to Jesus Christ.

MORNING ☼ INCLUSION EXCLUDES EXCLUSION

Scripture contains two fundamental principles when it comes to the eating of sacred meals. The first principle concerns what we eat, and the second principle concerns with whom we eat. The answers to these questions for Christians are, respectively, bread and wine, and with all who call upon the name of the true God. Excluded are nonbelievers and false believers.

Nonbelievers do not present a problem usually, because they eat from their own table. They do not want to share with us here. But false brothers are a different matter. They creep in to spy out our liberty.

We can welcome them to the true Table of the Lord only to the extent that they are willing to drop their false standards of exclusion. But dropping those false standards is the same thing as repentance. The message of unity that Paul insists on in Galatians does not permit a barrier at this Table between men and women, or Jews and Gentiles, slave or free, and so forth. But it necessitates a barrier between the gospel and the anti-gospel. Paul says that in Christ there is neither Jew nor Greek . . . he does not say that in Christ there is neither brother nor false brother.

This means that if one of the central meanings of this meal is that of inclusion, it must be a principled inclusion — meaning that it must exclude all those who would preach another gospel. This is no contradiction except of those who contradict the message of grace.

So come, and welcome, to Jesus Christ.

EVENING ◐ THE DEVIL'S MIRACLE-GRO

Resentments have a tendency to accumulate. Bitterness is a settled negative disposition *that feeds and grows*. If you once fired an employee for laziness or dishonesty, that might represent a settled negative disposition toward him, in that you would never hire him again. That is not bitterness, but rather simple wisdom. However, if you seize eagerly on new information about that person, information that reflects badly on him, then *that* is bitterness.

"Looking diligently lest any man fail of the grace of God; lest any root of bitterness springing up trouble you, and thereby many be defiled" (Heb. 12:15). Bitterness is described here as a root. It is underground, and what it does down there is gather up nutrients. Those nutrients are supplied by various talkers and gossips, or perhaps Facebook updates, and so the store of negativity grows. Bitterness can grow on negative reports that happen to be true or false. But the longer the process continues, the less the truth is necessary. After the roots grow to a certain size, the lies are, in fact, preferable — sort of the devil's Miracle-Gro. Notice also that roots have a tendency to come to the surface. The writer here describes them as "springing up." Roots lead to fruit, and the fruit here is corruption and defilement. When a bitter root springs up, when the nastiness goes public, the end result is that *many* are defiled.

The last point to realize about this is that bitterness has a tendency to look away from itself to the real or imagined offense of the other. If you tell a lie, you cannot think about the situation without thinking of your own lie. If you lose your temper, to think about it at all reveals your own offense to you. But when you are bitter, every time you think of the situation, your roots are eager to do so.

By way of contrast, when you come to this Table honestly, the Lord uses it to uproot every form of bitterness and resentment from your life.

So come, and welcome, to Jesus Christ.

MORNING ☼ A MOUTHFUL OF GRACE

This is the Table of grace, and God has set it down in the midst of a sinful world. Sinful unrighteousness knows enough to stay away, but sinful righteousness is constantly trying to figure out ways to turn this into a Table of law. But God reigns on His throne, and His determinative Word cannot be altered by our confusions. You don't have to be good to come here — you just have to know that you're bad. You cannot save up enough money to buy a ticket to this banquet. This is the place where all petty scruples are to be set aside. Your manners may be uncouth, but if your heart loves true grace, this is a sign that God has invited you here.

When you take this bread and put it in your mouth, and you taste and swallow this wine, know this. Your mouth has been filled with grace. This is what forgiveness tastes like. You must be done with your pitiful attempts to be accepted on the basis of your merits. If you are in bondage, then come. If you are in bondage, but do not yet know the Lord, then come through the water. If you have been baptized, and you do know the Lord, but have fallen for any of the enslaving lies that the enemy of our souls loves to tell, then just come. If you are in bondage about the food you eat, then come — here is the place where you must learn to eat and drink.

Here is the place where you acknowledge your liberation. This is a Table for free sons and true daughters.

So come, and welcome, to Jesus Christ.

The grace of God enables us to see and savor the grace of God everywhere. This happens in the created order, in the ordinances of worship, in the Scriptures, in the bread and wine, and in the law of God. For the gracious, everything is grace.

When someone does not know the grace of God, they do not know the grace of God anywhere. They do not know it in the gospel, or in the Scriptures, or in the bread and wine, or in the gospel. For the lawless, everything is law.

What is more gracious than the grace of the gospel? But for those who do not know Jesus, it is the aroma of death. The grace of God toward sinners in the gospel is a message of death — it is condemning law.

What is more demanding than "do this and you shall live"? And yet, for the gracious heart, this word is near you, in your mouth and in your heart. Jesus is Lord, and this is the grace of God toward all men.

It is the same here. Come to this Table in grace, and you receive nothing but grace. Come to this Table with merit in mind and all you take away are demerits. Come to this Table with legal scruples, and you are convicted as a lawless one. This is a place of grace. That grace extends to all of you, and you must acknowledge that it extends to everyone else who comes as well.

Here is bread and wine. And here you are.

So come, and welcome, to Jesus Christ.

MORNING ☼ NOTHING BUT GRACE AND GRATITUDE

Here is bread and wine. Here is the grace of God. Come as supplicants; come as those who know that they need nothing but the sheer, unadulterated grace of God.

Grace, if it is to remain grace, must be received as gift. We can be worthy of a gift after the fact, but if we try to be worthy of it beforehand, we are corrupting and insulting the very concept of gift.

What we bring to a gift beforehand is simply and solely need. What we bring to a gift before it is given is the need to have it given. That is all that we contribute.

What we do with a gift afterward is simply show our gratitude, our thanksgiving. Gratitude does not purchase a gift, but gratitude is worthy of the gift. Gratitude is appropriate to the gift.

Now it is fitting that this Table is a Eucharistic Table, that is, a Table of thanksgiving. There is a reciprocal motion here. God gives His grace to us, and we render our gratitude to God. Remember that in this moment, you give as well as receive. But what you give does not take away from the graciousness of the gift—gratitude can never do that.

God offers you the bread of life, and what you return is gratitude for that bread. God gives you the wine of the new covenant, and you return gratitude for it.

So come, and welcome, to Jesus Christ.

EVENING ◐ ACTIVE OBEDIENCE IN THE BREAD AND WINE

It is significant that we come here for bread and wine, and not for the raw products that are used in the production of bread and wine. We eat the bread and drink the wine, and we do not eat a handful of raw grain as the disciples did once, and we do not eat grapes.

In both cases, we are consuming the product of labor. We do not consume the product of nature, straight from nature. Man's industry is involved in the processing of this food — in the grinding, kneading, baking, crushing, fermenting, and so forth.

This provides us with a wonderful picture of the entire life of Jesus Christ. We are not simply saved on the basis of His sinless death, but His entire obedience is imputed to us. More than the end result of a crucified and resurrected Lord is imputed to us. We don't eat bread that just mysteriously appears, and we don't drink wine that is sent to us directly from Heaven.

In Jesus, mankind finally did it right. In Jesus, Israel obeyed the way Israel was called to obey. In our participation here, we are participating with the entire process that brought it here. So as you eat this bread, you are resisting the temptation to turn the stones to bread in the wilderness. When you eat the bread and drink the wine, you are eating and drinking its entire history. In the same way, when you eat and drink here, you are eating and drinking all four gospels. You are eating and drinking the Lord's biography. It is all yours.

So come, and welcome, to Jesus Christ.

MORNING ☼ EATING GRACE BY GRACE

One of the glories of the new covenant is that we get to eat and drink our salvation. In the Garden of Eden, our first parents were privileged to eat their communion with God in the tree of life. And after our fall into sin, it is significant that the gospel is presented to us as a restoration to that same tree of life.

"In the midst of the street of it, and on either side of the river, was there the tree of life, which bare twelve manner of fruits, and yielded her fruit every month: and the leaves of the tree were for the healing of the nations" (Rev. 22:2).

But how do we eat this salvation? How do we bite, chew, taste, and swallow? How is that done? The biblical answer is that we do all this by believing. We do this by *faith*.

As Jesus introduces His discussion of what the manna in the wilderness represented, which was the bread of life that Jesus Himself was, He said this. "Jesus answered and said unto them, This is the work of God, that ye believe on him whom he hath sent" (John 6:29).

Biting, chewing, tasting and swallowing are the work of God. And how do we do this work of God? We believe in Jesus. How can we do that? We cannot do that unless God gives us the gift of faith. Faith is not something we can generate on our own steam. Faith is not something we can pull up by some kind of self-effort. Faith is grace. You eat grace, and you eat by grace. And this is why we say grace.

So come, and welcome, to Jesus Christ.

EVENING ◐ WHAT THE DISCIPLINE IS FOR

We have gathered here at a meal, the Lord's Meal, and so we should want to be aware of anything that might get between us and the food.

Table manners can present that kind of barrier. This happens when you don't have any manners, and you have Table anarchy, or if you have a complex set of rigorist manners which don't let people come to the Table unless they have passed a series of high level tests. In the former situation, you have a condition of bedlam — quarrels and fights get in the way of Table fellowship. In the latter, you have a rigorist purity, which also gets in the way of Table fellowship. The devil's strategy is manifested in both situations — to keep God's people away from the food.

The discipline that surrounds this Table is important and significant. You ought not to approach God this way if you are engaged in blasphemy or adultery. The discipline that surrounds this Table also warns us . . . by means of gracious invitation . . . to refrain from endless bouts of introspection, and perpetual motive-scratching. The discipline here is a servant — bringing the food to us, and us to the food.

Discipline guards the fellowship; that is what it is for. The oath-taking aspect of this meal guards the fellowship, since fellowship with God is the point. The fact that some are excluded from the Table is regrettable, but the point is to make sure the Table remains a place of sweet fellowship for all those who love the Lord of the Table. You are among those people.

So come, and welcome, to Jesus Christ.

MORNING ☼ CHRIST IS YOUR CHRIST

This is, of course, a covenant meal. This is the cup of the new covenant. Christ is the covenant, and this is His body, and this is His blood.

But the word covenant is not just an all-purpose religious word, signifying something vaguely spiritual. A covenant is formed by an oath, a bond, between persons. This participation in this meal is a renewal of that oath, a renewal of that bond.

The covenant is renewed weekly, not because it was going to expire, like a lease, but because it is a form of life that is renewed by nourishment, by food. But as a covenant form of life, part of this nourishment is the renewal of the promises—again, not because the promises were going to expire, but rather because the promises and our faith in the promises need to be fed.

So as we eat and drink, God is undertaking to be our God. As we eat and drink, we are undertaking to be His people. We are doing so, not on the basis of law, but in a thorough-going dependence upon His grace. How do we receive that grace? By faith, by believing. Here is one of the places where God calls us to this faith, to this belief.

Take and receive. God is your God. Eat and drink. Christ is your Christ. Join together with all God's people. You are His people, the sheep of His pasture. Commit yourself entirely, body and soul, into the care of the God who receives you so kindly.

So come, and welcome, to Jesus Christ.

You have all heard the truism that you are what you eat. This is true on a number of levels, and of course it is also false in other ways. No matter how carelessly you eat, you are not going to turn into high fructose corn syrup. And no matter how finicky you are when you eat, you are not going to turn into a bean sprout. So it is not true that "you are what you eat" on that level, for which we may thank the Lord.

However, there are ways in which it is true. Scripture teaches that we become like what we worship, and if you worship your food, there will be transformations in accordance with this principle. Eating and drinking is not simply a matter of refueling. Far more is involved than this, and a fussy eater is a fussy worshiper. A careless eater is a careless worshiper. In both instances, the behavior reinforces itself, and a downward spiral sets in.

But if you worship Jesus Christ, the true calling of every Christian, you become more and more like Jesus Christ. Here is another way to think of it. This bread, this wine, set on this Table, is the grace of God. You are invited now to come and eat and drink that grace. Now if you become what you eat, what should be happening? You should be turning into the grace of God.

This is the grace of God to you, which feeds you, and you become the grace of God that feeds others. You receive gracious food so that you might become gracious food.

So come, and welcome, to Jesus Christ.

MORNING ☼ RECEIVING AND GRABBING

The Bible teaches that there are only two tables in the world—the Table of the Lord and the table of demons. Corresponding to this, there are only two kinds of table manners. One kind of person receives what is passed to him, and another kind grabs what he wants. The former is suitable for the Table of the Lord, and the latter is hellish, and corresponds to Belial.

When Elkanah and his family worshiped before the Lord, he would give Hannah a blessed portion, and she received it. Hophni and Phinehas would take the kind of portion they demanded. And this tells you everything you need to know about the difference between faith and unbelief. Faith receives and unbelief grabs.

As you come to this Table, you are invited to come expectantly. God is a God who gives, and it is not wrong for us to expect Him to give. That is not demanding—that is faith. It is when you start to think that He might not give that you are tempted to grab.

His Word is here, and His Word has promised an abundant portion for all His sons and daughters. Are you a son or daughter? Then there is no need to grab. The blessing of bread and wine will be brought to you. If you are not a true son or daughter, then grabbing won't help. Grabbing doesn't work.

Before you can rest while waiting for the bread and wine, you must first rest in His gospel grace.

So come, and welcome, to Jesus Christ.

EVENING ◐ THAT OUR EYES MIGHT BE OPENED

Biblical scholars have pointed to a striking parallel between the fall of our first parents and one of the resurrection accounts. In Gen. 3:7, it says "And the eyes of them both were opened, and they knew . . ." In Luke 24:31, it says, "And their eyes were opened, and they knew . . ."

Knew what? In the first instance, they knew that they were naked, and they were ashamed. In the second instance, they knew that Jesus was risen, and they were overjoyed.

We have learned before from Scripture that the tree of the knowledge of good and evil was a tree that represented maturity, and preparation for judgment rule. It was not a tree that represented moral consciousness, as though Adam and Eve were amoral before this. It was withheld from them because they needed to pass this test before they were ready for the regal authority that God was going to bestow on them. But they fell into sin and impotence, and so God had to send His Son the Messiah in order to correct the dislocations we had introduced into His plan. But when Jesus was raised, everything that was out of joint was put back where it belonged.

We know that through the gospel the tree of life is restored to us. But we should also know that through the very same gospel, the tree of the knowledge of good and evil is restored to us—our maturities and infantilism overcome. Christ is both trees, and when we come here to partake of Him, we are partaking of His kingly maturity. When we partake in true evangelical faith, our eyes are opened, and we know.

So come, and welcome, to Jesus Christ.

MORNING ☼ CHRIST IS NOT FOOD TO THE FAITHLESS

Fathers feed their children. One of the ways we know that we are children of God is that He provides food for us here. We come in faith rejoicing at what He has provided for us here.

Now some might wonder if this is really true. Do not hypocrites join churches? Don't they participate in this meal? How could God be telling them that they belong to Him when they clearly don't?

Well, the answer is that God never tells lies, but men do. Since Christ is only food for those who come in faith, He is not food for those who don't. What is He for them then? He is Christ to all, but Christ is food to the faithful and poison to the unfaithful. This image is not intended to be disrespectful — it is an image straight from Scripture. The Corinthians are warned against falling into the same sin committed by the Jews in the wilderness — the sin of drinking from Christ in such a way as to die (1 Cor. 10:2–5). The Israelites in the wilderness ate and drank Christ, but God was not pleased with many of them, and their bodies were scattered over the desert.

As the Puritans were fond of saying, not everyone who hangs around the court speaks with the king. Not everyone who touches this meal eats it as food. Not everyone whose lips touch the cup drink nourishment from the cup. But no one is just going through the motions. Everyone is here. There is no neutrality anywhere, especially here.

So come, and welcome, to Jesus Christ.

In Leviticus 23, the weekly sabbath is listed along with the rest of Israel's festivals as a feast, as a festival. The weekly sabbath was a day of rejoicing, not a day of gloom. The Jews had only one penitential day out of the year — their Good Friday, Yom Kippur, the day of atonement.

But for some, that is not nearly enough gloom. There is something in the religious heart that wants to locate affliction and trouble where the God of all grace has located none. When we say that we are sabbatarians, the mind and heart leap immediately to what we have to give up. It has been easy for us to see Lenten excesses in what other communions say and do, but the conservative Reformed view of the sabbath is often like Lent without any Easter to mitigate the sorrow.

The joy of the Lord is our strength. We have been laboring for many years to turn around this common error concerning the Lord's Day. More is involved in this than might initially appear, and so we give ourselves to it.

What must you give up in order to come to this Table? What must you leave behind? Only your sorrow. Only your guilt. Only your gloom.

So come, and welcome, to Jesus Christ.

MORNING ☼ SITTING OR RECLINING

You have heard many times that there is no neutrality, not anywhere, and not in anything. This is not the same thing as saying there is only one way to do something, but it does mean that we should think about everything that we do.

For example, we are seated as we partake of this Supper. That is not an incidental detail. There are other possible postures that would be fine, and there are postures that would not be. If we knelt as we took the Supper, that is a posture of reverence and prayer that is not fitting when we approach bread and wine. There have been times and places in the Church when the elements have been inappropriately adored, and posture was part of that.

But when Jesus instituted the Supper, He and His disciples were reclining at table — the custom in that generation. Sitting was the more ancient biblical practice, while reclining was a Hellenistic custom — the posture of the symposia — that the Jews of that day had picked up. The fact that Jesus did it means that it was okay, obviously, but it was different from sitting. Nevertheless, it was the posture for eating a meal, and there was more than one such posture. This is an example of "no neutrality" not excluding various approaches and options.

So when we gather, the fact that it is a spiritual meal does not keep it from being a meal. But the fact that we are with Christ in the heavenly places does not mean that the posture of our bodies is irrelevant. Rather, it means that we are eating a meal of communion with someone, and not adoring an object.

So come, and welcome, to Jesus Christ.

One of the more striking aspects of Christ's ministry was His willingness to eat with sinners. In fact, that is what He doing here, now, in this meal. He is eating with sinners.

But we have to be careful to understand this properly. Some have taken His willingness to associate with the lowly as an example of Him being, as one scholar put it, "the consummate party animal." But a faithful Christian laboring in an inner city soup kitchen is also eating with sinners, and we would scarcely think of that as being a "party animal." There is eating with sinners, calling for another round for the house, the way the prodigal son ran down his bank account, and then there is a ministerial eating with the outcast, in order to establish a new kingdom, a new way of doing things. This latter approach is what Jesus was doing.

But at the same time, there is eating and drinking. There is thanksgiving. There is a celebration. But it is on *God's* terms, as He fashions us into a new humanity. It is not on our terms — whether the old style respectability or the old style orgiastic revelry. God upends everything about the old humanity — its sanctimoniousness and its lasciviousness both.

Christ established a new humanity centered on a Table of grace. This grace is not proud, and this grace is not unclean. This is an accomplishment that only God could bring about, and He did it through the death and resurrection of His Son.

So come, and welcome, to Jesus Christ.

MORNING ☼ FEEDING THE DISREPUTABLE

In the gospel of Mark, when Jesus calls Levi or Matthew to follow Him (Mark 2:14–17), He does so by calling him from his vocation as tax collector. The fact that Levi was no mere functionary or drudge is seen in the fact that afterwards, Levi is able to throw a banquet, which Jesus attends, as do many others. It says that many publicans and sinners sat down with Jesus. Not only so, but Mark then repeats the fact that there were many, thus emphasizing it. When this happens, we see not only that Jesus is eating with sinners, but with quite a few of them. Quite naturally, Jesus is challenged on the point by the pious. How is it that Jesus eats with disreputable people?

It is worth noting that the disreputable people include categories that the super-pious still find offensive. Jesus associated with prostitutes, tax collectors, and centurions. Conservative Christians stumble over the prostitutes, and "social justice" Christians stumble over the rich tax collectors and the Marine colonels. But however we describe the disreputable, the fact remains that Jesus associated with them. When confronted with what He was doing, He replied that those who are whole don't need a physician, but those who are sick.

What does this mean? It means that when Jesus sits and eats with sinners, as He is doing right now, He is doing the work of a physician. You are in the role of a patient. So when you show up here with your troubles, you shouldn't feel apologetic about that. Grieve for your sins, certainly, but don't grieve over the fact that you have made it to the doctor. When Jesus accepted the invitation to Levi's house, He knew who was going to be there. When He decided to sit down with the sinners, that decision was well-informed. That is precisely what He had come here to do.

Are you struggling? Are you dealing with a trouble? This meal is for you.

So come, and welcome, to Jesus Christ.

EVENING ◐ METAMORPHOSIS

Eating is a great mystery, a mystery of metamorphosis. Whenever we eat, something is turning into something else. Eating is all about transformation. Not only is it true that you become what you eat (in one sense), what you eat becomes you. More peanut butter sandwiches turn into little boys than little boys turn into peanut butter sandwiches.

A little boy eating that sandwich doesn't turn into a sandwich, that is true enough. But a little boy who eats sandwiches *does* turn into something else — the nourishment means that he turns into a man. God has framed the world in such a way as to enable us to take an edible substance, ingest it, and use it to become something much greater than the sum of the parts.

And so we have gathered to eat bread and to drink wine. In doing this, we do not turn into bread and wine. The transformation does not work that way. Neither do we eat it to remain just what we were. The transformation — or rather, non-transformation — does not work that way either. Rather, by gathering here to eat this bread and drink this wine (assuming always a true and evangelical faith), the Holy Spirit takes this event as a means of growing us up into the perfect man, who is Jesus Christ.

We are being grown up into maturity. We are being established. We are being nourished. But in order to be nourished this way, we have to take the nourishment in fully. If we are living in flagrant, unrepentant sin, and you come to this Table, you are engaging in a form of spiritual bulimia. If you receive this bread and wine, and you keep what you receive by a simple and living faith, the transformation will continue on in your life, mysteriously and inexorably. Be reassured. God knows how to nourish His people. He knows how to grow them up. He knows what to feed them. So put away all thoughts of merit or inadequacy, and come to be fed.

So come, and welcome, to Jesus Christ.

MORNING ✹ NOT WHERE YOUR MOUTH IS

In the Sermon on the Mount, Jesus says to "take no thought for your life, what ye shall eat" (Matt. 6:25). He is talking about physical life and physical food, and the obvious relationship between the two. He is telling us not to chase after our physical lives in the first instance, and that chasing after food is the way that this would be done.

In another place, He tells us that He offers Himself as living bread (John 6:51). Unless we partake of this living bread, we have no life in ourselves (John 6:53). Just as physical life is sustained by physical food, so also spiritual life is sustained by spiritual food.

We cannot get nourishment from food when the nourishment is not there, which is why we cannot eat rocks or plastic. We can eat fruit, and meat, and vegetables, and they offer up what they contain. But they don't transmit what they contain automatically, no matter what we do. Smearing food on our foreheads is not eating.

In the New Jerusalem, we are invited to eat from the tree of life (Rev. 2:7). This means that the fruit is life, and that we get to chew and swallow life. We eat, and we take life into ourselves. We do this because Christ is life itself. But you cannot come to this Table, you cannot come to church and get blessing from it regardless of your behavior. If you take the life that is here and smash it on your forehead, you are not eating. And since this is spiritual food and drink, the warning has to be against smearing food on your spiritual forehead. That is not where your mouth is.

What is your spiritual mouth? It is your faith. And just as the food is living, so must the mouth be. As God has quickened you, and given you a true and living faith, then come.

So come, and welcome, to Jesus Christ.

EVENING ◐ ACTING LIKE THERE WILL BE LEFTOVERS

One of the characteristics of a Jesus meal is the astonishing level of leftovers. In the feeding of the five thousand, there were twelve baskets of leftovers (Mk. 8:19). In the miracle of the four thousand, there were seven baskets of leftovers (Matt. 16:10). We see this foreshadowed in the miracle of Elijah's as well.

"And there came a man from Baalshalisha, and brought the man of God bread of the firstfruits, twenty loaves of barley, and full ears of corn in the husk thereof. And he said, Give unto the people, that they may eat. And his servitor said, What, should I set this before an hundred men? He said again, Give the people, that they may eat: for thus saith the Lord, They shall eat, and shall leave thereof. So he set it before them, and they did eat, and left thereof, according to the word of the Lord" (2 Kings 4:42–44).

Notice that in all three instances, the leftovers are pointed to. They are a major part of the point. This is in contrast to the manna from Heaven given under Moses, where there were no leftovers day to day, but only on the weekends, to prevent labor on the Sabbath.

What are we to make of the leftovers? When we are done each Sunday, there are broken loaves here on the Table. What is the point of that? Like everything else about this meal, this is significant. This is an emblem of the grace of God for the world. We are reminded by the leftovers, each Sunday, that the world has not yet been fed, and that there is plenty and to spare.

This is an image of the atonement. We know that Jesus died to secure the salvation of His elect, but we also know that as the disciples fed the multitudes, there was no danger of running out. The reality of what we call definite atonement must not make us reluctant to take up our basket as we head out into the world to serve. We will not run out. We should act like there will be leftovers.

So come, and welcome, to Jesus Christ.

MORNING ✹ NO SHORTAGE OF BREAD

When Jesus fed the multitudes, He did so in desolate places — in the wilderness, in effect. The thousands that He fed were a motley group, a mixed multitude, just like Israel was when they came out of Egypt. And so when manna fell from heaven, it fed both the full-blooded Israelites and the mixed multitude with them. They all were fed.

When Jesus fed the multitudes when and where He did, given the crowd's composition, and the lack of facilities for washing, the whole thing had to be ritually unclean. Any Pharisees there would have been in trouble. Their inability to partake would have been because of the presence of scruples, and not because of the absence of bread.

The bread from Heaven is here. The grace of God is here. Forgiveness of sin is proclaimed here. Your scruples might keep you away, but do not pretend that there is a shortage of bread. A surplus of scruples is not the same thing as a shortage of bread. An abundance of law is not a deficiency of grace.

Christ offers to feed you here. Come. God offers the goodness of His grace to you here. Come. But you come to receive it. The one thing you cannot do is receive it without receiving it. Come. The grace of God deals with you. The grace of God gets in your midst, and will not leave things alone. So come.

Your scruples say that you do not deserve to come. Well, of course not. Whoever said that you did deserve it? Not deserving it is really the central point. The only thing the multitude in the wilderness contributed to the meal was their hunger . . . their need. So come. Are you hungry? Come. Are you thirsty? Come.

There is food enough here, on this Table, for the whole world.

So come, and welcome, to Jesus Christ.

When we come to this Table, we do so as forgiven sinners. Grace has dealt with the past, and has done so in such a way as that the past no longer matters. Under the blood of Christ, God doesn't care what you have done. As grace has washed away every stain, it follows that every stain has been washed away. The gospel invitation has gone out to all men, and every kind of sinner has responded to it. This includes adulterers, murderers, thieves, drunks, liars, pornographers, prostitutes, embezzlers, con artists, fornicators, skeptics, and every other kind of sinner that there might be. This grace means we come to this Table just as though not one of those sins had been committed.

What is to keep a sinner from abusing this system of grace? Why not sin that grace may abound (Rom 5:20)? Here's why: God never takes up our past by His grace without simultaneously taking up our future. When God picks up a human life, He picks it up by both ends. This is what He always does, and in every instance.

If He does not pick up the future, predestining us to holiness, then this means that He has not picked up the past. If He picks up the past, forgiving every last sin we have ever done, this means that He is engaged to do exactly the same thing with our future. God is not a system that can be worked. God is not gullible.

As we come to this Table, we are testifying to our confidence that God has engaged to be a God to us. And this means that ten years from now, twenty years, and fifty, He will still be our Savior. He will still be the one who cleanses us from all unrighteousness. His work is ongoing. His forgiveness is eternal. He never performs the work of salvation piecemeal. When it comes to the restoration of a fallen human life, God is a systematician — He methodically begins at one end, and leads us through to glory at the other.

So come, and welcome, to Jesus Christ.

MORNING ☼ HASTENING THE DAY

We noted at the beginning of the service that by receiving the bread rightly, you are loving your people. You are making a solemn pledge to love each other. You are renewing a most gracious oath, an oath that binds you together with everyone here, not to mention God's people all over the world. You are being knit together.

But the Spirit wants this knitting project to cooperate with what is being done. We are not simply passive; we are not inert. No, the Spirit calls us to active cooperation with His purposes and plans — for your marriage, for your family, for your parish, for this congregation, for this town, for this state, for the nation, and of course for the world. Lift up your heads! Enlarge your hearts! Something great is coming down.

Do you want to hasten that time? You certainly should. Do you want that time of glory to come soon? Why wouldn't you? What can you do that will hasten that day? Well, there is some bread here to eat. There is some wine here for you to drink. There is a neighbor here to love.

So come, and welcome, to Jesus Christ.

The Supper we partake of here is, among other things, a glorious foreshadowing of the great eschatological banquet. This is the time at the culmination of history, when all God's people sit down together in the Marriage Supper of the Lamb.

In the course of history, before that time, there is a winnowing — which foreshadows those who are excluded, and there is a great gathering — foreshadowing those who are brought in, from every tribe and nation. This is that great banquet in microcosm. This is that great banquet foretold. This is that great banquet in a sign.

We see this in Matthew 8:11–12, for example. Jesus tells us that many will come from east and west, and these summoned Gentiles will sit down in the kingdom with Abraham, Isaac, and Jacob. Not only so, but the natural heirs of the kingdom, those who ought to have understood all these things, will be ejected from the banquet hall, and exiled to the outer darkness.

How do you know if you are invited to that great banquet at the end of history? It is simple — by whether or not you are invited to this one. How do you know if you are invited to this one? The bread and wine are here, the gospel is here, and the invitation is declared. I have just declared it. How do you rsvp to God's gracious invitation to sit down with Him at the Last Day? You do that, now, by eating and drinking, now, in true and living evangelical faith.

So come, and welcome to Jesus Christ.

MORNING ☼ A TRUE FORETASTE

When Jesus tells His disciples that many will come from east and west to sit down in the great Messianic banquet (Matt. 8:11–12), we heard echoes of the great promise found in Isaiah 25:6–8.

"And in this mountain shall the LORD of hosts make unto all people a feast of fat things, a feast of wines on the lees, of fat things full of marrow, of wines on the lees well refined. And he will destroy in this mountain the face of the covering cast over all people, and the vail that is spread over all nations. He will swallow up death in victory; and the Lord GOD will wipe away tears from off all faces; and the rebuke of his people shall he take away from off all the earth: for the LORD hath spoken it."

There is a veil covering all the nations, including ours, and faithful gospel proclamation, followed by faithful gospel worship, are instruments in the hands of a holy God who is in the process of fulfilling these great and ancient promises. These are His promises, not ours, and He will do it. He is doing it. The mouth of the Lord has spoken it.

You have a seat at this Table — it is a feast of fat things, with rich wine. As we come in true faith, this has the effect of pulling the covering back, the covering that shrouds all the nations. It hastens the day when death is swallowed up in the victory of Christ's return. Our celebration of this meal, with a true and robust evangelical understanding, is a means by which the Lord God will wipe away every tear. Moreover, as a reproach lies upon His people, this is the way that the reproach will be removed. So come in faith, come with nothing but faith.

As often as we eat and drink, we proclaim Christ's death until He returns. What does the proclamation of this gospel do? Why it is the salvation of the world.

So come, and welcome, to Jesus Christ.

EVENING ◐ CHALICES AND PLATTERS I NEVER ASKED FOR

We have before us bread and wine. We also have before us the choice of whether to renew our covenant oaths with God honestly or not. Never forget that the principle issues are not the bread and wine.

"For John the Baptist came neither eating bread nor drinking wine; and ye say, He hath a devil. The Son of man is come eating and drinking; and ye say, Behold a gluttonous man, and a winebibber, a friend of publicans and sinners! But wisdom is justified of all her children" (Luke 7:33–35). John the Baptist came, not eating or drinking, yet he is in fellowship with us here at this Table. He was accused of demonism by the respectable. The Lord Jesus came, both eating and drinking, and He was accused of excessive partying by the fastidious. In effect, they were accusing Him, the faithful Son, of being the faithless son of Deuteronomy 21:20 and Proverbs 23:20–21.

So John the ascetic had a message of real repentance and true faith, and Jesus the celebrant had a message of . . . true repentance and true faith. The kingdom of God is not a matter of eating and drinking, but of righteousness, peace, and joy in the Holy Spirit (Rom. 14:17).

Do we then despise the sacrament? Never, as Paul would say — rather, we uphold it. How so? Jesus taught us to cleanse the inside of the cup first in order that the outside of the cup might be clean also (Matt. 23:25–26). Do you want to eat this bread rightly? Then eat the bread of repentance first in your heart. Chew inside first. Do you want to drink this cup rightly? Then drink the blood-bought faith in your soul first. In that frame of heart you may then come to the sacrament to have the sacrament strengthen your heart.

The Lord has been meeting with His people for thousands of years. And He says, have I been so long with you? Do you not know? Sacrifices and burnt offerings I do not require, chalices and platters I never asked for — but rather a humble and a contrite heart.

So come, and welcome, to Jesus Christ.

MORNING ✹ A TABLE FOR THE RIFF-RAFF

This is a Table set for sinners. But because "sinners" is a Bible word, many of us slip into our church-going trance, and we don't rightly consider the ramifications of such a statement. This is a Table for riff-raff. This is a Table for losers. This is a Table for self-righteous fussers. Are you all screwed up? That is good news indeed — you *qualify*!

"Jesus saith unto them, Verily I say unto you, That the publicans and the harlots go into the kingdom of God before you. For John came unto you in the way of righteousness, and ye believed him not: but the publicans and the harlots believed him: and ye, when ye had seen it, repented not afterward, that ye might believe him" (Matt. 21:31b-32).

If you are here, if you have come, this means that you are presenting yourself here as someone who does *not* deserve to be here. The world has its tables for the deserving, but you cannot find that here.

Grace is not a theology-word only, grace is a reality that invites you to drop everything and come. You must drop your sins, which is what repentance is, but having sins to drop is not a disqualification in the slightest. Are you an adulterer? Then come. Are you a thief? Then come. Have you had an abortion? Then come.

"Wait, wait," someone will say. "Don't you need to say 'drop your sin' with every invitation?" Don't you need to mention true repentance every other sentence? Not really. Grace is not something you can turn to without simultaneously turning away from that which is not grace. And all sin is not grace. You cannot turn toward the north wall without turning away from the south wall. You cannot turn toward the Mt. Gerizim without turning away from Mt. Ebal. You cannot turn toward this Table without turning away from the table of demons.

So come, and welcome, to Jesus Christ.

Allow me to speak a word of exhortation to the covenant children who are growing up in this church. For as long as you can remember, you have been welcome here at this Table. You are baptized, and you are invited to be here, invited to partake. This means that you are just as much a Christian as the adults who are partaking of the bread and wine around you. You are fellow Christians with us — our shared communion means that we are brothers and sisters.

The Bible teaches us that Jesus is our elder Brother. He is also here with us, and He is also involved in this. The Bible also says that coming to eat and drink here is a reciprocal thing — all that means is that it goes both ways. If Jesus receives you here, then you must receive Jesus here. If Jesus receives your brothers here, then you must receive your brothers here. If Jesus receives your sisters here, then you must receive your sisters here. If Jesus receives all of us here, and He does, then we all must receive Him . . . and one another.

This means that every time you are counting on Jesus accepting you, you also accept Him. And just as you count on Him accepting all of you, just as you are, so also you accept all of Him, just as He is. This is just another way of saying that this Table helps you to grow up into faithful Christians, who will walk with Jesus Christ in the power of His Spirit all your lives.

It is not complicated. Love God, love His Word, love His Spirit. As He brings you closer to Him, He also gives you neighbors to love, neighbors to accept just as God has accepted you. Most often, for younger children, these neighbors will be your physical brothers and sisters. We all need to learn how to love, and so God gives us older brothers, and younger brothers, and older sisters, and younger sisters . . . to practice on. And He gave us to them so that they would have someone to practice on.

So come, and welcome, to Jesus Christ.

MORNING ☼ FEED AND RESTORE

In John 21, Jesus shares breakfast with His disciples on the beach. This is one of His resurrection appearances, and it is quite a striking circumstance.

For our purposes here, note two things. The first is that the Lord shares a meal with His disciples, as He is doing here, and secondly, that it is in the context of this meal that He restores Peter. This is something the Lord loves to do. He loves to eat with us, and He loves to restore us to full and complete fellowship.

If you are like every other Christian in the world, this last week you had to struggle against lust, envy, pride, deception, and so on. When you fell into sin, you denied the Lord, claiming not to know Him. You may not have done it to a servant girl at the high priest's house, and you may not have heard a rooster crow right after you did it, but all sin is at heart a denial of the Lord.

And when you have done this, what does Jesus do? He invites you to come and dine with Him. And when you receive that invitation by faith, what is Jesus going to do as you come? The answer of Scripture is plain. He is going to receive you. He is going to nourish you, He is going to restore you.

So come, and welcome, to Jesus Christ.

As you all know, we meet together every Lord's Day. We do this in joyful recognition that Jesus rose from the dead. In this sense, every week contains an Easter. We declare this by our actions. And of course, all of the story of Christ must be present in order for us to understand any of it — from the Incarnation through to the Ascension.

But in this narrative, one element of this story is always to be emphasized and placed in high relief. The apostle Paul once said that he had resolved to know nothing except Christ and Him crucified. One of the things we do, and we do it every week, is break the bread which is the body of Christ, and drink the wine, which is the cup of His blood. Every week, we declare the Lord's death until He comes (1 Cor. 11:26). This proclamation of His death is most necessary, because it is this which will draw all men to Himself.

This is the heart of any robust evangelicalism. The evangel is the good news of the death of Jesus, a death in which He suffered so that we could die to our old way of life in Him. Of course, we assume the resurrection. Without the resurrection, we never would have heard of His death. Without the resurrection, His death would have been meaningless. But precisely because He rose, we are liberated to gather on the weekly anniversary of His resurrection in order to commemorate . . . His death. And so that is what we do.

Would you be free?

So come, and welcome, to Jesus Christ.

MORNING ☼ JESUS IS THE CONTAGIOUS ONE

In the Old Covenant, we learn that sin is contagious (Hag. 2:13–14). We see that if a clean object comes into contact with an unclean one, it is the clean object that becomes unclean. We recognize that this principle continues to apply in certain ways in the New Covenant as well, which is why we are supposed to avoid evil companions and why we are supposed to beware of the leaven of the Pharisees. But nevertheless, something is different now.

The ministry of the Lord Jesus shows us a form of powerful, and contagious, holiness. When the woman with the flow of blood (making her unclean) touched the hem of Christ's garment, she was made whole (Luke 8:44). The contagion did not go the other way. When Jesus took the little dead girl by the hand and told her to rise, the dead body did not make Jesus unclean (Mk. 5:41). Rather, He made her come alive.

Now we are coming to a holy Table, but not to a holy defenseless Table. You have confessed your sins. You are not coming here with hypocritical high-handedness.

Jesus was sent into the world to be the life of the world, but we must remember He was sent to be the life of a dead world. His life spreads to our death. His righteousness spreads to our wickedness. His holiness spreads to our contagion. Here, in this setting, with this gospel set before you, remember that Jesus is the contagious one, not you.

So come, and welcome, to Jesus Christ.

EVENING ◐ A GOOD PACE

Careful study of the gospels shows us five distinctive characteristics of Christ's Table fellowship. First, He consistently sought out fellowship with outcasts. Secondly, those outcasts responded to Him with joy. Third, the religious establishment routinely grumbled about it. Fourth, the Table fellowship was preceded by a call to radical discipleship. And fifth, such incidents frequently conclude with Jesus talking about His redemptive mission.

There are many lessons here that could fill up many books, and we could all profit by them. But we should draw our attention to only one of them right now. We are feeble, and one at a time is a good pace.

As we embrace Table fellowship with the Lord here — for this is what we are doing — we have to be careful to remember all five aspects of His kindness to us. In particular, we should be careful not to let our embrace of His call to radical discipleship in the fourth point turn us into the grumblers of the third point.

Radical discipleship is not radical fussing. Radical discipleship does not mean hyper-scrupulosity. Radical discipleship does not mean wagging a bony finger under the noses of others. Radical discipleship means that you come here to consume the body of another, imitating Him, and therefore you are learning how to be consumed for others. This too is grace.

So come, and welcome, to Jesus Christ.

MORNING ☼ THE TABLE OF FORGIVENESS

We have gathered here at the Table of Christ's body, and we are offered the cup of the new covenant, which is the cup of Christ's blood. This means that we have gathered at the Table of Forgiveness. Forgiveness was right at the center of the new covenant, and integral to it. We cannot celebrate the new covenant without celebrating the internalization of God's law, and without receiving the forgiveness promised in Jeremiah's famous prophecy of the new covenant.

So, then, this is a Table of Forgiveness. It is therefore not surprising that when we gather here we do something that is alien to other man-made religions. This is a Table of Forgiveness, and therefore we *sing* at it. Muslims do not sing in their worship. Buddhists do not sing in theirs. But Christians have been singing so long that we have started to take it all for granted. But singing is not something that unforgiven people do when they worship. Singing is an overflow of grace.

Think of it for a moment. We are gathered here in the presence of the God we have all offended in various ways. How could we sing unless we had been forgiven? At the Lord's Table, the Lord's forgiven ones gather, and they pass the bread, and they drink the wine. And as we do these glorious things, we sit up straight — for we are forgiven — and we sing.

So come, and welcome, to Jesus Christ.

John tells us that if any man pretends to himself that he has no sin, he deceives himself. We are to confess our sins and, according to His promise, He will forgive us our sins and cleanse us from all unrighteousness. But we need regularly to be reminded of several things concerning this.

The first is that this is not the place for confession of sin. Here is not the place we have assigned for self-examination and confession. Such self-examination is preparation for coming to the Table, but while you are at the Table, you should be receiving the food. Of course, if some sin arises right when you are coming to the Table — some prideful thought, say — of course you are to repent of it immediately, even if you are at the Table. I am simply saying that this is not the time or place for self-examination.

But here is the second thing. Telling you not to confess your sins here is only safe or wise if you are the kind of Christian who confesses his sins regularly before the Lord. Ideally, sin should be confessed immediately upon recognition of that sin. If you say something unkind to your wife on Tuesday, you shouldn't wait until the time of confession on Sunday to put it right. Because of how easy it is for sin to get by us, we have placed a time of reflection and confession at the first part of the service, right after we come into the Lord's presence. Any unfinished business should be finished there.

That is how it is possible for sinners, completely forgiven, to come to this Table here and hold their heads up. It is all the grace of God, and He is kind.

So come, and welcome, to Jesus Christ.

MORNING ☼ HOLINESS AND HOSPITALITY

This is a holy Table, to be sure, but it is the holiness of hospitality — not the holiness of separation and distance. The Bible teaches us both kinds of holiness. In the Old Testament, the first lesson was the lesson of consecration and holy separation. Holiness was set apart; holiness was not contaminated with common things. With holiness understood in this way, whenever contact occurred between the two, the common would contaminate the holy. This is one aspect of holiness — given to us so that we might come to understand that light has no fellowship with darkness. This was enacted so that we would never be tempted to blur the lines between evil and righteousness.

But if that were the only picture we drew, we could come to the mistaken conclusion that holiness was fragile. God wanted us to have another picture, one that completes our vision. This is the vision of a triumphant holiness, a conquering holiness. When Jesus touched a dead body, the holiness of His life was transmitted to the death, not the other way around. When Jesus came into contact with lepers, it was His health that was contagious.

Hospitality must exhibit this second kind of holiness. When people come to your home, they track things in. Hospitality receives that; holiness conquers it. We can understand this about our own instances of hospitality by looking at this Table here — where God is showing the kindness of hospitality to us here, and where we showed up, having tracked in all kinds of stuff. His holiness deals with us.

So come, and welcome, to Jesus Christ.

The bread and wine on this Table are simple fare. But appearances can be deceiving.

In the course of His ministry, Jesus declared all foods to be clean. Just as the two great commandments encompass all the law and the prophets, so also this bread and wine encompasses every form of food found in the world. Because we eat here, as disciples of Jesus, we are freed to eat anything. When you go out from this Table, and you approach any other earthly table, you are perfectly free to suit yourself. Where the Spirit of the Lord is, there is liberty, and that liberty includes both tofu and Velveeta, though perhaps not together.

And why is this? It is not what goes into a man that defiles a man, but what comes out of him. Snark, gossip, lies, and more all come out of our mouths, and represent the abundance of our hearts. What goes into our mouths here at this occasion represents the abundance of God's heart.

It is not what goes into a man's mouth that defiles a man, but when we eat and swallow, drink and swallow, in evangelical faith, what goes into a man does cleanse a man. It does strengthen a man. This Table is a means of sanctifying grace. God multiplies grace to you here. God is giving to you. God is rooting you in His love. God is establishing you. God is nourishing you.

And what is your role? Your role is to believe that He is doing so. We approach this sacrament by faith.

So come, and welcome, to Jesus Christ.

MORNING ☼ SUNDAY BY SUNDAY

The world as it will be unfolds slowly. The leaven works through the loaf slowly and quietly. The mustard seed grows silently and takes its sweet time. The world to come is in fact coming, but not on our timetable.

There are two kinds of unbelief. One doesn't want the new world to come at all—and tries to keep or retain the old ways. The other is the revolutionary form of unbelief, which demands that its particular fevered utopia must come by this time tomorrow. The first error is that of the pagan past, the second error is that of the futuristic heretic. Both of them hate wisdom, and therefore are worldviews that love and embrace death.

One wants to keep us in the death from which Jesus delivered our world, and the other wants to introduce a new form of death. In contrast to this, Jesus, the Lord of life, came into this world to transform it. Jesus came to bring everlasting life, a life which has been spreading slowly (but steadily) since it was first introduced just outside Jerusalem, that first resurrection morning. That life has been growing ever since—Sunday by Sunday, the worship of the true God has been expanding.

But this is not a quantitative expansion. It is qualitative. The kingdom is alive. The kingdom teems with life. Because the people of the kingdom will live forever, and are alive now, it follows that they will eat. What nourishes us? The answer is the body of the Lord Jesus, and the blood of the new covenant.

So come, and welcome, to Jesus Christ.

The Supper before us is a dramatic meal, at least if we understand it correctly. Jesus eats with us here, and He sits in the mercy seat. He offers His body, broken for us. He offers His cup, the cup of the new covenant in His blood.

In the Old Covenant, the Holy of Holies was entered by only one man, and he only did it once a year. To transgress at this point would have been to make himself susceptible to the penalty of death. As you know, when Jesus died, the curtain that marked the Holy of Holies was torn in two, from top to bottom (Mark 15:38).

This means that God has opened the way for us, and we are invited to come in, all of us. All of us, that is, that believe in Him. The trembling boldness that walks up to this Table is the boldness of faith. In faith, all may come. On account of faith in the crucified one, all must come.

Apart from faith, the grace of God is as dangerous as it ever was. Just as Uzzah died for touching the ark — the ark that was covered with the *mercy* seat — so also a number of Corinthians had become sick and had died because of their abuse of the cup of *blessing*. God doesn't change the names of His gifts to accommodate our sinfulness. Rather, He invites us to repent of our sinfulness so that we might enjoy the blessings of His grace.

So here it is — forgiveness, justification, reconciliation, mercy, goodness, kindness, and more. So in true evangelical faith, come.

So come, and welcome, to Jesus Christ.

MORNING ☼ THE TABLE AS WINNOWING FAN

In Romans 16, the apostle Paul tells us to note those who cause divisions, and to mark and avoid them. He says in the next breath that one of the things that such divisive people do is "deceive the hearts of the naïve" (Rom. 16:18, ESV). This kind of smooth (and sophomoric) talk is very easy to spin out when the faithful are busy trying to divide from the divisive. "Isn't that a contradiction?" is very easy to say, and the simple fall for it.

But the point here is to consider one step before this. The great Augustine once famously prayed, "Lord, give what you command, and command what thou wilt." God asks nothing from us but what His Spirit is active in our midst to do already. What He commands of us, He gives to us. If He commands separation from divisiveness, and He does, then *He* is at work constantly to accomplish separation from divisiveness.

This Table is a winnowing fan, and the wind that comes from it is the Spirit of God. Some of God's saints do understand that winnowing must happen, but they try to separate the wheat and chaff all by themselves, bringing the grain to the winnowing fan, pre-separated for God's convenience. And others deny the need for separation, insisting that the Table be offered in absolute stillness, with no wind at all, lest the Spirit give us a disruptive gift we do not want — the gift of shaking us down, *dealing* with us, causing some to withdraw.

You are the saints of God. You are welcome here. Not only are you welcome here, you are most welcome here. As the Holy Spirit works, let His winnowing wind separate your wheat from your chaff, in order to blow the chaff away. The alternative is to be the chaff. We are convinced of better things in your case.

So come, and welcome, to Jesus Christ.

EVENING ◐ SPIRITUAL DROPSY

In Luke 14, we read an account of a time when Jesus was invited to share table fellowship with Pharisees at a Sabbath meal. He accepted the invitation even though they arranged to have a man with dropsy there, a man with an unquenchable thirst. They did this as a trap at a meal of rest. Jesus walked right into the trap, and healed the man of his dropsy—that man's desire was fulfilled. His thirst was quenched.

Jesus then turned to address the spiritual dropsy of all the other guests. He noticed that they were positioning themselves to land in the seats of honor. But this thirst for honor is just like dropsy. The more you drink, the thirstier you get.

We are gathered here, on the Lord's Day, sharing a meal with Jesus. This is a Table of *koinonia* fellowship, which means that we partake of it as those who have been welcomed into a love of all our brothers and sisters in Christ. Whatever the lowest place is here, we should want to take that place. Whatever the place of honor is, we should want that place to go to another.

There is no problem having dropsy and being at a meal with Jesus. That, by itself, is no defilement. Just know that it is His intent to heal you of it. Do you have burning ambitions? Are you thirsty for honor? Has every honor you have ever received only inflamed that thirst even more? Come, and rest. Come, and have your thirst quenched.

So come, and welcome, to Jesus Christ.

MORNING ✲ FUSSERS AND LADDER KICKERS

We have a strong religious tendency to get things backwards. We have a strong religious tendency to keep things exclusive. We have a strong religious tendency to want to climb up on the high platform of grace, and then to kick the ladder away, so that the riffraff cannot follow us up. This tendency is a wicked tendency, and it must be mortified.

On one occasion Jesus caused a Pharisee to marvel because He had not washed before dinner (Luke 11:38). The Lord interpreted this as a particular method for kicking the ladder away. He said that the Pharisees would load men up with impossible burdens, and would somehow magically exempt themselves (Luke 11:46). He said that the lawyers had taken away the key of knowledge, had not entered themselves, and had tried to hinder those who wanted to enter (Luke 11:52). This is right out of Aesop. It is dog in the manger religiosity.

God's standards are high indeed—but they are not just higher than the standards of the mob, the dregs, the rabble. God's standards are higher than the standards of the fussers and ladder kickers. All of us must die; that is the way the rsvp for the invitation is registered. We die, which means that we intend to come. And quickened by the power of the Spirit, we do in fact come. We are here now, gathered as forgiven sinners all. You name it, God forgives it. He forgives theft, hatred, fornication, and smug pharisaism.

So come, and welcome, to Jesus Christ.

EVENING ◐ WHAT ARE THEY DOING HERE?

Jesus regularly redraws religious boundaries, and He does so by means of table fellowship. But when we do what He has commanded, and we observe what He has established — as we are doing right now — there is a constant temptation to reestablish the old boundaries, the boundaries that He abolished.

This is a Table for cleansed sinners. There is no food here for those who are not cleansed. But here is the point where we veer off. We tend to morph this observance into a meal where, instead of celebrating the cleansing, we celebrate the fact that we don't need cleansing. But there is a vast difference between those who have been forgiven and cleansed, their sins and lawless deeds remembered no more, and those who believe they are in no need of cleansing. Both come before God in the conviction that He requires us to be clean.

But self-righteousness is not clean. Table fellowship with Christ is conducted with a demeanor of repentance, not a demeanor of being above it all. The table conversation sounds like humility and love, and does not sound like the tones heard in an exclusive club.

But ironically, it is an exclusive club. This is because a humble and contrite heart is a rarity, and it is so rare because we tend to focus on how humble and contrite everybody else's hearts are. How did those *others* get in here? The real question is how did *I* get in here, and to ask that question with trembling boldness.

So come, and welcome, to Jesus Christ.

MORNING ☼ A SPIRITUAL MEAL

The Scriptures teach us that this is a spiritual meal, but we must exercise great caution as we think of it this way. This is not because there is a problem with how the Bible describes it — obviously not — but rather because a number of false assumptions about the nature of spirituality have crept into our thinking over the centuries.

A spiritual meal is not an ethereal meal. It is not an intangible meal. What does it mean to be spiritual then? The answer is that the spiritual man is the obedient man, not a ghostly man. A carnal man is a disobedient man, not a material man.

The Christian faith is by no means earthly — but it is extraordinarily earthy. The Lord Jesus is at the right hand of God the Father in the heavens, and He rules all things from there. Because Heaven and earth have been joined back together in Him, we can rejoice in the materiality of that which He has given us. He has given us the world, and it is precisely for this reason that we are not to be worldly.

The world does not contain the principles for its own organization, and whenever it tries to organize itself, the results are worldliness, carnality, earthly-mindedness. But when the world surrenders to Heaven, the Lord of Heaven gives us the world.

We see this in the bread and wine. This is material bread, and material wine — just like bread and wine everywhere. We in the Church have the authority to take bread and wine from absolutely anywhere, and to pronounce the words of institution over them. When we do, it becomes a spiritual meal, that is, a meal brought to the obedience of Christ — just as you partakers are being brought to the obedience of Christ.

Every time we partake of this meal, we are engaging in a solemn oath, in which we recognize that God has laid claim to us, and by which we also declare that that Lord Jesus has laid claim to the entire world. That is what He was born into the world to do.

So come, and welcome, to Jesus Christ.

The accounts of the Lord's behavior in the gospels tell us repeatedly that He would eat with outcasts. This included Gentiles outside the covenant of Israel, and we sometimes might assume that this was the point. But while Jesus did have "other sheep" that were not from the Jewish fold (John 10:16), He also would share table fellowship with outcasts within Israel. He summoned Gentiles who didn't know, but He also invited Jews, who knew better than what they were doing.

Take the example of Zacchaeus. Jesus calls him a son of Abraham, meaning that he was Jewish. At the same time, he was engaged in a practice that gouged his countrymen — and he knew that he owed restitution, however legal his practices might have been. At the same time, Jesus invited Himself to sit down with Zacchaeus in order to break bread together.

Every week I say, "Come, and welcome, to Jesus Christ." This invitation is extended to every creature. It is an evangelistic invitation to those who are not yet baptized — come to the bread and wine through the water. But it is also an invitation to those who are baptized, and who have openly backslidden into some spiritual condition that is not honoring to God. Come, and welcome. Repent your sins, and just come. But the invitation is also extended to any who are backslidden, but no one else really knows about it. Externally you are a faithful Christian, but internally, your heart is far away from Him. Repent, turn away, confess . . . and hear this.

So come, and welcome, to Jesus Christ.

MORNING ☼ CHRIST IS NOT AT THE END OF A SUPPLY CHAIN

The Puritan William Bridge noted that it is "man's disposition to come to God at the second hand." As we approach the Supper, we are sometimes tempted to think of God as the wholesaler, and the minister of the particular church as the retailer. But that is not how this is at all.

God is not off at a distance. This is a meal with Him, and we are not receiving something from Him at the end of a long supply chain. God is with us in the creation — in Him we live and move and have our being — but more than this, He is with us in the covenant of grace. God is present, here, now.

When we partake of this meal in faith, we are partaking of Christ. He does not keep us at a distance. He is present here, according to His Word. Sometimes we feel that presence, and sometimes we don't. When we feel His presence with us, this is a testimony of His love for us. When we don't feel His presence in the same way, it is a testimony of our love for Him — we long to be with Him, and to know that we are with Him.

God interrupts our peace sometimes so that we will know more deeply what a great gift of grace that peace was. We long for it to return, knowing more fully what blessing it was. All these things are offered here, in this meal, and by a God who is present with us. We used to be far off, but no longer. We are celebrating the birth of Immanuel, remember, which means God with us.

So come, and welcome, to Jesus Christ.

This is the Table of the Lord, just as the Bible is the Word of the Lord. Both the Table and the Word contain great and precious promises. But here is the question, one that has troubled many (in one sense) and not troubled near enough (in another). Are these promises for you? Is your name on them? As you walk up to this Table, can you make a name tag in the divine handwriting? When you read a promise in Scripture, such as "I will never leave you or forsake you," does that promise have your name attached to it?

The answer is no in one sense, and emphatically yes in another. No, you cannot read a name tag here with your physical eyes, and no matter how many times you type your name into your Bible search program, you will not come up with any results. So, there it is — no. But this just means you cannot read your name with your physical eyes. You are invited to read your name, however.

This is what faith does. God's promise as externally stated is general, and faith makes it particular. Now faith doesn't create that particular reality, but rather reveals what God's secret decrees were all along. Before the foundation of the world, God determined by name who would respond to Him in faith, and here you are. God issues a general invitation to all, along with the authorization to act upon that invitation. It is therefore not presumption to come, act like you read your name on a name tag, and sit down. It is actually presumption not to.

So come, and welcome, to Jesus Christ.

MORNING ☼ A TWO-FOLD VIRTUE

The principle of new life is given instantaneously. There is no middle ground between death and life. Once a man is regenerated, he is no longer dead in his sins. Until he is quickened, he is entirely dead. There is no gradation between death and life. This is why the Scripture teach us plainly that we must be born again.

But once we are born again, there are gradations. We are not instantaneously there. We have not arrived. God's intent is for us to grow, and to grow slowly and steadily. He is fitting us for Heaven.

As we come to Him at this Table, we come seeking nutrition. We seek to grow. We should seek this growth in patience. You may not see the difference between this week and last week, just as you do not measure the height of your growing children on a weekly basis. Growth is rarely explosive.

This means that in the course of your sanctification, patience is a two-fold virtue. It is of course one of the virtues that God is folding into you. But it is also the virtue that makes it possible for you to understand what is happening.

The arrival of life is dramatic, but the tending of life rarely is. As you come here in faith, you are seeking to be built up and strengthened over time. The one who calls you is faithful, and He will do it.

So come, and welcome, to Jesus Christ.

EVENING ◐ SETTING DOWN YOUR DISPUTES

This Table is a place where you should set aside all disputes when you come.

In the first place, set aside any disputes you have with God. If you dispute with God, you will be confounded. Will the one who is made say to Him who is His maker, why have you made me like this?

What disputes might you have with God? You might dispute with Him over how much money you have, or your height and weight, or your birth order, or your sexual nature. This is His Table; do not come to it with any disputes in your heart.

Also set aside any disputes you have with the devil. If you dispute with the devil, you will be deceived. With him it is a loss even to enter into the conversation.

What disputes might you have with the devil? Remember that he is the accuser; he is the prosecutor. Your disputes with him have to do with what a great sinner you are. He accuses, and you try to agree and make excuses at the same time. Drop it, and cling to the righteousness of Jesus Christ.

And set aside any disputes you have with your fellow man. This can include many subjects of dispute, so let me mention just one. If you are disputing with your spouse and you are coming to this Table, then stop it. Drop it. Let it go. Leave it on the floor, and don't come back for it later. If you think that the other person has to go first, if the other person has to repent, if the other person is the problem, then set that disputing spirit aside, put that critical spirit down. Your hands can receive this bread and wine, but you have to set down your disputes first.

So come, and welcome, to Jesus Christ.

MORNING ☼ COMMUNION AS COMFORT FOOD

Our God is the God of all comfort. His Table is the Table of peace. We know that we are to confess and set aside our sins before we come, but we also need to be reminded that we should confess and set aside our fears.

This is a holy Table, and so we know that we are not to bring unholy things to it. But we need to reflect more on how this is a peaceful Table, and so we are not to bring our anxieties, fears, emotional tumults, or worries.

The Lord Jesus is the one who looked at the waves on Lake Galilee and said, "Peace, be still," and the wind and the waves obeyed Him. How big are your waves? How unsettled is your heart? You come here, among other reasons, so that the Lord can say to you, "Peace, be still." When He did this to the waves, the disciples' response was to ask who He was. What kind of man is this? We know who He is, and so we should be looking to Him in expectation, waiting for Him to speak. Your heart may be in a tempest, but you are Christian, and the Lord is in your boat. To change the metaphor back again, the Lord who can speak with such authority is at the head of His Table, which is this Table. He invites you to sit by saying, "Peace."

The bread and the wine that is offered here is sacramental food. It is holy food. It is the food of love. But never forget that in the most fundamental way possible, it is also comfort food.

So come, and welcome, to Jesus Christ.

EVENING ◐ A LARGE BOWL OF MERCY

When we think of manna, we tend to think of daily provision, or the fact that manna was the Lord Jesus in a type. This is all good, but there is a good deal more. Recall also that when the manna was gathered, it was to be gathered for that day — sufficient unto the day is the *grace* thereof.

But there was one place where the manna would last, where it would not rot the same way it would in the tents of the Israelites. That place was inside the ark of the covenant, under the mercy seat. There, in that place, the bowl of manna was a bowl of mercy (Ex. 16:33). And it was not a small bowl either; it was not a small museum piece morsel, kept for sentimental reasons. God had them store up about three-fifths of a bushel within the ark of the covenant. His grace is sufficient.

God's provision comes to you where you are, and the grace He provides is to be used by you as it comes. But never forget that there is a store of it, a plentiful store of it, inside the ark of the covenant. Never forget that God can keep what you need, and you cannot — even if you got it from God originally. In this life, grace comes on the fly and you may use it as it comes. But in your inheritance, grace is stored up, and it does not diminish.

When you pray on Tuesday afternoon for grace, that is your daily manna. Here, at this Table, we are at the mercy seat, and our provision does not and cannot fail.

So come, and welcome, to Jesus Christ.

MORNING ☼ BREAD AND WINE MULTIPLY

The Lord Jesus enacted the true nature of the world for us when He fed the five thousand and the four thousand. In both cases, He refuted the central tenet of unbelief, which is that resources are scarce, and that God must be a skinflint. Zero-sum thinking is the idea that more for one person means less for somebody else.

In a closed system, say one run by a den of thieves, zero sum games can and do exist. But in God's green world, He spends a great deal of time teaching our flinty hearts that the universe is governed by a generous Father. This Supper is like the feeding of the multitudes in this respect. This meal is intended to teach us more than that the bread and wine are good, but also that the bread and wine grow.

It is not the case that more for one means less for another. At this Table, more for one means more for everyone. Grace and peace be multiplied to you.

As we partake of this grace, look around. The more you share with God's people, the more you have. Your love grows as you give it away, just like the loaves and fish. As God's people give to you the more they have.

Life is a mystery, but not a contradiction.

So come, and welcome, to Jesus Christ.

EVENING ◐ SACRIFICE AND LOVE, GRACE AND GIFT

The prophet Habakkuk tells us in a certain place that though earthly food may fail us, God will remain our portion. He says it this way:

> Although the fig tree shall not blossom,
> Neither shall fruit be in the vines;
> The labour of the olive shall fail,
> And the fields shall yield no meat;
> The flock shall be cut off from the fold,
> And there shall be no herd in the stalls:
> Yet I will rejoice in the Lord,
> I will joy in the God of my salvation. (Hab. 3:17–18)

This is how we may apply these words here. Though earthly food may fail you, this heavenly food will never fail you. Though your table at home may be scantily set, though you are struggling with thin commons, this Table is always set. Though you have abundant food of an earthly sort, such that you are stuffed with it, surfeited in an unhealthy way with it, this food remains, simple and wholesome—bread and wine, sacrifice and love, grace and gift.

Though you don't know how to eat, this Table will teach you to eat. Though you tend to think that it is all about the substance of what you put in your mouth, the Spirit will teach you that it is more about with whom you eat. This is a *fellowship* meal.

You are here. You are welcome. Rejoice in the God of your salvation, and rejoice in the Lord always. He is here. You fellowship with Him. His bread is for you. This wine is His gift. Your sins are forgiven. Your past is wiped away. His kindness lies before you, and does so everlastingly. His goodness is from generation to generation. He knows how to be kind to His people, and you are His people.

So come, and welcome, to Jesus Christ.

MORNING ✵ GOD KNOWS YOUR WORKS

We know the gospel well enough to know that we are not in any way saved or justified by our works. We are saved to good works, and not by them (Eph. 2:8–10). At the same time, we know that God is mindful of our works, placing them at the point of fruit on the branches, and not at the point of the roots in the ground.

With that understanding, the apostle Paul commends those who by patient labor or work seek for glory, honor, immortality, and eternal life (Rom. 2:7). This Table is the Table of your salvation, it is the food and drink of salvation, and we may apply Paul's words from another context — the one who refuses to work should not eat (2 Thess. 3:10).

When the Lord speaks to the seven churches of Asia, He says to them all that He knows "their works." To five of the churches, the word is spoken as a kind encouragement, and it is stern to only two of the churches — Smyrna and Laodicea.

God knows your works. God knows your labors. He knows the weight you carry. He knows what about your tasks is a temptation to great discouragement. In that condition, He offers you this cordial. He knows you, and He set this Table. You are resting in the finished work of Christ alone, and yet at the same time — indeed, because of Christ's work — God knows your works.

So come, and welcome, to Jesus Christ.

EVENING ◐ EXHORTATION

In a time like ours, one of the fundamental distinctions we must master is the distinction between a sin and a crime. This is more complicated than it looks or sounds. A crime is something outlawed by the civil authorities, and in what they have done, they may have behaved wisely or foolishly. For example, sometimes they outlaw things that biblical law would also outlaw (e.g. murder), sometimes they outlaw things that the Bible defines as sin but not as criminal (e.g. hatred), and other times they outlaw things that the Bible defines as righteousness (e.g. disapproval of sodomy).

The one thing we must banish from our minds is the idea that legality defines righteousness. *It does not.* A legal divorce can be wicked before God, for example. And at the same time, we must banish the idea that many Christians have that if something is sinful in the eyes of God that there ought therefore to be a law against it. This is absurd also. Covetousness is a great sin, but it cannot be made illegal.

The way we should navigate this is by remembering that as Christians we always answer to God and His Scriptures in the first instance. If any conflict ever arises between a course of action required by the Word and a course of action required by the magistrate, we must always obey God rather than men.

The first step in doing this is to be severe on your own sin first. One of the reasons why we have such bizarre moralistic crusades in the public square is that individuals refuse to mortify their own sin first. We would always rather start with our neighbor. But this edifying procedure must be rejected every time the tempter suggests it to you.

Making this distinction can be hard work. You will need strength for the labor involved in it, and the nourishment is here.

So come, and welcome, to Jesus Christ.

MORNING ☼ NOT A TIER OF LOOSE KNOTS

This is a Table of promise, and because it is a gospel Table, this means that the promise is what God promises to us. The initiative is entirely His. Now if we receive what God promises us, then we must necessarily have it. We cannot receive His promise without having His promise. We are bound by His oath when we accept by faith what He has done. The strength of the oath is His grace.

Grace ties the oath tight; grace is not a tier of loose knots.

Because of our sinful confusions, we think that being under law means distance from sin, and that being under grace means that God is somehow okay with sin. No, it is the other way around. Being under law means being under continual condemnation because of an inability to stop sinning. Being under grace means that sin is no longer your master, and you can begin the very real process of walking in the light — a real walk in real light.

We know that Jacob saw a vision of a glorious ladder, with angels ascending and descending on it. The Lord Jesus tells us in John 1:51 that He is that ladder. He is the true connection between Heaven and earth and, as He has promised, He is here now. Come to Him in true faith, and you will ascend.

So come, and welcome, to Jesus Christ.

EVENING ◐ DECORATED DAMNATION

The apostle Paul speaks of how the Corinthians came together at the Table in such a fashion as to do more harm than good (1 Cor. 11:17). How are we to understand this? How may we prevent falling into this sin ourselves?

God has created us as material creatures, and so we cannot worship Him in a way that does not use matter. There is no such thing as purely spiritual worship for us. At the same time, there is such a thing as pure spiritual worship for us, and so that should be our great interest.

Pure spiritual worship is not that which does not involve bodies and matter, but rather the use of all the matter that forms us and which we touch in a way that proceeds from true, regenerate hearts. Without that new heart, without true conversion to Jesus, a man defiles all that he touches. With it, he consecrates all that he touches.

The human heart is therefore the catalyst in every kind of worship that God receives. The human heart is what proves the will of God, what is good, and acceptable, and perfect. But we cannot do this to or for ourselves — our own hearts are out of our reach. And so this is why the Scriptures teach us that regeneration is the work of the Spirit, and it is a work out of the control of mediating priests. Without the Spirit of God, the only thing a priest can do is decorate your damnation.

So come, and welcome, to Jesus Christ.

MORNING ☼ THE PROMISE COMES FIRST

One of the things we should gather from this Table is a right grasp of the relationship between promise and trouble. God's saints do go through troubles, but they are like a cloud that passes over the sun. Nonbelievers have their troubles as well, but theirs are like the pitch of night that is a type of the coming darkness, what the Lord called the outer darkness. That won't be the kind of night that anyone can dance away.

So how can you rightly identify your troubles as a passing cloud, as a brief interruption of sunlight. You can tell by whether or not God has bound Himself with a promise first. Joseph spent some time in a jail in Egypt, but it was a passing cloud. Why? He had the promise first, in the dream that God had given him. David spent a good deal of time running from Saul, hiding in the wilderness. But that was a passing cloud as well — Samuel had anointed him first. Furthermore, Samuel had anointed David after being taught not to judge by appearances, a fact that David should have noted. He was going to be confronted with distracting appearances himself. But when you have the promises, ignore the passing cloud.

But what of you? What are your troubles? A passing cloud, or the darkness of night? If the darkness of night, then call on the Lord Jesus and you will be saved, you and your household. But for many of you, your troubles are a passing cloud — you have all God's promises, gathered and summed up, here. Here is where God has bound Himself with a great oath. You have received the promise of that oath by evangelical faith if you know in your heart that His oath has gathered you up, and bound you in His love.

So come, and welcome, to Jesus Christ.

EVENING ◐ RECEIVING YOUR TOKEN

Are you discouraged? Do you have troubles pressing in on you? Are some of your troubles of such a nature that you can see no possible way out?

God is still your Father, and God wants you to learn how to remember in the dark what you knew in the light. God wants you to trust Him in the midst of discouragement. That is how He grows His saints — through difficulties and trials. As one Puritan put it, God had one Son without sin, but He had no sons without adversities.

Troubles come in various ways, and under differing circumstances. The envelopes that contain your troubling news are all different sizes and colors. But the seal on the envelope is always the same — it is from the Lord. Look at it. Examine the seal before you panic over the letter.

While you are in trouble, God gives you lesser deliverances to give you confidence that a greater deliverance is coming. Rise up, stepping on the kindnesses He shows you in the midst of your difficulties.

But you may wonder what lesser deliverance I could be talking about . . . you still have that debt, your child is still wayward, your friendship is still being threatened . . . what lesser deliverance? What token do you have that God is with you, and that He will in fact deliver you?

What token? Here — it is the broken body of Jesus (broken for you) and the shed blood of Jesus (shed for you). The only problem with this image is that of calling this a "lesser" deliverance. Call it an earlier deliverance, and trust Him for the final deliverance.

So come, and welcome, to Jesus Christ.

MORNING ☼ LEARNING TO LEAN

When you are discouraged, as one of God's saints, you should strengthen your hands and weak knees. Whatever your circumstances, God has received you. See? You are here at this Table. You are *welcome.*

This is the opposite of the condition of a man outside of Christ. Whatever encouragements he might have, day to day, they are worthless in the light of God's displeasure with him. What does the Scripture say? "God is angry with the wicked every day" (Ps. 7:11). He is angry with them when the sun is shining, and when the weather is nice. He is angry with them when they have plenty of food and money. He is angry with them when they seem to run everything, when they are lords on the earth . . . at least in their own minds. There is a serious disconnect between their actual condition and their perceived condition.

It is the same with discouraged saints, only running the other way. God has forgiven you. He has received you. He has brought trouble into your life so that you might learn to lean on Him in all your doing. He has you carrying the weight you are carrying in order to make you stronger. And He has done all this without abandoning you.

See? You are here. The Table is set, and if you are baptized and not under church discipline, this bread is for you. This wine is for you. So do you have troubles and discouragements? Then you need nourishment.

So come, and welcome, to Jesus Christ.

EVENING ◐ THE DEATH SPECIALIST

This Table is emblematic of the death of Jesus, and yet it is by this means that God enables us to partake of the living Christ. Christ is risen; He is not dead. And yet here is His body, and here is His blood. These emblems are dead, and yet through them we are being knit together with Life itself. How can that be?

If God had a workshop, the prime materials stacked up in piles in that workshop would all be the wreckage of death. This is what He specializes in, which is why the apostle Paul said this — "But we had the sentence of death in ourselves, that we should not trust in ourselves, but in God which raiseth the dead" (2 Cor. 1:9). While there is what we think is life in us, there is what we think is hope in us. But God is not an energy drink for our life; He is living water for our death.

I have been speaking over the last few weeks to those of you with troubles, which is to say, all of you. One of our difficulties is that we want to make these troubles smaller so that God might be willing to lend a helping hand with them, when we really need to see them as bigger. God deals with death. The Lord Jesus, now the steward of the whole universe, holds in His hands the keys of death and Hades.

So when we struggle against admitting death into our lives, we are actually struggling against the opportunity to see what God — who raises the dead — can do. The doors of every form of death have a key, and Jesus holds it.

So come, and welcome, to Jesus Christ.

MORNING ☼ SWEETNESS AND SEVERITY

The Puritan William Bridge once said, "It is our duty to behold things as God presents them." He was talking about how God loves to present severity and sweetness together. If we extract the severity alone, and try to live by that, we labor under a cloud of condemnation. If we extract the sweetness alone, and try to live by that, we become effeminate in our faith, and have no structure for our faith. Behold, the apostle says, both the kindness and severity of God (Rom. 11:22).

The ark of the covenant was crowned with the mercy seat, and Uzzah was struck dead because he touched that ark (2 Sam. 6:7). The cup of blessing was given to the Corinthians, and many of them were dead or sick because they tried to drink both it and their selfishness together (1 Cor. 10:16).

Only true evangelical faith can grasp both of these poles. The terrible God, shrouded in the darkness of ineffable holiness, is filled to overflowing with tender mercies. The God of all comfort and kindness throws down empires, judges the hypocrite and pretender, and lays waste to the pretensions of the scholar and wise man.

We capture both elements when we refer to our Lord and Savior, Jesus Christ. We have gathered to Him here; this is His Table, is it not? He is Lord, He is the everlasting Lord, with authority over absolutely everything that can be named. He is also the Savior of the wicked, the helpless, the lost.

So come, and welcome, to Jesus Christ.

EVENING ◐ LET THE WORD APPLY IT TO THE WOUND

The Word that accompanies the sacrament here is a Word that should be spoken to the occasion, to the circumstance. The bread and wine are constant; we have no authority to substitute other elements. We have no authority to adjust the sacrament itself.

But do we speak words of warning or words of comfort? Do we fence the Table, keeping some away, or do we seek to gather up the reluctant?

This depends entirely on whether we are observing the service in Thyatira, or Pergamum, or Ephesus, or Laodicea. The Word is what applies the sacramental service as it ought to be applied. To simply go through motions involving bread and wine is to invite a covenantal disaster. This is a meal with our Lord; it is not a liturgical drill.

If all we had were certain pronounced words, the words of institution, and the distribution of the elements, we would be treating this meal with disrespect. It is not a one-size-fits-all sort of thing.

Are you troubled? Are you complacent? Are you living with hidden sin? Are you walking in the light? Are you living in high presumption? Have you committed a sin that you have confessed a hundred times? If this meal is the poultice, then you must let the Word apply it to the wound. Nothing else will do this for you.

So come, and welcome, to Jesus Christ.

MORNING ☼ THE SEAL ON DAMNATION'S VAULT

Everyone gathered here, although we are gathered in Christ, is still aware of our remaining sinfulness. We are, in addition to this, aware of our sins, those which we have committed, and which we have confessed at the beginning of this service. Some of those sins are egregious, as man reckons them, and all of them are egregious in the sight of a holy God.

Because of those sins, we are often tempted to shrink back from this Table, as though we do not deserve to come. Of course we do not deserve to come — that is the whole point. Anybody here who thinks he deserves this meal has wandered into the wrong building, the wrong service, the wrong religion.

We know that we have sinned against God's laws and precepts, and so we want to shrink back. But having sinned against His law is no basis for sinning against His grace and His gospel. Do not compound your rebellion. You are invited to come. You are summoned.

No man was ever condemned for his sin. The condemnation always falls because of a refusal to turn from it. The seal on the vault of damnation bears this imprint — "I will not turn." The sealing of damnation is complete when the wax on that seal hardens, just like the heart it represents. God is angry with the wicked every day *"if he turn not"* (Ps. 7:11–12). This means that the damning sin, the only damning sin, is stubbornness. It is not so with you.

So come, and welcome, to Jesus Christ.

We are the people of God, and so of course He promises to feed us. We are the sheep of His pasture, and He also promises to feed us in the presence of our enemies (Ps. 23:5).

And while we are being fed, our enemies are not silent about it. While we are being fed by the Lord, we hear their commentary about what is going on. They have opinions about our food, just as we are instructed to have opinions about theirs.

While Hezekiah and his people were besieged in Jerusalem, Rabshakeh, their adversary, taunted them about their food. He said that Hezekiah (and by implication, the Lord) would only be able to provide them with the loathsome food and drink of their own bodily waste (Is. 36:16). But if they listened to him, and surrendered, they would be led to a land of "corn and wine, bread and vineyards" (Is. 36:17). He would provide them with a *true* feast, and there they would be able to serve a "*great* king, the king of Assyria (Is. 36:4)."

God counters with a promise to Hezekiah (Is. 37:30) that they will be fed, and Sennacherib will come to nothing. There is a twofold refutation. What they say about our Table is false, and will be shown to be false. Secondly, what they claim about their promised food is also false. Why spend money for bread that is not bread (Is. 55:1–2). Come, let your soul delight in fatness.

The great king, the king of Assyria, was about to encounter an epic disaster, and that would be crowned with the indignity of being murdered by his own son. This, in contrast with the great king of Heaven and earth, who gave up His Son, who willingly laid down His life for us, that we might have the food and drink of everlasting life. And here it is now, the bread and wine of true grace.

So come, and welcome, to Jesus Christ.

MORNING ☼ THE SUPPER AS RAINBOW

The world has sinned since the time of Noah, and there have been times when the world has sinned most grievously. But though the world has sinned, the Lord has nevertheless promised that this sinful world will never again be under water.

In an analogous way, the saints of God have sinned since their conversion — and again, sometimes most grievously. At the same time, for the true saints of God, just like the world will never be under water again, so the converted sinner will never be under wrath again.

It is possible for a baptized covenant member to be under the wrath of God, but this only happens when he has always been under the wrath of God. It is not possible for a baptized covenant member to be truly delivered from the wrath of God, and then returned to it again. The apostle Peter tells us that baptism is an antitype of the flood (1 Pet. 3:20–21), and after that flood, we were given a sign of His commitment to never do that again.

So here is Jesus Christ. He is your ark, and He is your rainbow. You are not saved by admiring the ark from a mountain top, with water lapping at your feet. You are saved by getting in it. You may look to the rainbow of promise in faith, but only after you have left the ark, after the flood. For those truly regenerate, the judgment of God can never fall again, having fallen completely on Jesus.

So come, and welcome, to Jesus Christ.

EVENING ◐ A THOUSAND LIVES OF SIN

In our confusion, we tend to use the greatness of our sin as an argument against receiving the mercy of God. But that is not how the Bible reasons. Isaiah says that though our sins are as scarlet, they shall be as white as snow. And David prays this way — "pardon mine iniquity, for it is great" (Ps. 25:11).

Your sin might be great indeed. It might be shocking to others, and scandalous. But all this is an argument that cuts in the opposite direction than we want to think.

Yes, your hidden sin, your hypocrisy, might be a very great sin. But there is more mercy on this Table than there is sin in you. Take whatever sin it is that is troubling you, whatever heinous thing you did, give you a thousand lives in which to engage in that same sin over and over, and take into account the fact that each repetition of the sin makes it more grievous still, it remains a fact that there is mercy here for you, and to spare.

Our Savior is mighty to save. The Scripture teaches us that He saves to the uttermost. The one doing the forgiving here is Almighty. The one sinning against His kindness is a vapor.

Never forget there is more mercy in Christ than there is sin in you. This is a fundamental axiom in all evangelical religion.

So come, and welcome, to Jesus Christ.

MORNING ☼ PROVE IT

In the Old Testament law, because of man's hardness of heart, it was possible for a man to put away his wife for trivial reasons. When men and women become bitter, every trivial thing rises to intolerable proportions, and the thing cannot be resolved. But when a woman was put away by a man for trivial reasons, it was required that he give her a bill of divorce, so that she could prove she was no longer bound to such a man.

When we drift away from God, and are unfaithful to Him, we sometimes assume that a divorce has happened because that is what we deserve. But God does not treat us according to our merits, which are actually demerits, but rather in accordance with the obedience of His Son, Jesus Christ.

So when say that we are separated from God, He often surprises by asking us to prove it. We are emotionally estranged from Him, on our side of things, but He asks us to prove that He divorced us. "Where is the bill of divorce?" the Lord asks in Isaiah 50:1. Your sins have separated you, but do not pretend that He has acted the part of an irritable husband.

So if you are a Christian who feels distant from God, all you must do is surrender that distance — you are the one who embraced it — repent of it, and come, return.

So come, and welcome, to Jesus Christ.

EVENING ◐ JUST BREAD AND WINE

This is a humble meal, offered to us by God through the humble obedience of Jesus Christ, even to the point of death on a cross. This meal came from humility, and proceeds to humility.

The elements are humble — simple bread and wine. It is a plain meal, not one calculated to make us think of rich banqueting halls. At the same time, the Bible does describe it as a feast, but this must mean an abundance of something other than Nebuchadnezzar's kind of feasting. Just bread and wine.

We have a white table cloth, and trays and platters that are silver in color, but we should make sure to understand this rightly. We are not trying to adorn this meal by making it more glorious. We do not have that ability. We are seeking to show honor, but we want to do it in a way that is understated, not distracting us from the glory of humility that is there. If we were all hiding in catacombs, and someone crept out at night to buy some bread and wine, and we observed the Supper under such circumstances, with rats scurrying in the background, all the glory that is here, would also be there. The difference is that we might be more aware of it there because it is the glory of humility.

But be aware that humility is called for in every condition of life, and not just times of persecution. Humility is a constant need. So we should not cultivate artificial humiliation, but rather clothe ourselves with the real thing.

So come, and welcome, to Jesus Christ.

MORNING ☼ HUMBLED OR DISCOURAGED?

What is the difference between being humbled and being discouraged? This is an important question as we prepare ourselves to come to this meal. Humbling ourselves is how we wash up for this meal, and discouragement is a counterfeit form of washing up.

So what is the difference? The Puritan William Bridge is a great help here. A discouraged saint is thinking about his own condition — it is all about his own condition. A humbled saint is concerned for the dishonor done to God by his sin, and not primarily concerned with the trouble he himself is in as a result of it.

It is possible to be discouraged, but not humbled, as Cain was when he complained that his punishment was more than he could bear. The point of grief was what was happening to him. It is possible to be humbled, but not discouraged, as the prodigal son was when he decided to return home. In that case, his discouragement brought him to humility, and humility brought him home, willing to be received as a servant.

Humbling results in a glad reception. Discouragement spirals downward, ever downward, and does not end unless it is repented. This is a meal for the humbled, not for the discouraged. If you are discouraged, you may certainly come, but set aside your discouragement first — it is a sin, remember — and accept the humbling instead.

So come, and welcome, to Jesus Christ.

We have asked what the difference is between being humbled and being discouraged. The first thing we considered is the difference between thinking about dishonor to God and discomfort for oneself. But there is more to this.

Another difference is that we find truth in the gospel paradox that teaches us to respond to them quite differently. A godly man can be humbled for sin, however small it is, and a godly man will not be discouraged for sin, however great it is. In the other direction, an ungodly man will be discouraged over sin, however small, and he will not be humbled for sin, however great.

The Holy Spirit is called the Comforter by the Lord Jesus, and one of the central offices of this Comforter is to convict men of sin (John 16:7–8). But this means that true conviction of sin is a comfort. It means that humbling for sin and rejoicing over forgiveness go quite well together. But a man cannot be discouraged and rejoice at the same time — they are polar opposites. The Bible teaches this plainly. There is sorrow that leads only to death, and there is sorrow that leads to a regret-free forgiveness (2 Cor. 7:10). One of those sorrows is the gift of the Spirit, and the other is entirely of the flesh. God did not send His Spirit into the world so that we might learn how to feel sorry for ourselves. We already had that down.

The more you are humbled for sin, the more joy you have. The more you are discouraged over sin, the less joy you have.

So come, and welcome, to Jesus Christ.

MORNING ☼ REMEMBERING THE BASICS

We have considered the importance of reading the story we are in. In doing this, we avoid the trap of being like brute beasts — like pigs under an oak tree, eating all the acorns, but never, ever, looking up. The acorns are just there, taken for granted.

But as we read the story, we must also take care not to "soar too high into God's prerogative," as one Puritan put it. We can tell what kind of story we are in, and we can know what we are doing in it, and we can know whether or not we are here in order to receive God's blessing. When Cain and Abel departed from making their offerings, they both knew where they stood. That does not mean that they (or we) can know all the details involved. But we can certainly know the basics.

The basics are these. Christ shed His blood and His body was broken for all who come to Him in true humility and faith. As we break this bread and pass around the cup, God is knitting us together in love. Are there interruptions and obstacles? Of course. This is a sinful world. But God is determined to restore this world, and to do so by this means — by gathering a people to Himself, to be called by His name.

As He does this, we are to look to Him, and not to ourselves. When we look to ourselves, we start to fail, or perhaps to panic. When we look to Him, we have it all.

So come, and welcome, to Jesus Christ.

EVENING ◐ THE ROOT OF UNBELIEF

We have been considering how to cultivate a humble spirit without falling into discouragement. The way to approach this is by naming your sins rightly, and by tracing our sins back to the root sin, and identifying that root sin correctly.

Whenever you sin, whatever the sin is, the root of it is unbelief. If you find and identify that root, you will be humbled in the way that you ought to be, and you will not be discouraged — because repenting of unbelief means that you are turning into faith. All other forms of beating yourself up are actually forms of doubling down on the actual sin, which is unbelief.

This also helps us to grow in mercy towards others, and the sins they commit. When someone else sins, it is unbelief, and when I am exasperated with their sins, my sin is unbelief — the very same sin. This means that my exasperation is misplaced. How can I act superior when I am doing the very same thing?

When I correct the sin of unbelief in my heart, I cannot do it by turning to another place in my heart, and looking to something called "faith." Faith does not look at faith. Faith looks to Jesus. Faith looks away. This is why the preaching of the gospel is so encouraging. It invites you to look up, and to look away. This is why the Lord's Table is such an encouragement. You are invited to come and sit, to eat and to drink. You are invited to look away from yourself and all your troubles.

So come, and welcome, to Jesus Christ.

MORNING ☼ SMALL BUT SIGNIFICANT

Solomon tells us that there are four creatures that are apparently insignificant, but yet are extraordinarily wise. This is one of God favorite devices in telling His stories. Those four creatures are the ant, the rock badger, the locust, and the lizard (Prov. 30:24ff). Despite their smallness, they provide food and shelter for themselves, showing up in unexpected places, and they do so without the apparent resources to do so. But it still happens.

Locusts swarm together, ants work together, rock badgers can make their homes in towering cliffs, and lizards can make their way into kings' palaces. In God's economy, the sum is routinely greater than the sum of the parts. Birds wheel in the sky as though they were one organism, and schools of fish can function the same way. The mystery of small entities cooperating is actually a staggering mystery.

In the same way, local churches can appear to be insignificant, far away from anything that matters really. Our observance of the Supper here now can look like a collection of people in a room eating bread and drinking wine. But keep in mind that every Lord's Day, all over the world, millions of men and women, boys and girls, are all doing the same thing — worshiping God, hearing His Word, and partaking of these elements. At the end of the process, the entire world will be shaped and discipled by this reality.

If we could see the church as she actually is, extending throughout all history, encompassing centuries, spanning continents, growing into her full strength, not by by-passing her weakness, but by embracing it, we would all marvel at the greatness of God's wisdom and glory. We are invited to see that reality by faith right now. God is at work, and God is at work in the way He usually goes about it.

So come, and welcome, to Jesus Christ.

EVENING ◐ WEAK FAITH STAGGERS UNDER PROMISES

God promises to meet us here in this meal, enabling us to partake of the Lord Jesus Christ by faith. Note that we chew and swallow by faith, and the blessing that comes to us is in accordance with our faith. Grace comes to us through means such as bread and wine, but the catalytic means for us in this is our faith. Grace does not come into us as though we were filling up a little bucket with a garden hose. Two men can come and receive the same amount of bread and the same amount of wine, and yet be strengthened in varying degrees.

This is because the Bible teaches that faith is variable. It is possible to have little faith, weak faith, and it is possible to have more faith than Jesus saw anywhere else in Israel.

Now how does faith relate to the Supper? This is a Table laden with promises, and different kinds of faith react differently to promises. Strong faith feeds on promises, and weak faith staggers under them. The promises that are present here are enormous, and it is God's intention to feed our faith with them so that our faith may grow and feed even more.

The body of Christ is life for the world. The death of Jesus is forgiveness for the world. The blood of Jesus is cleansing for the world. The resurrection of Jesus is justification for the world. And the church of Jesus Christ is the place where these realities are enacted, and where these promises are believed and set forth so that the world may come to them.

Is your faith weak, then? Pray that the Lord of the Table would strengthen you, so that you do not stagger. Is your faith strong? Then trust God to make it stronger. But in either case, come.

So come, and welcome, to Jesus Christ.

MORNING ☼ INVINCIBLE GRACE

Eating in the presence of God is a glorious privilege. Drinking in the presence of God is a glorious privilege.

But God is not just present with us in the person of Christ at this Table. He is also present around this Table, in the hearts of all His saints, and He is present in the sacrificial food which was prepared for us by His faith, and which is only received for blessing by our faith, which in turn is a gift to us from God.

So everything about this meal is gift; everything about it is grace. The grain was grace, and the flour, and the bread. The grapes were grace, and the fermentation, and the wine. The host at the head of the Table is grace, and every last one of the guests, and the faith, hope, and love that bring us all together like this. There is not anything here that is given that was not given by Him — and all of it is given.

What do you have that is not a gift? And if it is a gift, then why should we boast as though it was not? Grace is a true conqueror. Grace is invincible.

So come, and welcome, to Jesus Christ.

When the Lord Jesus preached His famous sermon, the Sermon on the Mount, He began with the Beatitudes. Too many people read these as though they were a set of impossible hurdles. But Jesus was beginning His message as God loves to begin all His gospel work — with promises.

We are told in Scripture that the one who begins a good work in us will also be faithful to fulfill it. But we may also reason backwards — the one who will fulfill the good work is the one who began it. If He gives us the gift of seeing Himself, He also gives the gift of enabling us to be peacemakers. If He gives us the filling, He also gave us the hunger and thirst for righteousness to begin with.

This is the work that God gives us to do — that we believe in the one He has sent. The beginning, middle and end of all our duties is to trust in Him, to believe in Him, to rest in Him. Why? Because the just shall live by faith.

God is at work here. God offers Himself here. If He is doing it at all, He is doing it all. This means that if the grace in you is true grace, it does not matter how tiny it is. And if it is not true grace, it does not matter how strong it appears to you to be.

We are here as guests, as supplicants. We ask for and we receive the body and blood of Jesus by faith alone. Treasure those words, for they are your gospel, they are your salvation.

So come, and welcome, to Jesus Christ.

MORNING ☼ WHY DID YOU NOT BELIEVE?

Jesus used to ask His disciples "why" questions. When they were afraid of their boat sinking, and Christ was asleep in the boat, He asked them why they were afraid (Matt. 8:26). When they were anxious about not having brought bread, He asked them why (Matt. 16:8). When Peter began to sink into the water he had been walking on, Jesus asked him why (Matt. 14:31).

Jesus asks us about our doubts in order to show that there is no real reason for them. When we doubt Him, He asks us why, and then we say *ummmm*.

You are Christian disciples, which means that you should be all in. You call yourself by His name, which means that you are holding nothing back. But because our circumstances, because of the world, the flesh, and the devil, we will sometimes discover that we were not as all in as we thought we were.

In that shape, we come to this Table. We do not find ourselves banned from the Table for the faltering, but rather we encounter a gentle admonition. Why did you take so long to come? In this context, the chiding of Jesus is encouragement.

So come, and welcome, to Jesus Christ.

EVENING ◐ LIKE BEING WATERBOARDED

When we come to this Table, we are often mindful of our own weakness. This is good. We are weak, and we know that we must be made strong. One of the things God does for us to make us strong is that He feeds us.

But God does not just feed us, He also exercises us. He puts us into situations where we must act on the basis of the strength we have been given — even if we feel as though it is not very much.

This is why God gives us troubles, to grow us in our strength. He does not overtax us, but He does tax us. On top of that, we often feel as though we have been overtaxed. But God knows our frame, and He knows how to test and grow us in a way that does not truly overwhelm. It is like being waterboarded — you are not drowning, but you can feel like it.

And in His providence, because this is how He tells stories, it is often the case that the strong fall, while the weak stand. This is why all of us, strong and weak, must confess our weakness and come to Him. This is why all of us, in Christ, are strong and able to stand.

So come, and welcome, to Jesus Christ.

MORNING ☼ ELMS AND OLIVES

We have here gathered around the Table of the Lord. As the bride of Christ, we are like a fruitful vine, growing around the sides of His house. As the children of God, we are like olive shoots, growing up around His Table.

We often come here, mindful of how weak and small we are. But here is something that we need to remember. God does not measure things as we do. What is more impressive — a small grape vine, or a stately elm? What is more striking — two rows of grape vines, or two rows of majestic oaks? Well, the trees are more impressive, but the vines are more fruitful.

And compare the great trees with the olive trees. The olive trees are much smaller, and more gnarly-looking. But they are also more fruitful.

God delights in bringing fruit out of small vines. He delights in the olive shoots around His Table, and it should delight us to gather there in that capacity. That is what we are, and we must not chafe at what we are.

You are here at His Table, and He nourishes you here. He does not do it to turn you into a majestic tree. He does it to make you fruitful.

So come, and welcome, to Jesus Christ.

EVENING ◐ **LITTLE GRACE, GREAT GRACE**

Growing in grace is like climbing a tree, as the Puritan William Bridge once observed. When you want to grow in grace, what do you do? Well, you start with the lowest branches, those which are close to the ground. This is another way of saying that you start where you are.

There are doctrines near the top, and there are doctrines right next to the ground — where a child can climb. The doctrines near the top would be those issues that roil theologians of various traditions. The doctrines near the ground would be the fact that God loves you, and invites you to partake with one another in love. Another doctrine near the ground is that you cannot deserve to climb — climbing is a gift, not a reward. Another branch next to the ground is that all of us are climbing together.

As you begin, meditate on those things you understand. Reflect on them, chew on them, give thanks for them. You can be assured that nothing you learn here will conflict with anything you will learn later. Small achievements in grace will never collide with great achievements in grace. The beginning of a task is not contradictory to the completion of it.

Little grace is not contradicted by great grace.

So come, and welcome, to Jesus Christ.

MORNING ☼ A DIME-STORE OZYMANDIAS

For the last two thousand years, the Christian Church has been toppling tyrants. This started when the kings of the earth and the rulers of the former age banded together and decided that they were going to throw off the Messiah's chains. They had Him in the grasp, and so they killed Him.

But Jesus rose from the dead, which did more than disrupt their plans — it absolutely destroyed their plans. Since that time, the Lord has told us to counter every attempt to bring back the old order by similar means. We are to imitate the Lord's way of doing this. We are commanded to destroy their plans . . . how? By gathering together to sing psalms and hymns, hear the Word declared, and to eat bread and drink wine. What kind of battle plan is that? I'll tell you . . . it has overthrown more despots than all the armies of the world combined. We wonder what kind of threat that kind of behavior could be, but note — how do totalitarians treat free and unrestricted Christian worship? Right . . . as the ultimate threat to everything they want to do.

Now one writer accurately described our current president as a "dime-store Ozymandias." Sometimes the strength of unbelief looks more powerful, sometimes less powerful. But regardless, overthrow their pretended strength with gospel weakness. Take note — any weakness brought in by our sin overthrows nothing. But the weakness that is the result of obedience is something that the devil and all tyrannical rulers fear. Such obedience is resurrection fodder. Such obedience is seed in the ground. This is what God uses.

So come, and welcome, to Jesus Christ.

As we come to this Table, week after week, we know that the Lord is feeding us. And we should take note of all the different ways Scripture talks about the feeding of us.

In the famous passage at the end of the gospel of John, where Jesus asks Peter three times if he loved Him, much attention is paid to the different words used there for the word love. But not as much attention is paid to the fact that in the first exchange, after Peter answered the Lord affirmatively, the Lord responded with "feed my *lambs*." The last two times, He tells Peter to feed His sheep, but the first time it is "feed my lambs" (Jn. 21:15–17).

As has often been pointed out, being a sheep is not the most flattering metaphor in the world. Sheep are not the super-heroes of the animal kingdom. But lambs are a weak version of that. And Jesus tells Peter to feed my lambs. This means that Jesus *has* lambs, and it means that they are to receive food. It also means that the food we receive is all grace—it must not be any kind of achievement award, or "best in show" ribbon.

You are here, and perhaps you feel your weakness. Perhaps you feel it acutely. Know that this food is for you. Jesus did not come to this earth for all those (non-existent) people who had their act together. He traveled through the land, seeking out the weak and the diseased. He is the great Healer, not the Giver of gold medals.

There will come a time in redemptive history when He does say, "Well done, good and faithful servant" (Matt. 25:23). That does happen, and we should yearn for it. But He does not say that to us yet. What does He say to us now? He says, "Take, and eat." He says, "Take, and drink."

So come, and welcome, to Jesus Christ.

MORNING ☼ EDIBLE THEOLOGY, LIQUID DOCTRINE

We sometimes divide up things that ought not to be divided. Just because we can distinguish them does not mean that they should be separated. We can distinguish height, breadth, and depth, but we cannot remove one without removing all of them. We can distinguish soul and body, but to separate them is to die. We can distinguish Word and sacrament, but it is utter folly to try to separate them.

We are given a Word and a Table. God intends for the Word to accompany the sacrament, and for the sacrament to accompany the Word. To have theological lectures alone is like gathering your family around a table every night for words coming out of mouths, but with nothing coming out of the oven. To have the sacrament alone is like having a family that shovels the food in, but cannot be prevailed upon to converse with one another. Do you want to be in a family that talks, but never eats? Or in a family that eats, but never talks? How about neither?

We gather to hear the Word, and we gather to feed upon the Word we have been given. What do we have on this Table before us? Edible theology, that's what. Liquid doctrine. Love, doctrine, peace, conversation.

What God has joined together, no man should separate. Talk with God, partake with one another, share with one another, give to one another, and receive from one another. The Word informs us that this is what we are doing. The sacrament gives us opportunity to do. But without the Word, the sacrament does more harm than good. Without the sacrament, the Word doesn't get down into your bones.

So come, and welcome, to Jesus Christ.

EVENING ◐ COMING NEAR TO HEAR

When we gather at the Lord's Table, we are coming near to Him. We are approaching Him. How could we be partaking of Him and not be coming near? From the vantage of the holy things, our worship is a coming. From the vantage of our daily lives, our worship is a going. Come, let us go to worship the Lord.

Now in Isaiah 48, the Lord has a word for those who would come unto Him. He says, "Come ye near unto me, *hear ye this*" (v. 16).

What does He want us to hear? Among other things, He says, "I am the Lord thy God which teacheth thee to profit." In this context, it means that He wants our observance of this Supper to edify us, to build us up, to establish us. But it doesn't do this automatically. Paul tells the Corinthians that their observance of the Supper is not profiting them; it is doing more harm than good.

God teaches us to profit, but we learn to profit when we hear what He is teaching us. As we see the Lord in and through the entire service, we stop attributing a mere earthly value to it.

So God is here. And so are you — because He has summoned you. He has summoned you because He has something to say to you, and He wants you to hear it. You may hear it, by a true and lively faith, as you approach this Table to eat and to drink.

So hear what He says to you.

So come, and welcome, to Jesus Christ.

MORNING ☼ ACCEPTING WHAT HE GIVES

In just a few moments we are going to be eating and drinking the good news of our salvation. Before we do that, let us hear the good news of our salvation.

Our salvation, the whole thing, is God's gift to us. He is our righteousness, our justification, and our sanctification. He gives Himself to us completely, and so it is that we are saved. We do not commend ourselves to Him on the basis of our performance. Rather, He gives us all things, including our performance.

The Puritan William Bridge said it this way: "He will require no more than He gives; He will give what He requires, and He will accept what He gives." This is complete grace; this is secure salvation. We might protest there is chaff with our wheat. There most certainly is, but do you not think that God knows about this? And don't you think that He knows how to keep the wheat and get rid of the chaff? He certainly doesn't it do it the other way.

In Revelation 8, after the seven angels are mentioned, "another angel" comes, and I take this angel to be the Lord Jesus — because of what He is described as doing. The prayers of the saints are incense and they ascend up to God from that angel's hand (Rev. 8:4). If our prayers ascended from our own hands, we would be in trouble. If our prayers were their own smoke and that alone, we would all be lost. But our prayers are presented to the Father from the hand of Christ.

This means that you don't need to come to this Table cringing, wondering if "it" is good enough. In your own name, of course it is not good enough. But if you are here in the name of Jesus, then everything you show up with is part of what God gave you to come here with. And if He gave it to you, of course He will receive it back from you. So hear these blessed words.

So come, and welcome, to Jesus Christ.

In partaking of this meal, we are recognizing that the Lord Jesus is our ruler and sovereign. We rejoice in His righteousness, and we exult in His care for us. That care is manifested in a glorious way, here, at this Table.

"For the Lord your God is God of gods, and Lord of lords, a great God, a mighty, and a terrible, which regardeth not persons, nor taketh reward: He doth execute the judgment of the fatherless and widow, and loveth the stranger, in giving him food and raiment" (Dt. 10:17–18).

Our God is the God of gods. He is the Lord of lords. He is mighty and terrible, and cannot be bought off with human bribes. The only payment He has ever received concerning His judgment of us was the payment of His Son's blood, which is the memorial before us now. He is the one who defends the fatherless and widow, rising up to destroy all those who would show contempt to them.

Our God loves the stranger — which is what we were before His kindness brought us near. And what does He do for the stranger? He provides him with raiment, which in our case was the perfect white robe of Christ's righteousness. We were naked and He clothed us.

What else does He do? He provides us with food. Here before us is the body of Jesus Christ, broken for sinners, and the blood of Jesus Christ, shed for sinners. May you come to this meal? Well, are you a sinner? Have you recognized that sin by receiving the washing represented in baptism? If you have, then you may come. Anyone may come on this basis. Anyone may respond to this invitation. And all who may come on this basis *must* come.

So come, and welcome, to Jesus Christ.

MORNING ☼ AND EATS HATE

God does not just feed us when times are easy. He feeds us when we are at home and at peace, He feeds us on the road, and He feeds us when we are at war. He sets a Table for us, David says, in the presence of our enemies.

There are two ways this could go. One way would represent a wavering of faith on our part. The presence of our enemies, and their awareness of us, could cause us to lose our appetite. We might come to think it was somehow not appropriate for us to eat—even though God prepared the food—when we were in such a circumstance. But to state this plainly shows us what we ought to do. The Lord prepared the Table for a reason, after all.

The other way it can go is this. Our enemies see what God has done for us, and the incongruity of the whole thing is not lost on them either. But their response is rage. We can know this, and refuse to alter our enjoyment of God's kindness to us, and yet remain free from spite.

If any of them set down their weapons of rage, and petition the Lord of the Table for a seat at it, He would provide one—a seat purchased by His own blood, just as our seats were purchased. No, we are driven by joy, and not by spite. How could we begrudge such a thing, after what it took to get us here?

No, this is the Table that feeds love, and eats hate. The world, and all it contains, will go down before it.

So come, and welcome, to Jesus Christ.

This is a meal indeed, but it is also preparation for the Meal. It is a true Supper, but it is not the final Supper. All of history is God's preparation for the final Table of rejoicing, the great Supper of the Lamb.

In one way we certainly are at the Table. Sit and eat, sit and drink. But in another sense we are all still in the kitchen. We take a morsel on the run, the way a cook might taste how the food is coming along. We are still pilgrims, and this is why it is a privilege to snitch from the hors d'oeuvres tray, sitting there by the kitchen door. There is food here, there is camaraderie here, but there is also a mess and quite a bit of hurly burly. If you are frazzled, or distracted, calm your spirit. Quiet your heart. Peek out the door — the ultimate Table is set, and it is waiting for us there.

We must always remember that history is fluid, not static, and this means remembering that God is taking us somewhere. An understanding of where He is taking us, and all human history, and all the nations of men, is an eschatological understanding. One of the reasons conservations discourage so easily is that they don't have a robust eschatology. Without a robust eschatology, every battle becomes the whole war. But this is not how God is governing things at all.

So come, and welcome, to Jesus Christ.

MORNING ☼ BEING FITTED

The Puritans used to speak of improving their baptisms. By this they did not mean that the sacrament of baptism had any deficiencies, but rather that the sacrament of baptism was a beginning.

God is easily pleased with us, and with our improvements, but He is not easily satisfied. In fact, because we will live forever, and because He is always the infinite God, and we will always be finite, the process of growing up into Him will never be done. Because it will never be done, He will never be satisfied with us in that sense, as though we had somehow arrived. But every step along that way will be pleasure and satisfaction in another sense. This Table here is one of those steps. So come, improve your baptism.

As you do, never forget the actual journey you are on. Jonathan Edwards once said that for the unbeliever, this world will be as close to Heaven as he will ever get, while for the believer this world will be as close to Hell as he will ever get. Everything comes down to what it is we are becoming. We are being fitted for Heaven, or we (in rebellion) are insisting on being unfitted for it. Note the passive voice — we are *being fitted*. We are not *earning*.

So we improve our baptisms as we come to worship the Lord, as we hear His Word proclaimed, as we sing praises to Him, as we partake of His body and blood here at this Table, and as we walk in newness of life in the course of each week.

So come, and welcome, to Jesus Christ.

EVENING ◐ UNCLEAN CROWS ALL OVER IT

In Genesis 15, Abraham is told to offer a sacrifice in which the sacrificial animals were divided in two. This was a time when God was going to give him a great promise concerning his posterity, and it was a numinous and holy moment.

But when birds came down upon the sacrifice, they were treating it as just so much carrion — and so Abram drove the birds away. They were unclean birds, and they had no business desecrating a clean sacrifice.

In the same way, as we approach this Table, which is a Table of sacrificial praise, lifted up on the thanksgiving of God's people, do not let any unclean birds near your heart and mind. Come with forgiven hearts, and clean hands. Come with a song in your heart, and a song in your mouth.

Centrally, put away the vulture of envy and snark. If there is anyone in this room that you harbor malice toward, then when you look down at the bread in your hand, you should see unclean crows all over it. Imitate our father Abram, and scatter them.

How? Forgive one another. Love one another, Forebear with one another. Let it go. Whatever they did to you, it was a lot less than what you did to Jesus, and He let it go. So we have gathered to partake in love and joy, and to chase off the birds.

So come, and welcome, to Jesus Christ.

MORNING ☼ DEWS AND DOWNPOURS

As we come to this Table week after week, we are approaching the Lord Jesus. We are partaking of Him, and being knit together with one another in love. But sometimes, it might not feel that way to us. Sometimes we are tempted to be discouraged because we don't sense the progress strongly enough.

But as one wise old Puritan taught, God's answers to our prayers are both visible and invisible. Our prayers rise to Him, as water vapor rises from the earth. Sometimes our prayers return to us as in a thundershower, and you can hear it pounding on the roof. But other times God returns our prayers to us in the dew, which we cannot hear at all, and which we discover later.

As we gather together, we consistently pray that the Lord would protect us, and that He would use us in this state of protection to be able to offer the way of life to those who are still under His judgments. In effect, we are praying the sentiment of Zephaniah 2:3 — "Seek ye the Lord, all ye meek of the earth, which have wrought his judgment; seek righteousness, seek meekness: it may be that ye shall be hid in the day of the Lord's anger."

The answer to this prayer may be dramatic and visible, like the Hebrew children protected in the land of Goshen, or like Noah in the ark, or it may be quiet and mysterious, like the working of providence that delivered Mordecai from Haman.

So come, and welcome, to Jesus Christ.

EVENING ◐ DEFERRED GLORY IS GREAT GLORY

Every week, when I read the words of institution for this Supper, it includes the phrase "you show the Lord's death till He comes." This means that this meal has two elements in it—consummation and delay. We commune with the Lord now, and we show the Lord's death until He comes. The showing of the Lord's death is a present proclamation. This word "comes" means that there is a sense in which He is not here now; that is the delay.

This Table is a place of training. We learn how to receive God's gifts here, but we also learn how to wait patiently. God does not answer all our prayers in the instant we offer them. He sometimes does this for younger Christians, in much the same way that little ones have their plates filled up first at the dinner table. The older children have enough strength and wit to wait more patiently.

Why does God delay in the answering of our prayers? The reason is because there is a much greater blessing in it for us if He does it that way. He receives more glory, and we receive more good. One of the goods is that we learn endurance and patience. We learn how to wait upon Him; we learn how to trust Him.

Every week that goes by in which the Lord has not come is a deferred glory. God wants us to become long-term thinkers, not short-range thinkers. Deferred glory is great glory.

So come, and welcome, to Jesus Christ.

MORNING ☼ GOD PREPARES BOTH MEALS AND EATERS

At this Table, God delights to feed us. But God does not just feed us, He prepares us to be fed. He undertakes the feeding, and He undertakes the preparation for feeding.

Of course, the preparations began before the foundation of the world, when God the Father elected a people for Himself. And the preparations continued when the Lord Jesus gave Himself on the cross two thousand years ago. But what role in preparation does the Holy Spirit have? He was the one who converted you, and He is the one working in your heart in the course of every week, preparing you for this meal.

"Lord, thou hast heard the desire of the humble: Thou wilt prepare their heart, thou wilt cause thine ear to hear" (Ps.10:17).

Not only does God respond to us here, but He also prepares our hearts for us — so that He might respond to us as we offer up this sacrifice of praise. This means you did not just wander in. If you are baptized, you are invited. If you are not baptized, you are invited to be baptized — and the water brings with it an invitation to the Table. In short, one way or another, absolutely everyone is invited here. God prepared the meal, and in your heart, God prepared the one who would come and eat.

So come, and welcome, to Jesus Christ.

EVENING ◐ AND WE ALL QUALIFY

We serve a merciful God, but one who does not trifle with sin. When we come before Him, forgetful of our sins, in that self-serving and convenient way we have, He remembers them. In Hos. 8:13, when the worshipers came to offer their sacrifices, there God promised to remember their iniquity. But this is the same God who promises to forget our sins. The psalmist prays that God would not remember his sins (Ps. 25:7). As far as the east is from the west (Ps. 103:120, so far our sins are removed from us. He throws all our sins into the depths of the ocean (Micah 7:19).

So then, if we forget our sins, God does not forget them. If we remember them, confessing them (1 John 1:9), God forgets them. This is simply another way of saying that the man who worships God must do so honestly, and not be trying to work some game or other.

But this is why we can come to this Table with confidence. The Table is set with the body and blood of Jesus. The body was broken for sinners, and all of us here qualify. The blood was shed for sinners, and every last one of us qualifies.

So come, and welcome, to Jesus Christ.

MORNING ✹ KEEPING IT ALL

This Table embodies one of the central realities of the Christian life, which is the glory of *my life for yours*.

Of course, it doesn't seem that way. It is designed to seem different than it is, so that we can walk by faith, and not by sight. How can breaking bread make it whole? How can drinking the wine keep the blood of Christ from disappearing? How can giving things away, your own life especially, ensure that you keep it all?

This is gospel logic. One kind of worldling says that you must keep it to keep it. Another kind of worldling says that you must give it away because God doesn't want you to have it. But the way of the cross is that you must give it away because God wants you to have it forever.

In this meal, Jesus gives Himself to us, and God has therefore given Him the name that is above every name. We receive what He gives, and along with this is the privilege of imitating Him. And when we offer our own bodies and our own blood for one another, in imitation of this, God sees. And when God sees what He delights in, He honors it.

So some, and welcome, to Jesus Christ.

EVENING ◑ DONE WITH ACCUSATION

This Table goes by various names, like the Eucharist, which means thanksgiving, or by the Lord's Supper, or the Lord's Table. One of the common names for it is communion. In this meal, we have communion with the Lord Jesus, and with one another. But communion entails more than a nebulous spirit of unity. Christian unity always involves propositional content, which means conversation. That is why this meal is at the conclusion of a long conversation we have had with God—we have offered prayers and psalms to Him, and He has spoken to us through His Word. This is the climax of that conversation—it not a distinct or separated element.

If we are conversing with God, this means that we should be conversing a lot less with the devil. God's conversations are filled with comfort, and the devil's conversation is filled with accusation. That is what he does, that is what he is. And the only real spirit that is unable to receive God's comfort here is the spirit that wants to make room for accusation—whether it is accusation of self, or of others. Put another way, the one thing you may accuse here, in your own heart, is that spirit of accusation. This is because conviction at this point does not condemn—just the reverse.

So come, and welcome, to Jesus Christ.

MORNING ☼ TO UNTIE EVERY KNOT

The Puritan William Bridge once said that "the word 'father' is a sweet word, for it sweetens all our duties." So it is here. We have a duty or an obligation to come here to the Supper, but at the same time, it is a sweet duty. The Lord Jesus is here, His Spirit is here, and it is therefore the Father's Table.

One of the reasons why our generation is so neurotic about food issues is because we are a fatherless generation. We don't know, down in our bones the way we ought to, that fathers nourish, fathers provide, fathers feed. This Table is therefore a model for us.

The duty of calling God your Father is a fundamental duty. We cannot do this except through the blood and body of the Lord Jesus, displayed for us here. Neither can we do it except through the work of the Spirit of all love, displayed for us in the congregation, as we partake of all good things, including the gifts of one another.

So if your life is one of anxiety over food and drink, if your soul is tied up in knots, then come. This is the meal that unties every knot. Your Father is here.

So some, and welcome, to Jesus Christ.

When I lift up the loaf and break it, this fraction of the bread is a key element of our observance of the Supper here. It is not just important because Jesus broke the loaf He had, and we are to mimic everything without understanding. No, there is a world of glory in everything here.

Just as Adam was broken in two so that God could fashion Eve out of the rib, so also the Lord's body is broken so that God may present Him with a bride. God made Adam into two, so that He could take those two and make them one.

The Lord's body was broken so that we might be made whole, and we cannot be made whole unless we are made one with Him. But when we are made one with Him, we are enabled to imitate Him. We are equipped to die for one another. We are blessed with brokenness, and when we are blessed with brokenness, we are blessed with unity.

If we are stiff and unyielding, we don't usually break in this way — we shatter. But when the Lord holds the one loaf up and breaks it, He does it with this higher unity in mind.

So come, and welcome, to Jesus Christ.

MORNING ☼ WHAT ELSE WAS BROKEN?

The words of institution say that this bread is the body of Christ, which is broken for you. But that is not the only thing that is broken. Scripture says, "We know that we are from God, and the whole world lies in the power of the evil one" (1 John 5:19, ESV).

When Christ was broken on the cross, the power of the devil was also broken. His claims were all shattered. His accusations fell impotent to the ground. The body of Christ was broken under the condemnation of sin, and the condemnation of sin was thereby broken.

This is the mystery of the cross. This is the power of the cross. It is not for nothing that we are told to proclaim the death of Jesus until He comes again, because the death of Jesus is the death of everything that needs to die and must die. The death of Jesus is the death of accusation, the death of condemnation, the death of finger-pointing, the death of recriminations, and the death of returning evil for evil. The death of Jesus is the death of death.

But in order for this to be made manifest in your life, what must happen? It is not enough for you to watch me lift the loaf and break it. It is not enough for you to be a spectator of these marvels. No, you are summoned to come. You are summoned to eat this broken bread. And this eating means that you are invited to partake in the death of all condemnation.

So come, and welcome, to Jesus Christ.

The words of grace that surround this Table of grace are glorious words. The great Augustine once said that if God gave what He commanded, He could command whatever He wanted.

This Table has conditions — the unholy are not welcome. This Table contains a promise — the unholy are most welcome. Scripture frequently assigns conditions to us. If we will do this, He will do that. But Scripture in other places frequently teaches us that our fulfillment of such a condition is the very thing promised.

In one place we are told that true repentance is the condition of the promise (2 Chron. 6:36–39; Joel 2:15–19). In another place we are told that our true repentance is the very thing promised (Eze. 36:26). What are we to make of this?

What this means is that if you come to God in true evangelical faith, if you come to Him with humility of heart, you are invited to apprehend every conditional promise in the Bible, though you have met none of those conditions, because you have come in the name of the one who met all of them, the Lord Jesus Himself. Now I just used the phrase "true evangelical faith." What about that condition? That condition also is a gift from God, lest any should boast. Jesus was the only one with true evangelical faith. Jesus was the only Christian who ever lived — and so it is that the only true taunt of the unbelievers is the only true hope of believers. This is why we must take refuge in Him.

So come, and welcome, to Jesus Christ.

MORNING ☼ THREAT AND PROMISE

The Bible describes God has one who sometimes repents, sometimes changing His mind (Gen. 6:7). The Scripture also describes God as one who does not do so (1 Sam. 15:29). How are we to harmonize this? We know that with regard to His eternal decrees God freely and unalterably ordains whatsoever comes to pass. But in the course of our stories, within human history, from our vantage point, how are we to understand this?

One way of processing this is to realize that God relents when it comes to His threats, as the inhabitants of Nineveh discovered. But God never relents with regard to His promises. If God made the promise, and you are the recipient of it, then it is going to happen. God's word of grace always stands sure.

This is the Table of promise. We have here the bread and wine, the body and blood of Jesus. What are these, if not all the promises of God? And are they for you? God receives everyone who comes to Him, trusting in His promises.

But don't come here double-thinking yourself. Distinguish doubts from questions. If you commune while thinking what if you really don't mean it, that is a doubt and should be banished. But if you commune while wondering if this is consistent with all your lying, cheating, stealing, and fornicating, well, then, that would be a question. And a good one too. Answer it in repentance, and come.

So come, and welcome, to Jesus Christ.

EVENING ◐ GOD DOESN'T CARE

Given the grace and goodness of God the Father in giving us the sacrifice of Jesus, and given the work of the Holy Spirit in the gospel offer to all men, the only sin that is damnable is the sin of perpetual hardheartedness — the sin of rejecting grace, and willfully remaining in unbelief. The wrath of God remains on the one who stubbornly remains in his unbelief (John 3:36).

But even here, the grace of God extends an invitation to the hardhearted. "Hearken unto me, ye stouthearted, that are far from righteousness: I bring near my righteousness; it shall not be far off, and my salvation shall not tarry" (Is. 46:12–13):

Now there is a way for the hardhearted to twist what I am about to say in order to put a religious veneer over their hardheartedness, which is not the same thing as the blood of Christ applied to it. But God wants His grace stated this way regardless.

Because of the blood of Jesus Christ, the only sin that can keep you from this Table is the sin of refusing to come (by various proud devices) to this Table.

Hear me carefully. Have you used pornography? God doesn't care. Are you a thief? God doesn't care. Have you told clusters of lies? God doesn't care. Are you lazy? God doesn't care. Are you addicted to self-pity? God doesn't care. Have you been given to drunkenness? God doesn't care. Are you an adulterer? God doesn't care. Has your language been profane? God doesn't care. Here you may find full, free, and complete forgiveness.

But here is the potential deal-breaker. Are you being hardhearted? Even here, listen to the invitation of Isaiah. God will bring His righteousness to you, *even to you*. Do you want it?

So come, and welcome, to Jesus Christ.

MORNING ☼ WHEN AFFLICTION FLOATS

The grace of God is not just given to us in forgiveness of sin, although that is certainly an important part of it. The grace of God also equips and strengthens us to do things that we did not think we were going to be able to do. In short, the grace of God is not just given to us to fill up holes. The grace of God is also constructive, positive, and capable of getting us through great challenges.

Sin brings trouble, of its own kind, but not all trouble is the result of sin. In this world, trouble is God's testing ground. He wants to see what is in our hearts (Dt. 8:2). And whether it is affliction because of sin, or affliction because God is promoting us, we must take care. This is not surefire, but the very best way to perpetuate affliction is to chafe and grumble under it. The grace of God is here to enable you to rejoice under it.

You might say that your trial is great, your affliction is heavy. It wants to sink straight to the bottom as the borrowed ax head of the nameless prophet did (2 Kings 6:6). But remember that the God who made the ax head float is fully capable of making your afflictions float. That is something that afflictions don't ordinarily do, any more than ax heads do, but the God who gives grace to you here has promised that He will intervene in your life to make every affliction float. Now, keep in mind that making an affliction float is not the same thing as making it vanish. It is like the peace of God, passing understanding. It is that peace, passing understanding.

So come, and welcome, to Jesus Christ.

We are summoned to this Table in faith. Without faith it is impossible to please God, and we want our time here to be entirely pleasing to Him, as well as to ourselves. This means that we must come with full, complete, entire, evangelical faith in Jesus.

We may come with our sins, because that means we are coming to lay them down. But we may not come in our sins. If we come in our sins, which is to say, if we come in our unbelief, then this has the effect of turning this bread into a crust and the wine into vinegar. This is why Paul could say of some Corinthians that their approach to the Supper was doing more harm that good.

Note that the contrast is not between imperfect sinners coming and perfect saints coming. No, the contrast is between imperfect sinners coming in humility and imperfect sinners coming in insolence and pride. The issue is not the fact of sin — we all confess sin at the beginning of our service for a reason. Any man who says he does not have sin deceives himself.

But any man who says that he must continue to hold onto that sin also deceives himself. Christ came to cleanse sin, forgive it, eradicate it . . . He did not come to move it around in our lives. He did not take up residence in your life and heart in order to rearrange the furniture there. He came to remake all. Our presence here should say that this is exactly what we want Him to be doing.

So come, and welcome, to Jesus Christ.

MORNING ☼ THE SPIRIT BRINGS US

Christ is everything to us. We were saved by Christ, we are being saved in Christ, and we will be saved to the final image of Christ. Christ is the way to the Father, and we all, like lost children, must be brought to the Father.

This is the Father's Table. He set it — it was His will that issued the invitation, and to which the Lord submitted in the Garden. This is the Lord's Table — His is the body we partake of, and His is the blood we drink. This is the Spirit's Table, for He is the one who brings each of us here.

Christ brings us to the Father, and He does so by the power of the Spirit. This is all done on the basis of His death, burial and resurrection, embodied here for us. These emblems of bread and wine are the ground of our confidence. The instrument of our confidence is our evangelical and living faith. The object of our confidence is Christ and Him crucified, and we may have confidence for we know that Christ was impaled in that way in submission to the will of the Father, and brought to that point of extreme obedience by the Holy Spirit of God.

We do not have faith in God on autopilot. We are not permitted to just close our eyes and go. We see and believe. We hear and believe. We come because we believe. We are assembled here in faith, are we not?

So come, and welcome, to Jesus Christ.

God promises us times of refreshing in the gospel, but He always does it on His terms—never on ours. If the arrangement were to be made on our terms, it wouldn't be gospel at all. Repent, He says. Be converted, He says, which means to be turned . . . away from self and toward Him.

The times of refreshing that are promised come from the presence of the Lord, and we cannot enjoy any of it if we are engaged in fleeing from the presence of the Lord. The Lord Himself is present with Himself, and the Lord Himself is our refreshment. There is no other way.

Our joy is God Himself. Our salvation is God Himself. Salvation is not a commodity that the Lord would have us purchase. Salvation is of the Lord, but it is also important to say that salvation is the Lord. Thus, it is not possible to be saved if you detest Him. To detest Him is to detest salvation.

In this sense, repentance and faith are the same thing. If you turn away from the east, you are turning toward the west. The same motion can be described in two different ways. Repentance describes what we turn away from. Trust describes what we are turning toward.

Further, what we turn away from is personal, and what we turn toward is personal. We do not repent of impersonal sin substance, and we do not turn toward an impersonal righteousness substance. We repent of our very personal addiction to self, and we turn toward a very personal, our tri-personal, God.

The phrase that summons us to "personal relationship with Jesus" is hackneyed and clichéd, but never forget that this fact never made anything untrue. Truths never wear out because they have been repeated often.

So come, and welcome, to Jesus Christ.

MORNING ☼ REAL TEMPTATIONS

God's saints are often troubled by the mere *fact* of their temptations. Sin is one kind of trouble, but we know how to seek forgiveness for sin committed in the past. But what about the constant volley of suggestions that seem more than a little attractive, to which you have not given way, but which trouble you nonetheless? How could a real Christian be anything but repulsed by the thought of that, or *that*?

The only sin that Jesus ever repented of was our sin. He never had to repent of any iniquity that He himself had committed. But as a public person, He repented as only a true man could. Beginning with His baptism by John — a baptism of repentance — He identified with the sins of His people, and He repented perfectly. As a perfect man, He did not need to repent, but also as a perfect man, He could repent, which He did on our behalf.

But returning to the issue of temptation, the Lord experienced true temptation in His own right. He was buffeted by suggestions from the devil, and He experienced them as true temptations, meaning that they were things He wanted to do. He wanted to turn the stones to bread, He wanted to throw Himself off the temple, and He wanted to bow down and worship the devil. But, glory to God, He submitted Himself to the words of God as they are found in the book of Deuteronomy.

But this means that for you to feel disqualified from this Supper because of your many temptations means that you are trying to be holier than Jesus. Your sins do not keep you back, because the broken body and shed blood are here for just that reason. And your temptations do not forbid you because since temptations did not corrupt the sacrifice itself, how much less would they corrupt the ones for whom the sacrifice was made?

So come, and welcome, to Jesus Christ.

This Table is set for you as a means of grace. God intends to strengthen you, not only in terms of your endurance, but also in your wits. The serpent, it says, was craftier than all the other creatures. And the Lord Jesus teaches us to keep our innocence, but to grow in our wisdom. Be wise as serpents, He says (Matt. 10:16). This Table is here to help equip you in growing up into that wisdom.

Know that Satan often tempts you to one sin in order to tempt you to another. He is the master of misdirection. He tempts you to sin against the law at some point, and if you fall for it, so much the better. But the real game is to get you to sin against the gospel.

How could a true Christian have thoughts like *that* in his breast? Even if they were only there for a moment? In other words, he tempts you in order that he may use the fact that he has tempted you against you. He suggests the first thing, in order that he may suggest the second.

The broken body here, and the spilt blood here, are the only appropriate answer to any of this. Whether it is the first temptation — to lust, to anger, to avarice — or the second — self-doubts, melancholy, morbid introspection — what we have here on this Table is the only answer that suffices.

I may be a poor Christian, but this body here says that I am one. I may have stumbled and fallen just this last week, but blood was shed outside Jerusalem two thousand years ago so that this wine would be sitting here for me, and anybody else just like me.

And for all those who fear that such freedom in grace may led some to abuse it, the reply to that is let them go. We know that grace can do far more damage to sin than sin can do to grace. And is that not the point?

So come, and welcome, to Jesus Christ.

MORNING ☼ SO LOOK AROUND IN LOVE

One of the central things we are called to remember in this Supper is the fact that God has brought us to one another, and not just to Himself. Now He has brought us into fellowship with Him, and we rejoice in it, but He never does this in isolation. "The Lord gave the word: Great was the company of those that published it" (Ps. 68:11).

One of our responsibilities in the Supper thereof, is to see one another, to look at one another. This is a participation together.

Try to avoid looking just to the front of the church, as though all the action were down here, or on this Table. No, your love for one another is a great part of what we are enacting. So look around — this is not a lecture hall, or a concert. This is a great company, and we are called to love one another. We are called to be aware of our presence together. Feel free to speak to one another as we commune.

Look around, and pray for those with cancer. Look around, and pray for those who struggle with financial hardship. Look around, and ask God to fill your heart with love for those you believe have wronged you, or who have slighted you, or who do not appear to be aware you exist. Love them in your glance. Looking around in this way is not "being distracted." It is true fellowship.

Now it is true that there is a kind of looking around that is not love, but rather just gawking. If you are checking out the girls, you need to be more spiritually minded. If you are wondering if she noticed that you got new shoes, then your heart is not where it ought to be. Feel free to look back to the front again for a moment. But do that to calibrate your heart with this mystery — which is not the same thing as parking your heart here.

So come, and welcome, to Jesus Christ.

Our corporate participation in this meal, together with all other saints in the world, is a corporate participation in one person, the Lord Jesus. This means, obviously, that He is no ordinary person, but rather is an Adam.

Adam was a public person — that is, we were in him when he sinned. His sin was ours, and was justly reckoned to us. But the last Adam is also a public person — we believers were in Him, and were justly represented in Him, when He refused sin. His obedience was ours, and was justly reckoned or imputed to us.

When Adam reached for the fruit, in that fatal moment, the hand and arm which reached out toward it were your hand and arm. The fact that you were entailed in sin from the moment of your conception is no injustice to you. Adam represented you well. But there is glory on the flip side of this as well. When Jesus extended His hands and arms so that He might be bound and led away (Matt. 27:2), those were your hands and arms as well. His obedience in His suffering is imputed to you as well.

This is why you can come to partake of this meal at all. You come to partake of Jesus Christ in the name of Jesus Christ, and on the basis of His perfect obedience which has been credited, reckoned, and imputed to you. Our salvation is necessarily corporate. We must partake of Jesus Christ in order to be able to partake of Jesus Christ.

You must be worthy to come, but your worth is found in coming. You must be clean to come, but the cleansing is here. You must partake in faith, but faith comes by hearing and hearing by the Word of God. Listen then to the Word of God.

So come, and welcome, to Jesus Christ.

MORNING ✵ THOSE DARTS ARE DOUBTS

This meal is offered to you as a means of grace. It is one of God's great instruments for building your faith, for encouraging you in your walk, for establishing your assurance. Ah, there's the problem, some of you might be saying . . . assurance. If only I had it.

You think you need assurance to come to the Table, when actually you need to come to the Table for assurance. We do not come to this Supper because we have achieved something, but rather to receive something.

But should you not have assurance? Of course you should. "These things have I written unto you that believe on the name of the Son of God; that ye may know that ye have eternal life, and that ye may believe on the name of the Son of God" (1 John 5:13). This is why God offers to give it to you . . . by various means. The gospel preached, the gospel enacted, as here, the gospel embodied in the fellowship of the saints — these are all ways that God gives you assurance.

But, you might argue, if you were a true Christian, you could never entertain any doubts on the subject, right? Wrong. Think for a moment. When Jesus was tempted in the wilderness, two out of the three temptations were assaults on His identity. If you are the Son of God . . .

Try your form of argument on Him. If He were truly the Messiah, then He could never be tempted to doubt it, right? Now mark me well — I do not say that Jesus doubted who He was. I say that He was tempted to doubt it, and I also say that no servant is greater than his master. If Jesus could not walk through this world without this kind of assault, why on earth would we be immune from it?

The shield of faith extinguishes the flaming darts of the evil one (Eph. 6:16), and the nature of the shield tells us what the darts must be. Those darts are doubts, and what else is new?

So come, and welcome, to Jesus Christ.

EVENING ◐ HOW THE SIN ARGUMENT CAN'T WORK

This meal is a meal of all grace. When we shrink back from it, we do so (most often) because of our sins. But because it is a meal of grace, all the arguments we might construct out of our sins do not and cannot work.

This is because grace is there because of our sins, it *presupposes* them. Just as a bath presupposes someone in need of a bath, so also the blood of Jesus Christ here presented is the blood that cleanses us from all unrighteousness. The body of Jesus Christ here presented is the body that was broken on account of all unrighteousness. What argument fashioned from sins can you bring to this Table that is not quickly, thoroughly, and wonderfully refuted?

There is a convoluted way to turn a Table of grace into a table of judgment, and some have done it, but they have only succeeded in doing it by ignoring almost everything that is said about it. Some have gotten sick and died because of how they approached the cup of *blessing*, but their mistake was not a minor one, and their rebellion was not a subtlety.

We are convinced of better things concerning you. You cannot argue from your sins and shrink back, and you cannot argue from the magnitude of your sins and shrink back, because this Table is set with grace enough for the world. Neither can you argue from the secret decrees of God — because you don't know them. God does know His decrees, and He has authorized His ministers to summon you to come.

This is why, at the end of the day, the only reason people do not come to Christ is because of the sin they are committing at that very moment. They are refusing to repent. They are refusing to bow down. They are refusing to be a supplicant.

But you are not so.

So come, and welcome, to Jesus Christ.

MORNING ☼ HYPOCRITES DON'T CARE

The Lord Jesus warned us about the sin against the Holy Spirit, a sin that could not be forgiven (Matt. 12:31). We are approaching a Table laden with forgiveness, and some tender believers worry about whether they have a right to come, whether they have a right to be here.

Before considering what that sin might be, let us take a very important moment to recognize what it cannot be. There are hypocrites who are utterly deceived about their condition, but one of their most notable characteristics is that they do not worry about this possibility. There are those who have been guilty of the blasphemy against the Holy Spirit — these are those who don't care about whether they have or not. So one of the distinguishing marks of those who cannot have fallen into this sin is the feature of worrying that you might have fallen into it. Hypocrites don't care about whether or not they are hypocrites — that is why they are.

So what is the sin of blaspheming against the Spirit? In context, Jesus had been accused of casting out demons by the spirit of the devil. His accusers had completely inverted the categories of righteousness and unrighteousness, saying that God was the devil and implying that the devil was God. Even here, Jesus doesn't say that they had committed the unforgivable sin, but He does warn them that they are getting close. There comes a point where that inversion hardens completely, and the sin is everlastingly committed. There is perpetual lack of forgiveness because there is perpetual sin.

But you? You confessed your sin earlier this week, right after you committed it. You confessed your sin honestly and fully at the beginning of this service. You were cleansed, and ushered into the presence of God. And now, just in case, you acknowledge your fallenness and faults — you have let it all go. You trust in the broken body and shed blood of Jesus Christ, and in that alone.

So come, and welcome, to Jesus Christ.

One of the things that God wants to do for you here at this Table is *encourage* you. This is a Table of thanksgiving, which you cannot properly offer when you are *discouraged*.

When we are discouraged, it is often because of affliction around us, or sin within us.

Affliction is God's crucible, it is what God uses to purify His saints. To object to affliction is to object to that process of purifying. God removes the dross from the silver by means of smelting, and that means heat. You might like all your dross, and think you are doing quite well, considering. You are a rock in the rough, and the silver sparkles are obvious to anyone who knows you. But God refuses to leave you there. You want to be a rock with sparkles, while He intends an ingot, refined seven times. Hence the affliction, hence the smelting.

But what about sin within—including the sin of murmuring under the processes of smelting? What if you are discouraged because of that? Keep in mind that there is a difference between being defeated in the skirmish and defeated in the battle. You may have had a bad go of it. But is your weapon still in your hand? Are you here, worshiping the Lord? Do you want the next round to be better? Take heart. God has forgiven your sins, and His Spirit is with you here, teaching you to fight against the world, the flesh, and the devil more capably than you have done in the past.

So come, and welcome, to Jesus Christ.

MORNING ☼ BECAUSE HE BLED

We are gathered at this Table in a world that has been fundamentally transformed by the resurrection of Jesus. The world can never be the same as it was before because this is a world in which a man has come back from the dead. And so we believe in the resurrection, we declare and preach it, and we number it as being among the things that are of first importance.

But at this weekly meal, we commemorate and memorialize the death of Jesus. This is His body, broken on the cross. This is His blood, shed on the cross. And Paul tells us that as often as we eat and drink, we declare the Lord's death until He comes. In this meal, we participate in a living Christ, an alive Christ, a resurrected Christ. He would be no Savior at all had He not risen, and if He were not at the right hand of the Father. We ascend to Him there, in the power of the Spirit, as we partake of Christ. But it is the very fact of this life that enables us to extend the power of His death, the efficacy of His death, and offer it to a defiled world.

What can wash away my sin? Nothing but the blood of Jesus.

Jesus died once in history, and we can say that He died once for all because He is risen. Because He is risen, He can apply the potency of His blood to those who were not to be born for two thousand years after the death of Jesus. That death, two thousand years ago, is applied to you, here, now, because He has given gifts to men. One of those gifts is His Spirit, and He is the one who applies that remedy to your sore. Because He bled, He can stop your bleeding. Because He was broken, He can bind up what is broken in you. Because He died, He is the remedy. Because He lives, He can apply it.

So come . . . in faith. Come, in gratitude. Come, with as many needs as you might have.

So come, and welcome, to Jesus Christ.

EVENING ◐ THE TABLE OF NO COMPARISONS

This is a gospel Table, a good news Table. This is a Table that presents the broken body and shed blood. This means it cannot contain a hard message for anyone who partakes of it in living evangelical faith. This makes it the Table of no condemnation.

Because God is here, with no condemnation, this means that He wants you to be done with comparisons. You have to be perfect to be here at all, and that perfection is found in Jesus. The broken body is perfect. The shed blood is perfect. The salvation that God offers in the cross is sufficient, and cannot be supplemented with anything that we might bring here.

The only thing we bring here is the need to be here. That's it, and that's all.

So when you come before the Lord, no comparisons. No one here should be worried about how other moms have their act together more than you do. No one here should be tormented by the sins of their youth. No one here should be afflicted by your unworthiness. Of course we are not worthy—that is the whole point. What makes us think the Lord wanted us to establish another Pharisee awards banquet? The world is crammed full of those. The Lord did not come because we were running short of those. That is the world system, a system which Jesus came to push clean over. He toppled it. In that defeated system, a few get the choice portion and the medal, and everyone else chews on their dry bones of envious comparison and self-accusation, resolving to strive harder next time. But that is not what we have here. This is the Table of no condemnation. It is the Table of no comparisons. Jesus died once for all, the righteous for the unrighteous. There *is* no next time.

So come, and welcome, to Jesus Christ.

MORNING ☼ YOU ARE FREE TO GO

In the older covenant, when a man had the misfortune of killing another man by accident, the law made a provision for him to help him evade the avenger of blood. He could flee to one of the designated cities of refuge. In order to remain safe, he had to remain in that city until the death of the high priest. When the high priest died, he was at liberty to go, and the blood avenger could not touch him.

This is an odd picture. A man is bound to a particular city, and for him, the death of the high priest — ordinarily a time of grief and lamentation — would have been unmitigated good news. The high priest has died . . . you are free to go.

We are in that same position. Our high priest has died, and the fact that He rose again did not alter the fact that He died. Because the high priest died, we are free to go. The accuser has nothing to say to us, for we may simply reply that "the high priest has died." The blood avenger might want to do us harm, but we are secure — the high priest has died. This is a plea for which there is no answer, no comeback.

We commemorate this reality every week. This is His body, broken for you. This is His blood, shed for you. This Table is located in the heavenly places, set up in great sanctuary there, and we know that the Father looks on what we are doing with pleasure. We are free to go anywhere, including there, because the High Priest has died.

So come, and welcome, to Jesus Christ.

EVENING ◐ THE EXIT MAY BE BEHIND YOU

The Puritan William Bridge once said that whenever Satan builds a temptation, God is sure to build a door in the side of it. This is a great and wonderful truth, but we must not be simplistic in our attempts to grasp it.

As the flight attendants always remind us, in case of an emergency landing, remember that the exit may be *behind* you.

The way of escape, in other words, may not be immediately obvious. The strength you are receiving here, now, may be the deliverance from a temptation that is coming two days from now. The word you store up in your heart today may be the word that comes back unbidden at just the right time. The brother you encourage today may be the brother who encourages you just days from now. The exit may be behind you.

We are at a Table of rejoicing and thanksgiving, which means that our posture is fundamentally that of those who have already gone through the door of escape. We have been delivered, we are saved, we are forgiven — and so we rejoice. At the same time, we are still in the days of our pilgrimage, and God summons us to go through little doors of deliverance, lesser doors of escape, so that our entire lives might be a testimony to what God has done for us, what He is doing for us, and what He will do for you.

So come, and welcome, to Jesus Christ.

MORNING ✹ ALWAYS PUT YOURSELF FIRST

We are all coming to this Table for grace. We come together, but we also come individually. The meaning of communing together is seen when all of us do something individually. We give you bread, and *you* eat it. We give you a cup and *you* drink it. At the same time, all over the congregation, your brothers and sisters are doing the same thing.

Tending to the state of your own soul is not selfish; it is required. Tending to the state of your own soul *first* is not selfish; it is required. In the airline safety instructions, they tell you that when the oxygen masks drop out of the overhead, you are to put your own on *first* before helping others. The reason is obvious, is it not? If you do not do this, you will very rapidly be no help to others at all.

Jesus explicitly teaches us to do this. Getting the beam out of your own eye before trying to help others *is not selfish* (Matt. 7:3–5). The apostle Paul says the same. Correcting someone who is overtaken in a fault must not be done unless you have dealt with your own issues *first* (Gal. 6:1).

Of course, there is always a ditch on the other side of the road. Someone who spends forty years getting the beam out of his own eye (unsuccessfully), and who uses that as an excuse for staying holed up in his very own pietistic cocoon, never helping anyone else, is obviously missing the point.

But even with this granted, it is a glib mistake to think that we must always think of others first. When it comes to dealing with sin (which is the great adversary for us here on this sorry planet), we are commanded *always* to think of ourselves first. You can see how "always putting others first" could become an easy cloak for hypocrisy. The serpent was more subtle than all the beasts of the field.

So come, and welcome, to Jesus Christ.

EVENING ◐ THE GRACE OF SEEKING GRACE

This meal is one of God's appointed means of grace. We come to Him wanting that grace to be multiplied to us. But as it is multiplied, one of the things we must remember is that what is multiplied must come in a certain order. As a multiplication problem, if we just throw things down on the paper in random order, we are not good enough students to prevent ourselves from getting hopelessly confused.

So as we are seeking God's grace, the first grace we must seek is the grace of understanding just how much we need His grace. Grace is foundational. Grace is at the root. Grace pervades everything. Grace is not an add-on extra; grace is not a decorative fillip at the end.

When we delight in grace, that is the only time when we can rejoice in being overwhelmed. And God frequently leads us into situations where we are overwhelmed precisely so that we may learn this lesson.

So look at the week ahead of you. Look at your challenges, any one of which could bring you down if it went the wrong way. What can sustain you? The grace of God. The morsel of bread in your hand. The small cup of wine. Is that enough? More than sufficient, more than enough. It is the grace of God.

So come, and welcome, to Jesus Christ.

MORNING ☼ AND WE SING

One of the great blessings that accompanies coming to this Table every week is the blessing of being able to sing at this Table. One of the names for this meal comes from the Greek word for giving thanks — this is the Eucharist, a true sacrifice of praise.

The 22nd Psalm says that God inhabits the praise of His people, and this is yet another way in which Christ is present here with us as we partake. Think of it. Christ is contained in the emblems of bread and wine. Christ is manifested in the word of institution that is spoken over this bread and wine — it is the presence of that word that distinguishes sacramental bread from ordinary bread, and sacramental wine from ordinary wine. Christ is present in your neighbor, Christ is in your brothers and sisters all over the room. He is the one loaf, and we are the one loaf. We commemorate the broken body here, and we, because of that brokenness, are His restored body. So Christ is there in your brothers and sisters as well, and His Spirit of love that binds us all together.

And we sing. Christ is in the praise that we lift up to God. Remember that faith has two offices — one is to receive Christ from God, and the other is to offer Christ to God. When we sing around the Table, we are lifting Christ up to God because we are singing — just as we pray — in the name of Jesus Christ. All things, everywhere, are done in His name, but especially here.

So come, and welcome, to Jesus Christ.

EVENING — SWEET CONVICTION

The Scriptures teach us that we must not automatically assume that affliction is the result of God's chastisement for sin. The friends of Job made a serious mistake in this matter, and the disciples of the Lord, who wanted to know who had sinned — this man or his parents — such that he was born blind, made the same mistake.

So we must not reason simplistically in a straight-across fashion like this. But when we learn that affliction is sometimes not the result of sin, we leap to the false conclusion that affliction is never the consequence of sin. That is not true either. God is not mocked and a man reaps what he sows.

But you are a child of God. If you are here under affliction, and you suspect that unconfessed sin may be at the bottom of it, never forget that the love of God is at the ultimate bottom of it.

When we are behaving foolishly, God uses all manner of things to get our attention. If you avoid the sin of morbid introspection, it is never out of place to run a spiritual inventory. It is never out of place to surrender everything in principle — God can be trusted with that. It is never out of place to ask God to minister His grace to you here, through the bread and wine, in such a way as to reveal to you anything you have not yet understood about yourself.

We sometimes hang back from praying that way because we are afraid of the answer. But remember, the love and mercy of God is always at the bottom of it. The Spirit of God leads you into sweet conviction, never into horrendous condemnations. You are in Christ. There is no condemnation. This is a Table of consolation, not condemnation. But if you treat sweet conviction as if it had to be condemnation, then perhaps that defensive spirit is the thing that God's grace is removing from you. And love is at the bottom of it.

So come, and welcome, to Jesus Christ.

MORNING ✵ MANAGING THE BRAND

The Scriptures instruct us about the spiritual condition of the early church in Jerusalem, during the time when great grace was upon them.

"And they, continuing daily with one accord in the temple, and breaking bread from house to house, did eat their meat with gladness and singleness of heart, Praising God, and having favour with all the people. And the Lord added to the church daily such as should be saved" (Acts 2:46–47).

They gathered with one accord. They broke bread from house to house. They ate together with gladness and simplicity of heart. They did not over-engineer it. They just ate together, loving each other. As they lived in good fellowship this way, they had good favor from those who were outside the church. This good favor is not something you can get by "managing your brand" — it has to be the gift of God. And as a consequence of this, the Lord added to their number those who were being saved.

True evangelism is the result of a contagious holiness. Untrue evangelism is simply marketing or recruiting. Because there is some overlap between the two (in both, the word goes out by physical means), the way we keep our evangelism from deteriorating into a scramble for market share is by loving Jesus, and loving our neighbor. We are called to do this, as we partake of the bread and wine, in gladness and simplicity of heart.

And this is only possible as we grasp the gospel. That means, of course, that we see how the gospel has actually grasped us.

So come, and welcome, to Jesus Christ.

Before the Lord's Supper each week, we present our tithes, offerings, and gifts. We know of no better way to tangibly express our gratitude Table of thanksgiving. He loved us to the breaking of His body and the shedding of His blood, so we make an *imitative* sacrifice here.

What is the difference between tithes, offerings, and gifts? The tithe is God's tax — and the fact that it is likely the only *just* tax you have ever paid should not make you shy away from calling it a tax. God requires ten percent of your increase as His tribute; the fact that the state demands much more tells you who they think they are. We will know that our leaders are repentant when they refuse even to think about taking more than God requires.

You may think of offerings as votive gifts. You have made a vow, and God blessed you, and you offer a gift in fulfillment of the vow. This can sound mercenary, but it is a perfectly biblical thing to do. You are starting a business, let us say, and you vow to God that if He blesses it with *x*, you will respond with *y*. But make sure that you really do *y*, just like you said you would (Deut. 23:21).

And gifts are simply gifts — in response to a particular need or just because you are grateful. Offerings and gifts are given on top of the tithe, and should never be thought of as a substitute for it.

This raises a host of practical questions — do I tithe off net or gross? — but these are not inconsistent with a spirit of gratitude, because you tithe off the *increase,* that which God actually gave you. A farmer doesn't tithe off the crops that the locusts ate, and this includes the locusts that work for the Department of the Treasury.

We are not here at this Table to crunch numbers, but if we love the Lord with all our minds, we should ask and answer these questions so that we may come with the intent to *overflow* with gratitude, joy, love, and whatever we put in the offering box that is placed on this Table.

So come, and welcome, to Jesus Christ.

MORNING ✹ AS NEW AS THE EVERLASTING HILLS

As we come to this Table, remember — as you always should — that it is the Table of the new covenant. We talk a great deal about what is meant by *covenant*, but we should also reflect on the meaning of *new*. How can a ritual that we perform every week remain fresh? The answer is found in that word *new*. In one sense it means that something just arrived. It is a chronological term. The dress or the book you bought yesterday is new. The used car is new to you. But if something is three hundred years old, very rarely will you call it new.

But the new covenant is two thousand years old. If it extends for thousands of years more, such that it becomes older than the old covenant ever was, will that change anything? The answer is no, it will not. In Scripture, *new* can refer to the quality of something, and not just its age. For example, in the vision of heavenly worship, what are they singing before the throne? It is described in two ways. It is called the song of Moses — "And they sing the song of Moses the servant of God, and the song of the Lamb, saying, Great and marvellous are thy works, Lord God Almighty; just and true are thy ways, thou King of saints" (Rev. 15:3) — and it is also called the new song (Rev. 5:9; 14:3).

We are here at the Table of the Lord, who is able to make all things new. Indeed, that is why He came. "And he that sat upon the throne said, Behold, I make all things new" (Rev. 21:5). His mercies are new every morning. He has given you a new heart, and that heart is getting newer every day, as your inner man is being renewed (2 Cor. 4:16). So, come to this Table weekly, as your inner man is being renewed, knowing that the new covenant and the cup of the new covenant and the bread that is broken as the manna of the new covenant, are not intended to ever get old. As you come in faith, these blessings come to you as new, and are experienced by you in that way.

So come, and welcome, to Jesus Christ.

Our task is to gather, to worship, to listen, to take, and to eat and drink. This is how God has determined to give the nations of the world to His Son, and so we should be about His business.

The world was conquered in the death, burial, resurrection, and ascension of Jesus. The world was given to Jesus by the Father on that basis, and for that reason. Our worship, our evangelism, our commission is all part of the giving, and not part of the conquering. The conquest is done, and Jesus is Lord.

He is crowned as the King of all kings, and as the Lord of all lords. He is not campaigning for support. He is not angling for some parliamentary position. Jesus is *Lord,* I tell you.

Scripture tells us that every time we partake of this bread and wine, we are proclaiming His death until He comes again. That proclamation is authoritative. It is not seeking to make something so, but rather is seeking to make more manifest something that was accomplished outside Jerusalem two thousand years ago, a glorious triumph which was, in its turn, grounded on the eternal decrees of our God and Father. This was all established before ancient times, and so we are not to go out into the world in a spirit of timidity.

You eat the manna from Heaven here. You drink from the Rock that is Christ here. You partake of the body broken here. You drink the wine of His sacrifice here. The emblems we handle — body and blood — are emblems of defeat, surely. But they display God's ultimate wisdom. Jesus took defeat and death and destruction and despair, gathered them all to Himself, and sank down into the grave. And when He came back from the grave, He brought none of those things back with Him. He did not remain dead — but they sure did.

So come, and welcome, to Jesus Christ.

MORNING ✹ WHAT YOUR HANDS ARE HOLDING

We are to avail ourselves of the means of grace that God sets before us, and as we do, we are to wait on God to perform what He intends to perform. We have come to this Table having confessed our sins, having sung our gratitude to God, and having heard His Word proclaimed. We now come to the next means of grace, which is the Table before us now.

Since His purpose is the salvation of the world, and since His Spirit is gathering multitudes into His church, we can trust that His purposes are for our good and not for our destruction. We come, as we are told, and we wait for God to do what only God can do. We wait on Him in faith, and He strengthens us. God wants us to have assurance of our eternal life (1 John 5:13). But this assurance cannot be had through close introspection of our own hearts — all we will find there is reason to be unsettled in our assurance. At the same time, we know Christ is present in those He is saving.

We reject moralism — good deeds don't put us in with God. We reject liturgicalism — prancing in God's courts doesn't please Him. We reject doctrinalism — mouthing the right words doesn't do it. We are saved by the instrumentality of faith. We are justified by faith alone. We come before God in trust. But how do we detect the presence of this faith? Faith makes its presence known through good deeds, through worship that is acceptable to God, and through affirmation of the truths that God has given.

When you look to see the evidence of that faith, this is fine, but never make the mistake of thinking that your faith is the object of your faith. Jesus is the object of your faith. When you hold the bread, and when you hold the cup, you are doing so with your hand. Faith is your hand, and it is all right to notice it there. But the object of your meditation is the broken body, and the shed blood.

So come, and welcome, to Jesus Christ.

We come to this meal in grateful anticipation of what God has in store for all those who love Him, and who love His appearing. In this meal, God gives us Himself, but He does it by giving us tokens of what shall be.

The marriage supper of the Lamb, at the great consummation of all things, will be a meal that we will experience with all five senses, and probably some other senses we didn't know we had. God is giving us Himself here, and we rejoice in it, but in another important sense, He is just tiding us over. The meal that is to come will be staggering beyond anything we could hope to comprehend now.

God doesn't give that to us now, because if He did, the weight would crush us. But He offers enough of it here to prepare us, to help us get accustomed to the way He works. God feeds us, and He is doing this because He has a larger end in view.

The Old Testament is an anticipatory book, looking and longing for the day when the Messiah would come, the day of the New Testament. But the New Testament is an anticipatory book also — its pages are rustling, as C.S. Lewis once put it, with the idea that we shall one day get in. All the way in.

So these tokens are not the wages of a day laborer, a poor man who has to be paid daily. No, these are signs to us of a monumental grace, a grace so great that when we finally see how much God is giving to us, all thoughts of deserving any of it will be banished finally, and completely, forever and ever.

So come, and welcome, to Jesus Christ.

MORNING ☼ A RANSOM MEAL

The Lord has prepared a Table for us, and this Table is like all His other works — beyond marvelous. The Table is set simply — red wine and simple bread.

The Lord teaches us that this bread represents His body, broken for us. This wine represents His blood, shed for us. His physical body was broken outside Jerusalem two thousand years ago, but His mystical body is gathered here in this room. We are knit more closely together in that body as we, in love, partake of these elements that are, strictly speaking, not His body. But we are, strictly speaking, His body, and He is the Head of it.

The Bible also teaches that the body and blood of the Lord was a ransom payment (Mark 10:45; 1 Tim. 2:6). This payment was made, not to the devil, but rather to the holy wrath of the Father. This is how we were redeemed. "Forasmuch as ye know that ye were not redeemed with corruptible things, as silver and gold, from your vain conversation received by tradition from your fathers; But with the precious blood of Christ, as of a lamb without blemish and without spot" (1 Pet. 1:18–19). So Jesus Christ died as a propitiation, turning aside the wrath that we entirely deserved (1 John 2:1–2). But then, when God the Father received this payment, what did He do with it? He received what Jesus presented to Him in the courts of Heaven, *and then He made a meal out of it*. Not only so, but the meal is a celebratory meal, a meal of thanksgiving, a meal of Eucharistic thanks. There is no better evidence of the fact that the sting of death is over and done, that the curse of the law has passed far away from us, as far as the east is from the west. Think of it. The ransom payment was made, God's wrath was satisfied, and then God prepared a meal out of the ransom payment, and told the ransomed to eat it in the fullness of gratitude.

So come, and welcome, to Jesus Christ.

We must never forget that this meal is a meal, designed to nourish us, and given to us for that purpose and end. The bread and the wine are given to strengthen, build up, and fortify you. This is God's dining room in the first instance, and not a medical clinic.

But God's food is also medicine. If we think of it as *only* medicine we will go far astray, and will miss the center of what is happening here, which is Table fellowship with Jesus and all His people.

At the same time, the Bible teaches that this is food that affects people differently as they come to it — and this is not true of what we might call "regular" food. Some of the Corinthians were sick and some had died because of their abuse of this meal. It is a covenant meal, and God dispenses His blessings and chastisements covenantally through it.

But we should make a further distinction. Sometimes sickness is sickness proper, and other times it is only apparent "sickness" that is the result of medicine. What happens feels like sickness, but what is actually happening is healing that feels like sickness. If you are given a purgative, what happens feels like sickness, but it can actually be helpful in healing. A regimen of chemo can feel like terrible sickness, but that is not what it actually is.

Remember that this is a place where God *deals* with us. If you find yourself not liking that very much, and you find yourself shrinking away from this Table, or finding excuses to avoid it, or postpone it, consider that this is what might be happening. Rationalizations usually mean that *something* else is going on.

If God is dealing with you, if God is seeking the surrender of something, the best thing in the world for you to do is . . . deal with it. And you can deal with it here.

So come, and welcome, to Jesus Christ.

MORNING ☼ PROXIMITY & COMMUNION

There is a crucial distinction to be made between proximity to Jesus and communion with Jesus. Remember that the Lord's brothers did not believe in Him, even though they grew up right next to Him. They had proximity. It was not until later that they had faith.

As one Puritan noted, not everyone who hangs around the court speaks with the king. You are here in His court. You have been seated at His Table. Do not neglect the opportunity.

You are here at the Table of a king. You have every right to be here, provided you are trusting in Him. He has welcomed you. He sits at the head of the Table, and He has provided His own body and blood for the meal. He waits for you to speak to Him. You are here in order to commune with Jesus.

You are not here to commune with yourself. So do not curl up into a little spiritual ball in order to gaze at your sins. Do not close your eyes in order to reflect on what a bad person you are. We do not deny the fact of our sinfulness, but we have come to God through the gospel in order to be delivered from that sinfulness. That is why this is good news.

Look up. Look out. Look to Jesus, and speak with Him. Look around at His body, and rejoice that you have been incorporated into it.

When you meditate, mediate on your deliverance. When you reflect, remember that God did not send His Son into the world — which we are in the midst of celebrating — in order to condemn the world. In order for the world to be condemned, nothing whatever needed to be done. The world was condemned already. In order to be saved, Jesus needed to come, and that is why He came. He came for salvation, not condemnation.

So come, and welcome, to Jesus Christ.

We are creatures, and so it is that we must be fed. When we have food, it can simply seem like part of the framework of life, and we take it for granted. But when we miss a meal, or on a grander scale, if there is a famine, we know acutely what we are missing. As the old saying has it, you don't miss your water till the well runs dry.

We are accustomed to partake of this meal every week, and we have been doing this for a decade or so. It might be easy for those of you who worship here every week — or those of you who are less than ten years old and have never known anything else — to assume that this is just what we do. It is what we do, but it is not just what we do.

We are being fed and strengthened weekly. Perhaps you have missed a few Sundays because of illness, or perhaps you have had to travel, and you have worshiped with saints who don't practice weekly communion. All of a sudden, you become aware of something missing. That thing that is missing is what we are being given here.

This is the communion of the saints. It is no good raw — apart from the Word, the sacrament is just bread and wine. Apart from love of the saints, the sacrament is a vain and harmful show. Apart from the mouth of faith, this wine and bread cannot be chewed and swallowed.

Something really happens here, and if you miss it, you miss it. This does not mean that the sovereign God is limited by His gifts, and cannot bless you extraordinarily if you are providentially hindered or prevented from coming. But while there can be compensation for not being able to come, there is no substitute for coming.

So avoid a superstitious dependence. Avoid a cavalier disregard. Avoid an approach that is just doing the drill. Meditate upon Jesus, the author and finisher of your faith.

So come, and welcome, to Jesus Christ.

MORNING ☼ WHEN TROUBLES COME THICK

There are times — and this may be one of them for you — when troubles come thick, and there seems to be no end, and you cannot touch the bottom with your feet. Man is born to trouble, as Scripture says, as the sparks fly upward (Job 5:7). But here is the encouraging word.

"I waited patiently for the Lord; And he inclined unto me, and heard my cry. He brought me up also out of an horrible pit, out of the miry clay, And set my feet upon a rock, and established my goings" (Ps. 40:1–2).

God hears us when we cry out to Him. When it seems that He does not it is because He wants to deliver us from our troubles in a fashion that will glorify His name more, and which will be a greater delight to us when it happens. He is good, He is sovereign, and He is your God. This means that your troubles are perfectly suited to you. They are tailor-made, hand-stitched.

But we are not Stoics. The fact that all our troubles are perfect for us does not mean that we are to pretend that they are not troubles. No, they are troubles, but we are to receive them from the hand of the only wise God. But we do this by seeking the deliverance that is just as perfect for us as the troubles.

God writes perfect stories, and really good stories are full of troubles. Nobody would take the trouble to read *The Lord of the Rings* if the Council of Elrond had determined to have the eagles fly Frodo into Mordor to drop the ring into Mt. Doom as they flew over. A book without troubles is a book that no one would take the trouble to read. God brings you through troubles so that He might be glorified when He brings you out of them. He is glorified when He takes you out of the horrible pit, and sets your feet on the rock. This Table is that Rock. It is here that God will establish your goings.

So come, and welcome, to Jesus Christ.

When we come to this Table, we are, most of us, coming to it again. God not only feeds us, but He feeds us continually, regularly. And even if you are coming here for the first time, it is the first time of many.

God's purpose is to sustain you. He is the Creator of all things, but He is also the sustainer of all things. He feeds the beasts of the field, He feeds all the fish in the sea, He feeds all the sparrows in the parking lot at MacDonald's, and He provides you with your physical food. God brings into existence, and then nourishes what He has brought into existence.

It is the same with your spiritual life. He summoned you into that life, and, now that you are here, He feeds you. Not only does He feed you, but He feeds you every week. Here are your provisions — the body of Christ as food and the blood of Jesus as drink. This is more than enough. When you need more, it will be next Lord's Day.

When you need more, it will be important for you to be here. But note that you are not coming here to a Table only. You are coming together with the saints of God, who are bread and wine and for you. Unless providentially hindered, there is no way that you can stay away from the bread and wine without also avoiding the people that the bread and wine embody.

And when you stay away, you are saying that you don't need your brothers and sisters in Christ, which is false. When your attendance at worship is intermittent, you are drifting away from the gathering of ourselves together, which was the manner of some as early as the first century. But not only are you saying that you don't need them, which is false, you are also saying that they don't need you, which is equally false. Remember, you are part of the body of Christ. This means that when you do not come, it is not just a failure to be fed — it is a failure to feed.

So come, and welcome, to Jesus Christ.

MORNING ☼ THAT KIND OF FRIEND

You are here, an invited guest, because you are a friend of God. This great banquet is a banquet with assigned seating. There are place cards at every seat. You are invited. You are *welcome*.

Now the New Testament is filled with warnings about those who forge their own place cards, and counterfeit their invitations. That is a grim reality, and there are people who are bound hand and foot in order to be pitched out of the wedding banquet. But we are convinced of better things in your case. You are here because you have come in genuine evangelical faith.

I said that you are here as a friend of God, and so I want to emphasize that — unlike what we sometimes are — God is no piecemeal friend. When you have a true friend in this world, you know what it is like. You do not just have a warm place in his heart. If he is your real friend, then all that he has is your friend also. His house is your friend, his guest room is your friend, his checkbook is your friend, his weapons are your friend. If he is your friend, then all that he has comes with him.

God is that kind of friend. Now — you are here, as I said, because you are a friend of God. This means that the Table set before you is a true encouragement. You are a friend of God. That means that all of Christ is here. This is not some of Jesus.

He does not know how to give grace and goodness without giving Himself. There is no grace, there is no goodness, outside of Him. This means that if He has given you anything, He has also given you everything. All things are yours, whether things present or things to come. They are offered to you here, but because of the kind of friend that Jesus is, they are not offered to you piecemeal. They cannot be received piecemeal.

So come, and welcome, to Jesus Christ.

This is a Table of grace. This bread and this wine are means of grace.

But God has determined a spiritual law for the world. Grace is organic, and it grows and flourishes. Grace is alive, which is why it can multiply, according to its kind. Grace and peace can be added. Grace and peace can be multiplied.

As with other forms of life, it does not grow into newer life unless and until the older life is *expended*. We are given new grace as the older grace is used. We are given grace so that we may lay it out. When we have done so, *as* we are doing so, God is continually gracious to us. It is given to us, not to hoard, but to spend.

In your natural life, the point is not to walk back and forth between the dining table and the couch. So it is here. God strengthens you for the task. He equips you for the work of His kingdom. As you spend yourself—for the grace given becomes part of you, and to spend it means to spend yourself—you need to be restored. You need nourishment. You need strength. You need more grace.

Well, here it is. But this grace that is before you now had better not be here next week. It needs to be clean gone out of this world, and laid up as treasure in Heaven. As this happens, God is pleased to give you more. He who is faithful in little will be made faithful over much. He who is faithful in little grace, not trying to save it, but rather to expend it all in kingdom work, will be faithful over much.

Do you need more grace? Of course, we all do. Well, here it is.

So come, and welcome, to Jesus Christ.

MORNING ☼ GOD'S SOAP

This is a Table of rejoicing and peace. We have gathered here in order to overflow with thanksgiving.

But what of sin? Shouldn't we examine ourselves as we come to the Table? No, but not because we shouldn't examine ourselves. While we are here, we are to be singing, rejoicing, thanking God, and looking around at our brothers and sisters in love. In order to do this, we do have to deal with sin, but that should have happened a bit earlier. We wash up for dinner, but not at the table.

So how does God deal with our sin? The Puritan William Bridge rightly said that affliction is God's soap. The martyrs who gathered before the throne did so in white robes, and the robes were white because of Christ's blood, but it also said that they had come out of the great tribulation. Affliction is one of the ways God uses to apply Christ's blood to us. "Forasmuch then as Christ hath suffered for us in the flesh, arm yourselves likewise with the same mind: *for he that hath suffered in the flesh hath ceased from sin*" (1 Pet. 4:1).

So affliction is God's soap, and when we confess our sins, whether at the time, or at the beginning of the service here, we are rinsing off what God has done. Sin is abandoned in repentance, and God is marvelously wise in all the ways He brings repentance to us. The center of our problems is always pride, and nothing gets to pride in the heart of a saint like affliction does.

And when this happens, we are truly humbled. Humility is consistent with abundant fruit. When a branch is laden with heavy fruit, that is when it bows down the lowest. When a perky little branch is sticking up out of the top of the tree, as jaunty as anything, the one thing we can be sure of is that there is little or no fruit on it.

So come, and welcome, to Jesus Christ.

EVENING ◐ NOT ONE SIN

This Table represents two things that the world considers inconsistent. First, it is a Table of thanksgiving. It represents an overflow of joy, and love, and peace. This is a Table of fellowship, and mutual life. That is one thing.

But the second thing, just as real, is that this is a Table that proclaims death. The apostle says that every time we partake, we proclaim the Lord's death until He comes again.

How can these two things be consistent with one another? In their consistency, we see the wisdom of God, and we should also see the folly of man.

We proclaim a death that is the life of the entire world. What is it that died? Our old Adamic man died in the death of Jesus. In the death of Jesus Christ we rejoice in the death of death, and in the death of all things that lead to death. As one old Puritan noted, there are only two things that cause pain — sin and suffering. Christ took our sin upon Himself, and therefore can give us the privilege of partaking in His sufferings. Because of the death of Jesus, we do not even have *one* sin to bear. Shall we not then carry the lighter portion, and accept any sufferings that come to us with joy? Count it all joy, we are told, when we encounter sufferings?

How? The sting of sin is gone, and so if our comforts die, if our reputation dies, if our estate dies, if our bodies die — it is well. When the sin is dealt with, death must be followed by resurrection. This is the Table of that hope. It is a Table of the gospel. It is Table of life-giving transformation.

We proclaim that death until He comes again because for our lost and sorry world, death is the only possible way out.

So come, and welcome, to Jesus Christ.

MORNING ☼ AN HONOR TO HONOR

This is a Table of fellowship, and so we call it communion. This is a Table of gratitude and thanksgiving, and so we call it the Eucharist. But another important function of a meal like this is the giving of honor.

This meal is a place of sacrifice, but we do not sacrifice the blood of animals, for that system was prophetic, looking forward to the time of Christ (Heb. 10:4). This meal is a place of sacrifice, but we do not sacrifice Christ here because Scripture tells us that His death was a death that was offered once for all (Heb. 10:10)—and that happened two thousand years ago. So what kind of sacrifice do we offer? Not only at this Table, but throughout the worship service, and throughout the course of our lives, we lift up the sacrifice of praise (Heb. 13:15).

In this meal, we give honor and glory to God who established this meal. We declare the praises of the one who enabled us to declare His praises in this way. But there is more, and there is a Latin phrase that expresses it well. *Honor est in honorante*. There is honor in giving honor.

The more clearly we honor God above all things here, the more He takes care to honor those who do so. He says that the one who honors God is the one whom God will honor (1 Sam. 2:30).

We do not come here to honor ourselves, but rather to honor God. But we should do this knowing how He works. What is He like? He is the God who gives, the God who overflows, the God who *bestows*.

So come, and welcome, to Jesus Christ.

EVENING ◐ A CLEAN CONSCIENCE AT THE TABLE

As you have been told a number of times, this is not a Table of introspection and morbid confession. Confession is relevant to what we do here, but it should not be what we do here. You wash up before you come to the Table, but the Table is not the designated place for washing up. Of course, if the Spirit brings something to mind while you are here, simply confess it and return to the subject at hand. But don't go hunting for things to confess. You are not to be curled up in an introspective ball, but rather singing to the Lord, looking around at your people, the people you love.

As you prepare for this Table by means of confession, either at the time or during our time of confession in the liturgy, remember the difference between confessing that you are a sinner and confessing your sins. The former is the foundation of orthodoxy, while the latter is the foundation of a clean conscience before God.

When Paul was giving his defense before Felix (Acts 24:16), one of the things he said was that he labored to live before both God and men with a clean conscience. This involves much more than simply acknowledging the doctrinal truth that we all have sinned. That is a truth. It is an important truth. But it is not the truth that we confess when we are confessing our sins.

Confessing sins is specific. It names names. It deals with what must be put right — because the end result is what Paul mentions here, a clean conscience. And real confession, at the right time and done in the right way, is not a cause of morbidity. It is actually the opposite. It enables you to come to this Table already clean. It enables you to sit down to fellowship with your companions and to enjoy the food provided. And the food provided is the bread and wine of your forgiveness — the basis of your clear conscience.

So come, and welcome, to Jesus Christ.

MORNING ✹ AN EDIBLE OATH

The apostle tells us that every time we come to this Table we do so in order to make a proclamation. Every time we eat and drink here, we proclaim the Lord's death until He comes. Now this proclamation is something that occurs among the Lord's people, for we are the ones invited to this Table, but the proclamation is meant to be heard by all that has breath. Every living thing is invited to worship the Lord.

We don't need to know *how* God arranges for nonbelievers to hear this proclamation, or how they come to learn of it, but fortunately, we don't have to. All we have to do is eat and drink with sincere love for God and for our brothers and sisters. God takes care of the rest. He is the one who called it a proclamation, and who called all of us His messengers.

One reason the proclamation is heard is because when we do this we are taking a blood oath — and this is a blood oath that obligates us to break down all the altars of all the gods in the land. The caretakers of these altars are not oblivious to our presence; they are not ignoring what we are doing.

We are renewing covenant with the God who calls us into His salvation, and we do not do this because the covenant was going to expire, like a lease. We don't renew anything that way. We renew our covenant obligations the way food renews the body, the way sexual union renews marriages, and the way laughter and fellowship around meals renew family ties.

This meal is the way God has arranged for us to declare our allegiance. He invites us to His Table, and He also tells us that to try to eat from two tables is incoherent. Look at the bread. That is your only food. Look at the wine. That is your only drink.

So we declare our allegiance by renewing it. We renew our allegiance by declaring it. So here it is — an edible oath.

So come, and welcome, to Jesus Christ.

We are gathered here as a portion of the Lord's little flock. His flock universal is a little flock, and we are just a small part of that. But what is His purpose for that little flock? He says this: "Fear not, little flock; for it is your Father's good pleasure to give you the kingdom" (Luke 12:32).

It is the purpose of God to give His little flock a big kingdom.

The Puritan William Bridge once observed that in Scripture we read many times of people who were too mighty, or too numerous, or too rich, or too proud, or too powerful, to be used by God. But we never read of a people who were too little to be used by Him.

When Gideon was called, he protested that his family was poor in the tribe of Manasseh. The angel of the Lord cajoled him into service. And then, when he had finally mustered his army, God decided that it was far too big. We know the end of that story, however much consternation Gideon had to go through on the way.

We are told in Scripture not to despise the day of small beginnings (Zech. 4:10). Because this instruction is plain, we must take care that we do not despise the day of small beginnings. God loves to start with little acorns. It is the wisdom of this world to laugh at mustard seed beginnings. It is God's declared intention to inundate the world with something that began as the most humble trickle.

So we are the little flock, and we have gathered here to be fed. God strengthens us for the task, He is preparing us for the work, and He is fitting us for the kingdom. How He will accomplish this is His business. It is our business to come and eat, to come and drink.

So come, and welcome, to Jesus Christ.

MORNING ✵ JUST A TASTE

We are gathered here for a meal, but it is not the final or ultimate meal. We are not yet at the time for the marriage supper of the Lamb. We are not yet ready for the feast at the consummation of all things. We are still living in the shadow lands, and the ultimate banquet has not yet happened.

At the same time, God does not want us to grow discouraged as we are preparing for that great day. And that is why we are offered foretastes of glory. That is what we are doing here, week after week. God nourishes us and feeds us with appetizers.

But to keep us from becoming too settled here, to prevent us from forgetting that we are still a pilgrim church, He makes sure that the food He gives us only creates in us a desire for more of it. We have a taste now to keep us longing. When you come into the kitchen half an hour early, and the very kind cook gives you a morsel of meat, this should only make you look forward to dinner more.

The Puritan Thomas Brooks put it like this: "Here God gives his people *some* taste, that they may not faint; and he gives them *but a taste*, that they may long to be at home."

We must love where we are in the story, but we must also love where the story is going. We live in time, but we live in a time that is moving. We do not ever have the option of hitting pause. We are going somewhere, and what we do here should be preparation for what we will encounter then. And that is exactly what this is.

So come, and welcome, to Jesus Christ.

EVENING ◐ HUMBLE FARE

As we look at this Table, we see humble fare. What God has set before us here is simple — it is bread for food, and wine for drink. What could be simpler? There is little that could be done to make it a humbler meal.

It is designed this way — humble fare for humble wayfarers. The apostle Paul teaches that we not only eat this food, we are this food. We are one body, one loaf. The bread represents the body of Christ, which body we are. The wine embodies the blood of Christ, by which blood we are cleansed and brought into fellowship with one another. There are many rich applications, but this is one of them. Humble fare for humble wayfarers.

The Puritan Thomas Brooks once said that faith was the champion of grace, and that love was the nurse of grace. But humility, he said, was the *beauty* of grace.

Humility is the foundation of all honor. The only way that resurrection honor can be straight and true is if the foundation of humility is straight and true. And Scripture teaches plainly that humility comes *before* honor (Prov. 15:33; Prov. 18:12; Prov. 22:4). Some want to by-pass the cross — that everlasting testimony of ultimate humility — in order to go straight to the honors. But no cross, no crown. Others want a false, perpetual humility, a demeanor that refuses to be raised into glory, honor, and dominion. But how is rebellion against the purposes of God in any way humble?

So we sit down at this meal as peasants, and we rise from it as princes. We are washed before we come, but we are nonetheless seated in the full realization that we do not deserve to be here. We still remember what we were like before the cleansing. So when we are seated here in true humility, that seating is beautiful. When we are raised from our place at this Table, that raising is glorious.

So come, and welcome, to Jesus Christ.

MORNING ☼ GRACE IS HIGH WHEN HEARTS ARE LOW

This meal presents God's answer to the problem of evil. It does this in at least two respects. The first thing God wants to do with evil is forgive it, cleanse it, wash it away. His eternal design, established before all worlds, was to populate the resurrection with untold millions of forgiven sinners. The apostle John saw a multitude that no one could number standing before the throne. And here on this Table we see the foundation of that forgiveness. If Christ had not died under the wrath of God, as a propitiation for our sins, we would all be utterly lost. And that is the meaning of this broken bread. That is the meaning of this red wine. Christ died in the place of sinners.

But a second answer to the problem of evil concerns the mere existence of evil. Why did God allow evil to come into existence at all? The answer is that so we might come to understand in practice how the lowliness of humility overthrows the greatness of the proud. We overcome evil when our graces are high, but our graces are only high when our hearts are low.

When our hearts are low, we see things in a spiritual light. A humble man will never think that anything is little or small if Christ is there. And that man, if Christ is not there, will laugh at every pretended greatness. Now — is Christ here now? Is this a little thing? You will shortly have a morsel of bread in your hand, and you will have a taste of wine on your lips. What will that do? It throws down the principalities and powers, and it does so because Christ is here — as we see in evangelical faith. It does so because it embodies the gospel of grace, and that grace means that God was at work in the cross. What did He do? In humility, Christ became a propitiation, and we were forgiven. In humility, He modeled that humility for us to follow after we were forgiven, so that we might become the agents of extending His kingdom from the river to the ends of the earth.

So come, and welcome, to Jesus Christ.

As we come to this Table, we are coming to the Table of the only true Victim. Only Jesus was entirely innocent, only Jesus had an absolute right to complain — which is why He didn't.

We can certainly *harm* one another. We can certainly bite and devour and betray one another. There are many tragic tales in this world, and there have been many tears. But whenever we are wronged by others, we will always be tempted to "work it." There are those of us who play at being the victim. There are those of us who were truly wronged, but who then inflate the wrong for the sake of our own pride. Any response that don't involve turning to Jesus will turn the wrongs of others against us into "our precious."

The way out is not simply to "stop it." The Eagles told us to "get over it," but that is not something we are capable of doing. The only way out of nursing our own victimhood is turning to Jesus, the only true Victim, who will put it all right by forgiving our sins and giving us forgiveness for those who have wronged us. This is what the Christian faith is all about. This is what the covenant of grace entails. This is the heart of the new covenant — their sins and their iniquities will I remember no more (Heb. 8:12). There are only two ways — the way of forgiveness which leads to Heaven, and the way of tangled recriminations, which leads every accuser straight to Hell.

Forgiveness does not whitewash sin or turn it into a trifle. Sin is why the beloved Son of God died, under the fury of God the Father. Do you really want to say that you believe that God's response to sin was inadequate? And that you think He should have been tougher? Sin is a liar, and so if you choose this way of recrimination, you will simply multiply the kind of sin you say you oppose, and you will bequeath that terrible legacy to your children.

But we are convinced of better things in your case. You have forgiven one another.

So come, and welcome, to Jesus Christ.

MORNING ☼ THE FOOD OF HUMILITY

God has designed this Table so that it feeds and nourishes our souls. But we should want to inquire into what this means a bit more. Otherwise we will come to think that the point of the sacrament is to make our souls grow "bigger," and that's all.

But God is after more than just quantitative growth. The issue is quality first. What is the nature of the soul that is growing? If the soul is proud and stubborn, we don't want a bigger one. If the soul is humbled under the grace of God, we want every such soul to flourish and grow.

Within the church, we are tempted to surround our pride with the barricades of our rationalizations. We don't listen to others because we are too busy calling our stubbornness "standards," or "backbone," or "self-respect," or "true insight." All the other soldiers in the army are out of step. But that kind of conceit is not fed here — although it is *dealt* with here.

Think about what you are eating. A broken body given over to injustice, and the Lord did this without opening His mouth in protest. What are you drinking? You are drinking the cup of the new covenant, shed by someone who was willing to be blamed for things He did not do. Contrast this with our tendency, which is the refusal to be blamed for things that we did in fact do. You eat this bread and drink this cup, and you should do it with the knowledge that your food is designed to break down your arrogance, and build up true humility in its place.

A good diamond can glitter in a darkened room, and so can a humble soul in a proud generation. For God's true children, this meal feeds their humility — and does nothing with graceless pride except doom it.

So as you reach for the bread, and as you reach for the cup, recognize that you are reaching for the food that all true humility needs.

So come, and welcome, to Jesus Christ.

EVENING ◐ A TABLE SETTING OF FAITH, HOPE AND LOVE

We come to this Table and find that it has been set in faith, hope, and love.

We come in faith because God has promised to meet us here, and we believe Him. The entire worship service crescendos at this meal. God has been present with us all along, but He is present in a special way here. It is here that we are privileged to partake of Him. Do you believe? I know you do.

In the Scriptures, hope is grounded—it is not hope against hope. We have an assurance of things hoped for. Hope is assured, settled. When we hope in the promises of God, it is not like saying "I hope that it won't rain today," or "I hope that I win the lottery." No, we have the blessed hope of our Lord's return, a sure and certain thing. The grass withers, the flower fades, but the Word of the Lord lasts forever. Our hope is in Him.

Love is straightforward—love for God and love for his people. This meal is given to us so that we might be knit together in love. That is the purpose, that is the intent. That is the whole point of gathering together like this.

Faith, hope, and love meet together in this meal, just as they are the triad that crown the entire Christian life. We rejoice in them all, and receive them all as gifts from the hand of God. But remember that the apostle Paul taught us that the greatest of the three is love. With the bread in your hand, love God and love your neighbor. With the cup in your hand, love God and love your neighbor.

It doesn't matter whether they are sitting right behind you or across the room. This meal knits all of us together in love. God is doing it, and we pray for Him to do it by the means He has adopted.

So come, and welcome, to Jesus Christ.

MORNING ☼ JUST ENOUGH

This Table has been set for us by God as a means of grace. The bread and the wine are for us rations of grace.

One of the remarkable things about these rations is that they are exactly suited to the difficulties that each one of you will encounter in the coming days. Some of you are in great affliction, some of you are going through significant trials, while others of you are enjoying times of relative ease and prosperity. Some of you are struggling to find work, while others have more business than you know what to do with.

You all need grace, but you need it in differing degrees and amounts. Everything you need will be in your hand shortly. But when I say it will be in your hand shortly, I am speaking to you by way of emblems and signs. It will *not* be in your hand, and then in your mouth.

Your strength is actually at the right hand of the Father, and your hand and mouth are actually to be found in your heart. Your God is your grace, and your faith is the way you receive Him.

As you come to Him in faith — by the appointed means of taking, receiving, chewing, and swallowing — you are receiving your appointed rations of grace. It will not be deficient grace, and it will not be a giant mountain of surplus grace. God does not feed you with grace for the next year, and God does not give you thin rations.

His grace is always sufficient. But take note — sufficient grace does not always *feel* like it is sufficient. "And he said unto me, My grace is sufficient for thee: for my strength is made perfect *in weakness*. Most gladly therefore will I rather glory in *my infirmities*, that the power of Christ may rest upon me" (2 Cor. 12:9). So what will you have in a moment? The answer is just enough.

So come, and welcome, to Jesus Christ.

EVENING ◑ AN UNWORTHY OBJECTION

We are told in Scripture to walk worthy of the calling we have received. We do this by knowing that we are unworthy, and have been made fit to approach God in this fashion by the grace that He offers us in Jesus Christ. We are to walk worthy *in the Lord Jesus*.

If you try to walk worthy in your own name, you will have to resort to walking on the spindly stilts of your own self-righteousness — and they will bend, break, and snap at every attempted step. Your self-righteousness cannot hold you.

Those who are unworthy are so because they think they are worthy. Those who are worthy are so because they know they are unworthy. God opposes the proud but gives grace to the humble. But this knowledge of unworthiness is a gift of God, and the one who is given it is raised up by God. Christians are not to wallow in their depravity. Christians are not to remain stuck in sin. Christians know the gospel, and the cross is always followed by resurrection.

So to hang back from this Table because you are unworthy is itself an unworthy objection. The premise is true, but the reasoning flawed. You are unworthy to come to the blood and body of the perfect sacrifice, but the perfect sacrifice was made so that unworthy sinners could come to Him in faith.

"As the body lives by breathing, so the soul lives by believing." Believe what God has promised, and come to Him in faith. Do not look around at your own life and conclude that you are a mess. As the Puritan Thomas Brooks put it, if you are swayed by carnal reason, you will prefer to believe your five senses rather than the four evangelists. Do not give way to that temptation. You are invited by the goodness and kindness and graciousness of God.

So come, and welcome, to Jesus Christ.

MORNING ✵ THE LORD IS YOUR CUP

The message of Psalm 16 is one that speaks clearly of Christ, but also of His people.

The New Testament tells us plainly that God's promise to Christ in the grave was given in this psalm. God would not allow His holy one to see corruption, which is why Christ was in the grave for only three days (Ps. 16:10). But notice that this promise presupposes that the holy one would die. This promise assumes that the holy one would come to the grave, but would not be abandoned there.

The psalm also exults in God's goodness and kindness to us, His people. It says that the lines have fallen to us in pleasant places, and that we have a goodly heritage (Ps. 16:6). In the midst of affliction and trial we may want to murmur and complain. We might want to play the hermeneutics game, and say that the lines had fallen in pleasant places for David, the one who originally wrote these lines. Yes, but Scripture commands all God's people to sing these psalms as our corporate expression. The lines have fallen for *us* in the pleasant places.

But why is this? How does it work? The answer is found here, at this Table. "The Lord is the portion of mine inheritance *and of my cup . . .*" (Psalm 16:5a). This cup is the cup of the new covenant, and you are the new covenant people of God. This is your inheritance. This is your goodly heritage. The wine is the sacrament of Christ's blood, shed for you, and you partake of the benefit of that sacrifice as you partake in evangelical faith. And, as you see in this psalm, the Lord is your portion. The Lord Himself is your cup.

Your affliction is the Lord's affliction. Your suffering is the Lord's suffering. When you come to the grave, you have come to a place where the Lord has gone ahead of you. And because of that you know that you will not be left there. You have a good inheritance, and here it is, right in front of you.

So come, and welcome, to Jesus Christ.

This is a Eucharistic meal, and that word comes from the Greek word for thanksgiving. This is our weekly thanksgiving meal.

Because this meal is offered us by the sovereign Lord over all things, we must not think of it as an oasis of thanksgiving in the midst of a wilderness of grumbles. It is not an island of thanks in the middle of an ocean of trials and complaints.

No, we are giving thanks here for a broken body and shed blood, which illustrates how God governs the entire world. Remember that Jesus took the bread in His own hands, said this is my body, gave thanks, and broke it. He was giving thanks *for* the affliction; He was not just giving thanks *in* the affliction.

And this is why we are told: "In everything give thanks: for this is the will of God in Christ Jesus concerning you" (1 Thess. 5:18). And again, "Giving thanks always for all things unto God and the Father in the name of our Lord Jesus Christ;" (Eph. 5:20). God is sovereign, and this is why we are to learn to give thanks in our afflictions, and also for them. This meal equips us for that. Remember, you are thanking the God who saved the world through the tortured death of Jesus, whose body is represented here. We are His servants, and a servant is not greater than his master. If this happened to Jesus, what may happen to us?

Strengthened by this meal, if we are in darkness, we will bless the Lord. If we are in the sunny uplands, we will bless Him. If we are sick, we will bless His name. If we are without the money we need, we will bless Him. If we have an abundance, we will rejoice and bless Him. If He gives us great mercy, we will bless Him. If He gives us the scrapings of His mercy, we will bless Him even more. However empty you feel your hands to be, in a moment they will be holding the fullness of Christ.

So come, and welcome, to Jesus Christ.

MORNING ✺ WHAT WE ARE IN FOR

This is a meal, and so one of the things we do here is *taste*. "O taste and see that the Lord is good: Blessed is the man that trusteth in him" (Ps. 34:8). As we see in this passage, to taste the Lord is to trust Him. It is to believe Him. This is another way of saying that tasting is *sola fide*, by faith alone.

There are two levels here. We either taste or we do not. If we taste, we taste by faith. If we do not taste Christ here, if the ordinances are to us like the white of an egg, then we are gaining no profit. Without Christ, all the churchy things in the world are as nothing.

But suppose we taste Christ, as I am sure you are doing. This is the next truth, the next level, the next lesson. We taste but little. We taste little compared to what we should taste. We taste little compared to what others have tasted. We taste little compared to what we desire to taste. We taste little compared to what we shall taste.

Substitute the word *trust*, and you will see what I mean. We trust but little. We trust little compared to how we should trust. We trust little compared to how others have trusted. We trust little compared to how we desire to trust. We trust little compared to how we *shall* trust.

When we come to this Table, the fleeting experiences of spiritual tasting that we have here, in which we taste Christ, but not as fully as we would, should be an *encouragement* to you. You experience in such events the fact that the Holy Spirit is taking you somewhere. These fleeting "glimpses" are designed to bring you on. Come. The Spirit and the bride say, *come*.

God sanctifies us by enticing us. He is leading us on. He is preparing us for a meal that we could not come to without preparation. He is letting us now, little by little, what we are in for.

So come, and welcome, to Jesus Christ.

EVENING ◐ THE BACKDROP OF RESURRECTION

This meal commemorates the *death* of Jesus Christ. This bread represents His body, and this wine represents His blood. This Table is all about the crucifixion. The cross is what we are talking about. The affliction He went through on our behalf is the message.

But we have to presuppose the resurrection in order to be able to do this. If Jesus had not come back from the dead, then His death would have been just one more obscure execution, wherein a prophet was swallowed up by the system—devoured by the cruel machinery of death. We have the privilege of proclaiming the Lord's death two thousand years later because we are proclaiming the death of one who *rose*.

This dark world was utterly transformed by the resurrection. In the very middle of history—necessarily transforming the very meaning of history—Jesus came out of the tomb. This world is now a world in which the first man rose from the dead.

What this does is liberate us, so that we can proclaim the Lord's death as full of gospel meaning, instead of forgetting it as necessarily meaningless. Jesus was raised for our justification (Rom. 4:25), which means, in part, that He was raised so that we could declare that He died.

Further, this declaration helps keep the sap of grace flowing out to our leaves. Whenever affliction blows someone off the tree, it is a withered leaf that blows off. Afflictions test your graces. You should be strengthened in those graces by this. This Table is a Table of affliction, and it is simultaneously a Table of thanksgiving. Affliction because He died, thanksgiving because He rose. We imitate Him, then, in our afflictions. We see them all against the backdrop of resurrection.

So come, and welcome, to Jesus Christ.

MORNING ☼ LITTLE PLASTIC CUPS

The bread and wine here represent and embody the most precious gift that has ever been given to anyone. You were redeemed, Peter says, not with gold or with silver, but with the precious blood of Jesus Christ (1 Pet. 1:18–19). This is a precious gift indeed. What kind of vessel should this be put in then? The biblical answer is that *you* are that vessel.

Just as the bread and wine have a representative meaning, so do the trays and cups here. They contain the sacrament, and learn a lesson from it. They are clean, they are prepared with care beforehand, they are set apart for this use . . . and they are humble. These vessels didn't cost very much, but nevertheless they represent us, the vessels about to receive the elements of the sacrament.

God does not mind putting His precious things into humble vessels, but He does mind putting them into foul, putrid, unclean, and proud vessels. Remember what the apostle said — we have this treasure in *earthen* vessels. That is fine, that is a design feature (2 Cor. 4:6–7). But a humble vessel can be clean and prepared, just as a rich, ornamented vessel can be full of blasphemies, abominations, and the filthiness of fornication (Rev. 17:4).

As you prepare yourself to be a fit vessel of the gift you are about to receive, do not think that God requires spiritual ostentation. He actually requires the opposite. He requires care, thoughtfulness, and love. That is what it means to come to Him in a worthy fashion. Don't try to encrust your cup with diamonds — as though He needed anything decorated with self-righteousness. He doesn't mind that you are a little plastic cup. Just be a clean one.

We have this treasure in a little plastic vessel, that the excellency of the power may be of God, and not of us. You don't have to earn what you contain — but you do have to *contain* what you contain.

So come, and welcome, to Jesus Christ.

What we are doing here involves our minds, but it is not what we would call a mental exercise. It involves our mouths and throats, but it is not just ordinary eating. What we do here engages our hearts, but it is not meal of sentiment. So what are we doing then?

The apostle Paul describes this as a partaking of Christ, but this is not because this is a "special" supernatural meal in sharp contrast to a natural world. It is not as though we have the backdrop of the black night of nature, with a tiny spark of grace here.

No, God created the world to function in covenantal categories. So the thing that happens here at this Table is the same thing that happened in the Old Testament when priests partook of the altar. More than that, it is the same thing that happened when pagans partook of the altars they had erected to their demons. The world functions covenantally. This is not just something that happens in the spiritual world; it is how the whole world runs. Whatever we do, wherever we go, we are partakers.

So it is quite true that we partake of Christ in this meal, and that we do so spiritually. But take care what you mean by that word *spiritually*. When you give your physical body over to the control of God, it is, the apostle says, your *spiritual* worship. A spiritual man is not an ethereal man. A spiritual man is an obedient man.

As you present yourselves here to be fed, to be strengthened, to be built up, to be nourished, to be given wisdom, you are doing so because you have been *summoned*. There has been a call to worship, has there not? You have been invited, have you not? This bread and this wine is being offered to you, is it not? Jesus said that His crucified body would draw all men to Himself. This is the divine order—He has died, and we have come.

So come, and welcome, to Jesus Christ.

MORNING ☼ SEE YOUR NEIGHBOR IN THE SUPPER

We are here to discern the Lord's body. We are not here to do metaphysical speculations about what might be happening to the bread and wine on the subatomic level — although we do confess that God ministers to us spiritually with these material elements. We are not here to go spelunking in the deep caverns of our mysterious lusts, although healthy self-examination should be a normal and healthy prelude to our enjoyment of the Supper. We are not here to fight with other Christians who understand this meal differently than we do, although it is important for us to understand it as biblically as we can.

Our central task is to discern the Lord's body, and to see that this body is seated all around you. This means that the meal is given to us so that we might understand that we are the meal. There is one loaf, and you are that loaf. We partake of the body of Christ which means that we must be the body of Christ. But there is no way for you to be the body of Christ without coming to the conclusion that your neighbor is also part of that body.

You cannot partake of Him without also partaking of him, and him, and her, and them. This is why this meal knits us together. We are eating, drinking, meditating, listening, and singing, and we are doing it all in love for God, and in love for one another.

Some of the things we have made the Lord's Supper into are things which can exclude little children — just like the disciples did when they kept little children away from the Lord. The Lord didn't like it at all and said that coming to the kingdom involved becoming more like them. It is not like insisting that they become more like us — which is to say, clueless. Children may not be good at metaphysics, or at morbid introspection, but they can see their neighbor as well as you can. So love God, and love your neighbor.

So come, and welcome, to Jesus Christ.

EVENING ◐ JUST ONE SIN

We come to the Table in order to be nourished. We need to be nourished and strengthened so that we might have grace in our spiritual limbs when we come to do battle. And when we come to do battle, it should be directed against sin. The author of Hebrews exhorts his readers to be willing to commit themselves to the point of bloodshed in their fight against sin (Heb. 12:4).

And so our celebration of this Supper does have something important to do with sin, but not because it is a time for morbid introspection. We are to examine ourselves, we are to cultivate a tender conscience, but the time we have set apart for that is at the beginning of the service, when we first come into the presence of God. This Supper is about temptation and sin, but it is more about next week's temptation than last week's. The body and blood of Jesus do not just forgive past sin, they also equip us for our fight against future sin.

And you need to be strengthened against one sin, not against all of them. You will not be tempted to commit all of them. You will be tempted to be undone by just one. So put on the full armor of God. Noah, the most righteous man, was undone by one sin. Moses, the meekest of men, was shut out of the promised land by one sin. David, the best of kings, was taken down by one sin. Job, the most patient of men, was convicted of one sin, and repented in dust and ashes. Adam, the father of us all, plunged the world into the morass of sins by just one sin.

There is grace in this bread and in this wine. It is not grace that can be tasted with the tongue, but you all have a spiritual tongue that can taste and see that the Lord is good. That spiritual tongue is living faith, active faith, evangelical faith. When you believe in your heart, you are tasting with your tongue. And when you do that, you are being equipped for this coming Tuesday.

So come, and welcome, to Jesus Christ.

MORNING ✹ TO LIVE AND DIE AS CHRISTIANS

We gather at this Table weekly. As we do, we should remember that there are three elements to what we do. The first is *invocation*. We acknowledge God's presence here with us, and indeed, we invite it. We call upon Him. Second, we rejoice before Him with *thanksgiving*. This is a Table of thanksgiving and gratitude. And third, there is an element of binding ourselves with an *oath*.

We are renewing covenant with God here, but not because our covenant with Him was set to expire, like a lease. Rather, we renew our vows before Him, acknowledging to Him, with solemn and deep joy, our intention to live and die as Christians. This is a deep oath, solemn and glad, and so we return to it weekly.

This is not because the oath is weak, and needs shoring up weekly. Rather, it is because we are weak, and we need to be reminded. This is our life. This is our song. This is our connection to all our brothers and sisters throughout the world, and throughout history, who have loved the name of Jesus. This is the body of Jesus, and this is the blood of Jesus. This is our creed, an edible creed. This is our oath, and in gladness we drink all of it.

We have invoked the name of God, showing that we know what we are doing here. We have expressed our joy and gladness. Because of this body and blood, you are no longer in your sins. And by eating and drinking in faith, you are saying that you will be here next week, eager to say again that your intention is to live and die a Christian.

We are mindful of our sins, the sins we already confessed at the beginning of the service. But rather than making us morbid and introspective, our recognition of our sins here at this Table should simply add to the gratitude. Should it not? Sin at *this* Table is met by the blood of Jesus, which washes them all away.

So come, and welcome, to Jesus Christ.

EVENING ◐ WHERE THE TRANSFORMATION OCCURS

As you know, you are worshiping God in a Protestant church. This means, of course, that we deny certain things, and this lines up with the common modern understanding of the word *Protestant*. It is thought of as a variant of *protester*. But the term was originally more of an affirmation than a denial—think of a word like *pro-testimony*.

Now of course when you affirm one thing you must of necessity deny its opposite. If you face the east, your back is to the west. If you affirm that two and two make four, you deny that it is three. So in this sense, we do deny the doctrine of transubstantiation. We deny that this bread and wine turn into the actual body and blood of the Lord. But it would be a mistake to think that this denial does not have a corresponding affirmation. We do believe in transubstantiation, just not transubstantiation of the bread and wine.

We affirm and rejoice in the *transubstantiation of the congregation*. The process started when we were born again unto God, and as we gather week after week we continue to be transformed from one degree of glory to another (2 Cor. 3:18). While our outer man is decaying and withering, our inner man is being renewed daily (2 Cor. 4:16). We all together are being grown up into a perfect man, and that perfect man is Jesus Christ (Eph. 4:13). We are united to Christ, and we are being knit together in Him (Col. 2:2).

This is a transformation of entities who were far apart from Christ, but who are now being made partakers of the divine nature (2 Pet. 1:4). This is glory—that which was far away from Christ has been brought near. Not only have we been brought near, but we have been made one. It is glory, but it is glory that is the result of a miraculous transformation. When a heart of stone is made into a heart of flesh, what is this? When a valley of dry bones is raised up into a living congregation, what is this? It is the work of the Spirit of God.

So come, and welcome, to Jesus Christ.

MORNING ☼ THE HOUSEHOLD OF FAITH, HOPE AND LOVE

One of the ways we diminish our understanding of the Lord's Supper is through saying that it is just a metaphor. In the first place, the world is more mysterious than that and there is no such thing as "just" a metaphor. God created the cosmos by speaking, and words are not impotent little labels. But even using the common language of metaphor, the Lord's Supper would be a complex metaphor, not a simple one. There are *many* things going on here — thanksgiving, proclamation, longing for the day of redemption, and more.

One of those elements is underscored by our practice of celebrating this Supper weekly. What this accomplishes — among other things — is the creation of a household. Households eat together. Companions are those who share bread together — the word *panis*, bread, helps to form the word *companion*.

Because we observe this Supper weekly, this means that, with the exception of your immediate family, in many instances you eat and drink together here more often than you eat and drink with anyone else. This has the decided practical effect of shaping you into a *household*. That is what we are, right? The Bible describes us as the household of faith (Gal. 6:10). We belong to the household of God (Eph. 2:19). And what do households do? They eat and drink together. The prodigal son wanted to return to his father's household, where there was enough to eat. The Lord Jesus, in His Upper Room discourse, told us how He was going to His Father's *house* (John 14:2), in order to prepare many rooms.

A key element of the potency of this Supper has to do with your companions. It is not just you and the elements — the elements represent the body, and that Body is seated all around you. That Body is the household of God — the household of faith, hope, and love.

So come, and welcome, to Jesus Christ.

EVENING ◐ WINE IN A CUP, AND BLOOD SPILLED

There is a striking similarity between the bread we see here and the body of Jesus Christ. There is also a striking similarity between the wine in the cup and the blood of Jesus. If there were no similarity it could not work as a sacrament — it could not even work as a metaphor.

But there are dissimilarities as well, and we do well to keep them in mind. The bread we break here is bread on a Table, on a tray, with a white cloth beneath. The body that was broken was laid out on a cross and nailed there. The wine we drink is wine in a *cup*. The blood that was shed was blood that was *spilled*.

The sacramental meal we observe is a ritual, a religious ceremony. It is obviously civilized. It is contained, bounded, focused. The reality that it represents was brutal, and despite the efforts of the Sanhedrin to keep their minutes in order, lawless.

These dissimilarities are not limitations or faults in the Supper — this is all apparently a design feature. When the Lord instituted the Supper with His disciples, He used a cup to contain the wine that embodied the blood that the world itself could not contain. The blood of Christ contains the world, not the other way around.

We use particular words to declare universal and timeless truths. Here is an example. Jesus Christ died for the sins of the world. That is a simple declarative sentence, but the reality it references is cosmic. This is a particular cup on a particular Table in a particular town. What does it mean? It means that God saves sinners anywhere, in whatever tattered condition they might come. This is a particular loaf on a particular tray, but it speaks of the universal church, and God's infinite love.

We remind ourselves of these dissimilarities by means of words, so that we may grasp the instructive point of the dissimilarities by a living faith, the way God intended.

So come, and welcome, to Jesus Christ.

MORNING ☼ NO PICKY EATERS

The apostle Paul teaches us that we are all one loaf (1 Cor. 10:17). We are one body, one loaf, one congregation. We symbolize this by symbolically partaking of one loaf. Now if it happens that we have more saints gathered than can be fed by one loaf, no matter. The Lord once took five loaves to feed the multitude, so we shouldn't worry about it.

At the same time, there are other actions that are filled with symbolic meaning, they are freighted with meaning, and we cannot just arbitrarily say that they are not a big deal. Make sure you understand that the Bible makes a big deal out of eating together, and the unity this displays.

There are two common ways of disrupting this — one is by dividing the guest list, and the other is by dividing the menu. The first says that you may come, and you may not, and this — outside of Christ, or outside the lawful discipline of the church — is a huge deal. The apostle Paul confronted Peter over just this thing at Antioch. What some might have described as just the seating arrangements at the potluck, the apostle Paul took as an assault on the gospel. So if you divide the guest list here racially, or tribally, or with regard to income bracket, it is an awful sin.

Another way of disrupting fellowship is by inviting everybody, and dividing the menu. Paul says here that we are making a statement that we are one body because we have one food — in this case, bread and wine. We are Christians, which means we must not be picky eaters.

So come, and welcome, to Jesus Christ.

This Supper of the Lord is not limited in its signification to just one or two things. It is richly laden with meaning on multiple levels. But two of them might appear to be in tension.

The Lord's Supper is a memorial of what Christ has done for us, and the Lord's Supper is a communion in what Christ has done for us. This Supper is a memorial of the Lord and it is communion with the Lord. In the former sense, it would appear to assume the Lord's absence, and in the latter sense it would appear to assume the Lord's presence. Both are true, but in different senses.

The Lord is not present with us physically. His body has ascended into Heaven, and is there, not here. His body was nailed to a tree two thousand years ago, laid in a tomb, and was raised from the grave three days later. That same body ascended into Heaven where it now is. In that sense, this meal is a memorial of His sacrifice for us, reminding us of what He did, as well as a memorial of His sacrifice for God, reminding Him to receive us for Jesus' sake. In all this, we are presupposing His absence, and we long for His coming again.

But the Lord promised us that if He went away, He would send His Spirit to be present with us. In that sense, because the Holy Spirit of Christ is here with us, Christ is here with us. Christ promised to be wherever two or three are gathered, and so this would certainly include two or three hundred. The Spirit is not only present, but the Spirit is active, knitting us together in love. This is His appointed work, and He does it by creating *koinonia* or fellowship. Another English word for what is happening in this is communion, which also happens to be a name for the Supper itself.

So Christ is absent, and we remember Him. Christ is present and we commune with Him.

So come, and welcome, to Jesus Christ.

MORNING ☼ WHAT FLOWS FROM HERE

This is a time of year when many people are decorated up in frightening ways, running around saying frightening things, trying to scare other people. But take heart; the elections will be over on Tuesday. Coincidentally, today is also Halloween, when many are trying to frighten people in *other* ways. But how are we to respond to what unsettles or panics unbelievers? We are to summon them to a life of faith, outside of which is only alternative is fear.

In just a moment we will be singing the great battle psalm of the Huguenots, Psalm 68. God shall arise, and He will scatter His enemies according to His Word, according to His promises, according to His assigned means, and by the power of His Spirit. Unbelievers should therefore leave all their fears, and turn in wholesome fear to the one who can throw both body and soul into Hell.

There is no problem with giving candy to the kids who come to your door tonight. Go ahead, enjoy yourself, and bless their evening. There is no problem with going to the polling place this Tuesday and casting a responsible Christian vote. That is your civic duty, and a great privilege. But the world is being actually transformed *here*. God in the folly of His wisdom, in the wisdom of what men call folly, has determined to remake humanity in the image of Jesus Christ, and to do so by means of words, water, bread, and wine. We are equipped, blessed, strengthened, and made wise here. We then take it out into the world. The living water flows over the threshold of the Temple, and it flows outward from the Church for the healing of the nations.

But these things require a catalyst. We do not think that words mumbled, or holy water, or bread on a priestcraft table, or wine in a superstition cup can themselves change the world. *We* are the body of Christ, and because that body is not dead, the catalyst is a living, conquering, and glorious evangelical faith given by the Holy Spirit.

So come to this Table as you must come — *believing in Jesus. So come, and welcome, to Jesus Christ.*

Our God is a Savior, and because our need of salvation is something that is expressed in history, our God is the God of saving acts. God establishes the story, the end from the beginning, but God has also written in the story in such a way that requires Him to intervene in it.

When God told Noah to build an ark, and told him to retreat with his family into it, that was a saving act. When God intervened with Abraham, and pointed him to the ram in the thicket, that was a saving act. When God rained down destruction upon Egypt, and then led Israel through the cloud and the sea, that was a saving act. When God took Israel into Babylon for their sins, and brought them back to the land again, that was a saving act.

All these were precursors and types of the ultimate saving act, the death and resurrection of Jesus Christ. It is that saving act that we are memorializing here as we eat the bread and drink the wine. As we do so, we are partaking of God's great saving act through Jesus, and if we do so in genuine and sincere faith, we are partaking of that saving act.

Now it is not possible to partake of that saving act—really, genuinely—without being saved. If you are in the ark, you are not drowning. If you are on the far side of the Red Sea, then you are not under the Red Sea.

Our intent here is not to partake of a little ceremony. Our intent is to gather, as a people overflowing with faith, in order to partake in the salvation of the world. When you chew and swallow the bread, that is what the salvation of the world tastes like. When you take a drink of the wine, what you are tasting is God's kindness to sinners.

So we do not call God our Savior because that is a Bible word. We call Him Savior because He saves. We call Him that because we have gathered here to the salvation of mankind.

So come, and welcome, to Jesus Christ.

MORNING ☼ THE CENTRAL POINT

This meal is a sacrament. But what is a sacrament? Where does this use come from? The answer to that question — given the nature of what we are doing here — cannot be confined to one simple answer, but it does have an answer.

The use of the Latin word *sacramentum* was introduced by the early father Tertullian, who took it from the oath of allegiance that a Roman soldier would swear upon enlistment. This element is certainly present — at the sacrament of baptism, the one baptized is being bound by oath to serve Christ for the rest of his or her life. Every time we take the sacrament of the bread and wine, we are again swearing our allegiance to Christ. But there is more to it.

The word *sacramentum* came to be the word used to translate the Greek word *mysterion*. What to the Greeks were mysteries were to the Romans sacraments. Augustine took Tertullian's concept and developed it further, and defined a sacrament as an outward and visible sign of an interior and invisible grace. The oath is objective; the person is bound whether or not he meant it when he made it. But the oath includes the assumption that the profession is sincere. When it is not sincere, when the outward and visible sign does not line up with a heart-felt desire to follow Jesus Christ, then the sacrament is being defiled.

Note that the sacrament is not a nullity. Unbelief cannot undo God's Word. It is the other way around. God's Word is what undoes unbelief, destroying the hypocrisy, either by judging it or converting it. Abuse of the Supper was why many of the Corinthians were sick and dying. Their sin could not make the Supper get sick and die. Christ already died, and has risen to everlasting life. Death cannot touch Him, which is the central point, is it not?

So come, and welcome, to Jesus Christ.

EVENING ◐ EAT YOUR WISDOM

This meal consists of an edible word, a drinkable word. That word is, of course, the Lord Jesus, who is the eternal Word of the eternal Father. This is His body, and this is His blood. We do not just treat the bread and wine as a visible word and as visible drink, but as a word that we are called to take into our mouths, and to swallow it down in faith.

This is not faith in mere bread, or trust in wine. We do not think that any created thing has power in itself to do anything. But God uses instruments. The receptive instrument that He gives us is faith — living, vibrant, evangelical faith. But He also wields other instruments that this faith responds to, seeing the work of God in and through them — sermons and sacraments, for example.

So this meal is an edible word, a drinkable word, and this Word is the Lord Jesus. But what does the apostle John mean when He calls Jesus the Word of God. The Word is not a single mystic syllable of the sort you find in eastern mysticism. No, the Word of God is the eternal and everlasting Wisdom of God. When men reject the word of God, what *wisdom* is in them (Jer. 8:9)? We are told to let the word of Christ dwell in us richly, in all *wisdom* (Col. 3:16). The mouth of the righteous speaks *wisdom* (Ps. 37:30).

This is the edible word of God, it is edible drink from Him. This means that it is the edible wisdom of God. It is the wisdom of God in a cup.

Of course, to expect to find wisdom in these elements autonomously is to descend into superstitious folly. That is not wisdom at all. You are not an empty receptacle and this is not a spiritual commodity to put into it. No, you cannot come here a fool and go away wise. But if the word is in your heart and in your mouth already, then you may come here to put this wisdom into your heart and mouth. You are invited to eat your wisdom.

So come, and welcome, to Jesus Christ.

MORNING ☼ MORE THAN A WARP SPASM OF DEVOTION

The Bible contains different kinds of literature, which means that it also contains different approaches to theology. Because these theologies are ultimately harmonious, it is obviously our task to be students of them all. But part of this task means mastering them on their own terms *before* the harmonization is attempted.

For example, the psalms of David represent a devotional literature, which means that they shape a devotional theology of personal piety, heart religion. The proverbs of Solomon represent a wisdom literature, which means that they shape a wisdom theology. The two must go together, but they must be themselves in order to go together rightly. Wisdom theology isolated turns into an arid moralism. Devotional theology isolated turns into rationalism and egoism. We must be shaped by the entire Bible, but we do not do this by throwing the entire Bible into a blender, reducing it to biblical molecules. No, Scripture is assembled out of some great blocks of granite, and those blocks must be respected.

What does this have to do with the Supper? You must come here loving Jesus Christ, the way David loves God in the Psalms. There needs to be an existential encounter. We are not playing church; we are loving God. We *sing* to Him. But evangelical religion must not be limited to some kind of warp spasm of devotion. It must grow up into thoughtful, reflective, studious *wisdom*. But if we grow up into wisdom and get stuck there, the result is that we become a bunch of studious, learned, academic *duds*.

So there is something beyond wisdom, which is glory. "But we speak the wisdom of God in a mystery, even the hidden wisdom, which God ordained before the world *unto our glory*:" (1 Cor. 2:7). So come in faith to this edible glory, the glory of sacrifice vindicated, and grow up into what you eat and drink.

So come, and welcome, to Jesus Christ.

EVENING ◐ EMPOWERED, ENLIGHTENED, ENLIVENED

This meal is not a propitiatory sacrifice. We are not offering Christ to God — rather, God is offering Christ to us. He is able to do this because Christ's blood was spilled in the crucifixion, and applied to the heavenly altar in the Ascension. The offering of Christ to God was a singular event, and in the words of Hebrews it was "once for all." It does not need to be repeated, and indeed, in the very nature of the case, it *cannot* be repeated.

But Christ can be offered to sinners as long as we still have sinners — and we still do. They are being born all the time. We are still needy. We are still broken. We are still in need of being grown up into the perfect man. Christ need never again be offered to the Father. Christ must be offered to the world until the world is remade in Him, and is fit to be offered to the Father. Christ was offered to the Father once for all. Christ is offered to the world repeatedly.

Christ is offered to His people in the church repeatedly, multiple times. We hear the Word of God read in this service, we pray the Word of God in this service, we sing the Word of God in this service, and we hear the Word of God proclaimed in this service. In the Supper we have the privilege of sealing all of that by eating and drinking the very Wisdom of God.

As we do so, we are being transformed, from one degree of glory to another. We are empowered by it, we are enlightened by it, and we are enlivened by it. None of this happens because we simply go through the motions, but when we come to this Table in a lively and evangelical faith, it *does* happen. Christ is offered to us, again and again, and we receive Him again and again. We don't receive Him as though we never had Him; we receive Him in His fullness because we already have His fullness. We receive Him, all of Him, more and more.

So come, and welcome, to Jesus Christ.

MORNING ☼ NOT AN ESCAPE, BUT A CLEANSING

This meal is the Wisdom of God. But you do not come here to do things with that Wisdom, but rather so that God's infinite Wisdom will do things to you. The Wisdom of God is infinite and personal. Only the Spirit of God can plumb the depths of that infinite Wisdom, and that is because the infinite Wisdom is the person of Christ.

When you come to this Table, you are coming to Christ, the Wisdom of God, the amen of God, the fulfillment of every *yes* from the Father, He whose very nature is *yes*.

And Wisdom aims at righteousness. We live in a fallen world, and so we are sometimes led astray by counterfeit knockoffs of wisdom—academic and very turgid headiness being one of them. You are not coming here to learn how to theorize in ways detached from the world, but rather to learn how to think about the world in ways that enable you to live in it with righteousness.

Another way of saying this is that you are not communing here in order to be liberated from the flesh. You are not communing in order to detach yourself from the material world. This is not about escaping from the flesh, this is about the *sanctification* of the flesh. You are not here to eat and drink the Spirit, but rather, in the power of the Spirit, to partake of the body and blood of the Lord Jesus.

That body is not located here on this Table, but rather at the right hand of God the Father in Heaven. So we do not partake of a dead Christ, but rather of the living Christ, and we do it by means of the faith that the Spirit of God generates within us. The Spirit pervades Heaven and earth, and by the gift of faith He gives, He unites us to the Lord's risen body. This does not erase our bodies, but rather purifies them. And this is all the Wisdom of God, which draws us further and further into His holiness.

So come, and welcome, to Jesus Christ.

The sacraments are not a thing in themselves. The sacraments are what they are because they are an instrument or tool in the hand of God. And the way God wields His instrument or ministry of this Supper is through the agency of the Holy Spirit.

There is therefore no blessing here apart from a relationship between persons — the communicant and the Spirit who is using these means to build up and confirm the faith of that communicant. Everything always begins with God, so He gives us faith in the first place. In that faith, we come here, and because we come in the faith that was designed to enable us to commune with Him, He communes with us here. In meeting us here, He then uses these elements to confirm and nurture us in our faith so that we go out to live our daily lives strengthened by Him, and be better equipped to come back here in growing faith next week.

So the work that is done externally is the eating of bread and the drinking of wine. The work that is done internally, subjectively, by the Spirit, is the work of uniting us with Christ for blessing. Apart from Him doing that, there is no blessing at all.

Now the thing that causes the inside and the outside of the sacrament to line up properly is faith. Not faith in ourselves, not faith in the bread or wine, not faith in the church, and certainly not faith in our own faith. We are called to faith in our Father, who sent His Christ, and after that it is faith in the Father and the Son, who sent their Spirit.

It is not superstition to meet God where He said to meet Him. The sacraments work — when they work — the same way that sermons do. Nothing happens automatically. This Supper doesn't *contain* Christ, the way the cup contains the wine. But this Supper most certainly *ministers* Christ. And whenever a worshiper meets with His God, everything is transformed.

So come, and welcome, to Jesus Christ.

MORNING ☼ LOYALTIES

There are many aspects to this Supper, but one of them is that it is an expression of loyalty. In this meal, the Lord offers Himself to all who come to Him in faith, and all who come to Him in faith offer themselves in return, in a devout imitation.

Christ offers Himself. We may describe this doctrinally, but He does not offer us a mere doctrine. We may enact this liturgically, but He does not offer a liturgical shell. God offers us Himself. He gives Himself, and in the power of the Spirit, He gives Himself wholly.

We are to act as dearly beloved children, which means that we are to imitate Him in this. We come here to express our all-in loyalty. There are to be no double loyalties here — nothing else can be permitted to compete with the place of Christ in our hearts.

We do this fully aware of all the distractions that pull at our sleeves on a daily basis. We know of our faults and failings, and our propensity to wander. But that does not exclude us from this meal — God knows what kind of world we live in, and He knows what kinds of temptations we face. What we are dealing with is "common to man," and God has provided us with Word and sacrament. But note that these are merely instruments by which He provides us with Himself.

If you would profit by this — and why would you not want to profit by it — then you must receive what is actually being offered. When you do this, your loyalties are aligned with His, and His Spirit equips you fully.

So come, and welcome, to Jesus Christ.

The Lord is present through the Supper because the Lord is presented in the Supper. The Lord ascended into Heaven two thousand years ago, and His body is at the right hand of the Father. Since His body is there, it follows — since He has a true human body — that it is not here.

The Lord is not physically present in the elements of bread and wine; rather, the Lord is physically presented by means of the bread and wine. God has created the world with a host of covenantal interconnections, and this is one of the central ones. The Lord is physically present in Heaven, and we are physically present here. How can this distance be bridged?

The answer given in Scripture is the answer provided by the Holy Spirit of God. When these words are spoken, when bread and wine are received in obedient faith, the Holy Spirit knits us together with Christ, drawing the bonds of love ever tighter. Our unity with Christ is a unity of love. Because it is love between persons, it can obviously grower deeper and richer. But the fact that it is growing does not mean that we were not united before.

The union we have with Christ through the Supper is a union that is true, from the start, and yet is a union that can grow truly richer as time passes. We are being transformed from one degree of glory to another, and it is the gracious work of the Spirit.

So come, and welcome, to Jesus Christ.

MORNING ✹ A TABLE, AND NO ALTAR

We have before us a Table, *not* an altar. The distinction is not a slight one. We have gathered to offer a sacrifice of praise thanksgiving, not a of propitiation. Our propitiation was accomplished on the altar of the cross — prefigured throughout the Old Testament by the altars upon which sacrificial animals were slain.

Offering up true thanksgiving is possible only if propitiation has already been accomplished elsewhere and applied to us. Having been set free by Christ's once-for-all sacrifice, we sit down at this Table and lift up a liberated sacrifice, gratitude and harmony together, a spiritual sacrifice that is the consequence of all that has gone before.

This spiritual sacrifice supplants some of the tangible helps that our Old Covenant brothers and sisters employed as they looked forward to the time of our liberation. "Let *my prayer be set forth before thee as incense*; And the lifting up of my hands as the evening sacrifice" (Ps. 141:2). Prayer replaces incense, and lifted hands replace blood. Song fills all the space that bloody altars used to occupy. "The one who offers *thanksgiving as his sacrifice* glorifies me; to one who orders his way rightly I will show the salvation of God!" (Ps. 50:23, ESV). We are privileged to live in the day when we may, without a qualm, offer thanksgiving as our sacrifice. And that is what *eucharist* means — thanksgiving, not propitiation, thanksgiving *because* of the propitiation.

A definitive sacrifice of propitiation happens only once, and it provides a sure foundation for a continual sacrifice of another kind. "By him therefore let us offer the sacrifice of praise to God *continually*, that is, the fruit of our lips giving thanks to his name" (Heb. 13:15). And this is why I am no priest, offering up a victim. I, and the men here with me, are set apart to the privilege of being table waiters. We come to you in joy, bearing joy, and we call upon you to respond in joy.

So come, and welcome, to Jesus Christ.

EVENING · YOU MAY PUT THEM IN YOUR MOUTH

This Supper is all about the future. This is an eschatological meal that we are privileged to share in now. Just as the Spirit of God escorts us all into the heavenly places to partake of the living Christ there, so also the Spirit unites past, present, and future to enable every *true* Christian to partake of eternal life now. It is a present possession. "Whoso eateth my flesh, and drinketh my blood, hath eternal life; and I will raise him up at the last day" (John 6:54).

There is a mystery here because false Christians can certainly partake of the Supper in some fashion, which is why Paul says that their unbelief makes them guilty of the body and blood of Christ (1 Cor. 11:27). You can't defile something you have no connection with. They have some sort of union with Christ (John 15:1–6), and some way of trampling the blood of the covenant by which they were sanctified (Heb. 10:29). There is a connection there, but it is not life-giving.

There are Christians and then *real* Christians, partaking and *real* partaking. Real partaking is by faith alone and is efficacious. Going back to John 6:54, if someone eats Christ's body and drinks His blood, we may say that he *has*, right now, eternal life, and we may say that God has *promised* to raise him up at the last day. God breaks all kinds of things — worlds and kingdoms, heads and hearts, princes and presidents, and the pride of man, *but He never breaks a promise*. This means that someone who is not so raised is someone *who never had* that eternal life.

We are convinced of much better things in your case. This meal is offered to you here as an earnest on your final inheritance. If you receive it in true evangelical faith, with a humble heart, and without blowing any smoke at God, then you may marvel at what you are being given. This bread and this wine are eternal life. They are being given to *you*. They are yours. You may put them in your mouth.

So come, and welcome, to Jesus Christ.

MORNING ☼ ALL KERNEL, NO SHELL

Faith sees. Faith knows. Faith apprehends.

We know that without faith it is impossible to please God, and the converse is also true. Whenever genuine faith is present and active, that faith is a gift from God, and God is always pleased with His own gifts. If He stirs us up to something, then He will always take pleasure in His own work.

Faith is the gift that God gives us that enables us to see what He is up to. When we do not have that gift, we see nothing more than the skin of divine mysteries. We see the shell, the outside. If you would crack open the shell to obtain the kernel, then you must have faith.

This is important because without faith, everything presented to us presents only the shell. Preaching, attending church, singing psalms and hymns, receiving the waters of baptism, partaking of the bread and wine . . . all of it is simply the external shell.

But with faith, the metaphor becomes glorious. When faith cracks open the shell and obtains the kernel, all the bits of shell become the kernel also. Without faith, the nut is a solid shell, all the way through. With faith, the nut is nothing but kernel, all the way out.

This is why men of faith can sound like superstitious idolaters in how they speak of the sacraments — but they only sound that way to superstitious idolaters. And this is also why men of faith can sound like iconoclastic rebels, but they only sound that way to superstitious idolaters.

Bread and wine do you did not require, but a humble and a contrite heart. And whoever partakes of the bread and wine is partaking of Christ Himself. How can these paradoxes be resolved? Only by faith, by faith alone, *sola fide*.

So come, and welcome, to Jesus Christ.

As the Old Testament saints looked forward into the future, as Abraham did, rejoicing to see the day of Christ, they were looking forward to the times of refreshing, the times of the regeneration. But we must not think of this regeneration simply as an event, or the arrival of an era. There is a sense in which that is true, but there is another element to it all. We need more than just a line of regeneration, descending from Heaven to cross the line of history.

We need an axis of regeneration. From the perspective of the older covenant, there was a time coming when God's intervention was going to close off the times of unregeneration, and inaugurate the times of the regeneration. This is true. A time was coming when all the bodies in Ezekiel's boneyard were going to come to life, and were going to stand and live, in accordance with the sovereign Word of the sovereign God. Israel was going to be born again.

But there was always another line, and always will be, equally established in the will of God, a line that ran down the middle of human history, including the middle of the historical church, the covenant people of God. This *also* was a line of regeneration, separating the sons of Belial from the sons of Abraham.

Now when you come to this Table, you are called to come in true faith. And when you come in true evangelical faith, this Table is, for you, the point of intersection on this axis of regeneration. On the one hand, God's purpose for all history is slicing clean through it, from top to bottom. Christ is present, here. This Table is life in the regeneration. On the other hand, the fact that you are partaking *sincerely* separates you from all false and hypocritical professors. The fact that we are in the regeneration does not make being a son of Belial impossible. Far from it.

So come, and welcome, to Jesus Christ.

MORNING ☼ ROOM AND BOARD

When Nicolas Ridley was Bishop of London, he undertook the important reform of "stripping the altars." Churches then had multiple altars, in the front of the church and in many side alcoves. Ridley ordered these all be removed, and replaced with a wooden table, a "decent table."

He referred to this as the "Lord's board," taking that language from the translation of 1 Cor. 10:21 found in the Geneva Bible. Where our translations say the "Lord's table," the Geneva rendered it as *board*. We still have forms of this usage in expressions like "room and board," or "boarders." But whatever expression is used, the point was to replace an instrument for sacrificing with an instrument for eating.

In the times of the Old Testament, men of God built altars on the earth, and they were right to do so. They built altars because *the* altar had not yet been established. In the times of the new covenant, the earth itself has become an altar (Rom. 12:1–2), such that *anything* we do is to be offered up as a living sacrifice. Because Christ died once for all, the building of altars is no longer necessary, and, more than that, building altars is forbidden. We are summoned to come, take our place, in order to eat and drink.

So you are adopted into the family of God. You have every right to be here. God has given you His Spirit, the Spirit who calls out *Abba, Father*. This means that, unlike a renter, you may simply sit down to eat and drink. The costs are completely covered. No one would say of their toddler, except as a joke, that we decided to "give him room and board." But the reason we wouldn't say that is not because it isn't true. He *is* being given room and board. But grace is so much a part of everyone's thinking that the idea of making him *pay* for it never enters anyone's head.

So come, and welcome, to Jesus Christ.

One of the great doctrines of Scripture is the doctrine of union with Christ. The phrase *in Christ* or related phrases occurs in Paul's letters over 170 times. It occurs in the book of Ephesians over thirty times. Now for those who are Christ's this union is the case all the time. But Scripture also teaches us that there are occasions when that union is realized more fully, more richly, more deeply.

The Lord's Supper is intended to be just such an occasion. You are a Christian all the time. You bear the name of Christ all the time. But to paraphrase one Puritan — in other places we have His Word, in the sacrament we have His kiss.

Now when we partake of Christ this way, take care to remember that Christ is not being parceled out to you. You are receiving a little bit of bread, and a small cup of wine, that is true, but this is a sacramental synecdoche. A synecdoche is a figure of speech where we speak of the whole in terms of the parts or vice versa. For example, when we say many hands make light work, and we are referring to all the people connected to those hands, that is synecdoche.

I bring this up, not as a point of grammar trivia, but so that you might know that you are being presented with the whole Christ. You are not receiving a fraction of Christ here. You are in communion with Jesus Christ Himself. He is a person, and when He engages with you, He is engaged with you. When you partake of Him, you are partaking of *Him*.

And of course, you cannot be united to the whole Christ without being united to His people. His people are the body of Christ; they are part of the whole Christ. This is why we are called to partake of this sacred meal in faith, hope, and love — but love mostly.

So come, and welcome, to Jesus Christ.

MORNING ☼ EATING AND DRINKING THEIR FORGIVENESS

One of our great responsibilities in the Lord's Supper is to look around. By this I mean looking around metaphorically and looking around actually. We would encourage you not to stare at the bread and the wine, and we would encourage you not to curl up into a little ball of pious thoughts. Look around.

Look around the world. All over this globe, the saints of God are worshiping Him, ascending into the heavenly places in the power of the Holy Spirit. A swath of worship is sweeping around the globe at a steady rate, just like sunrise and sunset do. You are together with all of them. See that by faith, and make sure you look around.

Look around your town. There are many believing churches on the Palouse, and these saints are your brothers and sisters. You don't worship together with them, but you work together with many of them in the course of the week — sometimes in ministry and sometimes in your regular jobs — and so you know them, and love them. And even though you don't worship together with them, if you look around, you will see that you *do* worship together with them.

Look around this room. These are the saints that are together with you in one congregation. You all live together, worship together, educate your kids together, car pool together, and work together. What this means is that you have, with regard to those closest to you, the most opportunities for both gratitude and complaining. Isn't it odd that in the place where God has given us the most, and so we should be most thankful, we tend in that place to do most of our complaining? So as you look around the room, think of the offenses against you. Then look on the bread and wine, and realize that you are privileged to eat and drink their forgiveness.

So come, and welcome, to Jesus Christ.

EVENING ◐ UNSPEAKABLE JOY AND FULLNESS OF GLORY

We have not yet seen Jesus Christ in the body, and through the grace of God, this is a great blessing and glory for you. While that fact has led many into a ho-hum profession of the Christian faith, cruising along on autopilot, that is not how the Spirit intends to use the fact that we have not seen Jesus Christ. "Whom *having not seen*, ye love; in whom, though now *ye see him not*, yet believing, ye rejoice with joy unspeakable and full of glory:" (1 Peter 1:8). God wants the fact that we have not seen Jesus with our eyes to be something that faith lifts up into unspeakable joy and fullness of glory.

Ineffable joy is therefore something that is part of normal Christian living. It should be part of the baseline. This is not an over-enflamed condition of uber-saints; these are words written to ordinary Christians such as yourselves. "Joy unspeakable and full of glory" is not a private reserve for mystics. And this is what enables you, as you have gathered together in this way, coming to the Table of the Lord with that unspeakable joy, to then discern the body of the Lord Jesus in your brothers and sisters all around you. Just a few verses down, Peter says this: "Seeing ye have purified your souls in obeying the truth through the Spirit unto unfeigned love of the brethren, see that ye love one another with a pure heart fervently: Being born again, not of corruptible seed, but of incorruptible, by the word of God, which liveth and abideth for ever" (1 Pet. 1:22–23).

When there is an unfeigned love for the brethren, when we love one another from the heart fervently, this is the Spirit's seal upon us. It means that our joy unspeakable is not a sham, not a front, not a super-spiritual substitute for actually loving other people.

You have not seen Jesus Christ — joy unspeakable, full of glory. You have seen Jesus Christ in your brothers and sisters — unfeigned love, fervent love.

So come, and welcome, to Jesus Christ.

MORNING ☼ HIGH HEARTED

One of the great blessings of the covenant is that when we come to the Table of the Lord, the Lord is dealing with us. We partake of Christ in a special way here, and there is no way to partake of Christ with nothing happening. Christ is present here and He *deals* with us.

But He deals with us according to His grace, and not in a spirit of severity. This part of the service, where I say a few words just before the Supper, is called the Invitation. And it is a *true* invitation. *Come, and welcome, to Jesus Christ* is the constant theme.

We know that tolerating known sin in our lives is inconsistent with partaking of the Supper, but we need to think of this in more complete terms. Suppose you had that known sin in your left hand, and the bread that we pass out to you in your right. Look down at them both. Everyone knows that one or the other has to go, and that is quite true. One or the other has to go, but the next truth is just as important: It may not be the bread.

We are Christians, which means that we don't have the right to not partake of the bread and the wine. This is not something we are allowed to opt out of. We must come. The Invitation is an urgent one.

So this means that we are, all of us, called to come to this Table in a spirit of repentant gratitude. Sinners may come. Sinners must come. Defiled Christians are required to come. Rebels may not come while in that condition, but they must come as well. And that is why we come to the broken bread with broken hearts. A humble and a contrite spirit God will not despise. He binds up the brokenhearted.

This is a high Table, but it is not for the high hearted. But if the high hearted are baptized Christians, they are forbidden to come as they are in one sense, and required to come, just as they are in another sense.

So come, and welcome, to Jesus Christ.

In discussions of the sacrament, the distinction between sign and thing signified goes back to the great Augustine. This is a distinction that is essential for us to maintain if we are to keep ourselves out of superstition and idolatry. At the same time, we must make this distinction without dividing or separating the sign and thing signified. If we break the sign and thing signified in two, the only thing we will find ourselves holding is the mangled sign, with the reality long gone. They cannot be there together, except as God has appointed.

The appointed instrument that God has given that enables us to hold sign and thing signified together is *faith* — the kind of faith given by Him, which means that it necessarily is vibrant, alive, receptive, eager or, to use the word that sums it all up, *evangelical*.

Simple faith can see at a glance things that unconverted philosophers and theologians with bulging foreheads cannot figure out. Faith does not create mysteries on a *table*, with what is going on inside the bread or inside the wine. Faith receives the mystery into the body of Christ — you are that body — and there sees what God intends when He speaks of greater things under the form of the lesser.

What is offered here, in words and actions, is the body of Jesus, the blood of Jesus. But what is *actually* being offered is *totus Christus*, all of Christ, the entire Jesus. This is all about union with Christ, and remember that union with Christ is only effectual when received by faith, and it is not possible for a true faith to receive a partial Christ.

Similarly, you receive these emblems, these elements, with your hands and your mouth. But your hands and your mouth also represent something. They are also a lesser thing that represents, necessarily, *all* of you — body, soul, and spirit — and they represent you resting in Christ forever and ever, world without end.

So true faith receives the true and entire Christ into the true and new humanity, being grown up into the perfect man.

So come, and welcome, to Jesus Christ.

MORNING ☼ SUN'S PRESENCE

The sun is ninety-three million miles away. It would be fair to say that the sun is *distant*. But for everyone who has eyes to see, the sun is very much *present*.

The Lord Jesus Christ is seated at the right hand of the Father. He is there, not here. As a true man, He is located in the heavenly places. And yet, God has established the kingdom of His Son in such a way that the radiance of the Son's glory extends throughout that entire kingdom, which is done through the power of the Spirit.

That radiance of glory is not felt equally by all. If you were to bury a pebble in your garden and a seed in your garden right next to the pebble, you would get very different results from them. The seed contains life, and so can respond to the gift presented by the distant sun now present. The pebble contains no life, and is insensible to whether the sun is distant or present.

When the Word is preached to you, and when the bread and wine are presented to you, you are called to respond in faith to the felt presence of Christ. This is possible because the Spirit has quickened you — you are a seed, not a pebble. You are green shoot, struggling up through the soil, beginning a glorious journey for such a small plant. You are three inches tall and you plainly want to make a journey of ninety-three million miles.

The glory of grace is this — that distance is traveled, not by us, but rather by the sunlight. That gap is overcome by the power of the Spirit. The glory of grace is found in how it enlivens our lives here, how life is initially given and then turned into a life that is an abundant life. He comes to us, and we ascend toward Him.

So Christ is here. He is *present*. If you are alive in Him, you can feel the warmth, you can feel the strength, you can feel the glory.

So come, and welcome, to Jesus Christ.

EVENING ◐ MERCY IN HIS RIGHT HAND

As we gather here, we are partaking of Christ. This is presented to us under the forms of bread and wine, representing His passion on our behalf. But we are not being presented with a momentary Christ, a Christ limited to those few days at the end of His life.

No, we are presented with everything Christ is and has. We are presented with everything He has done in history, what He did for us on the cross, the glory of the moment when He left the tomb, the wonder of His ascension into Heaven and presentation before the Ancient of Days, His gracious outpouring of His Spirit, which brought His bride into union and communion with Him. Not only that, but we are united with Him in His glorious Second Coming.

As we consider the world outside of Christ, we see with them the perennial desire to be free of this Jesus. They do not want Him to rule over them. But we do want that, and we bring it to pass by worshiping His Father through Him and in His name, in the power of the Spirit. As we do this, we are anticipating by faith.

Anticipating what? We long for the day when Christ will be revealed to the entire created order as the one who has been given universal dominion. Every eye will see Him, and they mourn the one whom they pierced. They will acknowledge Him, with every tongue confessing that Jesus Christ is Lord, to the glory of God the Father. They will bend the knee before Him, because He sits on a throne looking down upon the sons of men, and as He does so, by faith we see righteousness in His left hand and — glory to God — mercy in His right. Because mercy is in His right hand, we have good news to proclaim to a world that has not been consumed.

We are not coming here to a partial Jesus, or an incomplete Christ.

So come, and welcome, to Jesus Christ.

MORNING ☼ THOUGH THE DEVIL SAY CONTRARY

This is the time in our weekly worship when we come to the Supper. But the connotations might be different for us if we simply said that this is Suppertime. This is the point where the Holy Spirit of God, who is the Comforter, offers us His food, but the connotations are different when we acknowledge that it is comfort food.

This is all true because Christ is here, Christ is here *seeking* you. As Samuel Rutherford put it, wonderfully, "Christ seeks you in the sacrament, seek ye Him again, and though the devil should say the contrary, there shall be a meeting."

There shall be a meeting because this meal is not a haphazard affair. It was not thrown together. In Proverbs 9, we see how Lady Wisdom sets her Table, and we see that she sets out bread and wine, as we have right here. "Come, eat of my bread, And drink of the wine which I have mingled" (Prov. 9:5).

And Jesus very much had this banquet in mind in the gospel of Luke when He told the story of a man who prepared a great feast, and, like Lady Wisdom before him, sent out messengers to invite to the feast people who were too wise in their own pursuits to come (Luke 14:15–24). But of course, to be too wise in your own pursuits to come to Jesus is to be a fool.

Like Lady Wisdom, like the man in the parable, Christ has done everything. He has prepared the meal. He has set the Table. He has appointed the time. He has sent out the invitations. "Ho, every one that thirsteth, come ye to the waters, And he that hath no money; Come ye, buy, and eat; Yea, come, buy wine and milk without money and without price" (Is. 55:1).

The only thing that is left for you to do is to sit, and eat. All you must do is sit, and drink, and to do so in grateful faith.

So come, and welcome, to Jesus Christ.

We might describe the marriage between the Lord Jesus Christ and His bride, the Christian church, as a community property marriage. This way of saying it might jar us at first, but it points to an important aspect of our faith that is often neglected.

What we have in this meal is a representation of *koinonia*, mutual partaking. In this meal, Christ offers Himself to us. In this meal, we offer ourselves to Him. In this meal, we offer ourselves to one another in koinonia love. And last, in this meal, we offer Christ (and ourselves with Him) to an aching, lost, miserable, and sin-torn world. As often as we partake here, we proclaim Christ's death until He comes.

Our understanding of this mutual partaking is an understanding that grows over time. In the Song of Songs, the bride at first mentions how her beloved belongs to her, and follows it up with the fact that she belongs to him. "My beloved is mine, and I am his: He feedeth among the lilies." (Song 2:16). But later in the book, this is reversed. She begins with the fact that He possesses her, and then goes on to rejoice in the fact that He belongs to her. "I am my beloved's, and my beloved is mine: He feedeth among the lilies" (Song 6:3).

We begin with the knowledge of what we are receiving, but we know that we are also giving. We grow up into the knowledge that we have given ourselves away, and in that knowledge, we know that we have received everything. Whoever loses everything for Christ's sake is one who has gained everything. He who grasps to keep what cannot be kept is forfeiting what, if received, could never be lost.

At this Table we are reminded—and we are reminded every week—that Christ is everything to us, and everything that He is and has is now our possession by right. That right was not bought through any merit of ours, but rather through the sheer and quite outrageous and completely scandalous grace of God.

So come, and welcome, to Jesus Christ.

MORNING ☼ TRUE NONETHELESS

As a proclamation of the gospel, this meal represents the great exchange. We were dead in our sins, and in Christ God exchanges us His life for our death. We were in abject poverty, and so in Christ God exchanges us His riches for our rags. We were slaves, chained to the dungeon walls of our own selfishness and pride, and so in Christ God exchanges us His liberty for our slavery.

He took our curses, and we walked away with His blessings. He took our iniquity, and we walked away with His righteousness. He took our guilt, and so we walked away with a song in our hearts and on our lips. He took our shame, and we walked away with His glory.

God made the one who had never known sin to be sin on our behalf, so that in Him we might become the righteousness of God. *That* is what this meal declares, embodies, and enacts. As often as we partake of this meal, we declare the Lord's death until He comes, and that is what our declaration is talking about. That is what His death, burial and resurrection mean.

So the Lord Jesus is at the head of the Table, and the lowliest Christian seated at the foot of the Table is in full possession of all the riches of this great house. Another way of saying this is that there *is* no foot to this Table. In Christ, we are all seated at the head. In Christ, nothing is withheld. In Christ, we do not lack for any good thing.

In Christ, we have far more than the blessing of what He took from us. He never takes anything from us, however tawdry, without replacing it with something glorious.

So this is the Table of the great transaction. This is glory through vicarious substitution. This is staggering wealth through sheer and infinite grace. This is too good to be true . . . but it is true nonetheless.

So come, and welcome, to Jesus Christ.

Sacraments can only be created by God Himself. A sacrament always has promises annexed to it, and they are the kind of promises that only God can make. Under the new covenant, we find that God has established two sacraments in the church — baptism and the Lord's Supper.

These sacraments have three elements to them. The first is the Word that accompanies them. If there is no Word declared, then all we have is water, bread or wine, and no sacrament. The second element is the sign. In order to be a sacrament, it is necessary to have a physical thing that is consecrated and set apart to a holy use. The water is a sign. The bread is a sign. The wine is a sign. The third element is the thing signified, which is Christ Himself — Christ and all His benefits, Christ and all His promises, Christ and all His grace.

Now in order for the sacrament to be a blessing to us, all three of these elements must be bound together. They cannot be detached from one another and enjoyed separately. They must come together — Word, sign, and thing signified — and in order to get this we need a divine bonding agent. Only one thing can tie these three things together, and the Bible teaches that this one thing is faith. Faith is something that the Holy Spirit gives us by generating it within us, as fruit of His activity and presence.

When the Holy Spirit is at work in this way, you hear the Word, you see and taste the sign, and you partake of the Lord Jesus Christ. When this happens, we come to understand that in faithful observance of the sacraments, *something happens*. God is at work.

So this is how the Scripture speaks of sacraments as signs *and seals* (Rom. 4:11). The sealing is an accomplishment. We are doing more here than thinking thoughts in our heads, and using these indicators as mere audio-visual aids. No — Christ ministers to you here *with effect*.

So come, and welcome, to Jesus Christ.

MORNING ☼ GROUND, INSTRUMENT, MEANS

The central point of the Lord's Supper is union with Christ. If we want to be nourished in our understanding of this, and indeed in our experience of it, we have to distinguish between the instrument for receiving this grace, and the means of receiving it.

The *ground* of your justification is the work of Christ on the cross, culminating in His resurrection and ascension. That is the ultimate foundation.

The *instrument* of your justification is your faith, but which is only yours because it was granted to you as a gift by the Spirit of God. God gave you a new heart, a heart that was capable of believing Him. In fact, the new heart that He gives is incapable of not believing Him.

And last, and most varied, there are various means of God's grace to us. These are presented to us, in line with God's Word, and if we have true, evangelical faith, we use such means to strengthen and nourish us in our union with Christ. Such means of grace would be worship, listening to sermons, improving your baptism by faith, singing and praying, and coming to the Lord's Table. So Christ is objectively offered here, but the only way to receive Him is through the subjective experience of trusting Him.

Some have made the mistake of thinking that because such faith is essential, it can therefore operate all on its own — without any need for preaching, or music, or prayer, or sacraments, and so on. But this is foolish — the verb *believe* requires a direct object. When we believe, we must believe *God,* and if we believe God, then we have to believe that He will in fact present Himself to us in those places where He promised to meet us.

The ground is Christ Himself. The instrument is living faith. The means are before you now.

So come, and welcome, to Jesus Christ.

Because Christ is the Head of the Church, it means that He is the one presiding at this Table. He is the Head which is why He is seated at the Head. It also means that He is the one who established the ritual for us, and so this is why we keep the ceremony at the same level of simplicity as when He instituted it.

There are only two elements, bread and wine. They are common elements, not exotic. We do only three things with the bread — we bless it, we break it, and we eat it together. We do two things with the wine — we bless it, and we drink it together.

To overcomplicate it would be to take it from the Lord's hands, wresting it all away from Him, in order to replace it with a ceremony more to our liking. But God knows what we need, and He has provided for us exactly what we need.

If Jesus required his itinerant ministers to eat whatever was set before them (Luke 10:8), then how much more should all God's servants eat what is set before *us*. We are quite clever enough to observe sacraments, but we are not nearly clever enough to invent them. Whenever we try to invent them, we come up short.

God says here is the bread. Bless it, break it, eat it, and love each other. Here is the wine. Bless it, and drink it and love each other. Next week we are called to exactly the same thing, with the same bread and wine. The bread and wine never change. What changes is the love — as we are being grown up into the perfect man, our love for God grows deeper and richer, and our love for one another does the same.

In other words, we don't say words over the elements in order to change them. They don't need changing. We say words over the elements because they will be instruments in the hands of God for changing us. *We* are what changes.

So come, and welcome, to Jesus Christ.

MORNING ☼ PLEDGE OF ALLEGIANCE

The sun is ninety-three million miles away, and yet every day we enjoy its warmth and light here. The Lord Jesus is at the right hand of God the Father, yet He is present here with us, now.

His warmth and presence comes to us in the person of the Holy Spirit, and so if anyone asks if we believe in the real presence of the Lord in the Supper, the answer is of course. We don't believe in His real absence. God is present here in and through the work of the Holy Spirit. We do not look for a physical presence in the elements of bread and wine, but rather a covenantal presence of Christ, manifested in His energy and power.

Christ is present in the participles — He is present in our praying, singing, breaking, eating and drinking. The catalyst for all this is our faith, and even that faith is a gift from God so that no one can boast.

So the bread and wine are evangelical types. They represent God's offer of Christ to us, and in faith, as we receive them (in the participles) we are gratefully accepting what is offered.

The Reformers lived in a time when the works of the early church father Tertullian were recovered, and it is from Tertullian that they learned that the word *sacramentum* referred to an oath that a soldier took upon his enlistment. As such, it is a most fitting word for this covenantal meal — we are taking a covenantal oath, and we are doing so as the ultimate pledge of allegiance.

We live in a world that is constantly trying to lure us away from this allegiance, but we want nothing to do with that. So we come here every week to renew our vows, and we are privileged to do so in the presence of Jesus Christ Himself.

So come, and welcome, to Jesus Christ.

When it comes to observance of the Lord's Supper, and especially when it comes to regular, weekly observance of the Lord's Supper, there are a number of questions that we have to address and answer. One of them is what devout preparation for participation looks like.

Paul teaches us that we do have a duty to examine ourselves. He uses the same word—*anakrisis*—in a couple of different places. "But let a man examine himself, and so let him eat of that bread, and drink of that cup" (1 Cor. 11:28). "Examine yourselves, whether ye be in the faith; prove your own selves. Know ye not your own selves, how that Jesus Christ is in you, except ye be reprobates?" (2 Cor. 13:5).

This means that the issue is not *whether* preparation for the Supper consists of self-examination. Of course it does. The problem is that a great deal of confusion exists over what constitutes lawful and sane self-examination. We must take it as a given that self-examination is necessary for every approach to the Table. We must not take it as a given that we have a good grasp of what healthy self-examination looks like.

Too often the people who try to examine themselves give way to morbid introspection, and the people who are not given to morbid introspection are only free of this vice because they have never attempted to obey Paul's requirement in any way.

When you examine yourself, you are not looking for sin. If the presence of sin disqualified us from the Supper, then no one could partake. What you are looking for is love of sin, devotion to it. If you examine yourselves and find that Jesus Christ is in you, you will not find loyalty to the world, the flesh and the devil. You will see your sins, but you will also see, by the grace of God, your hatred of them.

So come, and welcome, to Jesus Christ.

MORNING ☼ SEATING AT TABLE

We come to the Lord's Table every week, but what are the seating arrangements? What should our posture be, and how is the Supper laid out?

In the aftermath of the Reformation, this is one of the things that came to be reformed. Previously, the people would come to the Table rarely, they would come down a long nave, and they would kneel to receive just one of the elements. That is hardly a posture of Table fellowship. After the Reformation, the statement made by the seating was strikingly different. The Scots and the Dutch particularly wanted to have the statement be that of a family seated at a table together, and they went so far as to have a very large Table made, at which the congregation could sit down together. But then, as a congregation grows, you have to eat in shifts, and you are losing some aspects of that wonderful picture.

Another device that developed — the one we are using here — is the device of having the congregation seated on three sides of the Table. We are gathered at Table throughout the service, and we, as a family, are gathered around that Table. This is one of the reasons we decided to move from portrait seating to landscape seating. We are all here together.

The minister consecrates the elements, and officiates at the Table. The elements are distributed by elders, deacons, and sometimes when we are short-handed by men from the congregation. But liturgically, the waiters are the elders of the church. When the elements come to you, all of you pass them up and down the rows, and you do it family style.

And why family style? We are the household of faith, and so it is that we are privileged to give the body and blood of the Lord Jesus to one another.

So come, and welcome, to Jesus Christ.

EVENING ◐ CREATION ALL OVER AGAIN

When we come to the Table, the entire congregation is proclaiming the death of Jesus until He comes again. Faithful observance of the Supper is therefore an evangelistic act. Even though participation in the Supper is limited to baptized Christians, the import of the Supper is for all the children of men.

So when we proclaim the death of Jesus as the very center of the mighty acts of God, we are doing it context. We rejoice in our subjective experience of salvation, but we do not begin and end there. The experience of salvation is driven by the objective reality of it. God has done marvelous things in the world, and because we look at them and believe, the Spirit continues His work in us.

We declare, therefore, the mighty acts of God—what He has done in the creation—and we rejoice in how He delivered His people over and over again throughout the Old Testament period. He delivered Israel from Egypt, struck down Sennacharib, and brought His people back from Babylon. God is to be praised for all His works.

When the time was right, He sent His Son, born of a woman, born under the law. He lived a perfect, sinless life, doing so on our behalf, representing us as Israel, finally obedient. He went to the cross to have our sins laid upon Him and there judged. He was laid in the grave so as to taste death fully. He was raised to live for our justification. And all this is what we declare in our observance of the Supper.

What do we say then? We say that God is the creator of all things and the sovereign Lord who decreed that the created order would fall under the disobedience of Adam. He then promised that the dire blow of wrath from a holy God would in fact fall, but would fall upon Himself, in the person of the incarnate Son. We say further that God vindicated His wisdom in doing all of this by raising His Son Jesus from the dead. And so it is that we declare the three mighty acts of God—creation, redemption, and creation all over again.

So come, and welcome, to Jesus Christ.

MORNING ☼ EXERCISING OURSELVES IN THE TRUTH

When we come to the Table, we are being given the privilege of exercising ourselves in the truths of the gospel. One of the ways that God enables us to do this is through the establishment of memorials, and this memorial is one of them.

When God wanted us to exercise ourselves in the truth of creation, He gave us the Sabbath day as a memorial. When God wanted the Israelites to remember their deliverance from Egypt, He gave them a memorial in the Passover feast. When God wanted us to exercise our understanding of resurrection life, He transferred the memorial of the Sabbath Day to the first day of the week, the Lord's Day (Heb. 4:9–10; Rev. 1:10).

And when He wanted us to exercise ourselves in our knowledge of the shed blood of Jesus, and of His broken body, He gave us this memorial. When we do this, we do it in remembrance of Him, but because it is a covenantal memorial we have to remember also that we are lifting it up into the presence of God so that He will remember.

When we call upon God to remember, this is not because we are afraid that He was going to forget. He does not need our reminders. Rather, this is how memorials work — we need to remind Him for our sake, not for His. God places a rainbow in the sky as a memorial, testifying that He will never again flood the world. This is something that we need to remember. We must remember, but we must also remember to remind God. But this is because we need to be constantly reminded that God is the source of all things, and that when He is blessing us, He is doing so by keeping covenant.

And so, here is the bread. Here is the wine. Here is the gospel. Strengthen yourselves in it.

So come, and welcome, to Jesus Christ.

An older English word for *offer* is the word *tender*. The great theologian John Owen said that in the Lord's Supper, the Lord Jesus tenders an offer of Himself, inviting us to receive him. We have echoes of this older use of the word here and there, as in the phrase *legal tender* on your money.

This meal consists of the shed blood and broken body of the Lord Jesus. We are proclaiming His death until He comes, the apostle says. But we are also proclaiming everything about that death. We do not proclaim His death in isolation, but rather in concert with everything the Scriptures teach us about that death. And one of those things is the love of Jesus Christ for us. "And from Jesus Christ, who is the faithful witness, and the first begotten of the dead, and the prince of the kings of the earth. *Unto him that loved us*, and washed us from our sins in his own blood" (Rev. 1:5). Any exhibition of the death of Christ is necessarily an exhibition of the love of Christ. It says here that He loved us, and in that love He washed us from our sins in His own blood.

Too many times we are as Jacob was. "And Jacob awaked out of his sleep, and he said, Surely the Lord is in this place; and I knew it not" (Gen. 28:16). But the Lord is here, and He offers Himself now to you. He tenders His love, and He does it tenderly. The only appropriate response in receiving Him is to love Him in return. He gives His love, and we return it. We love Him because He first loved us, but we do love Him. This meal is a covenantal transaction. He gives us His love, and this creates love in us. That love, so created, must be tendered in return.

So come, and welcome, to Jesus Christ.

MORNING ☼ SO EXHIBITED

Even though a great deal of historic Reformed theology was written in English, our native language, we do have to take care to note certain changes in the meanings of some words.

When it comes to the Lord's Supper, the great theologian John Owen said that Christ was *exhibited* in it. That same word is used with regard to the baptism in the Westminster Confession, where it says that in baptism the grace promised is "not only offered, but really exhibited, and conferred, by the Holy Ghost" (WCF 28.6).

If you go to an *exhibition* at a modern museum, you are going to *look* at something behind a velvet rope. You go to an exhibition in order to see things, and then to go home. But in the seventeenth century, to exhibit meant something much stronger. To exhibit meant to hold something out in order that it might be received.

It is in this older sense that Christ is exhibited here at the Table. He is offered, He is conferred, He is extended to you. Part of that exhibition is found in the fact that the bread and wine are visible, but this offer goes far beyond the fact — true enough as far as it goes — that this sacrament is a visible Word. It *is* a visible Word, but when you sit down at your ordinary meals you do not dwell on the fact that your food is visible. It is visible, but, being food, it is also edible. The fact that it is visible helps you to find it, but it is not how you use it. The Lord says *take and eat*, not *watch and think*.

So this is the edible Word, and it is the *exhibited* Word. So God exhibits Himself so that you might receive Him in the person of His Son. What is the spiritual member you have that enables you to receive Him so exhibited? That member, that grace, that kindness is living and evangelical faith.

So come, and welcome, to Jesus Christ.

When Jesus said that the cup we drink was the new covenant in His blood, He was opening up a world of wisdom to us. So many truths are set before us that it is difficult to know where to begin, or what to do with them all.

Because of this we sometimes give up, and simply return time and again to two or three truths related to the Supper. Those truths are true, and so we are edified to meditate on them, but because this meal sets before us the wisdom, kindness and grace of God, we should also remember that we are being invited to know the unknowable, to grasp the ungraspable, and to enter into the height and breadth and depth of God's purposes for us.

What do we learn about covenants here? One of the things we learn is that a covenant is something you can drink. Jesus said plainly that the cup is the new covenant in His blood. And when Jesus gives it to us, He says, "Drink ye all of it" (Matt. 26:27). A covenant is something we can drink, and it is something we are summoned to drink down. Drink all of it.

This covenant contains all of God's purposes for us. And all of those promises — through the power and wisdom of God — can fit in that tiny little cup you will hold in your hand. Not only that, but all those promises, when you drink all of it in faith, fit inside you. When the Lord tells us that a covenant is something we can drink, He is telling us that we can be saved. The covenant is objective, and outside us. Nevertheless, when He gives the gift of faith we come in order to receive. And what do we receive? All of it.

So come, and welcome, to Jesus Christ.

MORNING ☼ HOT FOOD OR COLD

A popular salvation text is Rev. 3:20. "Behold, I stand at the door, and knock: if any man hear my voice, and open the door, I will come in to him, and will sup with him, and he with me." But this is not the door of an unconverted man, deciding whether to ask Jesus in. This is, in the first instance, the door of the church at Laodicea, and then by extension, any church that has people who have drifted into a lukewarm approach to Jesus. It is not the door of a man's heart; it is a church door.

If we respond to His call, to His voice, we are responding to the one who is the Amen, the faithful Witness, and we do so in a way that strengthens and establishes us. If we do this, we are opening the door of the *church*. We are inviting Jesus to come in and do what? We are ushering Him in so that He will sit down, it says, and sup with that man, and that man will sup with him.

We see here an exquisite balance of the individual and corporate. The faithful believer is not the one who opens the door of his heart in some place distinct from the church. No, he hears the knock of the faithful witness in the church, and goes and opens the door of the church, and Christ comes in and sups with the one who answered the door.

But what about the one who ignores the presence of Christ at the door of the church? He is tepid, lukewarm. Christ says that He will spit that food out. He is a room temperature Christian.

Through the covenant glory of *koinonia*, we partake of Christ, certainly. We also partake of one another, certainly. But Christ is at the Table, seated. He is the president of communion, but is also a participant in communion. He partakes of us. And when He does, we want to be either cold and refreshing, or hot and reassuring. The way to be that is to listen intently for the knock at the door.

So come, and welcome, to Jesus Christ.

Let us begin by acknowledging an unfortunate reality. The apostle Paul warns Christians not to bite and devour one another (Gal. 5:15), and he does this because this is what we are sometimes tempted to do. Christians are never warned of sins that they were never going to be an issue. The warning says that we are not to bite and devour because the end result will be that we are consumed. So in this sense, Paul says not to eat one another in this way.

The only alternative to this kind of quarrelsome devouring is to learn how to partake of one another in love. In the verse just prior to this warning (Gal. 5:14), Paul says that the entire law is summed up in the command to love our neighbor. We must love our companions, and companions are those with whom we break bread.

So Christ eats with us here, and we eat with Him. But the Bible teaches us that when we eat together with others in love, this is a covenant love, and covenants depend on what is called partaking. This is *koinonia*-partaking. We do not just eat with Christ; He offers us His body and blood to eat and to drink. And Christ does not just eat with us; He partakes of us just as we partake of Him. This is a sacramental enactment of what is described throughout the New Testament as union with Christ. We are not just with Him; we are *in* Him.

Now if you are not learning Christ in this way, if you are not growing in Him in this way, there is only one other way to be—and that is the kind of person who bites, devours, quarrels, accuses. If that is what your home is like, then you are not partaking rightly here. If you are partaking rightly here, if you eat in faith here, you are learning how to resist biting and devouring in another way, in an entirely destructive way.

So come, and welcome, to Jesus Christ.

Just as it is false to say that the tabernacle in the wilderness had no artistic representations of spiritual things, so also it is false to say that new covenant church has no portrayals in it. From blue pomegranates to cherubim covering the mercy seat, the tabernacle contained such images. But they were prohibited from making certain representations, and whenever the Israelites were faithful, they guarded that empty space above the mercy seat with a jealous and fierce love.

In a similar way, new covenant worship is filled with icons — but as committed Protestants, we insist that the icons have to be given to us, assigned to us. For example, this church has hundreds of icons in it — you all are created in the image of God, and this is in fact an image of God. Moreover, Christ is faithfully portrayed in the preaching of the gospel (Gal. 3:1), or in the reading of Scripture (Rev. 1:16). Such portrayals *must* occur in Christian churches, which means God has decreed that the image of God in Christ be painted with words as brushes. He gives us baptism, an enacted image of the death of Christ and our death in Him, a representation of His substitutionary death, into which we all enter. And then every week we come to the image of bread and wine. Christ has given us an image of His broken body, and an image of His shed blood, and we look on this image every week. But looking on it is just the beginning.

When we are obedient and carefully limit ourselves to the portrayals that God has required and assigned, we are given the great privilege of partaking in those portrayals. But when we invent our own icons, the promised partaking evaporates. Not only does the blessing not happen, a curse comes in, down to the third and fourth generations. We cannot meet with God unless we meet Him at the appointed places.

Faithful Christian worship must therefore have images. But it is equally crucial that we limit ourselves to the images we were given.

So come, and welcome, to Jesus Christ.

We are instructed by Scripture to think of this meal in multiple ways. It is not just "one thing." And four of the central aspects of this meal should be treasured in our hearts regularly.

First, it is a *commemoration*. Jesus established this pattern when He said that we were to observe the meal as a memorial (Luke 22:19). This memorial works in two directions—it reminds us and, like the rainbow, it reminds God. Second, it is a *confession*. Not a confession of sin, but of our *faith*. As often as we observe this meal, we proclaim the Lord's death (1 Cor. 11:26). Third, it is *communion*. When we come to this Table in evangelical faith, we are privileged to commune with Christ, to partake of Him and of one another (1 Cor. 10:16). The word for this is *koinonia*, and the Lord's Supper is how God knits us together. And last, it is a *covenant*. Again, the Lord taught us this when He called this cup the cup of the new covenant (Luke 22:20). This does not mean that the meal is somehow obliquely related to the covenant, but that the entire covenant is *in* the cup, and that you cannot drink it without taking the most solemn oath known to man.

In all these aspects, the Lord's Supper is the complete fulfillment of the Passover meal, first given to the Israelites on Exodus Eve. Remember that pattern. First the meal, then the actual deliverance, and afterward the series of meals looking back in gratitude. The Lord did the same—instituted the meal, accomplished the actual salvation, and then invited to look back in true Eucharistic gratitude.

So you have bread and wine before you now. But also remember you have been delivered from your sins—a wall of water is on either side of you. When Jesus was transfigured on the mount, and He was there communing with Moses and Elijah, that communion was with two men who had parted the waters, just as He was going to do at Jerusalem. The word used there for what Jesus was going to accomplish is the word *exodus* (Luke 9:31).

So come, and welcome, to Jesus Christ.

MORNING ☼ MEDITATION AND PRAYER

As we come to this weekly meal, we are to come in order to meditate and pray. And as Matthew Henry put it, meditation is conversing with yourself, and prayer is conversing with God.

Both are necessary, but whenever you converse, whether with yourself or with God, it is necessarily to converse intelligently. In other words, we have a responsibility in these conversations to do more than jabber thoughtlessly, or moan and complain, or accuse. When we converse with ourselves, and when we converse with God, particularly around the topic of the broken bread and poured out wine, we should be careful to speak in wisdom. In order to do this, we must hear the echoes of Scripture throughout everything we say.

Only this will protect us when we come to the perilous duty of self-examination. "But let a man examine himself, and so let him eat of that bread, and drink of that cup" (1 Cor. 11:28). Because this duty is positively commanded, many have given themselves over to it. But the standards for examination have often been grossly unscriptural, given over to a spirit of condemnation, others have reacted away from this duty, and have assumed that any self-examination at all is some sort of spiritual pathology.

But surely there is an alternative to some Christians tormenting themselves with imaginary sins while other Christians go from angry shouting at family members and participation in the sacrament without a second thought. We should not have to choose between diligent hunting of non-existent sins and a let-sleeping-dogs-lie approach to very glaring sins.

So when you meditate, converse with yourself in all wisdom. Stop listening to yourself, and start talking to yourself. And when you pray, don't assume that you know what God wants to hear. Pray to Him in accordance with His Word. He wants you here. He invited you. He understands all about it.

So come, and welcome, to Jesus Christ.

As we heard in the message today, we are called to live from faith to faith. The just shall live by faith. But living is an all-encompassing verb. Living by faith means walking by faith, singing by faith, fellowshipping by faith, eating and drinking by faith, reflecting by faith, and meditating by faith.

And faith requires an object. When you believe, you are believing someone, something. Biblical faith means apprehending, grasping, holding on to what God has spoken to us.

To attempt to have faith by cultivating a faithy sensation down in your heart is not dispensing with the need for an object. That is not an objectless faith; rather, it is faith trying to believe in itself.

Ultimately, there are only two choices — faith in God or faith in yourself. You know from experience how reliable *you* are, and so the word of the gospel comes to you as sweet relief. Lay it all down. Set it down. Take off your burdens. Trust in Christ.

He is set before you now. He is offered to you now. How can you know that you are *genuinely* trusting in Him? By knowing that you have abandoned all hope in yourself. Repentance turns away from self and, in that same motion, turns to God. That is what it means to repent and believe.

God's devices for building us up in the faith are simple and subtle, warm and unyielding, accepting and holy. All this is only possible because Jesus died on a cross as a substitute for all our sin, sinfulness, and sinning. This He did wholeheartedly, because He wanted to make sure that you would be able to come here today.

Turn. Come. Accept. Repent. Believe.

So come, and welcome, to Jesus Christ.

MORNING ☼ JOY AND EXASPERATION

Thanksgiving is a time — all over our nation — when people sit down to a feast with people who are dear to them, and who are also exasperating to them. This is why holidays like Thanksgiving are often filled with joy — and with tension. This is why our reunions contain both laughter and quarrels.

This meal is one we partake of every week, because we need to learn the discipline of loving sinners, and the even deeper discipline of doing so while being a sinner. Every week you sit down at this meal with people who are dear to you, and who are exasperating to you. And things get complicated fast.

Think of this meal as a pitch pipe. Let it tune your heart, as the hymn says, to sing God's praise, and to sing His praise in all kinds of challenging circumstances. We do not come to this meal as a statement that we, all of us together, have attained perfection. We come in the full understanding that we have not. We do not come to this meal with a requirement that all the other communicants must no longer need the grace of God. We come with the knowledge that all of us need it. We do not confess that those who exasperate us must deserve to come here. We know that not one of us deserves to come here as a result of our own performance. But if they don't deserve to come, then their ill-desert does not disqualify them from fellowship with God. And if God welcomes them, then of course, so do you — both today and Thursday.

So then, come, and welcome, to Jesus Christ.

Not only is this a covenant meal, with all the parties to the covenant alive and present, Scripture gives us another image to use with our grasp of the word testament. "For a testament is of force after men are dead: otherwise it is of no strength at all while the testator liveth" (Heb. 9:17). Here we have the image of a reading of a will. Our elder brother has died, and we have gathered to hear what He has left for us. Now of course, these images complement each other, and we do this in the full and certain knowledge of His resurrection. But even though He is risen, we remain His heirs. *That* part of this image is true enough.

In thinking about this, we can rely on the insights of the old Scots Reformed preacher John Willison. He points out that the executor of this will and testament in this world is the Holy Spirit. And as we have gathered to learn what we have received, we may learn it under the figure of a meal with seven dishes. This is a seven-course meal, and when you come in faith, you cannot leave hungry.

What are these seven dishes? First, you have pardon for sin sealed to the one who believes. The second course is peace and friendship with God. The third dish is the fact that we have been given adoption as heirs. After that comes peace of conscience. And then He gives to us comforting and strengthening graces. Then we are given the presence of Christ Himself, and communion with Him. The seventh is the outpouring of the Holy Spirit.

We are Christians. We live in this world, but we have not been left to languish.

So come, and welcome, to Jesus Christ.

MORNING ✵ ENGAGED TO FRESH OBEDIENCE

By the time we come to this point in the service, we have already confessed our sins. We did that at the beginning of the service, which means that we have already lamented and repented any disobedience. We wash up before we come to dinner, and dinner does not consist of constant introspection, trying to wash up while you eat.

At the same time, it would be a mistake to assume that partaking of this meal has nothing to do with matters of obedience. Not at all. This is a solemn meal, one in which we are engaging ourselves to fresh obedience.

This obedience is fresh in at least two senses. The first is that it is an obedience that starts here, starts now. We are taking in nourishment in order that we might go out from this place equipped to live according to His purposes for us. It is fresh in the sense that the moment is now. A new week lies before you. Obey Him by His grace. In Scripture, *works* are autonomous, proud, and inadequate. But *obedience* is a gift. Obedience is a good word — receive it fresh.

But the ways of God are also *qualitatively* fresh. We are communing together with Him; we have been united to Him as the Spirit works in us. But do not make the mistake of thinking you have been intruded on the divine nature, as though we as creatures have been metaphysically united to His triune nature. No, the Creator/creature distinction is one that will never be bridged that way. What we have been given is the opportunity to be united to God *covenantally*; we are united to God through covenantal fellowship with Christ, the union between God and man is found in Him, and by His Spirit we are in complete fellowship and union with Him. That fellowship is enacted here, in this meal. As we partake of it by faith, the Spirit works in us, and His work is always qualitatively new. It never ages.

So come, and welcome, to Jesus Christ.

Sometimes people tend to think that the Lord's Supper consists simply of the bread and the wine, and then the eating and drinking. But more elements are involved than just that. There is the prayer of consecration, there is the word that sets these elements apart to a holy use, then the breaking of the bread, and the distribution of the elements. Today I want to focus on this last thing, the distribution.

You notice that a minister is presiding over the meal, and this is because the elders of the church hold the keys. When the bread and wine are consecrated, the men then distribute the elements to you in the congregation. They do this with you *seated*, and you pass the elements up and down the rows, family style.

You are seated because this is a feast. The early Israelites were told to eat the Passover meal standing, to symbolize their pilgrimage out Egypt. They were to eat while ready to go. Years later, after they had entered the land of Canaan, the Israelites began to eat it sitting down, to symbolize that they had come into their inheritance. And so it is that we find Jesus and the disciples eating the meal in the common posture of the household meal. We are seated here the same way we would be seated if we came to a great banquet, for that is what this is.

And you pass the elements to one another. We do that on purpose as well. We are the household of faith (Gal. 6:10). We are all brothers and sisters in Christ Jesus (1 Pet. 3:8). We are to serve one another in love. The consideration you show in handing the tray to the one next to you is as much part of the meal as the bread and the wine are.

We are seated together in the great household of faith, accepted as sons and daughters of God, brothers and sisters to one another. Accept the seat that is offered to you. Serve one another in love.

So come, and welcome, to Jesus Christ.

MORNING ✵ HOW OBEDIENCE TASTES

When we come to this Table, we are doing as we have been instructed. We observe communion because the Lord established the meal, and instructed us to observe it. This is one reason for coming, and of course it is the foundational one. Partaking of this meal is an act of glad obedience.

But part of the reason the obedience is glad is that the more we observe it, the more we have an understanding of what obedience is like. When the apostle Peter tells us to desire the milk of the Word, he tells us to do it the way a newborn infant does. When a newborn is rooting for milk, he is doing it in obedience, but he is not following orders in some stoic fashion, bound to his duty. But he is obeying a deeper law.

And then, Peter adds, we are to keep coming, now that we have tasted that the Lord is good. When we discover that obedience is delightful, this does not make the obedience evaporate. No, it means that our obedience is maturing, growing up.

And it is the same with this ingestible Word as it is for the Word preached, or the Word read. Come to Jesus Christ, here presented to you, as a newborn infant, instinctively seeking out your life. And after you have been coming for a time, after you have tasted that the Lord is good, keep coming, keep returning. Obedience keeps tasting better.

So come, and welcome, to Jesus Christ.

Although your soul is not a body, it nevertheless has eyes, hands, and mouth. I am speaking here of more than the eyes, hands, and mouth that it possesses through possessing your actual physical body. No, the Bible teaches that you can see without physical eyes, hold without physical hands, and eat apart from a physical mouth.

Paul prays that the Ephesians would have the eyes of their heart enlightened (Eph 1:18). He wants this so that they might grasp with spiritual hands what was theirs in Christ Jesus. And when we partake of one another in love, we are eating life, but not physically.

This ability is called faith. Faith would be the two eyes of the soul, discerning Christ when and where He is offered. Faith would also be the two hands of the soul, enabling you to receive Christ as offered. Faith is the mouth of the soul, making it possible for you to feed on Him, to the satisfaction that brings life.

You come here body and soul, but you come here so that both body and soul might partake. Bread is offered to you. You see it, you reach out your hand, and you put it into your mouth. This is to teach you that your soul is doing the same thing. But where your eyes see bread, your spiritual eyes are to see Christ. Where your hands hold bread, your spiritual hands are to hold Christ. Where your mouth tastes bread, your spiritual mouth tastes Christ. The same thing is true of the wine.

So come. See with your soul. Take with your soul. Eat and drink with your soul. Your ability to do this is found in the gift of faith. God equips us, by His grace, to commune with Him. He gives us what we need to receive Him.

So come, and welcome, to Jesus Christ.

MORNING ☼ THE RETURN OF LOVE

We come here as Christians, which means that we come as those who are followers of Jesus Christ. We do not follow Him because we happened to be a crowd that happens to be going that way. We follow Him because He has called each of us, individually. We have heard His voice, according to the Lord's teaching, because we are His sheep. We recognize His voice and want to be there (Jn. 10:27). We follow Him because we love Him.

This Table of communion is therefore to be thought of as a way of displaying that love. We are not working our way through a liturgical checklist, we are communing with God the Father through our communion with His Son, and that communion with His Son is only possible because the Spirit of both Father and Son has been poured out upon us.

That is how it happens, but let us never forget what is happening. God is offering us His appointed tokens of His everlasting love for us, and we are responding by taking those tokens for ourselves, while at the same time returning the love. He gives us the bread and wine, but we do not return the bread and wine. We simply receive it. He gives us His love, but we are to return that.

That return is what makes this Table fellowship what it is. That is what communion is. If God loved us, and we were cold toward Him, that would not be communion, but rather ingratitude. If we loved God, but He did not love us, besides being impossible, that would be desperation. But He has offered His love to us, here. He has authorized His ministers to bid you welcome. When we invite you to be seated here, we are not taking anything upon ourselves. We are simply stewards of the feasts, inviting you to be seated and to partake, all in accordance with the covenant. You have been baptized, you are invited. You have true evangelical faith, which means you have accepted the invitation.

So come, and welcome, to Jesus Christ.

The Lord has prepared a Table for us here, in the presence of our enemies. This means that we dine while they rage. The Lord has taken us into His pavilion, while outside is the strife of tongues. There was this thing called the strife of tongues, even before the Internet. The strife of tongues is like a monkey scribbling with a crayon, and all the Internet did was give the monkey superpower speeds. But still the Lord is with His people. The Lord has accompanied us in the boat, even though a great storm rages outside the boat. We do not need to worry because we seek to be where Jesus is.

And where "Jesus is" can be found, according to His promise, in the Word and sacrament. He is presented to us in the declaration of His gospel, and He is presented to us in and through the bread and wine, according to His covenant. Where Christ is, everything is secure, settled, permanent, grounded. To borrow the words of the poet, He is the still point of the turning world.

Away from Christ is tumult. Away from Christ is necessary tumult. The roil of unbelief does not know how to trust, how to rest, how to settle. True faith, evangelical faith, rests in Him. He is present — as He has promised — here. If He is present, and if you approach Him in faith, you understand that presence. You feel it. You grasp it. You are alive in it.

No wonder you are alive in it. It is your life. Here is your life.

So come, and welcome, to Jesus Christ.

MORNING ☼ PROVISIONS

The doctrine of God's providence is a doctrine of a Father's love, care, mercy, and protection. God looks down the course of our journey and anticipates on our behalf. At every stop along that journey we find provisions waiting for us. This is one of the stops, and here are the provisions.

We are cared for. We are provided for. God has given us everything we need for life and for godliness. We are never stranded or marooned. There are times when we are stretched, when we might *feel* stranded, but we never are. The provision is always present.

Because the Father is a Father, He provides. This is what fathers do. And this is how we should understand the presence of God in this Supper. The Holy Spirit of God is the Spirit of both the Father and the Son, and the Holy Spirit is the one who is present here, knitting us together in love. Love, fellowship, kinship, community, affection — this is the true nature of the provision, and it all comes to us in the form of bread and wine.

We are not to look for Christ in the nouns, but rather in the adverbs. We are not to look at a fragment of bread under a microscope, or analyze a drop of wine, looking for Christ in the bread or wine. Christ *is* in the bread and wine, as we *gratefully* receive it from the Father, and as we *lovingly* pass it to our neighbor.

We have all been given provisions, and the more we share them, the more we will all have. Love is a grace that grows.

So come, and welcome, to Jesus Christ.

We have been emphasizing the relationship of personal self-control to larger political issues. A people enslaved to their own passions will soon face a larger and more sinister enslavement.

A lack of self-control can most obviously be seen with something like alcohol. When someone drinks too much, the symptoms are evident. Something similar can happen with food—and it happens in both directions. Just as teetotalers think of every drink as excessive and unnecessary, so also some want to say that a second helping of mashed potatoes at Thanksgiving, or a superfluous Snickers bar, are plain evidences of gluttony. But that is not correct.

The sins of drunkenness and gluttony are parallel. Scripture addresses them in the same breath and in the same way: "And they shall say unto the elders of his city, This our son is stubborn and rebellious, he will not obey our voice; he is a glutton, and a drunkard" (Deut. 21:20). "For the drunkard and the glutton shall come to poverty: And drowsiness shall clothe a man with rags" (Prov. 23:21).

What this is referring to is an orgiastic way of living. Someone is out of control. He throws himself into a pattern of sensual excess. Generally it is a life that involves sex, drunkenness, drugs, music, and food. He is the kind of person who participates in raves. Paul flatly prohibits such revelry and carousing (Rom. 13:13). Scripture prohibits raves (*komos*) and drinking parties (*potos*).

Peter makes a similar point: "For the time past of our life may suffice us to have wrought the will of the Gentiles, when we walked in lasciviousness, lusts, excess of wine, revellings, banquetings, and abominable idolatries: Wherein they think it strange that ye run not with them to the same excess of riot, speaking evil of you" (1 Pet. 4:3–4). Those who throw themselves into dissipation will not inherit the kingdom of God. And they *will* inherit political despotism. But we are training for something else entirely.

So come, and welcome, to Jesus Christ.

MORNING ✺ EUCHARISTIC COMMONWEALTH

This is the place where we glory in Christ, and we glory in what He has given us. We do not glory in the fact that He has everything and we have nothing. Rather, we glory in the fact that we *had* nothing, He had everything, He came and sacrificed everything, so that He might give us everything.

"Therefore let no man glory in men. For all things are yours; Whether Paul, or Apollos, or Cephas, or the world, or life, or death, or things present, or things to come; all are yours; And ye are Christ's; and Christ is God's" (1 Cor. 3:21–23).

The kingdoms and commonwealths of man are all built on the foundation of ingratitude. In the gospel, in the death, burial and resurrection of the Christ, God has sent an earthquake designed to shake everything temporal. His design is to replace it all with that which cannot be shaken. This Table, and the proclaimed gospel it is based on, is therefore the epicenter of His eucharistic commonwealth. All ingratitude must topple, and it must be replaced with countless forgiven sinners, all of them giving thanks.

The thanksgiving is based on the fact that we are invited *in,* we are asked to *partake,* we are *members* of Christ. In Christ, everything is now ours — the world and all it contains. Christ owns the world — for He purchased it with His blood — and we are in Christ. We are saying many things here when we partake, but that is one of them.

If there is no gratitude, it is because there *is* unrepented iniquity. The two displace each other. And those who live in iniquity will not inherit the kingdom (1 Cor. 6:9–10; Gal. 5:21) — they will not inherit the wealth of the commonwealth. Who will not inherit? The envious, the malicious, fornicators, adulterers, sodomites, drunkards, partiers, and the like. When you walk away from that, you are walking away from the poverty of death.

So come, and welcome, to Jesus Christ.

EVENING ◐ WHAT GRACE WAS MADE FROM

This Table represents to us the death of Jesus Christ. Because the death of Jesus was the death of all accusation, and the peculiar kind of envy that fuels so much accusation, this means that the sins that betrayed Jesus to the cross were actually sins that were being themselves led to the cross, there to be crucified.

The Jewish leaders turned Jesus over to Pilate because of their envy, and because that, and through that, their kind of envy was turned over to God. So when Pilate under pressure turned Jesus over to the executioners, God in that same event, under no pressure at all, but all through His free grace, took our accusations, our malice, our envy, our bitterness, and our self-righteousness, and turned them over to the executioners.

Isn't this a glory? Your innate sense of moral superiority and accusation was killed by Roman soldiers.

So then what do we eat? We are eating dead accusation. This is the way of life. The only alternative to this — apart from the cross of Jesus — is to have accusations eat you. Either you come to Christ, and in glad triumph eat and drink the death of sin, or you refuse to come to Christ, and the death of sin eats you.

The grain of recriminations has been ground to flour, and God has transformed it into the bread of life. The grapes of sour bitterness have all been crushed, and Jesus has done yet another miracle resulting in wine. The cup is now the cup of the new covenant, made such by the crushing of all the arguments we might level against our neighbors.

The grace of God was made out of the wrath of man. And this is why the bread is offered to us, and cup is offered to us, in the times of refreshing. This is the miracle of grace — death comes to life.

So come, and welcome, to Jesus Christ.

MORNING ☼ SONGS OR SNARLS

This Table is a Table of love and fellowship. God has set it so that we may sit around it and willingly (that is, lovingly) partake of it. In partaking of it in faith, we are partaking of Christ, partaking of one another, and partaking of the bread and wine. When we are done, Christ is not diminished. When we are done, we are not diminished but rather we have grown. The bread and wine are not gone, but rather we find an abundance of bread and wine always around us, with which we are enabled to go out and feed the world. When we partake in this way, the blessings are added and multiplied. God is the one who gives the *increase*.

This is what love always does. But when Christians turn away from the kind of love which partakes, they find that they are not able to turn away from eating. But the nature of the eating is entirely transformed. In Galatians 5, Paul tells the saints not to use their liberty as a way of serving their own flesh, but rather to serve one another in love (v. 13). He then says that they are called to love their neighbors as they do themselves (v. 14). The alternative to this, he says, is biting and devouring, with the end result of being consumed (v. 15).

The word for consumed means destroyed, annihilated, done away with, *utterly* consumed. It has the opposite effect that partaking does. When we partake of one another, sacrificing ourselves to one another, offering ourselves to one another, there is always more when we are done. When we bite and devour, when we are done, we are *done*.

We grow through sacrifice, gift, and grace. We shrink and diminish through grasping. These two ways of eating are entirely at odds. They are at war with one another. But one goes into battle with songs, and the other with snarls.

So come, and welcome, to Jesus Christ.

Through the course of church history, some have wanted to treat the communion of the Lord's Table as a penitential discipline, instead of what the New Testament sets it out to be, which is that of a Eucharistic celebration. We are not here to get forgiven; we are here because we have been forgiven. This is a sacrifice of praise, the fruit of lips giving *thanks* to His name (Heb. 13:15).

Now whenever sin has been committed, there is no problem whatever with repentance. Repentance is a good thing, but when penitence becomes a constant frame of mind, it is very difficult to keep the whole thing from turning into an ongoing exercise in penance. And it is terribly hard to keep that from turning into a form of works righteousness.

The Old Testament sacrificial system was described as deficient because it kept having to be repeated (Heb. 10:1–4). When we confess particular sins in the course of our lives, or at the beginning of the service, we are not doing it to improve on our justification. Justification, from the first moment of imputation, is perfect. It is the imputation of the obedience of Jesus Christ, so how could it be less than perfect?

We confess our sins in order to keep our relationship with God *honest*, and refusal to confess sins to Him is nothing less than dishonesty farming. Whether we are doing that in the right spirit can be measured by how we approach Him at His Table here. If this is a time of joy, gladness, refreshment, peace, gratitude, and hope, then you have been confessing your sins rightly. If this is a time of self-accusation, sternness, or grim resolve, then you are not coming in the right spirit.

You are sons and daughters of the Most High. You have been forgiven for everything. Come then.

So come, and welcome, to Jesus Christ.

MORNING ☼ COSTLY PREPARATION

The feasts of the Old Testament are full of gospel. The promised feasts that were coming were overflowing with gospel (Is. 25:6). The Lord's Supper, now before us, *is* gospel.

Scripture invites us to think of the Lord's Table in the category of a feast. Now a feast has many characteristics, but one of them is that feasts are very expensive, both with regard to time and money. "Wisdom hath builded her house, She hath hewn out her seven pillars: She hath killed her beasts; she hath mingled her wine; She hath also furnished her table" (Prov. 9:1–2). In other words, a feast requires thoughtful preparation and it requires great expense. We see both of these elements in the Table before us now.

First, the thoughtful preparation. When God established the gospel for us, and ordained a ministry to declare it, and grounded a church to gather around both Word and sacrament, He did so in accordance with what? "In whom also we have obtained an inheritance, being predestinated according to the purpose of him who worketh all things after the counsel of his own will" (Eph. 1:11). Every aspect of our salvation was worked out by God beforehand. Every detail was anticipated by Him. He works all things according to the counsel of His own will.

So this was planned, down to the last detail. What did it cost Him? The answer here is that this cost Him the blood of Jesus His Son. We were not redeemed by anything so inexpensive as silver or gold (1 Pet. 1:18), Peter tells us, but by the precious blood of Christ (v. 19).

But the fact that the feast is inexpensive does not mean that ministers of the gospel are to go out into all the world to sell tickets. No, not at all. This meal is beyond expensive; the price was staggering. But this was so that it might be made free for you. The Spirit and the bride both together invite "whosoever will" to come to the water of life in order to drink *freely* (Rev. 22:17).

So come, and welcome, to Jesus Christ.

EVENING ◐ GRACE TO EXPEND

One of the indicators that God is truly at work is the *vitality* of His people. But that vitality, the kind the world can see, is the second thing. The first thing is communion with God. Either we are brought into communion as we are first born again, or we are renewed in communion as we fellowship with Him, as we are doing here in the Lord's Supper. This is where God restores us, renews us, and nourishes us.

We are saved by grace through faith, and not by works. But we are saved to good works, which God prepared beforehand for us to do. We do not work salvation into our own hearts. God works salvation into us, but when He does so, the first thing that starts to happen is that we work it out. God establishes the principle of new life in the soul, but what this means is that the soul must therefore act the way a living soul does. When God pours life into us, life pours out of us.

This is why God's people should be characterized by vitality. And this helps us place this meal in an appropriate context. This is like an early breakfast, with a full day of work ahead of us. We are being fed, but we are being fed so that we might expend the grace we have been given.

We are hoses, not jars. God pours His grace into us so that it might flow through us, and out toward others in love and good works. He doesn't fill you up with grace, seal the lid, and put you in a storage unit. The grace of God is to be expended in the world. Whatever you receive here—and what you are receiving here is beyond all mortal reckoning—you are to take with you in order to leave it out there in the world. When you run out, you can come back for more next week.

So come, and welcome, to Jesus Christ.

MORNING ☼ HOLINESS, HUMILITY, HELP

We do not come here to grovel, but to glory. We are instructed as Christians to glory in another, in the Lord, but we do in fact glory. This is done on the basis of the Lord's free gift of justification. Without that gift, we can do nothing. With it, we are liberated, turned loose to glory. "In the Lord shall all the seed of Israel be justified, and shall glory" (Is. 45:25). What do we glory in? We could spend the rest of our lives investigating the Scriptures in order to answer that question, so let us limit ourselves to three things today. We glory in God's holiness, we glory in His humility, and we glory in His help.

This is a memorial of a blood sacrifice. A blood sacrifice was necessary because a holy God cannot look on sin, cannot fellowship with it, and cannot acquit the guilty by simple fiat. He is absolutely holy, and holiness requires death for sin. But God in His grace provided a faultless sacrifice in Jesus Christ, such that His holiness could be displayed in His wrath against sin, but without violating that holiness through selection of an irrelevant victim. He was an innocent victim, but a true member of the race that deserved to die. So in this meal we are confirmed in our understanding of God's holiness.

In Christ, God was reconciling the world to Himself. The apostle sets the Incarnation before us as a grand demonstration of Christ's true humility. He then enjoins us to imitate that humility in our own lives. Let this mind be in you which was also in Christ Jesus (Phil. 2:5).

But we are not called to imitate Him from a distance. We have been brought near, meaning that in this meal we partake of Him, which means partaking of His humility. In that partaking, He helps us. We are not left to strive on our own, or yearn from afar. No, God is a present help.

And all of this is sealed to us in the Supper. As Jonathan Edwards once put it, "Christ sealing the covenant with His blood is the greatest seal that ever was."

So come, and welcome, to Jesus Christ.

The foundation of every form of free government — whether in the family, or in civil affairs, or in the government of the church — is self-government. If the people do not have self-control, then you may depend upon it that they will be controlled by outside forces.

It is easy to lament despotism when it pinches, when the taxes are due, when the regulations are onerous. When Pharaoh demands the bricks but supplies no straw, all the slaves lament their slavery. Whenever the bills come due, the whole world is libertarian.

So we need to place two teachings from Scripture side by side. First, liberty is the work of the Spirit: "Now the Lord is that Spirit: and where the Spirit of the Lord *is*, there *is* liberty" (2 Cor. 3:17). Second, "the fruit of the Spirit is . . . self-control" (Gal. 5:22–23). A central way the Spirit brings about true liberty is by freeing the slaves of immorality. He strikes off their chains. The hymn writer knows what necessarily results from that: "I rose, went forth, and followed thee." A generation of slaves to sin *cannot* be free. They don't know what liberty is. It frightens them. If they were given it, they would have no idea how to preserve it. "A man without self-control is like a city broken into and left without walls" (Prov. 25:28, ESV). This is why drunkenness is a political issue. This is why pornography is such a problem. A generation of pot smokers cannot be free.

If some despot offered to chain you to a dungeon wall, but promise to implant an electrode in the pleasure center of your brain such that you would have constant euphoria until the day of your death, would you even think about it? But if you wouldn't take that massive bribe, why are you fooling about with the little bribes? If you wouldn't take great pleasure in exchange for your freedom, why are you settling for the petty pleasures in exchange for it?

There is only one way for men and women to be free, and that is if they are *upright*. And here at this Table God equips us to be that way.

So come, and welcome, to Jesus Christ.

MORNING ☼ A NO THAT PREPARES FOR YES

We have noted that the foundation of every form of free government is self-government. Fools and blockheads cannot build a free society. We cannot govern ourselves collectively unless we know how to govern ourselves individually. And we cannot learn self-government apart from a work of the Spirit of God.

This applies to every area where self-indulgence is a temptation. Paul highlights the principle while talking about wine: "And be not drunk with wine, wherein is excess; but be filled with the Spirit; Speaking to yourselves in psalms and hymns and spiritual songs, singing and making melody in your heart to the Lord" (Eph. 5:18–19). Notice how he reasons in a "this, not that" kind of way. Where the Spirit works, the result is joy and music. Where the Spirit is absent or grieved, the human heart wants some kind of exhilaration and will seek out ways of buying it in a bottle.

The prohibition is not a killjoy prohibition. We are told not to be drunk with wine in the same spirit that a mother would tell her son not to eat a bag of chips a half an hour before dinner. She has been preparing a meal that she knows will be a joy to him. She doesn't want him to come in right before the meal to wreck it with some poor substitute. She says *no*, not because she loves saying *no*, but rather because she is offering something far better.

This is how God speaks to us. He says no to drunkenness because He is offering us something far better. The Bible teaches us a *lot* about delayed gratification. "For the moment all discipline seems painful rather than pleasant, but later it yields the peaceful fruit of righteousness to those who have been trained by it." (Heb. 12:11, ESV). The wise embrace this principle — they would rather have great joy in the harvest than the easy pleasures of laziness in the time of plowing.

God has said no to many things this week — it was because He was preparing this meal for you.

So come, and welcome, to Jesus Christ.

EVENING ◐ NO OCCASION FOR THE FLESH

We have been looking at self-control as the foundation of all civic and political liberty. Living as we do in a time when such liberty is eroding at alarming rates, we need to make sure that when we run our spiritual inventories we do not do what sinners always love to do, which is to blame someone else.

While Scripture warns us against the abuse of alcohol, it sets alcohol before us as a legitimate gift from God — an aesthetic gift, a gift for your thirst, a sacramental gifts, and so on. Note that the only thing that pot does for you — get you buzzed — is the one use prohibited concerning alcohol. When Paul tells us not to be drunk with wine, he does not mean that getting drunk with beer or scotch is acceptable. The problem is not the wine, but rather the loss of self-control. Because such mental impairment is the whole *point* of smoking pot, recreational marijuana use is a serious sin, from the very first toke on down. No one smokes pot because it pairs nicely with the fish.

We live just a few miles from a town where recreational pot use is legal. Shops there are doing a brisk business, and the tax man has stars in his eyes. The statist thieves who would take all our liberties can kill two birds with one stoner — rake in money from lotus-eating fools, and simultaneously advance the kind of fuzzy and self-indulgent thinking that makes their style of despotic governance possible.

God gives the liberty to do right. "For, brethren, ye have been called unto liberty; only *use not liberty for an occasion to the flesh*, but by love serve one another." (Gal. 5:13). The Spirit does not bring us into liberty so that we might suit ourselves. And He did not grant us liberty so that we might sell it to socialist planners. A free man has calluses on his hands from honest work, and not brown stains on his fingers from rolling up our liberties and blowing them into thin air.

This is not a Table that encourages debauchery. This is the Table of sober-minded joy.

So come, and welcome, to Jesus Christ.

MORNING ✹ CHALCEDON & COMMUNION

When we come here to partake of the body and blood of the Lord, we use that language—because Scripture does. But at the same time, we want to guard against a crass literalism that throws out something else that the Bible teaches with equal clarity.

Christ assumed a human body, and He did so forever. The Incarnation was not a temporary adoption of a "man suit," but rather it was the stupendous miracle by which the second Person of the Godhead joined Himself to our human nature forever. This human body was not swallowed up by Christ's divinity, but rather was joined to the divinity in the one Person of Savior and Lord, Jesus of Nazareth.

This is one Person, and two natures. These two natures are joined in the miracle of the Incarnation—which we are celebrating again in this Advent season—and they are joined without confusion or muddle. The attributes of one nature do not alter the nature of the other, and yet this happens without making Jesus the ultimate schizophrenic.

But what does this mean at this Supper? It means that Christ's physical body is no more resting on this Table physically than your body is in China right now. A true human body, which Christ has, has defined limits. That's the way bodies are. So how do we partake of Christ's body? We do so through the power of the Holy Spirit, who weaves us into the Head by this sacramental means. Come then, and welcome to this glorious union.

So come, and welcome, to Jesus Christ.

EVENING ◐ THE EMPTY CHAIR

In their celebration of Passover, the Jews keep an empty chair for Elijah, the forerunner of the Messiah. As Christians, we confess that both Elijah and the Messiah have come, and in faith we mark that coming by our participation at this Table. So in a very real sense, this Table has no empty chair. Christ has come, and has brought us to sit down with Him, and with Abraham, Isaac, and Jacob, and with all the Gentiles who are streaming in from the east and the west (Matt. 8:12).

Now Christ died once for all, and yet we still proclaim His death and resurrection by this meal. Christ was born only once, to his mother Mary, and yet we commemorate this every year in our celebration of Christmas. In the same way, although there is no empty chair of expectation at this Lord's Table, yet we frame our hearts now to proclaim what that longing was like, before He came. This is the significance of Advent, a season of joyful expectation, full of faith and longing.

When we are solemn on Good Friday, for example, it is not because we do not know the end of the story — we most certainly do. And when we long for the coming of the Christ now, it is not because we have forgotten that He already came. We are proclaiming history, telling a story. God's people waited patiently in the pre-dawn, longing for sunrise. Now that Christ has come, we tell this story in our calendar so that non-believers around us, who are still living in darkness, may see how they might be included. We summon them urgently — *come!*

So Advent is not a time where the people of God return to temporary darkness. Rather, it is a time when the entire Christian church, in true evangelical fashion, gives its testimony. "God brought us out of darkness, and into His marvelous light. Here, let us tell you the story."

So come, and welcome, to Jesus Christ.

MORNING ☼ THE SENSATION OF LIBERTY

Without self-government, no other form of righteous government is possible. The only way to balance form and freedom in any larger society is for the individuals in that society to balance form and freedom in their own lives. The framework of structured liberty is freedom from vice on the individual level.

Would-be despots know this as much as lovers of liberty do. That is why they offer bribes. Sexual license, pot-smoking, porn use, drunkenness create the *sensations* of liberty, but can all be indulged in a prison cell. Truncated sensations of liberty are offered, and massive restraints on external liberty are imposed, so today we have a society that is simultaneously licentious and legalistic.

It is appropriate for a free republic to elect a *president* to represent them. But when a republic starts to turn into a collectivist hive, as ours has done, a more appropriate name for the its head would be something like "beekeeper." The bees are externally constrained, and internally antinomian.

It is easy to think of legalism as one end of the spectrum and licentiousness at the other, with liberty occupying some kind of a middle position, an average of legalism and license. But liberty is not a matter of Aristotle's golden mean. Legalism and license are conjoined Siamese twins at one end, and liberty is at the other. Liberty is the only alternative to *both* legalism and license.

Jesus said that our righteousness needed to exceed the righteousness of the Pharisees (Matt. 5:20). They were a mass of rules, restrictions, and touch-nots (legalism) but they were also a seething mass of lusts (Matt. 23:25). Internally it was all self-indulgence. They were not too righteousness, but rather not nearly righteous enough.

The liberty of the free man is only possible as the liberty of a Christian man. And that means grace and gospel down in the bones. And to get them there, it is necessary to come to the Table.

So come, and welcome, to Jesus Christ.

EVENING ◐ THE LIBERTY TO DO RIGHT

The theme we have been developing is that self-government is the ground of all other government. Men and women who cannot govern themselves will in fact be governed by others. The less government they have at home, in the heart, the more government from the outside will necessarily be imposed.

This liberty we are speaking of—at this individual level—is the liberty to do right, which is not the same thing as the liberty to do as you please. But we must be careful here. Augustine said that we could love God, and then do as we please. This makes sense because when we love God first, our desires will be rightly ordered. Delight yourselves in the Lord, and He will give you the desires of your heart (Ps. 37:4). This is a safe promise for God to make, because when you delight in Him, your desires are not demented. Seek first the kingdom, and a number of other things of a more pedestrian and earthly nature will be added to you (Matt. 6:33). We may obtain these other things, but only as a function of living in such a way that seeks first the kingdom. Love God all out and *then* do as you please.

So if you are loving God, what you please to pursue will be hard work, laughter and joy with your family, self-discipline, a decidedly uncool life, and the resultant blessings of God. This will bring you into a real collision with tyrants, with those who take away your liberty.

But if you are loving *self* first then you will also come into conflict with tyrants, and serves you right. If liberty makes you think of nothing but opportunities for dissolute living, then you are the slave masters' best friend. This is why so many on the libertarian alt-right are nothing but sub-contractors making chains for the statists to use.

If it is not consumed with a love for God and His Word, then it is a political theory that is worse than useless. And all right-minded political theory begins here at this Table.

So come, and welcome, to Jesus Christ.

MORNING ☼ AT HIS TABLE

We have been addressing the theme of self-government as the foundation of every other form of lawful and limited government. A nation of slaves to sin and vice can never be a free people. They are far too easily threatened, manipulated, seduced, and bribed. They will trade away precious liberties for contemptible baubles and trifles.

I have been speaking of various external vices in this regard — smoking dope, using porn, drunkenness, and so on. But we also need to reflect on the need for self-control where the lack of self-control first begins to manifest itself — in the realm of the emotions.

Our generation measures truth by what the loudest and shrillest *feel* should be true. So our culture is now dominated by the offended, the hurt, and the aggrieved. Before developing this, an important boundary has to be set. Those who have *truly* been abused deserve nothing from us but compassion. Those who have endured the cruelties of the wicked should not have to contend against the cruelties of the church, as well. I make this distinction because we have to deal with the fact that we live in a time when "abused" and "feeling abused" are treated as the same thing. A true victim and a false victim are merged into one; objective realities don't matter anymore.

Children who are spoiled with regard to their passions are being catechized in this approach. Instead of bringing their emotions in line with God's Word and the hard realities of God's world, the world, and then the Word, must cater to their passions. With fits of temper tolerated, bursts of passion bribed and bought off, and petulant selfishness indulged, what will happen when such children grow up into overwhelming adult passions? If they can't run with men, how will they run with horses? So if you want to know what it would be like to be governed by toddlers out of temper, look around.

We don't want that to continue, and so we seek to grow up into Christ. He feeds us here at His Table.

So come, and welcome, to Jesus Christ.

We have been addressing the issues surrounding self-government, and this includes our emotional deportment towards others. People without self-control collide with one another, because their vices collide and because their emotions follow suit. In a selfish world, people often grab for the same thing.

This leads to the plainest and most obvious litmus test for us — our willingness to extend forgiveness. Self-absorbed people cannot forgive, and forgiven people necessarily forgive. The Lord Jesus laid it down in the plainest possible way that those who refuse to forgive wrongs against them are not forgiven themselves.

So it would be good for us to dwell for a moment on what forgiveness is. This is a central aspect of our faith — we say every week when we recite the creed that we believe in "the forgiveness of sins." Do we? When we ask for God to forgive us, are we actually doing so? Or are we asking God to accept our excuses? These are very different. When we say that we forgive our brother, are we just accepting his excuses, agreeing not to examine them too closely? But this is not forgiveness at all. Forgiveness only occurs with the inexcusable.

You can pardon someone who bumps into you accidentally. That is why they say "pardon me." But someone who sees you standing there, lowers his head, and runs over the top of you would not say "pardon me" unless he was adding insulting sarcasm to his other sins. His behavior is inexcusable, and is therefore forgivable.

We seek forgiveness for our sins, not our blunders and miscalculations. Others seek forgiveness from us for their sins, not their mistakes and infelicities. And how we respond tells us where we are spiritually. Self-control is one of the Spirit's graces that enable you to both seek and extend forgiveness when you need to.

To extend that kind of forgiveness, we need more strength than we have. That strength is here, offered to you.

So come, and welcome, to Jesus Christ.

MORNING ✹ HONEST AS AN EVANGELICAL

We have been talking about the importance of self-government when it comes to temptations, emotions, and passions. Self-control often also goes missing in the area of work, vocational competence, and delivery of goods.

There is a distinction between hard work and honesty. During the Reformation, one common phrase in France was "honest as a Huguenot." How long do you think it will before "honest as an evangelical" will catch on here in North America? Hustling is essential, but a man who hustles without integrity is simply exhibiting lack of self-control at high rates of speed. Many Christians flatter themselves about their own business acumen because they are intense and read business guru books. Yeah, well, "He that trusteth in his own heart is a fool: But whoso walketh wisely, he shall be delivered" (Prov. 28:26).

A clear-headed thief steals on purpose. He jimmies open the window, and runs off with the stereo. But a muddle-headed entrepreneur or businessman steals in a cloud of confusion driven by lack of self-control. "Things are busy, Murphy's on vacation, nobody told me, where'd that invoice go?" This applies to everything on your to-do list: writing deadlines, software programing, video projects, call-backs, owed emails, product delivery, everything.

In the world, the creditor has to chase the debtor, and far too often Christians simply duplicate this worldly pattern. We don't deliver what we promised, and we respond with a shrug and the business equivalent of "Christians aren't perfect, just forgiven." Perhaps you cannot deliver because someone let you down. It is a fallen world. But a Christian who owes must pursue the one who is owed. Diligent communication is free. The only thing preventing that is lack of self-control, not lack of money.

We come and sit down at this Table because we must be fed. We need strength. We must be grown up into a self-disciplined honesty.

So come, and welcome, to Jesus Christ.

EVENING ◐ WHEN YOUR NERVES ARE YELLING AT YOU

Communion is a meal that feeds us spiritually, and we should make a point of understanding how this relates to something we call stress. At this time of year, most of us have additional responsibilities, and some of us have quite a few. This might be a function of Christmas preparations, or finals, or both. So all of us have quite a bit of additional stress. That can be good or bad, depending.

This is spiritual food and food feeds you so that you can work. The expenditure of energy, spiritual or otherwise, is not possible apart from stress. Muscles that are totally relaxed cannot do anything. This same thing is true of your spiritual muscles — you are fed so that you alternate between stress and relaxation in a rhythmical way, which is what work is. But this kind of stress is what enables you to sleep well, to sit down at a meal with gratitude. Godly stress makes you tired and hungry, which is a good thing to be. It is a great condition to be in, and it is all because of stress.

But the other kind of stress is just another name for worry or anxiety — as when we say someone is stressed out. That's not so good, being a sin. Muscles can't work when they are tight all the time, and when you are stressed in this way, you are approaching paralysis. Feeding spiritually, or trying to give yourself over to sabbath rest, or trying to sleep, won't work because your body, and your emotions, and your nerves, are all yelling at you. The only thing that can be done about this kind of stress is repentance.

Confess it like you would any other sin. Resist the temptation to get spun tight the same way you would resist any other temptation. After all, it is no fun and does absolutely no good. Not only does it not do any good, it usually makes things worse and gives you more to get stressed about. And having confessed the sin, sit down to feed spiritually here so that God can give you the right kind of stress.

So come, and welcome, to Jesus Christ.

MORNING ☼ TWO PIECES OF FUDGE

As we celebrate the Lord's Supper in the Advent season, we should note that word "celebration." When we celebrate God's grace to us here, we are learning how to celebrate His goodness in every aspect of our lives, and that includes our orientation to festivals like Christmas. In *The Lion, the Witch and the Wardrobe,* Father Christmas appears in the book to give gifts and to destroy winter. He distributes his gifts and moves on. We should learn to be much more like him. And who comes next, and what does she say? Correct, the White Witch comes next, and she says, "What is the meaning of all this gluttony, this waste, this self-indulgence?" In the White Witch's words we hear all the echoes of the pious fussers, and stewardship-mongers, and finger-under-the-nose-waggers, and anti-consumerism advocates.

But what do we learn in this meal, set before us? We learn of God's extravagance. We learn of His prodigality. We learn of His overflow. We learn that He doesn't know how to stay with respectable limits. Do you call saving us staying within respectable limits? Not a bit of it.

Now He did not do all that so that we would learn how to show our gratitude to Him by imitating the devil. We do not imitate Father Christmas by acting like the White Witch. And so, if you are hearing these words of grace, then all through Advent, when given the opportunity to have a piece of fudge, you should make a point of having *two*. And why? Because you have come to this Table, and you have been welcomed here.

So come, and welcome, to Jesus Christ.

EVENING ◐ DISCIPLINED FEELINGS

The great enemy of self-control is feeling. Not feeling as rightly ordered sentiment, which is an essential part of what it means to be human, but to the pernicious habit of making *feelings* foundational to all arguments — political arguments, family arguments, business arguments, and, underneath it all, theological arguments.

One of the most obvious things about feelings is that they vary. They go up and down. They slide back and forth. They are rickety. If you build your life, your family, your business, your convictions on the wobbly surface of these feelings, what happens? When your feelings go up and down, absolutely everything goes up and down. We see this problem in how moderns hold their wedding vows. They promised to be faithful, regardless of feelings, and they keep their promises . . . until their feelings change. Then they are in a whole new world, and the world applauds them for treachery, just so long as the feelings that led them into treachery were sincerely felt.

Your life should be built on fact. Theological fact first. The way the world actually, meaning natural revelation, second. I would put math third. Such facts are just the way a foundation ought to be — hard, cold, rigid concrete. Feelings anchored to such facts will be disciplined by them, and you will be able to enjoy your feelings. Feelings are like children — when they are wild and undisciplined they are no fun at all. Little hellions is what they are.

Jesus is Lord whether or not you are grumpy this morning. Theological fact. Men are supposed to be attracted to women and vice versa, not to members of the same sex. Natural fact. Your checking account has less money in it than that shiny new toy costs. Math fact.

Feelings are therefore what need to be disciplined. Feelings must never be made the taskmaster.

One of the ways we discipline our feelings is by coming here, sitting at the Table of Jesus, and being taught by Him.

So come, and welcome, to Jesus Christ.

MORNING ☼ FED WITH TRUE GLORY

We have been considering the relationship between self-discipline and the possibility of free and responsible government in other areas. Men and women who are slaves to their vices are not going to be capable of creating or sustaining the various forms of public liberty that God wants us to enjoy. It is not possible to make a good omelet with rotten eggs, regardless how good your kitchen equipment is. It is not possible to build a firm and sturdy building with shoddy bricks.

But what lies behind the lack of self-control? Scripture teaches us throughout that we become like what we worship. This means that when we unravel into various kinds of indiscipline, the culprit behind it all is some form of idolatry.

There are many aspects to this, but let us just consider one. The difference between God and all the idols is this. God is a covenant-keeping God, and He is the one who blesses and curses. Idols are slave-masters, and so they bribe and threaten.

Let us compare the first part of this. God blesses and idols bribe and seduce. It is the difference between a cheesemaker rejoicing in the wheel of premium cheese he just made, and a mouse rejoicing in the little bit of cheese he just found for free on that little wooden tray. There are deep thinkers who want to reduce it all to the same thing because cheese involved in both.

God blesses with faith, obedience, long obedience, and then glory. Idols bless with a momentary glory, and then a sharp *snap*. A blessing is the reward for those who have been led out of bondage. A bribe is a tidbit that entices those who are moving into bondage. The difference between the two is the difference between gold and glitter, between day and night, between honest labor and shoplifting, between Heaven and Hell. The differences are not subtle.

And here, at this Table, God is feeding us with true glory.

So come, and welcome, to Jesus Christ.

Self-control cannot be tucked away in one small portion of our lives. It applies everywhere, and that when a people are self-governed, they are in a position to enjoy free government. It should be self-evident that a huge collection of slaves to sin are not going to be free citizens. Slavery breeds slavery, and freedom breeds freedom.

A key area for us to examine whether we are self-controlled is the tongue. James draws a straight line between governance of the tongue and governance of everything else. He compares self-control here to a bit and bridle that enables a rider to direct a horse. "If any man among you seem to be religious, *and bridleth not his tongue*, but deceiveth his own heart, this man's religion is vain" (Jas. 1:26). "For in many things we offend all. If any man offend not in word, the same is a perfect man, *and able also to bridle the whole body*" (Jas. 3:2).

But there are two reasons why we want to be able to direct a horse we are riding. The first is to prevent it from going where we don't want to go. The first is to keep us on the trail, to keep us from arriving at a destination we do not want. The second is to direct us positively, to actually arrive where we need to be.

When we think of sins of the tongue, and of a lack of self-control there, they almost invariably think of the things they wish they hadn't said. When horse and rider are off in the bracken, everyone knows about the poor horsemanship. But what about an inability to get a horse to take more than several paces in *any* direction?

Men will not be able to speak the truth to governors, congressmen, and presidents when they cannot tell their wives that they love them, their children that they are proud of them, or their parents how grateful they are. Control of the tongue includes much more than an ability to say *whoa*—it requires also a mastery of *giddyup*.

When God invites us to this Table, it is not just to teach us how to eat and drink. It is to teach us how to talk.

So come, and welcome, to Jesus Christ.

MORNING ☼ SHADOWS OF THE PYRAMIDS

We have been considering the importance of self-control, and how it is the key to responsible governance in every larger societal grouping. Slaves to vice individually do not deserve liberty on a larger scale, and whether they deserve it or not, they do not know how to defend it or how to fight for it with a clean conscience. This is why the forms of libertarianism that have abandoned social conservatism are such a snare and delusion. Here is how Bunyan voiced this kind of snare in *The Pilgrim's Progress*: "Then it came burning hot into my mind, whatever he said, and however he flattered, when he got me home to his House, he would sell me for a Slave."

The trees of liberty can only grow in the soil of personal governance, responsibility, and self-control. But self-control is something that we cannot generate on our own. It is among the fruit of the Spirit (Gal. 5:22–23), and *the Spirit never operates independently of the gospel*. It follows that political liberty cannot be sustained where the gospel does not have significant influence. The fact that our society is now declaring its open hostility to that gospel, and to any who openly embrace it, means that our society has opened up hostilities on the very idea of liberty. And by this I do not mean simply religious liberty — I mean *every* form of liberty.

Put another way, we are being led back into Egypt, back to the house of bondage, because for a number of generations now we have allowed Egypt to be led back into us. When the tyrannies of Egypt have sway *within* us, it will not be long before they have sway *over* us.

"He that hath no rule over his own spirit is like a city that is broken down, and without walls" (Prov. 25:28). If the idols of Egypt are casting shadows in your heart, it will not be long before you are living in the shadows of the pyramids.

We do well if we ask the Lord to deal with our secret idols as we come to commune with Him. We come to His Table now.

So come, and welcome, to Jesus Christ.

As we continue to meditate on the importance of self-control, we have to do more than consider control of our false virtues as well as the appetites and emotions that we know to be a problem.

One of the false virtues of the modern evangelical church is softness. Now of course *gentleness* is a fruit of the Spirit, but it is sign of our decadence that we have confounded it with softness. Of *course* we are to cultivate gentleness, but Christian men are to be, as the phrase goes, velvet-covered bricks. Men are called by the Spirit of God to be *hard*. Self-control therefore calls us to embark on the process of pursuing and growing up into our masculinity and our femininity respectively. It is a mark of how much we in the church have been affected by the propaganda of our diseased culture that this is going to *sound* hokey and lame: Boys need to learn how to be manly. Girls need to learn how to be womanly. Only Spirit-given self-control can equip us for this, particularly in the face of unrelenting pressure from the world. But that world has abandoned its knowledge of masculinity and femininity *only because the evangelical church abandoned it first*.

This all sounds like a cartoon, right? Objections start to fly immediately. All the boys have to play football and work on cars? The girls need to concentrate on their cross-stitch? The boys have to cultivate a gruff voice? The girls have to make us all some biscuits? The fact that *this* paragraph resonates more with us than the previous one is why we have to meditate on this as we come to this Table to be strengthened. This has been one of our fundamental compromises—the evangelical church is still (thank God) predominately heterosexual . . . but our *culture* of evangelical leadership is thoroughly gay.

We have chosen as our spokesmen who would be better suited by their softness (*malakos*) to be in Herod's courts (Matt. 11:8). We have ignored the apostle's solemn charge in 1 Cor. 16:13 literally to "play the man" (*andrizomai*). And why? Lack of self-control.

So come, and welcome, to Jesus Christ.

MORNING ✹ LOADING THE RIGHT TRUCK

It is easy to relegate self-control issues to sins and peccadilloes of the flesh, strive for above average respectable in *that* department, and call it self-control. Now of course it is important to have the appetites under control, but for most Christians today, the central self-control issue is that of managing the schedule.

Part of this problem is that this evokes the standing question — *by what standard?* Peter Drucker taught us to distinguish efficiency from effectiveness: "Efficiency is doing things right; effectiveness is doing the right things." It is far better to load the right truck slowly than the wrong truck swiftly.

When we talk about control over our schedules and priorities, it is easy to get distracted into massive guilt over our inefficiencies. So we ought first to run an inventory on *what* we are doing to ensure that we are addressing the tasks assigned to us by God. Moms, are these your kids? Dads, is this your job? Students, are these your classes? In short, are you facing *your* responsibilities squarely? Are you refusing to be distracted by things that are not your responsibilities? Have you learned the gift of a Spirit-inspired *no*? As Oswald Chambers once put it, the need is not the call. And as someone else less spiritual-sounding once put it, "not my circus, not my monkeys."

Are you loading the right truck? If you are, thank God and make sure you *stay at that truck*. As you limit yourself to that truck, you will find that some of your inefficiencies have disappeared by themselves. And as you carry on faithfully, you will begin to remove your own inefficiencies. And when that has happened, as you have learned to bear your own burden (Gal. 5:5), you will find that you have a genuine surplus of time and competence, which means you will be in a position to help others bear their burden (Gal. 5:2).

As you do the right thing, the thing assigned to you, the thing in front of you, you will need strength for the task.

So come, and welcome, to Jesus Christ.

This is the Table where suffering makes sense. We are not just being nourished — we are also being nourished through a broken body and shed blood. This sacrifice, which we are privileged to partake of here, was not pointless. If it had been pointless, it could not have been a sacrifice. This whole gospel endeavor is filled with meaning. His body was broken *for you*. His blood was shed *for you*.

What is meant by that small word for? We mean that God did this *with the intent that*. He did it *for the purpose of obtaining*. He gave His Son *in order to secure the salvation of*. In short, the death of Jesus had a *telos*, it had a purpose, there was a divine intention behind it.

But while it was not pointless suffering, it was suffering. There has been no greater instance of suffering in the annals of all mankind. No man ever suffered the way the Lord Jesus did. He suffered the physical stripes and wounds, He suffered the indignity of being treated as a criminal by a race of criminals, He suffered the insults of being treated as a traitor by the treacherous and, most of all, He suffered unspeakable horror at the moment when the Father's wrath for all our sins was placed squarely on His shoulders. No one ever suffered as our Lord suffered.

Now if His suffering was not pointless, we can come to this Table knowing that our sufferings cannot be pointless. Why is this? We are in Him. We have been gathered up in Him. If Jesus is the point, and we are in Him, then all that we undergo is part of the point. This is why we can say in all confidence that all things work together for good for those who love God and are called according to His purpose.

You are called here according to His purpose. God is sovereign, which means that when His purposes are laid on top of your life, there is no remainder. Everything makes sense. But make no mistake about it. It can only make sense *here*.

So come, and welcome, to Jesus Christ.

MORNING ☼ THE PRESENCE OF OUR ENEMIES

Self-control is also greatly needed in the area of mockery and scoffing, because mockery is a deadly weapon, and a lot depends on where it is aimed. Mockery is inescapable — it is not whether you mock, but what you mock, when you mock it, and why. The Lord holds rebels in derision (Ps. 2:4). Elijah mocked the priests of Baal, cutting themselves with knives that way (1 Kings 18:27). At the same time, we are told not to sit in the seat of scoffers (Ps. 1:1). We must not mock *what* they do, or in the *way* they do. Whether or not mockery is godly or ungodly is a function of *direction* and *motive*.

This is why self-control in the matter of entertainment standards is so important. The entertainment industry is the Catechesis Department for the humanist state — the ones responsible for teaching you what is ridiculous, instructing you when to distance yourselves from someone who is being laughable. And the laugh track for all their vacuous sitcoms is that great comedic cattle prod, telling you when the hapless conservative is being a buffoon. *Ha ha ha!* — all the independent thinkers laughed together independently.

Christian parents who allow their kids to imbibe a steady diet of worldly entertainment, but who expect them to turn out as rock-solid evangelicals are like that Catholic family who had their kids memorize the Westminster Shorter Catechism, or the Lutheran family who sent their children to the VBS sponsored by the Jehovah's Witness, or the farmer who planted barley in high pursuit of a lentil crop.

With this said, Christians have done some decent work in trying to protect their children from overt filth in entertainment. But cuss counts, nudity, and violence are not the main thing. The main thing is who we are being trained to laugh at. Who is being made wince-worthy? And there we have done virtually no creative work at all.

Remember that this Table is set for us in the presence of our enemies.

So come, and welcome, to Jesus Christ.

EVENING ◐ JOY THAT CRANES ITS NECK

As we come to celebrate the Supper during the season of Advent, it is necessary to remind you of the temptations that come with "penitential" seasons like Advent and Lent.

This is a meal closely associated with the death of our Savior. The wine is the blood, and the bread is the body of the Lord, as we all know. But though it is associated with a death, this is not a sparse little meal at a wake. We are not nibbling at food absent-mindedly, consumed by our grief. We are not weeping for Tammuz, but rather celebrating the forgiveness that has been purchased for us in the death, burial, and resurrection of Jesus Christ.

We are partaking of the body and blood of Christ, but we do not partake of a dead Christ. He is risen. We know this, and are not permitted to forget about it during the course of the church year. In each portion of the church year, as we reenact a particular aspect of Christ's life, we also remember the whole story. This means that in every season of the church, the bedrock is always joy.

As we approach Christmas, the principal emotion we should feel is that of anticipatory joy, expectant joy, joy that cranes its neck. As we come to Christmas Day, our emotion will be that of joy satisfied, joy fulfilled, and joy that looks forward, with Mary, to the day when her heart would be pierced with many sorrows, and the day, three days after that, when all things in heaven and earth were put right. So come, eat and drink the joy before you.

So come, and welcome, to Jesus Christ.

MORNING ☼ RITUAL TRANSLATION

This meal is a ritual that was established by the Lord Jesus the night He was betrayed. We observe it as a ritual — which is not the same thing as an attempted reenactment. In a reenactment, everything is essential. In a ritual, only the essential things are essential. But what are those? How much sand can you put in the sugar bowl before it is no longer a sugar bowl?

Some of the differences are in fact sand in the sugar bowl. When we discover what those differences are, we should attempt to get rid of them. But other differences are not sand at all. They have no significance — they just come with the exigencies of translation. How do you tell the difference? Well, the first rule would be to avoid dogmatism. *Nothing* blinds in discussions of the Lord's Supper like unwarranted dogmatism.

Suppose someone observed the Lord's Supper with orange juice and potato chips. Suppose someone else did it sitting up straight, instead of reclining at Table. Suppose the ritual is separated from an accompanying meal. Suppose there is no foot washing beforehand. Suppose some use grape juice instead of wine. Suppose some wait for one another before partaking while others partake as they go.

The New Testament account (informed by Old Testament practices) was originally conducted in Aramaic. Our canonical source documents are a translation. The background assumptions governing a first century meal, and particularly a Passover meal, are lost on all of us. If you were magically transported back there to sit among them as a thirteenth disciple, you would have no idea of what the table etiquette was supposed to be, and what you were supposed to do next. They lost you when you couldn't find the salad fork.

All that doesn't matter. But that does not mean that nothing matters. Keep it simple. Here is bread. Here is wine. Here are all the promises of God.

So come, and welcome, to Jesus Christ.

At the end of human history, at the end of time as we know it, the Lord Jesus teaches us to anticipate the great marriage Supper. God has chosen and identified the bride that He desires for His Son, the engagement has been sealed, and the preparations are well underway. Messengers have been sent out into all the corners of the earth in order to invite men, women, and children to this feast. A good response to this invitation is actually a response which incorporates the one invited into the bride.

As these individuals grow in holiness, and as the bride herself grows in holiness, we yearn for the day when all the preparations are completed. We long for the time when the bride will finally be presented, when she will come down the aisle, glorious, and without any spot or blemish. The preparation time was hectic, the work was considerable, but it all came off. Everything came together. Everyone came together. Everyone who was appointed to be part of the bride is there, and everyone who identified with the spots and blemishes has been removed. The great marriage Supper will be the glory of all human history.

I said a moment ago that preparations for this wedding, for this feast, were hectic. The labors were significant. There was an overwhelming amount of work to do. But so that we would not forget that this was labor in preparation for a feast, God gives us regular foretastes of what He is up to. We have gathered here in a respite from our work of preparation, and God is giving us bread and wine. These are *hors d'oeuvres* of the Eschaton.

Not only are you strengthened by them for the work, you are also reminded by them of the *nature* of the work. This is given so that we might anticipate a feast.

So come, and welcome, to Jesus Christ.

MORNING ☼ COUNTING AND DANCING

Whenever a people regularly gather, they will fall into certain customs — what they do or don't do, what they say or do not say, what they enact or do not enact — things they will get accustomed to. Once they are accustomed, their minds may start to drift elsewhere while they enact the ritual, or their minds may seize on the central intention and meaning behind the custom. Those are the choices. To develop C.S. Lewis's illustration, when a man is learning to dance, he is not really dancing but rather counting. One, two, three, one, two, three. Once he has learned the dance, he can do it without thinking about the steps. He can now dance without counting, and focus his attention on his partner. But — and here is the perennial danger — he can also dance with her while thinking of another woman.

If our rituals are biblically grounded, we have a duty to learn the pattern and thereafter use the occasion properly — to set our minds on things above, not on things below. During a worship service, all that we say, think, or do must be focused on approaching God the Father through the name of Christ in the power of the Holy Spirit.

Some try to avoid heart-drift by constantly changing the dance. They want to keep us always counting so we will not think about the wrong woman during the dance. Or they ban all customs, all rituals. If there is no dancing at all, nobody will ever think of anything wrong. But this underestimates the nature of our circumstances. We will always be tempted to drift into the wrong patterns of thought. We can always sin with what God requires of us, but if we abandon those things for the sake of "purity," we will just sin *quicker*. You can refuse to go to any dances, and still think of the wrong woman.

What we must therefore do is enact the requirements of Scripture, knowing that we will regularly be tempted to approach God with our lips though our hearts are far from Him. Knowing that, we do not lean on our own understanding, but rather on the Spirit.

So come, and welcome, to Jesus Christ.

EVENING ◐ CHRISTMAS AND THE SUPPER

In the next few weeks comes one of our culture's high feasts. We may lament that many do not know what Christmas really means, or they have bent it into some other strange meaning, but the fact remains quite a striking one — this time of year, every year, the birth of Jesus Christ is marked and celebrated. Other contenders and Johnny-come-latelies like Kwanzaa don't really know what to do. Christmas really has a lot of momentum behind it.

One of the reasons our culture has drifted from a right understanding of Christmas is that the Church has drifted from a right celebration of this meal here. As Christians we have the privilege of feasting in the presence of God every week. When we come to other annual celebrations, like Thanksgiving or Christmas, we are not out of shape. We know, and practice, the reality of celebrating before God.

Now this is not to say that the Lord's Supper is simply training for events like Christmas — not at all. The Lord's Supper is central, not the other way around. But it is to say that this kind of memorial meal, that we are privileged to partake of every week, shapes and drives our behavior the rest of the week, and the rest of the time. Culture really is religion externalized. It is here, in the worship of God, that your religion is shaped and formed. It is there, out in the world that the cultural forms grow up around the real faith of God's people. If we have a problem with how badly the whole thing out there has gone off the rails, then the first place to address the problems is here. So come in true faith, eat and drink.

So come, and welcome, to Jesus Christ.

MORNING ☼ IN THE LIGHT

As we confess weekly, we believe in the communion of saints. This is enacted and embodied in what we do here in the Supper, but what does it mean? What does it entail?

We are gathered together in a particular congregation, and we are celebrating the Supper as we believe the Scripture instructs us to. But we are not doing this by ourselves. Because we are joined to Christ by faith, our fundamental unity is found there, and not in the fact that we are gathered in the same room. This means that we are joined together with anyone else who is joined together with Christ by faith. Time and place do not place any limitation on this.

We are united with the great cloud of witnesses, those believers who have gone before us. We are united with the immense gathering of believers alive today, all over the globe. And just as Abraham looked forward to the day of Christ and was glad, we also look forward to our unity with the saints who will live centuries from now and who will rejoice in their unity with us, when we have become part of that great cloud of witnesses.

Our unity is in Christ. He is the head, and we are the body. As the body grows, our unity grows. As blemishes are removed from the body over time, in such a way as to ensure that by the last day there will not be any spot or blemish, our unity grows in its holiness. If we walk in the light as He is in the light, we have fellowship with one another. We have communion with one another.

No limitation is placed on this communion, fellowship, or *koinonia* by geographical boundary or era. But at the same time, this communion occurs in one "place" only. The one place that communion cannot be observed is in hatred of a brother. This meal takes place in the light.

So come, and welcome, to Jesus Christ.

We come to this Table as summoned, but we often need to be reminded of the purpose of the summoning. This Table represents and enacts the favor of God. We come to this sacrament to receive God's grace, God's favor.

This is the place where we are intended to experience the friendliness of God. Does that phrase strike you? God receives us here warmly. God welcomes us. God wants us here.

Now the tension we feel is because we know that we — in our own persons, in our own names — have not been loyal to Him in the same way that He is loyal to us. He is our friend, but have we been His? He receives our presence warmly — have we shrunk from His presence? He delights to have us speak with Him? Do we hesitate at the prospect of prayer?

Another way of putting this is that we don't deserve to be here. We don't deserve God's friendliness. We do not merit the favor or grace of God. If we know anything at all about the mysteries of God, we know this.

The answer to this is found in what is on the Table. We don't deserve to be at the Table, and in fact could not come, but for what meets us at the Table. The broken body of Jesus, and the shed blood of Jesus, is the only answer we need. We do not come here because we are worthy; we are made worthy as we come.

But one other thing must be said about this. In order to experience God's favor rightly, we have to understand that it is through the work of the Holy Spirit, who is a person. And so we must not understand this as a mere ceremonial powered by an impersonal kind of electricity. Warmth, friendliness, welcome — these are all aspects of a relationship. So come now to the Father, in the strength of the Spirit, through the work of the Son.

So come, and welcome, to Jesus Christ.

MORNING ☼ WORKS THE OTHER WAY

We are blessed to partake in this meal weekly, and as we approach it with a careful biblical understanding, we realize that there is a profound Christian mysticism here.

"The cup of blessing which we bless, is it not the communion of the blood of Christ? The bread which we break, is it not the communion of the body of Christ? For we being many are one bread, and one body: for we are all partakers of that one bread" (1 Cor. 10:16–17).

We are not just forgiven because we have been cleansed by the blood of Jesus Christ. We are also told here that we have *koinonia-fellowship* together in the blood of Christ. We are joint-partakers of that blood. We are not simply united together because we have a common religious interest and shared theological opinions. We are one, united together, because we have koinonia-fellowship together in the body of Christ.

All of this happens through the agency and work of the Holy Spirit. The Son of God dwells in Heaven. His Spirit has been poured out on us here. That Spirit is what empowers us to be united with God through faith in His declared Word, and to be woven together with Him in the koinonia-sharing of His body and blood.

Some have been tempted to think that we become the body of Christ through eating and drinking the body of Christ in communion. It would be more to the point to realize that ordinary bread and wine is taken up into this mystery because the body and blood of Christ eats the bread and drinks the wine. How does wine become Christ? As the body of Christ drinks it. How does bread become Christ? As the body of Christ eats it.

So come, and welcome, to Jesus Christ.

We are told that as often as we partake of this meal, we proclaim (*katangello*) the Lord's death, and we are also told that this reality will be in force until He comes again. In this sense, the entire Christian church is a herald, an ambassador, a preacher. We announce, we declare, we proclaim. What we are proclaiming is the death of Jesus. His shed blood for us, and His broken body for us, are the subject of the declared message.

How does the resurrection fit into this? We know that if Christ were not raised from the dead, we Christians of all men are most to be pitied (1 Cor. 15:19). The resurrection is what brings the account of Christ's passion to a glorious fruition. We know that Christ was raised to life for our justification (Rom. 4:25).

So the resurrection is crucial, but let us remark on that word *crucial*, which comes from the Latin word for cross.

We break bread together on the Lord's Day, which is the weekly commemoration of His resurrection. But what we do on that day of resurrection is focus on the *death* of Jesus. The wine is His blood and the bread is His broken body. When Paul was reminding the Galatians of his preaching to them, he emphasized how pronounced his emphasis had been on the crucifixion (Gal. 3:1). Christ as crucified had been placarded before them, He had been bill-boarded in their presence as crucified. Paul says the same thing to the Corinthians. He resolved to know nothing among them except Christ and Him crucified (1 Cor. 2:2).

Now to enable us to do this faithfully, God did not give us a crucifix. We are not to try to portray the depth of what God did for us in the cross of Jesus with our own invented means for doing it. We are given two central instruments by God. One is the proclamation of the gospel, the preaching of the announced Word. The second is this enacted meal.

So come, and welcome, to Jesus Christ.

MORNING ☼ THE IDENTITY OF THE VICTIM

We come to this Table in order remember certain things, and to remember them by means of an enacted memorial. The two principal things we are to remember have to do with the person and work of our Lord Jesus Christ.

His work is more obvious to us because of the nature of this meal. We have bread to represent His broken body, and we have wine to represent His shed blood. His work was the work of His passion and suffering as He died on a cross of wood in order to satisfy the justice of God.

But we also remember the person of Jesus Christ, meaning that we must also remember who He is. It is not just that a man named Jesus died, but that the one who died was God enfleshed. The one who died was the God/man. "To [the Jews] belong the patriarchs, and from their race, according to the flesh, is the *Christ, who is God over all,* blessed forever. Amen" (Rom. 9:5, ESV).

According to His human nature, He was descended from David. But there was far more to it than that. "And was declared to be the Son of God in power according to the Spirit of holiness by his resurrection from the dead, Jesus Christ our Lord" (Rom. 1:4, ESV).

Now when we partake of this meal, we are partaking of Christ. And when we partake of Christ, we never partake of a partial Christ. In the gospel, in the proclamation of the Word, and in the sacrament, God gives us Himself through Christ. In a sense, God never gives us anything but Himself, and when He does it, He gives Himself fully.

So as we come here in true and living faith, we rejoice that the Creator/creature distinction is never done away with. We will always be finite. But at the same time the Creator and the creature have been miraculously joined in Jesus of Nazareth, and we are privileged to participate in that glorious union by faith alone.

So come, and welcome, to Jesus Christ.

As we come to this meal, there are a number of things we do together. We sit, we reflect, we observe, we take and eat, we take and drink, and we love one another. This is a meal of covenant partaking, and the Greek word that sums up that partaking, that sharing, that blending, is the word *koinonia*.

But there is something else we do together in this meal that typifies the whole thing wonderfully. When Jesus instituted this meal with His disciples, He also did this same thing. "And when they had sung an hymn, they went out into the Mount of Olives." (Matt. 26:30).

This is a *musical* meal. We sing together as we pass the elements to one another. And there are few things that provide a better specific instance of the whole meal than what happens in congregational singing. We have many voices and just one song. These voices are all voices together, but the timbre of each voice also varies. We have bass and baritone, tenor, alto and soprano. We also have the voices of children. Just as the one loaf is broken into many pieces in order to come back together into a different kind of unified loaf, so also many disparate voices were created in order unite together again in one song.

But the unity is even deeper and richer than that. Christian unity is not a monolithic slab, but rather something that is textured and intricately woven. The one song has different parts written for it, parts that are designed to receive the contribution of each kind of voice, and at the same time to blend with and complement what the other voices are doing as they bring their contributions.

Now just as the emblems of bread and wine are supposed to picture this kind of unity, so also singing in harmony embodies it. But this also is simply a sign pointing to something else. That something else is the love you actually have for one another.

So come, and welcome, to Jesus Christ.

MORNING ☼ PASSOVER

When Christians come to this Table, in faith they are partaking of the very same thing that the Jews partook of in the Passover meal. We are taught explicitly that Christ was the Passover Lamb, slain for us. He was executed on the cross at the same time as Passover. The blood of the lambs was sprinkled on the wood of Israelite doorways just as the blood of Jesus was smeared on the wooden cross— which is why the cross of Jesus Christ is for us the only doorway through which we may escape the wrath of God. And when Jesus instituted the Lord's Supper among His followers, which we are faithfully observing to this day, He instituted it at a Passover meal with His disciples.

Old Testament believers partook of the altar, looking forward in faith to the time when all the sacrifices of the Old Testament economy would be completed and fulfilled. They were looking forward to Christ, partaking of Him by faith. We are looking backward to the once-for-all sacrifice that Christ offered, and we are partaking of the same Christ.

Now the death of Jesus on the cross was the hinge upon which all of world history turns. There has never been a more completed event. If the Lord Jesus cries out it is finished, then as believers we must treat it as *finished*. The propitiatory sacrifice is over and done. Once for all, Christ died for sinners.

That aspect of the sacrifice is *not* being repeated here, nor could it be. What we are doing here is remembering and rejoicing. This is a eucharistic sacrifice, not a blood sacrifice. Because of the once-for-all blood sacrifice, we have been brought near so that we are united with Christ. United with Him, we partake of Him, and we do so as a forgiven and cleansed people. That is the foundation of our joy.

So come, and welcome, to Jesus Christ.

Word and sacrament are offered to us together. In what we are offered, we do have a glorious repetition, but we do not have redundancy. Never think that you are offered something in the sacrament that the Word has already completely supplied. The Word prepares us for the sacrament; it does not displace it. The sacrament feeds and nourishes us, but never think that the Word does not nourish us. We are Christians, and so we do feed on the words of Christ. But because we are Christians we also feed on our participation in the gospel of the Lord's death and resurrection.

God wants to come at us in two ways. He feeds the mind and heart with His Word. We listen and understand. We hear the terms and we acknowledge them. We agree that these things are all true. We rejoice to hear that they are all true. And when this is done, He slides the papers across the desk and asks us to sign.

Participation in the sacrament is partaking of Christ. It does this in an intensely personal way, and this is why it has the force of a mystical oath. You partake of this meal here today in a way that says, "I am all in." Next week you will do the same, saying, "I am *still* all in."

Some might wonder why God has us renew our vows this frequently. Is He that insecure that He needs to be reassured of our love for Him, on this kind of a weekly basis? Not a bit of it. Not surprisingly, we have it backwards. How could an infinite fortress be insecure? *We* are the frail ones. We are the ones following our guide through a dangerous and very treacherous world. Our guide is in front of us. He is sure-footed and knows the way. Periodically He reassures us. "I will never leave you." And so we partake — "Still here. Thank you."

So come, and welcome, to Jesus Christ.

MORNING ☼ SANCTIFYING GRACE

If we remember two import things about this meal, we will better understand the place of this memorial in the history of the church.

First, this is the *Lord's* Supper, not our own. The meal belongs to Him. He instituted it, and He sits at the head of the Table. He said the first blessing over it, a blessing that still remains, and He is offers His own body and blood as the ground of our covenant partaking. He is the principal actor. This is not something we do in order to offer to Him; rather this is something He invites us into. This is not the Christian supper. This is the Lord's Supper.

Second, this meal, wielded by Him, is a sanctifying grace. We understand this when it comes to our individual lives — we know that we are strengthened and encouraged by it. But this meal is also an instrument of His for sanctifying the church through history.

So we may not assign meanings to the Supper that the Scriptures do not teach. When we have done so — and Christian history is replete with examples — one of God's principal methods for removing those errors is found in the Supper itself. He uses the Supper to sanctify the church corporately, including our Eucharistic theology.

The two great errors that faithful partaking will sanctify over time are rationalism and superstition. Rationalism treats the elements of the Supper as propositions in 3D. The Supper is an audiovisual aid to help us think certain thoughts, and if we were to think those thoughts without the bread and wine, that would be just as good. Superstition wants to control spiritual forces, tying them down to one spot to better manipulate them. Priestcraft tends to want to reduce the mysteries of Christ so that they can fit on the god-shelf in the sacerdotal warehouse and can be shared with the people piecemeal.

But we are here to observe the Lord's Supper. Our demeanor should be as Mary's was in her reply to the angel. Be it unto me according to thy word (Luke 1:38).

So come, and welcome, to Jesus Christ.

EVENING ◐ EVERLASTING WAYBREAD

When cultural observers fret over the disintegration of once-intact families in our culture, one of the things they point to is how often people eat their meals separately, or eat them in haste, having breakfast over the sink. This concern is well-grounded — there is something to it. We *should* focus on table fellowship, both here and in our homes.

At the same time, we should know that this is not the entire picture. For example, what did God tell the Israelites when He established the Passover?

"And thus shall ye eat it; with your loins girded, your shoes on your feet, and your staff in your hand; and ye shall eat it in haste: it is the Lord's passover" (Ex. 12:11).

There is a time and a place for us to eat our meals in haste, and there is a sense in which this meal should remind us that we are pilgrim people. This is not only the bread of life, it is bread for the *way*. But do not worry over it. God has prepared us. Our shoes will not wear out. The Rock that accompanies us is Christ. We have been given everlasting waybread.

"When I remember these things, I pour out my soul within me. For I used to go with the multitude; I went with them to the house of God, With the voice of joy and praise, With a multitude that kept a pilgrim feast" (Ps. 42:4, NKJV).

We are a pilgrim people, and this also is a pilgrim feast. The apostle Peter reminds us that this is part of what reminds us to stay on a wartime footing. The fact that God prepares a table for us in the presence of our enemies should not make us forget that we have enemies.

"Dearly beloved, I beseech you as strangers and pilgrims, abstain from fleshly lusts, which war against the soul" (1 Pet. 2:11).

So come, and welcome, to Jesus Christ.

MORNING ☼ PROFESSION OF FAITH

One of the concerns expressed about bringing young children to the Table, as we do, is the concern that we are neglecting the important element of having every communicant make a profession of faith. Are we not minimizing the importance of personal faith by doing this?

Now it is possible for bad things to come out of child communion coupled with weekly observance, but not if we remember what it is we are actually doing. A profession of faith is not necessary prior to coming to this Table because coming to this Table *is* a profession of faith. As we bring our children up in the nurture and admonition of the Lord, we are not bypassing the need to profess our faith. Rather, we are professing our faith together, in the most solemn and regular way possible. As our children join us, they are being trained to profess their faith together with us.

The Lord's Supper is not just an event where we *receive* something from God. We do receive the bread and the wine, and the grace carried by them, but we also *render* something to God. He gives us grace, and with that grace we return our profession of loyalty, allegiance, fidelity and faith. We are not coming to this Table to receive our reward, but rather we are coming here to transact the realities of our covenantal engagements with Him.

Another way of saying this is that the bread is an edible oath. The wine is an oath in a cup. We have no power to take on such a solemn oath in our own strength or in our own power. We would be fools to do so. But we believe in Jesus Christ, crucified and raised, and we trust Him with the security of all these engagements. We come to this Table with great joy, and we do so in order to profess our faith.

So come, and welcome, to Jesus Christ.

One of our great privileges in this congregation is the privilege of coming to the Lord's Table weekly. When we come to the Lord's Table, we are coming to the Lord Himself, and why wouldn't we? We are evangelicals; we believe in coming to Jesus.

In the midst of the great Reformation, the great John Calvin wanted to institute monthly communion (moving from quarterly), but was prevented by political forces. He had to settle for writing down in their public acts that their "custom was defective," and that the Supper should be "in as frequent use as practicable in His Church, according to His own institution, and as it was observed in the Ancient Church." Sadly, the resistance that Calvin met with remained the norm. About the only one of Calvin's heirs who was able to successfully move to weekly communion was the great Baptist preacher, Charles Spurgeon. As one historian notes, "he was a vigorous promoter of celebrating Holy Communion each Lord's Day."

To be invited to share Table fellowship with the Lord Jesus is to be invited to be His friend (John 15:15). Why wouldn't we come, as often as we worship Him? This coming is not merely intellectual. We sit, we sing, we eat, we drink. We are members of the same household as Jesus Christ is. He calls us *friends*.

This is why we call it communion. We are sharing together. We are partaking together. We come because we have communion with God, and because we have communion with God we have communion with one another. We love God, and so it is that we love our neighbor as well.

This is great privilege indeed, especially when we are mindful of our own infirmities. Like that poor woman with the long hemorrhage in the gospels, you come here in order to *touch* Jesus Christ. You *have* come, trembling in your infirmity, and are released from here as His friend, trembling for joy.

So come, and welcome, to Jesus Christ.

MORNING ☼ THE FIRST SUPPER

The meal where this sacrament was instituted is commonly called the Last Supper. It is called *last* because it was the last meal that Jesus ate before His arrest, and of course this attribution makes sense at that level.

But there is also a real sense in which we ought to think of it as the *First* Supper. This was the meal where Christ instituted this memorial. It was the first observance of countless millions of observances. The Passover that Moses had the people celebrate was their last meal in Egypt, but it was the first Passover. The meal that Jesus established was His last meal before His death, but it was also the last true meal of the old creation.

Of course, both *first* and *last* remain fitting terms for it. Christ is Himself the First and the Last, and this is the foundational meal (first) and the ultimate, eschatological meal (last). Christ is everything to us—He is the cornerstone, and He is the capstone. He is the one who strengthens us for our journey and pilgrimage the day we begin it, and He is the one welcoming us home when we arrive there. He is the one in whom we live and move and have our being.

So not only does He commission and send us, and then welcome and receive us, so also He is present with us every step of the way, accompanying us through His Spirit. We affirm the real presence of Christ here because the Spirit of Christ indwells every faithful believer who partakes of this meal in faith.

The Lord offers Himself in the gospel and in the bread and wine, and the Lord, dwelling in us by His Spirit, receives what is offered by stirring up true faith within us. He offers Himself, He is what is offered, and He receives what is offered, equipping us as He does so. He does this through the instrumentality of living faith, which lives and abides in you.

So come, and welcome, to Jesus Christ.

We partake of the Lord's Supper — on the physical level — by means of our mouths and throats. As we do this, we want to make sure we are not highlighting any radical inconsistency. Mouths and throats are used in other ways: "Their throat is an open sepulchre; with their tongues they have used deceit; the poison of asps is under their lips: Whose mouth is full of cursing and bitterness: Their feet are swift to shed blood" (Rom. 3:13–15).

And James tells us that brackish and fresh water don't flow from the same spring. "Doth a fountain send forth at the same place sweet water and bitter?" (Jas. 3:11).

If that is the case, then it is also inconsistent to have brackish water flowing out, and broken bread and sacrificial wine being taken in. There is an inconsistency between foul and fair words traveling in the same direction on this road, but there is also an inconsistency between foul traffic coming out and fair traffic going in.

When we recognize the fact of this inconsistency, and repent of it, we may then in true faith be looking to God to strengthen us, by mortifying sin in us, and quickening us in our walk with God. Remember, always remember, that you cannot eat this body and drink this blood without simultaneously eating and drinking *the death of sin*. If you eat and drink that which is designed to mortify sin, overthrows sin, annihilate sin, then you should be aware of what you are doing.

Hypocrites love to twist words. "All day they twist my words; All their thoughts are against me for evil" (Ps. 56:5, NKJV). Among the words they seek to twist are these — *Christ died for our sins according to Scripture*. So when you come, as you are summoned to come, know what you are coming to. Do you really want the elements to slay any of your favorite ways of speaking on the way down?

So come, and welcome, to Jesus Christ.

MORNING ☼ DEALING WITH DULLNESS

The spiritual realm is the realm of ultimate realities. The material realm that you see and experience around you is certainly real *materially*, but it draws its ultimate being and reality from the will of God the Father, and this God must be known in spirit and in truth. This means that matter is the shadow, and the realm of the spirit the true object.

If we are being held captive by our senses, we have a tendency to think that this here is the reality, and that the spiritual realm is ephemeral. And thus, if we want this Supper to display a "real presence" of Christ, we want to locate it on the Table. But the real presence of Christ is spiritual, ministered to us by the Holy Spirit, and is a presence not composed of atoms and molecules. For people who think materially, the real presence of the Lord depends upon the corporeal presence of the Lord. But this is to ignore the splendid *reality* of the spiritual world.

Another stumbling block for us is that even if we grant that the spiritual world is real, we assume that it must be *distant*. Heaven is real, but I can't see it, so it must be distant — the way a planet in another solar system would be. But there is no reason for assuming this. Charles Spurgeon put it this way: "I am persuaded that there is no great actual distance between earth and heaven: the distance lies in our dull minds." Mark that — the distance is in our dullness.

One of the things that is happening in this Supper is that God is dealing with that dullness. In Christ, all things are being gathered together, whether things in heaven or on earth (Eph. 1:10). This worship service, this observance of the sacrament, is part of that gathering, part of that knitting together, part of that assembling of heaven and earth. The dullness is being removed.

So come, and welcome, to Jesus Christ.

EVENING ◐ HUNGER FOR THE REAL THING

This is a meal, and physically speaking it is a very plain meal. We have simple bread and red wine set before us. At the same time, you are invited to get a great deal out of it. You are summoned to feed upon Christ here, and all that Christ contains — and He is infinite — is available to you here. How can this be?

The best way to understand this is through our proverb *hunger is the best sauce.* Because this is a spiritual meal, and not an ordinary one, that hunger must be a spiritual hunger. The Lord instructs us that those who hunger and thirst for righteousness shall be filled (Matt. 5:6). What a *glorious* promise.

Notice that He places no limit on this. If we hunger and thirst for righteousness — the real thing — there is no such thing as gluttony. Over-indulgence is an impossibility. We may have as much as we want.

When the preacher in Ecclesiastes tells us not to be righteous over-much (Ecc. 7:16), he is not talking about an acceptance of infinite joy. He is there speaking of the petty fastidiousness that we frequently display in the name of religion, with biblical justifications gummed on the outside of it. Whenever we are overly-righteous it is because we have slapped together some kind of cardboard cut-out morality meant to approximate the glory of the Godhead, and the fact that we fail to represent Him (and fail spectacularly) should come as no surprise.

But here is the bread of life. The more you eat, the more you are filled, and the more you are filled, the more you are able to eat. Here is an infinite amount of the most intoxicating wine that ever was, and the more you drink it, the more sober-minded and clear-headed you become.

So come, and welcome, to Jesus Christ.

MORNING ✲ AN INVITATION TO MESS WITH IT

We have a meal here that entails consecration. All of Christ is offered to you, and in natural return, you are summoned to come. But when you are summoned to come, this means that *all* of you is summoned to come.

The cup of blessing is here, set before you. But we want always to remember what the Scriptures teach about the nature of blessing. "Blessed are they that keep his testimonies, and that seek him *with the whole heart*" (Ps. 119:2). So you are invited to come, and you are being exhorted to come with an entire heart.

The underlying cause of great affliction for many struggling Christians is partialism. They want to have God in their lives, but they want to hold back something for themselves in reserve. God can have that, but we want to retain this. Thus we parcel ourselves out, and are surprised when nothing works as it ought. God is happy to work with the fragments of your life, but He insists on having all of them.

Different people want to retain different things, but the results are always some sort of dislocation. Some want to keep control of their money, others of private lusts, and others of their position in the community. If we turn whatever it is over to God, He might mess with it.

But God's people are, always and everywhere, exhorted to deal with God in bulk. "Therefore also now, saith the Lord, Turn ye even to me *with all your heart*" (Joel 2:12). So what you are saying by approaching this Table — since it is governed by the words of Scripture, and not our own private desires — is that you want God to take whatever it is . . . and mess with it.

So come, and welcome, to Jesus Christ.

In order for this to be a meal of true fellowship, it must be a meal of perfect fellowship. God is the God of all perfections, and He cannot look upon evil. He cannot fellowship with sin, or countenance iniquity.

How then is possible for *us* to be here? We are fallen, sinful, and corrupt. You knelt in confession earlier in this service. You know that. And yet this is a meal of perfect fellowship. Not only do we praise the bridegroom seated at the head of the Table, He also praises. Notice this. Not only do we praise the Lord in our worship of Him, but He also praises His bride. How could a perfect bridegroom be so churlish as to not praise his bride?

The lover in Song of Solomon says that his bride is the "fairest among women." He finds all perfection in her. This is certainly God's intention concerning us. Paul says this in Ephesians: "That he might present it to himself a glorious church, not having spot, or wrinkle, or any such thing; but that it should be holy and without blemish" (Eph. 5:27). And he says of the Colossians that God intends to "present you holy and unblameable and unreproveable in his sight:" (Col. 1:22).

We know that in ourselves we are only sinners. This kindness is only possible because of His grace in justification, that grace which has imputed to us all the righteousness of Jesus Christ, and only the righteousness of Jesus Christ. But to say that it is only possible through Christ is not to say that it is impossible. Those are very different things.

God does not gaze on His own work of redemption and see shoddy work. He sees the same perfections that He has declared, and as He has declared it, we must believe it. As the bride of Christ we must learn to take His compliments with a good grace. It is not humility to refuse them. This is the ground of perfect fellowship.

So come, and welcome, to Jesus Christ.

MORNING ☼ MUCH OF OUR LITTLES

The reason it is possible for God to pronounce the glorious vindication of "no condemnation" over us is because of the imputation of the perfect obedience of Jesus Christ to us. This is our justification, this is our exoneration, this is our judicial deliverance. The Lord is our righteousness.

But when we move from the subject of justification to that of our day-to-day sanctification, we sometimes forget the *spirit* of free grace that animated the former, and that it is the same spirit. When God looks at us in Christ, He sees no fault or sin of any kind. That is why there is no condemnation — that is our justification. But when He looks at us with our sanctification in view, we know that He can see sin (which He does not "see" in our justification). But when we realize that He can see sin in us at all, we tend to assume He can see nothing but sin in us.

The grace of God which bestows on us the sentence of "not guilty" is not a grace that is looking for excuses to condemn elsewhere. It is not the case, in other words, that God says *no condemnation* in justification and *all condemnation* in our sanctification.

Put another way, do not simply assume that God's eye can see the smallest sin, and so that is all He cares to look at in you. God's eye can see the stirrings of His grace in you. He sees and rejoices in the smallest beginnings. God not only sees the fruit, He also sees the smallest bud. As one great preacher once put it, He makes much of our littles.

As we partake of this bread and this wine, we sing to God gratefully. But never forget that God, knowing what we are like, receives us here with infinite gladness. He rejoices over us with singing (Zech. 3:17).

So come, and welcome, to Jesus Christ.

The Lord Jesus is present here with us now, and He is altogether lovely. He visits us in our imperfections, but in the grace of God He does so in His perfections. God has not given us an *adequate* savior. He has not given us a "good enough" redeemer. The salvation that has been brought to us, and which is set before us on this Table in its appointed emblems, is a salvation that saves to the *uttermost*.

We are not just barely saved. Because we are saved in and through the perfections of Christ, it follows that we are perfectly saved. If you are saved at all, you are *perfectly* saved.

This can only be true because our salvation originates from outside us. If it had to arise from within, it could not arise at all. We know this as the wholesome doctrine of Scripture, but we also know it in our hearts. In our flesh, we all confess, dwells no good thing. We are corrupt in our nature, and so deliverance must come another place. This is the place we must be saved *from*, not the place where we can cobble together a salvation from surrounding materials.

We are taken out of the dungeon. We do not build a sky palace out of the rocks of the dungeon.

All of this is true because Jesus is a sufficient savior. Not barely sufficient, and not minimally adequate. He is infinitely and ultimately beautiful. He is altogether lovely. And not in some sentimental or effeminate way either. No, He is the precise image of His infinite Father, and if we have beheld Him, we have beheld His Father. And of course, this is only possible if His Holy Spirit works in us to give us the eyes to see, the hands to receive, and the mouths to taste.

So come, and welcome, to Jesus Christ.

MORNING ☼ MISERS AND MEDDLERS

A common name for this meal that we share together weekly is communion. This is a rendering of the Greek word *koinonia,* which has a range of meanings and possible translations.

God gives to us in this meal, and, ultimately, He has nothing to give but Himself — so that is what He in fact gives. He gives us Himself, and we celebrate *koinonia* by giving and receiving. We are participating in what He does, and we are imitating what He does. This is right at the center of the Christian life, this giving and receiving.

The idea is to have this giving and receiving at the center spread out into the corners. Notice this: "For it hath pleased them of Macedonia and Achaia to make a certain contribution for the poor saints which are at Jerusalem" (Rom. 15:26). The word rendered *contribution* is *koinonia.* "But to do good and to communicate forget not: for with such sacrifices God is well pleased" (Heb. 13:16). The word translated *communicate* is related to *koinonia.* "Whiles by the experiment of this ministration they glorify God for your professed subjection unto the gospel of Christ, and for your liberal distribution unto them, and unto all men" (2 Cor. 9:13). The word *distribution* is *koinonia.*

Notice all the ways that the giving and receiving extends out to the edges: We encourage one another, babysit, mow a lawn, donate to the deacons' fund, volunteer, attend a dull committee meeting for Jesus, and so on. That is, this is what we are doing when we are walking in faith. If we do not grasp the heart of *koinonia,* we will either give or not give to others externally. If we do not give, then we are being misers, skinflints, pinchfisted, and will call it all prudence. If we do give, but not in the Spirit of Christ, then we will be meddlers, busybodies, uplifters, and will call it love. But Paul insisted you could give absolutely everything away to the poor, and be a spiritual zero (1 Cor. 13:3). Outside of the kindness and *koinonia* of Christ, it will be misers or meddlers. But what is set before us is body life.

So come, and welcome, to Jesus Christ.

EVENING ◐ EVERYTIME PRESENCE

The Incarnation was an event in history. So was the crucifixion, as also the resurrection. They happened, and they happened in the same way that other historical events happened. Christ was born at a point in time, and He died at a point in time, and He rose from the dead. All these things happened at particular times of the day, on particular days, at a particular time of the year.

In one respect, the day of Pentecost was like the first Christmas, or the day of resurrection. There was a particular day when the Holy Spirit was poured out upon the disciples in Jerusalem. But something else was going on there too. A great deal more was involved than something the Spirit decided to do one day.

The Spirit was poured out upon "all flesh" (Acts 2:17), and what that means has relevance for us here, gathered around this Table today. The meaning of Christ's birth, death, and resurrection needs to be applied to us. The efficacy of His work must be mediated to us. Otherwise, it is removed from us by the passage of years, and the more time goes by, the more removed Christians will be from it.

And this means that when the Spirit was poured out on all flesh, He was poured out on *everytime*. He is present here with us now. In fact, it is His presence with us that enables us to partake of Jesus Christ in the way we do. If it were not for the Spirit's work, we could no more partake of Christ's work than we could leap to the moon.

And with the Spirit's work, we are *as much partakers* of the resurrected Christ as were the disciples who first broke bread together on the day of Pentecost (Acts 2:46). We are not partaking at a far remove. We are not sitting in the back corner of an enormous banqueting hall. We are present with an immediate mediator because the Spirit is present in *everytime*, and we are present in His Spirit—and so the Spirit and the Son bring us into the presence of the Father.

So come, and welcome, to Jesus Christ.

MORNING ☼ **HOST, GUEST, FOOD**

In this meal we eat family style. We both receive the food and pass the food. In additions, because it is a covenant meal, we consume the food that is made up of all the others, and we offer ourselves to be consumed to all the others. We are enabled to do this because the Head of the church is seated at the head of the Table, and He is simultaneously the food offered, the Host offering, and the guest receiving it. Everything we do here is modeled for us by Him.

This makes no sense if we are thinking of it mechanically, or even magically. This can only make sense if we have been shown the secrets of the covenant. Covenantal realities overlap in ways that other realities do not.

Let us start with the fact that Jesus is the Host. In the establishment of the meal, He fulfills that role perfectly, wonderfully. He is the one who has His disciples make arrangements for the room (Mark 14:15). He is right at the center of all that happens in the meal — He is definitely the host.

Second, and most familiar, He offers Himself as the food. "And as they did eat, Jesus took bread, and blessed, and brake it, and gave to them, and said, Take, eat: this is my body" (Mk. 14:22).

And last, a guest. Jesus Himself ate at the Last Supper. Note that he identified Judas as His betrayer by saying that the treacherous man would be the man who dipped "with me" in the dish (Mk. 14:14). Jesus was, and is, a full participant in this meal. That is the only way that *we* can be full participants in this meal. Without Him, without Jesus, this is all meaningless mumbo jumbo.

But He is here. He is present. He is ready to bless. The blessing will be at its fullest when you imitate Him in what he is doing. Pass the food as though you were the host. Receive it as though you were the guest. Offer yourself to God and to your neighbor as though you were ready to be consumed for the sake of the others.

So come, and welcome, to Jesus Christ.

EVENING ◐ NO PERPLEXITY AT ALL

We know that when we sit down to partake of this meal, we are partaking of our forgiveness. The broken body and blood of Christ are the meal, and our resurrected and forgiving Lord is seated at the head of the Table. We also know that when we partake of this meal we are partaking of our deliverance from all our afflictions. We are fellowshipping with the one who delivers.

But we are also sitting down to eat and drink with our *answers*. All of us here have sins to be forgiven, and we all have afflictions to be lifted. But it is also the case that we all have our perplexities.

An affliction is a trouble where you see no way out. A perplexity is when you know there is a way out, or perhaps many ways out, but you don't know what they are or how to discover them. You don't know what to *do*.

Many Christians in such straits pray earnest to discover God's will, as though He would send you a text or an email. "Here, do this." But that is not how it works. That is not how God guides you through your perplexities.

There are many aspects to this, but the first thing is for you to sit down and have true fellowship with one who knows your situation perfectly, and who is not perplexed at all. He knows exactly what to do. And because you have come to be with Him you may have every assurance that He was already with you.

Whatever your perplexity, you are in it together, and the one who is with you—and you know He is with you for you just shared a meal together—knows everything that can be known about that perplexity. And for Him, it is no perplexity at all.

So come, and welcome, to Jesus Christ.

MORNING ✹ EACH MORSEL CONTAINS WORLDS

When we partake of this meal, we are partaking of both the Lord's disgrace, and His promised glory.

"Behold, my servant shall deal prudently, He shall be exalted and extolled, *and be very high*. As many were astonied at thee; His visage was so *marred more than any man*, and his form more than the sons of men" (Is. 52:13–14).

Our Lord embraced His sufferings in obedience to His Father, and He was embraced by the pleasure and glory of God in His resurrection. And because of our union with Christ, both are ours. His agony is ours and His glory is ours. We partake of His sufferings; our sufferings and our sins were all imputed to Him. We partake of His glory; His obedience and righteousness were imputed to us.

"For he hath made him to be sin for us, who knew no sin; that we might be made the righteousness of God in him" (2 Cor. 5:21).

We partake of both. When Jesus died, marred beyond all recognition, all His elect died there with Him, also marred beyond all recognition. All of our wretchedness was all there — the outer darkness was nailed to a stake of wood. And when Jesus rose to glory, brighter than ten thousand suns, we rose with Him to partake of *that* glory. Jesus is not imputed to us on a piecemeal basis. All that He is, all that He ever did, all that He ever suffered, all that He ever inherited, is bequeathed to you.

As an emblem of all this, as a token of all the promises, God this morning offers you a morsel of bread and a swallow of wine. But as with all such things, God is not offering you a tiny fraction of His grace. Every morsel of bread, and every small cup of wine, contains worlds. And as you eat and drink in genuine faith, you inherit.

So come, and welcome, to Jesus Christ.

The neck of the Church is that which attaches her to her Head, the Lord Jesus Christ. And what is it that brings us into union with the Lord? Is it not our faith? Living and evangelical faith is therefore the neck of the bride, without which there can be no bride at all.

We are told that the just shall live by faith (Hab. 2:4; Rom. 1:17). By this, of course it is meant that we live day-to-day trusting in God — we live our lives by faith. But it also means that we stay alive by faith. Without connection to the Head, we would all simply die. The Head is that which supplies the spiritual nourishment necessary for us to flourish. "And not holding the Head, from which all the body by joints and bands *having nourishment ministered*, and knit together, increaseth with the increase of God." (Col. 2:19). That connection is our life, our source of life.

But of course faith comes by hearing and hearing by the Word of God proclaimed. We may therefore say in a figure that the necklace of the bride of Christ is the preaching of the gospel. "Thy neck is like the tower of David builded for an armoury, Whereon there hang a thousand bucklers, all shields of mighty men" (Song 4:4).

The Church is beautiful in the world, terrible as an army with banners, when the neck is joined to the Head, when the Head is thereby lifted up, and the necklace of the Word is proudly displayed like the shields of warriors, arrayed around the tower.

From Chrysostom to Spurgeon, from Knox to Whitefield, from Augustine to Edwards, the Word has been proclaimed in truth. There are many shields on the tower. Precisely because it has been faithfully proclaimed for two thousand years, precisely because the Word which defines the sacrament has been faithfully preached, you may come to be nourished by it now.

So come, and welcome, to Jesus Christ.

MORNING ☼ THE BAKERY OF GOD

The Word of life, bread for the world, was born in Bethlehem. The word *Bethlehem* means "House of Bread." So Bethlehem was the bakery of God, and that is where the ovens of God were located. This bread, like all true offerings to God, was a sweet-smelling savor.

When we are *done* with the process, there is a sweet-smelling savor, but you might not guess the results if you were unacquainted with the process and saw it for the first time. We get a glimpse of this right at the end, where the loaf is broken in order to represent how the Lord's body was broken in the crucifixion. The loaf is broken, distributed, and then consumed.

But this reality is manifest earlier. This is God's way. The seed must first be cast away, thrown into the soil. When it grows up, it must be cut. When it is cut, it must be threshed, to separate the kernels of wheat from the husks. Then, when it is just wheat, it must be ground into flour. When it is ground into flour, it is mixed into dough, and after that, it is placed in the oven. All this preparation so that it might be broken.

This is God's way. He makes us whole by breaking us. And lest that seem harsh to us, He showed us how it is to be done. The Incarnate Son served as the preeminent example. He went first so that we could see. He was a man of sorrows, acquainted with grief—because He was sown in the ground, cut down in obedience, threshed in affliction, ground in submission, kneaded as one entirely submissive, and then cooked in the furnace of the devil's spite, the Father's wrath, and the Father's culminating and sovereign mercy.

And the loaf is before us now, so that it might be broken. And as it is broken, we have something to eat, and something to imitate.

So come, and welcome, to Jesus Christ.

EVENING ◐ A BODY THAT COULD DIE

The body that was broken for you was a body broken on the cross. But the body that was broken on the cross was the same body that was formed in the womb of the virgin. And that body was taken on by the eternal Word in order that it might be broken. The blood that began to circulate in the veins of Jesus before He was even born was the same blood that was to be shed for you many years later.

Christmas is the opening move in God's salvation of His people. Communion causes us to reflect on the closing moves, the Lord's passion and death. Meditate on the fact that Christmas and communion are to be understood together, as part of the same story.

So come, and welcome, to Jesus Christ.

MORNING ☼ A MEAL THAT MEANS

As we gather repeatedly for this meal, you may have noticed that the portions are small. You receive a morsel of bread, and you receive a small cup of wine, a bit larger than a thimble.

In one respect this is simply a function of what is necessary when hundreds of people partake together on a weekly basis. This is a meal, and that means that logistical considerations matter. But there is more to it than that.

If there were only ten of us partaking, we still would not have the portions be as large as they would be if you were having lunch. When the early church used to partake of communion in conjunction with what they called their love feasts, and which we would call a church potluck, Paul took care to have them disassociate the communion amounts from the amounts they ate in their "regular" meal.

"What? have ye not houses to eat and to drink in? or despise ye the church of God, and shame them that have not? What shall I say to you? shall I praise you in this? I praise you not" (1 Cor. 11:22).

If you are eating to satisfy physical hunger, Paul says, then do it somewhere else. That is not the point of this meal. But then what is the point of this meal?

This is *a meal that means*. The bread is an edible noun, and the cup is a drinkable verb. This means that what you eat and drink is measured by what it means, and not how much it weighs, or how much space it occupies in your hand. When it comes to this kind of communication, you don't calculate by volume. The word rubbish has significantly more letters than the word gold. And when you look at a check, you look at where the decimal point is placed, and not how much ink was used in writing the check.

And so what does your morsel of bread mean? What does your ounce of wine mean? It means all of Christ, and all He possesses. It means that there are no limits to what He will give to you in His Son.

So come, and welcome, to Jesus Christ.

EVENING ◐ A SINGING CHRIST

When the Lord instituted this meal, it was in the context of a Passover supper. At the conclusion of the meal they sang a hymn, and then went out (Matt. 26:30). It is almost certain that they followed the Jewish custom of singing the *Hallel* psalms, six psalms starting at 113.

Remember that this is shortly before the Lord's arrest. In a brief time, He is going to plead to have the cup pass from Him. In a matter of hours, Judas will kiss Him, the soldiers flog Him, the leaders of Israel reject Him, and His Father in Heaven turn His face away.

And what was the hymn selection for that occasion? "Praise ye the Lord. Praise, O ye servants of the Lord" (Ps. 113:1). "Tremble, thou earth, at the presence of the Lord" (114:7). "Not unto us, O Lord, not unto us, But unto thy name give glory" (115:1). "O Israel, trust thou in the Lord: He is their help and their shield" (115:9). "I love the Lord, because he hath heard My voice and my supplications" (116:1). "I will walk before the Lord In the land of the living" (116:9). "O praise the Lord, all ye nations: Praise him, all ye people" (117:1). "O give thanks unto the Lord; for he is good: Because his mercy endureth for ever" (118:1).

If the Lord sang on that night, would He not sing together with us now? Two thousand years into His reign, all is unfolding according to the perfect counsel of God's will. In this circumstance, the Lord rejoices over us with singing. "The Lord thy God in the midst of thee is mighty; He will save, he will rejoice over thee with joy; He will rest in his love, he will joy over thee with singing" (Zep. 3:17).

So we come to partake of Christ, but not a dead Christ. He is alive forevermore, and is seated at the right hand of the Father. This Table has a white cloth on it, but it is not a winding sheet. We are the living body of the living Christ because we partake of Him, and we are not a corpse because He is not a corpse. The Christ we partake of is a *singing* Christ.

So come, and welcome, to Jesus Christ.

MORNING ☼ SOMEBODY TOUCHED ME

In Luke 8, we are told the story of the woman with a hemorrhage who approached Christ in the press of the crowd, touched Him, and was healed. She came to him in true faith, but as she thought, anonymously, and yet was healed. But it was not a secret to Christ. He felt the healing power as it went out of Him.

As we come to this Table, we do so in order to touch Christ. We handle the bread, and eat it, and we drink down the wine. We come to do this in the middle of a great throng. But regardless of the crowd, your purpose in it should be to touch Him individually. You should want more than to be among those who jostle Him. According to the disciples, there were many that day who pressed in on Him—He was touched in *that* way by a lot of people.

But in the midst of that press, Jesus suddenly asked, "Who touched me?" He asked this because He felt power (*dunamis*) go out of Him. Everyone denied it, and Peter expostulated with Him. Look at the crowd. But Jesus said, "Somebody touched me."

And somebody had. More than that, a *nobody* touched Him. We are not even given her name. And yet the power of Christ came to her in the middle of that crowd, healing an affliction she had suffered for years.

You are here to worship the Father in the name of Jesus in the power of the Spirit. The first thing to remember is this. When you come, you should want to come in such a way as to *touch* the Lord. The hand you are to use to reach out is your faith, which is given to you that you may touch Him. You are here because you want to have personal contact with Him. Second, when you do, then you will be a recipient of His grace. Power, virtue, strength will be given to you, flowing from Him to you. And third, Jesus knows about it. There are no secrets here. The grace you desperately need is here, but *none* of it is given by accident.

So come, and welcome, to Jesus Christ.

We are instructed in Scripture to examine ourselves as we come to this Table. But because we are instructed to do so, we must also follow instructions in the *way* we do so.

"Wherefore whosoever shall eat this bread, and drink this cup of the Lord, unworthily, shall be guilty of the body and blood of the Lord. But let a man examine himself, and so let him eat of that bread, and drink of that cup. For he that eateth and drinketh unworthily, eateth and drinketh damnation to himself, not discerning the Lord's body" (1 Cor. 11:27–29).

Over the years, many saints have stumbled over that word unworthily. They shrink back from the Supper, saying that they know themselves to be utterly unworthy. They know what their life was like before their conversion, and since their conversion there have been numerous unworthy moments as well. If I really examine myself, they think, how could I possibly come?

But before you examine your heart, take care to examine the text. As Spurgeon pointed out many years ago, the word "unworthily" is an adverb, not an adjective. It is not describing a man who has behaved in unworthy ways in time past. It is describing a man who, in his manner of coming right this minute, is doing so flippantly, or contemptuously, or with complacency. It is an adverb that describes the coming, not an adjective describing a sinner who needs to come.

So the emptier you feel, the greater the need to come. There is fullness here, fullness for your emptiness. So the weight of your sin bears you down, but there is one here who will lift all of your burdens and will bear them away. So you feel sometimes as though your heart is black as hell, but here is edible light.

Humble yourself, and do not fear that adverb. Come.

So come, and welcome, to Jesus Christ.

MORNING ☼ COMMUNION IS THE POINT

Those who are lost in this world are characterized by a bewilderment concerning whether or not there is any point to life. If they knew there was one, and if they knew what it was, they wouldn't be lost. But here they are, and lost is the best word we might use to describe them.

Suppose them to be here, and suppose one of them asked us what the point of life was. The answer to that question — the greatest of all questions — is right here in front of us. This is. Here, the bread of life and the wine of forgiveness are set on the Table in front of us as the entire point of our lives. How is that?

This Table is all about communion with God, and that is why God created us — to have communion with Him. If He created us to have communion with Him, then having communion with Him is the point of life. This Table, set before us weekly, is our sacramental reminder that apart from communion with God, the image of God necessarily has no point.

If we are not created in the image of God, we have no purpose, no point. If we are created in His image, but are estranged from Him, then we find our lives to be pointless also. The only way to be oriented rightly is to be oriented while in fellowship with Him. And that is what this Table is for. This is to remind you, to refurbish you, to strengthen you, to nourish you, to speak to you, to commune with you.

This is communion, and the reason human beings were created by God was to live in communion with Him. This is what He desires, and as His minister I am authorized to invite you into what He desires. I am inviting you to desire it too.

So come, and welcome, to Jesus Christ.

This is a meal, and we know that we are to wash up for meals. It is the same with this sacramental meal as it is with any meal. Before you eat, you wash up. That is just what you do.

We understand this by how we place our time of confession at the beginning of the service and the meal at the end of it. We wash up first, and then we eat.

But we want to make sure we truly understand how this "washing up" actually works. When the Lord instituted the Supper, this is one of the things He taught on. When the Lord had come to wash Peter's feet, Peter naturally objected. It was not fitting that the Lord take the position of a slave. After a brief exchange, the Lord said this: "He that is washed needeth not save to wash his feet, but is clean every whit: and ye are clean, but not all. For he knew who should betray him; therefore said he, Ye are not all clean" (John 13:10–11).

Jesus has not yet washed Peter's feet, but He says that Peter was already clean (and the others also, Judas only excepted). This clearly means that the foot-washing was a metaphor for what might be called the incidental cleansing of sanctification, and not the foundational cleansing of justification. Judas was wrong at the root, but the others were true followers of Christ.

Peter and the others were *clean*, the Lord said. He said this, despite knowing and predicting that they would all be scattered shortly. Peter's betrayal is just hours in the future . . . and yet he was declared to be *clean*.

When you confess your sins at the beginning of the service, you are not accomplishing the actual cleansing that is necessary. You are rather testifying to the fact that you know that Christ is the only one who cleanses. And you, having been justified by faith alone, have been declared *clean*.

So come, and welcome, to Jesus Christ.

MORNING ☼ SATAN AT THE SUPPER

When the Lord first instituted this meal, He was greatly troubled in His spirit because there was treachery at the Table: "When Jesus had thus said, he was troubled in spirit, and testified, and said, Verily, verily, I say unto you, that one of you shall betray me" (John 13:21). Asked who it would be, Jesus said that the one He would give a morsel of bread to was the one who would betray Him (John 13:25). Judas took the morsel, Satan entered into him, and Jesus told him to do immediately whatever it was he was going to do. When Judas went out into the night, he went out into everlasting night.

Note that Satan was *present* at the institution of this meal. No doubt, in some way, shape, or form, he is present now. Also note that Judas went out into the night with that morsel, from the hand of Jesus Himself, in his hand, or in his mouth, or in his stomach. And as the everlasting bread entered him . . . Satan entered him.

This is disconcerting to us. Why did Jesus let Judas participate? Especially since Satan himself was right there at his elbow? Once again we start wondering about Jesus and His low standards.

Some Christians want to insist that *their* observance of the Supper be more pure than Jesus managed to keep His observance. They set up guards and hurdles and interviews and clearances — as though that by itself could ever be successful. Others just take the presence of treachery in stride, serenely administering communion to apostates and libertines, hypocrites and scoundrels because, they say, they are a church and not a sect. Jesus gave the bread to *Judas*, they say. Yes, but Jesus was greatly troubled by the treachery, and they are not troubled by it at all. Indeed, they want actively to encourage it.

So as we gather, the question should never far away from us — "Lord, is it I?" And at the same time, in a church that is cultivating warm affection for the Lord Jesus, the answer comes back overwhelmingly — "No, it is not."

So come, and welcome, to Jesus Christ.

EVENING ◐ IMPUTING MOTIVES

Imputation is a glorious part of our salvation. Through imputation, God credits us with the complete and untouchable righteousness of Jesus Christ. His obedience is reckoned as ours. There are times and places in our lives where we are invited to imitate Him in this — imputation occurs in every wedding, for example.

But there are many other times when we think we can accomplish something by imputation, and we really cannot. Chief among these would be our tendency to impute motives to others. We know what they did, we know that we don't like what they did, and we also know what our motives would have had to have been if we had done it. And so we "impute motives." We don't know why they did that, and the only reasons that occur to us are nefarious.

Often the energy of our response comes not from the fact that we disagree, but from the assumption that we are fighting the forces of evil. But in many instances, the "forces of evil" were things that we made up in our own heads, in our own imaginations. Conflicts escalate so quickly because our imputation of motives transforms the nature of the conflict. The problem is not their sin, but our own.

This is a bad approach everywhere, but it is particularly troublesome in marriages and in families. The family provides the close quarters, and the differences between men and women provide the inability to understand the motives of the other, and the sin provides the illusion that you do understand the motives of the other.

This is what it looks like. "If I had done that, my motives would have been thus and such. So and so did thus and such. Therefore his motives are what mine would have been." This is a bad business, guaranteed to generate conflict. And unnecessary conflict with those you love is not what you want. The very worst place to impute motives is when you are seated around a Table with companions that God has welcomed together with you. So set all that aside.

So come, and welcome, to Jesus Christ.

MORNING ✹ PARTAKING OF ALL

As we come to this Table in true evangelical faith, we partake of Jesus Christ. We also partake of one another, and we do this through the power and activity of the Holy Spirit of God. We are covenantally united, and the Spirit of God is the Spirit of the covenant.

Now Jesus teaches us that if we see Him we have seen the Father (John 14:9). No one comes to the Father except through Him (John 14:6), and it is not possible to have the Son without also having the Father (1 John 2:23). This means that as we partake of the Lord Jesus, we are also in some sense partaking of the Father. We are only able to do this through the work of the Holy Spirit, who is the Spirit of Christ and the Spirit of His Father also.

When Jesus offered His body and blood, which are the basis of this communion, He was submitting to the will of His Father. When He sent His disciples out to proclaim the reality of this restorative sacrifice to a wasting-away world, He specifically told them to wait until the Spirit had been poured out upon them. On the day of Pentecost, when that Spirit was poured out, they preached the Word powerfully, and afterward they broke bread together.

The Word comes in power. The bread comes in power. The wine comes in power. This is possible because the entire Godhead is involved in it. We do not manipulate Him by these means, but rather we meet Him here. We can meet Him here in faith because He promised to be here.

The persons of the Trinity can be distinguished — and must be distinguished — but they cannot be separated. If you don't partake of them all, according to their roles, you aren't partaking of any of them. If you come to one in reality, you have come to them all. The Father is the destination, the Lord Jesus is the road, and the Holy Spirit is the vehicle.

So come, and welcome, to Jesus Christ.

In this meal we sit down to eat with Jesus Christ, we feed on Jesus Christ, and we are fed by Jesus Christ.

First, what do we mean by *with*? In the Great Commission, Jesus promised to be with His followers until the end of the age (Matt. 28:20). He does this by means of His Holy Spirit, which He poured out on His people on the day of Pentecost.

How do we feed *on* Jesus Christ? Jesus said that unless we feed on Him, we have no life within us (John 6:54). And how do we feed on Him, as He presents Himself to us as the bread of life? He explains the hard saying to His disciples by saying that His words are spirit and life (John 6:63). We feed on those words by the Holy Spirit also.

How are we fed *by* Jesus Christ? Jesus saw the multitudes (John 6:6), He tested Philip, but He already knew what He was going to do. He was going to feed those who had flocked to Him. How could He not? He is the chief shepherd, and this is what shepherds do—they protect the flock as they lead the flock to green pastures.

This is not all that is occurring in this gracious meal, but this is right at the heart of what is occurring. You are Christian people, and because you are alive in Christ, it follows that you are hungry in Christ. But there is no way to be hungry in Christ without being hungry for Him.

So come, and welcome, to Jesus Christ.

MORNING ☼ OUR LOYALTY LESSONS

God has fashioned the world in such a way that table companionship is filled with meaning. And it is not just one meaning, but a multitude of meanings, running in every direction. But one of those meanings is the implied pledge of mutual fidelity.

We can see this in the implications found in the words of the psalmist, "Yea, mine own familiar friend, in whom I trusted, which did eat of my bread, Hath lifted up his heel against me" (Ps. 41:9). The complaint here depends upon an understanding of the treachery involved. How is it possible for a good friend, one who had shared bread with the psalmist, to turn away in betrayal? The words are made even more poignant when Jesus quotes them in application to Judas (John 13:18). In other words, what was the case with ordinary table fellowship remains the case with sacramental Table fellowship.

And so we have gathered here, friends and Table companions to the Lord. By coming here, we are accepting this standard — that those who break bread together should be *loyal* to one another — and we are imitating the standard as it is found in the one who is seated at the head of the Table. The Lord Jesus embodies everything that anyone who is seated here should always embody. In other words, *He* will never play the role of Judas — not in great things, and not in small things. He is the ultimate example of loyalty.

We, on the other hand, confess our sins at the beginning of every service. We know that whenever we sin, we are lifting up our heel against Christ. We do confess those sins, and the tendencies we have to commit them, and seek God's forgiveness. He knew we would be like this when He saved us, and He nevertheless receives us gladly, constantly, warmly. Even with the fact of our sins and waywardness, He still *wants* us to come.

And so we come here weekly because we are greatly in need of our loyalty lessons.

So come, and welcome, to Jesus Christ.

We have come here to eat and drink; we have come here to be nourished. Now one of the central reasons why God nourishes us is that He wants us to bear fruit. His intention for us is fruitfulness. Nutrition is not a dead end process. He nourishes us so that we might flourish and grow. The prophet Isaiah expresses an element of this in this way: "My wellbeloved hath a vineyard *in a very fruitful hill*" (Is. 5:1b).

You are here, in the presence of the Lord. The Lord sets the fellowship of His sufferings before you so that you might partake of them. You partake of His sufferings in this way so that you might also be partakers of the fruit. In this place, in this manner, all year long, God has been equipping you.

But He is equipping you right where you are. You are planted, along with the rest of all God's people in *a very fruitful hill*. The entire vineyard, made up of all God's people, is situated on a southern slope. The soil is rich, and the exposure to the sun of righteousness is wonderful.

Now some of you may struggle with this, but I want to encourage you. Your situation is ideal for you. God has chosen for you the very best place for you to be fruitful. If being somewhere else, in another situation, would bring Him greater glory, and you more good, then you may rest assured that that is where you would be.

This is nourishment that enables you to be fruitful where you are. This is an exercise in growth, and not an exercise in transplanting. Your trials, your afflictions, your challenges, are the best opportunity that you will ever have to rejoice in God's goodness and to bear fruit before Him. They are also, given the reality of temptation, the best place for you to turn away from that privilege. But we have a better expectation concerning you.

So come, and welcome, to Jesus Christ.

Made in the USA
Monee, IL
10 October 2024

66924717R00433